Steps to Writing Well

with Additional Readings

TENTH EDITION
2020 APA UPDATE EDITION

Jean Wyrick

Professor Emerita of English
Colorado State University

Australia • Brazil • Canada • Mexico • Singapore • United Kingdom • United States

CENGAGE

Steps to Writing Well with Additional Readings, **Tenth Edition**

2020 APA Update Edition

Jean Wyrick

Product Director: Monica Eckman

Product Manager: Laura Ross

Senior Content Developer: Leslie Taggart

Content Developers: Lynn Huddon and Phoebe Matthews

Associate Content Developer: Rachel Smith

Product Assistant: Claire Branman

Media Developer: Cara Douglass-Graff

Marketing Director: Stacy Purviance

Content Project Manager: Rebecca Donahue

Senior Art Director: Marissa Falco

Manufacturing Planner: Betsy Donaghey

IP Analyst: Ann Hoffman

IP Project Manager: Betsy Hathaway

Production Service and Compositor: Lachina Publishing Services

Text and Cover Designer: Deborah Dutton

Cover Image: Blooming Erpart, 2006 (oil on board), Martonfi-Benke, Marta (Contemporary Artist)/Private Collection/Bridgeman Images.

Feature Boxes: Practicing What You've Learned: Shutterstock.com

Assignment: Shutterstock.com

Applying What You've Learned: Shutterstock.com

Essay Topics: Getty Images

Revision Worksheet: Shutterstock.com

For product information and technology assistance, contact us at **Cengage Customer & Sales Support, 1-800-354-9706**

For permission to use material from this text or product, submit all requests online at **www.cengage.com/permissions** Further permissions questions can be emailed to **permissionrequest@cengage.com**

Library of Congress Control Number: 2015953932

Student Edition:

ISBN: 978-1-337-28094-5

Loose-leaf Edition:

ISBN: 978-1-337-28095-2

Cengage
200 Pier 4 Boulevard
Boston, MA 02210
USA

Cengage is a leading provider of customized learning solutions with employees residing in nearly 40 different countries and sales in more than 125 countries around the world. Find your local representative at **www.cengage.com**.

To learn more about Cengage platforms and services, register or access your online learning solution, or purchase materials for your course, visit **www.cengage.com**.

Printed in the United States of America
Print Number: 09 Print Year: 2020

Brief Contents

Part One: The Basics of the Short Essay

Part Two: Purposes, Modes, and Strategies

Part Three: Special Assignments

Part Four: A Concise Handbook

Part Five: Additional Readings

Detailed Contents

6   Effective Sentences 129

7   Word Logic 158

14 Causal Analysis 291

15 Argumentation 306

MindTap®
Online Chapter
Writing about Visual Arts

MindTap®
Online Chapter
Writing about Film

LIST OF ARTWORKS

LIST OF ADVERTISEMENTS

To the Teacher

With the most extensive coverage of the writing process and a wealth of professional readings, student models, and assignments, *Steps to Writing Well with Additional Readings* has been used by thousands of teachers and has helped thousands of students learn to write effective academic essays. This text is written for composition teachers who want a writing guide that students can easily read and understand. Too many writing texts are unnecessarily dry, complex, or massive. Written simply, in an informal, friendly style directly addressed to the student, *Steps to Writing Well with Additional Readings* offers a step-by-step guide to writing a variety of academic essays. The combination of practical advice; more than 70 student and professional samples; hundreds of short, long, and collaborative assignments; and a brief handbook should provide more than enough helpful guidance for students, without intimidating them.

About the New Edition

New discussions, student and professional writing samples, classroom activities, and assignments appear throughout this tenth edition, in addition to updated and expanded features that are popular with instructors and students who have used previous editions. This edition features useful new visual learning aids; 50% new student sample essays; more than 25% new professional readings and visual selections; all new essay assignments that promote using sources and using multiple rhetorical strategies; a new organization for expository writing assignments and for writing researched essays; and all new coverage of how to read multimodal texts.

Once again, readers of this edition may note an occasional attempt at humor. The lighthearted tone of some samples and exercises is the result of the author's firm belief that while learning to write is serious business, solemn composition classrooms are not always the most beneficial environments for anxious novice writers. The author takes full responsibility—and all of the blame—for the bad jokes and even worse puns.

New to This Edition

New Visual Learning Aids. New flowcharts have been added to this edition to summarize key processes and to help students who may be visual learners. These new "Visualizing the Process" flowcharts highlight the steps in the writing and revision process in Part One, the key steps in the composing process for each type of rhetorical essay featured in Part Two, as well as important research strategies in Chapter 19.

New Stand-Alone Exposition Chapters in Part Two. Chapters 9–14 in this new edition focus on individual exposition strategies (exemplification, process analysis, comparison/contrast, definition, division/classification, and causal analysis) and allow students and instructors to more easily find the rhetorical strategies that they need.

New Sample Student Essays. Eight new student essays (of 16 total) in Parts One, Two, and Three offer new models for drafting, composing, and researching. New student samples include a draft and revised essay in Chapter 5; new exemplification, process analysis, comparison/contrast, and argument essays; new MLA and APA research papers; and a new summary response essay in Chapter 21. Topics of the new essays include the fear of success, finding the best place to study, why campus food establishments should use food calorie labels, and the perils of computers that monitor people's emotions.

New Professional Readings. *Steps to Writing Well with Additional Readings* includes a great wealth of professional reading selections (51 in all, with more than 25% new to this edition) offering students numerous models for their own writing. New selections feature work by well-known contemporary authors such as David Sedaris, Rhina Espaillet, Jessica Lahey, and David Brooks, and touch on issues such as the rhetorical reasons why some advertising slogans work and others don't, whether voting should become mandatory for all citizens, and why college may be better suited for "grown-ups" than for young adults right out of high school.

New Coverage of Reading Multimodal Texts. Chapter 8 includes an all new section on reading multimodal texts, offering strategies to help students analyze visual and multimedia texts, and also includes an all new sample annotated advertisement that demonstrates how to use these analytic strategies.

New Assignments Offer Practice with Research and Multiple Modes. New end-of-chapter "Using Strategies and Sources" assignments in Part Two offer new opportunities for students to practice using multiple rhetorical strategies and using secondary sources to explore topics and develop an essay.

Chapter 5 Offers More on Drafting. Chapter 5 now includes an all new draft and revised version of a student essay, to better demonstrate the composing process for students, as well as a revised and expanded discussion of drafting.

Research Is Now Discussed in Two Chapters. Coverage of writing a research project is now divided into two chapters (Chapter 19, "Conducting Research and Using Sources," and Chapter 20, "Documenting Sources"), to allow students and instructors to more easily navigate the research process. Chapter 20 also includes a new sample student research paper: "Pervasive Computing and Privacy Rights: Who Owns Your Emotions?"

New Online Chapters. Two chapters are now available only online in the MindTap˙ for *Steps to Writing Well with Additional Readings*—"Writing about Visual Arts" and "Writing about Film."

Organizational Overview

Although many parts of the book have been revised or expanded for this edition, its organization remains the same. The book still begins with the essay "To the Student," which not only argues that students can learn to write better with practice and dedication but also gives them a number of practical reasons why they *should* learn to write better. Part One offers advice on "The Basics of the Short Essay"; Part Two discusses "Purposes, Modes, and Strategies"; Part Three focuses on "Special Assignments"; and Part Four presents "A Concise Handbook." Part Five contains thirty-one additional readings. A diamond-shaped reference symbol ◆ often appears within discussions, alerting readers to related information or exercises in other parts of the book.

Part One: The Basics of the Short Essay

Part One, containing eight chapters, guides students through the process of writing the short essay. Each chapter concludes with a summary of the most important points.

Exercises and Assignments

Each chapter in Part One contains exercises, activities, and assignments, many new to this edition. As in the previous editions, the "Practicing What You've Learned" exercises follow each major section in every chapter so that both teacher and students can quickly discover if any particular material needs additional attention. Moreover, by conquering small steps in the writing process, one at a time, students should feel more confident and should learn more rapidly. The Practices and the Assignments, which also follow each major section in these chapters, offer opportunities for both individual and collaborative work. Activities called "Applying What You've Learned to *Your* Writing" encourage students to "follow through" by incorporating into a current draft the skill they have just studied and practiced. By following a three-step procedure—reading, practicing, and then applying the advice directly to their own prose—students should improve their writing processes.

Part One includes the following chapters:

Chapter 1, Prewriting

Chapter 1, on prewriting, stresses finding the proper attitude ("the desire to communicate") and presents helpful suggestions for selecting a subject. This chapter then offers students ten methods for finding a significant purpose and focus for their essays. In addition, a section on using a journal explains more than a dozen ways students can improve their skills through a variety of nonthreatening—and even playful—assignments. The section on audience awareness should help student writers identify and communicate effectively with their particular readers.

Chapter 2, The Thesis Statement

After considering their essay's purpose, focus, and audience, students are ready for Chapter 2, which first explains the role of a "working thesis" in early drafts and then discusses in detail the usefulness of a clear thesis statement by presenting a host of examples to illustrate the advice. Also included in this chapter is an explanation of the "essay map," an organizational tool that can help students plan and structure their essays.

Chapter 3, The Body Paragraphs

Chapter 3 presents over forty samples to illustrate the qualities of effective body paragraphs: topic sentences, unity, order and coherence, adequate development, use of specific detail, and logical sequence. This chapter provides opportunities for students to see how a topic can progress from a working thesis statement to an informal essay outline, which in turn helps produce well-developed paragraphs in the body of an essay.

Chapter 4, Beginnings and Endings

To complete the overview of the short essay, Chapter 4 explains, through dozens of examples, the creation of good introductions, conclusions, and titles.

Chapter 5, Drafting and Revising: Creative Thinking, Critical Thinking

Chapter 5 begins by clarifying the revision process. Because too many students still think of revision as merely proofreading their final drafts rather than as an essential, recursive activity, this chapter emphasizes the importance of revision in all stages of good writing. Updated and expanded tips for efficient drafting practices appear next, and a section on procrastination explains why this bad habit interferes with a writer's critical thinking process and suggests practical ways to challenge this behavior. These pages then offer a system for revising drafts in stages to avoid overload that might result in Writer's Block, a malady helpfully addressed at the end of this chapter. Chapter 5 now includes an all new draft and revised version of a student essay ("The Fear No One Talks About") to better demonstrate the composing process for students.

Chapter 5 also presents an expanded section on critical thinking and visual literacy; this discussion encourages students to analyze and evaluate their ideas and those of others as they read, write, and select evidence for any writing assignment. Shaped by current composition research, a section in Chapter 5 on collaborative activities explains the value of peer workshops, small-group exercises, and team projects to foster discussion and new ideas, encourage audience awareness, teach critical thinking, promote revision, and polish editing skills. Students receive practical advice here to help them gain the most benefit from various kinds of paired peer-work and group activities.

Chapter 6, Effective Sentences

Chapter 6, on effective sentences, emphasizes the importance of clarity, conciseness, and vividness, with nearly one hundred fifty samples illustrating the chapter's advice. A section addressing fused sentences, comma splices, and fragments offers additional help resolving these common problems.

Chapter 7, Word Logic

Chapter 7, on word choice, presents suggestions for selecting accurate, appropriate words that are specific, memorable, and persuasive. This chapter also contains advice for avoiding sexist language and "bureaucratese," as well as commentary on the importance of understanding appropriate audiences for texting and Internet language.

Chapter 8, The Reading–Writing Connection

Chapter 8 points out that by learning to read analytically, students can improve their own writing skills. The chapter contains step-by-step directions for reading and annotating essays, suggesting ways students can profit from studying the rhetorical choices of other writers. A new annotated professional essay ("College for Grown-Ups") demonstrates how to use these critical reading strategies. Chapter 8 also includes an all new section on reading multimodal texts, offering strategies to help students analyze visual and multimedia texts, and an all new sample annotated advertisement that demonstrates how to use these analytic strategies. Guidance on how to write effective summaries and how to participate in class discussions concludes the chapter.

Part Two: Purposes, Modes, and Strategies

Part Two discusses the most useful organizational patterns, or strategies, for short essays whose primary purposes are exposition, argument, description, and narration. Each discussion in this Part follows a similar format by offering students (a) a clear explanation of the strategy's purpose; (b) practical advice for developing each essay; (c) identification of common problems; (d) suggested essay topics; (e) a topic proposal sheet; (f) sample student essay(s) with marginal notes; (g) professional essay(s) with questions and additional writing suggestions; (h) a revision worksheet; and (i) new "Using Strategies and Sources" assignments that offer opportunities for using multiple rhetorical strategies and secondary sources to explore topics and develop essays.

Professional and Student Essays

The sixteen student essays (eight of them new to this edition) in Parts One, Two, and Three of this text should encourage student writers by showing them that their peers have indeed composed organized, well-developed essays. The student essays here are not perfect and, as such, provide opportunities for classroom discussion of further revision. Fifteen essays (and five literary selections) by professional writers illustrate the rhetorical principles and stylistic advice presented throughout the chapters; seven new essays are included in this edition.

Suggestions for Writing

Nine lists, each containing twenty suggested essay topics, appear throughout the chapters in Part Two. These lists of possible topics, updated for this edition, offer students a wide range of choices that may draw on their academic, professional, or personal interests. Students who are visual learners will always find options for writing about images reproduced in this book. (For quick reference, complete lists of the artworks and advertisements appear at the end of the Detailed Table of Contents.) Other suggestions for writing follow each professional essay in Chapters 9–18.

Part Two contains the following chapters:

Exposition (Chapters 9–14)

Chapters 9–14 in this new edition focus on individual exposition strategies (exemplification, process analysis, comparison/contrast, definition, division/classification, and causal analysis). Formerly all contained in one chapter, the separate chapters in the new edition allow students and instructors to more easily find the rhetorical strategies that they need. New "Practicing What You Learn" assignments have been added to each of these chapters, along with new end-of-chapter "Using Strategies and Sources" assignments. New exemplification, process analysis, and comparison/contrast student essays are included in these chapters, along with a new professional causal analysis essay.

Chapter 15, Argumentation

Chapter 15 discusses the argumentative essay and includes a new student essay, as well as a new pair of professional essays that take different views on whether voting should become mandatory for all U.S. citizens. In addition, a series of advertisements, many new to this edition, offer opportunities for students to improve their critical thinking skills through analysis of the various appeals used in the ads. New suggestions for writing include many current topics of controversy relevant to students' lives.

Chapter 16, Description, and Chapter 17, Narration

Chapters 16 and 17, on writing description and narration, may be assigned prior to the expository strategies or may be used as supplementary material for any kind of writing incorporating descriptive language or extended example. Both chapters include new professional reading selections and contain visual art selected to stress the importance of vivid details in support of a dominant effect.

Chapter 18, Writing Essays Using Multiple Strategies

Although this text shows students how to practice individual rhetorical strategies, one pattern at a time, writers often choose a combination, or blending, of strategies to best accomplish their purpose. Chapter 18 concludes Part Two by offering advice to writers ready to address more complex topics and essay organization. This chapter also contains both a student essay and a new professional article to illustrate different uses of multiple strategies to accomplish the writer's purpose.

Part Three: Special Assignments

Part Three, "Special Assignments," allows instructors to design their composition courses in a variety of ways, perhaps by adding a research paper, a literary analysis, an in-class essay, a classroom presentation, or a business-writing assignment. Coverage of writing a research project is now divided into two chapters (Chapters 19 and 20) to allow students and instructors to more easily navigate the discussions of conducting research and documenting sources.

Part Three contains the following chapters:

Chapter 19, Conducting Research and Using Sources

Chapter 19 focuses on the research process and follows a student from her topic selection to the final essay. This chapter shows students how they can focus on a subject, search for information in a variety of ways, evaluate the sources that they find, paraphrase and quote sources, avoid plagiarism, and effectively incorporate source material in their essays. This edition includes three new visual flowcharts that summarize and highlight key steps in the research process, and it emphasizes the role critical thinking plays in evaluating sources, especially those found online. In addition, this chapter includes practical advice for how to conduct primary research, with specific guidance on collecting material through interviews and questionnaires.

Chapter 20, Documenting Sources

Chapter 20 contains updated and expanded coverage of the very latest guidelines for both MLA and APA documentation formats, including citations for a variety of online and multimedia sources. The new approach to MLA documentation reflects the guidelines put forth in the eighth edition of the *MLA Handbook* (2016). MLA style has been simplified to emphasize a common approach to a wide variety of source types, and the updated chapter introduces the new method while continuing to offer numerous citation examples for students. New indexes to the MLA Works Cited and APA Reference List citation models included in the chapter will help students more easily find the models that they need to document their sources. A new sample student research paper, presented in two forms to model both MLA and APA styles ("Pervasive Computing and Privacy Rights: Who Owns Your Emotions?"), concludes the chapter.

Chapter 21, Classroom Writing: Exams, Timed Essays, and Presentations

Chapter 21 begins with advice designed to help students respond quickly, accurately, and calmly to a variety of in-class writing assignments by understanding their task's purpose and by recognizing key directional words. Because many composition courses today include some variation of the "summary-and-response" assignment (often as a timed placement or exit test), this chapter specifically addresses that kind of writing and offers a new sample student essay. A final section of the chapter discusses various kinds of in-class presentations and suggests ways writing assignments can be best shaped for listeners, as well as offering hints for effective classroom delivery.

Chapter 22, Writing about Literature

Chapter 22 discusses ways literary selections can be used as prompts for personal essays or for papers of literary analysis. Students are offered suggestions for close reading of both poetry and short fiction, advice illustrated through an annotated poem, an annotated short story, and two student essays. Two additional poems and a brief story are presented for classroom discussion or for writing assignments.

Chapter 23, Writing in the World of Work

Chapter 23 allows students to practice composing business letters, office memos, electronic mail, and résumés. This edition also contains expanded advice for writing effective cover letters to accompany job seekers' résumés.

Two chapters are now available online in the MindTap® for *Steps to Writing Well with Additional Readings*:

MindTap® Online Chapter, Writing about Visual Arts

This chapter encourages critical thinking and good writing practice in discussions of paintings, photographs, and sculptures. To illustrate the guidelines for analysis, this chapter includes a student's prewriting notes and subsequent essay on Edward Hopper's well-known painting *Nighthawks*. Composition students may choose their own subject matter from more than twenty artworks reproduced in this chapter and others throughout the text. Artists such as Vincent van Gogh, Frida Kahlo, Claude Monet, Dorothea

Lange, Ansel Adams, Francisco Goya, Salvador Dali, and many others offer a variety of styles from social realism to abstract expressionism. The art in this chapter and throughout the print text can provide effective prompts for other assignments, such as descriptive paragraphs or comparison/contrast essays.

MindTap' Online Chapter, Writing about Film

This chapter offers an opportunity for students to practice good writing skills in essays using movies as subject matter in a variety of ways. Suggestions for critical thinking and writing about films and a glossary of cinematic terms are included, as well as a student essay and a new movie review (of "The Theory of Everything") that can be critiqued in class.

Part Four: A Concise Handbook

Part Four presents a concise handbook with accessible explanations and examples showing how to correct the most common errors in grammar, punctuation, and mechanics. Brief discussions on the parts of speech and sentence components preface the three chapters; exercises throughout the Handbook provide ample opportunities for practicing its advice. Each chapter begins with unique diagnostic tests for students to self-score; by comparing their corrections to the answers provided, students can assess their strengths and their needs for reviewing handbook material.

Part Five: Additional Readings

Part Five gives instructors the opportunity to choose among thirty-one additional professional readings. These selections—some serious, some humorous, some classic, some contemporary—offer a variety of ideas, structures, and styles to consider. There are ten new readings in this Part, touching on issues as diverse as how to protect oneself from identity theft, the rhetorical reasons why some advertising slogans work and others don't, a look at homelessness among college students, and the pros and cons of mandating that police officers use body cameras. Studying the professional selections from diverse writers such as David Sedaris, Brent Staples, Judith Ortiz Cofer, and Martin Gansberg should expand novice writers' awareness of rhetorical choices and can suggest additional topics for writing.

Instructor and Student Supplements

MindTap® English

MindTap' English for *Steps to Writing Well with Additional Readings*, tenth edition, engages your students to become better thinkers, communicators, and writers by blending your course materials with content that supports every aspect of the writing process.

- Interactive activities on grammar and mechanics promote application in student writing.
- Easy-to-use paper management system helps prevent plagiarism and allows for electronic submission, grading, and peer review.
- A vast database of scholarly sources with video tutorials and examples supports every step of the research process.

- Professional tutoring guides students from rough drafts to polished writing.
- Visual analytics track student progress and engagement.
- Seamless integration into your campus learning management system keeps all your course materials in one place.

In addition, instructors and students will find this content in MindTap° English for *Steps to Writing Well with Additional Readings*:

- eBook for *Steps to Writing Well with Additional Readings*, tenth edition. The acclaimed MindTap° Reader boasts a multimedia-rich experience with tagged note-taking, highlighting, and bookmarking for easy study guide creation.
- Video Tutorials and Quizzes. New short videos provide examples of students using each of the rhetorical strategies discussed in Part Two of the text to give students additional help with these key strategies.
- MindTap° Online Chapters in Part Three. "Writing about Visual Arts" and "Writing about Film" are online-only chapters that offer instructors additional assignment options for their course.
- Chapter Learning Objectives. These Learning Objectives are linked to the key points in each chapter to keep students focused on the important learning outcomes.
- Homework Assignments. Interactive assignments give students the practice they need with grammar and writing.
- Writing Assignments. Papers can be assigned and graded online via a writing app that also features peer review, sample rubrics, and an originality checker.
- Reflection Activities. These activities, styled like notebook entries, encourage students to think deeply about what they've learned in each part of the book and apply that knowledge to future skills.
- Resources for Teaching. A separate folder on the learning path contains additional instructor materials, including the instructor's manual.

MindTap° lets you compose your course, your way.

Instructor's Companion Site and Instructor's Manual

For additional instructor support materials, including PowerPoint slides and the instructor's manual, go to login.cengage.com. The instructor's manual provides teaching suggestions, suggested answers to exercises, and a sample course syllabus to assist instructors in teaching the course.

Concluding Thoughts

Although a new edition of this textbook has allowed its author to make changes and additions, the book's purpose remains as stated in the original preface: "While there are many methods of teaching composition, *Steps to Writing Well* tries to help inexperienced writers by offering a clearly defined sequential approach to writing the short essay. By presenting simple, practical advice directly to the students, this text is intended to make the demanding jobs of teaching and learning the basic principles of composition easier and more enjoyable for everyone."

Acknowledgments

I want to express my appreciation to many people at Cengage Learning for their help with this new edition. Many thanks to Product Manager Laura Ross for her unfailing support of the book and its author. I am indebted beyond measure to Content Developers Leslie Taggart and Lynn Huddon, whose helpfulness and efficiency guided this project every step of the way. Thank you, Lynn, for all the hard work—for your expertise and thoroughness, for your tireless searches and evaluation of just the right material, and for your always on-target suggestions. Many thanks to Betsy Hathaway and Ann Hoffman at Cengage and the permission specialists at Lumina Datamatics for negotiating the text's complex text and image permission rights.

Special thanks to Joel Henderson of Chattanooga State Community College; Scott Douglass of Chattanooga State Community College; Kathleen Flynn of Glendale Community College; and Anthony Sovak of Pima Community College for their extensive help updating and improving this new edition. I greatly appreciate their creative ideas and thoughtful work on the new discussions, assignments, examples, and reading selections found throughout the book.

I'm grateful to Senior Project Manager Jill Quinn at Cengage and Project Managers Chris Black and Molly Montanaro of Lachina for smoothly guiding the book through the production process. I'm indebted to the copyeditors for their careful work and good suggestions and to Elizabeth Rice for her fine proofreading. As always, I extend my ongoing gratitude to the students at Colorado State University and at other colleges who allowed me to reprint their words and to the many teachers who through the years have contributed to the Instructor's Manual, supervised this edition by Rachel Smith, Associate Content Developer, with additional material provided by Kathleen Smith.

I continue to be assisted by colleagues around the country whose helpful feedback informed many parts of this new edition:

Michael Alleman, *Louisiana State University, Eunice*

Emily Baldys, *Zane State College*

Sandra Cusak, *Heald College*

Ashley Dugas, *Copiah-Lincoln Community College*

Rima Gulshan, *Northern Virginia Community College*

Kenneth Harrison, *Florissant Valley Community College*

Caren Kessler, *Blue Ridge Community College*

Darrell Lagace, *Zane State College*

Robin Lyons, *Mississippi Gulf Coast Community College*

James McCachren, *Halifax Community College*

Cynthia McDaniel, *Southwestern College*

Pamela McGlynn, *Southwestern College*

Pat McGrath, *Kaua'i Community College*

Richard Middleton-Kaplan, *Harper College*

Natasha Whitton, *Southeast Louisiana University*

No acknowledgment is complete without mentioning my family—Sarah, Kate, and Austin—to whom this book has always been dedicated. Finally, I would like to give a last, heartfelt thanks to all the teachers who have chosen to use my work in their classrooms through the years.

To the Student

Finding the Right Attitude

If you agree with one or more of the following statements, we have some serious myth killing to do before you begin this book:

1. I'm no good in English—never have been, never will be.

2. Only people with natural talent for writing can succeed in composition class.

3. My composition teacher is a picky, comma-hunting old fogey/radical who will insist I write just like him or her.

4. I write for myself, not for anyone else, so I don't need this class or this book.

5. Composition classes are designed to put my creativity in a straitjacket.

The notion that good writers are born, not made, is a widespread myth that may make you feel defeated before you start. But the simple truth is that good writers *are* made—simply because *effective writing is a skill that can be learned*. Despite any feelings of insecurity you might have about composition, you should realize that you already know many of the basic rules of good writing; after all, you've likely been writing since you were six years old. What you need now is some practical advice on composition, some coaching to sharpen your skills, and a strong dose of determination to practice those skills until you can consistently produce the results you want. Talent, as the French writer Flaubert once said, is nothing more than long patience.

Think about learning to write well as you might consider your tennis game (or some other sport). No one is born a tennis star. You first learn the basic rules and movements and then go out on the court to practice. And practice. No one's tennis will improve if he or she stays off the court; similarly, you must write regularly and receive feedback to improve your composition skills. Try to see your teacher not as Dr. Frankenstein determined to reproduce his or her style of writing in you, but rather as your coach, your loyal trainer who wants you to do the very best you can. Like any good coach, your teacher will point out your strengths and weaknesses; she or he will often send you to this text for practical suggestions for improvement. And while there are no quick, magic solutions for learning to write well, the most important point to remember is this: with this text, your own common sense, and determination, *you can improve your writing.*

Why Write?

"OK," you say, "so I can improve if I try—but why should I bother? Why should I write well? I'm not going to be a professional writer."

In the first place, writing helps us explore our own thoughts and feelings. Writing forces us to articulate our ideas, to discover what we really think about an issue. For example, let's suppose you're faced with a difficult decision and that the arguments pro and con are jumbled in your head. You begin to write down all the pertinent facts and feelings, and suddenly, you begin to see that you do, indeed, have stronger arguments for one side of the question than the other. Once you "see" what you are thinking, you can then scrutinize your opinions for any logical flaws or weaknesses and revise your argument accordingly. In other words, writing lays out our ideas for examination, analysis, and thoughtful reaction. Thus when we write, we (and the world at large) see who we are, and what we stand for, much more clearly. Moreover, writing can provide a record of our thoughts that we can study and evaluate in a way that conversation cannot. In short, writing well enables us to see and know ourselves—our feelings, ideas, and opinions—better.

On a more practical level, we need to write effectively to communicate with others. While some of our writing might be done solely for ourselves, the majority of it is created for others to share. In this world, it is almost impossible to claim that we write only for ourselves. We are constantly asked to put our feelings, ideas, and knowledge in writing for others to read. During your college years, no matter what your major, you will be repeatedly required to write essays, tests, reports, and exercises (and possibly e-mail home). Later, you might need to write formal letters of application for jobs or graduate training; your writing might make that important first impression. At work, you might have to write numerous kinds of reports, proposals, analyses, and requisitions. To be successful in any field, you must make your correspondence with business associates and co-workers clearly understood; remember that enormous amounts of time, energy, and profit have been lost because of a single unclear office memo.

There's still a third—more cynical—reason for studying writing techniques. Once you begin to improve your ability to use language, you will become more aware of the ways others write and speak. Through today's mass media and electronic highways, we are continually bombarded with words from politicians, advertisers, scientists, preachers, teachers, and self-appointed "authorities." We need to understand and evaluate what we are hearing, not only for our benefit but also for self-protection. Language is frequently manipulated to manipulate us. For example, the CIA has long referred to the "neutralization" of enemies, and the former Bush-Cheney administration authorized "enhanced interrogation techniques" on suspects, which others saw as torture. On occasion, Pentagon officials have carefully soft-pedaled discussion of misdirected "physics packages" (bombs) falling on "soft targets" (civilians). (One year not so long ago, the National Council of Teachers of English gave their Doublespeak Award to the U.S. officers who, after accidentally shooting down a plane of civilians, reported that the plane didn't crash—rather, it had "uncontrolled contact with the ground.") Some members of Congress have seen no recessions, just "meaningful downturns in aggregate output," so they have treated themselves to a "pay equalization concept," rather than a raise. Advertisers frequently try to disguise their pitches through "infomercials" and "advertorials"; realtors may promote dumps as "designer-ready" houses; the television networks treat us to "encore presentations" that are the same old summer reruns. And "fenestration engineers" are still window cleaners; "environmental superintendents" are still janitors; "drain surgeons" are still plumbers.

By becoming better writers ourselves, we can learn to recognize and reject the irresponsible, cloudy, or dishonest language of others before we become victims of their exploitation.

A Good Place to Start

If improving writing skills is not only possible but important, it is also something else: hard work. H. L. Mencken, American critic and writer, once remarked that "for every difficult and complex problem, there is an obvious solution that is simple, easy, and wrong." No composition textbook can promise easy formulas guaranteed to improve your writing overnight. Nor is writing always fun for everyone. But this text can make the learning process easier, less painful, and more enjoyable than you might anticipate.

Written in plain, straightforward language addressed to you, the student, this book will suggest a variety of practical ways for you to organize and write clear, concise prose. Because each of your writing tasks will be different, this textbook cannot provide a single, simple blueprint that will apply in all instances. Later chapters, however, will discuss some of the most common methods of organizing essays, such as development by example, definition, classification, causal analysis, comparison/contrast, and argument. As you become more familiar with, and begin to master, these patterns of writing, you will find yourself increasingly able to assess, organize, and explain the thoughts you have about the people, events, and situations in your own life. And while it might be true that in learning to write well there is no free ride, this book, along with your own willingness to work and improve, can start you down the road with a good sense of direction.

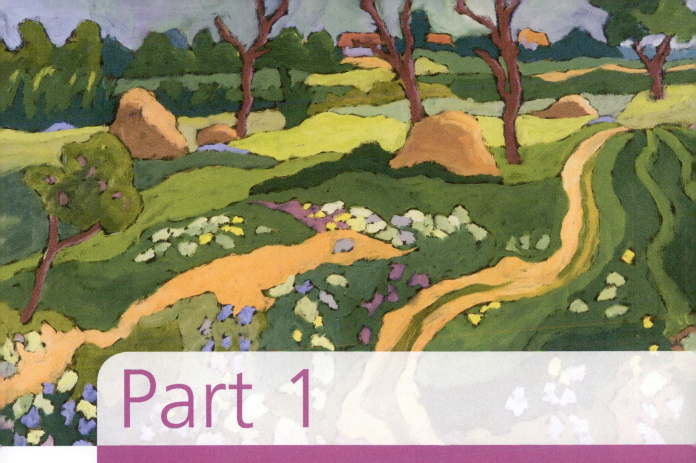

Part 1

The Basics of the Short Essay

The first section of this text is designed to move you through the writing process as you compose a short essay, the kind you are most likely to encounter in composition class and in other college courses. Chapters 1 and 2, on prewriting and the thesis statement, will help you find a topic, purpose, and focus for your essay. Chapter 3, on paragraphs, will show you how to plan, organize, and develop your ideas; Chapter 4 will help you complete your essay. Chapter 5 offers suggestions for revising your writing, and Chapters 6 and 7 present additional advice on selecting your words and composing your sentences. Chapter 8 explains the important reading–writing connection and shows how learning to read essays and other kinds of texts analytically can sharpen your writing skills.

Prewriting

Getting Started (or Soup-Can Labels Can Be Fascinating)

For many writers, getting started is the hardest part. You may have noticed that when it is time to begin a writing assignment, you suddenly develop an enormous desire to straighten your books, water your plants, or clean out your closet. If this situation sounds familiar, you may find it reassuring to know that many professionals undergo these same strange compulsions before they begin writing. Jean Kerr, author

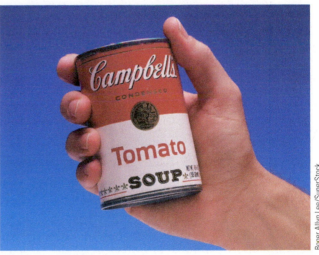

Roger Allyn Lee/SuperStock

of *Please Don't Eat the Daisies*, admitted that she often found herself in the kitchen reading soup-can labels—or anything—to prolong the moments before taking pen in hand. John C. Calhoun, vice president under Andrew Jackson, insisted he had to plow his fields before he could write, and Joseph Conrad, author of *Lord Jim* and other novels, is said to have cried on occasion from the sheer dread of sitting down to compose his stories. Writer Ernest Hemingway once confessed that the most frightening thing he ever confronted in his life of adventures was "a blank sheet of paper," and contemporary horror writer Stephen King agrees that the "scariest moment" of all occurs just before one starts writing.

To spare you as much hand-wringing as possible, this chapter presents some practical suggestions on how to begin writing your short essay. Figure 1.1 summarizes some of the prewriting tips and techniques discussed in this chapter. Although all writers must find the methods that work best for them, you may find some of the following ideas helpful.

Figure 1.1 VISUALIZING THE PROCESS: PREWRITING

Prewriting
Chapter 1

Drafting
Chapters 2, 3, 4, 5

Revising
Chapter 5

Editing/
Proofreading
Chapters 6, 7

Tips for Selecting Your Subject

1. Start early.
2. Find your best space.
3. Select something in which you have a strong interest.
4. Narrow your subject.

Techniques for Priming the Pump

1. Listing
2. Freewriting
3. Looping
4. The Boomerang
5. Clustering
6. Cubing
7. Interviewing
8. The Cross-Examination
9. Sketching
10. Dramatizing the subject
11. Keeping a journal

Identify and Analyze Your Audience

1. Check to see if the assignment specifies an audience.
2. Question your audience's motivation for reading your essay.
3. Discover your audience's subject knowledge.
4. Consider your audience's attitudes and emotional states.
5. Evaluate any special qualities your audience might have.

© Cengage Learning 2017

No matter how you actually begin putting words on paper, it is absolutely essential to maintain two basic ideas concerning your writing task. Before you write a single sentence, you should always remind yourself that:

1. You have some valuable ideas to tell your reader, and

2. More than anything, you want to communicate those ideas to your reader.

These reminders may seem obvious to you, but without a solid commitment to your own opinions as well as to your reader, your prose will be lifeless and boring. If *you* don't care about your subject, you can't very well expect anyone else to. Have confidence that your ideas are worthwhile and that your reader genuinely wants, or needs, to know what you think.

Equally important, you must also have a strong desire to tell others what you are thinking. One of the most common mistakes inexperienced writers make is failing to move past early stages in the writing process in which they are writing for—or writing to—themselves only. In the first stages of composing an essay, writers frequently "talk" on paper to themselves, exploring thoughts, discovering new insights, making connections, selecting examples, and so on. The ultimate goal of a finished essay, however, is to communicate your opinions to *others* clearly and persuasively. Whether you wish to inform your readers, change their minds, or stir them to action, you cannot accomplish your purpose by writing so that only you understand what you mean. The burden of communicating your thoughts falls on *you*, not the reader, who is under no obligation to struggle through unclear prose, paragraphs that begin and end for no apparent reason, or sentences that come one after another with no more logic than lemmings following one another to the sea.

Therefore, as you move through the drafting and revising stages of your writing process, commit yourself to becoming increasingly aware of your readers' reactions to your prose. Ask yourself as you revise your drafts, "Am I moving beyond writing just to myself? Am I making myself clear to others who might not know what I mean?" Much of your success as a writer depends on an unflagging determination to communicate clearly with your readers.

Selecting a Subject

Once you have decided that communicating clearly with others is your ultimate goal, you are ready to select the subject of your essay. Here are some suggestions on how to begin:

Start early. Writing teachers since the earth's crust cooled have been pushing this advice—and for good reason. It's not because teachers are egoists competing for the dubious honor of having the most time-consuming course; it is because few writers, even experienced ones, can do a good job when rushed. You need time to mull over ideas, organize your thoughts, revise and polish your prose. Rule of thumb: Always give yourself twice as much time as you think you'll need to avoid the 2:00-A.M.-why-did-I-come-to-college panic. (◆ For help overcoming procrastination, see pages 103–104.)

Find your best space. Develop some successful writing habits by thinking about your very own writing process. When and where do you usually do your best composing? Some people write best early in the morning; others think better later in the day. What time of day seems to produce your best efforts? Where are you working? At a desk? In your room or in a library? Do you start drafting ideas on a computer, or do you begin with notes on a piece of paper? With a certain pen or sharpened pencil? Most writers avoid noise and interruptions (the lure of social media sites, phone calls or texts, TV, friends, etc.), although some swear by playing music in the background. If you can identify a previously successful writing experience, try duplicating its location, time, and tools to help you calmly address your new writing task. Or consider trying new combinations of time and place if your previous choices weren't as productive as you would have liked. Recognition and repeated use of your most comfortable writing "spot" may shorten your hesitation to begin composing; your subconscious may recognize the pattern ("Hey, it's time to write!") and help you start in a positive frame of mind. (Remember that it's not just writers who repeat such rituals—think of the athletes you've heard about who won't begin a game without wearing their lucky socks. If it works for them, it can work for you.)

Select something in which you currently have a strong interest. If the essay subject is left to you, think of something fun, fascinating, or frightening you've done or seen lately, perhaps something you've already told a friend about. The subject might be the pleasure of a new hobby, the challenge of a recent book or movie, or even the harassment of registration—anything in which you are personally involved. If you aren't enthusiastic enough about your subject to want to spread the word, pick something else. Bored writers write boring essays.

Don't feel you have nothing from which to choose your subject. Your days are full of activities, people, joys, and irritations. Essays do not have to be written on lofty intellectual or poetic subjects—in fact, some of the world's best essays have been written on such subjects as china teacups, roast pig, and chimney sweeps. Think: what have you been talking or thinking about lately? What have you been doing that you're excited about? Or what about your past? Reflect a few moments on some of your most vivid memories; special people, vacations, holidays, childhood hideaways, your first job or first date—all are possibilities.

Still searching? Make a list of all the subjects on which you are an expert. None, you say? Think again. Most of us have an array of talents we hardly acknowledge. Perhaps you play the guitar or make a mean pot of chili or know how to repair a sports car. You've trained a dog or become a first-class house sitter or gardener. You know more about computers or old baseball cards than any of your friends. You play soccer or volleyball or Ping-Pong. In other words, take a fresh, close look at your life. You know things that others don't . . . now is your chance to enlighten them!

If a search of your immediate or past personal experience doesn't turn up anything inspiring, try looking in your local or campus newspaper for stories that arouse your strong feelings; don't skip the editorials or "Letters to the Editor" column. What are the current topics of controversy on your campus? How do you feel about a particular graduation requirement? Speakers or special-interest groups on campus? Financial aid applications? Registration procedures? Parking restrictions? Consider the material you are studying in your other classes: reading *The Jungle* in a literature class might spark an investigative essay on the hot dog industry today, or studying previous immigration laws in your history class might lead you to an argument for or against current immigration practices. Current news magazines or Internet news blogs might suggest timely essay topics on national or international affairs that affect your life. In addition, there were, according to the search engine Technorati in 2009, over 200 million individual English-language blogs; more recent estimates now put that number at over 450 million. Personal Web logs today may offer information and opinions (often controversial) on almost any subject one can name, with topics including politics, cultural trends, business, travel, education, entertainment, and health issues, to name only a few examples. Some blogs are directed to specific groups with shared interests or professional objectives, while others may have more in common with personal diaries or daily logs. Although all readers should always carefully evaluate any information provided online, a professional or personal blog might present an idea or argument that invites your thoughtful investigation and response.

In other words, when you're stuck for an essay topic, take a closer look at your environment: your own life—past, present, and future; your hometown; your campus and college town; your state; your country; and your world. You'll probably discover more than enough subjects to satisfy the assignments in your writing class.

Narrow a large subject.   Once you've selected a general subject to write on, you may find that it is too broad for effective treatment in a short essay; therefore, you may need to narrow it somewhat. Suppose, for instance, you like to work with plants and have decided to make them the subject of your essay. The subject of "plants," however, is far too large and unwieldy for a short essay, perhaps even for a short book. Consequently, you must make your subject less general. "Houseplants" is more specific, but, again, there's too much to say. "Minimum-care houseplants" is better, but you still need to pare this large, complex subject further so that you can treat it in depth in your short essay. After all, there are many houseplants that require little attention. After several more tries, you might arrive at more specific, manageable topics, such as "houseplants that thrive in dark areas" or "the easy-care Devil's Ivy."

Then again, let's assume you are interested in sports. A 500- to 800-word essay on "sports" would obviously be superficial because the subject covers so much ground. Instead, you might divide the subject into categories such as "sports heroes," "my years on the high school tennis team," "women in gymnastics," "my love of running," and so forth. Perhaps several of your categories would make good short essays, but after looking at your list, you might decide that your real interest at this time is running and that it will be the topic of your essay.

Finding Your Essay's Purpose and Focus

Even after you've narrowed your large subject to a more manageable topic, you still must find a specific *purpose* for your essay. Why are you writing about this topic? Do your readers need to be informed? Persuaded? Entertained? What do you want your writing to accomplish?

In addition to knowing your purpose, you must also find a clear *focus* or direction for your essay. You cannot, for example, inform your readers about every aspect of running. Instead, you must decide on a particular part of the sport and then determine the main point you want to make. If it helps, think of a camera: you see a sweeping landscape you'd like to photograph, but you know you can't get it all into one picture, so you pick out a particularly interesting part of the scene. Focus in an essay works in the same way; you zoom in, so to speak, on a particular part of your topic and make that the focus of your paper.

Sometimes part of your problem may be solved by your assignment; your teacher may choose the focus of your essay for you by asking for certain specific information or by prescribing the method of development you should use (compare running to aerobics, explain the process of running properly, analyze the effects of daily running, and so forth). But if the purpose and focus of your essay are decisions you must make, you should always allow your interest and knowledge to guide you. Often a direction or focus for your essay will surface as you narrow your subject, but don't become frustrated if you have to discard several ideas before you hit the one that's right. For instance, you might first consider writing on how to select running shoes and then realize that you know too little about the shoe market, or you might find that there's just too little of importance to say about running paths to make an interesting 500-word essay.

Let's suppose for a moment that you have thought of a subject that interests you—but now you're stuck. Deciding on something to write about this subject suddenly looks as easy as nailing Jell-O to your kitchen wall. What should you say? What would be the purpose of your essay? What would be interesting for you to write about and for readers to hear about?

At this point, you may profit from trying more than one prewriting exercise designed to help you generate some ideas about your topic. The exercises described next are, in a sense, "pump primers" that will get your creative juices flowing again. Because all writers compose differently, not all of these exercises will work for you—in fact, some of them may lead you nowhere. Nevertheless, try all of them at least once or twice; you may be surprised to discover that some pump-primer techniques work better with some subjects than with others.

Pump-Primer Techniques

1. Listing

Try jotting down all the ideas that pop into your head about your topic. Free-associate; don't hold back anything. Try to brainstorm for at least ten minutes.

A quick list on running might look like this:

fun	training for races
healthy	both sexes
relieves tension	any age group
no expensive equipment	running with friend or spouse
shoes	too much competition
poor shoes won't last	great expectations
shin splints	good for lungs
fresh air	improves circulation
good for heart	firming
jogging paths vs. streets	no weight loss
hard surfaces	warm-ups before run
muscle cramps	cool-downs after run
going too far	getting discouraged
going too fast	hitting the wall
sense of accomplishment	marathons

As you read over the list, look for connections between ideas or one large idea that encompasses several small ones. In this list, you might first notice that many of the ideas focus on improving health (heart, lungs, circulation), but you discard that subject because a "running improves health" essay is too obvious; it's a topic that's been done too many times to say anything new. A closer look at your list, however, turns up a number of ideas that concern how *not* to run or reasons why someone might become discouraged and quit a running program. You begin to think of friends who might have stuck with running as you have if only they'd warmed up properly beforehand, chosen the right places to run, paced themselves more realistically, and so on. You decide, therefore, to write an essay telling first-time runners how to start a successful program, how to avoid a number of problems—from shoes to track surfaces—that might otherwise defeat their efforts before they've given the sport a chance.

2. Freewriting

Some people simply need to start writing to find a focus. Facing a blank page, give yourself at least ten to fifteen minutes, and begin writing whatever comes to mind on your subject. Don't worry about spelling, punctuation, or even complete sentences. Don't change, correct, or delete anything. If you run out of things to say, write, "I can't think of anything to say" until you can find a new thought. At the end of the time period you may discover that by continuously writing you will have written yourself into an interesting topic.

Here are examples of freewriting from students who were given ten minutes to write on the general topic of "nature."

Student 1:

I'm really not the outdoorsy type. I'd rather be inside somewhere than out in nature tromping through the bushes. I don't like bugs and snakes and stuff like that. Lots of my friends like to go hiking around or camping but I don't. Secretly, I think maybe one of the big reasons I really don't like being out in nature is because I'm deathly afraid of bees. When I was a kid I was out in the woods and ran into a swarm of bees and got stung about a million times, well, it felt like a million times. I had to go to the hospital for a few days. Now every time I'm outside somewhere and something, anything, flies by me I'm terrified. Totally paranoid. Everyone kids me because I immediately cover my head. I keep hearing about killer bees heading this way, my worst nightmare come true.

Student 2:

We're not going to have any nature left if people don't do something about the environment. Despite all the media attention to recycling, we're still trashing the planet left and right. People talk big about "saving the environment" but then do such stupid things all the time. Like smokers who flip their cigarette butts out their car windows. Do they think those filters are just going to disappear overnight? The parking lot by this building is full of butts this morning where someone dumped their car ashtray. This campus is full of pop cans, I can see at least three empties under desks in this classroom right now.

These two students reacted quite differently to the same general subject. The first student responded personally, thinking about her own relationship to "nature" (defined as being out in the woods), whereas the second student obviously associated nature with environmental concerns. More freewriting might lead student 1 to a humorous essay on her bee phobia or even to an inquiry about those dreaded killer bees; student 2 might write an interesting paper suggesting ways college students could clean up their campus or easily recycle their aluminum cans.

Often freewriting will not be as coherent as these two samples; sometimes freewriting goes nowhere or in circles. But it's a technique worth trying. By allowing our minds to roam freely over a subject, without worrying about "correctness" or organization, we may remember or discover topics we want to write about or investigate, topics we feel strongly about and wish to introduce to others.

3. Looping*

Looping is a variation on freewriting that works amazingly well for many people, including those who are frustrated rather than helped by freewriting.

Let's assume you've been assigned that old standby, "My Summer Vacation." Obviously, you must find a focus, something specific and important to say. Again, face a blank page and begin to freewrite, as described previously. Write for at least ten minutes. At the end of this period, read over what you've written and try to identify a central idea that has emerged. This idea might be an important thought that occurred to you in the middle or at the end of your writing, or perhaps it was the idea you liked best for whatever reason. It might be the idea that was pulling you onward when time ran out. In other words, look for the thought that stands out, that seems to indicate the direction of your thinking. Put this thought or idea into one sentence called the "center-of-gravity sentence." You have now completed loop 1.

To begin loop 2, use your center-of-gravity sentence as a jumping-off point for another ten minutes of freewriting. Stop, read what you've written, and complete loop 2 by composing another center-of-gravity sentence. Use this second sentence to start loop 3. You should write at least three loops and three center-of-gravity sentences. At the end of three loops, you may find that you have focused on a specific topic that might lead to a good essay. If you're not satisfied with your topic at this point, by all means try two or three more loops until your subject is sufficiently narrowed and focused.

Here's an example of one student's looping exercise:

Summer Vacation

Loop 1   I think summer vacations are very important aspects of living. They symbolize getting away from daily routines, discovering places and people that are different. When I think of vacations I think mostly of

---

* This technique is suggested by Peter Elbow in *Writing Without Teachers* (Oxford UP, 1975).

traveling somewhere too far to go, say, for a weekend. It is a chance to get away and relax and not think about most responsibilities. Just have a good time and enjoy yourself. Vacations can also be a time of gathering with family and friends.

Center-of-gravity sentence

Vacations are meant to be used for traveling.

Loop 2

Vacations are meant for traveling. Last summer my family and I drove to Yellowstone National Park. I didn't want to go at first. I thought looking at geysers would be dumb and boring. I was really obnoxious all the way up there and made lots of smart remarks about getting eaten by bears. Luckily, my parents ignored me and I'm glad they did, because Yellowstone turned out to be wonderful. It's not just Old Faithful—there's lots more to see and learn about, like these colorful boiling pools and boiling patches of mud. I got interested in the thermodynamics of the pools and how new ones are surfacing all the time, and how algae make the pools different colors.

Center-of-gravity sentence

Once I got interested in Yellowstone's amazing pools, my vacation turned out great.

Loop 3

Once I got interested in the pools, I had a good time, mainly because I felt I was seeing something really unusual. I knew I'd never see anything like this again unless I went to Iceland or New Zealand (highly unlikely!). I felt like I was learning a lot, too. I liked the idea of learning a lot about the inside of the earth without having to go to class and study books. I really hated to leave—Mom and Dad kidded me on the way back about how much I'd griped about going on the trip in the first place. I felt pretty dumb. But I was really glad I'd given the Park a closer look instead of holding on to my view of it as a boring bunch of water fountains. I would have had a terrible time, but now I hope to go back someday. I think the experience made me more open-minded about trying new places.

Center-of-gravity sentence

My vacation this summer was special because I was willing to put aside my expectations of boredom and learn some new ideas about the strange environment at Yellowstone.

At the end of three loops, this student has moved from the general subject of "summer vacation" to the more focused idea that her willingness to learn about a new place played an important part in the enjoyment of her vacation. Although her last center-of-gravity sentence still contains some vague words and phrases ("special," "new ideas," "strange environment"), the thought stated here may eventually lead to an essay that not only will say something about this student's vacation but may also persuade readers to reconsider their attitude toward taking trips to new places.

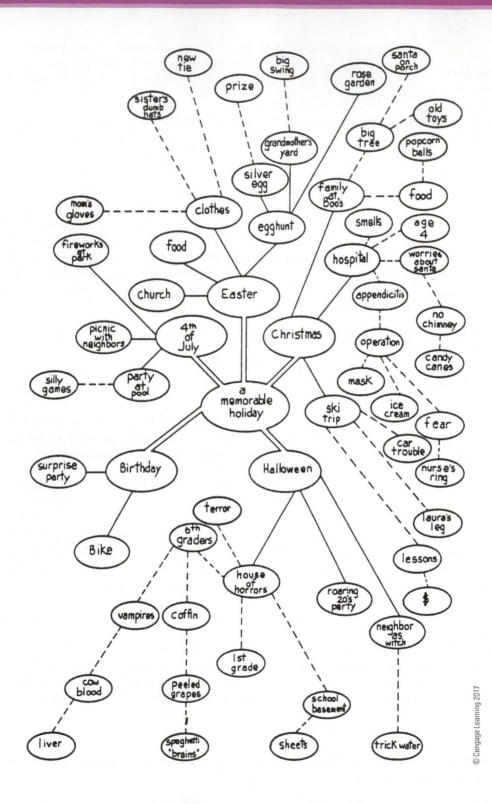

4. The Boomerang

Still another variation on freewriting is the technique called the "boomerang," named appropriately because, like the Australian stick, it invites your mind to travel over a subject from opposite directions to produce new ideas.

Suppose, for example, members of your class have been asked to write about their major field of study, which in your case is Liberal Arts. Begin by writing a statement that comes into your mind about majoring in the Liberal Arts, and then freewrite on that statement for five minutes. Then write a second statement that approaches the subject from an opposing point of view, and freewrite again for five minutes. Continue this pattern several times. Boomeranging, like looping, can help writers see their subject in a new way and consequently help them find an idea to write about.

Here's an abbreviated sample of boomeranging:

1. Majoring in the Liberal Arts is impractical in today's world.
   [Freewrite for five minutes.]

2. Majoring in the Liberal Arts is practical in today's world.
   [Freewrite for five minutes.]

3. Liberal Arts is a particularly enjoyable major for me.
   [Freewrite for five minutes.]

4. Liberal Arts is not always an enjoyable major for me.
   [Freewrite for five minutes.]

And so on.

By continuing to "throw the boomerang" across your subject, you may not only find your focus but also gain insight into other people's views of your topic, which can be especially valuable if your paper will address a controversial issue or one that you feel is often misunderstood.

5. Clustering

Another excellent technique is clustering (sometimes called "mapping"). Place your general subject in a circle in the middle of a blank sheet of paper and begin to draw other lines and circles that radiate from the original subject. Cluster those ideas that seem to fall together. At the end of ten minutes, see if a topic emerges from any of your groups of ideas.

Ten minutes of clustering on the subject of "A Memorable Holiday" might look like the drawing on page 12.

This student may wish to brainstorm further on the Christmas he spent in the hospital with a case of appendicitis or perhaps on the Halloween he first experienced a house of horrors. By using clustering, he has recollected some important details about a number of holidays that may help him focus on an occasion he wants to describe in his paper.

6. Cubing

Still another way to generate ideas is cubing. Imagine a six-sided cube that looks something like the figure on page 14.

Mentally, roll your subject around the cube and freewrite the answers to the questions that follow. Write whatever comes to mind for ten or fifteen minutes; don't concern yourself with the "correctness" of what you write.

a. **Describe it:** What does your subject look like? What size, colors, and textures does it have? Does it have any special features worth noting?

b. **Compare or contrast it:** What is your subject similar to? What is your subject different from? In what ways?

c. **Free-associate it:** What does this subject remind you of? What does it call to mind? What memories does it conjure up?

d. **Analyze it:** How does it work? How are the parts connected? What is its significance?

e. **Argue for or against it:** What arguments can you make for or against your subject? What advantages or disadvantages does it have? What changes or improvements should be made?

f. **Apply it:** What are the uses of your subject? What can you do with it?

A student who had recently volunteered at a homeless shelter wrote the following responses about her experience:

a. **Describe it:** I and five other members of my campus organization volunteered three Saturdays to work at the shelter here in town. We mainly helped in the kitchen, preparing, serving, and cleaning up after meals. At the dinners we served about forty homeless people, mostly men but also some families with small children and babies.

b. **Compare or contrast it:** I had never done anything like this before so it's hard to compare or contrast it to anything. It was different though from what I expected. I hadn't really thought much about the people who would be there—or, to be honest, I think I thought they would be pretty weird or sad and I was kind of dreading going there after I volunteered. But the people were just regular normal people. And they were very, very polite to us.

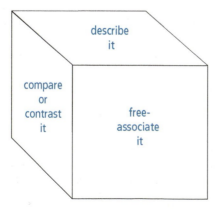
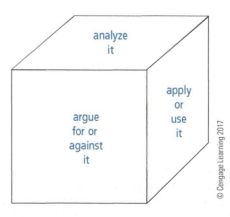

© Cengage Learning 2017

c. **Free-associate it:** Some of the people there reminded me of some of my relatives! John, the kitchen manager, said most of the people were just temporarily "down on their luck" and that reminded me of my aunt and uncle who came to stay with us for a while when I was in high school after my uncle lost his job.

d. **Analyze it:** I feel like I got a lot out of my experience. I think I had some wrong ideas about "the homeless," and working there made me think more about them as real people, not just a faceless group.

e. **Argue for or against it:** I would encourage others to volunteer there. The work isn't hard and it isn't scary. It makes you appreciate what you've got and also makes you think about what you or your family might do if things went wrong for a while. It also makes you feel good to do something for people you don't even know.

f. **Apply it:** I feel like I am more knowledgeable when I hear people talk about the poor or the homeless in this town, especially those people who criticize those who use the shelter.

After you've written your responses, see if any one or more of them give you an idea for a paper. The student who wrote the preceding responses decided she wanted to write an article for her campus newspaper encouraging people to volunteer at the shelter not only to provide much-needed help but also to challenge their own preconceived notions about the homeless in her college town. Cubing helped her realize she had something valuable to say about her experience and gave her a purpose for writing.

7. Interviewing

Another way to find a direction for your paper is through interviewing. Ask a classmate or friend to discuss your subject with you. Let your thoughts range over your subject as your friend asks you questions that arise naturally in the conversation. Or your friend might try asking what are called "reporter's questions" as she or he "interviews" you on your subject:

Who?	When?
What?	Why?
Where?	How?

Listen to what you have to say about your subject. What were you most interested in talking about? What did your friend want to know? Why? By talking about your subject, you may find that you have talked your way into an interesting focus for your paper. If, after the interview, you are still stumped, question your friend: if he or she had to publish an essay based on the information from your interview, what would that essay focus on? Why?

8. The Cross-Examination

If a classmate isn't available for an interview, try cross-examining yourself. Ask yourself questions about your general subject, just as a lawyer might if you were on the witness stand. Consider using the five categories described on the next page, which are adapted from those suggested by Aristotle centuries ago to the orators of his day. Ask yourself as many questions in each category as you can think of, and then go on to the next category. Jot down brief notes to yourself as you answer.

Here are the five categories, plus six sample questions for each to illustrate the possibilities:

1. Definition
   a. How does the dictionary or encyclopedia define or explain this subject?
   b. How do most people define or explain it?
   c. How do I define or explain it?
   d. What do its parts look like?
   e. What is its history or origin?
   f. What are some examples of it?

2. Comparison and Contrast
   a. What is it similar to?
   b. What does it differ from?
   c. What does it parallel?
   d. What is its opposite?
   e. What is it better than?
   f. What is it worse than?

3. Relationship
   a. What causes it?
   b. What are the effects of it?
   c. What larger group or category is it a part of?
   d. What larger group or category is it in opposition to?
   e. What are its values or goals?
   f. What contradictions does it contain?

4. Circumstance
   a. Is it possible?
   b. Is it impossible?
   c. When has it happened before?
   d. What might prevent it from happening?
   e. Why might it happen again?
   f. Who has been or might be associated with it?

5. Testimony
   a. What do people say about it?
   b. What has been written about it?
   c. What authorities exist on the subject?
   d. Are there any relevant statistics?
   e. What research has been done?
   f. Have I had any direct experience with it?

Some of the questions suggested here, or ones you think of, may not be relevant to or useful for your subject. But some may lead you to ideas you wish to explore in more depth, either in a discovery draft or by using another prewriting technique described in this chapter, such as looping or clustering.

9. Sketching

Sometimes when you have found or been assigned a general subject, the words to explain or describe it just won't come. Although listing or freewriting or one of the other methods suggested here work well for some people, other writers find these techniques intimidating or unproductive. Some of these writers are visual learners—that is, they respond better to pictorial representations of material than they do to written descriptions or explanations. If, on occasion, you are stuck for words, try drawing or sketching or even cartooning the pictures that are in your mind.

You may be surprised at the details that you remember once you start sketching. For example, you might have been asked to write about a favorite place or a special person in your life or to compare or contrast two places you have lived in or visited. See how many details you can conjure up by drawing the scenes or the people; then look at your details to see if some dominant impression or common theme has emerged. Your Aunt Sophie's insistence on wearing two pounds of costume jewelry might become the focus of a paragraph on her sparkling personality, or the many details you recalled about your grandfather's barn might lead you to a paper on the hardships of farm life. For some writers, a picture can be worth a thousand words—especially if that picture helps them begin putting those words on paper.

10. Dramatizing the Subject

Some writers find it helpful to visualize their subject as if it were a drama or play unfolding in their minds. Kenneth Burke, a thoughtful writer himself, suggests that writers might think about human action in dramatists' terms and then see what sorts of new insights arise as the "drama" unfolds. Burke's dramatists' terms might be adapted for our use and pictured like the diagram on the next page.

Just as you did in the cubing exercise, try mentally rolling your subject around the star and explore the possibilities that emerge. For example, suppose you want to write about your recent decision to return to college after a long period of working, but you don't know what you want to say about your decision. Start thinking about this decision as a drama and jot down brief answers to such questions as these:

Action: What happened?

What were the results?

What is going to happen?

Actors: Who was involved in the action?

Who was affected by the action?

Who caused the action?

Who was for it and who was opposed?

Motive: What were the reasons behind the action?

What forces motivated the actors to perform as they did?

Method: How did the action occur?

By what means did the actors accomplish the action?

Setting: What were the time and place of the action?

What did the place look like?

What positive or negative feelings are associated with this time or place?

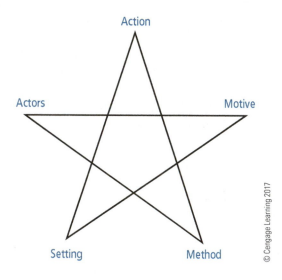

© Cengage Learning 2017

These are only a few of the dozens of questions you might ask yourself about your "drama." (If it helps, think of your "drama" as a murder mystery and answer the questions the police detective might ask: what happened here? To whom? Who did it? Why? With what? When? Where? and so on.)

You may find that you have a great deal to write about the combination of actor and motive but very little to say in response to the questions on setting or method. That's fine—simply use the "dramatists' approach" to help you find a specific topic or idea you want to write about.

REMEMBER: If at any point in this stage of the writing process you are experiencing Writer's Block, you might turn to the suggestions for overcoming this common affliction that appear on pages 125–128 in Chapter 5. You might also find it helpful to read the section "Keeping a Journal," pages 27–30, because writing in a relaxed mood on a regular basis may be the best long-term cure for your writing anxiety.

After You've Found Your Focus

Once you think you've found the focus of your essay, you may be ready to compose a *working thesis statement,* an important part of your essay discussed in great detail in the next chapter. If you've used one of the prewriting exercises outlined in this chapter, by all means hang on to it. The details and observations you generated as you focused your topic may be useful as you begin to organize and develop your body paragraphs.

Practicing What You've Learned

A. Some of the subjects listed below are too broad for a 500- to 800-word essay. Identify those topics that might be treated in short papers and those that still need to be narrowed.

1. The role of the modern university

2. My first (and last) experience with skateboarding

3. The characters of William Shakespeare

4. Solar energy

5. Collecting baseball cards

6. Gun-control laws

7. Down with throwaway bottles

8. Computers

9. The best teacher I've ever had

10. Selecting the right bicycle

B. Select two of the large subjects that follow and, through looping or listing details or another prewriting technique, find focused topics that would be appropriate for essays of three to five pages.

1. Music

2. Cars

3. Education

4. Jobs

5. Television commercials

6. Politics

7. Animals

continued on next page

8. Childhood

9. Smartphones

10. Athletics

Discovering Your Audience

Once you have a focused topic and perhaps some ideas about developing your essay, you need to pause a moment to consider your *audience*. Before you can decide what information needs to go into your essay and what should be omitted, you must know who will be reading your paper and why. Knowing your audience will also help you determine what *voice* you should use to achieve the proper tone in your essay.

Suppose, for example, you are attending a college organized on the quarter system, and you decide to write an essay arguing for a switch to the semester system. If your audience is composed of classmates, your essay will probably focus on the advantages to the student body, such as better opportunities for in-depth study in one's major, the ease of making better grades, and the benefits of longer midwinter and summer vacations. However, if you are addressing the Board of Regents, you might emphasize the power of the semester system to attract more students, cut registration costs, and use professors more efficiently. If your audience is composed of townspeople who know little about either system, you will have to devote more time to explaining the logistics of each one and then discuss the semester plan's advantages to the local merchants, real estate agents, restaurateurs, and so on. *In other words, such factors as the age, education, profession, and interests of your audience can make a difference in determining which points of your argument to stress or omit, which ideas need additional explanation, and what kind of language to adopt.*

How to Identify Your Readers

To help you analyze your audience before you begin writing your working thesis statement and rough drafts, here are some steps you may wish to follow:

1. **First, see if your writing assignment specifies a particular audience or a general audience of your peers**. A specific audience could be a person like the editor of a particular magazine or a group like the Better Business Bureau of your town, while a more general audience could include all your classmates or all readers of the campus newspaper. Even if your assignment does not mention an intended audience, try to imagine one anyway. Imagining specific readers will help you stick to your goal of communicating clearly, in engaging detail.

2. **If a specific audience is designated, ask yourself some questions about their motivation or *reasons for reading* your essay.**
   - What do these readers want to learn?
   - What do they hope to gain?
   - Do they need your information to make a decision? Formulate a new plan? Design a new project?
   - What action do you want them to take?

The answers to such questions will help you find both your essay's purpose and its content. If, for example, you're trying to persuade an employer to hire you for a particular job, you certainly would write your application in a way that stresses the skills and training the company is searching for. You may have a fine hobby or a wonderful family, but if your prospective employer-reader doesn't need to hear about that particular part of your life, toss it out of this piece of writing.

3. **Next, try to discover what *knowledge* your audience has of your subject.**

   - What, if anything, can you assume that your readers already know about your topic?

   - What background information might they need to know to understand a current situation clearly?

   - What facts, explanations, or examples will best present your ideas? How detailed should you be?

   - What terms need to be defined? Equipment explained?

   Questions like these should guide you as you collect and discard information for your paper. An essay written to your colleagues in electrical engineering, for instance, need not explain commonly used technical instruments; to do so might even insult your readers. But the same report read by your composition classmates would probably need more detailed explanation for you to make yourself understood. Always put yourself in your readers' place and then ask: what else do they need to know to understand this point completely?

4. **Once you have decided what information is necessary for your audience, dig a little deeper into your readers' identities.** Pose some questions about their *attitudes* and emotional states.

   - Are your readers already biased for or against your ideas in some way?

   - Do they have positive or negative associations with your subject?

   - Are they fearful or anxious, reluctant or bored?

   - Do they have radically different expectations or interests?

   Let's suppose you are arguing for the adoption of a new, wholly organic food service provider by a local school system, and your audience is the parent-teacher organization. Some of your readers might be concerned or even hostile because of perceptions about increased costs and limited menu choices. Knowing this, you would wisely begin your argument with a disarming array of information showing that the health benefits of eating organic foods outweigh the minimal costs associated with the new food service provider. You might also provide a sample menu that illustrates the creative variety that comes with organic cooking. In other words, the more you know about your audience's attitudes before you begin writing, the more convincing your prose, because you will make the best choices about both content and organization.

5. **Last, think of any *special qualities* that might set your audience apart from any other.**

   - Are they older or younger than your peers?

   - Do they share similar educational experiences or training?

- Are they from a particular part of the world or country that might affect their perspective? Urban or rural?
- Are they in positions of authority?

Knowing special facts about your audience makes a difference, often in your choice of words and tone. You wouldn't, after all, use the same level of vocabulary addressing a group of fifth graders as you would writing to the children's teacher or principal. Similarly, your tone and word choice probably wouldn't be as formal in an e-mail to a friend as in a letter to a credit card company protesting your most recent bill.

Without question, analyzing your specific audience is an important step to take before you begin to shape your rough drafts. And before you move on to writing a working thesis, here are a few tips to keep in mind about *all* audiences, no matter who your readers are or what their reasons for reading your writing.

1. Readers don't like to be bored. Grab your readers' attention and fight to keep it. Remember the last dull movie you squirmed—or slept—through? How much you resented wasting not only your money but your valuable time as well? How you turned it off mentally and drifted away to someplace more exciting? As you write and revise your drafts, keep imagining readers who are as intelligent—and busy—as you are. Put yourself in their place: would you find this piece of writing stimulating enough to keep reading?

2. Readers hate confusion and disorder. Can you recall a time when you tried to find your way to a party, only to discover that a friend's directions were so muddled you wound up hours later, out of gas, cursing in a cornfield? Or the afternoon you spent trying to follow a friend's notes for setting up a chemistry experiment, with explanations that twisted and turned as often as a wandering stray cat? Try to relive such moments of intense frustration as you struggle to make *your* writing clear and direct.

3. Readers want to think and learn (whether they realize it or not). Every time you write, you strike a bargain of sorts with your readers: in return for their time and attention, you promise to inform and interest them, to tell them something new or show them something familiar in a different light. You may enlighten them or amuse them or even try to frighten them—but they must feel, in the end, that they've gotten a fair trade. As you plan, write, and revise, ask yourself, "What are my readers learning?" If the honest answer is "nothing important," you may be writing only for yourself. (If you yourself are bored rereading your drafts, you're probably not writing for anybody at all.)

4. Readers want to see what you see, feel what you feel. Writing that is vague keeps your readers from fully sharing the information or experience you are trying to communicate. Clear, precise language—full of concrete details and specific examples—lets your readers know that you understand your subject and that you want them to understand it, too. Even a potentially dull topic such as tuning up a car can become engaging to a reader if the right details are provided in the right places: your terror as blue sparks leap under your nose when the wrong wire is touched, the depressing sight of the screwdriver squirming from your greasy fingers and disappearing into the oil pan, the sudden shooting pain when the wrench slips and turns your knuckles to raw hamburger. Get your readers involved and interested—and they'll listen to what you have to say. (Details also persuade your reader that you're an authority on your subject; after all, no reader likes to waste time listening to someone whose tentative, vague prose style announces, "I only sort of know what I'm talking about here.")

5. Readers are turned off by writers with pretentious, phony voices. Too often, inexperienced writers feel they must sound especially scholarly, scientific, or sophisticated for their essays to be convincing. In fact, the contrary is true. When you assume a voice that is not yours, when you pretend to be someone you're not, you don't sound believable at all—you sound phony. Your readers want to hear what *you* have to say, and the best way to communicate with them is in a natural voice. You may also believe that to write a good essay it is necessary to use a host of unfamiliar, unpronounceable, polysyllabic words gleaned from the pages of your thesaurus. Again, the opposite is true. Our best writers agree with Mark Twain, who once said, "Never use a twenty-five-cent word when a ten-cent word will do." In other words, avoid pretension in your writing just as you do in everyday conversation. Select simple, direct words you know and use frequently; keep your voice natural, sincere, and reasonable. (◆ For additional help choosing the appropriate words and the level of your diction, see Chapter 7.)

Don't Ever Forget Your Readers!
Thinking about them as you write will help you choose your ideas, organize your information effectively, and select the best words.

Practicing What You've Learned

A. Practice identifying intended audiences by analyzing, first, the Geico insurance advertisement that appears on the next page and then at least two additional advertisements reprinted in other pages of this text, such as "Gas Heat Makes Me Nervous" (page 337) or PETA's "Go Vegan" ad (page 343). (A list of the ads in this text follows the Detailed Table of Contents.)

In each case, first determine the purpose of the ad and then describe the ad's target audience, explaining your reasons for your response. You may find it helpful to consider some of the following questions:

1. What age group does the ad target? Does it appeal primarily to males, females, or both? Is the intended audience of a particular social or economic class?

2. What concerns or strong interests might this audience have?

continued on next page

Courtesy of Geico, Inc.

3. What kinds of arguments are used in the ad to persuade its intended audience?

4. What specific words or phrases are chosen to appeal to this particular audience?

B. Select an essay or feature story from a magazine or journal of your choosing and identify the intended audience. Explain how you arrived at this conclusion by showing ways the writer effectively addresses his or her audience.

C. Find two advertisements for the same kind of common product (car, cell phone service, shoes, cosmetics, etc.) but with different brands (e.g., Ford and Toyota, AT&T and Verizon). Do the ads you have selected have different or similar target audiences? How do you know? Does one ad more effectively address its audience than the other, and if so, why?

Assignment

A. The article that follows appeared in newspapers across the country some time ago. Read about the diet called "Breatharianism" and then write one or more of the assignments that follow the article.

The Ultimate in Diet Cults: Don't Eat Anything at All

1   Corte Madera, Calif.—Among those seeking enlightenment through diet cults, Wiley Brooks seemed to have the ultimate answer—not eating at all. He called himself a "Breatharian" and claimed to live on air, supplemented only by occasional fluids taken to counteract the toxins of urban environments.

2   "Food is more addictive than heroin," the tall, gaunt man told hundreds of people who paid $500 each to attend five-day "intensives," at which he would stand before them in a camel velour sweatsuit and talk for hours without moving, his fingers meditatively touching at their tips.

3   Brooks, 46, became a celebrity on the New Age touring circuit. ABC-TV featured him in October, 1980, as a weight lifter; he allegedly hoisted 1,100 pounds, about 10 times his own weight. He has also been interviewed on radio and in newspapers.

4   Those who went to his sessions during the past six months on the West Coast and in Hawaii were not just food faddists, but also physicians and other professionals who—though not necessarily ready to believe—thought this man could be onto something important. Some were convinced enough by what they saw to begin limiting their own diets, taking the first steps toward Breatharianism.

5   In his intensives, Brooks did not recommend that people stop eating altogether. Rather, he suggested they "clean their blood" by starting with the "yellow diet"— 24 food items including grapefruit, papaya, corn products, eggs, chicken, fish, goat's milk, millet, salsa piquante (Mexican hot sauce) and certain flavors of the Häagen Dazs brand ice cream, including "rum raisin." These foods, he said, have a less toxic effect because, among other things, "their vibrational quality is yellow."

6   Last week, however, aspirants toward Breatharianism were shocked by reports that Brooks had been eating—and what's more, eating things that to health food purists are the worst kind of junk.

7   Word spread that during an intensive in Vancouver, Brooks was seen emerging from a 7-Eleven store with a bag of groceries. The next morning there were allegedly room service trays outside his hotel room, while inside, the trash basket held empty containers of chicken pot pie, chili and biscuits.

8   Kendra Wagner, regional Breatharian coordinator, said she herself had seen Brooks drinking a Coke. "When I asked him about it he said, 'That's how dirty the air is here,'" she explained. "We (the coordinators) sat down with Wiley after the

continued on next page

training and said, 'We want you to tell us the truth.' He denied everything. We felt tricked and deceived."

9   As the rumors grew, some Breatharians confronted their leader at a lecture in San Francisco. Brooks denied the story and said that the true message of Breatharianism did not depend on whether he ate or not, anyway.

10   The message in his promotional material reads that "modern man is the degenerate descendant of the Breatharian," and that "living on air alone leads to perfect health and perfect happiness." Though followers had the impression Brooks has not eaten for 18 years, his leaflets merely declare that "he does not eat, and seldom drinks any fluid. He sleeps less than seven hours a week and is healthier, more energetic and happier than he ever dreamed possible."

11   In a telephone interview, Brooks acknowledged that this assertion is not quite correct. "I'm sure I've taken some fruit, like an apple or an orange, but it's better in public to keep it simple." He again staunchly denied the 7-Eleven story.

12   Among those who have been on the yellow diet for months is Jime Collison, 24, who earlier tried "fruitarianism," fasting and other special regimens, and moved from Texas to the San Francisco Bay area just to be around the Breatharian movement. "Now I'm a basket case," he said. "My world revolved around Wiley's philosophy." He had thought Wiley "made the jump to where all of us health food fanatics were going," Collison said.

13   Other Brooks disciples, though disappointed, feel they nevertheless benefited from their experience. Said a physician who has been on the yellow diet for four months: "I feel very good. I still don't know what the truth is, but I do know that Wiley is a good salesman. So I'll be patient, keep an open mind and continue to observe."

14   "Breatharianism is the understanding of what the body really needs, not whether Wiley eats or doesn't," said James Wahler, 35, who teaches a self-development technique called "rebirthing" in Marin County. "I'm realizing that the less I eat the better I feel." He also suggested that Brooks may have lied for people's own good, to get them to listen.

15   "Everyone has benefited from what I'm saying," Brooks said. "There will be a food shortage and a lot of unhappy people when they realize that I was trying to save their lives."

The assignments that follow are directed to different audiences, each unfamiliar with Breatharianism. What information does each audience need to know? What kinds of details will be the most persuasive? What sort of organization will work best for each purpose and audience?

1. Write a single-page flyer advertising the five-day intensives. What appeals might persuade people to pay $500 each to attend a seminar to learn to eat air?

2. Assume you are a regional Breatharian coordinator. Write a letter to your city council petitioning for a parade permit that will allow members of your organization to parade down your main street in support of this diet and its lifestyle. What do council members need to know before they vote on such a permit?

continued on next page

3. You are a former Breatharian who is now unhappy with the diet and its unful-filled promises. Write a report for the Better Business Bureau calling for an investigation into the organization. Convince the investigators that the organization is defrauding local citizens and should be stopped.

B. *Collaborative Activity:* In a small group of three or four classmates, exchange the assignments you have written. Which flyer, petition, and report does the group find most persuasive for its intended audience, and why? Present your group's analysis to the class.

Keeping a Journal (Talking to Yourself Does Help)

Many professional writers carry small notebooks with them so they can jot down ideas and impressions for future use. Still others write blogs, Web logs intended for public reading and commentary.

In your composition class, you may find it useful to keep a private journal or keep notes on your smartphone to help you with your writing process, or you may be assigned a journal or blog whose entries will be shared with your teacher or classmates. Whatever the exact medium, you might use a journal to explore your thoughts, experiment with prewriting techniques, save important ideas, respond to classroom readings or discussions, comment on other students' writing, remember important course material, or reflect on your own work, to name only a few possibilities. Devoting time to a journal can help you become a more confident, practiced writer.

Often, the journal is kept in a notebook you can carry with you (spiral is fine, although a prong or ring notebook allows you to add or remove pages when you wish); some writers prefer to collect their thoughts in designated computer files or Web logs. Even if a journal is not assigned in your composition class, it is still a useful tool.

Writers who have found journal writing effective advise trying to write a minimum of three entries a week, with each entry at least a half page. To keep a carry-around notebook organized, start each entry on a new page and date each entry you write. You might also leave the backs of your notebook pages blank so that you can return and respond to an entry at a later date if you wish.

Uses of the Journal

Here are some suggested uses for your journal as you move through the writing process. You may want to experiment with a number of these suggestions to see which are the most productive for you.

1. Use the journal, especially in the first weeks of class, to confront your fears of writing, to conquer the blank page. Write anything you want to—thoughts, observations, notes to yourself, letters home, anything at all. Best your enemy by writing down that witty retort you thought of later and wished you had said. Write about your ideal job, vacation, car, or home. Write a self-portrait or make a list of all the subjects on which you are (or would like to become) an "authority." The more you write, the easier writing

becomes—or at least, the easier it is to begin writing—because, like a sword swallower, you know you have accomplished the act before and lived to tell about it.

2. **Improve your powers of observation.** Record interesting snippets of conversations you overhear or catalog noises you hear in a ten-minute period in a crowded place, such as your student center, a bookstore, or a mall. Eat something with multiple layers (a piece of fruit such as an orange) and list all the tastes, textures, and smells you discover. Look around your room and write down a list of everything that is yellow. By becoming sensitive to the sights, sounds, smells, and textures around you, you may find that your powers of description and explanation will expand, enabling you to help your reader "see" what you're talking about in your next essay.

3. **Save your own brilliant ideas.** Jot down those bright ideas that might turn into great essays. Or save those thoughts you have now for the essay you know is coming later in the semester so you won't forget them. Expand or elaborate on any ideas you have; you might be able to convert your early thoughts into a paragraph when it's time to start drafting.

4. **Save other people's brilliant ideas.** Record interesting quotations, facts, and figures from other writers and thinkers. You may find some of this information useful in one of your later essays. It's also helpful to look at the ways other writers make their words emphatic, moving, and arresting so you can try some of their techniques in your own prose. (Important: Don't forget to note the source of any material you record, so if you do quote any of it in a paper later, you will be able to document it properly.)

5. **Be creative.** Write a poem or song or story or joke. Parody the style of someone you've heard or read. Become an inanimate object and complain to the humans around you (for example, what would a soft-drink machine like to say to those folks constantly beating on its stomach?). Become a little green creature from Mars and convince a human to accompany you back to your planet as a specimen of Earthlings (or be the invited guest and explain to the creature why you are definitely not the person to go). The possibilities are endless, so go wild.

6. **Keep pre- and post-reading notes.** As a composition student, you may be asked to read and analyze selections by professional writers, and your journal is a fine place to record your responses. In addition, many of the professional essays in this text have pre-reading/thinking questions designed to encourage your preliminary consideration of the writer's topic or point of view; you might reply to those questions in a journal entry or perhaps freewrite on a subject they suggest.

After you've read your assignment, try a split-page entry. Draw a line down the middle of a page in your journal, and on the left side of the page write a summary of what you've read or perhaps list the main points. Then on the right side of the same page, write your responses to the material. Your responses might be your personal reaction to the content (what struck you hardest? why?) or your agreement or disagreement with a particular point or two. Or the material might call up some long-forgotten idea or memory. By thinking about your class material both analytically and personally, you almost certainly will remember it for class discussion. You might also find that a good idea for an essay will arise as you think about the reading assignments in different ways.

7. Record responses to class discussions. A journal is a good place to note your reactions to what your teacher and your peers are saying in class. You can ask yourself questions ("What did Megan mean when she said . . .") or note any confusion ("I got mixed up when . . .") or record your own reactions ("I disagreed with Jamal when he argued that . . ."). Again, some of your reactions might become the basis of a good essay.

8. Focus on a problem. You can restate the problem or explore the problem or solve the problem. Writing about a problem often encourages the mind to flow over the information in ways that allow discoveries to happen. Sometimes, too, we don't know exactly what the problem is or how we feel about it until we write about it. Remember the encouraging words of the philosopher Voltaire: "No problem can withstand the assault of thinking." Writing *is* thinking.

9. Practice audience awareness. Write letters to different companies, praising or panning their product; then write advertising copy for each product. Become the third critic on a popular movie-review program and show the other two commentators why your review of your favorite movie is superior to theirs. Thinking about a specific audience when you write will help you plan the content, organization, and tone of each writing assignment.

10. Describe your own writing process. It's helpful sometimes to record how you go about writing your essays. How do you get started? How much time do you spend getting started? Do you write an "idea" draft or work from an outline? How do you revise? Do you write multiple drafts? These and many other questions may give you a clue to any problems you might have as you write your next essay. If, for example, you see that you're having trouble again and again with conclusions, you can turn to Chapter 4 for some extra help. Sometimes it's hard to see that there's a pattern in our writing process until we've described it several times.

11. Write a progress report. List all the skills you've mastered as the course progresses. You'll be surprised at how much you have learned. Read the list over if you're ever feeling frustrated or discouraged, and take pride in your growth.

12. Become sensitive to language. Keep a record of jokes and puns that play on words. Record people's weird-but-funny uses of language (overheard at the dorm cafeteria: "She was so skinny she was emancipated" and "I'm tired of being the escape goat"). Rewrite some of today's bureaucratic jargon or retread a cliché. Come up with new images of your own. Playing with language in fun or even silly ways can make writing tasks seem less threatening. (A newspaper recently came up with this language game: change, add, or subtract one letter in a word and provide a new definition. Examples: intoxication/intaxication—the giddy feeling of getting a tax refund; graffiti/giraffiti—spray paint that appears on tall buildings; sarcasm/sarchasm—the gulf between the witty speaker and the listener who doesn't get it.)

13. Write your own textbook. Take notes on material that is important for you to remember. For instance, make your own grammar or punctuation handbook with only those rules you find yourself referring to often. Or keep a list of spelling rules that govern the words you misspell frequently. Writing out the rules in your own words and having a convenient place to refer to them may help you teach yourself quicker than studying any textbook (including this one).

These suggestions are some of the many uses you may find for your journal once you start writing in one on a regular basis. Obviously, not all the suggestions here will be appropriate for you, but some might be. If it's helpful, consider using multiple files or, in a notebook, a set of divider tabs to separate the different functions of your journal (one section or file for class responses, one section for your own thoughts, one for your own handbook, and so on).

You may find, as some students have, that the journal is especially useful during the first weeks of your writing course, when putting words on a page is often hardest. Many students, however, continue to use the journal throughout the entire course, and others adapt their journals to record their responses to their other college classes and experiences. Whether you continue using a journal beyond this course is up to you, but consider trying the journal for at least six weeks. You may find that it will improve your writing skills more than anything else you have tried before.

Chapter 1 Summary

Here is a brief summary of what you should know about the prewriting stage of your writing process:

1. Before you begin writing anything, remember that you have valuable ideas to tell your readers.

2. It's not enough that these valuable ideas are clear to you, the writer. Your single most important goal is to communicate those ideas clearly to your readers, who cannot know what's in your mind until you tell them.

3. Whenever possible, select a subject to write on that is of great interest to you, and always give yourself more time than you think you'll need to work on your essay.

4. Try a variety of prewriting techniques to help you find your essay's purpose and a narrowed, specific focus.

5. Review your audience's knowledge of and attitudes toward your topic before you begin your first draft; ask yourself questions such as "Who needs to know about this topic, and why?"

6. Consider keeping a journal to help you explore good ideas and possible topics for writing assignments in your composition class.

Chapter 2

The Thesis Statement

The famous American author Thomas Wolfe had a simple formula for beginning his writing: "Just put a sheet of paper in the typewriter and start bleeding." For some writers, the "bleeding" method works well. You may find that, indeed, you are one of those writers who must begin by freewriting or by writing an entire "discovery draft" to find your purpose and focus—you must write yourself into your topic, so to speak.* Other writers are more structured; they may prefer prewriting in lists, outlines, or cubes. Sometimes writers find that they have to change composing methods to suit different kinds of projects. There is no right or wrong way to find a topic or to begin writing; simply try to find the methods that work best for you.

Let's assume at this point that you have identified a topic you wish to write about—perhaps you found it by working through one of the prewriting activities mentioned in Chapter 1 or by writing in your journal. Perhaps you had an important idea you had been wanting to write about for some time, or perhaps the assignment in your class suggested the topic to you. Suppose that through one of these avenues you have focused on a topic and you have given some thought to a possible audience for your paper. You may now find it helpful to formulate a *working thesis*.

What Is a Thesis? What Does a "Working Thesis" Do?

The thesis statement declares the main point or controlling idea of your entire essay. Frequently located near the beginning of a short essay, the thesis answers these questions: "What is the subject of this essay?" "What is the writer's opinion on this subject?" "What is the writer's purpose in this essay?" (To explain something? To argue a position? To move people to action? To entertain?) Figure 2.1 highlights some of the guidelines for developing a good thesis discussed in this chapter.

Consider a "working thesis" a statement of your main point in its trial or rough-draft form. Allow it to "work" for you as you move from prewriting through drafts and revision.

---

* ◆ If you do begin with a discovery draft, you may wish to turn at this point to the manuscript suggestions on pages 99–102 in Chapter 5.

FIGURE 2.1 VISUALIZING THE PROCESS: THESIS STATEMENTS

Prewriting
Chapter 1

Drafting
Chapters 2, 3, 4, 5

Revising
Chapter 5

Editing/
Proofreading
Chapters 6, 7

© Cengage Learning 2017

Your thesis statement is the main point of controlling idea of your entire essay.

Your "working thesis" is the draft of your thesis that will control the shape of your rough draft; expect it to evolve and change as your progress.

Guidelines for Writing a Good Thesis

A good thesis...

1. States the writer's opinion on some subject.
2. Asserts one main idea.
3. Has something worthwhile to say.
4. Is limited to fit the assignment.
5. Is clearly stated in specific terms.
6. Is recognized as the main idea and is often located in the first or second paragraph.

Five Common Errors in Thesis Statements

1. Don't merely announce your subject matter or describe your intentions.
2. Don't clutter your thesis with unnecessary phrases that make you sound timid.
3. Don't make irrational or oversimplified claims.
4. Don't merely state a fact.
5. Don't express your thesis in the form of a question.

An essay map, which briefly states in the introduction the major points of the essay, can be a useful supporting technique for your thesis.

Your working thesis may begin as a very simple sentence. For example, one of the freewriting exercises on nature in Chapter 1 (pages 9–10) might lead to a working thesis such as "Our college needs an on-campus recycling center." Such a working thesis states an opinion about the subject (the need for a center) and suggests what the essay will do (give arguments for building such a center). Similarly, the prewriting list on running (page 8) might lead to a working thesis such as "Before beginning a successful program, novice runners must learn a series of warm-up and cool-down exercises." This statement not only tells the writer's opinion and purpose (the value of the exercises) but also indicates an audience (novice runners).

A working thesis statement can be your most valuable organizational tool. Once you have thought about your essay's main point and purpose, you can begin to draft your paper to accomplish your goals. *Everything in your essay should support your thesis.* Consequently, if you write your working thesis statement at the top of your first draft and refer to it often, your chances of drifting away from your purpose should be reduced.

Can a "Working Thesis" Change?

It's important for you to know at this point that there may be a difference between the working thesis that appears in your rough drafts and your final thesis. As you begin drafting, you may have one main idea in mind that surfaced from your prewriting activities. But as you write, you may discover that what you really want to write about is different. Perhaps you discover that one particular part of your essay is really what you want to concentrate on (instead of covering three or four problems you have with your current job, for instance, you decide you want to explore in depth only the difficulties with your boss), or perhaps in the course of writing you find another approach to your subject more satisfying or persuasive (explaining how employees may avoid problems with a particular kind of difficult boss instead of describing various kinds of difficult bosses in your field).

Changing directions is not uncommon: *writing is an act of discovery.* Frequently, we don't know exactly what we think or what we want to say until we write it. A working thesis appears in your early drafts to help you focus and organize your essay; don't feel it's carved in stone.

A warning comes with this advice, however. If you do write yourself into another essay—that is, if you discover as you write that you are finding a better topic or main point to make—consider this piece of writing a "discovery draft," extended prewriting that has helped you find your real focus. Occasionally, your direction changes so slightly that you can rework or expand your thesis to accommodate your new ideas. But more frequently, you may find that it's necessary to begin another draft with your newly discovered working thesis as the controlling idea. When this is the case, don't be discouraged—this kind of "reseeing" or revision of your topic is a common practice among experienced writers. (◆ For more advice on revising as rethinking, see Chapter 5.) Don't be tempted at this point to leave your original thesis in an essay that has clearly changed its point, purpose, or approach—in other words, don't try to pass off an old head on the body of a new statue! Remember that ultimately you want your thesis to guide your readers rather than confuse them by promising an essay they can't find as they read on.

Guidelines for Writing a Good Thesis

To help you draft your thesis statement, here is some advice:

A good thesis states the writer's clearly defined opinion on some subject. You must tell your reader what you think. Don't dodge the issue; present your opinion specifically and precisely. For example, if you were asked to write a thesis statement expressing your position on the national law that designates twenty-one as the legal minimum age to purchase or consume alcohol, the first three theses listed here would be confusing:

Poor	Many people have different opinions on whether people under twenty-one should be permitted to drink alcohol, and I agree with some of them. [The writer's opinion on the issue is not clear to the reader.]
Poor	The question of whether we need a national law governing the minimum age to drink alcohol is a controversial issue in many states. [This statement might introduce the thesis, but the writer has still avoided stating a clear opinion on the issue.]
Poor	I want to give my opinion on the national law that sets twenty-one as the legal age to drink alcohol and the reasons I feel this way. [What is the writer's opinion? The reader still doesn't know.]
Better	To reduce the number of highway fatalities, our country needs to enforce the national law that designates twenty-one as the legal minimum age to purchase and consume alcohol. [The writer clearly states an opinion that will be supported in the essay.]
Better	The legal minimum age for purchasing alcohol should be eighteen rather than twenty-one. [Again, the writer has asserted a clear position on the issue that will be argued in the essay.]

If you want to write about a personal experience but are finding it difficult to clearly define your thesis idea, try asking yourself questions about the topic's significance or value. (Examples: Why is this topic important to me? What was so valuable about my year on the newspaper staff? What was the most significant lesson I learned? What was an unexpected result of this experience?) Often the answer to one of your questions will show you the way to a working thesis. (Example: Writing for the school newspaper teaches time-management skills that are valuable both in and out of class.)

A good thesis asserts one main idea. Many essays drift into confusion because the writer is trying to explain or argue two different, large issues in one essay. You can't effectively ride two horses at once; pick one main idea and explain or argue it in convincing detail.

Poor	The proposed no-smoking ordinance in our town will violate a number of our citizens' civil rights, and no one has proved that secondhand smoke is dangerous anyway. [This thesis contains two main assertions—the ordinance's violation of rights and secondhand smoke's lack of danger—that require two different kinds of supporting evidence.]
Better	The proposed no-smoking ordinance in our town will violate our civil rights. [This essay will show the various ways the ordinance will infringe on personal liberties.]

Better   The most recent U.S. Health Department studies claiming that second-hand smoke is dangerous to nonsmokers are based on faulty research. [This essay will also focus on one issue: the validity of the studies on secondhand smoke danger.]

Poor   High school athletes shouldn't have to maintain a "B" or better grade-point average in all subjects to participate in school sports, and the value of sports for some students is often overlooked. [Again, this thesis moves in two different directions.]

Better   High school athletes shouldn't have to maintain a "B" or better grade-point average in all subjects to participate in school sports. [This essay will focus on one issue: reasons why a particular average shouldn't be required.]

Better   For some students, participation in sports may be more valuable than achieving a "B" grade-point average in all subjects. [This essay will argue that the benefits of sports sometimes outweigh those of elective classes.]

Incidentally, at this point you may recall from your high school days a rule about always expressing your thesis in one sentence. Writing teachers often insist on this rule to help you avoid the double-assertion problem just illustrated. Although not all essays have one-sentence theses, many do, and it's a good habit to strive for in this early stage of your writing.

A good thesis has something worthwhile to say. Although it's true that almost any subject can be made interesting with the right treatment, some subjects are more predictable and therefore more boring than others. Before you write your thesis, think hard about your subject: Does your position lend itself to stale or overly obvious ideas? For example, most readers would find the following theses tiresome unless the writers had some original method of developing their essays:

Poor   Dogs have always been man's best friends. [This essay might be full of ho-hum clichés about dogs' faithfulness to their owners.]

Poor   Friendship is a wonderful thing. [Again, watch out for tired truisms that restate the obvious.]

Poor   The food in my dorm is horrible. [Although this essay might include some vivid and repulsive examples, the subject itself is old news and not likely to lend itself to an effective essay.]

Frequently in composition classes you will be asked to write about yourself; after all, you are the world's authority on that subject, and you have many significant interests to talk about whose subject matter will naturally intrigue your readers. However, some topics you might consider writing about may not necessarily appeal to other readers because the material is simply too personal or restricted to be of general interest. In these cases, it often helps to *universalize* the essay's thesis so your readers can also identify with or learn something about the general subject, while learning something about you at the same time:

Poor	The four children in my family have completely different personalities. [This statement may be true, but would anyone other than the children's parents really be fascinated by this topic?]
Better	Birth order can influence children's personalities in startling ways. [The writer is wiser to offer this controversial statement, which is of more interest to readers than the preceding one because many readers have brothers and sisters of their own. The writer can then illustrate her claims with examples from her own family, and from other families, if she wishes.]
Poor	I don't like to take courses that are held in big lecture classes at this school. [Why should your reader care one way or another about your class preference?]
Better	Large lecture classes provide a poor environment for the student who learns best through interaction with both teachers and peers. [This thesis will allow the writer to present personal examples that the reader may identify with or challenge, without writing an essay that is exclusively personal.]

In other words, try to select a subject that will interest, amuse, challenge, persuade, or enlighten your readers. If your subject itself is commonplace, find a unique approach or an unusual, perhaps even controversial, point of view. If your subject is personal, ask yourself if the topic alone will be sufficiently interesting to readers; if not, think about universalizing the thesis to include your audience. Remember that a good thesis should encourage readers to read on with enthusiasm rather than invite groans of "Not this again" or shrugs of "So what?"

A good thesis is limited to fit the assignment. Your thesis should show that you've narrowed your subject matter to an appropriate size for your essay. Don't allow your thesis to promise more of a discussion than you can adequately deliver in a short essay. You want an in-depth treatment of your subject, not a superficial one. Certainly you may take on important issues in your essays; don't feel you must limit your topics to local or personal subjects. But one simply cannot refight the Vietnam War or effectively defend U.S. foreign policy in Central America in five to eight paragraphs. Focus your essay on an important part of a broader subject that interests you. (◆ For a review of ways to narrow and focus your subject, see pages 7–18.)

Poor	Nuclear power should be banned as an energy source in this country. [Can the writer give the broad subject of nuclear power a fair treatment in three to five pages?]
Better	Because of its poor safety record during the past two years, the Collin County nuclear power plant should be closed. [This writer could probably argue this focused thesis in a short essay.]
Poor	The parking permit system at this college should be completely revised. [An essay calling for the revision of the parking permit system would involve

discussion of permits for various kinds of students, faculty, administrators, staff, visitors, delivery personnel, and so forth. Therefore, the thesis is probably too broad for a short essay.]

Better   Because of the complicated application process, the parking permit system at this college penalizes students with disabilities. [This thesis is focused on a particular problem and could be argued in a short paper.]

Poor   African American artists have always contributed a lot to many kinds of American culture. ["African American artists," "many kinds," "a lot," and "culture" cover more ground than can be dealt with in one short essay.]

Better   Scott Joplin was a major influence in the development of the uniquely American music called ragtime. [This thesis is more specifically defined.]

A good thesis is clearly stated in specific terms. More than anything, a vague thesis reflects lack of clarity in the writer's mind and almost inevitably leads to an essay that talks around the subject but never makes a coherent point. Try to avoid words whose meanings are imprecise and those that depend largely on personal interpretation, such as "interesting," "good," and "bad."

Poor   The women's movement is good for our country. [What group does the writer refer to? How is it good? For whom?]

Better   The Colorado Women's Party is working to ensure the benefits of equal pay for equal work for both males and females in our state. [This tells who will benefit and how—clearly defining the thesis.]

Poor   Registration is a big hassle. [No clear idea is communicated here. How much trouble is a "hassle"?]

Better   Registration's alphabetical fee-paying system is inefficient. [The issue is specified.]

Poor   Living in an apartment for the first time can teach you many things about taking care of yourself. ["Things" and "taking care of yourself" are both too vague. What specific ideas does the writer want to discuss? And who is the "you" the writer has in mind?]

Better   By living in an apartment, a first-year student can learn valuable lessons in financial planning and time management. [The thesis is now clearly defined and directed.]

A good thesis is easily recognized as the main idea and is often located in the first or second paragraph. Many students are hesitant to spell out a thesis at the beginning of an essay. To quote one student, "I feel as if I'm giving everything away." Although you may feel uncomfortable "giving away" the main point so soon, the alternative of waiting until the last page to present your thesis can seriously weaken your essay.

© The Metropolitan Museum of Art. Image source: Art Resource, NY

The Great Wave at Kanagawa, 1831, by Katsushika Hokusai

Without an assertion of what you are trying to prove, your reader does not know how to assess the supporting details your essay presents. For example, if your roommate comes home one afternoon and points out that the roof on your apartment leaks, the rent is too high, and the closet space is too small, you may agree but you may also be confused. Does your roommate want you to call the owner, or is this merely a gripe session? How should you respond? On the other hand, if your roommate first announces that he wants the two of you to look for a new place, you can put the discussion of the roof, rent, and closets into its proper context and react accordingly. Similarly, you write an essay to have a specific effect on your readers. You will have a better chance of producing this effect if readers easily and quickly understand what you are trying to do.

Granted, some essays whose position is unmistakably obvious from the outset can get by with a strongly *implied thesis*, and it's true that some essays, often those written by professional writers, are organized to build dramatically to a climax. But if you are an inexperienced writer, the best choice at this point still may be a direct statement of your main idea. It is, after all, your responsibility to make your purpose clear, with as little expense of time and energy on the readers' part as possible. Readers should not be forced to puzzle out your essay's main point—it's your job to tell them.

Remember: an essay is not a detective story, so don't keep your readers in suspense until the last minute. Until you feel comfortable with more sophisticated patterns of organization, plan to put your clearly worded thesis statement near the beginning of your essay.

Avoiding Common Errors in Thesis Statements

Here are five mistakes to avoid when forming your thesis statements:

1. Don't make your thesis merely an announcement of your subject matter or a description of your intentions. State an attitude toward the subject.

Poor	The subject of this essay is my experience with a pet boa constrictor. [This is an announcement of the subject, not a thesis.]
Poor	I'm going to discuss boa constrictors as pets. [This represents a statement of intention but not a thesis.]
Better	Boa constrictors do not make healthy indoor pets. [The writer states an opinion that will be explained and defended in the essay.]
Better	My pet boa constrictor, Sir Pent, was a much better bodyguard than my dog, Fang. [The writer states an opinion that will be explained and illustrated in the essay.]

2. Don't clutter your thesis with such expressions as "in my opinion," "I believe," and "in this essay I'll argue that . . ." These unnecessary phrases weaken your thesis statement because they often make you sound timid or uncertain. This is your essay; therefore, the opinions expressed are obviously yours. Be forceful: speak directly, with conviction.

Poor	My opinion is that the federal government should devote more money to solar energy research.
Poor	My thesis states that the federal government should devote more money to solar energy research.
Better	The federal government should devote more money to solar energy research.
Poor	In this essay I will present lots of reasons why horse racing should be abolished in Texas.
Better	Horse racing should be abolished in Texas.

3. Don't be unreasonable. Making irrational or oversimplified claims will not persuade your reader that you have a thorough understanding of the issue. Don't insult any reader; avoid irresponsible charges, name-calling, and profanity.

Poor	Radical religious fanatics across the nation are trying to impose their right-wing views by censoring high school library books. [Words such as "radical," "fanatics," "right-wing," and "censoring" will antagonize many readers immediately.]
Better	Only local school board members—not religious leaders or parents—should decide which books high school libraries should order.
Poor	Too many corrupt books in our high school libraries selected by liberal, atheistic educators are undermining the morals of our youth. [Again, some readers will be offended.]
Better	To ensure that high school libraries contain books that reflect community standards, parents should have a voice in selecting new titles.

4. Don't merely state a fact. A thesis is an assertion of opinion that leads to discussion. Don't select an idea that is self-evident or dead-ended.

Poor	Child abuse is a terrible problem. [Yes, of course, who wouldn't agree that child abuse is terrible?]
Better	Child-abuse laws in this state are too lenient for repeat offenders. [This thesis will lead to a discussion in which supporting arguments and evidence will be presented.]
Poor	Advertisers often use attractive models in their ads to sell products. [True, but rather obvious. How could this essay be turned into something more than a list describing one ad after another?]
Better	A number of liquor advertisers, well known for using pictures of attractive models to sell their products, are now using special graphics to send subliminal messages to their readers. [This claim is controversial and will require persuasive supporting evidence.]
Better	Although long criticized for its negative portrayal of women in television commercials, the auto industry is just as often guilty of stereotyping men as brainless idiots unable to make a decision. [This thesis makes a point that may lead to an interesting discussion.]

5. Don't express your thesis in the form of a question unless the answer is already obvious to the reader.

Poor	Why should every college student be required to take two years of foreign language?
Better	Chemistry majors should be exempt from the foreign-language requirement.

> REMEMBER: Many times writers "discover" a better thesis near the end of their first draft. That's fine—consider that draft a prewriting or focusing exercise and begin another draft, using the newly discovered thesis as a starting point.

Practicing What You've Learned

A. Identify each of the following thesis statements as adequate or inadequate. If the thesis is weak or insufficient in some way, explain the problem.

1. I think *Schindler's List* is a really interesting movie that everyone should see.

continued on next page

2. Which cars are designed better, Japanese imports or those made in the United States?

3. Some people think that the state lottery is a bad way to raise money for public schools.

4. My essay will tell you how to apply for a college loan with the least amount of trouble.

5. During the fall term, final examinations should be given before Winter Break, not after the holidays as they are now.

6. Raising the cost of tuition will be a terrible burden on the students and won't do anything to improve the quality of education at this school.

7. I can't stand to even look at people who are into body piercing, especially in their face.

8. The passage of the Affordable Healthcare Act will lead to socialized medicine in this country.

9. People over seventy-five should be required to renew their driver's licenses every year.

10. Having a close friend you can talk to is very important.

B. Rewrite the following sentences so that each one is a clear thesis statement. Be prepared to explain why you changed the sentences as you did.

1. Applying for a job can be a negative experience.

2. There are many advantages and disadvantages to the county's new voting machines.

3. Buying baseball tickets online is one big headache.

4. In this paper I will debate the pros and cons of the controversial motorcycle helmet law.

5. We need to do something about the billboard clutter on the main highway into town.

6. The insurance laws in this country need to be rewritten.

7. Bicycle riding is my favorite exercise because it's so good for me.

8. In my opinion, Santa Barbara is a fantastic place.

9. The Civil Rights Movement of the 1960s had a tremendous effect on this country.

10. All my friends like the band Thriving Ivory, and it's too bad they don't play more venues around here.

Assignment

Narrow the subject and write one good thesis sentence for five of the following topics:

1. A political or social issue

2. College or high school

3. Family

4. A hobby or pastime

5. A recent book or movie

6. Vacations

7. An environmental issue

8. A current fad or fashion

9. A job or profession

10. A rule, law, or regulation

Using the Essay Map*

Many thesis sentences will benefit from the addition of an *essay map*, a brief statement in the introductory paragraph introducing the major points to be discussed in the essay. Consider the analogy of beginning a trip by checking your map to see where you are headed. Similarly, an essay map allows the readers to know in advance where you, the writer, will be taking them in the essay.

Let's suppose you have been assigned the task of praising or criticizing some aspect of your campus. You decide that your thesis will be "The Study Skills Center is an excellent place for first-year students to receive help with basic courses." Although your thesis does take a stand ("excellent place"), your reader will not know why the Center is helpful or what points you will cover in your argument. With an essay map added, the reader will have a brief but specific idea where the essay is going and how it will be developed:

Thesis

Essay map
(underlined)

The Study Skills Center is an excellent place for first-year students to receive help with basic courses. <u>The Center's numerous free services, well-trained tutors, and variety of supplementary learning materials can often mean the difference between academic success and failure for many students.</u>

Thanks to the essay map, the reader knows that the essay will discuss the Center's free services, tutors, and learning materials.

---

*I am indebted to Susan Wittig Albert for this useful concept, introduced in *Steps to Structure: An Introduction to Composition and Rhetoric* (Winthrop Publishers, 1975).

Here's another example—this time let's assume you have been frustrated trying to read books your teacher has placed "on reserve" in your campus library, so you have decided to criticize your library's reserve facility:

Thesis	The library's reserve facility is badly managed. <u>Its unpredictable hours, poor staffing, and inadequate space discourage even the most dedicated students.</u>
Essay map (underlined)	

After reading the introductory paragraph, the reader knows the essay will discuss the reserve facility's problematic hours, staff, and space. In other words, the thesis statement defines the main purpose of your essay, and the essay map indicates the route you will take to accomplish that purpose.

The essay map often follows the thesis, but it can also appear before it. It is, in fact, frequently part of the thesis statement itself, as illustrated in the following examples:

Thesis with underlined essay map	<u>Because of its free services, well-trained tutors, and useful learning aids,</u> the Study Skills Center is an excellent place for students seeking academic help.
Thesis with underlined essay map	For those students who need extra help with their basic courses, the Study Skills Center is one of the best resources <u>because of its numerous free services, well-trained tutors, and variety of useful learning aids.</u>
Thesis with underlined essay map	<u>Unreasonable hours, poor staffing, and inadequate space</u> make the library's reserve facility difficult to use.

In addition to suggesting the main points of the essay, the map provides two other benefits. It will provide a set of guidelines for organizing your essay, and it will help keep you from wandering off into areas only vaguely related to your thesis. A clearly written thesis statement and essay map provide a skeletal outline for the sequence of paragraphs in your essay, frequently with one body paragraph devoted to each main point mentioned in your map. (Chapter 3, on paragraphs, will explain in more detail the relationships among the thesis, the map, and the body of your essay.) Note that the number of points in the essay map may vary, although three or four may be the number found most often in 500- to 800-word essays. (◆ More than four main points in a short essay might result in underdeveloped paragraphs; see pages 61–64 for additional information.)

Some important advice: although essay maps can be helpful to both writers and readers, they can also sound too mechanical, repetitive, or obvious. If you choose to use a map, always strive to blend it with your thesis as smoothly as possible.

Poor	The Study Skills Center is a helpful place for three reasons. The reasons are its free services, good tutors, and lots of learning materials.
Better	Numerous free services, well-trained tutors, and a variety of useful learning aids make the Study Skills Center a valuable campus resource.

If you feel your essay map is too obvious or mechanical, try using it only in your rough drafts to help you organize your essay. Once you're sure it isn't necessary to clarify your thesis or to guide your reader, consider dropping it from your final draft.

Practicing What You've Learned

A. Identify the thesis and the essay map in the following sentences by underlining the map.

1. *Citizen Kane* deserves to appear on a list of "Top Movies of All Time" because of its excellent ensemble acting, its fast-paced script, and its innovative editing.

2. Our state should double the existing fines for first-offense drunk drivers. Such a move would lower the number of accidents, cut the costs of insurance, and increase the state revenues for highway maintenance.

3. To guarantee sound construction, lower costs, and personalized design, more people should consider building their own log cabin home.

4. Apartment living is preferable to dorm living because it's cheaper, quieter, and more luxurious.

5. Not everyone can become an astronaut. To qualify, a person must have intelligence, determination, and training.

6. Through unscrupulous uses of propaganda and secret assassination squads, Hitler was able to take control of an economically depressed Germany.

7. Because it builds muscles, increases circulation, and burns harmful fatty tissue, weightlifting is a sport that benefits the entire body.

8. The new tax bill will not radically reform the loophole-riddled revenue system: deductions on secondary residences will remain, real estate tax shelters will be untouched, and nonprofit health organizations will be taxed.

9. Avocados make excellent plants for children. They're inexpensive to buy, easy to root, quick to sprout, and fun to grow.

10. His spirit of protest and clever phrasing blended into unusual musical arrangements have made Bob Dylan a recording giant for more than fifty years.

B. Review the thesis statements you wrote for the Assignment on page 42. Write an essay map for each thesis statement. You may place the map before or after the thesis, or you may make it part of the thesis itself. Identify which part is the thesis and which is the essay map by underlining the map.

C. *Collaborative Activity:* Write a thesis sentence with an essay map for an essay you might write for this or another class. Exchange your work with that of a classmate and, drawing on the advice of this chapter, reconfirm strengths or offer suggestions for revision.

Assignment

Use one of the following quotations to help you think of a subject for an essay of your own. Don't merely repeat the quotation itself as your thesis statement but, rather, allow the quotation to lead you to your subject and a main point of your own creation that is appropriately narrowed and focused. Don't forget to designate an audience for your essay, a group of readers who need or want to hear what you have to say.

1. "Opportunity is missed by most people because it is often dressed in overalls and looks like work."—Thomas Edison, inventor

2. "The world is a book and those who don't travel read only a page." —St. Augustine, cleric

3. "It is never too late to be what one might have been."—George Eliot (Mary Ann Evans), writer

4. "Sports do not build character. They reveal it."—Heywood Hale Broun, sportscaster

5. "Noncooperation with evil is as much a moral obligation as is cooperation with good."— Martin Luther King, Jr., statesman and civil-rights activist

6. "When a thing is funny, search it carefully for a hidden truth."—George Bernard Shaw, writer

Jackie Robinson, who with exemplary courage ended segregation of American pro-baseball, steals home plate during the 1955 World Series.

7. "I am a great believer in luck, and I find the harder I work the more I have of it."—Stephen Leacock, economist and humorist

8. "It is never too late to give up your prejudices."—Henry Thoreau, writer and naturalist

9. "When an old person dies, a library burns to the ground."—African proverb

10. "No person is your friend who demands your silence or denies your right to grow" –Alice Walker, writer

11. "Education is the most powerful weapon. You can use it to change the world." —Nelson Mandela, anti-apartheid activist and former president of South Africa

continued on next page

12. "The journey is the reward."—Taoist proverb

13. "You can discover more about a person in an hour of play than in a year of conversation."—Plato, philosopher

14. "Nobody can make you feel inferior without your consent."—Eleanor Roosevelt, stateswoman

15. "Never doubt that a small group of thoughtful, committed people can change the world. Indeed, it is the only thing that ever has."—Margaret Mead, anthropologist

16. "If you are patient in one moment of anger, you will escape a hundred days of sorrow."—Chinese proverb

17. "I took the [road] less traveled by, and that has made all the difference."—from "The Road Not Taken" by Robert Frost, poet (◆ For the complete poem, see page 516.)

Early Snow, ca. 1827, by Caspar David Friedrich

bpk, Berlin/Hamburger Kunsthalle/Art Resource, NY

continued on next page

18. "Let your hook be always cast; in the pool where you least expect it, there will be a fish."—Ovid, Roman poet

19. "Even if you are on the right track, you will get run over if you just sit there."—Will Rogers, humorist and writer

20. "No matter what accomplishments you make, somebody helps you." —Althea Gibson, tennis champion

21. "Only when the well runs dry do we learn the wealth of water." —Benjamin Franklin, statesman

22. "Pearls lie not on the seashore. If thou desirest one, thou must dive for it." —Chinese proverb

Chapter 2 Summary

Here's a brief review of what you need to know about the thesis statement:

1. A thesis statement declares the main point of your essay; it tells the reader what clearly defined opinion you hold.

2. Everything in your essay should support your thesis statement.

3. A good thesis statement asserts one main idea, is narrowed to fit the assignment, and is stated in clear, specific terms.

4. A good thesis statement makes a reasonable claim about a topic that is of interest to its readers as well as to its writer.

5. The thesis statement is often presented near the beginning of the essay, frequently in the first or second paragraph, or is so strongly implied that readers cannot miss the writer's main point.

6. A "working" or trial thesis is an excellent organizing tool to use as you begin drafting because it can help you decide which ideas to include.

7. Because writing is an act of discovery, you may write yourself into a better thesis statement by the end of your first draft. Don't hesitate to begin a new draft with the new thesis statement.

8. Some writers may profit from using an essay map, a brief statement accompanying the thesis that introduces the supporting points discussed in the body of the essay.

The Body Paragraphs

The middle—or *body*—of your essay is composed of paragraphs that support the thesis statement. By citing examples, explaining causes, offering reasons, or using other strategies in these paragraphs, you supply enough specific evidence to persuade your reader that the opinion expressed in your thesis is a sensible one. Each paragraph in the body usually presents and develops one main point in the discussion of your thesis. Generally, but not always, a new body paragraph signals another major point in the discussion. Figure 3.1 highlights some of the guidelines for developing effective body paragraphs discussed in this chapter.

Planning the Body of Your Essay

Many writers like to have a plan before they begin drafting the body of their essay. To help you create a plan, first look at your thesis. If you used an essay map, as suggested in Chapter 2, you may find that the points mentioned there will provide the basis for the body paragraphs of your essay. For example, recall from Chapter 2 a thesis and essay map praising the Study Skills Center: "Because of its free services, well-trained tutors, and useful learning aids, the Study Skills Center is an excellent place for students seeking academic help." Your plan for developing the body of your essay might look like this:

Body paragraph one: discussion of free services

Body paragraph two: discussion of tutors

Body paragraph three: discussion of learning aids

At this point in your writing process you may wish to sketch in some of the supporting evidence you will include in each paragraph. You might find it helpful to go back to your prewriting activities (listing, looping, freewriting, mapping, cubing, and so on) to see

Figure 3.1 VISUALIZING THE PROCESS: BODY PARAGRAPHS

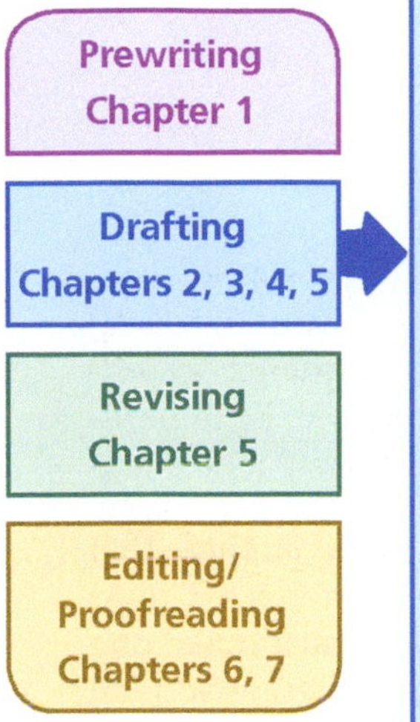

Prewriting
Chapter 1

Drafting
Chapters 2, 3, 4, 5

Revising
Chapter 5

Editing/
Proofreading
Chapters 6, 7

The body of your essay is composed of paragraphs that support your thesis statement. If you used an essay map, then the body paragraphs often correspond to the main points outlined in the essay map.

The Topic Sentence...

1. Supports the thesis by clearly stating a main point in the discussion.
2. Announces what the paragraph will be about.
3. Controls the subject matter of the paragraph.

Specific Supporting Evidence Ensures Effective Paragraph Development

1. The information in each paragraph must adequately support your topic sentence.
2. Paragraphs that lack adequate support are underdeveloped, a common mistake of novice writers.
3. Support, or evidence, can come from personal experiences, observations, facts, statistics, etc.
4. Vague generalities or repetitious ideas are not convincing.

Four means to achieving paragraph unity

1. Make sure every sentence in the paragraph relates to the topic sentence's main idea.
2. Avoid topic drift.
3. Beware the tendency to end your paragraph with a new idea.
4. The supporting sentences should support the topic sentence; the paragraphs support the thesis statement.

Five means to achieving paragraph coherence

1. A natural or easily recognized order (chronological, spatial, deductive, inductive)
2. Transitional words and phrases
3. Repetition of key words
4. Substitution of pronouns for key nouns
5. Parallelism

© Cengage Learning 2017

what ideas surfaced then. Adding some examples and supporting details might make an informal outline of the Study Skills paper appear like this:

I. Free services
   A. Minicourse on improving study skills
   B. Tutoring ⟨ composition
                 math
   C. Weekly seminars ⟨ stress management
                        test anxiety
                        building vocabulary
   D. Testing for learning disabilities
II. Tutors
   A. Top graduate students in their fields
   B. Experienced teachers
   C. Some bilingual
   D. Have taken training course at Center
III. Learning aids
   A. Supplementary texts
   B. Workbooks
   C. Audiovisual aids

Notice that this plan is an *informal* or *working outline* rather than a *formal outline*—that is, it doesn't have strictly parallel parts nor is it expressed in complete sentences. Unless your teacher requests a formal sentence or topic outline, don't feel you must make one at this early stage. Just consider using the informal outline to plot out a tentative plan that will help you start your first draft.

Here's an example of an informal outline at work: let's suppose you have been asked to write about your most prized possession, and you've chosen your 1966 Mustang, a car you have restored. You already have some ideas, but as yet they're scattered and too few to make an interesting, well-developed essay. You try an informal outline, jotting down your ideas thus far:

   I. Car is special because it was a gift from Dad
   II. Fun to drive
   III. Looks great—new paint job
   IV. Engine in top condition
   V. Custom features
   VI. Car shows—fun to be part of

After looking at your outline, you see that some of your categories overlap and could be part of the same discussion. For example, your thoughts about the engine are actually part of the discussion of "fun to drive," and "custom features" are what make the car look great. Moreover, the outline may help you discover

© Bettmann/Corbis

new ideas. For example, custom features could be divided into those on the interior as well as those on the exterior of the car. The revised outline might look like this:

I. Gift from Dad
II. Fun to drive
    A. Engine
    B. Steering
III. Looks great
    A. New paint job
    B. Custom features
        1. exterior
        2. interior
IV. Car shows

You could continue playing with this outline, even moving big chunks of it around; for example, you might decide that what really makes the car so special is that it was a graduation gift from your dad and that is the note you want to end on. So you move "I. Gift from Dad" down to the last position in your outline.

The important point to remember about an informal or working outline is that it is there to help you—not control you. The value of an outline is its ability to help you plan, to help you see logical connections between your ideas, and to help you see obvious places to add new ideas and details. (The informal outline is also handy to keep around in case you're interrupted for a long period while you're drafting; you can always check the outline to see where you were and where you were going when you stopped.) In other words, *don't be intimidated by the outline!*

Here's one more example of an informal outline, this time for the thesis and essay map on the library reserve facility, from Chapter 2:

Thesis–Essay Map: Unpredictable hours, poor staffing, and inadequate space make the library's reserve facility difficult for students to use.

I. Unpredictable hours
    A. Hours of operation vary from week to week
    B. Unannounced closures
    C. Closed on some holidays, open on others
II. Poor staffing
    A. Uninformed personnel at reserve desk
    B. Too few on duty at peak times
III. Inadequate space
    A. Room too small for number of users
    B. Too few chairs, tables
    C. Weak lighting

You may have more than three points to make in your essay. And, on occasion, you may need more than one paragraph to discuss a single point. For instance, you might discover that you need two paragraphs to explain fully the many services at the Study Skills Center. (◆ For advice on splitting the discussion of a single point into two or more paragraphs, see page 64.) At this stage, you needn't bother trying to guess whether you'll need more than one paragraph per point; just use the outline to get going. Most writers don't know how much they have to say before they begin writing—and that's fine because *writing itself is an act of discovery and learning.*

When you are ready to begin drafting, read Chapter 5 for advice on composing and revising. ◆ Remember, too, that Chapter 5 contains suggestions for beating Writer's Block, should this condition arise while you are working on any part of your essay, as well as some specific hints on formatting your draft that may make revision easier.

Composing the Body Paragraphs

There are many ways to organize and develop body paragraphs. Paragraphs developed by common patterns, such as example, comparison, and definition, will be discussed in Part Two; at this point, however, here are some comments about the general nature of all good body paragraphs that should help as you draft your essay.

> REMEMBER: Most of the body paragraphs in your essay will profit from a focused *topic sentence*. In addition, body paragraphs should have adequate *development*, *unity*, and *coherence*.

The Topic Sentence

Most body paragraphs present one main point in your discussion, expressed in a *topic sentence*. The topic sentence of a body paragraph has three important functions:

1. It supports the thesis by clearly stating a main point in the discussion.
2. It announces what the paragraph will be about.
3. It controls the subject matter of the paragraph. The entire discussion—the examples, details, and explanations—in a particular paragraph must directly relate to and support the topic sentence.

Think of a body paragraph (or a single paragraph) as a kind of mini-essay in itself. The topic sentence is, in a sense, a smaller thesis. It too asserts one main idea on a limited subject that the writer can explain or argue in the rest of the paragraph. Like the thesis, the topic sentence should be stated in as specific language as possible.

To see how a topic sentence works in a body paragraph, study this sample:

Essay Thesis: The Study Skills Center is an excellent place for students who need academic help.

Topic Sentence
1. The topic sentence supports the thesis by stating a main point (one reason the Center provides excellent academic help).

The Center offers students a variety of free services designed to improve basic skills. Those who discover their study habits are poor, for instance, may enroll in a six-week minicourse in study skills that offers advice on such topics as how to read a text, take notes, and organize material for review. Students whose math or writing skills are below par can sign up for free tutoring sessions held five days a week throughout each semester. In addition, the Center presents weekly seminars on special topics such as stress management and overcoming test anxiety

2. The topic sentence announces the subject of the paragraph (a variety of free services that improve basic skills).

for those students who are finding college more of a nerve-wracking experience than they expected; other students can attend evening seminars in such worthwhile endeavors as vocabulary building or spelling tips. Finally, the Center offers a series of tests to identify the presence of any learning disabilities, such as dyslexia, that might prevent a student from succeeding academically. With such a variety of free services, the Center can help almost any student.

3. The topic sentence controls the subject matter (all the examples—the minicourse, the tutoring, the seminars, and the testing—support the claim of the topic sentence).

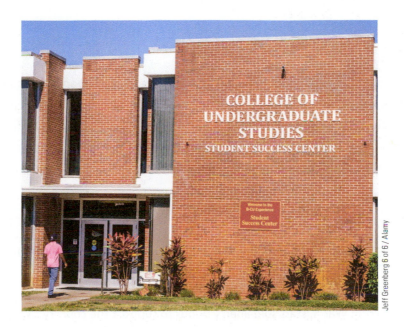

Jeff Greenberg 6 of 6 / Alamy

Here's another example from the essay on the library reserve facility:

Essay Thesis: The library's reserve facility is difficult for students to use.

Topic Sentence
1. The topic sentence supports the thesis by stating a main point (one reason the facility is difficult to use).

2. The topic sentence announces the subject of the paragraph (the unpredictable hours).

The library reserve facility's unpredictable hours frustrate even the most dedicated students. Instructors who place articles or books on reserve usually ask students to read them by a certain date. Too often, however, students arrive at the reserve desk only to find it closed. The facility's open hours change from week to week: students who used the room last week on Tuesday morning may discover that this week on Tuesday the desk is closed, which means another trip. Perhaps even more frustrating are the facility's sudden, unannounced closures. Some of these closures allow staff members to have lunch or go on breaks, but, again, they occur without notice on no regular schedule. A student arrives, as I did two weeks ago, at the desk to find a "Be Back Soon" sign. In my case, I waited for nearly an hour. Another headache is the holiday schedule, which is difficult to figure out. For example, this year the reserve room was closed without advance notice on Presidents' Day but open on Easter; open during Winter Break but closed some days during Spring Break, a time many students use to catch up on their reserve assignments. Overall, the reserve facility would be much easier for students to use if it adopted a set schedule of operating hours, announced these times each semester, and maintained them.

3. The topic sentence controls the subject matter (all examples—the changing hours, the sudden closures, the erratic holiday schedule—support the claim of the topic sentence)

Always be sure your topic sentences actually support the particular thesis of your essay. For example, the second topic sentence presented here doesn't belong in the essay promised by the thesis:

Thesis: Elk hunting should be permitted because it financially aids people in our state.

Topic Sentences

1. Fees for hunting licenses help pay for certain free, state-supported social services.

2. Hunting helps keep the elk population under control.

3. Elk hunting offers a means of obtaining free food for people with low incomes.

Although topic sentence 2 is about elk and may be true, it doesn't support the thesis's emphasis on financial aid and therefore should be revised or tossed out of this essay.

Here's another example:

Thesis: During the past seventy-five years, movie stars have often tried to change the direction of America's politics.

Topic Sentences

1. During World War II, stars sold liberty bonds to support the country's war effort.

2. Many stars refused to cooperate with the blacklisting of their colleagues during the McCarthy Era in the 1950s.

3. Some stars were actively involved in protests against the Vietnam War.

4. More recently, stars have appeared in Congress criticizing the lack of legislative help for struggling farmers.

Topic sentences 2, 3, and 4 all show how stars have tried to effect a change. But topic sentence 1 says only that stars sold bonds to support, not *change*, the political direction of the nation. Although it does show stars involved in politics, it doesn't illustrate the claim of this particular thesis.

Sometimes a topic sentence needs only to be rewritten or slightly recast to fit:

Thesis: The recent tuition hike may discourage students from attending our college.

Topic Sentences

1. Students already pay more here than at other in-state schools.

2. Out-of-state students will have to pay an additional "penalty" to attend.

3. Tuition funds should be used for scholarships.

As written, topic sentence 3 doesn't show why students won't want to attend the school. However, a rewritten topic sentence does support the thesis:

3. Because the tuition money will not be used for scholarships, some students may not be able to afford this higher-priced school.

In other words, always check carefully to make sure that *all* your topic sentences clearly support your thesis's assertion.

Focusing Your Topic Sentence

A vague, fuzzy, or unfocused topic sentence most often leads to a paragraph that touches only on the surface of its subject or that wanders away from the writer's main idea. On the other hand, a topic sentence that is tightly focused and stated precisely will not only help the reader to understand the point of the paragraph but will also help you select, organize, and develop your supporting details.

Look, for example, at these unfocused topic sentences and their revisions:

Unfocused	Too many people treat animals badly in experiments. [What people? Badly how? What kinds of experiments?]
Focused	The cosmetic industry often harms animals in unnecessary experiments designed to test products.
Unfocused	Grades are an unfair pain in the neck. [Again, the focus is too broad. All grades? Unfair how?]
Focused	A course grade based on two multiple-choice exams doesn't accurately measure a student's knowledge of the subject.
Unfocused	Finding the right job is important and can lead to rewarding experiences. [Note both vague language and a double focus: "important" and "can lead to rewarding experiences."]
Focused	Finding the right job can lead to an improved sense of self-esteem.

◆ Before you practice writing focused topic sentences, you may wish to review pages 33–40, the advice on composing good thesis statements, as the same rules generally apply.

Placing Your Topic Sentence

Although the topic sentence most frequently occurs as the first sentence in the body paragraph, it also often appears as the second or last sentence. A topic sentence that directly follows the first sentence of a paragraph usually does so because the first sentence provides an introductory statement or some kind of "hook" to the preceding paragraph. A topic sentence frequently appears at the end of a paragraph that first presents particular details and then concludes with its central point. Here are two paragraphs in which the topic sentences do not appear first:

Introductory sentence

Topic sentence

Millions of Americans have watched the elaborate Rose Bowl Parade televised nationally each January from Pasadena, California. *Less well known, but growing in popularity, is Pasadena's Doo Dah Parade, an annual parody of the Rose Bowl spectacle, which specializes in wild-and-crazy participants.* Take this year's Doo Dah Precision Drill Team, for instance. Instead of marching in unison, the members cavorted down the avenue displaying—what else—a variety of precision electric drills. In heated competition with this group was the Synchronized Briefcase Drill Team, whose members wore gray pinstripe suits and performed a series of tunes by tapping on their briefcases. Another crowd-pleasing entry was the Citizens for the Right to Bare Arms, whose members sang while carrying aloft unclothed mannequin arms. The zany procession, led this year as always by the All-Time Doo Dah Parade Band, attracted more than 150,000 fans and is already preparing for its next celebration.

In the preceding paragraph, the first sentence serves as an introduction leading directly to the topic sentence. In the following example, the writer places the topic sentence last to sum up the information in the paragraph:

Topic sentence

Rumors certainly fly around Washington's Capitol Building—but ghosts, too? According to legend, the building was cursed in 1808 by construction superintendent John Lenthall, who was crushed by a falling ceiling following a feud with his architect over the wisdom of ceiling braces. Some workers in the building swear they have heard both the ghostly footsteps of James Garfield, who was assassinated after only four months as president, and the spooky last murmurings of John Quincy Adams, who died mid-speech on the House floor. Others claim to have seen a demon cat, so large and terrifying that it caused a guard to suffer a fatal heart attack. Perhaps the most cheerful ghosts appear on the night of a new president's swearing-in ceremony when the statues in Statuary Hall are said to leave their pedestals and dance at their own Inaugural Ball. *Whether these stories are true or merely the products of rich imaginations, the U.S. Capitol Building boasts the reputation as one of the most haunted buildings in America.*

As you can see, the position of topic sentences largely depends on what you are trying to do in your paragraph. And it's true that the purposes of some paragraphs are so obvious that no topic sentences are needed. However, if you are a beginning writer, you may want to practice putting your topic sentences first for a while to help you organize and unify your paragraphs.

Some paragraphs with a topic sentence near the beginning also contain a concluding sentence that makes a final general comment based on the supporting details. The last sentence of the following paragraph, for example, reemphasizes the main point.

Topic sentence   *Of all nature's catastrophes, tornadoes may cause the most bizarre destruction.* Whirling out of the sky at speeds up to 300 miles per hour, tornadoes have been known to drive broom handles through brick walls and straws into tree trunks. In one extreme case, a Kansas farmer reported that his prize rooster had been sucked into a two-gallon distilled-water bottle. More commonly, tornadoes lift autos and deposit them in fields miles away or uproot trees and drop them on lawns in neighboring towns. One tornado knocked down every wall in a house

Concluding
sentence
but one—luckily, the very wall shielding the terrified family. *Whenever a tornado touches the earth, spectacular headlines are sure to follow.*

Warning: Although topic sentences may appear in different places in a paragraph, there is one common error you should be careful to avoid. Do *not* put a topic sentence at the end of one body paragraph that belongs to the paragraph that follows it. For example, let's suppose you are writing an essay discussing a job you held recently, one that you enjoyed because of the responsibilities you were given, the training program you participated in, and the interaction you experienced with your coworkers. The body paragraph describing your responsibilities may end with its own topic sentence or with a concluding sentence about those responsibilities. However, that paragraph should not end with a sentence such as, "Another excellent feature of this job was the training program for the next level of management." This "training program" sentence belongs in the *following* body paragraph as its topic sentence. Similarly, you would not end the paragraph on the training program with a topic sentence praising your experience with your coworkers.

If you feel that your paragraphs are ending too abruptly, consider using a concluding sentence, as described previously. Later in this chapter you will also learn some ways to smooth the flow from one paragraph to the next by using transitional devices and "idea hooks" (page 86). For now, remember: Do *not* place a topic sentence that introduces and controls paragraph "B" at the end of paragraph "A." In other words, always place your topic sentence in the paragraph to which it belongs, to which it is topic-related, not at the end of the preceding paragraph.

Practicing What You've Learned

A. Point out the topic sentences in the following paragraphs; identify those paragraphs that also contain concluding sentences. Cross out any stray topic sentences that belong elsewhere.

1.   Denim is one of America's most widely used fabrics. It was first introduced during Columbus's voyage, when the sails of the *Santa Maria* were made of the strong cloth. During our pioneer days, denim was used for tents, covered wagons, and the now-famous blue jeans. Cowboys found denim an ideal fabric for protection against sagebrush, cactus, and saddle sores. World War II also gave denim a boost in popularity when sailors were issued jeans as part of their dress code. Today, denim continues to be in demand as more and more casual clothes are

continued on next page

cut from the economical cloth. Because of its low cost and durability, manufacturers feel that denim will continue as one of America's most useful fabrics.

2.   Adlai Stevenson, American statesman and twice an unsuccessful presidential candidate against Eisenhower, was well known for his intelligence and wit. Once on the campaign trail, after he had spoken eloquently and at length about several complex ideas, a woman in the audience was moved to stand and cheer, "That's great! Every thinking person in America will vote for you!" Stevenson immediately retorted, "That's not enough. I need a majority!" Frequently a reluctant candidate but never at a loss for words, Stevenson once defined a politician as a person who "approaches every question with an open mouth." Stevenson was also admired for his work as the Governor of Illinois and, later, as Ambassador to the United Nations.

3.   Almost every wedding tradition has a symbolic meaning that originated centuries ago. For example, couples have been exchanging rings to symbolize unending love for over a thousand years. Most often, the rings are worn on the third finger of the left hand, which was thought to contain a vein that ran directly to the heart. The rings in ancient times were sometimes made of braided grass, rope, or leather, giving rise to the expression "tying the knot." Another tradition, the bridal veil, began when marriages were arranged by the families and the groom was not allowed to see his bride until the wedding. The tossing of rice at newlyweds has long signified fertility blessings, and the sweet smell of the bride's bouquet was intended to drive away evil spirits, who were also diverted by the surrounding bridal attendants. Weddings may vary enormously today, but many couples still include ancient traditions to signify their new life together.

4.   You always think of the right answer five minutes after you hand in the test. You always hit the red light when you're already late for class. The one time you skip class is the day of the pop quiz. Back-to-back classes are always held in buildings at opposite ends of campus. The one course you need to graduate will not be offered your last semester. If any of these sound familiar, you've obviously been a victim of the "Murphy's Laws" that govern student life.

5.   Want to win a sure bet? Then wager that your friends can't guess the most widely sold musical instrument in America today. Chances are they won't get the answer right—not even on the third try. In actuality, the most popular instrument in the country is neither the guitar nor the trumpet but the lowly kazoo. Last year alone, some three and one-half million kazoos were sold to music lovers of all ages. Part of the instrument's popularity arises from its availability, since kazoos are sold in variety stores and music centers nearly everywhere; another reason is its inexpensiveness—it ranges from the standard thirty-nine-cent model to the five-dollar gold-plated special. But perhaps the main reason for the kazoo's popularity is the ease with which it can be played by almost anyone—as can testify the members of the entire Swarthmore College marching band, who have now added a marching kazoo number to their repertoire. Louis Armstrong, move over!

6.   It's a familiar scenario: Dad won't stop the car to ask directions, despite the fact that he's been hopelessly lost for over forty-five minutes. Mom keeps

continued on next page

nagging Dad to slow down and finally blows up because your little sister suddenly remembers she's left her favorite doll, the one she can't sleep without, at the rest stop you left over an hour ago. Your legs are sweat-glued to the vinyl seats, you need desperately to go to the bathroom, and your big brother has just kindly acknowledged that he will relieve you of your front teeth if you allow any part of your body to extend over the imaginary line he has drawn down the backseat. The wonderful tradition known as the "family vacation" has begun.

B. Rewrite these topic sentences so that they are clear and focused rather than fuzzy or too broad.

1. My personality has changed a lot in the last year.

2. His date turned out to be really great.

3. The movie's special effects were incredible.

4. The Memorial Day celebration was more fun than ever before.

5. The evening with her parents was an unforgettable experience.

C. Add topic sentences to the following paragraphs:

1. Famous inventor Thomas Edison, for instance, did so poorly in his first years of school that his teachers warned his parents that he'd never be a success at anything. Henry Ford, the father of the auto industry, also had trouble in school with both reading and writing. But perhaps the best example is Albert Einstein, whose parents and teachers suspected that he was mentally disabled because he responded to questions so slowly and in a stuttering voice. Einstein's high school record was poor in everything but math, and he failed his college entrance exams the first time. Even out of school the man had trouble holding a job—until he announced the theory of relativity.

2. A 1950s felt skirt with Elvis's picture on it, for example, now sells for $150, and Elvis scarves go for as much as $300. Elvis handkerchiefs, originally 50 cents or less, fetch $150 in today's market; 1956 wallets imprinted with the singer's face have sold for over $400 each. Original posters from the Rock King's movies can sell for $750, and cards from the chewing gum series can run $30 apiece. Perhaps one of the most expensive collectors' items is the Emenee Elvis toy guitar that can cost a fan up to $1,000, regardless of musical condition.

3. When successful playwright Jean Kerr once checked into a hospital, the receptionist asked her occupation and was told, "Writer." The receptionist said, "I'll just put down 'housewife.'" Similarly, when a British official asked W. H. Auden, the award-winning poet and essayist, what he did for a living, Auden replied, "I'm a writer." The official jotted down "no occupation."

4. Cumberland College, for example, set the record back in 1916 for the biggest loss in college ball, having allowed Georgia Tech to run up 63 points in the first quarter and ultimately succumbing to them with a final score of 222 to nothing. In pro ball, the Washington Redskins are the biggest losers, going down in defeat 73 to 0 to the Chicago Bears in 1940. The award for the longest losing

continued on next page

streak, however, goes to Northwestern University's team, who by 1981 had managed to lose 29 consecutive games. During that year, morale was so low that one disgruntled fan passing a local highway sign that read "Interstate 94" couldn't resist adding "Northwestern 0."

D. Write a focused topic sentence for five of the following subjects:

1. Job interviews

2. Friends

3. Food

4. Money

5. Selecting a major or occupation

6. Clothes

7. Music

8. Dreams

9. Housing

10. Childhood

Assignment

Review the thesis statements with essay maps you wrote for the Practice "B" exercise on page 44. Choose two, and from each thesis create at least three topic sentences for possible body paragraphs.

Applying What You've Learned to *Your* Writing

If you currently have a working thesis statement that you have written in response to an assignment in your composition class, try sketching out an outline or a plan for the major ideas you wish to include. After you write a draft, underline the topic sentences in your body paragraphs. Do your topic sentences directly support your thesis? If you find that they do not clearly support your thesis, you must decide if you need to revise your draft's organization or whether you have, in fact, discovered a new, and possibly better, subject to write about. If the latter is true, you'll need to redraft your essay so that your readers will not be confused by a paper that announces one subject but discusses another. (◆ See Chapter 5 for more information on revising your drafts.)

Paragraph Development

Possibly the most serious—and most common—weakness of all essays by novice writers is the lack of effectively developed body paragraphs. The information in each paragraph must adequately explain, exemplify, define, or in some other way support your topic sentence. Therefore, you must include enough supporting information or evidence in each paragraph to make your readers understand your topic sentence. Moreover, you must make the information in the paragraph clear and specific enough for the readers to accept your ideas.

The next paragraph is *underdeveloped*. Although the topic sentence promises a discussion of Jesse James as a Robin Hood figure, the paragraph does not provide enough specific supporting evidence (in this case, examples) to explain this unusual view of the gunfighter.

> Although he was an outlaw, Jesse James was considered a Robin Hood figure in my hometown in Missouri. He used to be generous to the poor, and he did many good deeds, not just robberies. In my hometown, people still talk about how lots of the things James did weren't all bad.

Rewritten, the paragraph might read as follows:

> Although he was an outlaw, Jesse James was considered a Robin Hood figure in my hometown in Missouri. Jesse and his gang chose my hometown as a hiding place, and they set out immediately to make friends with the local people. Every Christmas for four years, the legend goes, he dumped bags of toys on the doorsteps of poor children. The parents knew the toys had been bought with money stolen from richer people, but they were grateful anyway. On three occasions, Jesse gave groceries to the dozen neediest families—he seemed to know when times were toughest—and once he supposedly held up a stage to pay for an old man's operation. In my hometown, some people still sing the praises of Jesse James, the outlaw who wasn't all bad.

The topic sentence promises a discussion of James's generosity and delivers just that by citing specific examples of his gifts to children, the poor, and the sick. The paragraph is therefore better developed.

The following paragraph offers reasons but no specific examples or details to support its claims:

> Living with my ex-roommate was unbearable. First, she thought everything she owned was the best. Second, she possessed numerous filthy habits. Finally, she constantly exhibited immature behavior.

The writer might provide more evidence this way:

> Living with my ex-roommate was unbearable. First, she thought everything she owned, from clothes to cosmetics, was the best. If someone complimented my pants, she'd point out that her designer jeans looked better and would last longer because they were made of better material. If she borrowed my shampoo, she'd let me know that it didn't get her hair as clean and shiny as hers did. My hand cream wasn't as

smooth; my suntan lotion wasn't as protective; not even my wire clothes hangers were as good as her padded ones! But despite her pickiness about products, she had numerous filthy habits. Her dirty dishes remained in the sink for days before she felt the need to wash them. Piles of the "best" brand of tissues were regularly discarded from her upper bunk and strewn about the floor. Her desk and closets overflowed with heaps of dirty clothes, books, cosmetics, and whatever else she owned, and she rarely brushed her teeth (when she did brush, she left oozes of toothpaste in the sink). Finally, she constantly acted immaturely by throwing tantrums when things didn't go her way. A poor grade on an exam or paper, for example, meant books, shoes, or any other small object within her reach would hit the wall flying. Living with such a person taught me some valuable lessons about how not to win friends or keep roommates.

By adding more supporting evidence—specific examples and details—to this paragraph, the writer has a better chance of convincing the reader of the roommate's real character.

Where does evidence come from? Where do writers find their supporting information? Evidence comes from many sources. Personal experiences, memories, observations, hypothetical examples, reasoned arguments, facts, statistics, testimony from authorities, many kinds of studies, and research—all these and more can help you make your points clear and persuasive. In the paragraph on Jesse James, for example, the writer relied on stories and memories from his hometown. The paragraph on the obnoxious roommate was supported by examples gained through the writer's personal observation. The kind of supporting evidence you choose for your paragraphs depends on your purpose and your audience; as the writer, you must decide what will work best to make your readers understand and accept each important point in your discussion. (◆ For advice on ways to think critically about evidence, see Chapter 5; for more information on incorporating research material into your essays, see Chapter 19.)

Having a well-developed paragraph is more than a matter of adding material or expanding length, however. The information in each paragraph must effectively explain or support your topic sentence. *Vague generalities or repetitious ideas are not convincing.* Look, for example, at the following paragraph, in which the writer offers only generalities:

We ought to ban the use of cell phones in moving vehicles. Some people who have them think that's a really good idea, but a lot of us don't agree. Using a phone while driving causes too many dangerous accidents to happen, and even if there's no terrible accident, people using them have been known to do some really stupid things in traffic. Drivers using phones are constantly causing problems for other drivers; pedestrians are in big trouble from these people, too. I think this is getting to be a really dangerous situation, and we ought to do something about it soon.

This paragraph is weak because it is composed of repetitious general statements using vague, unclear language. None of its general statements is supported with specific evidence. Why is phone use when driving not a "good" idea? How can it cause accidents? What are the "problems" and "trouble" the writer refers to? What exactly does "do something about it" mean? The writer obviously had some ideas in mind, but these ideas are not clear to the reader because they are not adequately developed with specific evidence and language.

By adding supporting examples and details, the writer might revise the paragraph this way:

> Although cell phones are a time-saving convenience for busy people, they are too distracting for use by drivers of moving vehicles, whose lack of full attention poses a serious threat to other drivers and to pedestrians. The simple act of answering a phone, for example, may take a driver's eyes away from traffic signals or other cars. Moreover, involvement in a complex or emotional conversation could slow down a driver's response time just when fast action is needed to avoid an accident. Last week, I drove behind a man using his phone. As he drove and talked, I could see him gesturing wildly, obviously agitated with the other caller. His speed repeatedly slowed and then picked up, slowed and increased, and his car drifted more than once on a street frequently crossed by schoolchildren. Because the man was clearly not in full, conscious control of his driving, he was dangerous. My experience is not isolated: a recent study by the Foundation for Traffic Safety maintains that using a cell phone is more distracting to drivers than listening to the radio or talking to a rider. With additional studies in progress, voters in our state should soon demand legislation to restrict phone use to passengers or to drivers when the vehicles are not in motion.

The reader now has a better idea why the writer feels such cell phone use is distracting and, consequently, dangerous. By using two hypothetical examples (looking away, slowed response time), one personal experience (observing the agitated man), and one reference to research (the safety study), the writer offers the reader three kinds of supporting evidence for the paragraph's claim.

After examining the following two paragraphs, decide which explains its point more effectively.

1. Competing in an Ironman triathlon is one of the most demanding feats known to amateur athletes. First, they have to swim many miles, and that takes a lot of endurance. Then, they ride a bicycle a long way, which is also hard on their bodies. Last, they run a marathon, which can be difficult in itself but is especially hard after the first two events. Competing in the triathlon is really tough on the participants.

2. Competing in an Ironman triathlon is one of the most demanding feats known to amateur athletes. During the first stage of the triathlon, the competitors must swim 2.4 miles in the open ocean. They have to battle the constantly choppy ocean, the strong currents, and the frequent swells. The wind is often an adversary, and stinging jellyfish are a constant threat. Once they have completed the ocean swim, the triathletes must ride 112 miles on a bicycle. In addition to the strength needed to pedal that far, the bicyclists must use a variety of hand grips to ensure the continued circulation in their fingers and hands as well as to ease the strain on the neck and shoulder muscles. Moreover, the concentration necessary to steady the bicycle, as well as the attention to the inclines on the course and the consequent shifting of gears, causes mental fatigue for the athletes. After completing these two grueling segments, the triathletes must then run 26.2 miles, the length of a regular marathon. Dehydration is a constant concern, as is the prospect

of cramping. Even the pain and swelling of a friction blister can be enough to eliminate a contestant at this late stage of the event. Finally, disorientation and fatigue can set in and distort the athlete's judgment. Competing in an Ironman triathlon takes incredible physical and mental endurance.

The first paragraph contains, for the most part, repetitious generalities; it repeats the same idea (the triathlon is hard work) and gives few specific details to illustrate the point presented in the topic sentence. The second paragraph, however, does offer many specific examples and details—the exact mileage figures, the currents, jellyfish, inclines, grips, blisters, and so forth—that help the reader understand why the event is so demanding.

Joseph Conrad, the famous novelist, once remarked that a writer's purpose was to use "the power of the written word to make you hear, to make you feel . . . before all, to make you *see*. That—and no more, and it is everything." By using specific details instead of vague, general statements, you can write an interesting, convincing essay. Ask yourself as you revise your paragraphs, "Have I provided enough information, presented enough clear, precise details to make my readers see what I want them to?" In other words, a well-developed paragraph effectively makes its point with *an appropriate amount of specific supporting evidence.* (Remember that a paragraph in a handwritten rough draft will look much shorter when it is typed. Therefore, if you can't think of much to say about a particular idea, you should gather more information or consider dropping it as a major point in your essay.)

Paragraph Length

"How long is a good paragraph?" is a question novice writers often ask. Like a teacher's lecture or a preacher's sermon, paragraphs should be long enough to accomplish their purpose and short enough to be interesting. In truth, there is no set length, no prescribed number of lines or sentences, for any of your paragraphs. In a body paragraph, your topic sentence presents the main point, and the rest of the paragraph must give enough supporting evidence to convince the reader. Although unnecessary or repetitious detail is boring, too little discussion will leave the reader uninformed, unconvinced, or confused.

Although paragraph length varies, beginning writers should avoid the one- or two-sentence paragraphs frequently seen in newspapers or magazine articles. (Journalists have their own rules to follow; paragraphs are shorter in newspapers, for one reason, because large masses of print in narrow columns are difficult to read quickly.) Essay writers do occasionally use the one-sentence paragraph, most often to produce some special effect, when the statement is especially dramatic or significant and needs to call attention to itself or when an emphatic transition is needed. For now, however, you should concentrate on writing well-developed body paragraphs.

One more note on paragraph length: sometimes you may discover that a particular point in your essay is so complex that your paragraph is growing far too long—nearly a page, for instance. If this problem occurs, look for a logical place to divide your information and start a new paragraph. For example, you might see a convenient dividing point in a series of actions you're describing or a break in the chronology of a narrative or between explanations of arguments or examples. Just make sure you begin your next paragraph with some sort of transitional phrase or key words to let the reader know that you are still discussing the same point as before ("Still another problem caused by the computer's faulty memory circuit is . . .").

Practicing What You've Learned

A. Analyze the following paragraphs. Explain how you might improve the development of each one.

1. Professor Wilson is the best teacher I've ever had. His lectures are interesting, and he's very concerned about his students. He makes the class challenging but not too hard. On tests he doesn't expect more than one can give. I think he's a great teacher.

2. Newspaper advice columns are pretty silly. The problems are generally stupid or unrealistic, and the advice is out of touch with today's world. Too often the columnist just uses the letter to make a smart remark about some pet peeve. The columns could be put to some good uses, but no one tries very hard.

3. Driving tests do not adequately examine a person's driving ability. Usually the person being tested does not have to drive very far. The test does not require the skills that are used in everyday driving situations. Supervisors of driving tests tend to be very lenient.

4. Nursing homes are often sad places. They are frequently located in ugly old buildings unfit for anyone. The people there are lonely and bored. What's more, they're sometimes treated badly by the people who run the homes. It's a shame something better can't be done for the elderly.

5. There is a big difference between acquaintances and friends. Acquaintances are just people you know slightly, but friends give you some important qualities. For example, they can help you gain self-esteem and confidence just by being close to you. By sharing their friendship, they also help you feel happy about being alive.

B. Practice developing paragraphs by choosing two of the following three topics, fleshing out each paragraph with an example from your own experience or that of a close friend. Use vivid, specific details to make each paragraph clear and interesting. (If you cannot think of an appropriate example, you may rework the topic sentence; for instance, in the first paragraph, you might change the topic to a product or service that exceeded your expectations rather than one that disappointed you.)

1. Too many products today have expensive advertising campaigns but simply don't live up to their claims. For instance,

2. Sooner or later, almost everyone experiences that dreaded moment when he or she suddenly forgets something familiar. Someone forgets a friend's name in the middle of an introduction; someone else experiences memory loss standing in front of the ATM or just after volunteering to answer a question in class. I,

continued on next page

too, have temporarily "gone blank," but eventually regained my composure. For example,

3. Unexpected help is a miracle that often comes just in time to prevent a disaster or foolish move. Such help can come from a variety of sources—from friends, family, or even strangers. For example,

Assignment

A. Find two well-developed paragraphs in an essay or book; explain why you think the paragraphs are successfully developed.

B. Select one of the paragraphs from Practicing What You've Learned, exercise "A" (page 65) and rewrite it, adding enough specific details to make a well-developed paragraph.

C. *Collaborative Activity:* Exchange paragraphs with a classmate. Mark any weaknesses you see in the topic sentence or in the paragraph's development. Rewrite at least one problematic area so that the paragraph is stronger, with enough appropriate supporting detail. In a sentence or two, explain why you made the changes you did.

Applying What You've Learned to *Your* Writing

If you are currently drafting an essay, look closely at your body paragraphs. Find the topic sentence in each paragraph, and circle the key words that most clearly communicate the main idea of the paragraph. Then ask yourself whether the information in each paragraph effectively supports, explains, or illustrates the main idea of the paragraph's topic sentence. Is there enough information? If you're not sure, try numbering your supporting details. Are there too few to be persuasive? Does the paragraph present clear, specific supporting material, or does it contain too many vague generalities to be convincing? Where could you add more details to help the reader understand your ideas better and to make each paragraph more interesting? (◆ For more help revising your paragraphs, see Chapter 5.)

Paragraph Unity

Every sentence in a body paragraph should relate directly to the main idea presented by the topic sentence. A paragraph must stick to its announced subject; it must not drift away into another discussion. In other words, a good paragraph has *unity*.

Examine the following unified paragraph; note that the topic sentence clearly states the paragraph's main point and that each sentence thereafter supports the topic sentence.

(1)Frank Lloyd Wright, America's leading architect of the first half of the twentieth century, believed that his houses should blend naturally with their building sites. (2)Consequently, he designed several "prairie houses," whose long, low lines echoed the flat earth plane. (3)Built of brick, stone, and natural wood, the houses shared a similar texture with their backgrounds. (4)Large windows were often used to blend the interior and exterior of the houses. (5)Wright also punctuated the lines and spaces of the houses with greenery in planters to further make the buildings look like part of nature.

Frank Lloyd Wright's Robie House in Chicago, IL

Grant Smith/VIEW Pictures Ltd / Alamy

The first sentence states the main idea, that Wright thought houses should blend with their locations, and the other sentences support this assertion:

Topic Sentences: (1) Wright's houses blend with their natural locations.

Supporting Sentences: (2) Long, low lines echo flat prairie.

(3) Brick, stone, wood provide same texture as location.

(4) Windows blend inside with outside.

(5) Greenery in planters imitates the natural surroundings.

Now look at the next paragraph, in which the writer strays from his original purpose:

(1)Cigarette smoke is unhealthy even for people who don't have the nicotine habit themselves. (2)Secondhand smoke can cause asthmatics and sufferers of sinusitis serious problems. (3)Doctors regularly advise heart patients to avoid confined smoky areas because coronary attacks might be triggered by the lack of clean air. (4) Moreover, having the smell of smoke in one's hair and clothes is a real nuisance. (5) Even if a person is without any health problems, exhaled smoke doubles the amount of carbon monoxide in the air, a condition that may cause lung problems in the future.

Sentence 4 refers to smoke as a nuisance and therefore does not belong in a paragraph that discusses smoking as a health hazard to nonsmokers.

Sometimes a large portion of a paragraph will drift into another topic. In the following paragraph, did the writer wish to focus on her messiness or on the beneficial effects of her engagement?

I have always been a very messy person. As a child, I was a pack rat, saving every little piece of insignificant paper that I thought might be important when I grew up. As a teenager, I filled my pockets with remnants of basketball tickets, hall passes, gum wrappers, and other important articles from my high school education. As a college student,

Note shift from the topic of messiness

I became a boxer—not a fighter, but someone who cannot throw anything away and therefore it winds up in a box in my closet. But my engagement has changed everything. I'm really pleased with the new stage of my life, and I owe it all to my fiancé. My overall outlook on life has changed because of his influence on me. I'm neater, much more cheerful, and I'm even getting places on time like I never did before. It's truly amazing what love can do.

This writer may wish to discuss the changes her fiancé has inspired and then use her former messiness, tardiness, and other bad habits as examples illustrating those changes; however, as presented here, the paragraph is not unified around a central idea. On the contrary, it first seems to promise a discussion of her messiness but then wanders into comments on "what love can do."

Also beware a tendency to end your paragraph with a new idea. A new point calls for an entirely new paragraph. For example, the following paragraph focuses on the *origins* of Muzak; the last sentence, on Muzak's *effects* on workers, should be omitted or moved to a paragraph on Muzak's uses in the workplace.

Breaks unity

Muzak, the ever-present background music that pervades elevators, office buildings, and reception rooms, was created nearly eighty years ago by George Owen Squier, an army general. A graduate of West Point, Squier was also an inventor and scientist. During World War I he headed the Signal Corps, where he began experimenting with the notion of transmitting simultaneous messages over power lines. When he retired from the army in 1922, he founded Wired Radio, Inc., and later, in 1934, the first Muzak medley was heard in Cleveland, Ohio, for homeowners willing to pay the great sum of $1.50 a month. That year he struck upon the now-famous name, which combined the idea of music with the name of the country's then-most popular camera, Kodak. *Today, experiments show that workers get more done when they listen to Muzak.*

In general, think of paragraph unity in terms of the following diagram:

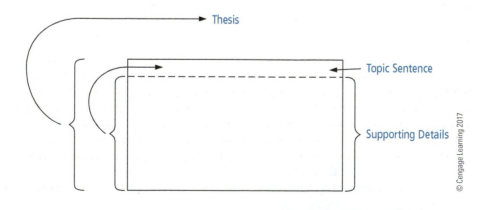

Thesis

Topic Sentence

Supporting Details

© Cengage Learning 2017

The sentences in the paragraph support the paragraph's topic sentence; the paragraph, in turn, supports the thesis statement.

Practicing What You've Learned

In each of the following examples, delete or rewrite any information that interferes with the unity of the paragraph or begins to drift off topic:

1. In the Great Depression of the 1930s, American painters suffered severely because few people had the money to spend on the luxury of owning art. To keep our artists from starving, the government ultimately set up the Federal Art Project, which paid then little-known painters such as Jackson Pollock, Arshile Gorky, and Willem de Kooning to paint murals in post offices, train stations, schools, housing projects, and other public places. During this period, songwriters were also affected by the Depression, and they produced such memorable songs as "Brother, Can You Spare a Dime?" The government-sponsored murals, usually depicting familiar American scenes and historical events, gave our young artists an opportunity to develop their skills and new techniques; in return, our country obtained thousands of elaborate works of art in over one thousand American cities. Sadly, many of these artworks were destroyed in later years as public buildings were torn down or remodeled.

2. After complaining in vain about the quality of food in the campus restaurant, University of Colorado students are having their revenge after all. The student body voted to rename the grill after Alferd Packer, the only American ever convicted of cannibalism. Packer was a Utah prospector trapped with an expedition of explorers in the southwest Colorado mountains during the winter of 1874; the sole survivor of the trip, he was later tried by a jury and sentenced to hang for dining on at least five of his companions. Colorado students are now holding an annual "Alferd Packer Day" and have installed a mural relating the prospector's story on the main wall of the restaurant. Some local wits have also suggested slogans for the bar and grill, including "Have a friend for lunch!" and "Serving our fellow man since 1874." Another well-known incident of cannibalism in the West occurred in the winter of 1846, when the Donner party, a wagon train of eighty-seven California-bound immigrants, became trapped by ice and snow in the Sierra Nevada mountain range.

3. Inventors of food products often name their new creations after real people. In 1896 Leo Hirshfield hand-rolled a chewy candy and named it after his daughter Clara, nicknamed Tootsie. In 1920 Otto Schnering gave the world the Baby Ruth candy bar, named after the daughter of former President Grover Cleveland. To publicize his new product, Schnering once dropped the candy tied to tiny parachutes from an airplane flying over Pittsburgh. One of our most popular soft drinks was named by a young suitor who sought to please his sweetheart's

continued on next page

physician father, none other than old Dr. Pepper. Despite the honor, the girl's father never approved of the match, and the young man, Wade Morrison, married someone else.

4.   States out West have often led the way in recognizing women's roles in politics. Wyoming, for example, was the first state to give women the rights to vote and hold office, back in 1869 while the state was still a territory. Colorado was the second state to grant women's suffrage; Idaho, the third. Wyoming was also the first state to elect a woman as governor, Nellie Tayloe Ross, in 1924. Montana elected Jeannette Rankin as the nation's first congresswoman in 1916. Former U.S. Representative from Colorado, Patricia Schroeder, claims to be the first person to take the congressional oath of office while clutching a handbag full of diapers. Ms. Schroeder later received the National Motherhood Award.

5.   Living in a college dorm is a good way to meet people. There are activities every weekend, such as game night and parties where one can get acquainted with all kinds of students. Even just sitting by someone in the cafeteria during a meal can start a friendship. Making new friends from foreign countries can teach students more about international relations. A girl on my dorm floor, for example, is from Peru, and I've learned a lot about the customs and culture in her country. She's also helping me with my study of Spanish. I hope to visit her in Peru some day.

Applying What You've Learned to *Your* Writing

If you have written a draft of an essay, underline the topic sentence in each body paragraph and circle the key words. For example, if in an essay on America's growing health consciousness, one of your topic sentences reads, "In an effort to improve their health, Americans have increased the number of vitamins they consume," you might circle "Americans," "increased," and "vitamins." Then look closely at your paragraph. All the information in that paragraph should support the idea expressed in your topic sentence; nothing should detract from the idea of showing that Americans have increased their vitamin consumption. Now study the paragraphs in your draft, one by one. Cross out any sentence or material that interferes with the ideas in your topic sentences. If one of your paragraphs begins to drift away from its topic-sentence idea, you will need to rethink the purpose of that paragraph and rewrite it so that the reader will understand what the paragraph is about. (◆ For additional help revising your drafts, turn to Chapter 5.)

Paragraph Coherence

In addition to unity, *coherence* is essential to a good paragraph. Coherence means that all the sentences and ideas in your paragraph flow together to make a clear, logical point about your topic. Your paragraph should not be a confusing collection of ideas set down in random order. The readers should be able to follow what you have written and see easily and quickly how each sentence grows out of, or is related to, the preceding sentence. To achieve coherence, you should have a smooth connection or transition between the sentences in your paragraphs.

There are five important means of achieving coherence in your paragraphs:

1. A natural or easily recognized order
2. Transitional words and phrases
3. Repetition of key words
4. Substitution of pronouns for key nouns
5. Parallelism

These transitional devices are similar to the couplings between railroad cars; they enable the controlling engine to pull the train of thought along as a unit.

A Recognizable Ordering of Information

Without consciously thinking about the process, you may often organize paragraphs in easily recognized patterns that give the reader a sense of logical movement and order. Four common patterns of ordering sentences in a paragraph are discussed here.

The Order of Time

Some paragraphs are composed of details arranged in chronological order. You might, for example, explain the process of changing an oil filter on your car by beginning with the first step, draining the old oil, and concluding with the last step, installing the new filter. Here is a paragraph on black holes in which the writer chronologically orders the details:

> A black hole in space, from all indications, is the result of the death of a star. Scientists speculate that stars were first formed from the gases floating in the universe at the beginning of time. In the first stage in the life of a star, the hot gas is drawn by the force of gravity into a burning sphere. In the middle stage—our own sun being a middle-aged star—the burning continues at a regular rate, giving off enormous amounts of heat and light. As it grows old, however, the star eventually explodes to become what is called a nova, a superstar. But gravity soon takes over again, and the exploded star falls back in on itself with such force that all the matter in the star is compacted into a mass no larger than a few miles in diameter. At this point, no heavenly body can be seen in that area of the sky, as the tremendous pull of gravity lets nothing escape, not even light. A black hole has thus been formed.

The Order of Space

When your subject is a physical object, you should select some orderly means of describing it: from left to right, top to bottom, inside to outside, and so forth. For example, you might describe a sculpture as you walk around it from front to back. In the following paragraph describing a cowboy, the writer has ordered the details of the description in a head-to-feet pattern:

Big Dave was pure cowboy. He wore a black felt hat so big that it kept his face in perpetual shade. Around his neck was knotted a red bandana stained with sweat from long hot days in the saddle. An oversized blue denim shirt hung from his shoulders to give him plenty of arm freedom, and his faded jeans were held up by a broad leather belt with a huge silver buckle featuring a snorting bronc in full buck. His boots, old and dirt-colored, kicked up little dust storms as he sauntered across the corral.

Deductive Order

A paragraph ordered deductively moves from a generalization to particular details that explain or support the general statement. Perhaps the most common pattern of all paragraphs, the deductive paragraph begins with its topic sentence and proceeds to its supporting details, as illustrated in the following example:

If a group of 111 ninth-graders is typical of today's teenagers, spelling and social science teachers may be in for trouble. In a recent experiment, not one of the students tested could write the Pledge of Allegiance correctly. In addition, the results showed that the students apparently had little understanding of the pledge's meaning. For example, several students described the United States as a "nation under guard" instead of "under God," and the phrase "to the Republic for which it stands" appeared in several responses as "of the richest stand" or "for Richard stand." Many students changed the word "indivisible" to the phrase "in the visible," and over 9% of the students, all of whom are Americans from varying racial and ethnic backgrounds, misspelled the word "America."

Inductive Order

An inductive paragraph begins with an examination of particular details and then concludes with a larger point or generalization about those details. Such a paragraph often ends with its topic sentence, as does the following paragraph on Little League baseball:

At too many Little League baseball games, one or another adult creates a minor scene by yelling rudely at an umpire or a coach. Similarly, it is not uncommon to hear adults whispering loudly with one another in the stands over which child should have caught a missed ball. Perhaps the most astounding spectacle of all, however, is an irate parent or coach yanking a child off the field after a bad play for a humiliating lecture in front of the whole team. Sadly, Little League baseball today often seems intended more for childish adults than for the children who actually play it.

Transitional Words and Phrases

Some paragraphs may need internal transitional words to help the reader move smoothly from one thought to the next so that the ideas do not appear disconnected or choppy.

Here is a list of common transitional words and phrases and their uses:

giving examples	for example, for instance, specifically, in particular, namely, another, other, in addition, to illustrate
comparison	similarly, not only . . . but also, in comparison
contrast	although, but, while, in contrast, however, though, on the other hand, nevertheless
sequence	first . . . second . . . third, finally, moreover, also, in addition, next, then, after, furthermore, and, previously
results	therefore, thus, consequently, as a result

Notice the difference the use of transitional words makes in the following paragraphs:

Working in the neighborhood grocery store as a checker was one of the worst jobs I've ever had. In the first place, I had to wear an ugly, scratchy uniform cut at least three inches too short. My schedule of working hours was another inconvenience; because my hours were changed each week, it was impossible to make plans in advance, and getting a day off was out of the question. In addition, the lack of working space bothered me. Except for a half-hour lunch break, I was restricted to three square feet of room behind the counter and consequently felt as if I were no more than a gerbil in a cage.

The same paragraph rewritten without transitional words sounds choppy and childish:

Working in the neighborhood grocery store as a checker was one of the worst jobs I've ever had. I had to wear an ugly, scratchy uniform. It was cut at least three inches too short. My schedule of working hours was inconvenient. My hours changed each week. It was impossible to make plans in advance. Getting a day off was out of the question. The lack of working space bothered me. Except for a half-hour break, I was restricted to three square feet of room behind the counter. I felt like a gerbil in a cage.

Although transitional words and phrases are useful in bridging the gaps between your ideas, don't overuse them. Not every sentence needs a transitional phrase, so use one only when the relationship between your thoughts needs clarification. It's also a mistake to place the transitional word in the same position in your sentence each time. Look at the paragraph that follows:

It's a shame that every high school student isn't required to take a course in first aid. *For example*, you might need to treat a friend or relative for drowning during a family picnic. Or, *for instance*, someone might break a bone or receive a snakebite on a camping trip. *Also*, you should always know what to do for a common cut or burn. *Moreover*, it's important to realize when someone is in shock. *However*, very few people take the time to learn the simple rules of first aid. *Thus*, many injured or sick people suffer more than they should. *Therefore*, everyone should take a first aid course in school or at the Red Cross center.

As you can see, a series of sentences each beginning with a transitional word quickly becomes repetitious and boring. To hold your reader's attention, use transitional words only when necessary to avoid choppiness, and vary their placement in your sentences.

Repetition of Key Words

Important words or phrases (and their synonyms) may be repeated throughout a paragraph to connect the thoughts into a coherent statement:

> One of the most common, yet most puzzling, phobias is the *fear* of *snakes*. It's only natural, of course, to be afraid of a poisonous *snake*, but many people are just as frightened of the harmless varieties. For such people, a tiny green grass *snake* is as terrifying as a cobra. Some researchers say this unreasonable *fear* of any and all *snakes* is a legacy left to us by our cave-dwelling ancestors, for whom these *reptiles* were a real and constant danger. Others maintain that the *fear* is a result of our associating the *snake* with the notion of evil, as in the Garden of Eden. Whatever the reason, the fact remains that for many otherwise normal people, the mere sight of a *snake* slithering through the countryside is enough to keep them city dwellers forever.

The repeated words "fear" and "snake" and the synonym "reptile" help tie one sentence to another so that the reader can follow the ideas easily.

Pronouns Substituted for Key Nouns

A pronoun is a word that stands for a noun. In your paragraph you might use a key noun in one sentence and then use a pronoun in its place in the following sentences. The pronoun "it" often replaces "shark" in the description that follows:

> [1]The great white shark is perhaps the best equipped of all the ocean's predators. [2]*It* can grow up to twenty-one feet and weigh three tons, with two-inch teeth that can replace themselves within twenty-four hours when damaged. [3]The shark's sense of smell is so acute that *it* can detect one ounce of fish blood in a million ounces of water. [4]In addition, *it* can sense vibrations from six hundred feet away.

Sentences 2, 3, and 4 are tied to the topic sentence by the use of the pronoun "it."

Parallelism

Parallelism in a paragraph means using the same grammatical structure in several sentences to establish coherence. The repeated use of similar phrasing helps tie the ideas and sentences together. Next, for example, is a paragraph predominantly unified by its use of grammatically parallel sentences:

> [1]The weather of Texas offers something for everyone. [2]If you are the kind who likes to see snow drifting onto mountain peaks, a visit to the Big Bend area may satisfy your eye. [3]If, on the other hand, you demand a bright sun to bake your skin a golden brown, stop in the southern part of the state. [4]And for hardier souls, who

ask from nature a show of force, the skies of the Panhandle regularly release fero-cious springtime tornadoes. (5)Finally, if you are the fickle type, by all means come to central Texas, where the sun at any time may shine unashamed throughout the most torrential rainstorm.

The parallel structures of sentences 2, 3, and 5 ("if you" + verb) keep the paragraph flowing smoothly from one idea to the next.

Using a Variety of Transitional Devices

Most writers use a combination of transitional devices in their paragraphs. In the following example, three kinds of transitional devices are circled: transitional words, repetition of pronouns, and repetition of key words. See whether you can identify each one.

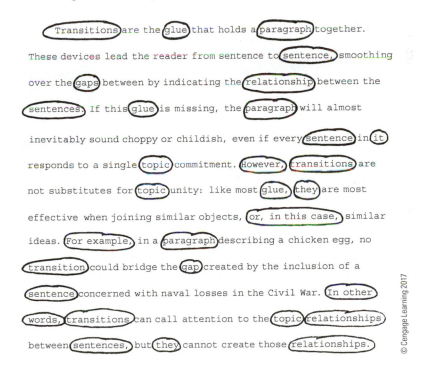

Transitions are the glue that holds a paragraph together. These devices lead the reader from sentence to sentence, smoothing over the gaps between by indicating the relationship between the sentences. If this glue is missing, the paragraph will almost inevitably sound choppy or childish, even if every sentence in it responds to a single topic commitment. However, transitions are not substitutes for topic unity: like most glue, they are most effective when joining similar objects, or, in this case, similar ideas. For example, in a paragraph describing a chicken egg, no transition could bridge the gap created by the inclusion of a sentence concerned with naval losses in the Civil War. In other words, transitions can call attention to the topic relationships between sentences, but they cannot create those relationships.

© Cengage Learning 2017

Avoiding Whiplash

The preceding example not only illustrates a variety of transitional devices but also makes an important point about their use—and their limitations. Transitional devices show connections between sentences, but they alone cannot create a logical flow of ideas if none exists. For example, notice in the following sample the "disconnect" between the first three sentences and sentence 4:

(1)Despite our growing dependency on computers, one of our most useful house-hold tools is still the lowly pencil. (2)Cheap, efficient, and long-lasting, the pencil may be operated by children and adults alike, without the necessity of a user's manual or tech support. [3]According to the Incense Cedar Institute, today's pencil can draw a line 70 miles long, be sharpened 17 times, and write an average of 45,000 words. [4]Chinese factories don't have to follow as many environmental regulations, and their workers are paid less than their American counterparts. [5]Many pencils used in this country are still manufactured in China because of the cheaper cost.

Did you suffer "reader's whiplash" as your mind experienced the sudden jerk from the discussion of pencil use to "Chinese factories"? No addition of a simple transitional word will fix this problem; the writer needs to revise the paragraph's internal logic and flow or perhaps even consider a new paragraph on cost or production. In other words, don't rely on transitional devices when deep-structure revision for coherence is needed. Make your reader's trip through your prose an enjoyable one by avoiding sudden stops and starts in thought, and then smooth that ride with appropriate transitional devices when they are necessary.

Practicing What You've Learned

A. Identify each of the following paragraphs as ordered by time, space, or parallelism:

1.   My apartment is so small that it will no longer hold all my possessions. Every day when I come in the door, I am shocked by the clutter. The wall to my immediate left is completely obscured by art and movie posters that have become so numerous they often overlap, even hiding each other. The adjoining wall has become home to a jumbled pile of my shoes; every time I get home, I kick off the pair I wore that day, and the mound has begun to impede movement across the room. The big couch that runs across the back of the room is always piled so high with schoolbooks and magazines that a guest usually ends up sitting on the floor. To my right is a large sliding glass door that opens onto a balcony—or at least it used to, before it was permanently blocked by my tennis gear, golf clubs, and bicycle. Even the tiny closet next to the front door is bursting with clothes, both clean and dirty. I think the time has come for me to move.

2.   Once-common acts of greeting may be finding renewed popularity after three centuries. According to one historian, kissing was at the height of its popularity as a greeting in seventeenth-century England, when ladies and gentlemen of the court often saluted each other in this affectionate manner. Then the country was visited by a strange plague, whose cause was unknown. Because no one knew how the plague was spread, people tried to avoid physical contact with others as much as possible. Both kissing and the handshake went out of fashion and were replaced by the bow and curtsy, so people could greet others without having to touch them. The bow and curtsy remained in vogue for over

continued on next page

a hundred years, until the handshake—for men only—returned to popularity in the nineteenth century. Today, both men and women may shake hands upon meeting others, and kissing as a greeting is making a comeback—especially among the jet-setters and Hollywood stars.

3.   Students have diverse ways of preparing for final exams. Some stay up the night before, trying to cram into their brains what they avoided all term. Others pace themselves, spending a little time each night going over the notes they took in class that day. Still others just cross their fingers, assuming they absorbed enough along the way from lectures and readings. In the end, though, everyone hopes the tests are easy.

B. Circle and identify the transitional devices in the following paragraphs:

1.   Each year I follow a system when preparing firewood to use in my stove. First, I hike about a mile from my house with my bow saw in hand. I then select three good-size oak trees and mark them with orange ties. Next, I saw through the base of each tree about two feet from the ground. After I fell the trees, not only do I trim away the branches but I also sort the scrap from the usable limbs. I find cutting the trees into manageable-length logs is too much for one day; however, I roll them off the ground so they will not begin to rot. The next day, I cut the trees into eight-foot lengths, which allows me to handle them more easily. Once they are cut, I roll them along the fire lane to the edge of the road, where I stack them neatly but not too high. The day after that, I borrow my uncle's van, drive to the pile of logs, and load as many logs as I can, thus reducing the number of trips. When I finally have all the logs in my backyard, I begin sawing them into eighteen-inch lengths. I create large piles that consequently have to be split and finally stacked. The logs will age and dry until winter, when I will make daily trips to the woodpile.

2.   Fans of professional baseball and football argue continually over which is America's favorite spectator sport. Though the figures on attendance for each vary with every new season, certain arguments remain the same, spelling out both the enduring appeals of each game and something about the people who love to watch. Football, for instance, is a quicker, more physical sport, and football fans enjoy the emotional involvement they feel while watching. Baseball, on the other hand, seems more mental, like chess, and attracts those fans who prefer a quieter, more complicated game. In addition, professional football teams play sixteen games a season, usually providing fans with a week between games to work themselves up to a pitch of excitement and expectation. Baseball teams, however, play almost every day for six months, so that the typical baseball fan is not so crushed by missing a game, knowing there will be many other chances to attend. Finally, football fans seem to love the halftime pageantry, the cheerleaders, and the mascots, whereas baseball fans are often more content to concentrate on the game's finer details and spend the breaks between innings filling out their own private scorecards.

continued on next page

C. The following paragraph lacks common transitional devices. Fill in the blanks with appropriate transitional words or key words.

Scientists continue to debate the cause of the dinosaurs' disappearance. One group claims the _____ vanished after an asteroid smashed into the earth; dust and smoke _____ blocked the sun for a long time. _____ of no direct sunlight, the earth underwent a lengthy "winter," far too cold for the huge _____ to survive. A University of California paleontologist, _____, disputes this claim. He argues that _____ we generally think of _____ living in swampy land, fossils found in Alaska show that _____ could live in cold climates _____ warm ones. _____ group claims that the _____ became extinct following an intense period of global volcanic activity. _____ to killing the _____ themselves, these scientists _____ believe the volcanic activity killed much of the plant life that the _____ ate and, _____, many of the great _____ who survived the volcanic eruptions starved to death. Still _____ groups of _____ claim the _____ were destroyed by acid rain, by a passing "death star," _____ even by viruses from outer space.

D. The sentences below are out of order. By noting the various transitional devices, arrange the sentences into a coherent paragraph.

How to Purchase a New Car

a. If you're happy with the car's performance, find out about available financing arrangements.

b. Later, at home, study your notes carefully to help you decide which car fits your needs.

c. After you have discussed various loans and interest rates, you can negotiate the final price with the salesperson.

d. A visit to the showroom also allows you to test-drive the car.

e. Once you have agreed on the car's price, feel confident that you have made a well-chosen purchase.

f. Next, a visit to a nearby showroom should help you select the color, options, and style of the car of your choice.

g. First, take a trip to the library to read the current auto magazines and consumers' guides.

h. As you read, take notes on models and prices.

E. *Collaborative Activity:* Rearrange a paragraph you have written so that your sentences are listed out of order, in similar fashion to those in the preceding exercise. Exchange your sentences with those of a classmate. If the original paragraphs were written with logical unity and enough transitional devices for a smooth flow, it

continued on next page

should be easy for both of you to reassemble the sentences into their proper cohesive order. If you cannot solve your classmate's paragraph puzzle or if you experience "reader's whiplash," explain the problem, offering suggestions for revision.

Paragraph Sequence

The order in which you present your paragraphs is another decision you must make. In some essays, the subject matter itself will suggest its own order.* For instance, in an essay designed to instruct a beginning runner, you might want to discuss the necessary equipment—good running shoes, loose-fitting clothing, and a sweatband—before moving to a discussion of where to run and how to run. Other essay topics, however, may not suggest a natural order, in which case you must decide which order will most effectively reach and hold the attention of your audience. Frequently, writers withhold their strongest point until last. (Lawyers often use this technique; they first present the jury with the weakest arguments, then pull out the most incriminating evidence—the "smoking gun." Thus, the jury members retire with the strongest argument freshest in their minds.) Sometimes, however, you'll find it necessary to present one particular point first so that the other points make good sense. Study your own major points, and decide which order will be the most logical, successful way of persuading your reader to accept your thesis.

Transitions between Paragraphs

As you already know, each paragraph usually signals a new major point in your discussion. These paragraphs should not appear as isolated blocks of thought but rather as parts of a unified, step-by-step progression. To avoid a choppy essay, link each paragraph to the one before it with *transitional devices.* Just as the sentences in your paragraphs are connected, so are the paragraphs themselves; ◆ therefore, you can use the same transitional devices suggested on pages 72–76.

The first sentence of most body paragraphs frequently contains the transitional device. To illustrate this point, here are some topic sentences lifted from the body paragraphs of a student essay criticizing a popular sports car, renamed the 'Gator to protect the guilty and to prevent lawsuits. The transitional devices are italicized.

Thesis: The *'Gator* is one of the worst cars on the market.

- When you buy a *'Gator,* you buy physical inconvenience. [repetition of key word from thesis]
- *Another* reason the *'Gator* is a bad buy is the cost of insurance. [transitional word, key word]
- You might overlook the *inconvenient* size and exorbitant *insurance* rates if the *'Gator* were a strong, reliable car, *but* this automobile constantly needs repair. [key words from preceding paragraphs, transitional word]
- When you decide to sell this car, you face *still another* unpleasant surprise: the extremely low resale value. [key word, transitional phrase]
- The most serious drawback, *however,* is the *'Gator's* safety record. [transitional word, key word]

---

* ◆For more information on easily recognized patterns of order, see pages 71–72.

Sometimes, instead of using transitional words or repetition of key words or their synonyms, you can use an *idea hook*. The last idea of one paragraph can lead you smoothly into your next paragraph. Instead of repeating a key word from the previous discussion, find a phrase that refers to the entire idea just expressed. If, for example, the previous paragraph discussed the highly complimentary advertising campaign for the 'Gator, the next paragraph might begin, "This view of the 'Gator as an economy car is ridiculous to anyone who has pumped a week's salary into this gas guzzler." The phrase "this view" connects the idea of the first paragraph with the one that follows. Idea hooks also work well with transitional words: "This view, however, is ridiculous. . . ."

If you do use transitional words, don't allow them to make your essay sound mechanical. For example, a long series of paragraphs beginning "First . . . Second . . . Third . . ." quickly becomes boring. Vary the type and position of your transitional devices so that your essay has a subtle but logical movement from point to point.

Applying What You've Learned to *Your* Writing

If you are currently working on a draft of an essay, check each body paragraph for coherence, the smooth connection of ideas and sentences in a logical, easy-to-follow order. You might try placing brackets around key words, pronouns, and transitional words that carry the reader's attention from thought to thought and from sentence to sentence. Decide whether you have enough ordering devices, placed in appropriate places, or whether you need to add (or delete) others. (◆ For additional help revising your drafts, turn to Chapter 5.)

Chapter 3 Summary

Here is a brief restatement of what you should know about the paragraphs in the body of your essay:

1. Each body paragraph usually contains one major point in the discussion promised by the thesis statement.

2. Each major point is presented in the topic sentence of a paragraph.

3. Each paragraph should be adequately developed with clear supporting detail.

4. Every sentence in the paragraph should support the topic sentence.

5. There should be an orderly, logical flow from sentence to sentence and from thought to thought.

6. The sequence of your essay's paragraphs should be logical and effective.

7. There should be a smooth flow from paragraph to paragraph.

8. The body paragraphs should successfully persuade your reader that the opinion expressed in your thesis is valid.

Beginnings and Endings

As you work on your rough drafts, you might think of your essay as a coherent, unified whole composed of three main parts: the introduction (lead-in, thesis, and essay map), the body (paragraphs with supporting evidence), and the conclusion (final address to the reader). These three parts should flow smoothly into one another, presenting the reader with an organized, logical discussion. The following pages will suggest ways to begin, end, and name your essay effectively. Figure 4.1 highlights the key ideas for developing good lead-ins and conclusions discussed in this chapter.

How to Write a Good Lead-In

The first few sentences of your essay are particularly important; first impressions, as you know, are often lasting ones. The beginning of your essay, then, must catch your readers' attention and make them want to keep reading. Recall the way you read a magazine: if you are like most people, you probably skim the magazine, reading a paragraph or two of each article that looks promising. If the first few paragraphs hold your interest, you read on. When you write your own introductory paragraph, assume that you have only a few sentences to attract your reader. Consequently, you must pay particular attention to making those first lines especially interesting and well written.

In some essays, your thesis statement alone may be controversial or striking enough to capture the readers. At other times, however, you will want to use the introductory device called a *lead-in*.* The lead-in (1) catches the readers' attention; (2) announces the subject matter and tone of your essay (humorous, satiric, serious, etc.); and (3) sets up, or leads into, the presentation of your thesis and essay map.

_____

* Do note that for some writing assignments, such as certain kinds of technical reports, attention-grabbing lead-ins are not appropriate. Frequently, these reports are directed toward particular professional audiences and have their own designated format; they often begin, for example, with a statement of the problem under study or with a review of pertinent information or research.

Figure 4.1 VISUALIZING THE PROCESS: INTRODUCTIONS AND CONCLUSIONS

Prewriting
Chapter 1

Drafting
Chapters 2, 3, 4, 5

Revising
Chapter 5

Editing/
Proofreading
Chapters 6, 7

The Parts of the Beginning or Introduction

1. Lead-in
2. Thesis
3. Essay Map

Suggestions for Writing a Good Lead-In

1. A paradoxical or intriguing statement
2. An arresting statistic or shocking statement
3. A question
4. A quotation from a recognized authority, historical figure, or literary source
5. A relevant story, joke, or anecdote
6. A description, often used for emotional appeal
7. A factual statement or a summary who-what-where-when-why lead-in
8. An analogy or comparison
9. A contrast or a before-and-after scenario
10. A personal experience
11. A catalog of relevant examples or facts
12. A statement of a problem or a popular misconception
13. A brief dialogue to introduce the topic
14. A proverb, maxim, or motto
15. A recognition, revelation, or insight
16. An appeal to a common or imagined experience

Avoiding Errors in Lead-Ins

1. Make sure your lead-in introduces your thesis.
2. Keep your lead-in brief.
3. Don't begin with an apology or complaint.
4. Don't assume your audience already knows your subject matter.
5. Stay clear of overused lead-ins.

Suggestions for Writing a Good Ending or Conclusion

1. A summary of the thesis and the essay's major points
2. An evaluation of the importance of the essay's subject
3. A statement of the essay's broader implications
4. A recommendation or call to action
5. A warning based on the essay's thesis
6. A quotation from an authority or someone whose insight emphasizes the main point

> 7. An anecdote or brief example that emphasizes or sums up the point of the essay
>
> 8. An image or description that lends finality to the essay
>
> 9. A rhetorical question that makes the reader think about the essay's main point
>
> 10. A forecast based on the essay's thesis
>
> 11. An ironic twist, witticism, pun, or playful use of words
>
> 12. Return to the technique used in your lead-in
>
> ### Avoiding Errors in Conclusions
>
> 1. Avoid a boring, mechanical ending.
>
> 2. Don't introduce new points or irrelevant material.
>
> 3. Don't tack on a conclusion.
>
> 4. Don't change your stance.
>
> 5. Avoid trite expressions.
>
> 6. Don't insult or anger your reader.

© Cengage Learning 2017

Here are some suggestions for and examples of lead-ins:

1. A paradoxical or intriguing statement

"Eat two chocolate bars and call me in the morning," says the psychiatrist to the patient. Such advice sounds like a sugar fanatic's dream, but recent studies have indeed confirmed that chocolate positively affects depression and anxiety.

2. An arresting statistic or shocking statement

One of every eight women in the U.S. will develop invasive breast cancer over the course of a lifetime, according to a recent report prepared by the American Cancer Society.

3. A question

What are more and more Americans doing these days to stay in touch with friends and family? Overwhelmingly, the answer is text messaging. An Experian report indicates that the average number of texts sent and received per month is nearly 4000 total messages per person for the 18–24 age group alone, a figure that has likely only increased in the years since the report's 2013 publication.

4. A quotation from a recognized authority, historical figure, or literary source

Confucius wisely noted that "our greatest glory is not in never falling, but in rising every time we fall." Despite a frustrating series of close losses, my soccer team faced every new game with optimism and determination. My teammates' never-give-up attitudes have shown me that the value of sport is not winning but learning how to face defeat and begin again.

Note, too, that sometimes writers may challenge the wisdom of authorities or use their words in humorous ways to introduce lighthearted essays:

> When Einstein wrote that the "most beautiful thing we can experience is the mysterious," I don't believe he was thinking about the mystery smell coming from our attic last summer.

5. A relevant story, joke, or anecdote

> Writer and witty critic Dorothy Parker was once assigned a remote, out-of-the-way office. According to the story, she became so lonely, so desperate for company, that she ultimately painted "Gentlemen" on the door. Although this university is large, no one on this campus needs to feel as isolated as Parker obviously did: our excellent Student Activity Office offers numerous clubs, programs, and volunteer groups to involve students of all interests.

6. A description, often used for emotional appeal

> With one eye blackened, one arm in a cast, and third-degree burns on both her legs, the pretty, blond two-year-old seeks corners of rooms, refuses to speak, and shakes violently at the sound of loud noises. Tammy is not the victim of a war or a natural disaster; rather, she is the helpless victim of her parents, one of the thousands of children who suffer daily from America's hidden crime, child abuse.

7. A factual statement or a summary who-what-where-when-why lead-in

> Texas's first execution of a woman in twenty-three years occurred September 14, 2005, at the Huntsville Unit of the state's Department of Corrections, despite the protests of various human-rights groups around the country.

8. An analogy or comparison

> The Romans kept geese on their Capitol Hill to cackle alarm in the event of attack by night. Modern Americans, despite their technology, have hardly improved on that old system of protection. According to the latest Safety Council report, almost any door with a standard lock can be opened easily with a common plastic credit card.

9. A contrast or a before-and-after scenario

> I used to search for toast in the supermarket. I used to think "blackened"—as in blackened Cajun shrimp—referred to the way I cooked anything in a skillet. "Poached" could only have legal ramifications. But all that has changed! Attending a class in basic cooking this summer has transformed the way I purchase, prepare, and even talk about food.

10. A personal experience

> I first realized times were changing for women when I overheard my six-year-old nephew speaking to my sister, a prominent New York lawyer. As we left her elaborate, luxurious office one evening, Tommy looked up at his mother and queried, "Mommy, can little boys grow up to be lawyers, too?"

11. A catalog of relevant examples or facts

A two-hundred-pound teenager quit school because no desk would hold her. A three-hundred-pound chef who could no longer stand on his feet was fired. A three-hundred-fifty-pound truck driver broke furniture in his friends' houses. All these people are now living healthier, happier, and thinner lives, thanks to the remarkable intestinal bypass surgery first developed in 1967.

12. Statement of a problem or a popular misconception

Some people believe that poetry is written only by aging beatniks or solemn, mournful men and women with suicidal tendencies. The Poetry in the Schools Program is working hard to correct that erroneous point of view.

13. Brief dialogue to introduce the topic

"Be bold! You can do it!" said my roommate again and again during the weeks before choir tryouts, despite my whimpering cries of "I can't, I can't." For a shy person like me, the thought of singing in a public audition was agony. But thanks to the ABC Relaxation Method suggested by the Counseling Center, I performed so well I was chosen for a solo. The ABC method, incorporating visualization and proper breathing techniques, is a helpful process every shy person should practice regularly.

14. A proverb, maxim, or motto

"One falsehood spoils a thousand truths," says the African proverb. Caught in the biggest lie of his political career, once-popular local mayor Paul TerGhist is learning the meaning of this old saying the hard way, as his former friends and supporters are now deserting him.

15. A recognition, revelation, or insight

As someone who earned "A's" throughout my Spanish classes, I thought I had a good grasp of the language. However, immersion in the Tres Amigos Building Project in Monterrey, Mexico, over Spring Break this year showed me I had much to learn about conversational speech patterns.

16. An appeal to a common or imagined experience

Come on, you know you've done it . . . in your bedroom, bathroom, car, wherever you've listened to hard rock music. You played your air guitar—and you're good, but maybe not great. If you keep practicing, though, you might be able to join the best air-shredders in the country as they compete annually in front of sold-out crowds at the national Air Guitar Championships.

Thinking of a good lead-in is often difficult when you sit down to begin your essay. Many writers, in fact, skip the lead-in until the first draft is written. They compose their working thesis first and then write the body of the essay, saving the lead-in and conclusion for last. As you write the middle of your essay, you may discover an especially interesting piece of information you might want to save to use as your lead-in.

Avoiding Errors in Lead-Ins

In addition to the previous suggestions, here is some advice to help you avoid common lead-in errors:

Make sure your lead-in introduces your thesis. A frequent weakness in introductory paragraphs is an interesting lead-in but no smooth or clear transition to the thesis statement. To avoid a gap or awkward jump in thought in your introductory paragraph, you may need to add a connecting sentence or phrase between your lead-in and thesis. Study the following paragraph, which uses a comparison as its lead-in. The italicized transitional sentence takes the reader from a general comment about Americans who use wheelchairs to information about those in Smallville, smoothly preparing the reader for the thesis that follows.

Lead-in	In the 1950s African Americans demanded the right to sit anywhere they pleased on public buses. Today, Americans who use wheelchairs are fighting for the right to board those same buses. *Here in Smallville,*
Transitional sentence	*the lack of proper boarding facilities often denies citizens with physical disabilities basic transportation to jobs, grocery stores, and medical cen-*
Thesis	*ters.* To give people using wheelchairs the same opportunities as other residents, the City Council should allocate the funds necessary to convert every bus in the public transportation system.

Keep your lead-in brief. Long lead-ins in short essays often give the appearance of a tail wagging the dog. Use a brief, attention-catching hook to set up your thesis; don't make your introduction the biggest part of your essay.

Don't begin with an apology or complaint. Such statements as "It's difficult to find much information on this topic . . ." and "This controversy is hard to understand, but . . ." do nothing to entice your reader.

Don't assume your audience already knows your subject matter. Identify the pertinent facts even though you know your readers know the assignment. ("The biggest problem with the new college requirement. . . ." What requirement?) If you are writing about a particular piece of literature or art, identify the title of the work and its author or artist, using the full name in the first reference.

Stay clear of overused lead-ins. If composition teachers had a nickel for every essay that began with a dry dictionary definition, they could all retire to Bermuda. Leave

Webster's alone and find a livelier way to begin. Asking a question as your lead-in is becoming overworked, too, so use it only when it is obviously the best choice for your opener.

Practicing What You've Learned

Describe the lead-ins in the following paragraphs. Did any of the writers blend more than one kind of lead-in?

1. In the sixth century, Lao-Tzu, the father of Taoism, described the "good traveler" as someone who has "no fixed plans and is not intent on arriving." If that ancient Chinese philosopher is correct, then my aimless but eventful wanderings across the South last fall qualify me as a World-Class Traveler.

2. Ever wonder if those long hours hitting the books are worth it? Do grades really matter to employers? According to a survey by the National Association of Colleges and Employers, the answer is . . . yes. Strong grades and a go-getter attitude are the keys to securing a good job after college.

3. An average can of soda may contain ten or more teaspoons of sugar. If you are one of the college students who drinks a can or two of soda every day, you could be consuming as much as thirty-two pounds of sugar every year! Cutting back on soft drinks is an easy way people can achieve a healthier diet.

4. I used to think bees were my friends. They make the honey I like to eat, and they help pollinate the flowers I like to smell. But after being stung multiple times and spending three days in the hospital last summer, I have come to see the little creatures in a totally different light. For those of us who are allergic to their venom, bees are flying killers whose buzz sends us scurrying for cover.

5. On May 6, 1937, the *Hindenburg*, a luxurious German airship with cabins for fifty, exploded into flames as it tried to land in New Jersey, killing thirty-six people and ending zeppelin passenger service forever. Theories about the cause of this mysterious explosion include lightning and static electricity, but the most intriguing explanation involves sabotage and betrayal.

© Bettmann/Bettmann Premium/Corbis

How to Write a Good Concluding Paragraph

Like a good story, a good essay should not stop in the middle. It should have a satisfying conclusion, one that gives the reader a sense of completion on the subject. Don't allow your essay to drop off or fade out at the end—instead, use the concluding paragraph to emphasize the validity and importance of your thinking. Remember that the concluding paragraph is your last chance to convince the reader. (As one cynical but realistic student pointed out, the conclusion may be the last part of your essay the teacher reads before putting a grade on your paper.) Therefore, make your conclusion count.

Some people feel that writing an essay shares a characteristic with a romantic fling—both activities are frequently easier to begin than they are to end. If you find, as many writers do, that you often struggle while searching for an exit with the proper emphasis and grace, here are some suggestions, by no means exhaustive, that might spark some good ideas for your conclusions:

1. A summary of the thesis and the essay's major points (most useful in long essays)

> The destruction of the rain forests must be stopped. Although developers protest that they are bringing much-needed financial aid into these traditionally poverty-stricken areas, no amount of money can compensate for what is being lost. Without the rain forests, we are not only contributing to the global warming of the entire planet, we are losing indigenous trees and plants that might someday provide new medicines or vaccines for diseases. Moreover, the replacement of indigenous peoples with corporation-run ranches robs the world of cultural diversity. For the sake of the planet's well being, Project Rainforest should be implemented.

2. An evaluation of the importance of the essay's subject

> These amazing, controversial photographs of the comet will continue to be the subject of debate because, according to some scientists, they yield the most important clues yet revealed about the origins of our universe.

3. A statement of the essay's broader implications

> Because these studies of feline leukemia may someday play a crucial role in the discovery of a cure for AIDS in human beings, the experiments, as expensive as they are, must continue.

4. A recommendation or call to action

The specific details surrounding the death of World War II hero Raoul Wallenberg are still unknown. Although Russia has recently admitted—after fifty years of denial—that Wallenberg was murdered by the KGB in 1947, such a confession is not enough. We must write our congressional representatives today urging their support for the new Swedish commission investigating the circumstances of his death. No hero deserves less.

5. A warning based on the essay's thesis

Understanding the politics that led to the destruction of Hiroshima is essential for all Americans—indeed, for all the world's peoples. Without such knowledge, the frightful possibility exists that somewhere, sometime, someone might drop the bomb again.

6. A quotation from an authority or someone whose insight emphasizes the main point

Even though I didn't win the fiction contest, I learned so much about my own powers of creativity. I'm proud that I pushed myself in new directions. I know now I will always agree with Herman Melville, whose writing was unappreciated in his own time, that "it is better to struggle with originality than to succeed in imitation."

7. An anecdote or brief example that emphasizes or sums up the point of the essay

Bette Davis's role on and off the screen as the catty, wisecracking woman of steel helped make her an enduring star. After all, no audience, past or present, could ever resist a dame who drags on a cigarette and then mutters about a passing starlet, "There goes a good time that was had by all."

8. An image or description that lends finality to the essay

As the last of the Big Screen's giant ants are incinerated by the Army scientist, one can almost hear the movie audiences of the 1950s breathing a collective sigh of relief, secure in the knowledge that once again the threat of nuclear radiation had been vanquished by the efforts of the U.S. military.

(◆ For another last image that captures the essence of an essay, see the "open house" scene that concludes "To Bid the World Farewell," page 231.)

9. A rhetorical question that makes the readers think about the essay's main point

No one wants to see hostages put in danger. But what nation can afford to let terrorists know they can get away with blackmail?

10. A forecast based on the essay's thesis

"Reality" TV shows that are competition-based (contestants singing, dancing, cooking, etc.) will continue to be popular not only because they invite viewers to imagine themselves as powerful judges but also because such shows are easier and cheaper for networks to produce than scripted dramas or comedies.

11. An ironic twist, witticism, pun, or playful use of words (often more appropriate in lighthearted essays)

After analyzing and understanding the causes of my procrastination, I now feel better, more determined to change my behavior. In fact, I've decided that today is the day for decisive action! I will choose a major! Hmmmm . . . or maybe not. I need to think about it some more. I'll get back to you, okay? Tomorrow. Really.

12. Return to the technique used in your lead-in (answer a question you asked, circle back to a story, extend a quotation, etc.)

So was Dorothy right in *The Wizard of Oz*? After the tough summer I spent on our ranch in Wyoming, mending barbed-wire fences and wrestling angry calves, I could think of nothing but Dorothy's words on the long bus ride back to school. As eager as I had been to leave, I couldn't wait to get back there. It wasn't Kansas, but Dorothy and I knew the truth: there's no place like home.

◆ **Hint:** After reading the preceding suggestions, if you are still struggling with your conclusion, turn back to the advice for writing lead-ins on pages 83–87. One of the suggestions there may trigger a useful idea for closing your essay. In fact, following a first draft, you may decide that the technique you chose to open your essay might be used more effectively to conclude it.

Avoiding Errors in Conclusions

Try to omit the following common errors in your concluding paragraphs:

Avoid a boring, mechanical ending. One of the most common weaknesses in student essays is a conclusion that merely restates the thesis, word for word. A brief essay of 500 to 750 words rarely requires a flat, point-by-point conclusion; in fact, such an ending often insults the readers' intelligence by implying that their attention spans are extremely short. Only after reading long essays do most readers need a precise recap of all the writer's main ideas. Instead of recopying your thesis and essay map, try finding an original, emphatic way to conclude your essay—or, as a well-known newspaper columnist described it, a good ending should snap with grace and authority, like the close of an expensive sports car door.

Jack Hollingsworth/keepsake RF/Corbis

Don't introduce new points or irrelevant material. Treat the major points of your essay in separate body paragraphs rather than in your exit. Stay focused on your essay's specific thesis and purpose; don't allow any unimportant or off-subject comments to drift into your concluding remarks.

Don't tack on a conclusion. There should be a smooth, logical flow of thought from your last body paragraph into your concluding statements.

Don't change your stance. Sometimes writers who have been critical of something throughout their essays will soften their stance or offer apologies in their last paragraph. For instance, someone complaining about the poor quality of a particular college course might abruptly conclude with statements that declare the class wasn't so bad after all, maybe she should have worked harder, or maybe she really did learn something after all. Such reneging may seem polite, but in actuality it undercuts the thesis and confuses the reader who has taken the writer's criticisms seriously. Instead of contradicting themselves, writers should stand their ground, forget about puffy clichés or "niceties," and find an emphatic way to conclude that is consistent with their thesis.

Avoid trite expressions. Don't begin your conclusion by declaring, "In conclusion," "In summary," or "As you can see, this essay proves my thesis that. . . ." End your essay so that the reader clearly senses completion; don't merely announce that you're finished.

Don't insult or anger your reader. No matter how right you feel you are, resist the temptation to set up an "either-or" conclusion in an argumentative essay: either you agree with me or you are an ignorant/wrong/selfish/immoral person. Don't exaggerate your claims or moralize excessively as you exit. Remember that your purpose is to inform and persuade your readers, not to annoy them to the point of rejecting your thesis out of sheer irritation. Conclude on a positive note, one that encourages readers to see matters your way.

Practicing What You've Learned

Identify the weaknesses you see in the following conclusions. How might these writers revise to create more satisfactory endings for their essays?

1. My thesis in this essay stated that I believe that having to change schools does not harm children for three reasons. Children at new schools learn how to make new friends. They learn how to get along with a variety of people. They also learn about different teaching styles. For these three reasons, I believe that having to change schools does not harm children.

2. "A journey of a thousand miles must begin with a single step" (Lao Tzu). As I discussed in this causal analysis essay, I would have never started painting again if I hadn't gone back to school. I'm the first to admit that it was a long, hard road to get my degree, and sometimes I really questioned the value of certain courses I had to take (like algebra, for example, which I think is a totally useless course for artists. The entire math requirement needs revision, in my opinion). But going back to school was the right choice for me and—who knows?—maybe it would be for others.

3. In conclusion, as I have shown here, our country's forest conservation policies are just plain stupid. If you don't stand up and join the fight against them, I hope you will enjoy living in a tent because pretty soon there isn't going to be any lumber for houses left. After selling out to the tree-huggers, will you be able to look at yourself in the mirror?

Assignment

Find three good concluding paragraphs. Identify each kind of conclusion, and tell why you think it is an effective ending for the essay or article.

How to Write a Good Title

As in the case of lead-ins, your title may be written at any time, but many writers prefer to finish their essays before naming them. A good title is similar to a good newspaper headline in that it attracts the readers' interest and makes them want to investigate the essay. Like the lead-in, the title helps announce the tone of the essay. An informal or humorous essay, for instance, might have a catchy, funny title. Some titles show the writer's wit and love of wordplay; a survey of recent magazines revealed these titles: "Bittersweet News about Saccharin," "Coffee: New Grounds for Concern," and "The Scoop on the Best Ice Cream."

On the other hand, a serious, informative essay should have a more formal title that suggests its content as clearly and specifically as possible. Let's suppose, for example, that you are researching the meaning of color in dreams, and you see an article in a database list titled merely "Dreams." You don't know whether you should bother to read it. To avoid such confusion in your own essay and to encourage readers' interest, always use a specific title: "Interpreting Animal Imagery in Dreams," "Dream Research: An Aid to Diagnosing Depression," and so forth. Moreover, if your subject matter is controversial, let the reader know which side you're on (e.g., "The Advantages of Solar Power"). Never substitute a mere label, such as "Football Games" or "Euthanasia," for a meaningful title. And never, never label your essays "Theme One" or "Comparison and Contrast Essay." In all your writing, including the title, use your creativity to attract the readers' attention and to invite their interest in your ideas.

If you're unsure about how to present your title, here are three basic rules:

1. Your own title should not be underlined, italicized, or put in quotation marks. It should be written at the top of page one of your essay or on an appropriate title page with no special marks of punctuation.

2. Capitalize the first, last, and important words of your title. Generally, do not capitalize such words as "an," "and," "a," or "the," or prepositions, unless they appear as the first or last words of the title or follow a colon within the title.

3. Sometimes writers craft a title that presents a word or phrase followed by a colon introducing a definition, a revealing image, a question, or some other kind of explanatory material to interest the reader.

Examples   "Stephen Crane: Daredevil Reporter"

"Memories Carved in Stone: Tennessee Pioneer Memorials"

"Intervention in Iran: A Recipe for Disaster"

"Yoga: Does Twisting Like a Pretzel Really Help?"

You may use such titles to clarify a work's scope or perhaps to set the appropriate tone for your reader, but be careful not to overuse this structure. (Note that the word after the colon is capitalized as if it were the first word of the title.)

Practicing What You've Learned

Describe any weaknesses you see in the following titles. How might each one be revised to clarify its essay's content and to attract more reader interest?

1. Advice for College Freshmen

2. Essay Assignment #3: "Review of a Favorite Movie"

3. Learning to Play Texas Hold'em

4. A Comparison of Two Heroes

5. The Problem of Abandoned Pets and Its Solution

6. Steroids and Athletes Today

7. The Effects of Three Popular Diets

8. The Best Tablet on the Market

9. An Explanation of the Human Genome Project

10. My Interpretation of Auden's "The Unknown Citizen"

Assignment

A. Read one of the student or professional essays in this text and evaluate the title. Explain why you think the title is or is not effective. Or, if you prefer, write a new title for one of the essays in this book. Why is your choice as effective as (or even better than) that of the original writer?

B. *Collaborative Activity:* Bring to class three titles or headlines from print or online articles. In a small group of classmates, compare all the samples. Which ones would encourage members of the group to read on? Which one is the least interesting or helpful? (If time permits, select one effective title to read to the class as a whole.) How might your choices influence your crafting of a title for your next essay?

Applying What You've Learned to *Your* Writing

Look at the draft of the essay you are currently working on, and ask yourself these questions:

- Does the opening of my essay make my reader want to continue reading? Does the lead-in smoothly set up my thesis, or do I need to add some sort of transition to help move the reader to my main idea? Is the lead-in appropriate in terms of the tone and length of my essay?

- Does the conclusion of my essay offer an emphatic ending, one that is consistent with my essay's purpose? Have I avoided a mechanical, trite, or tacked-on closing paragraph? Have I refrained from adding a new point in my conclusion that belongs in the body of my essay or in another essay?

- Does my title interest my reader? Are its content and tone appropriate for this particular essay?

If you have answered "no" to any of these questions, you should continue revising your essay. (◆ For more help revising your prose, turn to Chapter 5.)

Chapter 4 Summary

Here is a brief restatement of what you should remember about writing introductions, conclusions, and titles:

1. Many essays will profit from a lead-in, the first sentences of the introductory paragraph that attract the reader's attention and smoothly set up the thesis statement.

2. Essays should end convincingly, without being repetitious or trite, with thoughts that emphasize the writer's main purpose.

3. Titles should invite the reader's interest by indicating the general nature of the essay's content and its tone.

Chapter 5

Drafting and Revising: Creative Thinking, Critical Thinking

"There is no good writing, only rewriting."
— James Thurber, author and humorist

"When I say writing, O, believe me, it is rewriting that I have chiefly in mind."
— Robert Louis Stevenson, novelist and essayist

The absolute necessity of revision cannot be overemphasized. All good writers rethink, rearrange, and rewrite large portions of their prose. The French novelist Colette, for instance, wrote everything over and over. In fact, she often spent an entire morning working on a single page. Hemingway, to cite another example, rewrote the ending to *A Farewell to Arms* thirty-nine times "to get the words right." Although no one expects you to make thirty-nine drafts of each essay, the point is clear: writing well means revising. **All good writers revise their prose.**

What Is Revision?

Revision is a *thinking process* that occurs any time you are working on a writing project. It means looking at your writing with a "fresh eye"—that is, reseeing your writing in ways that will enable you to make more effective choices throughout your essay. Revision often entails rethinking what you have written and asking yourself questions about its effectiveness; it involves discovery as well as change. As you write, new ideas surface, prompting you to revise what you have planned or have just written. Or perhaps these new ideas will cause changes in earlier parts of your essay. In some cases, your new ideas will encourage you to begin an entirely new draft with a different focus or approach. Revision means making important decisions about the best ways to focus, organize, develop, clarify, and emphasize your ideas. Figure 5.1 summarizes some of the revision tips and techniques discussed in this chapter.

Figure 5.1 VISUALIZING THE PROCESS: DRAFTING AND REVISING

Revision is a thinking process that asks you to look at your draft with fresh eyes; as such, it should occur throughout your writing process.

Myths about Revision

1. Revision is not autopsy.
2. Revision is not limited to editing or proofreading.
3. Revision is not punishment or busywork.

Basic Tips for Drafting and Revising

1. Leave placeholders to mark spots for future revision.
2. Mark revised or omitted sections for potential later use.
3. Always keep your notes, outlines, drafts, and an extra copy of your final draft.
4. Don't get hung up on the details in your initial attempts.

Hints When Drafting and Revising on a Computer

1. Learn to use the editing tools that your word-processing program offers.
2. Learn to edit, question your word choice, and proofread carefully with your own eyes and brain.
3. Use the computer to help you double-check for your own common errors.
4. Even if you are comfortable drafting and revising on your computer, resist doing all your work there.

Hints When Handwriting a Draft

1. Write on one side of your paper only.
2. Leave big margins on both sides of your pages to allow for jotting down new ideas.
3. Devise a system of symbols to remind you of changes you want to make later.
4. Do eventually work on a computer-generated print copy.

A Revision Process for Your Drafts

1. Rethink purpose, thesis, and audience.
2. Rethink ideas and evidence.
3. Rethink organization.
4. Rethink clarity and style.
5. Edit for grammar, punctuation, and spelling errors.
6. Proofread the entire draft.

Prewriting
Chapter 1

Drafting
Chapters 2, 3, 4, 5

Revising
Chapter 5

Editing/
Proofreading
Chapters 6, 7

© Cengage Learning 2017

When Does Revision Occur?

Revision, as previously noted, occurs throughout your writing process. Early on, you are revising as you sort through ideas to write about, and you almost certainly revise as you define your purpose and audience and sharpen your thesis. Some revising may be done in your head, and some may be on paper or a computer screen as you plan, sketch, or "discovery-write" your ideas. Later, during drafting, revision becomes more individualized and complex. Many writers find themselves sweeping back and forth over their papers, writing for a bit and then rereading what they wrote, making changes, and then moving ahead. Some writers like to revise "lumps," or pieces of writing, perhaps reviewing one major idea or paragraph at a time. Frequently, writers discover that a better idea is occurring almost at the very moment they are putting another thought on a page. And virtually all writers revise after "reseeing" a draft in its entirety.

Revision, then, occurs before drafting, during drafting, between parts of drafts, and at the ends of drafts. You can revise a word, a sentence, a paragraph, or an entire essay. If you are like most writers, you sometimes revise almost automatically as you write (deleting one word or line and quickly replacing it with another as you move on, for example), and at other times you revise very deliberately (concentrating on a conclusion you know is weak, for example). Revision is "rethinking," and that activity can happen any time, in many ways, in any part of your writing.

Myths about Revision

If revision is rethinking, what is it not? Three misconceptions about revision are addressed here.

1. **Revision is not autopsy.** Revision is not an isolated stage of writing that occurs *only* after your last draft is written or right before your paper is due. Revising is not merely a postmortem procedure, to be performed only after your creative juices have ceased to flow. Good writing, as the popular writer James Thurber noted, *is* revision, and revision occurs throughout the writing process.

2. **Revision is not limited to editing or proofreading.** Too many writers mistakenly equate revision with editing and proofreading. *Editing* means revising for "surface errors"—mistakes in spelling, grammar, punctuation, sentence sense, and word choice. Certainly, good writers comb their papers for such errors, and they edit their prose extensively for clarity, conciseness, and emphasis, too. *Proofreading* to search out and destroy errors and typos that distort meaning or distract the reader is also important. Without question, both editing and proofreading are essential to a polished paper. But revision is not *limited* to such activities. It includes them but also encompasses those larger, global changes writers may make in purpose, focus, organization, and development. Writers who revise effectively not only change words and catch mechanical errors but also typically add, delete, rearrange, and rewrite large chunks of prose. In other words, revision is not cosmetic surgery on a body that may need major resuscitation.

3. **Revision is not punishment or busywork.** At one time or another, most of us have found ourselves guilty of racing too quickly through a particular job and then moving on. And perhaps just as often we have found ourselves redoing such jobs because the results were so disappointing. Some people may regard revising in a similar light—as the repeat performance of a job done poorly the first time. But that attitude isn't productive. Revising isn't punishment for failing to produce a perfect first draft. Rarely, if ever, does anyone—even our most admired professional writers—produce the results he or she wants without revising.* Remember that revising is not a tacked-on stage, nor is it merely a quick touch-up; it's an integral part of the entire writing process itself. It's an ongoing opportunity to discover, remember, reshape, and refine your ideas.

If you've ever created something you now treasure—a piece of jewelry, furniture, painting, or music—recall the time you put into it. You probably thought about it from several angles, experimented with it, crafted it, worked it through expected and unexpected problems, and smoothed out its minor glitches, all to achieve the results you wanted. Similarly, with each revision you make, your paper becomes clearer, truer, more satisfying to you and to your readers. With practice, you will produce writing you are proud of—and you will discover that revising has become not only an essential but also a natural part of your writing process.

Can I Learn to Improve My Revision Skills?

Because revision is such a multifaceted and individual activity, no textbook can guide you through all the rethinking you may do as you move through each sentence of every writing project. But certainly you can learn to improve your ability to think both creatively and analytically about your prose. To sharpen your critical thinking and revision skills, this chapter will suggest a step-by-step method of self-questioning designed to help you achieve your writing goals.

Preparing to Draft

Before you begin drafting (either a "discovery" draft or a draft from your working thesis), remember this important piece of advice: no part of your draft is sacred or permanent. No matter what you write at this point, you can always change it. Drafting is discovering and recollecting as well as developing ideas from your earlier plans. Take the pressure off yourself: no one expects blue-ribbon prose in early drafts. (◆ If you can't seem to get going or if you do become stuck along the way, reread pages 103–104 and 125–128 of this chapter for help triumphing over your procrastination or case of Writer's Block.) Figure 5.1 (see page 96) highlights some of the important drafting tips and techniques explained below.

---

*All of us have heard stories about famous essays or poems composed at one quick sitting. Bursts of creativity do happen. But it's also possible that authors of such pieces revise extensively in their heads before they write. They may rattle ideas around in their brains for such a prolonged period that the actual writing does in fact flow easily or may even seem "dictated" by an inner voice. This sort of lengthy internal "cooking" may work well at various times for you, too.

Some Basic Tips for Drafting

Because you will be making many changes in your writing, you may find revising less cumbersome and time-consuming if you keep in mind these basic tips for drafting as described here.

1. If your ideas are flowing well but you realize you need more supporting evidence for some of your points, consider leaving some blank spots or inserting a placeholder to fill in later. For example, let's say you are writing about the effects of social media campaigns on presidential elections; your ideas are good, but in a particular body paragraph you decide some statistics on Twitter use or Facebook posts would be most convincing. Or perhaps you need to cite an example of a particular Tweet, but you just can't think of a good one at that moment. Leave a spot for the piece of evidence with a key word or two to remind you of what's needed, and keep writing. Later, when you come back to that spot, you can add the appropriate support. If you can't find or think of the right supporting evidence to insert, you may decide to omit that point.

2. If you do decide to rewrite or omit something—a sentence or an entire passage—in a draft, mark it in some fashion, perhaps by highlighting it or italicizing it if using a computer or a single "X" or line through it lightly in a handwritten draft. Don't scratch it out or destroy it completely; you may realize later that you want to reinsert the material there or move it to another, better place. Or consider moving a larger chunk of prose to a "holding page" or to the end of the current draft so you can take another look at it later.

3. Always keep your notes, outlines, drafts, and an extra copy of your final paper. Never burn your bridges—or your drafts! Sometimes essays change directions, and writers find they can return to prewriting or earlier drafts to recover ideas, once rejected, that now work well. Drafts also may contain ideas that didn't work in one paper but look like great starts for another assignment. Tracking revisions from draft to draft can give writers a sense of accomplishment and insight into their composing processes. And drafts can be good insurance in case final copies of papers, either electronic or hard copy, are lost or accidentally destroyed.

4. Finally, don't get hung up on the details. Too many novice writers allow themselves to get bogged down in the details of word choice, sentence structure, or proper punctuation and lose track of their paper's larger mission. Remember that the drafting stage is about getting your ideas down in a coherent, organized, supported fashion. Save the sentence-level polishing for later. Almost no one can produce a "perfect" first draft, and trying to do so results in frustration and often surrender.

Some Hints When Drafting on a Computer

Most college students today are accustomed to using computers at school, home, or work, and feel quite comfortable drafting and revising at their keyboards. If this has been your experience, you probably already know how helpful computers can be in

Ermolaev Alexander/Shutterstock.com

all stages of the writing process. You can, for example, compose and store your pre-writing activities, journal entries, notes, or good ideas in various files until you need to recall certain information—and you can easily produce extra copies of your drafts or finished essays without having to search out a copy machine and correct change. Spell-checkers and dictionaries can help you correct many of your errors and typos.

But the most important use of the computer to a writer may be what it can do as you draft and revise your prose. A word-processing program enables you to add, delete, or change words easily; it allows you to move words, sentences, and even paragraphs or larger pieces of your essay. Tracking tools allow a record of changes, additions, and deletions. In other words, computers can help us as writers do the kind of deep-structure revision necessary to produce our best, most effective prose—the kind of major changes that, in the pre-computer era, students may have been hesitant to make because of the time involved in recopying or retyping major portions of their drafts. But computer drafting comes with its own set of special temptations and potential problems. Here, in addition to the hints in the previous section, are a few more suggestions for drafting and revising your essay on a computer:

1. To avoid the "agony of delete," always save what you have composed every ten minutes or so, and consider printing out your work (or copying it to a flash drive or e-mailing it to yourself) after each drafting session in case your system crashes or gobbles your pages. Remember that all sorts of events, from electrical storms to carpet cleaning, have caused the tiny leprechauns in computers to behave badly; having copies of your notes and latest revisions will help you reconstruct your work should disaster strike. If you have drafts in multiple files, add the date to each file name (Rafting 4-10); for multiple versions on the same date, add a letter (Rafting 4-10a, Rafting 4-10b). (Also, if you are working on multiple writing tasks, as most students are, or if you are just the forgetful type, develop the habit of noting on each print copy the name you have given the file. Doing so may save you from a frustrating search through your list of existing documents, especially if several days have elapsed between drafts.)

2. Do learn to use the editing tools that your word-processing program offers. In addition to allowing you to make changes and move text, most programs offer a dictionary to help you check the proper spellings, meanings, and uses of your words; a thesaurus can help you expand your vocabulary, avoid repetition of words, or find just the right word to express the shade of meaning you want. Even the "word count" command can help writers who want to trim the fat from their essays.

One of the most prized tools the computer offers writers is the spell-checker. For poor spellers and bad typists, the invention of the spell-checker ranks right up there with penicillin as a boon to humankind. The spell-checker performs minor miracles as it asks writers to reconsider certain words as typed on the page. If you have one available, by all means run it! But be aware of its limitations; though modern spell-checkers now recognize more sophisticated usage situations such as the correct use of the possessive case, they remain fallible.

Make sure to carefully review your document for common spelling and grammar mistakes. Learn to edit, question your word choice, and proofread carefully with your own eyes and brain. The same advice holds true for grammar-check and "style" programs, too. Such programs may help you take a second look at your grammar, punctuation, or word choice, but do not rely on *any* computer program to do your editing and proofreading work for you.

3. Use the computer to help you double-check for your own common errors. By using the "search," "find," or similar command, writers can highlight words they know they frequently misuse. For example, perhaps you have an ongoing struggle with the uses of "affect" and "effect" and know that you have used these words often in your essay. Reviewing your word-choice decisions in the proofreading stage could make an important difference to your readers, who wish to travel smoothly through the ideas in your essay without annoying errors flagging down their attention. Also consider searching for and replacing words that you know you overuse or those that are lazy or vague. For example, until you break yourself of the habit, highlight any use of the word "thing." In each case, are you really discussing an unknown quantity—or do you need to press yourself to find a more specific or vivid word to communicate what you mean?

4. Even if you are comfortable drafting on your computer, resist doing all your work there. It's a good idea from time to time to read your screen version in its printed form—the format your readers may see. Many effective writers move back and forth multiple times between the computer screen and printed copies of their drafts. Experiment to discover the best ways for you to revise. Remember that a neatly printed draft can look professional but may still need much rethinking, restructuring, and polishing!

Some Hints When Handwriting a Draft

While most students now prefer to perform their drafting tasks at the computer keyboard, good old-fashioned paper-and-pencil drafting can also be a useful method for many writers. Handwriting your draft requires a slower, more thoughtful approach to expressing your ideas, and this approach to drafting can reap great rewards for the patient student of writing. Here are some suggestions to keep in mind if you are handwriting your draft:

1. If you are handwriting your first drafts, always write on one side of your paper only, in case you want to cut and tape together portions of drafts or you want to experiment with interchanging parts of a particular draft. (If you have written

on both sides, you may have to copy the parts of your essay you want to save; your time is better spent creating and revising.)

2. Leave big margins on *both* sides of any handwritten pages so you can add information later or jot down new ideas as they occur. (Some writers also skip lines for this reason. If you choose to write on every other line, however, do remember that you may not be getting a true picture of your paragraph development or essay length. A handwritten double-spaced body paragraph, for example, may appear skimpy in your typed final copy.)

3. Devise a system of symbols (circles, stars, checks, asterisks, etc.) that will remind you of changes you want to make later. For example, if you're in hot pursuit of a great idea but can't think of the exact word you want, put down a word that's close, circle it (or type three XXXs by it), and go on so that your thinking is not derailed. Similarly, a check in the margin might mean "return to this tangled sentence." A question mark might mean a fuzzy idea, and a star, a great idea that needs expanding. A system of symbols can save you from agonizing over every inch of your essay while you are still trying to discover and clarify your ideas.

4. If you begin with a handwritten draft, do eventually work on a print copy. The more compact spacing of typed prose allows you to see more clearly the relationship of the parts in your essay, making it easier for you to organize and develop your ideas. It is also far more likely that you will catch spelling and other mechanical errors in a printed draft.

Writing Centers, Computer Classrooms, and Electronic Networks

Today, most schools have professionally staffed writing centers and/or computer labs open to composition students. The writing center or lab likely has print or electronic resources designed to help you brainstorm, focus your ideas, organize a working structure, compose your drafts, revise your essay, and proofread. These resources also can help you to research a topic by allowing you to check information available in your campus library as well as providing virtual access to other libraries and assorted Web sources. Many writing centers have special tutors on hand to answer your questions about your drafts as well as to explain effective uses of the available electronic tools. In addition, most schools now utilize a learning management system such as Canvas or Blackboard, which allow a specific group of writers to communicate with each other and/or with their instructor. In such a system's discussion forums, for example, students might read each other's drafts and make suggestions or post comments about a current reading assignment for their classmates to consider.

Whether the program you are using at home or at school is a series of simple commands or an elaborate instructional system, make a point of getting to know how to use the computer in the most effective ways. Study the advice that accompanies your word-processing program, and don't be afraid to ask your instructor or computer lab tutor for assistance. The more you practice using your available electronic resources to help you organize, develop, and revise your prose, the better your writing will be.

Procrastination: Enemy of Critical Thinking, Thief of Time

Now that you have a good understanding of the continual interplay between writing and revision and have your writing tools at hand, you are ready to get down to business, to begin that first draft. You're going to start this very afternoon. Or maybe early tomorrow morning would be better. Or in that free hour between classes on Tuesday. Or, let's see, over the weekend. Or . . .

Let's talk about *procrastination.* Yes, right now, not later.

Procrastination refers to the human practice of postponing action and/or thought. It's a common response; all of us at one time or another have put off activities—chores, jobs, confrontations, responsibilities—that we'd rather not do. So we stall, finding excuses, and often discover ourselves stressed out, doing poor last-minute work, sometimes taking longer to do the job than if we had just jumped in right away.

Although putting off an assignment may feel good temporarily, doing so may ultimately produce more time-wasting anxiety in the long run, as you guiltily fret and dodge each time thoughts of your project surface. As the famous psychologist William James once said, "Nothing is so fatiguing as the eternal hanging on of an uncompleted task."

But procrastination often produces a worse effect than creeping anxiety: it is likely to defeat your best chance of success. Waiting too long to begin means less time to think about what you are writing. Rather than thoroughly exploring your ideas and shaping them effectively for your purpose and audience, you may only skim your subject's surface or veer off course without time to revise. *Critical thinking*—the careful consideration of ideas, claims, and evidence—takes time, effort, and some objective distance, as will be discussed in more detail on pages 106–110. Even if your initial ideas are good ones, a last-minute draft may mean you have inadequate time for creating clear organization or careful editing of contorted sentences or distracting errors. Worst-case scenario: the pressure to produce prose at the eleventh hour is so great you develop paralyzing Writer's Block and can't finish your assignment at all.

So if you want to avoid self-sabotage, challenge yourself to overcome your procrastination. Avoid what we might call, using a football metaphor, the fourth down and long "desperation punt-draft." That is, don't get yourself into a crunch situation in which, facing the crashing onrush of a deadline, you sit at the computer, write whatever comes to mind, rip the draft from the printer, and turn in feeble drivel. Triumph unlikely.

Despite the lack of success it may bring, procrastination can be a hard habit to break. How can you change such a pattern? First, understand its causes. For many people, procrastination results from insecurity, the fear that we aren't up to the task at hand. The work is too hard; it won't be good enough. Arm yourself against these self-doubts by realizing that you do know how to begin a discovery draft (review earlier chapters in this book if necessary) and that you don't have to instantly produce perfect prose. Begin early and let it be a comfort that you have given yourself plenty of time to think, rethink, stop, start, and revise in stages (following the steps outlined in this chapter will help). If you are a habitual procrastinator in many areas of your life, focus on your larger, long-range goals rather than on short-term ease. Consider: If I want to be ultimately successful at "X," what choices today will best accomplish this? And remember, busy is not the same as productive.

Mental attitude is key, but here are some additional hints to help you conquer procrastination during your writing process:

1. As soon as you receive and understand your assignment, break your writing task into parts (working thesis, rough outline, first major point, etc.). Make a list of these parts and give yourself a specific deadline to accomplish each one ("Have draft of first body paragraph finished by Wednesday noon."). Be sure to set aside an extra day for time away from your last draft and enough time after that day to "resee" and polish your essay, however necessary. Check and revise your list each day; try to stay up with or even ahead of your schedule. Yes, Life Happens, but if you have started early enough, you can miss a deadline and still be all right.

2. Promise yourself a "carrot" or reward after you successfully complete an item on your list, even if the gift to yourself is as small as a coffee break or a short walk outside.

3. Procrastinators are often easily distracted. Leave your friends; close the door. Turn off your phone and TV; do not allow yourself to check e-mail or your social media pages while you are working. If you can't resist the sound of temptation, use your technology's mute button. (Your brain has a mute button, too; use it to silence non-writing thoughts and stay on task.)

4. Find a suitable place to work, one that is comfortable but not too cozy or near distractions. Although it may be tempting to write as you flop on a couch or prop up in bed, the time-to-begin function in your brain will probably turn on quicker if you are sitting upright at a desk or table, squarely facing the task at hand. (Hint: Some writers have discovered that they perform better on in-class exams and essays if they prepare in an environment similar to the classroom or testing center, such as a library or study room.)

5. Remember that no first draft is perfect and that revision is recursive; it occurs throughout your writing process in both large and small ways. As you move toward completion of a rough draft, familiarize yourself with the suggested six-stage revision procedure that follows this section to ensure that you do not derail yourself by trying to revise every part of your essay at the same time.

Conquering your procrastination should help you produce successful results: a thoughtful, well-written essay. If at any time during your drafting you do become temporarily stuck, don't panic—after all, you've left yourself plenty of time, right? ◆ Turning to the suggestions for beating Writer's Block, at the end of this chapter, will help you start moving again.

A Revision Process for Your Drafts

Let's assume at this point that you have completed a draft, using the first four chapters of this book as a guide. You feel you've chosen an interesting topic and collected some good ideas. Perhaps the ideas came quickly or perhaps you had to coax them. However your thoughts came, they're now in print—you have a draft with meaning and a general order, although it's probably much rougher in some spots than in others. Now it's time to "resee" this draft in a comprehensive way.

But wait. If possible, put a night's sleep or at least a few hours between this draft and the advice that appears on the next few pages. All writers become tired when they work on any project for too long at one sitting, and then they lose a sense of perspective. When you've looked at a piece of prose again and again, you may begin to read what's written in your head instead of what's on the page—that is, you may begin to "fill in" for yourself, reading into your prose what you meant to say rather than what your reader will actually see. Always try to start your writing process early enough to give yourself a few breaks from the action. You'll find that you will be better able to evaluate the strengths and weaknesses of your prose when you are fresh.

When you do return to your draft, *don't try to look at all the parts of your paper, from ideas to organization to mechanics, at the same time.* Trying to resee everything at once is rarely possible and will only overload and frustrate you. It may cause you to overlook some important part of your paper that needs your full attention. Overload can also block your creative ideas. Therefore, instead of trying to revise an entire draft in one swoop, break your revising process into a series of smaller, more manageable steps. Here is a suggested process:

I. Rethink purpose, thesis, and audience
II. Rethink ideas and evidence
III. Rethink organization
IV. Rethink clarity and style
V. Edit grammar, punctuation, and spelling
VI. Proofread entire essay

IMPORTANT: Please note that these steps are not necessarily distinct, nor must you always follow this suggested order. You certainly might, for instance, add details to a paragraph when you decide to move or reorder it. Or you might replace a vague word with a specific one after thinking about your audience and their needs. After strengthening a particular point, you might decide to offer it last, and therefore you rearrange the order of your paragraphs. In other words, the steps offered here are not part of a forced march—they are here simply to remind you to rethink and improve any part of your essay that needs work.

Now let's look at each of the steps in the revision process suggested here in more detail.

I. Revising for Purpose, Thesis, and Audience

To be effective, writers need a clear sense of purpose and audience. Their essays must present (or clearly imply) a main idea or thesis designed to fulfill that purpose and to inform their audience. As you reread your draft, ask yourself the following questions:

- Have I fulfilled the objectives of my assignment? (For example, if you were asked to analyze the causes of a problem, did you merely describe or summarize it instead?)

- Did I follow directions carefully? (If you were given a three-part assignment, did you treat all parts as requested?)

- Do I understand the purpose of my essay? Am I trying to inform, persuade, or amuse my readers? Spur them to action? Convince them to change their minds? Give them a new idea? Am I myself clear about my exact intent— what I want to do or say—in this essay?

- Does my essay reflect my clearly understood purpose by offering an appropriately narrowed and focused thesis? (After reading through your essay once, could a reader easily state its purpose and main point?)

- Do I have a clear picture of my audience—their character, knowledge, and expectations?

- Have I addressed both my purpose and my readers' needs by selecting appropriate strategies of development for my essay? (For example, would it be better to write an essay primarily developed with examples illustrating the community's need for a new hospital, or should you present a more formal argument that also rebuffs objections to the project? Should you narrate the story of your accident or analyze its effects on your family?)

If you feel that your draft needs work in any of these areas, make changes. ◆ You might find it helpful to review Chapters 1 and 2 of this text to guide you as you revise.

II. Revising for Ideas and Evidence

If you're satisfied that your purpose and thesis are clear to your readers, begin to look closely at the development of your essay's ideas.

You want your readers to accept your thesis. To achieve this goal, you must offer body paragraphs whose major points clearly support that main idea. As you examine the body of your essay, you might ask yourself questions such as these:

- Is there a clear relationship between my thesis and each of the major points presented in the body of my essay? That is, does each major point in my essay further my readers' understanding, and thus their acceptance, of my thesis's general claim?

- Did I write myself into a new or slightly different position as I drafted my essay? If so, do I need to begin another draft with a new working thesis?

- Have I included all the major points necessary to the readers' understanding of my subject or have I omitted pertinent ones? (On the other hand, have I included major ideas that aren't relevant or that actually belong in a different essay?)

- Are my major points located and stated clearly in specific language so that readers can easily see what position I am taking in each part of my discussion?

If you are happy with your choice and presentation of the major ideas in the body of your essay, it's time to look closely at the evidence you are offering to support those ideas (which, in turn, support the claim of your thesis). To choose the best supporting evidence for their major points, effective writers use *critical thinking skills.*

What Is Critical Thinking?

Critical thinking refers to the ability to reflect upon and evaluate the merits of our own ideas and those of others as we decide what to believe, what to do, or how to act. To think "critically" about ideas doesn't mean being hostile or negative; it means undertaking a close, reasonable examination of opinions, logic, and evidence before we accept certain claims or pass them along to others.

Critical thinking, in your classes, professional work, or personal life, calls for questioning and evaluation. Is the idea or claim under consideration clear, fair, relevant? Is the supporting evidence accurate, logical, reasonable? Is its source reliable, current, balanced? Critical thinking employs these and other similar questions as we examine various kinds of assertions and beliefs.

Here's a common situation in which critical thinking comes into play: two of your friends are arguing over the use of animals in medical research. Each friend has many points to offer; each is presenting statistics, case studies, the words of experts, and hypothetical situations that might arise. Many of the statistics and experts on one side of the argument seem to contradict directly the figures and authorities on the other side. Which side do you take? Why? Are there other points of view to consider? How can you know what to think?

Every day we are faced with just such decisions. Practicing critical thinking skills in your composition course will help you learn to judge what you hear and read, ultimately strengthening your confidence in your choice of beliefs and actions.

Thinking Critically as a Writer

As a writer, you will be thinking critically in two important ways. First, you will need to think critically about any information you may be collecting to use as evidence in your essay. You will, for example, need to be a critical reader as you consider information from books, journals, or electronic sources. (◆ For specific advice to help you become an effective critical reader, see the steps outlined in Chapter 8. For more discussion on the evaluation and selection of reliable print and online sources, turn to pages 414–417 in Chapter 19.)

As you draft and revise your essay, you must become a critical thinker in a second way: you must become your own toughest reader-critic. To convince your readers that your essay has merit, you must stand back and assess objectively what you have written. Are your ideas clear not only to you but to your readers as well? Will readers find your opinions well developed, logical, and supported? In other words, to revise more effectively, try role-playing one of your own most thoughtful critical readers, someone who will be closely examining the ideas and evidence in your essay before agreeing with its position.

Here are six suggestions to help you think critically as you draft and revise:

1. **Learn to distinguish fact from opinion.** A *fact* is an accepted truth whose verification is not affected by its source. No matter who presents it, a fact remains true. We accept some statements as facts because we can test them personally (fire is hot) or because they have been verified frequently by others (penguins live in Antarctica). We accept as fact, for example, that Martin Luther King, Jr., was murdered on April 4, 1968, at the Lorraine Motel in Memphis, Tennessee. However, even though much investigation and debate have focused on the assassination, the question of who was responsible for the murder is, for many people, still a matter of *opinion*. Although some people think that James Earl Ray was the lone gunman, a number of others

believe in other explanations, holding local racists, Memphis police, the FBI, or the Mafia responsible to varying degrees. Opinions are often based on one's awareness and interpretation of information and can often be influenced by personal feelings. Therefore, as you write, be careful that you don't present your personal opinions as facts accepted by everyone. Opinions are debatable, and therefore you must always support them before your readers will be convinced.

2. **Support your opinions with evidence.** To support your opinions, you must offer evidence of one or more kinds. You have a variety of options to choose from. You might support one idea by using personal experiences. Or you might describe the experiences of friends or family. In another place you might decide to offer detailed examples or to cite statistics or to quote an expert on your subject. You can also use hypothetical examples, researched material, vivid descriptions, reasoned arguments, revealing comparisons, case studies, or testimony of relevant participants, just to name a few other strategies. Consider your purpose and your audience, review the possibilities, and choose the most effective kind of support. The more convincing the support, the more likely your readers are to accept your opinions as true. (◆ If you need to review some sample paragraphs developed by various types of evidence, turn to pages 61–64 of Chapter 3.)

3. **Evaluate the strength and source of your evidence.** As you choose your evidence, you should consider its value for the particular point it will support. Use your critical thinking skills to scrutinize the nature and source of your evidence carefully. If you are using examples, do they clearly illustrate your claim? Does this example or a different one (or both?) provide the best illustration of your particular point? Is description alone enough support here? Are your statistics or researched material from a reliable, current source? Was information from your research collected in a careful, professional way? Are your experts unbiased authorities in the field under discussion? Where did your experts obtain their information? (For example, are you claiming that a certain vitamin drink possesses healing powers because a professional athlete said so and she sounded reasonable to you? Just how much do you know about the source of a particular Web site? Or the knowledge of a blogger?) Asking yourself the kinds of questions posed here will help you develop a critical eye for choosing the best evidence to support your opinions. (◆ For more discussion on choosing reliable sources, see pages 414–417.)

IMPORTANT REMINDER: If you decide to include the ideas, opinions, or research of others to support your ideas, you must not only use your critical thinking skills to evaluate the evidence but you must also cite the sources of your borrowed material carefully. ◆ For information on selecting and accurately documenting research data, such as studies, statistics, or the testimony of authorities, see Chapters 19 and 20 on using and documenting sources. Remember that if you include the specific ideas of others in your paper, you must give proper credit, even if you do not quote the material word for word. Learning to identify and document your sources correctly for your readers will strengthen your claims and also prevent any unintentional plagiarism.

4. **Use enough specific supporting evidence.** Readers need to see strong, relevant supporting evidence throughout your essay. You must be sure, therefore, that you have enough clearly stated evidence for each of your major points. If you present, for instance, too few examples or only a vague reference to an event that supports one of your ideas, a reader may remain unconvinced or may even be confused. As you revise, ask yourself questions such as these: "Do I need to provide additional information here?" "Do I need more details to clarify my supporting evidence?" "Is any of my evidence clouded by vague or fuzzy language?" If you feel additional supporting evidence or details are needed, take another look at any prewriting you did or use one of the "pump-primer" techniques described in Chapter 1 to discover some new creative thoughts. For some topics, you may need to do more research or interviewing to find the information you need. (Writers occasionally need to prune ideas too, especially if they're repetitious or off the topic. But, in general, most early drafts are thin or overly general and will profit from more, rather than less, specific supporting evidence.)

5. **Watch for biases and strong emotions that may undermine evidence.** As you think critically about evidence you are using, monitor any biases and emotional attitudes that may distort information you wish to incorporate into your essay. If you are using personal experiences, for example, have you calmed down enough from your anger over your landlord's actions to write about the clash in a rational, persuasive way? In an essay criticizing a particular product, are you so familiar with the frustrating item that you are making ambiguous claims? (If you write, "The new instructions for assembly are more confusing than ever," have you shown that they were confusing in the first place? Or why they are more so now?) Be sensitive to any racial, ethnic, cultural, religious, or gender-based assumptions you or your sources may have. Opinions based on generalizations and stereotypes ("Japanese cars are good buys because Asians are more efficient workers than Americans"; "Women should stay home and out of the workplace because they are better with children than men") are not convincing to thinking readers.

6. **Check your evidence for logical fallacies.** Thinking critically about your drafts should help you support your ideas with reasonable, logical explanations and arguments. Logical fallacies are common errors in reasoning that good writers try to avoid. ◆ Those fallacies found most often today are explained on pages 316–319 of this text; reviewing them will enable you to identify problems in logic that might appear in the writing of others or in your own drafts.

Critical thinking is not, of course, limited to the suggestions offered here. But by practicing this advice, you will begin to develop and sharpen analytical skills that should improve any writing project.

A Special Note: Critical Thinking and Visual Literacy

Using critical thinking to analyze and evaluate the written and spoken claims of others is an essential skill. In today's media-saturated world, however, you also need to sharpen your *visual literacy*—that is, your ability to "read" and assess the validity of messages presented through all kinds of images. In particular, photographs that may appear in newspapers, magazines, billboards, Web pages, blogs, and social media (to list only a few sources) may be altered in ways to manipulate your response. Most of us know that the faces of models in cosmetic ads are frequently airbrushed to lure us to a particular product and that tabloids have been routinely guilty of staging attention-grabbing pictures (space invaders? Big Foot?) to sell their newspapers. Photoshopped pictures making the rounds on the Internet may be silly fun (deer heads on humans) or wry satire (the California university police officer casually pepper-spraying protestors transported into other settings, including famous art works such as the signing of the Constitution).

But on a much more serious note, be aware that altered pictures have been used dishonestly as evidence for political and social claims in order to arouse fear, encourage prejudice, or substantiate false statements. For example, in recent years, a presidential candidate was "inserted" into a photo taken at a controversial rally he never attended, while, in another picture, a different candidate at a speaking event had soldiers magically cloned throughout the crowd in an attempt to exaggerate his support from military personnel. While some photos are just plain dishonest in their altered states, others lack validity because they are taken out of context or are not current.

Just as you would not accept all written or spoken communication as true or valid without thoughtful scrutiny, do not be taken in by visual images that also need your close, critical examination. Be especially careful with images circulated on the Internet, which, unlike many print sources, has no designated fact-checker or other methods of "quality control."

III. Revising for Organization

In reality, you have probably already made several changes in the order and organization of ideas in your draft. As noted before, it's likely that when you thought about your essay's meaning—its major points and their supporting evidence—you also thought about the arrangement of those ideas. As you take another look at your draft's organization, use these questions as a guide:

- Am I satisfied with the organizational strategy I selected for my purpose? (For example, would an essay developed primarily by comparison and contrast achieve your purpose better than a narrative approach?)

- Are my major points ordered in a logical, easy-to-follow pattern? Would readers understand my thinking better if certain paragraphs or major ideas were rearranged? Added? Divided? Omitted? Expanded?

- Are my major points presented in topic sentences that state each important idea clearly and specifically? (If any of your topic sentences are implied rather than stated, are you absolutely, 100% sure that your ideas cannot be overlooked or even slightly misunderstood by your readers?)

- Is there a smooth flow between my major ideas? Between paragraphs? Within paragraphs? Have I used enough transitional devices to guide the reader along?

- Are any parts of my essay out of proportion? Too long or too brief to do their job effectively?

- Do my title and lead-in draw readers into the essay and toward my thesis?
- Does my conclusion end my discussion thoughtfully, emphatically, or memorably?

Don't be afraid to restructure your drafts. Most good writers rearrange and recast large portions of their prose. Describing his writing process, the admired novelist Bernard Malamud once said, "First drafts are for learning what one's [writing] wants him to say. Revision works with that knowledge to enlarge and enhance an idea, to reform it." ◆ Reviewing Chapters 3 and 4 may help you address questions about organization, beginnings, or endings.

IV. Revising for Clarity and Style

As you've revised for purpose, ideas, and organization, you have also taken steps to clarify your prose. Making a special point now of focusing on sentences and word choice will help ensure your readers' complete understanding of your thinking. Read through your draft, asking these kinds of questions:

- Is each sentence as clear and precise as it could be for readers who do not know what I know? Are there sentences that contain misplaced words or convoluted phrases that might cause confusion?
- Are there any sentences that are unnecessarily wordy? Is there deadwood that could be eliminated? (Remember that concise prose is more effective than wordy, "fat" prose because readers can more easily find and follow key ideas and terms. Nearly every writer has a wordiness problem that chokes communication, so now is the season to prune.)
- Do any sentences run on for too long to be fully understood? Can any repetitive or choppy sentences be combined to achieve clarity and a pleasing variation of sentence style? (To help you decide whether you need to combine sentences, you might try this experiment: select a body paragraph and count the number of words it contains. Then, count the number of sentences; divide the number of words by the number of sentences to discover the average number of words per sentence. If your score is less than 15–18, you might need to combine *some* sentences. Good prose offers a variety of sentence lengths and patterns.)
- Are all my words and their connotations accurate and appropriate?
- Can I clarify and energize my prose by adding "showing" details and by replacing bland, vague words with vivid, specific ones? By using active verbs rather than passive ones?
- Can I eliminate any pretentious or unnecessary jargon or language that's inappropriate for my audience? Replace clichés and trite expressions with fresh, original phrases?
- Is my voice authentic, or am I trying to sound like someone else? Is my tone reasonable, honest, and consistent?

◆ The issues raised by these questions—and many others—are discussed in detail in Chapters 6 and 7, on effective sentences and words, which offer more advice on clarifying language and improving style.

V. Editing for Errors

Writers who are proud of the choices they've made in content, organization, and style are, to use a baseball metaphor, rounding third base and heading for home. But there's more to be done. Shift from a baseball metaphor to car maintenance for a moment. All good essays are not only fine-tuned but also waxed and polished—they are edited and proofread repeatedly for errors until they shine. To help you polish your prose by correcting errors in punctuation, grammar, spelling, and diction, here are some hints for effective editing:

Read aloud. In addition to repeatedly reading your draft silently, reading your draft aloud is a good technique because it allows your ears to hear ungrammatical "clunks" or unintended gaps in sense or sound you may otherwise miss. (Reading aloud may also flag omitted words. If, for example, the mother had reread this note to her child's teacher, she might have noticed a missing word: "Please excuse Ian for being. It was his father's fault.")

Know your enemies. Learn to identify your particularly troublesome areas in punctuation and grammar, and then read through your draft for one of these problems at a time: once for fragments, once for comma splices, once for run-ons, and so on. (If you try to look for too many errors at each reading, you'll probably miss quite a few.)

Read backwards. Try reading your draft one sentence at a time starting at the *end* of your essay and working toward the beginning. Don't read each sentence word-for-word backwards—just read the essay one sentence at a time from back to front. When writers try to edit (or proofread) starting at the beginning of their essays, they tend to begin thinking about the ideas they're reading rather than concentrating on the task of editing for errors. By reading one sentence at a time from the back, you will find that the sentences will still make sense but that you are less likely to wander away from the job at hand.

Learn some tricks. There are special techniques for treating some punctuation and grammar problems. ◆ If you have trouble with comma splices, for example, turn to the FANBOYS hint on page 151. If fragments plague your writing, try the "It is true that" test explained on page 134. Consider designating a special part of your journal or class notebook to record in your own words these tricks and other useful pieces of advice so that you can refer to them easily and often.

Eliminate common irritants. Review your draft for those diction and mechanical errors many readers find especially annoying because they often reflect sheer carelessness. For example, look at these frequently confused words: *it's/its, your/you're, there/their/they're, who's/whose* (◆ other often-confused words are listed on page 159). Some readers are ready for a national march to protest the public's abandonment of the apostrophe, the Amelia Earhart of punctuation. (Apostrophes *can* change the meaning of sentences: "The teacher called the students names." Was the instructor being rude or just taking roll?) It's a grammatical jungle out there, so be sensitive to your weary readers.

Use your tools. Keep your dictionary handy to check the spellings, usages, and meanings of words in doubt. A thesaurus can also be useful if you can restrain any tendencies you might have for growing overly exotic prose. If you are using a computer spell-checker, by all means run it after your last revisions are completed. Do remember, as noted earlier in this chapter, that such programs only flag words whose spelling they don't recognize; they will not alert you to omitted or confused words (*affect/effect*), nor will they signal when you've typed in a wrong, but correctly spelled, word (*form* for *from*).

◆ Use Part Four of this text to help resolve any questions you may have about grammar, mechanics, and spelling. Advice on untangling sentences and clarifying word choice in Chapters 6 and 7 may be useful, too.

VI. Proofreading

Proofread your final draft several times, putting as much time between the last two readings as possible. Fresh eyes catch more typographical or careless errors. Remember that typing errors—even the simple transposing of letters—can change the meaning of an entire thought and occasionally bring unintended humor to your prose. (Imagine, for example, the surprise of restaurant owners whose new lease instructed them to "Please sing the terms of the agreement." Or consider the ramifications of the newspaper ad offering "Great dames for sale" or the 1716 Bible whose advice "sin no more" was misprinted as "sin on more.")

Make sure, too, that any hard-copy paper looks professional before you turn it in. You wouldn't, after all, expect to be taken seriously if you went to an executive job interview dressed in scruffy jeans. Turning in a paper with a coffee stain or ink smear on it has about the same effect as a blob of spinach in your teeth—it distracts folks from hearing what you have to say. If your final copy has stains, smears, tears, or tatters, reprint or photo copy your pages for a fresh look.

Check to be sure you've formatted your paper exactly as your assignment requested. Some instructors ask for a title page; others want folders containing all your drafts and prewriting. Most teachers requiring print copy want essays with pages that are numbered, ordered correctly, and paper-clipped or stapled, with clean edges (no sheets violently ripped from a spiral notebook still dribbling angry confetti down one side; no pages mutilated at the corners by the useless "tear-and-fold-tab" technique). Putting your name on each page will identify your work if papers from a particular class are accidentally mixed up.

> As it's often been said, essays are never really done—only due. Take a last reading using the checklist that follows, make some notes on your progress as a writer and thinker, and congratulate yourself on your fine efforts and accomplishment.

A Final Checklist for Your Essay

If you have written an effective essay, you should be able to answer "yes" to the following questions:

1. Do I feel I have something important to say to my reader?
2. Am I sincerely committed to communicating with my reader and not just with myself?

3. Have I considered my audience's needs? (See Chapter 1.)

4. Do my title and lead-in attract the reader's attention and help set up my thesis? (See Chapter 4.)

5. Does my thesis statement assert one main, clearly focused idea? (See Chapter 2.)

6. Does my thesis and/or essay map give the reader an indication of what points the essay will cover? (See Chapter 2.)

7. Do my body paragraphs contain the essential points in the essay's discussion, and are those points expressed in clearly stated or implied topic sentences? (See Chapter 3.)

8. Is each major point in my essay well developed with enough detailed supporting evidence? (See Chapter 3.)

9. Does each body paragraph have unity and coherence? (See Chapter 3.)

10. Are all the paragraphs in my essay smoothly linked in a logical order? (See Chapter 3.)

11. Does my concluding paragraph provide a suitable ending for the essay? (See Chapter 4.)

12. Are all my sentences clear, concise, and coherent? (See Chapter 6.)

13. Are my words accurate, necessary, and meaningful? (See Chapter 7.)

14. Have I edited and proofread for errors in grammar, punctuation, spelling, and typing? (See Part Four.)

And most important:

15. Has my essay been effectively revised so that I am proud of this piece of writing?

Sample Student Essay

In the following draft of her expository essay, a student writer explores the idea that many college students fear success. As you read through this draft, note the decisions the writer makes regarding expository strategies, types and placement of support, and organization. Note, too, her thinking about the essay's development as evidenced by the annotations in the margin. Compare these annotations with the questions or ideas you employ when creating and revising a draft of your own work.

Draft Essay

Fear of Success

Can I start with a dramatic story to get readers hooked?

College students in the United States easily admit to a fear of failure but rarely confess to a fear of success. Most students would be embarrassed to admit that the thought of success scares them. It is important to recognize the reasons students fear success.

Tell why it's important.

Should I list the points I will cover in my paper here?

Chose order of impor-
tance for organizing
my main points.
Works OK.

Am I over explaining
this?

Example doesn't
say why the fire
made her give up
on college.

Need to connect
this example to
topic sentence.

Topic sentence not
the clearest. Reword?

I should tell
where I got the
dieting thing.

Maybe add some
actual directions
I gave my friend?

Kind of wordy and
confusing.

Some people who fear success believe they are not good enough. They let their negative view of their own value keep them from trying their best. They expect to fail, so they don't even try to succeed. This lack of self-esteem can come from a bad life event. My friend Olivia was getting ready to start college when a fire put her father in the hospital. Olivia decided not to go college.

People can fear success because they are afraid they won't be able to live up to it. When my mother was in preschool, her teachers decided to put her into a group with older kids. But she didn't know how to tie her shoes yet. When all the other kids took off their sneakers, she did also but then felt really dumb when it was time to tie them back up and she had to ask her teacher for help.

People can fear success because of change. Like some people who are overweight have trouble sticking to a diet. They have trouble imagining a newer, slimmer self. Another example is that many people who don't succeed are anxious about making others feel less than. When I worked at a fast food restaurant last summer, one of my friends from college was hired after me, and I was asked to train her. I had trouble giving her directions because I figured that she would think I was acting like I was better than she was.

So success can be frightening because it makes us think about being undeserving, not meeting new challenges, and that success will change us. *I like that I repeated my main points but still needs work. What do I want readers to remember or do after reading my essay?*

Revised Essay

The essay that follows reflects the author's subsequent revisions to her earlier draft above. Consider the ways in which the essay has been strengthened through revision. The annotations in this draft illustrate the changes made by the author. Note especially the changes that she has made to her title, her transitions, and her use of supporting details. How might these changes and revising decisions influence your own revision process?

Cordova 1

Ava Cordova

English 100

Prof. Henderson

28 March 2015

The Fear No One Talks About

1*   When my friend Victoria was a college sophomore, she won a contest put on by a local charity, and her logo was posted on its Web site. But when her art professor told the class, her stomach hurt and she felt panicky. College students in the United States easily admit to a fear of failure but rarely confess to a fear of success. After all, winning is everything. Most students would be embarrassed to say that the thought of wealth, responsibility, and fame makes them want to hide under the bed. Recognizing the reasons students fear success is the first step to solving this huge problem that can lead to terrible regrets in life. The main reasons people avoid success are because they don't think they deserve it, they don't know whether or not they can follow through, and they worry about how success will change them.

2   The first main reason for fear of success is feeling like you don't deserve it. The summer before my friend Olivia was going to start college, a skillet of grease she was heating on the stove caught fire. Her father put it out, was burned on his chest and arms, and was rushed to the hospital. Olivia blamed herself for the accident and decided not to go to college. She believed that she was an awful, careless, inferior person who didn't deserve to pursue her own goals.

3   The second main reason people fear success is that they are afraid they won't be able to keep on succeeding. When my mother was in preschool, her teachers moved her into a

Margin notes:

Starts with a dramatic story that shows, rather than tells, what fear of success is like.

Explanation of why understanding the fear of success is important.

The three main points Ava will cover in this paper.

Explains how the story about Olivia supports the topic sentence.

Uses strong adjectives to get across how Olivia felt.

---

* Paragraphs in the Sample Student Essays are numbered here and throughout this book for ease of discussion. Do not number paragraphs in your own papers.

Cordova 2

new group with older kids. At first she felt excited and proud. Unfortunately, she didn't know how to tie her shoes yet. When the older kids happily kicked off their sneakers during circle time, she did the same thing. Then she felt humiliated when she had to ask her teacher for help tying them again. In contrast, things are different now. My mother learned how to tie her sneakers, of course. And she is now a respected manager at a major scientific laboratory.

4   The final and most important reason that people fear success is that they think they will change for the worse. For example, some people who are overweight have trouble sticking to a diet, according to *Psychology Now*. They struggle with the idea of becoming a skinnier self because it is different. They probably wonder, "What would a thinner me be like, what would I wear, how would people treat me?" In addition, many people are terrified that success might turn them into a person they don't want to be. When I worked at a fast food restaurant last summer, a friend from college was hired after me, and I was asked to train her. I had trouble giving her directions about how she swept the floor or grilled burgers because I didn't want to sound like I was overly controlling or thought I was better than she was. After that, I believed success would turn me into the enemy.

5   So success can stand for something to be feared. We shiver at the thought of not deserving it, making mistakes, and most of all, that it will change us into someone we don't know any more. But if you keep in mind the three main reasons people are afraid to succeed, you can start letting your light shine. And that could show other people how they can shine, too.

Margin annotations:

Adding detail helps readers visualize the scene.

Transition sentence.

For this factual example, the writer gives her source. If her instructor requires it, she will also provide proper documentation.

Using dialogue enlivens and further supports the point.

More specific details added here.

Ava concludes with a persuasive statement that inspires readers to action.

Practicing What You've Learned

A. As you work on strengthening your own revision skills, you may find it easier in the beginning to practice on the writing of others. Assume the writer of the draft that follows is directing these comments to a group of high school students contemplating their college choices. By offering helpful marginal comments and questions, guide this writer to a revised draft with more effective arguments, organization, and clarity.

Maybe You Shouldn't Go Away to College

Going away to college is not for everyone. There are good reasons why a student might choose to live at home and attend a local school. Money, finding stability while changes are occurring, and accepting responsibility are three to consider.

Money is likely to be most important. Not only is tuition more expensive, but extra money is needed for room and board. Whether room and board is a dorm or an apartment, the expense is great.

Most students never stop to consider that the money that could be saved from room and board may be better spent in future years on graduate school, which is likely to be more important in their careers.

Going to school is a time of many changes anyway, without adding the pressure of a new city or even a new state. Finding stability will be hard enough, without going from home to a dorm. Starting college could be an emotional time for some, and the security of their home and family might make everything easier.

When students decide to go away to school, sometimes because their friends are going away, or maybe because the school is their parents' alma mater, something that all need to decide is whether or not they can accept the responsibility of a completely new way of life.

Everyone feels as if they are ready for total independence when they decide to go away to college, but is breaking away when they are just beginning to set their futures a good idea?

Going away to school may be the right road for some, but those who feel that they are not ready might start looking to a future that is just around the corner.

B. Practice your editing and proofreading skills by correcting all the errors you see in the paragraph that follows. Look carefully for problems in grammar, punctuation, spelling, word confusion, and sentence sense, as well as typos. Some proofreaders find it useful to place a blank piece of paper or index card under each line to help them focus as they read.

One fo the most interesting books I've read lately is Bold Spirit, by Linda Lawrence Hunt. Its the true story of Hega Estby's 1896 walk across america,

continued on next page

form Eastern Washingto to New york City; in order to win a $10,000 prize to save the family farm. Acompanied by her teen age daughter Clara the two sets out with only $5 dollars each and walked 3500 miles on foot in Victorian clothes. Despite alot bad wheather and dangerous encounter along the the way. Helga and her daughter did arrive safely, but, unfortunately they weren't never able too collect there prize money. Worse then that, tho, Helgas family afterwards r so embarrasssed about her walk that they burned her diary, her notes & newspaper clippings, her story only came to light recently be cause a daughter-inlaw had secretly saved and album of clippings from the fire.

Assignment

Select a body paragraph from "The Fear No One Talks About" (pages 116–117) or "Maybe You Shouldn't Go Away to College" (page 118) and revise it, making effective changes in focus, development, organization, sentence construction, and word choice. (Feel free to elaborate on or delete any supporting details to improve the paragraph's content.)

Applying What You've Learned to *Your* Writing

If you have completed a draft of an essay, you have already revised many parts of it—changing ideas, sentences, and words as you wrote. Now begin to revise by moving through the stages outlined in this chapter. Remember, you cannot revise for everything at once, so this process calls for multiple readings—and rewriting. After another look at your work, are you satisfied that it accomplishes your purpose, that it addresses the needs of your specific audience? Using your best critical thinking skills, strengthen any weak development of your ideas; then tackle questions of order and coherence. You may find that you need another draft at this point to accommodate new material or deep-structure changes.

Once you are happy with your essay's larger issues of content and organization, work on clarity by polishing rough sentences and substituting better words. Proofread your draft for surface errors at least twice! Until a revision process becomes second nature to you, use the checklist on page 113–114 as a guide.

Collaborative Activities: Group Work, Peer Revision Workshops, and Team Projects

Writers in both the business and academic worlds often consult their colleagues for advice; they might, for example, ask for help with a difficult explanation, a complex description, or a twisted sentence. Sometimes they may write together as part of a task force or committee. Similarly, you may find that working on composing and revising strategies with your colleagues—your classmates—can be enormously helpful.

You may have already noticed a practice exercise or assignment earlier in this text identified as a Collaborative Activity. "Collaborative" simply means working together, and these assignments are designed so you and your classmates can help each other improve particular writing skills. By offering reactions, suggestions, and questions (not to mention moral support), your classroom colleagues may become some of your best writing teachers.

Collaborative activities in composition courses take many forms and may occur in any stage of the writing process. Here are three of the most common types:

1. Group Work: Frequently in writing classes an instructor will ask three to five students to form a discussion or activity group. For example, students might be asked to evaluate a writing sample or to respond to an exercise or to ask for feedback on their own drafts. The possibilities are numerous, and small-group discussions can be especially useful early on as writers brainstorm on and focus their topics, as well as later in the writing process when they are striving for well-developed content and clear organization.

2. Peer Revision Workshops: On some days, instructors may ask students to respond to each other's drafts in writing. Sometimes teachers will give student-reviewers a list of tasks to perform ("Underline the thesis") or questions to answer ("How successful is the conclusion?"); at other times, the writers themselves will create the inquiries. Although many workshops are organized as one-on-one exchanges of papers in the classroom, most schools today employ some sort of learning management system (Blackboard, D2L, etc.) that allows students to exchange papers and provide feedback virtually. Structured in many effective ways, peer workshops allow writers to see their drafts from a reader's point of view.

Vitchanan Photography/Shutterstock.com

3. Team Projects: Sometimes students will be asked to work together to produce a single piece of writing. Because many organizations today require a set of members or employees to prepare such projects as proposals, position papers, or grants, the practice of writing together as a committee or team can provide a valuable experience. A "blended" project might call for members of a team to write individually and then compare their efforts, selecting and revising the best ideas and prose as they craft the final piece together. A "composite" approach might ask students to assign each team member a different task (investigate a problem, research a study, conduct an interview, etc.) or a particular section to write, with the group responsible for smoothly meshing the parts into a whole.

◆ Panel discussions, debates, and other kinds of oral presentations are often important parts of team-project assignments. For advice on preparing and delivering your written work or research in the classroom, turn to pages 491–494 in Chapter 21.

There are, of course, numerous other ways instructors may create collaborative activities, depending upon the lesson, goals, and logistics. In one format or another, working collaboratively can frequently help writers consider alternative ways of thinking and that, in turn, may encourage clearer, more effective prose.

Benefiting from Collaborative Activities

Collaborative activities can be extremely useful, but working with other writers may also present challenges. To receive the most benefit from interaction with your classmates, you'll need to develop both a sense of cooperation and good communication skills. The following section offers suggestions for gaining the most value from one-on-one revision workshops as well as some advice for successful participation in small-group discussions.

Guidelines for Peer Revision Workshops

Students taking part in revision workshops for the first time often have questions about the reviewing process. Some student reviewers may feel uneasy about their role, wondering, "What if I can't think of any suggestions for the writer? How can I tell someone that the essay is really terrible? What if I sense something's wrong but I'm not sure what it is—or how to fix it?" Writers, too, may feel apprehensive or even occasionally defensive about receiving criticism of their papers. Because these concerns are genuine and widespread, here is some advice for you in the roles of both writer and reviewer.

When you are the **writer**:

1. Develop a constructive attitude. Admittedly, receiving criticism—especially on a creation that has required hard work—can sometimes be difficult, particularly if your self-image has become mixed up with your drafts. Try to realize that your reviewer is not criticizing you personally but rather is trying to help you by offering fresh insights. All drafts can be improved, and no writer need feel embarrassed about seeking or receiving advice. (Take comfort in the words of writer Somerset Maugham: "Only the mediocre person is always at his best.") See the workshop as a nonthreatening opportunity to reconsider your prose and improve your audience awareness.

2. Come prepared. If your workshop structure permits, tell your reviewer what sort of help you need at this point in your drafting or revising process. Ask for suggestions to fix a particularly troublesome area, or ask for feedback on a choice you've made but are feeling unsure of. Don't hesitate to ask your reviewer for assistance with any part of your essay.

3. **Evaluate suggestions carefully.** Writing isn't math; most of the time there are no absolutely right or wrong answers—just better or worse rhetorical choices. That is, there are many ways to communicate an idea to a set of readers. You, as the writer, must decide on an effective way, the way that best serves your purpose and your readers' needs. Sometimes your reviewer will suggest a change that is brilliant or one so obviously right you will wonder why in the world you didn't think of it yourself. At other times you may weigh your reviewer's suggestion and decide that your original choice is just as good or perhaps even better. Be open to suggestions, but learn to trust thyself as well.

4. **Find the good in bad advice.** Occasionally, you may have a reviewer who seems to miss a crucial point or misunderstands your purpose entirely, whose suggestions for revising your paper seem uniformly unproductive for one reason or another. You certainly shouldn't take bad advice—but do think about the issues it raises. Although it's helpful to receive a dynamite suggestion you can incorporate immediately, the real value of a revision workshop is its ability to encourage you to rethink your prose. Readers' responses (yes, even the bizarre ones) challenge writers to take still another look at their rhetorical choices and ask themselves, "Is this clear after all? Does this example really work here? Did something in my essay throw this reader off the track?" Revision workshops offer you benefits, even if you ultimately decide to reject many of your reviewer's suggestions.

When you are the **reviewer**:

1. **Develop a constructive attitude.** Sometimes it's hard to give honest criticism—most of us are uncomfortable when we think we might hurt someone's feelings—but remember that the writer has resolved to develop a professional attitude, too. The writer expects (and is sometimes desperately begging for) sincere feedback, so be honest as you offer your best advice.

2. **Be clear and specific.** Vague or flippant responses ("Confusing"; "Huh?") don't help writers know what or how to revise. Try putting some of your comments into this format: your response to X, the reason for your response, a request for change, and, if possible, a specific suggestion for the change. ("I'm confused when you say you enjoy some parts of breakfast because this seems to contradict your thesis claim of 'wretched dorm food.' Would it be clearer to modify your thesis to exclude breakfast or to revise this paragraph to include only discussion of the rubbery eggs?")

3. **Address important issues.** Unless you have workshop directions that request certain tasks, read through the draft entirely at least once and then comment on the larger issues first. Writers want to know if they are achieving their overall purpose, if their thesis is clear and convincing, if their major points and evidence make sense, and if their paper seems logical and ordered. Editing tips are fine, too, but because workshops encourage authors to rewrite large portions of their prose, attention to minor details may be less valuable early on than feedback on ideas, organization, and development. (Of course, an editing workshop later in the revision process

might be exclusively focused on sentence, word, and mechanical errors. Workshops may be designed to specifically address any set of problems that writers face.)

4. **Encourage the writer.** Writers with confidence write and revise better than insecure or angry writers. Praise honestly wherever you can, as specifically as you can. When weaknesses do appear, show the writer that you know she or he is capable of doing better work by linking the weakness to a strength elsewhere in the draft. ("Could you add more 'showing' details here so that your picture of the dentist is as vivid as your description of the drill?") Substitute specific responses and suggestions for one-word labels such as "awk" (awkward) or "unclear." Even positive labels don't always help writers repeat effective techniques. ("Good!" enthusiastically inscribed in the margin by a well-developed paragraph feels nice but might cause the writer to wonder, "'Good' what? Good point? Good supporting evidence? Good detail? How can I do 'good' again if I don't know exactly what it is?")

5. **Understand your role as critical reader.** Sometimes it's easy for a reviewer to take ownership of someone else's paper. Keep the writer's purpose in mind as you respond; don't insist on revisions that produce the essay that's in *your* head. Be sensitive to your own voice and language as a reviewer. Instead of making authoritative pronouncements that might offend, ask reader-based questions ("Will all your readers know the meaning of this technical term?" "Would some readers profit from a brief history of this controversy?"). If you're unsure about a possible error, request verification ("Could you recheck this quotation? Its wording here is confusing me because . . ."). Practice offering criticism in language that acknowledges the writer's hard work and accentuates the positive nature of revision ("Would citing last year's budget figures make your good argument against the fish market even stronger?").

Last, always look over your own draft in light of the insightful suggestions you are offering your classmates. You may feel at first that it is far simpler to analyze someone else's writing than your own. As you participate in revision workshops, however, you will find it increasingly easy to transfer those same critical reading skills to your own work. Becoming a good reader-reviewer for your composition colleagues can be an important part of your training as a first-rate writer.

Guidelines for Small-Group Work

Much of the previous advice for participation in peer workshops holds true for student involvement in many kinds of classroom group activities. In addition, consider these suggestions for participation in groups of three to five members:

1. **Start informed.** Quickly acknowledge everyone's first name, and be sure everyone has a copy of the assignment or other materials necessary to the task at hand.

2. **Know your purpose.** Make sure everyone in your group clearly understands the goal of the activity. Consult your teacher if there are any questions about the instructions or the expected results.

3. **Create a plan with a time schedule.** In discussion groups that ask participants to give opinions or offer help, estimate the time allowed so that each person has an equal opportunity to talk. If your assignment has multiple parts, figure out how much time should be devoted to each task. (Larger team projects may call for an action plan that stretches over a number of days, with appropriate deadlines for the various jobs.)

4. **Consider appointing roles.** In some groups it's helpful to have a moderator or facilitator to keep participants focused and on track; sometimes it's useful to have a recorder to take notes, a timekeeper to call out when discussions need to move on, or a friendly "devil's advocate" to offer counter opinions. Some groups may designate a reporter to present the results of the activity to the class as a whole. Assigning roles or specific responsibilities may encourage each participant to remain engaged in the group's work.

5. **Stay focused.** It's easy to drift off topic or get bogged down. Keep yourself and your classmates on target; be polite but firm if one of your group begins to wander off task. At times it may be helpful to stop a discussion and summarize what has been done thus far and what has yet to be accomplished.

6. **Be a good listener as well as a good talker.** Be willing to entertain the opinions of others in your group; stay open to criticism, suggestions, and diverse approaches. If there are conflicting opinions in the group, note differences but avoid personal hostility or sarcastic remarks. Lively debates can be exhilarating, but heated arguments may become irrational and unproductive.

7. **Set a good example.** Model behavior that promotes the good of the group; always do your share of the work. Consider taking on a leadership role: encourage the quieter members of the group by asking questions to draw out more details. Be grateful for help you receive from your classmates, even if it only means taking a second hard look at your own opinions or prose choices.

Most importantly, after the activity is finished, think about what you have learned. Every group discussion or exercise is a lesson created to improve your thinking, writing, and reading skills. Ask yourself what ideas and strategies you can apply to your own writing to make it more effective—and then revise your work accordingly!

Practicing What You've Learned*

Collaborative Activity: Working with two or three classmates, first designate a recorder to take notes on the discussion of the following letter (if your group is larger, consider

continued on next page

---

*Special note: Many other peer-based exercises appear throughout this text. If you find working with classmates helpful, look in the index of this book under "collaborative activities" to discover more ideas for focusing and revising your prose.

appointing a facilitator and perhaps a timekeeper as well). Assist poor Bubba by compiling a list of five specific suggestions to help him revise this draft so that it better addresses his audience and accomplishes his purpose. Rank order your suggestions and be prepared to report them to the class as a whole.

Dear Mom and Dad,

This week at college has been very interesting.

My roommate is gone and so is my wallet and computer. I tried to tell the police that the stacks of phony $3 bills by his copier weren't mine but I don't know if they believed me.

And, hey, the car thing isn't my fault either. Despite the testimony of all those witnesses. Who knew the entire back end would crumple like that? The other guy's lawyer will be in touch.

Without any transportation, I don't know when I can come home. Maybe at Thanksgiving. The doctor says the rash shouldn't be contagious by then. The arm, after the fight at the party, is another matter altogether.

I have a new girlfriend! Bambi's real nice and the age difference between us is no big deal. I hope you like her, despite how you feel about tattoos. I have a funny story to tell you about how the stuff in her face set off the airport metal detector last weekend. I just wish her sick grandmother didn't need me to help out so much with her expensive operation. Bambi and her brother are pressuring me a lot.

As you can plainly see, I need more financial help! Please send money right away!

Your devoted son,
Bubba

Assignment

Collaborative Activity: Ask a classmate to read a draft on which you are currently working. Include at the end of the draft three questions you have about rough patches in your work—areas, for instance, where you think your ideas are fuzzy or your organization is unclear or your prose has missed the  mark. Ask your classmate to respond to your concerns as a reader-reviewer who can help you revise. Once you understand the suggestions for your paper, provide similar assistance to your classmate by changing roles. (If possible, in a later follow-up discussion, show each other the revised work, explaining what changes were incorporated and why.)

Some Last Advice: How to Play with Your Mental Blocks

Most writers, sooner or later, will suffer a form of Writer's Block, the inability to move forward in some stage of their drafting process. Writers may begin with creativity and enthusiasm, but then at some point become "stuck"; the necessary ideas or words to express them simply won't come no matter how hard they're called. Symptoms may include sweaty palms, pencil chewing, and a pronounced, sudden desire to organize a sock drawer or clean out a closet. Although not every "cure" works for everyone, here are a few suggestions to help minimize your misery:

Try to give yourself as much time as possible to write your essay. Don't try to write the entire paper in one sitting at the last minute. By doing so, you place yourself under too much pressure. Writer's Block often accompanies the "up against the wall" feeling that strikes at 2:00 A.M. the morning your essay is due at 9:00. Make a start on your assignment as soon as you can; prewriting, notes, and rough outlines are all good first steps. (*Special note:* ◆ If you are a habitual writing procrastinator—that is, if you are the king or queen of delaying tactics and have trouble getting started at all—turn back now to pages 103–104 in this chapter for encouragement and advice.)

Because most of us have had more experience talking than writing, try verbalizing your ideas. Sometimes it's helpful to discuss your ideas with friends or classmates. Their questions and comments (not to mention their sympathy for your temporary block) will often trigger the thoughts you need to begin writing again. In some cases, especially if you're stuck while drafting an argument or persuasive paper, it's useful to ask someone to role-play your Cranky Opposition. Forcing yourself to answer his or her objections to your position might lead you out of your bog-down into new or stronger points to include in your draft.

When an irresistible force meets an immovable object, something's going to give. Conquer the task: break the paper into manageable bits. Instead of drooping with despair over the thought of a ten-page research paper, think of it as a series of small parts (explanation of the problem, review of current research, possible solutions, etc.). Then tackle one part at a time, and reward yourself when that section is done.

Get the juices flowing and the pen (or keys) moving. Try writing the easiest or shortest part of your essay first. A feeling of accomplishment may give you the boost of confidence you need to undertake the other, more difficult sections. If no part looks easy or inviting, try more prewriting exercises, as described in Chapter 1, until you feel prepared to begin the essay itself.

Play "Let's Make a Deal" with yourself. Sometimes we just can't face the failure that we are predicting for ourselves. Strike a bargain with yourself: promise yourself that you are going to work on your paper for only twenty minutes—absolutely, positively only twenty minutes, not a second more, no sir, no way. If in twenty minutes, you're onto something good, ignore your promise to yourself and keep going. If you're not, then leave and come back for another twenty-minute session later. (If you started early enough, you can do this without increasing your anxiety.)

Give yourself permission to write garbage. Take the pressure off yourself by agreeing in advance to tear up the first page or two of whatever you write. You can always change your mind if the trash turns out to be treasure. If it isn't, so what? You said you were going to tear it up anyway.

Imagine that your brain is a water faucet. If you're like most people, you've probably lived in a house or apartment containing a faucet that needed to run for a few minutes before the hot water came out. Think of your brain in the same way, and do some other, easier writing task to warm up. Write a letter, send an e-mail, make a grocery list, copy notes, whatever, to get your brain running. When you turn to your essay, your ideas may be hotter than you thought.

Remove the threat by addressing a friendly face. Sometimes we can't write because we are too worried about what someone else will think about us, or maybe we can't write because we can't figure out who would want to read this stuff anyway. Instead of writing into a void or to an audience that seems threatening, try writing to a friend. Imagine what that friend's responses might be and try to elaborate or clarify wherever necessary. If it helps, write the first draft as a letter ("Dear Clyde, I want to tell you what happened to me last week."), and then redraft your ideas as an essay when you've found your purpose and focus, making whatever changes in tone or development are necessary to fit your real audience.

If Writer's Block does hit, remember that it is a temporary bog-down, not a permanent one. Other writers have had it—and survived to write again. Try leaving your draft and taking a walk outdoors or at least into another room. Think about your readers— what should they know or feel at this point in your essay? As you walk, try to complete this sentence: "What I am trying to say is . . ." Keep repeating this phrase and your responses aloud until you find the answer you want.

Sometimes while you're blocked at one point, a bright idea for another part of your essay will pop into your head. If possible, skip the section that has you stuck, and start working on the new part. (At least jot down the new idea somewhere so it won't be lost when you need it later.)

"Feelings, woo-o-o, nothing more than feelings . . . " You've hit a wall: you now despise your essay topic; you can't face that draft one more time. Turn that fear and loathing into something more positive. Put the draft away. Go to a blank page or screen and pour out your feelings toward your essay's *subject*. Why did you care about this topic in the first place? What's meaningful about it? Why did you want others to think about it? Reconnecting with your subject matter, rather than arm wrestling the same draft again and again, may suggest a new start with a clearer purpose. (And if this suggestion doesn't work, you may have at least helped yourself to a good night's rest. According to studies by James Pennebaker, a University of Texas psychology professor, writing about your feelings "reduces stress and allows for better sleep." A good snooze may be just what you need to tackle your essay with renewed energy.)

Change partners and dance. If you're thoroughly overcome by the vast white wasteland on the desk (or screen) before you, get up and do something else for a while. Exercise, balance your checkbook, or put on music and dance. (Mystery writer Agatha Christie claimed she did her best planning while washing the dishes.) Give your mind a break and refresh your spirit. When you come back to the paper, you may be surprised to discover that your subconscious writer has been working while the rest of you played.

Here's the single most important piece of advice to remember: relax. No one—not even the very best professional writer—produces perfect prose every time pen hits paper. If you're blocked, you may be trying too hard; if your expectations of your first draft are too high, you may not be able to write at all for fear of failure. You just might be holding yourself back by being a perfectionist at this point. You can always revise and polish your prose in another draft—the first important step is jotting down your ideas. Remember that once the first word or phrase appears on your blank page or screen, a major battle has been won.

Chapter 5 Summary

Here is a brief summary of what you should remember about drafting and revising your writing:

1. Revision is an activity that occurs in all stages of the writing process.

2. All good writers revise and polish their prose.

3. Revision is not merely editing or last-minute proofreading; it involves important decisions about the essay's ideas, organization, and development.

4. To revise effectively, novice writers might review their drafts in stages to avoid the frustration that comes with trying to fix everything at once.

5. Critical thinking skills are vitally important to all good readers and writers.

6. Collaborative activities can help writers draft and revise in a number of useful ways.

7. Most writers experience Writer's Block at some time but live through it to write again.

Effective Sentences

An insurance agent was shocked to open his mail one morning and read the following note from one of his clients: "In accordance with your instructions, I have given birth to twins in the enclosed envelope." However, he may not have been more surprised than the congregation who read this announcement in their church bulletin: "There will be a discussion tomorrow on the problem of adultery in the minister's office." Or the patrons of a health club who learned that "guest passes will not be given to members until the manager has punched each of them first."

Certainly, there were no babies born in an envelope, nor was there adultery in the minister's office, and no one believes the club manager was planning to assault the membership. But the implications (and the unintended humor) are nevertheless present—solely because of the faulty ways in which the sentences were constructed.

To improve your own writing, you must express your thoughts in clear, coherent sentences that produce precisely the reader response you want. Effective sentences are similar to the threads in a piece of knitting or weaving: each thread helps form the larger design; if any one thread becomes tangled or lost, the pattern becomes muddled. In an essay, the same is true: if any sentence is fuzzy or obscure, the reader may lose the point of your discussion and, in some cases, never bother to regain it. Therefore, to retain your reader, you must concentrate on writing informative, effective sentences that continuously clarify the purpose of your essay. Figure 6.1 highlights some of the tips and techniques for creating effective sentences that will be discussed in this chapter.

iStockphoto.com/PeopleImages

Figure 6.1 VISUALIZING THE PROCESS: EDITING SENTENCES

Develop a Clear Style

1. Give your sentences content.
2. Make your sentences specific.
3. Avoid overpacking your sentences.
4. Fix major sentence errors.
5. Pay attention to word order.
6. Avoid mixed constructions and faulty predication.

Develop a Concise Style

1. Avoid deadwood constructions.
2. Avoid redundancy.
3. Carefully consider your passive verbs.
4. Avoid pretentiousness.

Develop an Engaging Style

1. Use specific, descriptive verbs.
2. Use specific, precise modifiers.
3. Emphasize people when possible.
4. Vary your sentence style.
5. Avoid overuse of any one kind of construction in the same sentence.
6. Don't change your point of view between or within sentences.

Develop an Emphatic Style

1. Consider word order.
2. Use coordination to stress two closely related ideas equally.
3. Use subordination to connect a main idea and a less emphasized one.

Prewriting
Chapter 1

Drafting
Chapters 2, 3, 4, 5

Revising
Chapter 5

Editing/
Proofreading
Chapters 6, 7

© Cengage Learning 2017

Many problems in sentence clarity involve errors in grammar, punctuation, word choice, and usage; the most common of these errors are discussed in Chapter 7, "Word Logic," and throughout Part Four, the handbook section of this text. In this chapter you'll find some general suggestions for writing clear, concise, engaging sentences. However, *don't try to apply all the rules to the first draft of your essay.* Revising sentences before your ideas are firmly in place may be a waste of effort if your essay's stance or structure changes. Concentrate your efforts in early drafts on your thesis, the development of your important supporting points, and the essay's general organization; then, in a later draft, rework your sentences so that each one is informative and clear. Your reader reads only the words on the page, not those in your mind—so it's up to you to make sure the sentences in your essay express the thoughts in your head as closely and vividly as possible.

REMEMBER: All good writers revise and polish their sentences.

Developing a Clear Style

When you are ready to revise the sentences in your rough draft for clarity, consider the following six rules.

Give Your Sentences Content

Fuzzy sentences are often the result of fuzzy thinking. When you examine your sentences, ask yourself, "Do I know what I'm talking about here? Or are my sentences vague or confusing because I'm really not sure what my point is or where it's going?" Look at this list of content-poor sentences taken from student essays; how could you put more information into each one?

- If you were to observe a karate class, you would become familiar with all the aspects that make it up.
- The meaning of the poem isn't very clear the first time you read it, but after several readings, the poet's meaning comes through.
- One important factor that is the basis for determining a true friend is the ability that person has for being a real human being.
- Listening is important because we all need to be able to sit and hear all that is said to us.

Don't pad your paragraphs with sentences that run in circles, leading nowhere; rethink your ideas and revise your writing so that every sentence—like each brick in a wall—contributes to the construction of a solid discussion. In other words, commit yourself to a position and make each sentence contain information pertinent to your point; leave the job of padding to mattress manufacturers.

Sometimes, however, you may have a definite idea in mind but still continue to write "empty sentences"—statements that alone do not contain enough information to make a specific point in your discussion. Frequently, an empty sentence can be revised by combining it with the sentence that follows, as shown in the examples that follow. The empty, or overly general, sentences are underlined.

Poor	<u>There are many kinds of beautiful tropical fish</u>. The kind most popular with aquarium owners is the angelfish.
Better	Of the many kinds of beautiful tropical fish, the angelfish is the most popular with aquarium owners.
Poor	<u>D. W. Griffith introduced many new cinematic techniques</u>, Some of these techniques were contrast editing, close-ups, fade-outs, and freeze-frame shots.
Better	D. W. Griffith made movie history by introducing such new cinematic techniques as contrast editing, close-ups, fade-outs, and the freeze-frame shot.
Poor	<u>There is a national organization called The Couch Potatoes</u>, The group's 8,000 members are devoted television watchers.

Better   The Couch Potatoes is a national organization whose 8,000 members are devoted television watchers.

◆ For more help combining sentences, see pages 151–154.

Make Your Sentences Specific

In addition to containing an informative, complete thought, each of your sentences should give readers enough clear details for them to "see" the picture you are creating. Sentences full of vague words produce blurry, boring prose and drowsy readers. Remember your reaction the last time you asked a friend about a recent vacation? If the only response you received was something like, "Oh, it was great—a lot of fun," you probably yawned and moved on to a new topic. But if your friend had begun an exciting account of a wilderness rafting trip, with detailed stories about narrow escapes from freezing white water, treacherous rocks, and uncharted whirlpools, you'd probably have stopped and listened. The same principle works in your writing—clear, specific details are the only sure way to attract and hold the reader's interest. Therefore, make each sentence contribute something new and interesting to the overall discussion.

The following examples first show sentences that are far too vague to sustain anyone's attention. Rewritten, these sentences contain specific details that add clarity and interest:

Vague   She went home in a bad mood. [What kind of a bad mood? How did she act or look?]

Specific   She stomped home, hands jammed in her pockets, angrily kicking rocks, dogs, small children, and anything else that crossed her path.

Vague   His neighbor bought a really nice old desk. [Why nice? How old? What kind of desk?]

Specific   His neighbor bought an oak roll-top desk made in 1885 that contains a secret drawer triggered by a hidden spring.

Vague   My roommate is truly horrible. ["Horrible" in what ways? To what extent? Do you "see" this person?]

Specific   My thoughtless roommate leaves dirty dishes under the bed, sweaty clothes in the closet, and toenail clippings in the sink.

◆ For more help selecting specific "showing" words, see pages 146–147 in this chapter, pages 166–171 in Chapter 7, and pages 347–352 in Chapter 16.

Avoid Overpacking Your Sentences

Because our society is becoming increasingly specialized and highly technical, we tend to equate complexity with excellence and simplicity with simplemindedness. This assumption is unfortunate because it often leads to a preference for unnecessarily complicated and even contorted writing. In a recent survey, for example, a student chose a sample of bureaucratic hogwash over several well-written paragraphs, explaining his choice by saying that it must have been better because he didn't understand it.

Our best writers have always worked hard to present their ideas simply and specifically so that their readers could easily understand them. Mark Twain, for instance, once praised a young author this way: "I notice that you use plain simple language, short words, and brief sentences. This is the way to write English. It is the modern way and the best way. Stick to it." And when a critic asked Hemingway to define his theory of writing, he replied, "[I] put down what I see and what I feel in the best and simplest way I can tell it."

In your own writing, therefore, work for a simple, direct style. Avoid sentences that are overpacked (too many ideas or too much information at once) as in the following example on racquetball:

> John told Phil that to achieve more control over the ball, he should practice flicking or snapping his wrist, because this action is faster in the close shots and placing a shot requires only a slight change of the wrist's angle instead of an acute movement of the whole arm, which gives a player less reaction time.

To make the overpacked sentence easier to understand, try dividing the ideas into two or more sentences:

> John told Phil that to achieve more control over the ball, he should practice flicking or snapping his wrist, because this action is faster in the close shots. Placing a shot requires only a slight change of the wrist's angle instead of an acute movement of the whole arm, which gives a player less reaction time.

Don't ever run the risk of losing your reader in a sentence that says too much to comprehend in one bite. This confusing notice, for example, came from a well-known credit card company:

> The Minimum Payment Due each month shall be reduced by the amounts paid in excess of the Minimum Payment Due during the previous three months which have not already been so applied in determining the Minimum Payment Due in such earlier months, unless you have exceeded your line of credit or have paid the entire New Balance shown on your billing statement.

Or consider the confusion of soccer players whose coach warned them in this manner:

> It is also a dangerous feeling to consider that where we are in the league is of acceptable standard because standard is relevant to the standards we have set, which thereby may well indicate that we have not aspired to the standard which we set ourselves.

Try, too, for a straightforward construction. This sentence by Ronald Reagan early in his campaign for the presidency, for example, takes far too many twists and turns for anyone to follow it easily on the first reading:

> My goal is an America where something or anything that is done to or for anyone is done neither because of nor in spite of any difference between them, racially, religiously, or ethnic-origin-wise.

◆ If any sentences in your rough draft are overpacked or contorted, try rephrasing your meaning in shorter sentences and then combining thoughts where most appropriate. (Help with sentence variety may be found on pages 151–154 of this chapter.)

Fix Major Sentence Errors

Rather than creating overpacked sentences, some writers have the opposite problem. They write *sentence fragments*, dropping thoughts here or there without forming them into complete, comprehensible grammatical units. Such fragments are confusing to readers, who must struggle to fill in the connecting link between the writer's ideas.

A complete sentence has both a subject (the thing that performs the action or maintains the state of being) and a predicate (the verb and any modifiers or complements). A sentence fragment is often missing its subject, as shown in the following example:

Fragment	David bought a gopher ranch. *Hoping to strike it rich.*
Correct	David bought a gopher ranch, hoping to strike it rich.
Correct	David bought a gopher ranch. He hoped to strike it rich.

Other fragments have the essential sentence components but are considered fragments because they begin with a subordinating conjunction (such as "although," "if," or "when") or a relative pronoun (such as "who," "which," "whose," or "that").

Fragment	David bought a gopher ranch. *Although he knew nothing about rodents.*
Correct	David bought a gopher ranch, although he knew nothing about rodents.

Fragment	David bought a gopher ranch. *Which was for sale at a low price.*
Correct	David bought a gopher ranch, which was for sale at a low price.

If you are having problems recognizing whether a group of words is a fragment or a complete sentence, try the "It is true that" test. When you suspect a fragment, say, "It is true that" in front of the words in question. In most cases, a complete sentence will still make sense, but a fragment will not.*

- It is true that . . . David bought a gopher ranch. [Makes sense: complete sentence]
- It is true that . . . hoping to strike it rich. [No sense: fragment]
- It is true that . . . which was for sale at a low price. [No sense: fragment]

Although they can appear anywhere, fragments most often "belong" to the thought in front of them. To make a fragment fully meaningful, consider connecting it to the preceding or following sentence, as appropriate, or simply rewrite it as a complete sentence (for examples, see the first two "Correct" sentences in this section).

In some cases, a writer will intentionally use a fragment for a particular purpose, often for emphasis or to create a specific tone ("She felt rotten. Worse than rotten.

---

*The "It is true that" test does not work on questions, elliptical responses or exclamations (such as "Hello," "Yes," "Help!"), or commands ("Go to your room right now.").

Miserable-rotten."). But unless you clearly know how to use a fragment for effect and are certain that the tone it creates is appropriate for your essay and audience, stick to writing complete sentences.

◆ For more help with fragments, see pages 561–562 in the Handbook. See also pages 151–154 in this chapter, which will suggest ways to combine thoughts through coordination and subordination.

In addition to unintentional fragments, another construction that may confuse meaning for readers is called a *run-on* (or *fused*) sentence. Run-ons are most often two complete sentences joined together without any punctuation. Such sentences may be corrected by making separate sentences, by placing a semicolon between the complete thoughts, by using a comma plus a coordinating conjunction, or by subordinating one clause.

Run-on	Peter the Penguin was disappointed at the airport's security checkpoint he learned he was on the no-fly list.
Corrected with semicolon	Peter the Penguin was disappointed at the airport's security checkpoint; he learned he was on the no-fly list.
Corrected with subordination	Peter the Penguin was disappointed at the airport's security checkpoint when he learned he was on the no-fly list.

Don't, however, correct a run-on sentence by merely inserting a comma without a coordinating conjunction between the two sentences; doing so will likely result in another major sentence error called a *comma splice*.

Comma splice	My economics professor says success is a great teacher, my yoga teacher says adversity may be an even greater one.
Corrected with a comma and a coordinating conjunction	My economics professor says success is a great teacher, but my yoga teacher says adversity may be an even greater one.

The common coordinating conjunctions are "and," "or," "but," "for," "so," "nor," and "yet." ◆ For more information on coordination, turn to pages 151–152 in this chapter. (For more help correcting the run-on sentence and the comma splice, see pages 563–565 in the Handbook.)

Pay Attention to Word Order

The correct word order is crucial for clarity. Always place a modifier (a word or group of words that affects the meaning of another word) near the word it modifies. The position of a modifier can completely change the meaning of your sentence; for example, each sentence presented here offers a different idea because of the placement of the modifier "only."

   1. Eliza said she loves only me. [Eliza loves me and no one else.]

   2. Only Eliza said she loves me. [No other person said she loves me.]

   3. Eliza said only that she loves me. [Eliza said she loves me, but said nothing other than that.]

   4. Eliza said only she loves me. [Eliza said no one else loves me.]

To avoid confusion, therefore, place your modifiers close to the words or phrases they describe.

A modifier that seems to modify the wrong part of a sentence is called "misplaced." Not only can misplaced modifiers change or distort the meaning of your sentence, they can also provide unintentional humor, as illustrated by the following excerpt from the 1929 Marx Brothers movie *The Cocoanuts*:

Woman: There's a man waiting outside to see you with a black mustache.
Groucho: Tell him I've already got one.

Of course, the woman didn't mean to imply that the man outside was waiting with (that is, accompanied by) a mustache; she meant to say, "There's a man with a black mustache waiting outside."

A poster advertising a lecture on campus provided this opportunity for humor: "Professor Elizabeth Sewell will discuss the latest appearance of Halley's Comet in room 104." Under the announcement a local wit had scribbled, "Shall we reserve room 105 for the tail?" Or take the case of this startling headline: "Calf Born to Rancher with Two Heads."

Here are some other examples of misplaced modifiers:

Misplaced   Dilapidated and almost an eyesore, Shirley bought the old house to restore it to its original beauty. [Did the writer mean that Shirley needed a beauty treatment?]

Revised   Shirley bought the old house, which was dilapidated and almost an eyesore, to restore it to its original beauty.

Misplaced   Because she is now thoroughly housebroken, Sarah can take the dog almost anywhere. [Did the writer mean that Sarah once had an embarrassing problem?]

Revised   Because the dog is now thoroughly housebroken, Sarah can take her almost anywhere.

Misplaced   Three family members were found bound and gagged by the grandmother. [Did the writer mean that the grandmother had taken up a life of crime?]

Revised   The grandmother found the three family members who had been bound and gagged.

Misplaced   The lost child was finally found wandering in a frozen farmer's field. [Did the writer mean to say that the farmer was that cold?]

Revised   The lost child was finally found wandering in a farmer's frozen field.

In each of the preceding examples, the writer forgot to place the modifying phrase so that it modifies the correct word. In most cases, a sentence with a misplaced modifier can be easily corrected by moving the word or phrase closer to the word that should be modified.

In some sentences, however, the word being modified is missing entirely. Such a phrase is called a "dangling modifier." Think of these phrases as poor orphans, waiting out in the cold, without a parent to accompany them. Most of these errors can be corrected by adding the missing "parent"—the word(s) described by the phrase. Here are some examples followed by their revisions:

Dangling	Waving farewell, the plane began to roll down the runway. [Did the writer mean the plane was waving farewell?]
Revised	Waving farewell, <u>we</u> watched as the plane began to roll down the runway.
Dangling	After spending hours planting dozens of strawberry plants, the gophers came back to the garden and ate every one of them. [Did the writer mean that the gophers had a good meal after putting in such hard work?]
Revised	After spending hours planting dozens of strawberry plants, <u>Ralph</u> realized that the gophers had come back to the garden and eaten every one of them.
Dangling	While telling a joke to my roommate, a cockroach walked across my soufflé. [Did the writer mean that the cockroach was a comedian?]
Revised	While telling a joke to my roommate, <u>I</u> noticed a cockroach walking across my soufflé.
Dangling	Having tucked the children into bed, the cat was put out for the night. [Did the writer mean that the family pet had taken up nanny duties?]
Revised	Having tucked the children into bed, <u>Mom and Dad</u> put the cat out for the night.

Misplaced and dangling modifiers (and many other kinds of sentence errors) often occur as you write your first "idea" drafts. Later, when you are satisfied with your content and organization, you can smooth out these confusing or unintentionally humorous constructions. At first you may agree with well-known essayist Annie Dillard, who notes that writing sometimes feels like alligator wrestling: "With your two bare hands, you hold and fight a sentence's head while its tail tries to knock you over." By practicing good revision skills, however, you soon should be able to wrestle your sentence problems to the ground. (◆ For additional examples of misplaced and dangling modifiers, see page 560 in the Handbook.

Avoid Mixed Constructions and Faulty Predication

Sometimes you may begin with a sentence pattern in mind and then shift, midsentence, to another pattern—a change that often results in a generally confusing sentence. In many of these cases, you will find that the subject of your sentence simply doesn't fit with the rest of the sentence (the predicate). Look at the following examples and note their corrections:

Faulty	Financial aid is a growing problem for many college students. [Financial aid itself isn't a problem; rather, it's the lack of aid.]
Revised	College students are finding it harder to obtain financial aid.

Faulty   Pregnant cows are required to teach a portion of two courses in Animal Science, AS100 (Breeding of Livestock) and AS200 (Problems in Reproduction of Cattle). [Obviously, the cows will not be the instructors for the classes.]

Revised   The Animal Science Department needs to purchase pregnant cows for use in two courses, AS100 (Breeding of Livestock) and AS200 (Problems in Reproduction of Cattle).

Faulty   Love is when you start rehearsing dinner-date conversation before breakfast. [A thing is never a "when" or a "where"; rewrite all "is when" or "is where" constructions.]

Revised   You're in love if you start rehearsing dinner-date conversation before breakfast.

Faulty   My math grade is why I'm so depressed. [A grade is not a "why"; rewrite "is why" constructions.]

Revised   I'm so depressed because of my math grade.

Faulty   "Fans, don't fail to miss tomorrow's game." [A contorted line from Dizzy Dean, baseball star and sportscaster.]

Revised   "Fans, don't miss tomorrow's game."

Clear, straightforward sentences keep readers from feeling as though they are lost in an Escher maze. Convex and Concave, 1955, by M.C. Escher.

Many mixed constructions occur when a writer is in a hurry; read your rough drafts carefully to see if you have sentences in which you started one pattern but switched to another. (◆ For more help on faulty predications and mixed constructions, see pages 568–569 in Part Four.)

Practicing What You've Learned

A. In this exercise, you will find sentences that contain some of the problems discussed thus far in this chapter. Rewrite any sentences that you find vague, confusing, overly simplistic, or overpacked; correct any sentence fragments, run-ons, or comma splice errors. You may divide or combine sentences and replace vague words to improve clarity.

1. There's a new detective show on television. Starring Phil Noir. It is set in the 1940s. According to *TV Guide.*

2. Roger was an awesome guy he was really a big deal in his company.

3. I can't help but wonder whether or not he isn't unwelcome.

4. The book *Biofeedback: How to Stop It* is a good book because of all the good ideas the writer put into it.

5. His assistant stole the magician's bag of tricks. The magician became disillusioned.

6. Afraid poor repair service will ruin your next road trip? Come to the Fix-It Shop and be sure. If your car has a worn-out part, we'll replace it with one just like it.

7. I've signed up for a course at my local college, it is "Cultivating the Mold in Your Refrigerator for Fun and Profit."

8. I'm not sure but I think that Lois is the author of *The Underachiever's Guide to Very Small Business Opportunities* or is she the writer of *Whine Your Way to Success* because I know she's written several books since she's having an autograph party at the campus bookstore either this afternoon or tomorrow.

9. For some people, reading your horoscope is a fun way to learn stuff about your life. Although some people think it's too weird.

10. Upon being asked if she would like to live forever, one contestant in a Miss USA contest replied: "I would not live forever, because we should not live forever, because if we were supposed to live forever, then we would live forever, but we cannot live forever, which is why I would not live forever."

continued on next page

B. The following sentences contain misplaced words and phrases as well as other faulty constructions. Revise them so that each sentence is clear.

1. If you are accosted in the subway at night, you should learn to escape harm from the police.

2. The bride was escorted down the aisle by her stepfather wearing an antique family wedding gown.

3. Almost dead for five years now, I miss my dog so much.

4. For sale: unique gifts for that special, hard-to-find person in your life.

5. The reason why I finally got my leg operated on over Thanksgiving break is because it had been hanging over my head for years.

6. We need to hire two three-year-old teachers for preschool kids who don't smoke.

7. The story of Rip Van Winkle is one of the dangers endured by those who oversleep.

8. We gave our waterbed to friends we didn't want anymore.

9. People who are allergic to chocolate and children should not be given the new vaccine.

10. "I remember meeting a mother of a child who was abducted by the North Koreans right here in the Oval Office."—George W. Bush, 2008

Developing a Concise Style

Almost all writing suffers from wordiness—the tendency to use more words than necessary. When useless words weigh down your prose, the meaning is often lost, confused, or hidden. Flabby prose calls for a reducing plan: put those obese sentences on a diet by cutting out unnecessary words, just as you avoid eating too many fatty foods to keep yourself at a healthy weight. Mushy prose is ponderous and boring; crisp, to-the-point writing, on the other hand, is both accessible and pleasing. Beware, however, a temptation to overdiet—you don't want your prose to become so thin or brief that your meaning disappears completely. Therefore, cut out only the *unessential* words and phrases.

Wordy prose is frequently the result of using one or more of the following: (1) deadwood constructions, (2) redundancies, (3) passive constructions, and (4) pretentious diction.

Avoid Deadwood Constructions

Always try to cut empty "deadwood" from your sentences. Having a clear, concise style does not mean limiting your writing to choppy, childish Dick-and-Jane sentences; it only means that all unnecessary words, phrases, and clauses should be deleted. Here are some sentences containing common deadwood constructions and ways they may be pruned:

Poor	The *reason* the starving novelist drove fifty miles to a new restaurant was because it was serving his favorite chicken dish, Pullet Surprise. ["The reason . . . was because" is both wordy and ungrammatical. If you have a reason, you don't need a "reason because."]
Revised	The starving novelist drove fifty miles to a new restaurant because it was serving his favorite chicken dish, Pullet Surprise.
Poor	The land settlement *was an example where* my client, Ms. Patti O. Furniture, did not receive fair treatment.
Revised	The land settlement was unfair to my client, Ms. Patti O. Furniture.
Poor	Because *of the fact that* his surfboard business failed after only a month, my brother decided to leave Minnesota.
Revised	Because his surfboard business failed after only a month, my brother decided to leave Minnesota.

Other notorious deadwood constructions include the following:

regardless of the fact that	(use "although")
due to the fact that	(use "because")
the reason is that	(omit)
as to whether or not to	(omit "as to" and "or not")
at this point in time	(use "now" or "today")
it is believed that	(use a specific subject and "believes")
concerning the matter of	(use "about")
by means of	(use "by")
these are the kinds of . . . that	(use "these" plus a specific noun)
on account of	(use "because")

Watch a tendency to tack on empty "fillers" that stretch one word into a phrase:

Wordy	Each candidate will be evaluated *on an individual basis.*
Concise	Each candidate will be evaluated *individually.*
Wordy	Television does not portray violence *in a realistic fashion.*
Concise	Television does not portray violence *realistically.*
Wordy	The New York blackout produced a *crisis-type situation.*
Concise	The New York blackout produced a *crisis.*

To retain your reader's interest and improve the flow of your prose, trim all the fat from your sentences.

"There are," "It is." These introductory phrases are often space wasters. When possible, omit them or replace them with specific subjects, as shown in the following:

Wordy	*There are* ten dental students on Full-Bite Scholarships attending this university.
Revised	Ten dental students on Full-Bite Scholarships attend this university.

Wordy	*It is* true that the County Fair still offers many fun contests, including the ever-popular map fold-off.
Revised	The County Fair still offers many fun contests, including the ever-popular map fold-off.

"Who" and "which" clauses. Some "who" and "which" clauses are unnecessary and may be turned into modifiers placed before the noun:

Wordy	The getaway car, *which* was stolen, turned the corner.
Revised	The stolen getaway car turned the corner.

Wordy	The chef, *who* was depressed, ordered his noisy lobsters to simmer down.
Revised	The depressed chef ordered his noisy lobsters to simmer down.

When adjective clauses are necessary, the words "who" and "which" may sometimes be omitted:

Wordy	Sarah Bellam, *who* is a local English teacher, was delighted to hear that she had won the annual lottery, *which* is sponsored by the Shirley Jackson Foundation.
Revised	Sarah Bellam, a local English teacher, was delighted to hear that she had won the annual lottery, sponsored by the Shirley Jackson Foundation.

"To be." Most "to be" phrases are unnecessary and ought not to be. Delete them every time you can.

Wordy	She seems *to be* angry.
Revised	She seems angry.

Wordy	Herb's charisma-bypass operation proved *to be* successful.
Revised	Herb's charisma-bypass operation proved successful.

Wordy	The chef wanted his favorite horror movie, *The Texas Coldslaw Massacre*, *to be* awarded the film festival's top prize.
Revised	The chef wanted his favorite horror movie, *The Texas Coldslaw Massacre*, awarded the film festival's top prize.

"Of" and infinitive phrases. Many "of" and infinitive ("to" plus verb) phrases may be omitted or revised by using possessives, adjectives, and verbs, as shown here:

Wordy	At the time *of registration,* students are required *to make* payment *of their library fees.*
Revised	At registration students must pay their library fees.

Wordy	The producer fired the mother *of the director of the movie.*
Revised	The producer fired the movie director's mother.

Including deadwood phrases makes your prose puffy; streamline your sentences to present a simple, direct style.

Avoid Redundancy

Many flabby sentences contain *redundancies* (words that repeat the same idea or whose meanings overlap). Consider the following examples, currently popular in the Department of Redundancy Department:

- *In this day and age,* people expect to live at least seventy years. ["Day" and "age" present a similar idea. "Today" is less wordy.]

- He repeated the winning bingo number *over again.* ["Repeated" means "to say again," so there is no need for "over again."]

- The group consensus of opinion was that the pizza crust tasted like cardboard. ["Consensus" means "collective opinion," so it's unnecessary to add "group" or repeat "opinion."]

- She thought his hot-lava necklaces were really very unique. [Because "unique" means "being the only one of its kind," the quality described by "unique" cannot vary in degree. Avoid adding modifiers such as "very," "most," or "somewhat" to the word "unique."]

Some other common redundancies include the following:

reverted ~~back~~	~~new~~ innovation
reflected ~~back~~	red ~~in color~~
retreated ~~back~~	burned ~~down/up~~
fell ~~down~~	~~pair of~~ twins/~~two~~ twins
climb ~~up~~	~~resulting~~ effect (or "result")
a ~~true~~ fact	~~final~~ outcome
large ~~in size~~	at this point ~~in time~~ (or "now")
joined ~~up~~	8 P.M. ~~at night~~

Carefully Consider Your Passive Verbs

When the subject of the sentence performs the action, the verb is *active;* when the subject of the sentence is acted on, the verb is *passive.* You can recognize some sentences with passive verbs because they often contain the word "by," telling who performed the action.

Passive	The wedding date *was announced* by the young couple.
Active	The young couple *announced* their wedding date.
Passive	His letter of resignation *was accepted* by the Board of Trustees.
Active	The Board of Trustees *accepted* his letter of resignation.
Passive	The trivia contest *was won* by the popular Boulder team, The Godzillas Must Be Crazy.
Active	The popular Boulder team, The Godzillas Must Be Crazy, *won* the trivia contest.

In addition to being wordy and weak, passive sentences often disguise the performer of the action in question. You might have heard a politician, for example, say something similar to this: "It was decided this year to give all the senators an increase in salary." The question of *who* decided to raise salaries remains foggy—perhaps purposefully so. In your own prose, however, you should strive for clarity and directness; therefore, use active verbs as often as you can except when you wish to stress the person or thing that receives the action, as shown in the following examples:

- Their first baby was delivered September 30, 1980, by a local midwife.
- The elderly man was struck by a drunk driver.

Special note: Authorities in some professional and technical fields prefer the passive construction because they wish to emphasize the experiment or process rather than the people performing the action. If the passive voice is preferred in your field, you should abide by that convention when you are writing reports or papers for your professional colleagues.

Avoid Pretentiousness

Another enemy of clear, concise prose is *pretentiousness.* Pompous, inflated language surrounds us, and because too many people think it sounds learned or official, we may be tempted to use it when we want to impress others with our writing. But as George Orwell, author of *1984*, noted, an inflated style is like "a cuttlefish squirting out ink." If you want your prose easily understood, write as clearly and plainly as possible.

To illustrate how confusing pretentious writing can be, here is a copy of a government memo announcing a blackout order, issued in 1942 during World War II:

Such preparations shall be made as will completely obscure all Federal buildings and non-Federal buildings occupied by the Federal government during an air raid for any period of time from visibility by reason of internal or external illumination.

President Franklin Roosevelt intervened and rewrote the order in plain English, clarifying its message and reducing the number of words by half:

Tell them that in buildings where they have to keep the work going to put something across the windows.

By translating the obscure original memo into easily understandable language, Roosevelt demonstrated that a natural prose style can communicate necessary information to readers more quickly and efficiently than bureaucratic jargon. (◆ For more advice on ridding your prose of jargon, see pages 171–172.)

REMEMBER: In other—shorter—words, to attract and hold your readers' attention and to communicate clearly and quickly, make your sentences as informative, straightforward, specific, and concise as possible.

Practicing What You've Learned

The following sentences are filled with deadwood, redundancies, awkward phrases, and passive constructions. Rewrite each one so that it is concise and direct.

1. In point of fact, the main reason he lost the editing job was primarily because of his being too careless and sloppy in his proofreading work.

2. It was revealed to us by staff members today that there were many adults at the company picnic throwing their trash on the ground as well as their children.

3. My brother Austin, who happens to be older than me, can't drive to work this week due to the fact that he was in a wreck in his car at 2:00 A.M. early Saturday morning.

4. In this modern world of today, we often criticize or disapprove of advertising that is thought to be damaging to women by representing them in an unfair way.

5. When the prosecution tried to introduce the old antique gun, this was objected to by the attorney defending the two twin brothers.

6. It seems to me in my opinion that what the poet is trying to get across to the reader in the poem "Now Is the Winter of Our Discount Tent" is her feeling of disgust with camping.

7. We very often felt that although we expressed our deepest concerns and feelings to our boss, she often just sat there and gave us the real impression that she was taking what we said in a very serious manner although, in our opinion, she did not really and truly care about our concerns.

8. It is a true fact that certainly bears repeating over and over again that learning computer skills and word processing can help you perform in a more efficient way at work and school and also can save you lots of time in daily life, too.

9. Personally, I believe that there are too many people who go to eat out in restaurants who always feel they must continually assert their superior natures by acting in a rude, nasty fashion to the people who are employed to wait on their tables.

10. In order to enhance my opportunities for advancement in the workplace at this point in time, I arrived at the decision to seek the hand of my employer's daughter in the state of matrimony.

Assignment

Collaborative Activity: Write a paragraph of at least five sentences as clearly and concisely as you can. Then rewrite this paragraph, filling it with as many vague words, redundancies, and deadwood constructions as possible. Exchange this rewritten paragraph for a similarly faulty one written by a classmate; give yourselves fifteen minutes to "translate" each other's sentences into effective prose. Compare the translations to the original paragraphs. Which version is clearer? Why?

Developing an Engaging Style

Good writing demands clarity and conciseness—but that's not all. Good prose should also be appealing and interesting. Each line should encourage the reader to the next. Consider, for example, a dull article you've read recently. It may have been written clearly, but perhaps it failed to interest or inform because of its insufferably bland tone; by the time you finished a few pages, you had discovered a new cure for insomnia.

You can prevent your readers from succumbing to a similar case of the blahs by developing an inviting prose style that continually engages and pleases them. As one writer has pointed out, all subjects—with the possible exceptions of sex and money—are dull until somebody makes them interesting. As you revise your rough drafts, remember: bored readers are not born but made. As playwright Anton Chekov once said, "Don't tell me the moon is shining; show me the glint of light on broken glass."

To help you transform ho-hum prose into lively sentences and paragraphs, here are some practical suggestions:

Use specific, descriptive verbs. Avoid bland verbs that must be supplemented by modifiers.

Bland	His fist *broke* the window *into many little pieces.*
Better	His fist *shattered* the window.
Bland	Dr. Love *asked* his congregation about donating money to his "love mission" *over and over again.*
Better	Dr. Love *hounded* his congregation into donating money to his "love mission."
Bland	The exhausted runner *went* up the last hill *in an unsteady way.*
Better	The exhausted runner *staggered* up the last hill.

To cut wordiness that weighs down your prose, try to use an active verb instead of a noun plus a colorless verb such as "to be," "to have," "to get," "to do," and "to make." Avoid unnecessary uses of "got."

Wordy	At first the players and managers *had an argument* over the money, but finally they *came to an agreement that got* the contract dispute settled.
Better	At first the players and managers *argued* over the money, but finally they *settled* the contract dispute.
Wordy	The executives *made the decision* to *have another meeting* on Tuesday.
Better	The executives *decided to meet again* on Tuesday.
Wordy	The family *made many enjoyable trips* to Hawaii before their daughter *got married* there in 2009.
Better	The family *enjoyed* many trips to Hawaii before their daughter *married* there in 2009.

Use specific, precise modifiers that help the reader see, hear, or feel what you are describing. Adjectives such as "good," "bad," "many," "more," "great," "a lot," "important," and "interesting" are too vague to paint the reader a clear picture. Similarly, the adverbs "very," "really," "too," and "quite" are overused and add little to sentence clarity. The following are examples of weak sentences and their revisions:

Imprecise	The potion changed the scientist into a *really old* man.
Better	The potion changed the scientist into a *one-hundred-year-old* man.

Imprecise	Aricelli is a *very interesting* person.
Better	Aricelli is *witty, intelligent,* and *talented.*

Imprecise	The vegetables tasted *funny.*
Better	The vegetables tasted *like moss mixed with Krazy Glue.*

◆ For more advice on using specific, colorful words, see pages 166–170 in Chapter 7 and pages 347–352 in Chapter 16.)

Emphasize people when possible. Try to focus on human beings rather than abstractions whenever you can. Next to our fascinating selves, we most enjoy hearing about other people. Although all the sentences in the first paragraph that follows are correct, the second one, revised by a class of composition students at Brown University, is clearer and more useful because the jargon has been eliminated and the focus changed from the tuition rules to the students.

Original	Tuition regulations currently in effect provide that payment of the annual tuition entitles an undergraduate-degree candidate to full-time enrollment, which is defined as registration for three, four, or five courses per semester. This means that at no time may an undergraduate student's official registration for courses drop below three without a dean's permission for part-time status and that at no time may the official course registration exceed five. (Brown University course announcement)
Revised	If students pay their tuition, they may enroll in three, four, or five courses per semester. Fewer than three or more than five can be taken only with a dean's permission.

Here's a similar example with a bureaucratic focus rather than a personal one:

Original	The salary deflations will most seriously impact the secondary educational profession.
Revised	High school teachers will suffer the biggest salary reductions.

Obviously, the revised sentence is the more easily understood of the two because the reader knows exactly who will be affected by the pay cuts. In your own prose, wherever appropriate, try to replace vague abstractions such as "society," "culture," "administrative concerns," and "programmatic expectations," with the human beings you're thinking about. In other words, remember to talk *to* people *about* people.

Vary your sentence style. Don't force readers to wade through annoying paragraphs full of identically constructed sentences. To illustrate this point, the following are a few sentences composed in the all-too-common "subject + predicate" pattern:

Soccer is the most popular sport in the world. Soccer exists in almost every country. Soccer players are sometimes more famous than movie stars. Soccer teams compete every few years for the World Soccer Cup. Soccer fans often riot if their team loses. Soccer fans even commit suicide. Soccer is the only game in the world that makes people so crazy.

Excruciatingly painful, yes? Each of us tends to repeat a particular sentence pattern (though the choppy "subject + predicate" is by far the most popular); you can often detect your own by reading your prose aloud. To avoid overdosing your readers with the same pattern, vary the length, arrangement, and complexity of your sentences. Of course, this doesn't mean that you should contort your sentences merely for the sake of illustrating variety; just read your rough draft aloud, listening carefully to the rhythm of your prose so you can revise any monotonous passages or disharmonious sounds. (Try also to avoid the hiccup syndrome, in which you begin a sentence with the same word that ends the preceding sentence: "The first president to install a telephone on his desk was Herbert *Hoover*. *Hoover* refused to use the telephone booth outside his office.")

Avoid overuse of any one kind of construction in the same sentence. Don't, for example, pile up too many negatives, "who" or "which" clauses, and prepositional or infinitive phrases in one sentence.

- He *couldn't* tell whether she *didn't* want him to go or not.
- I gave the money to my brother, *who* returned it to the bank president, *who* said the decision to prosecute was up to the sheriff, *who* was out of town.
- I went to the florist *for* my roommate *for* a dozen roses *for* his date.

Try also to avoid stockpiling nouns, one on top of another, so that your sentences are difficult to read. Although some nouns may be used as adjectives to modify other nouns ("baseball bat," "gasoline pump," "food processor"), too many nouns grouped together sound awkward and confuse readers. If you have run too many nouns together, try using prepositional phrases ("an income tax bill discussion" becomes "discussion of an income tax bill") or changing the order or vocabulary of the sentence:

Confusing   The legislators are currently considering the *liability insurance multiple-choice premium proposal.*

Clearer   The legislators are currently considering the proposal that suggests *multiple-choice premiums* for *liability insurance.*

Confusing   We're concerned about the low *female labor force participation figures* in our department.

Clearer   We're concerned about the low *number of women working* in our department.

Don't change your point of view between or within sentences. If, for example, you begin your essay referring to students as "they," don't switch midway—or midsentence—to "we" or "you."

Inconsistent	Students pay tuition, which should entitle *them* to some voice in the university's administration. Therefore, *we* deserve one student on the Board of Regents.
Consistent	Students pay tuition, which should entitle *them* to some voice in the university's administration. Therefore, *they* deserve one student on the Board of Regents.
Inconsistent	*I* like my photography class because *we* learn how to restore *our* old photos and how to take better color portraits of *your* family.
Consistent	*I* like my photography class because *I'm* learning how to restore *my* old photos and how to take better color portraits of *my* family.

Perhaps this is a good place to dispel the myth that the pronoun "I" should never be used in an essay; on the contrary, many of our best essays have been written in the first person. Some of your former teachers may have discouraged the use of "I" for these two reasons: (1) personal opinion does not belong in the essay, and (2) writing in the first person often produces too many empty phrases, such as "I think that" and "I believe that." Nevertheless, if the personal point of view is appropriate in a particular assignment, you may use the first person in moderation, making sure that every other sentence doesn't begin with "I" plus a verb.

Practicing What You've Learned

Replace the following underlined words so that the sentences are clear and vivid. In addition, rephrase any awkward constructions or unnecessarily abstract words you find.

1. Judging from the <u>crazy</u> sound of the reactor, it isn't obvious to me that nuclear power as we know it today isn't a technology with a less than wonderful future.

2. The City Council felt <u>bad</u> because the revised tourist development activities grant fund application form letters were mailed without stamps.

3. To watch Jim Bob eat pork chops was <u>most interesting</u>.

4. For sale: <u>very nice</u> antique bureau suitable for ladies or gentlemen with thick legs and extra-large side handles.

5. We <u>don't want anybody to not</u> have fun.

6. My roommate is <u>sort of different</u>, but he's a <u>good</u> guy at heart.

7. After reading the <u>great</u> new book, *The Looter's Guide to Riot-Prone Cities*, Eddie <u>asked to have</u> a transfer <u>really soon</u>.

8. The wild oats soup was <u>fantastic</u>, so we drank <u>a lot of it very fast</u>.

9. When his new cat Chairman Meow won the pet show, owner Warren Peace got <u>pretty excited</u>.

10. The new diet <u>made me feel awful</u>, and it <u>did many horrible things</u> to my body.

Assignment

A. Find a short piece of writing you think is too bland, boring, vague, or confusing. (Possible sources: your college catalog, a business contract, a form letter, or your student health insurance policy.) In a well-written paragraph of your own, identify the sample's major problems, and offer some specific suggestions for improving the writing.

B. *Collaborative Activity*: Following your work on Assignment "A," you might participate in this peer activity. After the class has separated into small sets of three or four students, listen as each person in your group reads aloud his or her original sample. What makes each one so bland, boring, or confusing? Together, select the worst offender to share with the class as a whole. When all the groups have reported, vote one the winner of the Most Lifeless Prose Award. Vow to avoid any such blandness and/or vagueness in your own writing!

C. Continue working on a clear, concise style by writing a public service announcement (PSA) as a caption for the following photo. Think of a charity, service organization, or social program and use your words plus the picture to promote one of their goals (consider, for example, advertising a fund-raising activity, an awareness event, or an open house). Or, if you prefer, announce a new campus regulation or remind readers of a current policy. Assume your text and the picture will appear in a local or campus newspaper and, because print space is expensive, you must accomplish your task in three or four highly effective sentences. Be ready to read your caption to your classmates.

Blend Images/SuperStock

Developing an Emphatic Style

Some words and phrases in your sentences are more important than others and therefore need more emphasis. Three ways to vary emphasis are by (1) word order, (2) coordination, and (3) subordination.

Word Order

The arrangement of words in a sentence can determine which ideas receive the most emphasis. To stress a word or phrase, place it at the end of the sentence or at the beginning of the sentence. Accordingly, a word or phrase receives least emphasis when buried in the middle of the sentence. Compare the following examples, in which the word "murder" receives varying degrees of emphasis:

Least emphatic	For Colonel Mustard *murder* was the only solution.
Emphatic	*Murder* was Colonel Mustard's only solution.
Most emphatic	Colonel Mustard knew only one solution: *murder*.

Another use of word order to vary emphasis is *inversion*, taking a word out of its natural or usual position in a sentence and relocating it in an unexpected place.

Usual order	Parents who give their children both roots and wings are *wise*.
Inverted order	*Wise* are the parents who give their children both roots and wings.

Not all your sentences will contain words that need special emphasis; good writing generally contains a mix of some sentences in natural order and others rearranged for special effects.

Coordination

When you want to stress two closely related ideas equally, coordinate them.* In coordination, you join two sentences with a coordinating conjunction. To remember the coordinating conjunctions ("for," "and," "nor," "but," "or," "yet," "so"), think of the acronym FANBOYS; then always join two sentences with a comma and one of the FANBOYS. Here are two samples:

Choppy	The most popular girl's name in the U.S. last year was Sophia. The most popular boy's name in the U.S. last year was Jacob.
Coordinated	The most popular girl's name in the U.S. last year was Sophia, *and* the most popular boy's name was Jacob.
Choppy	The patient requested a chocolate I.V. The nurse said no.
Coordinated	The patient requested a chocolate I.V., *but* the nurse said no.

---

*To remember that the term "coordination" refers to equally weighted ideas, think of other words with the prefix *co* such as "copilots," "co-authors," or "cooperation."

You can use coordination to show a relationship between ideas and to add variety to your sentence structures. Be careful, however, to select the right words while linking ideas, unlike this sentence that appeared in a church newsletter: "The ladies of the church have discarded clothing of all kinds, and they have been inspected by the minister." In other words, writers often need to slow down and make sure their thoughts are not joined in unclear or even unintentionally humorous ways: "For those of you who have children and don't know it, we have a nursery downstairs."

Sometimes when writers are in a hurry, they join ideas that are clearly related in their own minds but whose relationship is confusing to the reader:

Confusing   My laboratory report isn't finished, and today my sister is leaving for a visit home.

Clear   I'm still working on my laboratory report, so I won't be able to catch a ride home with my sister who's leaving today.

You should also avoid using coordinating conjunctions to string too many ideas together like linked sausages:

Poor   We went inside the famous cave and the guide turned off the lights and we saw the rocks that glowed.

Revised   After we went inside the famous cave, the guide turned off the lights so we could see the rocks that glowed.

Subordination

Some sentences contain one main statement and one or more less emphasized elements; the less important ideas are subordinate to, or are dependent on, the sentence's main idea.* Subordinating conjunctions introducing dependent clauses show a variety of relationships between the clauses and the main part of the sentence. Here are four examples of subordinating conjunctions and their uses:

1. To show time

Without subordination   Superman stopped changing his clothes. He realized the phone booth was made of glass.

With subordination   Superman stopped changing his clothes *when* he realized the phone booth was made of glass.

2. To show cause

Without subordination   The country-western singer failed to gain success in Nashville. She sadly returned to Snooker Hollow to work in the sequin mines.

With subordination   *Because* the country-western singer failed to gain success in Nashville, she sadly returned to Snooker Hollow to work in the sequin mines.

---

*To remember that the term "subordination" refers to sentences containing dependent elements, think of such words as "a subordinate" (someone who works for someone else) or a post office "substation" (a less important branch of the main post office).

3. To show condition

Without subordination	Susan ought to study the art of tattooing. She will work with colorful people.
With subordination	*If* Susan studies the art of tattooing, she will work with colorful people.

4. To show place

Without subordination	Bulldozers are smashing the old movie theater. That's the place I first saw Roy Rogers and Dale Evans ride into the sunset.
With subordination	Bulldozers are smashing the old movie theater *where* I first saw Roy Rogers and Dale Evans ride into the sunset.

Subordination is especially useful in ridding your prose of choppy Dick-and-Jane sentences and those "empty sentences" discussed on pages 131–132. Here are some examples of choppy, weak sentences and their revisions, which contain subordinate clauses:

Choppy	Lew makes bagels on Tuesday. Lines in front of his store are a block long.
Revised	When Lew makes bagels on Tuesday, lines in front of his store are a block long.
Choppy	I have fond memories of Zilker Park. My husband and I met there.
Revised	I have fond memories of Zilker Park because my husband and I met there.

Effective use of subordination is one of the marks of a sophisticated writer because it presents adequate information in one smooth flow instead of in monotonous drips. Subordination, like coordination, also adds variety to your sentence construction.

Generally, when you subordinate one idea, you emphasize another, so to avoid the tail-wagging-the-dog problem, put your important idea in the main clause. Also, don't let your most important idea become buried under an avalanche of subordinate clauses, as in the sentence that follows:

> *When* he was told by his boss, *who* had always treated him fairly, *that* he was being fired from a job *that* he had held for twenty years at a factory *where* he enjoyed working *because* the pay was good, Henry felt angry and frustrated.

Practice blending choppy sentences by studying the following sentence-combining exercise. In this exercise, a description of a well-known movie has been chopped into simple sentences and then combined into one complex sentence.

1. *Psycho* (1960)
Norman Bates manages a motel.
It is remote.
It is dangerous.
Norman has a mother.
She seems overly fond of knives.
He tries to protect his mom.

In a remote—and dangerous—motel, manager Norman Bates tries to protect his mother, who seems overly fond of knives.

2. *King Kong* (2005)
A movie director goes to the jungle.
He captures an ape.
The ape is a giant.
The ape is taken to New York City.
He escapes.
He dies fighting for a young woman.
He loves her.
She is beautiful.

A movie director captures a giant ape in the jungle and takes him to New York City, where he escapes but dies fighting for the beautiful young woman he loves.

3. *Casablanca* (1942)
Rick is an American.
He is cynical.
He owns a café.
He lives in Casablanca.
He meets his former love.
She is married.
Her husband is a French resistance fighter.
Rick helps the couple.
He regains self-respect.

When Rick, a cynical American café owner in Casablanca, helps his former love and her husband, a French resistance fighter, he regains his self-respect.

Please note that the sentences in these exercises may be combined effectively in a number of ways. For instance, the description of *King Kong* might be rewritten this way: "After a movie director captures him in the jungle, a giant ape escapes in New York City but dies fighting for the love of a beautiful young woman." How might you rewrite the other two sample sentences?

Practicing What You've Learned

A. Revise the following sentences so that the underlined words receive more emphasis.

   1. A remark attributed to the former heavyweight boxing champion <u>Joe Louis</u> is "I don't really like money, but it quiets my nerves."

   2. According to recent polls, <u>television</u> is where most Americans get their news.

   3. Of all the world's problems, it is <u>hunger</u> that is most urgent.

   4. I enjoyed visiting many foreign countries last year, <u>Greece</u> being my favorite of all of them.

   5. The annoying habit of <u>knuckle-cracking</u> is something I can't stand.

continued on next page

B. Combine the following sentences using coordination or subordination.

1. The guru rejected his dentist's offer of novocaine. He could transcend dental medication.

2. John failed his literature test. John incorrectly identified Harper Lee as the author of the south-of-the-border classic *Tequila Mockingbird*.

3. Peggy Sue's house burned. She tapped a "9." She couldn't find "11" on the phone keypad.

4. The police had only a few clues. They suspected Jean and David had strangled each other in a desperate struggle over control of the thermostat.

5. Ken's favorite movie is *Sorority Babes in the Slimeball Bowl-O-Rama* (1988). A film critic called it "a pinhead chiller."

6. We're going to the new Psychoanalysis Restaurant. Their menu includes banana split personality, repressed duck, shrimp basket case, and self-expresso.

7. Kato lost the junior high spelling bee. He could not spell *DNA*.

8. Colorado hosts an annual BobFest to honor all people named Bob. Events include playing softbob, bobbing for apples, listening to bob-pipes, and eating bob-e-que.

9. The earthquake shook the city. Louise was practicing primal-scream therapy at the time.

10. In 1789 many Parisians bought a new perfume called "Guillotine." They wanted to be on the cutting edge of fashion.

C. Combine the following simple sentences into one complex sentence. See if you can guess the name of the book or movie described in the sentences. (Answers appear on page 157.)

1. A boy runs away from home.
    His companion is a runaway slave.
    He lives on a raft.
    The raft is on the Mississippi River.
    He has many adventures.
    The boy learns many lessons.
    Some lessons are about human kindness.
    Some lessons are about friendship.

2. A young girl and her brother live with their father.
    They live in a small town in Alabama.
    Their father is a lawyer.
    Their father defends an African-American against false charges.
    The African-American is convicted and shot.

continued on next page

The plaintiff's father attacks the brother and sister.
They are rescued by their reclusive neighbor.

3. A scientist is obsessed.
   He wants to re-create life.
   He creates a monster.
   The monster rebels against the scientist.
   The monster kills his creator.
   The villagers revolt.
   The villagers storm the castle.

Assignment

A. *Collaborative Activity:* Make up your own sentence-combining exercise by finding or writing one-sentence descriptions of popular or recent movies, books, or television shows. Divide the complex sentences into simple sentences and exchange papers with a classmate. Give yourselves ten minutes to combine sentences and guess the titles.

B. The following two paragraphs are poorly written because of their choppy, wordy, and monotonous sentences. Rewrite each passage so that it is clear, lively, and emphatic.

1. There is a new invention on the market. It is called a "dieter's conscience." It is a small box to be installed in one's refrigerator. When the door of the refrigerator is opened by you, a tape recorder begins to start. A really loud voice yells, "You eating again? No wonder you're getting fat." Then the very loud voice says, "Close the door; it's getting warm." Then the voice laughs a lot in an insane and crazy fashion. The idea is one that is designed to mock people into a habit of stopping eating.

2. In this modern world of today, man has come up with another new invention. This invention is called the "Talking Tombstone." It is made by the Gone-But-Not-Forgotten Company, which is located in Burbank, California. This company makes a tombstone that has a device in it that makes the tombstone appear to be talking aloud in a realistic fashion when people go close by it. The reason is that the device is really a recording machine that is turned on due to the simple fact of the heat of the bodies of the people who go by. The closer the people get, the louder the sound the tombstone makes. It is this device that individual persons who want to leave messages after death may utilize. A hypochondriac, to cite one example, might leave a recording of a message that says over and over again in a really loud voice, "See, I told you I was sick!" It may be assumed by one and all that this new invention will be a serious aspect of the whole death situation in the foreseeable future.

Applying What You've Learned to *Your* Writing

If you have drafted a piece of writing and are satisfied with your essay's ideas and organization, begin revising your sentences for clarity, conciseness, and emphasis. As you move through your draft, think about your readers. Ask yourself, "Are any of my sentences too vague, overpacked, or contorted for my readers to understand? Can I clarify any of my ideas by using more precise language or by revising confusing or fragmented sentence constructions?"

If you can't easily untangle a jumbled sentence, try following the sentence-combining exercise described on pages 155–156 of this chapter—but in reverse. Instead of combining ideas, break your thought into a series of simpler sentences. Think about what you want to say, and put the person or thing of most importance in the *subject* position at the beginning of the sentences. Then select a verb and a brief phrase to complete each of the sentences. You will most likely need several of these simpler constructions to communicate the complexity of your original thought. Once you have your thought broken into smaller, simpler units, carefully begin to combine some of them as you strive for clarity and sentence variety. (◆ If you are concerned about fragment sentences, use the "It is true that" test described on page 134.)

Remember that it's not enough for you, the writer, to understand what your sentences mean—your readers must be able to follow your ideas, too. When in doubt, always revise your writing so that it is clear, concise, and inviting. (◆ For more help, turn to Chapter 5, on revision.)

Chapter 6 Summary

Here is a brief summary of what you should remember about writing effective sentences:

1. All good writers revise and polish their sentences.

2. You can help clarify your ideas for your readers by writing sentences that are informative, straightforward, and precise.

3. You can communicate your ideas more easily to your readers if you cut out deadwood, redundancies, confusing passives, and pretentious language.

4. You can maintain your readers' interest in your ideas if you cultivate an engaging style offering a variety of pleasing sentence constructions.

Answers to sentence-combining exercise (pages 155–156):

1. *Huckleberry Finn*
2. *To Kill a Mockingbird*
3. *Frankenstein*

Word Logic

The English language contains nearly one million words—quite a selection for you as a writer to choose from. But such a wide choice can make you feel like a starving person confronting a six-page, fancy French menu. Which choice is best? How do I choose? Is the choice so important?

Word choice can make an enormous difference in the quality of your writing for at least one obvious reason: if you substitute an incorrect or vague word for the right one, you risk being misunderstood. Ages ago, Confucius noted the same point: "If language is incorrect, then what is said is not meant. If what is said is not meant, then what ought to be done remains undone." It isn't enough that you know what you mean; you must transfer your thoughts onto paper in the proper words so that others clearly understand your ideas.

To help you think critically about diction—that is, word choice—this chapter offers some practical suggestions for selecting words that are not only accurate and appropriate but also memorable and persuasive. Figure 7.1 highlights some of the tips and techniques for using and choosing effective words that are discussed in this chapter.

Selecting the Correct Words

Accuracy: Confused Words

- Unless I get a bank loan soon, I will be forced to lead an *immortal* life.
- Dobermans make good pets if you train them with enough *patients*.
- He dreamed of eating *desert* after *desert*.
- She had dieted for so long that she had become *emancipated*.
- The young man was completely in *ah* of the actress's beauty.
- Socrates died from an overdose of *wedlock*.

The preceding sentences share a common problem: each one contains an error in word choice. In each sentence, the italicized word is incorrect, causing the sentence to be nonsensical or silly. (Consider a sign recently posted in a local night spot: "No miners allowed." Did the owner think the lights on their hats would bother the other customers?

Figure 7.1 VISUALIZING THE PROCESS: EDITING WORDS

Selecting the Correct Words

1. Watch out for commonly confused words.

2. Use idiomatic phrases with caution.

3. Think carefully about the appropriate level of your language: colloquial, informal, or formal.

4. Avoid using words that give your writing these kind of tones: invective, sarcasm, irony, flippancy, sentimentality, preachiness, pomposity.

5. Be aware of a word's denotation and connotation.

Selecting the Best Words

1. Do make your words as precise as possible.

2. Do make your word choices as fresh and as possible.

3. Don't use trendy expressions or slang in your essays.

4. Refrain from using texting language and Web-speak in your academic or professional writing.

5. Do select simple, direct words your readers can easily understand.

6. Do call things by their proper names.

7. Avoid sexist language.

8. Do enliven your writing with figurative language, when appropriate.

9. Do vary your word choice so that your prose does not sound wordy, repetitious, or monotonous.

10. Do remember that wordiness is a major problem for all writers.

Prewriting
Chapter 1

Drafting
Chapters 2, 3, 4, 5

Revising
Chapter 5

Editing/
Proofreading
Chapters 6, 7

© Cengage Learning 2017

Did the student with "duel majors" imagine that his two areas of study were squaring off with pistols at twenty paces?) To avoid such confusion in word choice, check your words for *accuracy*. Select words whose precise meaning, usage, and spelling you know; consult your dictionary for any words whose definitions (or spellings) are fuzzy to you. As Mark Twain noted, the difference between the right word and the wrong one is the difference between lightning and the lightning bug.

Here is a list of words that are often confused in writing. Use your dictionary to determine the meanings or usage of any word unfamiliar to you.

its/it's	lead/led	choose/chose
to/too/two	cite/sight/site	accept/except
there/their/they're	affect/effect	council/counsel
your/you're	good/well	reign/rein
complement/compliment	who's/whose	lose/loose
stationary/stationery	lay/lie	precede/proceed
capitol/capital	than/then	illusion/allusion
principal/principle	insure/ensure	farther/further

Special note: Some "confused" words don't even exist! Here are four commonly used nonexistent words and their correct counterparts:

No Such Word or Spelling	Use Instead
irregardless	regardless
alright	all right
alot	a lot
its'	its or it's

Accuracy: Idiomatic Phrases

Occasionally, you may have an essay returned to you with words marked "awkward diction" or "idiom." In English, as in all languages, we have word groupings that seem governed by no particular logic except the ever-popular "that's-the-way-we-say-it" rule. Many of these idiomatic expressions involve prepositions that novice writers sometimes confuse or misuse. Some common idiomatic errors and their corrected forms are listed here.

Yellow Dog Productions/Riser/Getty Images

regardless ~~to~~ of	different ~~than to~~ from	relate ~~with~~ to
insight ~~of~~ into	must ~~of~~ have known	capable ~~to~~ of
similar ~~with~~ to	superior ~~than~~ to	aptitude ~~toward~~ for
comply ~~to~~ with	~~to~~ in my opinion	prior ~~than~~ to
off ~~of~~	meet ~~to~~ her standards	should ~~of~~ have

To avoid idiomatic errors, consult your dictionary and read your essay aloud; often your ears will catch mistakes in usage that your eyes have overlooked.*

Levels of Language

In addition to choosing the correct word, you should select words whose status is suited to your purpose. For convenience here, language has been classified into three categories, or levels, of usage: (1) colloquial, (2) informal, and (3) formal.

---

*You may not immediately recognize what's wrong with words your teacher has labeled "diction" or "idiom." If you're uncertain about an error, ask your teacher for clarification; after all, if you don't know what's wrong with your prose, you can't avoid the mistake again. To illustrate this point, here's a true story: A bright young woman was having trouble with prepositional phrases in her essays and, although her professor repeatedly marked her incorrect expressions with the marginal note "idiom," she never improved. Finally, one day near the end of the term, she approached her teacher in tears and wailed, "Professor Jones, I know I'm not a very good writer, but must you write 'idiot,' 'idiot,' 'idiot' all over my papers?" The moral of this story is simple: it's easy to misunderstand a correction or misread your teacher's writing. Because you can't improve until you know what's wrong, always ask when you're in doubt.

1) Colloquial language is the kind of speech you use most often in conversation with your friends, classmates, and family. It may not always be grammatically correct ("it's me"); it may include fragments, contractions, some slang, words identified as nonstandard by the dictionary (such as "yuck" or "lousy"), and shortened or abbreviated words ("grad school," "LOL"). Colloquial speech is everyday language, and although you may use it in some informal writing (text messages, personal e-mail and letters, social media, and so forth), you should think carefully about using colloquial language in most college essays or in professional letters or reports because such a choice implies a casual relationship between writer and reader. (◆ For more discussion of appropriate audiences for texting and Internet language, see pages 170–171.)

2) Informal language is called for in most college and professional assignments. The tone is more formal than in colloquial writing or speech, and no slang or nonstandard words are permissible. Informal writing consistently uses correct grammar; fragments are used for special effect or not at all. Authorities disagree on the use of contractions in informal writing: some say avoid them entirely; others say they're permissible; still others advocate using them only to avoid stilted phrases ("let's go," for example, is preferable to "let us go"). Most, if not all, of your essays in English classes will be written in informal language.

3) Formal language is found in important documents and in serious, often ceremonial, speeches. Characteristics include an elevated—but not pretentious—tone, no contractions, and correct grammar. Formal writing often uses inverted word order and balanced sentence structure. John F. Kennedy's 1960 Inaugural Address, for example, was written in a formal style ("Ask not what your country can do for you; ask what you can do for your country"). Most people rarely, if ever, need to write formally; if you are called on to do so, however, be careful to avoid diction that sounds pretentious, pompous, or phony.

Tone

Tone is a general word that describes writers' attitudes toward their subject matter and audience. There are as many different kinds of tones as there are emotions. Depending on how the writer feels, an essay's "voice" may sound lighthearted, indignant, sarcastic, or solemn, to name but a few of the possible choices. In addition to presenting a specific attitude, a good writer gains credibility by maintaining a tone that is generally reasonable, sincere, and authentic.

Although it is impossible to analyze all the various kinds of tones one finds in essays, it is nevertheless beneficial to discuss some of those that repeatedly give writers trouble. Here are some tones that should be used carefully or avoided altogether:

Invective

Invective is unrestrained anger, usually expressed in the form of violent accusation or denunciation. Let's suppose, for example, you hear a friend argue, "Anyone who votes for Joe Smith is a Fascist pig." If you are considering voting for Smith, you are probably offended by your friend's abusive tone. Raging emotion, after all, does not sway the opinions of intelligent people; they need to hear the facts presented in a calm, clear discussion. Therefore, in your own writing, aim for a reasonable tone. You want your readers to think, "Now here is someone with a good understanding of the situation, who has evaluated it with an unbiased, analytical mind." Keeping a controlled tone doesn't mean you shouldn't feel strongly about your subject—on the contrary, you certainly should—but you should realize that a hysterical or outraged tone defeats your purpose by causing you to sound irrational and therefore untrustworthy. For this reason, you should avoid using profanity in your essays; the shock value of an obscenity is probably not worth what you might lose in credibility. The most effective way to make your point is by persuading, not offending, your reader.

Sarcasm

In most of your writing you'll discover that a little sarcasm—bitter, derisive remarks—goes a long way. As with invective, too much sarcasm can damage the reasonable tone your essay should present. Instead of saying, "The last time we had a judge like him, people were burned at the stake," give your readers some reasons why you believe the judge is a poor one. Sarcasm can be effective, but realize that it often backfires by causing the writer to sound like a childish name-caller rather than a judicious commentator.

Irony

Irony is a figure of speech whereby the writer or speaker says the opposite of what is meant; for the irony to be successful, however, the audience must understand the writer's true intent. For example, if you have slopped to school in a rainstorm and your drenched teacher enters the classroom saying, "Ah, nothing like this beautiful, sunny weather," you know that your teacher is being ironic. Perhaps one of the most famous cases of irony occurred in 1938, when Sigmund Freud, the famous Viennese psychiatrist, was arrested by the Nazis. After being harassed by the Gestapo, he was released on the condition that he sign a statement swearing he had been treated well by the secret police. Freud signed it, but, as the story goes, he added a few words after his signature: "I can heartily recommend the Gestapo to everyone." Looking back, we easily recognize Freud's jab at his captors; the Gestapo, however, apparently overlooked the irony and let him go.

Although irony is often an effective device, it can also cause great confusion, especially when it is written rather than spoken. Unless your readers thoroughly understand your position in the first place, they may become confused by what appears to be a sudden contradiction. Irony that is too subtle, too private, or simply out of context merely complicates the issue. Therefore, you must make certain that your reader has no trouble realizing when your tongue is firmly embedded in your cheek. And unless you are assigned to write an ironic essay (in the same vein, for instance, as Jonathan Swift's "A Modest Proposal"), don't overuse irony, whose effectiveness may be reduced with overkill.

Flippancy or Cuteness

If you sound too flip, hip, or bored in your essay ("People with IQs lower than their sunscreen number will object . . ."), your readers will not take you seriously and, consequently, will disregard whatever you have to say. Writers suffering from cuteness will also antagonize their readers. For example, let's assume you're assigned the topic "Which Person Did the Most to Arouse the Laboring Class in Twentieth-Century England?" and you begin your essay with a discussion of the man who invented the alarm clock.

Although that joke might be funny in an appropriate situation, it's not likely to impress your reader, who's looking for serious commentary. How much cuteness is too much is often a matter of taste, but if you have any doubts about the quality of your humor, leave it out. Also, omit personal messages or comic asides to your reader (such as "Ha, ha, just kidding!" or "I knew you'd love this part"). Humor is often effective, but remember that the purpose of any essay is to persuade an audience to accept your thesis, not merely to entertain with freestanding jokes. In other words, if you use humor, make sure it is appropriate for your subject matter and that it works to help you make your point.

Sentimentality

Sentimentality is the excessive show of cheap emotions—"cheap" because they are not deeply felt but evoked by clichés and stock, tear-jerking situations. In the nineteenth century, for example, a typical melodrama played on the sentimentality of the audience by presenting a black-hatted, cold-hearted, mustache-twirling villain tying a golden-haired, pure-hearted "Little Nell" to the railroad tracks after driving her ancient, sickly mother out into a snowdrift. Today, politicians (among others) often appeal to our sentimentality by conjuring up images they feel will move us emotionally rather than rationally to take their side: "My friends," says Senator Stereotype, "this fine nation of ours was founded by men like myself, dedicated to the principles of family, flag, and freedom. Vote for me, and let's get back to those precious basics that make life in America so grand." Such gush is hardly convincing; good writers and speakers use evidence and logical reason to persuade their audience. In personal essays, guard against becoming too carried away by emotion, as did this student: "My dog, Cuddles, is the sweetest, cutest, most precious little puppy dog in the whole wide world, and she will always be my best friend." In addition to sending the reader into sugar shock, this description fails to present any specific reasons why anyone should appreciate Cuddles. In other words, be sincere in your writing, but don't lose so much control of your emotions that you become mushy or maudlin.

Preachiness

Even if you are so convinced of the rightness of your position that a burning bush couldn't change your mind, try not to sound smug about it. No one likes to be lectured by someone perched atop the mountain of morality. Instead of preaching, adopt a tone that says, "I believe my position is correct, and I am glad to have this opportunity to explain why." Then give your reasons and meet objections in a positive but not holier-than-thou manner.

Pomposity

The "voice" of your essay should sound as natural as possible; don't strain to sound scholarly, scientific, or sophisticated. If you write, "My summer sojourn through the Western states of this grand country was immensely pleasurable" instead of "My vacation last summer in the Rockies was fun," you sound merely phony, not dignified and learned. Select only words you know and can use easily. Never write anything you wouldn't say in an intelligent classroom conversation. (◆ For more information on correcting pretentious writing, see page 144 and pages 171–174.)

To achieve the appropriate tone, be as sincere, forthright, and reasonable as you can. Let the tone of your essay establish a basis of mutual respect between you and your reader.

Denotation and Connotation

A word's *denotation* refers to its literal meaning, the meaning defined by the dictionary; a word's *connotation* refers to the emotional associations surrounding its meaning. For example, "home" and "residence" both may be defined as the place where one lives, but "home" carries connotations of warmth, security, and family that "residence" lacks. Similarly, "old" and "antique" have similar denotative meanings, but "antique" has the more positive connotation because it suggests something that also has value. Reporters and journalists do the same job, but the latter name somehow seems to indicate someone more sophisticated and professional. Because many words with similar denotative meanings do carry different connotations, good writers must be careful with their word choice. *Select only words whose connotations fit your purpose.* If, for example, you want to describe your grandmother in a positive way as someone who stands up for herself, you might refer to her as "assertive" or "feisty"; if you want to present her negatively, you might call her "aggressive" or "pushy."

In addition to selecting words with the appropriate connotations for your purpose, be careful to avoid offending your audience with particular connotations. For instance, if you were trying to persuade a group of politically conservative doctors to accept your stand on a national health-care program, you would not want to refer to your opposition as "right-wingers" or "reactionaries," extremist terms that have negative connotations. Remember, you want to inform and persuade your audience, not antagonize them.

You should also be alert to the use of words with emotionally charged connotations, especially in advertising and propaganda of various kinds. Car manufacturers, for example, have often used names of swift, bold, or graceful animals (Jaguar, Cougar, Impala) to sway prospective buyers; cosmetics manufacturers have taken advantage of the trend toward lighter makeup by associating such words as "nature," "natural," and "healthy glow" with their products. Consumers are now deluged with "light" beverages, "organic" food, and "green" household products, despite the vagueness of those labels. Politicians, too, are heavy users of connotation; they often drop in emotionally positive, but virtually meaningless, words and phrases such as "defender of the American Way," "friend of the common man," and "visionary" to describe themselves, while tagging their opponents with such negative, emotionally charged labels as "radical," "elitist," and "anti-family."

Intelligent readers, like intelligent voters and consumers, want more than emotion-laden words; they want facts and logical argument. Therefore, as a good writer, you should use connotation as only one of many persuasive devices to enhance your presentation of evidence; never depend solely on an emotional appeal to convince your audience that your position—or thesis—is correct.

Practicing What You've Learned

A. Some of the following underlined words are used incorrectly; some are correct. Substitute the accurate word wherever necessary.

1. Vacations of <u>to</u> weeks with <u>to</u> friends are always <u>to</u> short, and although <u>you're to</u> tired <u>to</u> return <u>to</u> work, <u>your to</u> broke not <u>to</u>.

2. The professor, <u>whose</u> famous for his <u>photogenic</u> memory, graciously <u>excepted</u> a large <u>amount</u> of <u>complements</u>.

3. <u>Its to</u> bad you don't like <u>they're</u> brand of <u>genetic</u> paper towels since <u>their</u> giving six <u>roles</u> of it <u>to</u> you for <u>you're</u> camping trip.

4. The finances of the chicken ranch are in <u>fowl</u> shape because the hens <u>r</u> <u>lying</u> down on the job.

5. Sara June said she deserved an "A" in math, <u>irregardless</u> of her 59 average in the <u>coarse</u>, but her arguments were in <u>vein</u>.

6. Did <u>u</u> <u>chose</u> to put the pamphlet "Ridding Your Home of Pesky <u>Aunts</u>" in the domestic-relations area of the library?

7. Did the high school <u>principal</u> <u>loose</u> <u>you're</u> heavy <u>medal</u> CD and <u>it's</u> case <u>too</u>?

8. The new city <u>counsel</u> parade ordinance will <u>effect</u> everyone in the <u>capitol</u> city <u>except</u> members of the Lawn Chair Marching Band.

B. The following sentences contain words and phrases that interfere with the sincere, reasonable tone good writers try to create. Rewrite each sentence, replacing sentimentality, cuteness, and pretentiousness with more appropriate language.

1. The last dying rays of day were quickly ebbing in the West as if to signal the feline to begin its lonely vigil.

2. Because of seasonal unproductivity, it has been deemed an unfortunate fiscal necessity to terminate your valuable association with our store in order to meet our projected growth estimates.

3. I was desirous of acquiring knowledge about members of our lower income brackets.

4. If the bill to legalize medical marijuana is passed, we can safely assume that the whole county will soon be going to pot (heh, heh!).

5. I just love to look at those little critters with their itty-bitty mousey eyes.

C. In each of the following groups of words, identify the words with the most pleasing and the least positive (or even negative) connotations.

1. dull/drab/quiet/boring/colorless/serene

2. slender/slim/skinny/thin/slight/anorexic

continued on next page

3. famous/notorious/well-known/infamous

4. wealthy/opulent/rich/affluent/privileged

5. teacher/instructor/educator/professor/lecturer

D. Replace the underlined words in the following sentences with words that arouse more positive feelings:

1. The <u>stench</u> from Jean's kitchen meant that dinner was ready and was about to be served.

2. My neighbor was a <u>fat spinster lady</u> known for finding <u>cheap deals</u> on the Internet.

3. The coach had <u>rigid</u> rules for all her players.

4. His <u>obsession</u> with his yard pleased the city's beautification committee.

5. The <u>slick</u> car salesman made a <u>pitch</u> to the <u>old geezer</u> who walked in the door.

6. Textbook writers admit to having a few <u>bizarre</u> habits.

7. Carol was a <u>mediocre</u> student.

8. His <u>odd</u> clothes made Mary think he was a <u>bum</u>.

9. The High Priest explained his tribe's <u>superstitions</u>.

10. Many of the board members were amazed to see how Algernon <u>dominated</u> the meeting.

Selecting the Best Words

In addition to selecting the correct word and appropriate tone, good writers choose words that firmly implant their ideas in the minds of their readers. The best prose not only makes cogent points but also states these points memorably. To help you select the best words to express your ideas, the following is a list of do's and don'ts covering the most common diction (word choice) problems in writing today.

Do make your words as precise as possible. Consider choosing active verbs, specific nouns, and engaging modifiers. "The big tree was hit by lightning," for example, is not as informative or interesting as "Lightning splintered the neighbors' thirty-foot oak." *Don't* use words whose meanings are unclear:

Vague Verbs

Unclear	She *got involved* in a lawsuit. [How?]
Clear	She is suing her dentist for filling the wrong tooth.
Unclear	Tom can *relate* to Jennifer. [What's the relationship?]
Clear	Tom understands Jennifer's financial problem.

Unclear	He won't *deal* with his ex-wife. [In what way?]
Clear	He refuses to speak to his ex-wife.
Unclear	Clyde *participated* in an off-Broadway play. [How?]
Clear	Clyde held the cue cards for the actors in an off-Broadway play.

Vague Nouns

Unclear	The burglar took several valuable *things* from our house.* [What items?]
Clear	The burglar took a *television*, a *cell phone*, and a *microwave oven* from our house.
Unclear	When I have my car serviced, there is always *trouble*. [What kind?]
Clear	When I have my car serviced, *the mechanics always find additional repairs and never have the car ready when it is promised*.
Unclear	When I have *problems*, I always call my friends for advice. [What problems?]
Clear	*If my girlfriend breaks up with me, my roof needs repairing, or my dog needs surgery*, I always call my friends for advice.
Unclear	I like to have *fun* while I'm on vacation. [What sort of activities?]
Clear	I like to *eat in fancy restaurants, fly stunt kites*, and *walk along the beach* when I'm on vacation.

Vague Modifiers

Unclear	His *terrible* explanation left me *very* confused. [Why "terrible"? How confused?]
Clear	His *disorganized* explanation left me *too confused to begin the project*.
Unclear	The boxer hit the punching bag *really* hard. [How hard?]
Clear	The boxer hit the punching bag *so hard it split open*.
Unclear	*Casablanca* is a *good* movie *with something for everyone*. [Why "good" and for everyone?]
Clear	*Casablanca* is a *witty, sentimental* movie that *successfully combines an adventure story and a romance*.

To help you recognize the difference between general and specific language, consider the following series of words:

General → **Specific**

food→snack food→chips→potato chips→Red Hot Jalapeño Potato Chips

car→red car→red sports car→classic red Corvette→1966 red Corvette convertible

building→house→old house→big old fancy house→19th-century Victorian mansion

---

*Advice that bears repeating: banish the word "thing" from your writing. In nine out of ten cases it is a lazy substitute for some other word. Unless you mean a nameless inanimate object, replace "thing" with the specific word it represents.

The preceding examples illustrate varying degrees of generality, with the words becoming more specific as they move to the right. Sometimes in your writing you will, of course, need to use general words to communicate your thought. However, most writers need practice finding specific language to substitute for bland, vague, or overly general diction that doesn't clearly present the precise picture the writer has in mind. For instance, look at the difference between these two sentences:

- My date arrived at the restaurant in an older car and then surprised us by ordering snack food.
- My date arrived at the restaurant in a rusted-out, bumperless '52 Cadillac DeVille and then surprised us by ordering a large, expensive bowl of imported cheese puffs.

Which description better conveys the start of an unusual evening? Which sentence would make you want to hear more?

Not all occasions call for specific details, to be sure. Don't add details that merely clutter if they aren't important to the idea or mood you are creating. If all your readers need to know is "I ate dinner alone and went to bed early," you don't need to write "Alone, I ate a dinner of lasagna, green salad, and ice cream before putting on my Gap cowgirl pajamas and going to sleep under my yellow comforter at nine o'clock."

Most of the time, however, writers can improve their drafts by giving their language a close look, considering places where a vigorous verb or a "showing" adjective or a specific noun might make an enormous difference to the reader. As you revise and polish your own essays, ask yourself if you can clarify and enliven your writing by replacing dull, lifeless words with engaging, vivid, specific ones. Challenge yourself to find the best words possible—it's a writing habit that produces effective, reader-pleasing results. (◆ For more help in converting vague sentences to clear, inviting prose, see the discussion that starts on page 131 in Chapter 6.)

Do make your word choices as fresh and original as possible. Instead of saying, "My hometown is very quiet," you might say, "My hometown's definition of an orgy is a light burning after midnight." In other words, if you can make your readers admire and remember your prose, you have a better chance of persuading them to accept your ideas.

Conversely, to avoid ho-hum prose, *don't* fill your sentences with clichés and platitudes— overworked phrases that cause your writing to sound lifeless and trite. Although we use clichés in everyday conversation, good writers avoid them in writing because (1) they are often vague or imprecise (just how pretty is "pretty as a picture"?) and (2) they are used so frequently that they rob your prose style of personality and uniqueness ("It was raining cats and dogs"—does that phrase help your reader "see" the particular rainstorm you're trying to describe?).

Novice writers often include trite expressions because they do not recognize them as clichés; therefore, at the top of the next page is a partial list (there are literally thousands more) of phrases to avoid. Instead of using a cliché, try substituting an phrase to describe what you see or feel. Never try to disguise a cliché by putting it in quotation marks—a baboon in dark glasses and a wig is still a baboon.

crack of dawn	needle in a haystack	gentle as a lamb
a crying shame	bed of roses	blind as a bat
white as a sheet	cold as ice	strong as an ox
depths of despair	hard as nails	sober as a judge
dead of night	white as snow	didn't sleep a wink
shadow of a doubt	almighty dollar	face the music
hear a pin drop	busy as a bee	out like a light
blessed event	to make a long story short	the last straw
first and foremost	pale as a ghost	solid as a rock

It would be impossible, of course, to memorize all the clichés and trite expressions in our language, but do check your prose for recognizable, overworked phrases so that your words will not be predictable and, consequently, dull. If you aren't sure whether a phrase is a cliché, but you've heard it used frequently, your prose will probably be stronger if you substitute an original phrase for the suspected one.

Some overused words and phrases might better be called "Insta-Prose" rather than clichés. Similar to those instant "just add water and stir" food mixes on grocery shelves, Insta-Prose occurs when writers grab for the closest words within thought-reach rather than taking time to create an original phrase or image. It's easy, for example, to recognize such overused phrases as "last but not least," "easier said than done," and "when all was said and done." But Insta-Prose may pop up in essays almost without a writer's awareness. For instance, using your very first thoughts, fill in the blanks in the following sentence:

After years of service, my old car finally _____, _____, and
_____ by the side of the road.

If your immediate responses were the three words printed at the bottom of page 181, don't be surprised! Most people who have taken this simple test responded that way too, either entirely or in part. So what's the problem, you might ask. The writer describing the car wanted her readers to see *her* particular old car, not some bland image identically reproduced in her readers' minds. To show readers her car—as opposed to thousands of other old cars—she needs to substitute specific, "showing" language for the Insta-Prose.* (Retest yourself: what might she have said about this car that would allow you, the reader, to see what happend that day?)

As a writer, you also want your readers to "see" your specific idea and be engaged by your prose rather than skipping over canned-bland images. When you are drafting for ideas early in the writing process, Insta-Prose pours out—and that's to be expected because you are still discovering your thoughts. But, later, when you revise your drafts, be sensitive to predictable language in all its forms. Stamp out Insta-Prose! Cook up some fresh language to delight your reader.

---

*Some prose is so familiar that it is now a joke. The phrase "It was a dark and stormy night," the beginning of an 1830 novel by Edward George Bulwer-Lytton, has been frequently parodied (and pla-giarized without shame by Snoopy in the *Peanuts* comic strip). It has also prompted a bad-writing con-test sponsored since 1982 by the English Department at San José State University, in which entrants are challenged to "compose the opening sentence to the worst of all possible novels."

Don't use trendy expressions or slang in your essays. Slang generally consists of commonly used words made up by special groups to communicate among themselves. Slang has many origins, from sports to space travel; for example, surfers gave us the expression "to wipe out" (to fail), soldiers lent "snafu" (from the first letters of "situation normal—all fouled up"), astronauts provided "A-OK" (all systems working), and boxing managers contributed "throw in the towel" (to quit).

Although slang often gives our speech color and vigor, it is unacceptable in most writing assignments for several reasons. First, slang often originates as part of a private language understood only by members of a particular professional, social, or age group. Second, slang often presents a vague picture or one that changes meanings from person to person or from context to context. Different people may hold unique definitions for a particular slang expression, and although these definitions may overlap, they may not be precisely the same. Consequently, your reader could interpret your words in one way although you intend them in another—a dilemma that might result in total miscommunication (imagine, for example, the reaction of your grandmother who hears you say, "That's sick!").

Too often, beginning writers rely on vague, popular phrases ("The party was way awesome") instead of thinking of specific words to explain specific ideas. Slang expressions frequently contain nontraditional grammar and diction that are inappropriate for college work. Moreover, slang becomes dated quickly, and almost nothing sounds as silly as yesterday's "in" expressions. (Can you seriously imagine addressing a friend as "Daddy-O" or joyfully proclaiming "twenty-three skidoo"?)

Try to write so that your prose will be as fresh and pleasing ten years from now as it is today. Don't allow slang to give your writing a tone that detracts from a serious discussion. Putting slang in quotation marks isn't the solution—omit the slang and use precise words instead.

Refrain from using texting language and Web speak in your academic or professional writing. Millions of people worldwide are chatting daily online and through their cell phone screens, with the number of messages increasing with each technological advance. But the language often used there—with its shorthand spelling (GR8, C U 2morrow), abbreviations (BTW, IMO, IDK), pictograms (what's ^?, I <3 U), and incomplete or "imposter" words (txtspk, cuz)—is not appropriate for your college assignments or traditional business correspondence.

iStockphoto.com/apomares

Texting lingo thrives because it is fast and easy to type on a palm-sized keypad and quickly reduces content in small-screen messages that may be confined to a limited number of characters (for example, Twitter's 140-character cap for "tweets"). Despite its frequent use in casual messaging, such language is too informal for many other writing situations and audiences. More importantly, some readers may not understand all the acronyms, and even commonly used abbreviations may be misinterpreted. (Does LOL here mean "laughing out loud" or "lots of love"? Consider, too, that someone's failure to understand a message marked NSFW as "not suitable for work" might lead to a professional disaster.) In addition, some readers may see incomplete or misspelled words simply as errors or as indications of carelessness; other readers may wonder if a lack of proper capitalization or incorrect punctuation reveals ignorance rather than chat-style. Still others may regard such language as juvenile slang, since keyboard symbols and emoticons [:-)] are so frequently used by younger teens.

Good writers understand that standards and levels of English vary from situation to situation and that to be successful in their communications, all effective writers must both respect and respond to the needs of different kinds of readers. Keep your shorthand symbols in their appropriate informal places, not in your college and professional work. But anywhere, at any time, if there's a chance the meaning of your message might be lost, take the extra minute to write out those words!

   Do select simple, direct words your readers can easily understand. Don't use pompous or pseudo-sophisticated language in place of plain speech. Wherever possible, avoid *jargon*—that is, words and phrases that are unnecessarily technical, pretentious, or abstract.

   Technical jargon—terms specific to one area of study or specialization—should be omitted or clearly defined in essays directed to a general audience because such language is often inaccessible to anyone outside the writer's particular field. By now, most of us are familiar with bureaucratese, journalese, and psychobabble, in addition to gobbledygook from business, politics, advertising, and education. If, for example, you worry that "a self-actualized person such as yourself cannot transcend either your hostile environment or your passive-aggressive behavior to make a commitment to a viable lifestyle and meaningful interpersonal relationships," you are indulging in psychological or sociological jargon; if you "review existing mechanisms of consumer input, thruput, and output via the consumer communications channel module," you are speaking business jargon. Although most professions do have their own terms, you should limit your use of specialized language to writing aimed solely at your professional colleagues; always try to avoid technical jargon in prose directed at a general audience.

   Today the term "jargon" also refers to prose containing an abundance of abstract, pretentious, multisyllabic words. The use of this kind of jargon often betrays a writer's attempt to sound sophisticated and intellectual; actually, it only confuses meaning and delays communication. Here, for instance, is a sample of incomprehensible jargon from a college president who obviously prefers twenty-five-cent words to simple, straightforward, nickel ones: "We will divert the force of this fiscal stress into leverage energy and pry important budgetary considerations and control out of our fiscal and administrative procedures." Or look at the thirty-eight-word definition of "exit" written by an Occupational Safety and Health Administration bureaucrat: "That portion of a means of egress which is separated from all spaces of the building or structure by construction or equipment as required in this subpart to provide a protected way of travel to the exit discharge." Such language is not only pretentious and confusing, but almost comic in its wordiness.

Legal jargon, complicating even the smallest transaction, has become so incomprehensible that some lawmakers and consumers have begun to fight back. Today in Texas, for example, any firm lending $500 or less must use a model plain-English contract or submit its contract for approval to the Office of Consumer Credit. The new, user-friendly contract replaces "Upon any such default, and at any time thereafter, Secured party may declare the entire balance of the indebtedness secured hereby, plus any other sums owed hereunder, immediately due and payable without demand or notice, less any refund due, and Secured Party shall have all the remedies of the Uniform Commercial Code" with a clear, easy-to-understand statement: "If I break any of my promises in this document, you can demand that I immediately pay all that I owe." Hooray for the gobbledygook squashers in the Lone Star State!

To avoid such verbal litter in your own writing, follow these rules:

1. Always select the plainest, most direct words you know.

Jargon	The editor wanted to halt the proliferation of the product because she discovered an error on the page that terminates the volume.
Revised	The editor wanted to stop publishing the book because she found an error on the last page.

2. Replace nominalizations (nouns that are made from verbs and adjectives, usually by adding endings such as *-tion, -ism, -ness,* or *-al*) with simpler verbs and nouns.

Jargon	The departmental head has come to the recognition that the utilization of verbose verbalization renders informational content inaccessible.
Revised	The head of the department recognizes that wordiness confuses meaning.

3. Avoid adding *-ize* or *-wise* to verbs and adverbs.

Jargon	*Weatherwise*, it looked like a good day to *finalize* her report on wind tunnels.
Revised	The day's clear weather would help her finish her report on wind tunnels.

4. Drop out meaningless tack-on words such as "factor," "aspect," and "situation."

Jargon	The convenience *factor* of the neighborhood grocery store is one *aspect* of its success.
Revised	The convenience of the neighborhood grocery store contributes to its success.

Remember that good writing is clear and direct, never wordy, cloudy, or ostentatious. (◆ For more hints on developing a clear style, see pages 129–138.)

Do call things by their proper names. Don't sugarcoat your terms by substituting *euphemisms*—words that sound nice or pretty applied to subjects some people find distasteful. For example, you've probably heard someone say, "she passed away" instead of "she died" or "he was under the influence of alcohol" instead of "he was drunk." Flight attendants refer to a "water landing" rather than an ocean crash. "Senior citizens" (or, worse, the "chronologically advantaged") may receive special discounts. Often, euphemisms are used to soften names of jobs: "sanitary engineer" for garbage collector, "field representative" for salesperson, "information processor" for typist, "vehicle appearance specialist" for car washer, and so forth.

Some euphemisms are dated and now seem plain silly: in Victorian times, for example, the word "leg" was considered unmentionable in polite company, so people spoke of "piano limbs" and asked for the "first joint" of a chicken. The phrases "white meat" and "dark meat" were euphemisms some people used to avoid asking for a piece of chicken breast or thigh.

Today, euphemisms still abound. Though our generation is perhaps more direct about sex and death, many current euphemisms gloss over unpleasant or unpopular business, military, and political practices. Some stockbrokers, for example, once referred to an October market crash as "a fourth-quarter equity retreat," and General Motors didn't really shut down one of its plants—the closing was merely a "volume-related production schedule adjustment." Similarly, Chrysler didn't lay off workers; it simply "initiated a career alternative enhancement program." Nuclear power plants no longer have dumps; they have "containment facilities" with radiation "migration" rather than leaks and "inventory discrepancies" rather than thefts of plutonium. Simple products are now complex technology: clocks are "analog temporal displacement monitors," toothbrushes are "home plaque removal instruments," sinks are part of the "hygienic hand-washing media," and pencils are "portable handheld communications inscribers." Vinyl is now "vegetarian leather."

Euphemisms abound in governments and official agencies when those in charge try to hide or disguise the truth from the public. On the national level, a former budget director gave us "revenue enhancements" instead of new taxes, and a former Secretary of Health, Education, and Welfare once tried to camouflage cuts in social services by calling them "advance downward adjustments." Wiretaps once became "technical collection sources" used by "special investigatons units" instead of spies, and plain lying became on one important occasion merely "plausible deniability." Other lies or exaggerations have been "strategic misrepresentations" and convenient "reality augmentations." Interestingly enough, even Washington staff members in charge of prettying up the truth for the public have earned their own euphemistic title: "spin doctors."

In a large Southwestern city, people might have been surprised to learn that there were no potholes in the streets—only "pavement deficiencies." Garbage no longer stinks; instead, it "exceeds the odor threshold." In some jails, a difficult prisoner who once might have been sent to solitary confinement is now placed in the "meditation room" or the "adjustment center." In some hospitals, sick people do not die—they experience "negative patient care outcome"; if they died because of a doctor's mistake, they underwent a "diagnostic misadventure of a high magnitude." Incidentally, those patients who survive no longer receive greeting cards; instead, they open "social expression products." During their recovery, patients might watch the "choreographed reality" of TV wrestling, while their dogs enjoy "play activities" at a local "pet lodge."

Perhaps the military is the all-time winner of the "substitute-a-euphemism" contest. Over the years, the military has used a variety of words, such as "neutralization," "pacification," and "liberation," to mean the invasion and destruction of towns, countries, and governments. During the first Gulf War with Iraq, for example, bombs that fell on civilians were referred to as "incontinent ordnance," with the dead becoming "collateral damage." Earlier, to avoid publicizing a retreat, the military simply called for "backloading our augmentation personnel." On the less serious side, the Navy changes ocean waves into "climatic disturbances at the air-sea interface," and the Army, not to be outdone, transforms the lowly shovel into a "combat emplacement evacuator."*

Although many euphemisms seem funny and harmless, too many of them are not, because people—often those with power to shape public opinion—have intentionally designed them to obscure the reality of a particular situation or choice of action. Because euphemisms can be used unscrupulously to manipulate people, you should always avoid them in your own prose and be suspicious of them in the writing of others. As Aldous Huxley, author of *Brave New World*, noted, "An education for freedom is, among other things, an education in the proper uses of language."

In addition to weakening the credibility of one's ideas, euphemisms can make prose unnecessarily abstract, wordy, pretentious, or even silly. For a clear and natural prose style, use terms that are straightforward and simple. In other words, call a spade a spade, not "an implement for use in horticultural environments."

Avoid sexist language. Most people will agree that language helps shape thought. Consequently, writers should avoid using language that promotes any kind of exclusion or demeaning stereotypes. In particular, sexist language, by consistently identifying certain groups, jobs, or actions as male, subtly suggests that only men, rather than both men and women, appear in those roles. To make your writing as inclusive and unbiased as possible, here are some simple suggestions for writing nonsexist prose:

1. Try using plural nouns to eliminate the need for the singular pronouns "he" and "she."

Original	Today's *doctor* knows *he* must carry extra malpractice insurance.
Revision	Today's *doctors* know *they* must carry extra malpractice insurance.

2. Try substituting gender-neutral occupational titles for those ending in "man" or "woman."

Original	The *fireman* and the *saleslady* watched the *policeman* arrest the former *chairman* of the Physics Department.
Revision	The *firefighter* and the *sales clerk* watched the *police officer* arrest the former *chair* of the Physics Department.

3. Don't contribute to stereotyping by assigning particular roles solely to men or women.

Original	*Mothers* concerned about the possibility of Reyes syndrome should avoid giving aspirin to their sick children.
Revision	*Parents* concerned about the possibility of Reyes syndrome should avoid giving aspirin to their sick children.

---

* ◆ For more examples of euphemisms and doublespeak, see the "To the Student" section in the front of this text.

4. Try substituting such words as "people," "persons," "one," "voters," "workers," "students," and so on, for "man" or "woman."

Original	Any *man* who wants to become a corporation executive before thirty should buy this book.
Revision	*Anyone* who wants to become a corporation executive before thirty should buy this book.

5. Don't use inappropriate diminutives.

Original	In the annual office picture, the photographer asked the men to stand behind the *girls*.
Revision	In the annual office picture, the photographer asked the men to stand behind the *women*.

6. Consider avoiding words that use "man" to describe the characteristics of a group or that refer to people in general.

Original	Rebuilding the space shuttle will call for extra money and *manpower*, but such an endeavor will benefit *mankind* in the generations to come.
Revision	Rebuilding the space shuttle will call for extra money and *employees*, but such an endeavor will benefit future *generations*.

Similarly, substitute more specific words for "man" used as a verb or as an adjective.

Original	We needed someone to *man* the booth at the fair where we were selling *man-made* opals.
Revision	We needed someone to *staff* the booth at the fair where we were selling *synthetic* opals.

7. Be consistent in your treatment of men's and women's names, marital status, professional titles, and physical appearances.

Original	Neither Herman Melville, the inspired novelist, nor *Miss* Emily Dickinson, the *spinster poetess* of Amherst, gained fame or fortune in their lifetimes.
Revision	Neither Herman Melville, the novelist, nor Emily Dickinson, the *poet*, gained fame or fortune in their lifetimes.

8. If a situation demands multiple hypothetical examples, consider including or alternating references to both genders, when appropriate.

Original	In a revision workshop, one writer may request help with *his* concluding paragraph. Another writer may want reaction to *his* essay's introduction.
Revision	In a revision workshop, one writer may request help with *his* concluding paragraph. Another writer may want reaction to *her* essay's introduction.

Revising your writing to eliminate certain kinds of gender-specific references does not mean turning clear phrases into awkward or confusing jumbles of "he/she told him/her that the car was his/hers." By following the previous suggestions, you should be able to make your prose both clear and inoffensive to all members of your audience.*

Do enliven your writing with figurative language, when appropriate. Figurative language produces pictures or images in a reader's mind, often by comparing something unfamiliar to something familiar. The two most common figurative devices are the simile and the metaphor. A *simile* is a comparison between two people, places, feelings, or things, using the word "like" or "as"; a more forceful comparison, omitting the word "like" or "as," is a *metaphor.* Here are two examples:

Simile   George eats his meals like a hog.

Metaphor   George is a hog at mealtime.

In both sentences, George, whose eating habits are unfamiliar to the reader, is likened to a hog, whose sloppy manners are generally well known. By comparing George to a hog, the writer gives the reader a clear picture of George at the table. Figurative language not only can help you present your ideas in clear, concrete, economical ways but also can make your prose more memorable—especially if the image or picture you present is a fresh, arresting one. Here are some examples of striking images designed to catch the reader's attention and to clarify the writer's point:

- An hour away from him felt like a month in the country.
- The atmosphere of the meeting room was as tense as a hostage negotiation.
- The woman's earrings were as big as butter plates.
- The angry accusation flew like a spear: once thrown, it could not be retrieved and it cut deeply.
- Out of the night came the convoy of brown trucks, modern-day buffalo thundering single file across the prairie, eyes on fire.
- Behind her broad polished desk, Matilda was a queen bee with a swarm of office drones buzzing at her door.
- The factory squatted on the bank of the river like a huge black toad.

Sometimes, in appropriate writing situations, exaggerated similes and metaphors may be used humorously to underscore a particular point: "I felt so stupid that day. I'm sure my colleagues thought my brain was so small that if they placed it on the head of a pin, it would roll around like a marble on a six-lane highway."

Figurative language can spice up your prose, but like any spice, it can be misused, thus spoiling your soup. Therefore, don't overuse figurative language; not every point needs a metaphor or simile for clarity or emphasis. Too many images are confusing. Moreover, don't use stale images. (Clichés—discussed on pages 168–169—are often tired metaphors or similes: "snake in the grass," "hot as fire," "quiet as a mouse," etc.) If you can't catch your readers' attention with a fresh picture, don't bore them with a stale one.

---

* Some writers now use "s/he" to promote gender inclusivity in their informal prose. Be aware, however, that this usage is nontraditional and not accepted universally. Always check with your instructors, or the publication for which you are writing, for the appropriate and preferred style.

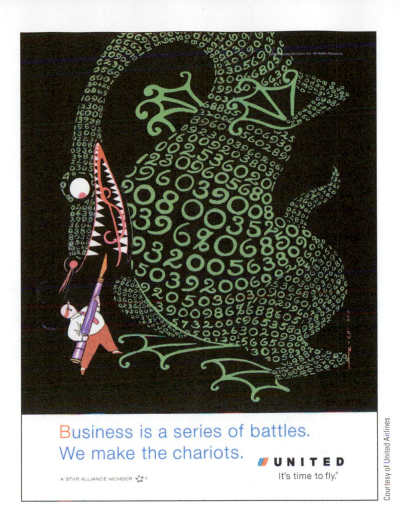

Business is a series of battles.
We make the chariots.   ✈ **UNITED**
                        It's time to fly.®

A STAR ALLIANCE MEMBER ✦ ®

Advertising often uses figurative language to sell products. What is the metaphor in this ad?

Finally, don't mix images—this too often results in a confusing or unintentionally comic scene. For example, a former mayor of Denver once responded to a question about city fiscal requirements this way: "I think the proper approach is to go through this Garden of Gethsemane that we're in now, give birth to a budget that will come out of it, and then start putting our ducks in order with an appeal and the backup we would need to get something done at the state level." Or consider the defense attorney who didn't particularly like his client's plea-bargaining deal but nevertheless announced, "Given the attitude of the normal jury on this type of crime, I feel we would be paddling up a stream behind the eight ball." Perhaps a newspaper columnist wins the prize for confusion with this triple-decker: "The Assemblymen also were miffed at their Senate counterparts because they have refused to bite the bullet that now seems to have grown to the size of a millstone to the Assemblymen whose necks are on the line."

Think of figurative language as you might regard a fine cologne on the person sitting next to you in a crowded theater: just enough is engaging; too much is overpowering.

(◆ For more discussion of similes, metaphors, and other figurative language, see pages 351–352 in Chapter 16.)

Do vary your word choice so that your prose does not sound wordy, repetitious, or monotonous. Consider the following sentence:

> According to child psychologists, depriving a child of sensory stimulation in the earliest stages of childhood can cause the child brain damage.

Reworded, the following sentence eliminates the tiresome, unnecessary repetition of the word "child":

> According to child psychologists, depriving infants of sensory stimulation can cause brain damage.

By omitting or changing repeated words, you can add variety and crispness to your prose. Of course, don't ever change your words or sentence structure to achieve variety at the expense of clarity or precision; at all times, your goal is to make your prose clear to your readers.

Do remember that wordiness is a major problem for all writers, even the professionals. State your thoughts directly and specifically in as few words as necessary to communicate your meaning clearly. ◆ In addition to the advice given here on avoiding wordy or vague jargon, euphemisms, and clichés, you might also review the sections on simplicity and conciseness in Chapter 6.

> THE MOST IMPORTANT KEY TO EFFECTIVE WORD CHOICE IS REVISION. As you write your first draft, don't fret about selecting the best words to communicate your ideas; in later drafts, one of your main tasks will be replacing the inaccurate or imprecise words with better ones. (Dorothy Parker, famous for her witty essays, once lamented, "I can't write five words but that I change seven.") All good writers rewrite, so revise your prose to make each word count.

Practicing What You've Learned

A. Underline the vague nouns, verbs, and modifiers in the sentences that follow. Then rewrite each sentence so that it says something clear and specific.

1. The experiment had very bad results.

2. The speaker came up with some odd items.

3. The house was big, old, and ugly.

4. The man was a nice guy with a good personality.

5. I felt that the whole ordeal was quite an experience.

continued on next page

6. The machine we got was missing a few things.

7. The woman was really something special.

8. The classroom material wasn't interesting.

9. The child made a lot of very loud noises.

10. The cost of the unusual meal was amazing.

B. Rewrite the following sentences, eliminating all clichés, slang, mixed metaphors, and euphemisms; change any texting or sexist language you find.

1. Anyone who wants to be elected the next congressman from our state must clearly recognize that our tourist industry is sitting on a launching pad, ready to flex its muscles and become a dynamo.

2. BTW, I thought the whole deal was sweet, but then my sister got a special delivery from the duh truck and 4gt 2 pick me ^. G2G, thx, Dude!

3. After all is said and done, agricultural producers may be forced to relocate to urban environments, settling in substandard housing with other members of the disadvantaged class until the day they expire.

4. Both Ron Howard and Shirley Temple were popular child actors; careerwise, Howard moved on to directing movies, but Shirley left show biz to serve Old Glory by becoming ambassadoress to Ghana and Czechoslovakia.

5. Each commander realizes that he might one day be called upon to use the peacekeepers to depopulate an emerging nation in a lethal intervention.

6. Although Jack once regarded her as sweet and innocent, he knew then and there that Jill was really a wolf in sheep's clothing with a heart of stone.

7. The city councilman was stewing in his juices when he learned that his goals-impaired son had been arrested for fooling around with the funds for the fiscal underachievers' home.

8. NVR rite lik ds n yr skool r prowork. Srsly. Tlk 2 u l8r.

9. The U.S. Embassy in Budapest once warned its employees: "It must be assumed that available casual indigenous female companions work for or cooperate with the Hungarian government security establishment."

10. At a press conference on the war in Iraq, former Defense Secretary Donald Rumsfeld announced the following: "Reports that say something hasn't happened are always interesting to me, because as we know, there are known knowns, there are things we know we know. We also know there are known unknowns; that is to say we know there are some things we do not know. But there are also unknown unknowns—the ones we don't know we don't know."*

*Incidentally, this comment won Rumsfeld the "Foot in Mouth" prize for the most confusing public statement of that year, awarded by Britain's Plain English Campaign, a group dedicated to ridding the language of jargon and legalese.

Assignment

A. Sometimes something as simple as changing your bland verbs to action words can make an enormous difference in creating prose that is interesting, lively, and emphatic. Practice such revision by first finding a sports section of a newspaper and circling any verbs in the headlines that you think help readers "see" the events. (Do teams *trounce* their opponents? *Charge, sneak,* or *sail* to victory? Does a contender *crumble* or *smash* a record?) Next, look at a current draft you are polishing, and take a second look at any sentences that might profit from replacing a "blah" verb (like "got" or "make") with a stronger one.

B. *Collaborative Activity:* In a group with three classmates, fill in the blanks with colorful words. You may make the paragraph as exciting or humorous as you wish, but avoid clichés and Insta-Prose (those predictable phrases that first come to mind). Work together to make your responses as and creative as possible. When your story is finished, select a member of the group to read your paragraph to the class as whole. After all the groups have read their versions of the story, which images or details remain the most memorable, and why?

As midnight approached, Janet and Brad _____ toward the _____ mansion to escape the _____ storm. Their _____ car had _____ on the road nearby. The night was _____, and Brad _____ at the shadows with _____ and _____. As they _____ up the _____ steps to the _____ door, the _____ wind was filled with _____ and _____ sounds. Janet _____ on the door, and moments later, it opened to reveal the _____ scientist, with a face like a _____. Brad and Janet _____ at each other and then _____

(complete this sentence and then end the paragraph and the story).

C. To continue practicing effective word choice, turn to one of the many paintings or photographs in this text. Write several sentences that vividly describe the image you see. For instance, how might you describe the scene in *The Subway* (page 267)? Or the woman's face in *Migrant Mother* (page 364)? What sensory details might be appropriate in a description of *Starry Night* (page 507)? (For a list of all artworks in this text, see the page following the Table of Contents.)

Applying What You've Learned to *Your* Writing

If you have drafted a piece of writing and you are satisfied with the development and organization of your ideas, you may want to begin revising your word choice. First, read your draft for accuracy, looking up in your dictionary any words you suspect may have been used incorrectly. Then focus your attention on your draft's tone, on the "voice" your words are creating. Have you selected the right words for your purpose, subject, and audience?

If you need a word with a slightly different connotation, use your thesaurus to suggest choices (for example, is the person you're discussing best described as smart, intellectual, studious, or wise?). Next, go on a Bland Word Hunt. Try to replace colorless verbs (such as "are," "get," or "make") with active, vivid ones. Revise vague nouns ("thing") and dull adjectives ("very," "really"); if you're stuck, think of words with strong sensory appeal (sight, smell, taste, sound, touch) to enliven your prose. Last, mine-sweep for any clichés, slang, or jargon. Make each word count: each choice should clarify, not muddy, your meaning.

Chapter 7 Summary

Here is a brief restatement of what you should remember about word choice:

1. Consult a dictionary if you are in doubt about the meaning or usage of a particular word.

2. Choose words that are appropriate for your purpose and audience.

3. Choose words that are clear, specific, and fresh rather than vague, bland, or clichéd.

4. Avoid language that is sexist or trendy or that tries to disguise meaning with jargon or euphemisms.

5. Work for prose that is concise rather than wordy, precise rather than fuzzy.

Answer for page 169:
Most people respond with "coughed, sputtered, and died."

The Reading–Writing Connection

It's hardly surprising that good readers often become good writers themselves. Good readers note effectiveness in the writing of others and use these observations to help clarify their own ideas and rhetorical choices about organization, development, and style. Analogies abound in every skill: singers listen to vocalists they admire, tennis players watch championship matches, actors evaluate their colleagues' award-winning performances, medical students observe famous surgeons, all with an eye to improving their own craft. Therefore, to help you become a better writer, your instructor may ask you to study some of the professional essays included in other sections of this text. Learning to read these essays analytically will help when you face your own writing decisions. To sharpen your reading skills, follow the steps suggested in this chapter. After practicing these steps several times, you should discover that the process is becoming a natural part of your reading experience.

How Can Reading Well Help Me Become a Better Writer?

Close reading of the professional essays in this text should help you become a better writer in several ways. First, understanding the opinions expressed in these essays may spark interesting ideas for your own essays; second, discovering the various ways other writers have organized and explained their material should give you some new ideas about selecting your own strategies and supporting evidence. Familiarizing yourself with the effective stylistic devices and diction of other writers may also encourage you to use language in ways you've never tried before.

Perhaps most importantly, analyzing the prose of others should make you more aware of the writing process itself. Each writer represented in this text faced a series of

Michael Newman/PhotoEdit

decisions regarding choice of ideas, organization, development of details, and style, just as you do when you write. By asking questions (Why did the writer begin the essay this way? Why compare this event to that one? Why use a personal example in that paragraph?), you will begin to see how the writer put the essay together—and that knowledge will help you plan and shape your own essay. Looking carefully at the rhetorical choices of other writers should also help you revise your prose because it promotes the habit of asking yourself questions that consider the reader's point of view (Does the point in paragraph 3 need more evidence to convince my reader? Will the reader be confused if I don't add a smoother transition from paragraph 4 to 5? Does the conclusion fall flat?).

In other words, the skills you practice as an analytical reader are those you'll use as a good writer.

How Can I Become an Analytical Reader?

Becoming an analytical reader may, at first, demand more time—and involvement—than you have previously devoted to a reading assignment. Analytical reading requires more than allowing your eyes to pass over the words on the page; it's not like channel surfing through late-night TV shows, stopping here or there as interest strikes. Analytical reading asks you not only to apply your critical thinking skills to understanding the writer's ideas, but also to consider *how* those ideas were presented, *why* the writer presented them that way, and whether that presentation was *effective*. To gain the most benefits from the reading–writing connection, plan on two readings of any assigned essay, some note-taking, and some marking of the text (called *annotating*). This procedure may seem challenging at first, but the payback to you as both reader and writer will be well worth the extra minutes. Figure 8.1 highlights some of the key steps to reading well discussed in this chapter.

Steps to Reading Well

1. Before you begin the essay itself, note the *title* of the selection. Does it draw you into the essay? Does it suggest a particular tone or image?

2. Note any *publication information* and *biographical data* about the author of the selection you are about to read. In this textbook, such information may be found in a paragraph that precedes each professional essay. Consider: Does the author seem qualified to write about this subject? Where and when was the essay originally published, and for what audience? Is the subject matter still timely, or is it now dated? Is there any other helpful introductory material? For example, many of the professional essays in Part Two of this book are accompanied by *pre-reading questions* designed to focus your connection to the essay's subject matter (and perhaps even suggest a topic for an essay of your own).

3. You're now ready to begin your first reading of the essay. Some readers like to read through the essay without stopping; others feel comfortable at this point underlining a few main ideas or making checks in the margins. You may also have to make a dictionary stop if words you don't know appear in key places in the essay. Many times you can figure out definitions from context—that is, from the

Figure 8.1 STEPS TO READING WELL

Pre-reading

1. Note the title of the selection.
2. Note the publication information of the selection and the biographical data of the author.

First Reading

1. a) Read continuously through without stopping.
   b) Write down your impression of the selection.
   c) Consider the author's purpose.

Second Reading

1. Take a closer look at the title and introduction.
2. Locate the thesis.
3. Identify the main points (usually topic sentences).
4. Consider the rhetorical strategies used by the writer.

Post-Reading

1. Look back over the selection's organization.
2. Consider the selection's unity and coherence.
3. Analyze the writer's style and tone.

© Cengage Learning 2017

words and ideas surrounding the unknown word—but don't miss the point of a major part of an essay because of failure to recognize an important word, especially if that word is repeated or emphasized in some way.

When you finish this reading, write a sentence or two summarizing your general impression of the essay's content or ideas. Consider the author's *purpose*: what do you think the writer was trying to do? Overall, how well did he or she succeed? (A typical response might be "argued for tuition hike—unconvincing, boring—too many confusing statistics.")

Now prepare to take another, closer look at the essay. Make some notes in the margins or in another convenient place as you respond to the following tasks and questions. Remember that analytical reading is not a horse race: there are no trophies for finishing quickly! Fight the bad habit of galloping at breakneck speed through an essay; slow down to admire the verbal roses the writer has tried to place in your path.

4. Look at the *title* (again) and at the essay's *introductory paragraph(s)*. Did they effectively set up your expectations? Introduce the essay's topic, main idea, tone? (Would some other title or introductory "hook" have worked better?)

5. Locate the writer's main point or *thesis*; this idea may be stated plainly, or it may be clearly implied. If you didn't mark this idea on your first reading, do so now by placing a "T" in the margin so you can refer to the thesis easily. (If the thesis is implied, you may wish to mark places that you think most clearly indicate the writer's stance.)

6. As you reread the essay, look for important statements that support or illustrate the thesis. (As you know, these are often found as *topic sentences* occurring near the beginning or end of the body paragraphs.) Try numbering these supporting points or ideas and jotting a key word by each one in the margin.

7. After you identify each important supporting point, ask yourself how the writer develops, explains, or argues that idea. For example, does the writer clarify or support the point by providing examples, testimony, or statistics? By comparing or contrasting one idea to another? By showing a cause-effect relationship? Some other method? A combination of methods? A writer may use one or many methods of development, but each major point in an essay should be explained clearly and logically. Make brief marginal notes to indicate how well you think the writer has succeeded ("convincing example," "generalization without support," "questionable authority cited," "good comparison," etc.). Practice using marginal symbols, such as stars (for especially effective statements, descriptions, arguments) or question marks (for passages you think are confusing, untrue, or exaggerated). Make up your own set of symbols to help yourself remember your evaluations of the writer's ideas and techniques.

8. Look back over the essay's general *organization*. Did the writer use one of the expository, descriptive, narrative, or argumentative strategies to structure the essay? Some combination of strategies? Was this choice effective? (Always consider alternative ways: would another choice have allowed the writer to make his or her main point more emphatically? Why or why not?)

9. Does the essay flow logically and coherently? If you are having trouble with *unity* or *coherence* in your own essays, look closely at the transitional devices used in a few paragraphs; bracketing transitional words or phrases you see might show you how the writer achieved a sense of unity and flow.

10. Consider the writer's *style* and the essay's *tone*. Does the writer use figurative language in an arresting way? Specialized diction for a particular purpose? Repetition of words or phrases? Any especially effective sentence patterns? Does the writer's tone of voice come through clearly? Is the essay serious, humorous, angry, consoling, happy, sad, sarcastic, or something else? Is the tone appropriate for the purpose and audience of this essay? Writers use a variety of stylistic devices

to create prose that is vivid and memorable; you might mark new uses of language you would like to try in essays of your own.

Now is also the time to look up meanings of any words you felt you could skip during your first time through the essay, especially if you sense that these words are important to the writer's tone or use of imagery.

Once you have completed these steps and added any other comments that seem important to the analysis of the essay, review your notes. Is this an effective essay? Is the essay's thesis explained or supported adequately with enough logically developed points and evidence? Is the essay organized as effectively as it could have been? What strengths and weaknesses did you find after this analytical reading? Has your original evaluation of this essay changed in any way? If so, write a new assessment, adding any other notes you want to help you remember your evaluation of this essay.

Finally, after this close reading of the essay, did you discover any new ideas, strategies, or techniques you might incorporate into *your* current piece of writing?

Sample Annotated Essay

Here is a professional essay annotated according to the steps listed on the previous pages.

By closely reading and annotating the professional essays in this text, you can improve your own writing in numerous ways. Once you have practiced analyzing essays by other writers, you may discover that you can assess your own drafts' strengths and weaknesses with more confidence.

College for Grown-Ups ———————————————

Mitchell L. Stevens

— *Provocative title*

Mitchell L. Stevens is the Director of the Scandinavian Consortium for Organizational Research, and he serves as an Associate Professor of Sociology and Organizational Behavior at Stanford University. Stevens is, by training, a sociologist with a strong interest in the study of higher education. His essay "College for Grown-Ups" first appeared online December 11, 2014 and then again as an op-ed piece in the December 12, 2014 print issue of the *New York Times*. The essay's appearance has generated hundreds of comments from all points on the opinion spectrum. Stevens's current research focuses on the ways in which universities are reorganizing themselves in response to current economic forces.

educator

general audience

Is this the thesis?

1   A cruel paradox of higher education in America is that its most coveted seats are reserved for young people. Four-year residential colleges with selective admissions are a privileged elite in the academic world, but their undergraduate programs effectively discriminate on the basis of age. Admissions officers typically prefer that the best and brightest be children.

Loaded term used for dramatic effect. Are 18-year-olds children?

2   Yet leaving home at a young age to live on a campus full-time is not without serious financial, psychological and even physical risk.

3 risks: financial, psychological, physical

People make major investment decisions when they are choosing colleges, but with minimal information about quality and fit. Meanwhile flagship public universities, which rely on tuition to offset diminished public subsidies, condone Greek systems that appeal to many affluent families but also incubate cultures of dangerous play. The <u>so-called party pathway</u> through college is an all-encompassing lifestyle characterized by virtually nonstop socializing, often on the male-controlled turf of fraternity houses. Substance abuse and sexual assault are <u>common consequences</u>.

Loaded language

According to whom? What source is this based on?

3   Even at the schools where the party pathway is carefully policed, life on a residential campus can be a psychological strain. A substantial body of research demonstrates that <u>first-generation college students, those from low-income families and racial minorities</u> are particularly at risk for feelings of exclusion, loneliness and academic alienation. The costs of leaving college can be large for everyone: lost tuition, loan debt and a subtle but consequential diminishment of self-esteem.

High-risk students

4   The source of these problems is baked into the current organization of residential higher education. Virtually all <u>selective schools</u> arrange their undergraduate programs on the <u>presumption</u> that teenagers are the primary clients. Administrators plan dormitory architecture, academic calendars and marketing campaigns to appeal to high school juniors and seniors. Again the cruel paradox: In the ever-growing number of administrators and service people catering to those who pay tuition, there are grown-ups all over campus, but they are largely peripheral to undergraduate culture.

As opposed to open enrollment

Source of the problem is that schools cater to teenage clientele

5   If we were starting from zero, we probably wouldn't design colleges as <u>age-segregated playgrounds</u> in which teenagers and very young adults are given free rein to spend their time more or less as they choose. Yet this is the reality.

More loaded language

6   It doesn't have to be that way. <u>Rethinking the expectation that applicants to selective colleges be fresh out of high school would go far in reducing risk for young people while better protecting everyone's college investment</u>. Some of this rethinking is already underway. <u>Temporarily delaying college</u> for a year or two after high school is now becoming respectable among the admissions gatekeepers at top schools. <u>Massive online open courses</u> (MOOCs) and other forms of online learning make it possible to experience fragments of an elite education at little or no cost.

I think <u>this</u> is the thesis

New alternatives to current "college age" model:
1. delay attendance
2. MOOCs

7   In the Bay Area, where I live, people are tinkering further with conventional campus models. <u>The Minerva Project</u>, a San Francisco start-up with offices two blocks from Twitter, offers classic seminar-style college courses via a sophisticated interactive online learning platform and accompanies them with residencies in cities all over the world. Nearby in the SoMa district, <u>Dev Bootcamp</u>, a 19-week

3. Online + residency

4. immersive curriculum

immersive curriculum that trains people of all ages for jobs in the tech industry, is a popular alternative. Some successfully employed graduates brag of bypassing college altogether.

8   At Stanford, where I teach, an idea still in the concept phase developed by a student-led team in the university's Hasso Plattner Institute of Design calls for the replacement of four consecutive college years in young adulthood with multiple residencies distributed over a lifetime. What the designers call Open Loop University would grant students admitted to Stanford multiple years to spend on campus, along with advisers to help them time those years strategically in light of their personal development and career ambitions. Today's arbitrarily segregated world of teenagers and young adults would become an ever-replenished intergenerational community of purposeful learners.

Biographical info about the author that establishes credibility

Are they traditional or nontraditional students?

Alternative 5: lifelong learning

(arbitrary: not based on reason)

9   This utopian ideal is admittedly quite a distance from the institutional arrangements we have inherited, which encourage the nation's most privileged young people to enter and finish college by the ripe old age of 22. But the status quo is not sustainable. Unrelenting demand for better-educated workers, rapidly developing technological capacity to support learning digitally and the soaring costs of conventional campus life are driving us toward substantial change.

3 forces that are challenging the status quo

10   While innovators continue to imagine more flexible forms of college, traditionalists might champion two proven models: community colleges, which were designed to educate people of all ages and walks of life together, and the G.I. Bill, which sent more than two million grown-ups to college, made campus culture much more serious and helped American higher education become the envy of the world.

Two traditional alternatives:
1. community colleges
2. the G.I. Bill

Conclusion is a little abrupt. No real summary statement on the essay as a whole.

First impression: Stevens argues that college is a poor fit for those to whom it's traditionally geared, students right out of high school. He contends that it creates financial, physical, and psychological damage. He believes that there are a number of alternatives that make more sense.

Notes: Even though this is an opinion piece written for a newspaper, the author's use of loaded language is pretty strong. He doesn't really acknowledge that college could be well suited to some teens, nor does he talk about why adults are better suited for college (despite the title). He also makes some big claims without providing specific evidence. I think his list of alternatives is really interesting, however, and they seem like viable choices.

Personal responses: Although I would like to have seen more evidence and less loaded language, I think Mitchell Stevens has assembled an interesting collection of alternatives to the traditional four years of college right after high school. I'm not necessarily persuaded by his unsupported reasons for why more students coming out of high school should pursue alternative education paths, though.

Practicing What You've Learned

Select one of the professional essays reprinted in this text, and annotate it according to the steps described in this chapter. Note at least one strength in the essay that you would like to incorporate into your own writing.

Assignment

Select one of the professional essays in this text to read analytically and annotate. Then write a one-page explanation of the essay's major strengths (or weaknesses), showing how the writer's rhetorical choices affected you, the reader.

How Can I Read Multimodal Texts Analytically?

When you visit a Web site, check out a magazine advertisement, play a video game, read a graphic novel, or even review the online components of your college textbook, you are engaging with multimodal texts. These types of texts include more than one communication strategy or "mode" and have elements such as visuals, hypertext, audio files, digital content, video clips, and more. Reading and interacting with multimodal texts require you to use critical thinking skills beyond those you use when reading a traditional essay. When reading an assigned multimodal text analytically, you will want to ask some of the same questions as when you are reading an essay, but you will also want to consider other questions about medium, genre, and design or composition.

Steps to Reading Multimodal Texts Well

1. To start, consider what *type,* or *genre,* of text you are reading. Is it an advertisement, a comic, a movie, a song? Is it a blog post, a tweet, a comment from Facebook? Is it a map, a chart, a table? Because each genre is associated with a specific set of assumptions and expectations, knowing the genre of the multimodal text you are reading will help you to more accurately evaluate its meaning. For example, you might expect more informal language from a Facebook post, more poetic language from a song, and more truncated language from a tweet.

2. Make note of the *publication information* of the multimodal text you are reading. When and where did this text appear? Is the publication date recent? Are you encountering the text in its original context? For example, people frequently e-mail or post articles on the Web that may have originated years earlier in a very different context. Accurate analysis of any text requires an understanding of when and where the text first appeared or was published.

3. Identify who *created* or *authored* the text. This information can be more difficult to discover with multimodal texts than with essays, but it's just as important. Is the author an individual? A nonprofit organization? An international corporation?

Is the author a known and credible person, group, or company? For example, when reading an advertisement, you would identify the company or organization behind the ad. What do you know about that company or organization? What other products do they sell besides the one presented in the advertisement? What is the organization's goal or mission? You can usually find some basic information about a company by visiting its Web site.

4. Consider the text's *medium*. The medium is the material, vehicle, or technology used to deliver the idea of the text. It's the physical method by which the text's content is presented to you as a reader. You are likely used to encountering essays in one or two mediums (print or online books or magazines), but multimodal texts can be delivered in a wide variety of formats. If it is an advertisement, then is it a print ad, a TV ad, or a Web ad? If it is a song, then is it a live performance, an audio recording, or a video from YouTube? A text's medium will determine whether it is composed of static or dynamic images, whether or not it includes audio, etc. As with genre, a text's medium carries with it both author assumptions and audience expectations.

5. Investigate who the *intended audience* is for the multimodal text you are reading. The audience of a text can be just as important as the author of the text. The format, the language and tone, and the venue of the text can all give you clues as to who the intended audience is. For example, when reading an advertisement, you can get some ideas about the intended audience by considering the format or place where you encountered the ad. If you see the advertisement in a magazine, consider the type of magazine in which the ad appears. Who usually reads that magazine? Men or women or both, and what ages? What other types of products appear in the magazine's ads? If the advertisement is a television commercial, during what program was the product advertised? What do these answers tell you about the target demographic of the product and the company's intentions? The answers to these questions will tell you much about the author's assumptions about you as the reader.

6. You are now ready to think about the text's meaning. What is the *subject*? What is this text about? What is the *purpose* of the text? What message is being communicated? Just as you think about the author's purpose when reading an essay, you will also want to ask yourself what the author of this multimodal text is trying to do. Is he or she trying to convince you to buy something or to take action in some way? Is the text presenting information? While an advertisement is often obviously trying to persuade you to purchase something, a map or chart may simply be providing information.

7. Consider the *design* or *composition* of the text. Thinking about design or composition is similar to thinking about the organization and style of an essay. With a multimodal text, you want to think about how the elements of the text are put together. You can ask questions such as the following: What is the focal point? What draws your eye or your attention when reading this text? What other details do you notice? Don't forget to think about what is missing or left out. Remember that, as with words, visual elements contain both literal meanings and associated meanings. In other words, if an advertisement features an image of a tree, the reader will likely see the image as a representation of a physical plant. However, the reader will also likely associate that image with the idea of nature as a whole.

If a tire swing is hanging from the tree in the image, then the tree may suddenly be associated with the idea of childhood. Authors of multimodal texts are extremely careful in selecting images for this very reason.

8. Finally, pay close attention to the *nonvisual elements* that are included. What kinetic or auditory elements are included? What impact does motion, voiceover, or musical accompaniment have on the presentation of the main idea or message? The author of a traditional essay uses style and tone to shape his or her meaning, and the author of a multimodal text is no different. Just as when selecting images, authors of multimodal texts carefully choose auditory elements that convey a desired mood or atmosphere. In a multimodal text, the inclusion of visual and nonvisual elements can be just as important as the textual elements. In other words, *how* text is presented can be as important as *what* is presented.

Once you have completed these steps and noted any other key elements, take a moment to review your notes. What conclusions can you draw about the multimodal text you've analyzed? Is it effective? Is the message clear? How persuasive or informative is it? What is the impact of the author's visual and nonvisual element choices? What have you discovered about the text as a whole? The answers to these questions can be consolidated into a written assessment of the text you've analyzed. Such a written analysis can be an extremely useful tool in helping you discover new techniques and approaches for your own writing.

Sample Annotated Advertisement

Below is a World Wildlife Fund advertisement and on the next page are one student's notes as she does a close reading of this ad.

What will it take before we respect the planet?

wwf.org

First Impressions: I am struck by the jarring nature of the graffiti on the elephant's side. Something so clearly unnatural on the side of something so clearly natural.

Notes:

1. I did a search and found out that this was created by an ad agency in 2010, but I'm not sure when or where this ad was originally published.

2. This ad is for WWF and I can go to their Web site (wwf.org) to learn more about them.

3. This is a print ad, and so it has no video or audio elements. Nevertheless, the picture conveys movement and vibrance.

4. The ad seems to be geared toward a general audience.

5. This ad is designed to be persuasive. The image and message are provocative, designed to create an emotional response.

6. The message of the ad is pretty straightforward. WWF is equating humanity's treatment of the earth with the intentional and disrespectful act of painting graffiti on someone else's property. The simple question ("What will it take before we respect the planet?") pushes me to consider what outrage will have to occur before I take some action to help protect the planet.

7. Design/composition:

   – My attention is drawn to the vivid colors of the graffiti on the elephant. These bright colors stand in stark contrast to the washed out colors of the background.

   – The organization's logo is small but easily located, and it does not detract from the impact of the ad as a whole.

   – The elephant is definitely the focal point; the graffiti contrasts sharply with the animal's natural majesty.

Personal Response: I think this ad works well. It combines the best elements of nature photography with a common symbol of urban decay. The simple text message that accompanies it made me stop to think about the implications of the idea of "respect" for the planet. Powerful.

Writing a Summary

Frequently writing teachers will ask students to read an essay and briefly summarize it. A *summary* is an objective, condensed version of a reading selection containing the author's main ideas. Although summaries are always more concise than the original texts, the length of a particular summary often depends on the length and complexity of the reading and the purpose of the summary.

Learning to summarize reading material is a valuable skill, useful in many classes and in professional work. In one of your college classes, for example, your instructor might ask you to summarize an article pertinent to an upcoming lecture or class discussion, thus ensuring that you have thoroughly understood the information; at other times, you may need to summarize material for your own research. On a job, you might want to

Figure 8.2 WRITING A SUMMARY

> Read and annotate the selection.

> Drafting Dos and Don'ts

- **DO** include the author's name and title of the selection in the first sentence.
- **DO** use your own words to present the thesis and other main points.
- **DO** use quotation marks if you decide to use exact words from the original text.
- **DO** provide an objective condensed overview of the selection.

- **DON'T** simply copy sentences from the original text.
- **DON'T** include references to supporting examples and details from the selection.
- **DON'T** overuse original wording from the selection.
- **DON'T** give your opinion or interpretation of the material.

© Cengage Learning 2017

share a summary of an important report with colleagues, or you might be asked to present a summary of project results to your boss.

Because summarizing is such a useful skill, here are a few guidelines (see also Figure 8.2).

1. Read the selection carefully, as many times as it takes for you to understand and identify the author's thesis and main ideas. You might underline or take notes on the key ideas as you read, using the suggestions in the previous pages of this chapter to help you.

2. When you begin to draft your summary, always include the author's name and the title of the original text in your first sentence. Many times it's important to include the source of the work and its publication date, too.

3. Using your own words, present the author's thesis and other main ideas in a few concise sentences. Do not merely copy sentences directly from the original text. Use your own words to convey the main ideas as clearly and concisely as possible.

4. Omit all references to the supporting examples and details in the selection, unless you have been instructed to include these.

5. If, for clarity or emphasis, you do need to include an exact word or phrase from the original text, be certain to enclose the words in quotation marks.

6. Do not give your own opinion or interpretation of the material you are summarizing. Your goal is an objective, accurate, condensed overview of the selection that does not reveal your attitude toward the ideas presented.

To illustrate the preceding guidelines, here is a brief summary of the essay that appears on pages 186–188 of this chapter.

> In the *New York Times* op-ed "College for Grown-Ups," Mitchell L. Stevens contends that college is a privilege wasted on the young. Stevens, a professor at Stanford University, argues that sending new high school graduates off to college places these students at great financial, psychological, and even physical risk. The source of these risks is "baked" into the existing setup in place at most traditional colleges and universities. Stevens suggests a number of alternatives, including a mandatory delay in enrollment after high school, MOOCs, immersive curricula, and lifelong education. He concludes that the "status quo is not sustainable."

Note that the writer of the summary did not offer her opinion of Stevens' proposal, but, instead, objectively presented the essay's main ideas.

◆ For additional discussion clarifying the difference between *summary* and *paraphrase*, see pages 419–420 in Chapter 19. ◆ For suggestions on writing the assignment known as the "summary-and-response essay," see pages 485–487 in Chapter 21; this section also contains a sample student paper written in response to Mitchell Stevens' essay, "College for Grown-Ups."

Practicing What You've Learned

Read one of the professional essays in this textbook, and annotate it according to the steps outlined earlier in this chapter. After you are sure you clearly understand the author's thesis and main ideas, write a one-paragraph summary of the essay. Use your own words to convey the essay's main ideas, but remember to remain objective in your summary.

Benefiting from Class Discussions

If you have been practicing the steps for close reading of essays, you are on your way to becoming a better writer. By analyzing the rhetorical choices of other writers, you are gathering new ideas and techniques as well as improving your ability to look thoughtfully at your own drafts. To continue this progress, your composition instructor may devote class time to discussing sample professional or student essays that appear in this text.

Active participation in these discussions will contribute to your growth as a writer as you share ideas about effective prose with your classmates. To benefit from such discussions, consider these suggestions for improving your classroom skills (see also Figure 8.3).

Try to arrive a few minutes before class begins so that you can look over the reading and your marginal notes (and any other homework assigned to accompany the essay, such as questions or a summary).* Remind yourself that it is time to become an "active listener," so if sitting by friends or near a window is a distraction, move to another seat. Sitting up

---

* ◆ If you're having a difficult time remembering details in the essays you've been assigned to read, try the split-page journal technique, described on pages 28–29.

Figure 8.3 BENEFITING FROM CLASS DISCUSSIONS

Before Class

1. Read the selection carefully and create annotations.
2. Complete any associated homework.
3. Prepare possible responses to questions at end of selection.
4. Arrive in class early to choose an optimal seat when possible.
5. Review your notes.
6. Prepare yourself mentally to be an "active listener."

During Class

1. Listen carefully.
2. Offer insights and opinions when appropriate.
3. Ask questions.
4. Take notes.
5. Be respectful of others' thoughts and opinions.

After Class

1. Staple handouts into your notes.
2. Review notes and highlight points of emphasis.
3. Consider the implications of the discussion.
4. Make connections to your own work.

© Cengage Learning 2017

front is encouraged not only because you can hear your instructor better, but also because he or she can see and hear you more clearly if you have questions. (Be sure you have turned off your cell phone, media player, or any other electronic device, and remember that gum popping, pencil tapping, pen clicking, and knuckle cracking may lead to bad-karma thoughts from nearby students who are also trying to listen without distraction.)

During the class period, your teacher may ask for responses to questions that follow selected essays in this text, or he or she may pose new questions. If you've prepared by closely reading and annotating the assigned essay as outlined on pages 183–186, you should be able to join these discussions. Listen carefully to your classmates' opinions; offer your own insights and be willing to voice agreement or polite disagreement. If participating in class makes you nervous, prepare one or two comments out of class in such clear detail that speaking about them will be easier for you, and then volunteer when those topics arise in the discussion. Don't hesitate to ask questions or request additional explanations; remember that if you don't understand something, it's a good bet others in the class are puzzled too.

As discussion of a sample essay unfolds, practice thinking critically on two levels. First, think of the essay as a draft in which the writer made certain choices to communicate meaning, just as you do in your essays. Trading ideas with your classmates may help you see why the writer chose as he or she did—and whether those decisions work effectively. As you gain a clear understanding of the strengths and weaknesses in the sample essay, move to the second level by considering the choices you are making in your own writing. For example, if you struggle with conclusions to your essays, listen attentively to the discussion of the writer's choice and then consider whether this kind of ending might work in your essay. If a writer has failed to provide enough examples or details to illustrate a particular point, think about a paragraph in your current rough draft. Do you now see a similar problem in need of revision? In other words, as you and your classmates analyze essays in class, *actively make the essential connection between the readings and your own work.*

To remember important points in any class discussion, sharpen your note-taking skills. If you use a paper notebook for this course, you may find it helpful to leave a wide margin on the left side of each page, giving yourself space to write key words, questions, or ideas for your own writing. Start each day's notes on a new page with the day's date to help you locate material later. Acquire the habit of stapling or taping handouts to blank pages that immediately follow notes from a particular class period (handouts stuck in your textbook or in your backpack are easily lost). As you take notes, pay special attention to any words your teacher considers significant enough to repeat in learning aids such as handouts, classroom or electronic boards, or slide presentations. Be sensitive to the verbal cues your instructor uses to emphasize essential material (words such as "key terms," "main reasons," and "central idea," as well as repetition or even a slightly louder tone of voice).

Because class discussion often moves quickly, you'll need to develop a shorthand method of note-taking. Some students write out an important term the first time (development) and then abbreviate it thereafter (dev). You can devise your own system of symbols, but included here are some abbreviations common to note-taking you may find handy. Most of these abbreviations are for notes only, although some (such as *e.g., i.e., cf.,* and *ca.*) may be used in college and professional writing; consult your instructor or the appropriate style manual if you are in doubt.

b/c = because	$\rightarrow$ = causes, leads to, produces
b/4 = before	cf. = compare
w/ = with	$\uparrow$ = increases, higher than
w/o = without	$\downarrow$ = decreases, lower than
w/i = within	esp. = especially
e.g. = for example	re = regarding
i.e. = that is	ca. = approximately (use with dates or figures)
& = and	$\therefore$ = therefore
@ = at	$\neq$ = not equal to, not the same, differs from
# = number	N.B. = "nota bene," Latin for "note well"

Later, after class, you may want to underline, star, or highlight important material. Fill in any gaps and rewrite any illegible words now before you forget what you meant. Make some notes about applying the ideas and techniques discussed in class to your own writing. Reread these notes before you begin drafting or revising your essay.

Here's the last, and possibly most important, piece of advice for every student of writing: *attend every class session!* There is a logical progression in all composition courses; each day's lesson reemphasizes and builds on the previous one. By conscientiously attending every class discussion and actively participating in your own learning process, you *will* improve your writing skills.

Practicing What You've Learned

Collaborative Activity: Listen attentively and take notes on a classroom discussion of a sample essay or on another lesson your instructor has just presented. In a group of two or three classmates, compare your notes. As a group, describe the lesson's purpose and determine which points in the discussion were the most important, and why. In what ways will this class lesson help you improve your writing? What questions, if any, do you still have about this particular lesson?

Chapter 8 Summary

Here is a brief summary of what you should remember about the reading–writing connection.

1. Reading and analyzing essays can improve your writing skills.

2. Learning to recognize and evaluate the strategies and stylistic techniques of other writers will help you plan and shape your own essays.

3. Reading analytically takes time and practice but is well worth the extra effort.

4. Learning to summarize reading material accurately and objectively is an important skill, useful in school and at work.

5. Active participation in class discussions of sample essays can help you strengthen your own writing.

Part One Summary: The Basics of the Short Essay

Here are ten suggestions to keep in mind while you are working on the rough drafts of your essay:

1. Be confident that you have something important and interesting to say.

2. Identify your particular audience and become determined to communicate effectively with them.

3. Use prewriting techniques to help you focus on one main idea that will become the thesis of your essay.

4. Organize your essay's points logically, in a persuasive and coherent order.

5. Develop each of your ideas with enough evidence and specific details.

6. Delete any irrelevant material that disrupts the smooth flow from idea to idea.

7. Compose sentences that are clear, concise, and informative; choose accurate, vivid words.

8. Improve your writing by learning to read analytically.

9. Revise your prose.

10. Revise your prose!

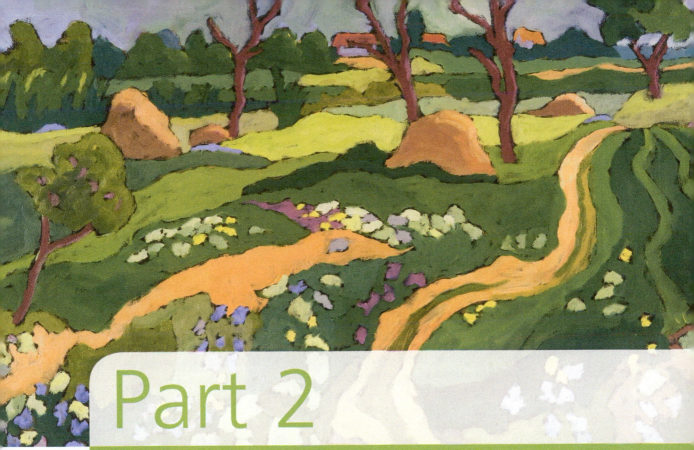

Part 2

Purposes, Modes, and Strategies

Communication may be divided into four types (or "modes" as they are often called): exposition, argumentation, description, and narration. Although each one will be explained in greater detail in this section of the text, the four modes may be defined briefly as follows:

Exposition
The writer intends to explain or inform. (See Chapters 9–14)

Argumentation
The writer intends to convince or persuade. (See Chapter 15)

Description
The writer intends to create in words a picture of a person, place, object, or feeling. (See Chapter 16)

Narration
The writer intends to tell a story or recount an event. (See Chapter 17)

Although we commonly refer to exposition, argumentation, description, and narration as the basic types of prose, in reality it is difficult to find any one mode in a pure form. In fact, almost all essays are combinations of two or more modes; it would be virtually impossible, for instance, to write a story—narration—without including description or to argue without also giving some information. Nevertheless, by determining a writer's main purpose, we can usually identify an essay or prose piece as primarily exposition, argumentation, description, or narration. In other words, an article may include a brief description of a new mousetrap, but if the writer's main intention is to explain how the trap works, then we may designate the essay as exposition. In most cases, the primary mode of any essay will be readily apparent to the reader.

In Part Two of this text, not only will you study each of the four modes in detail, but you will also learn some of the patterns of development, called *strategies*, that will enable you to write the kinds of prose most frequently demanded in college and professional work. Mastering the most common prose strategies in their simplest forms now will help you successfully assess and organize any kind of complex writing assignment you may face in the future. Chapter 18 concludes this section by discussing the more complex essay, developed through use of multiple strategies.

Chapter 9

Development by Example

Perhaps you've heard a friend recently complain about a roommate. "Tina is an inconsiderate slob, impossible to live with," she cries. Your natural response might be to question your friend's rather broad accusation: "What makes her so terrible? What does she do that's so bad?" Your friend might then respond with specific examples of Tina's insensitivity: she never washes her dishes, she ties up the bathroom for hours, and she borrows clothes without asking. By citing several examples, your friend clarifies and supports her general criticism of Tina, thus enabling you to understand her point of view.

Such a use of examples is one strategy of expository prose, writing whose primary purpose is giving information. Expository prose focuses on a clear thesis statement that conveys the writer's purpose and position followed by a succession of organized body paragraphs that further explain and support that thesis. An exemplification essay is simply an expository essay that relies chiefly on the use of examples to provide explanation and support for the thesis. This type of essay works in precisely the same way as the preceding hypothetical story: specific examples are used to *support, clarify, interest,* and *persuade.* Following a writing process like that represented in Figure 9.1 will help you develop an effective exemplification essay.

Why and How to Use Examples In Your Writing

In your writing assignments, you might want to assert that dorm food is cruel and inhuman punishment, that recycling is a profitable hobby, or that the cost of housing near campus is rising dramatically. But without some carefully chosen examples to show the truth of your statements, these remain unsupported generalities or mere opinions. Your task, then, is to provide enough specific examples to support your general statements; to make them both clear and convincing. Here is a statement offering the reader only hazy generalities:

> Our locally supported TV channel presents a variety of excellent educational shows. The shows are informative on lots of different subjects for both children and adults. The information they offer makes channel 19 well worth the public funds that support it.

Figure 9.1 VISUALIZING THE PROCESS: EXEMPLIFICATION

Prewriting

Identify possible subjects by considering the following questions:

- What topics are of interest to you?
- What topics are of interest to your audience?
- About what topics do you have sufficient knowledge to write a paper?

Drafting

Determine the effect you hope your essay will have on your audience by asking the following questions:

- What is your purpose? This will become your thesis statement.
- What do you want your audience to think, feel, or do about this topic?
- What examples can you collect from personal experience, research, or hypothetical situations to support the points you want to make about your topic?

Revising

Carefully review your thesis and the supporting examples you use by asking the following questions:

- Are all of your examples relevant to the points you're trying to make in your essay?
- Are the examples you have selected as support the best one for the audience to whom you're writing? Did your selection process involve a consideration of your audience?
- Are your examples specific, clear, and convincing?
- Did you use a sufficient number of examples? Did you use too many? Do you sacrifice depth for breadth in the number you use?

Editing/Proofreading

Consider the sentence-level issues of your exemplification essay by asking the following questions:

- Do your examples contain vivid details designed to capture the reader's interest?
- Have you reviewed your sentences for spelling, grammar, and punctuation errors?
- Is your paper formatted according to assignment guidelines?

Rewritten, the same paragraph explains its point clearly through the use of specific examples:

Our locally supported TV channel presents a variety of excellent educational shows. For example, young children can learn their alphabet and numbers from *Sesame Street*; imaginative older children can be encouraged to experiment, act, cook, or create by watching *Zoom*, a show filled with viewer-submitted recipes, jokes, plays, games, and ideas of all types. Adults may enjoy learning about antiques and collectibles from a program called *Antiques Roadshow*; each week the show features the stories and appraisals of family heirlooms, garage sale treasures, and forgotten knickknacks. Those folks wishing to become handy around the home can use information on repairs from plumbing to wiring on *This Old House*, while those interested in music can view a wide variety of performances from musical innovators and legends alike on the country's longest running music series, *Austin City Limits*. Budding chefs may profit from weekly instruction by America's hospitality expert on *Martha Stewart's Cooking School*. The information offered makes these and other educational shows on channel 19 well worth the public funds that support the station.

Although the preceding example is based on real shows, you may also use personal experiences, hypothetical situations, anecdotes, research material, facts, testimony, or any combination thereof, to explain, illustrate, or support the points in your essays.

In some cases you may find that a series of short examples fits your purpose, illustrating clearly the idea you are presenting to your reader:

In the earlier years of Hollywood, actors aspiring to become movie stars often adopted new names that they believed sounded more attractive to the public. Frances Ethel Gumm, for instance, decided to change her name to Judy Garland long before she flew over any rainbows, and Alexander Archibald Leach became Cary Grant on his way from England to America. Alexandra Cymboliak and Merle Johnson, Jr., might not have set teenage hearts throbbing in the early 1960s, but Sandra Dee and Troy Donahue certainly did. Although some names were changed to achieve a smoother flow (Frederic Austerlitz to Fred Astaire, for example), some may have also been changed to ensure a good fit on movie theater marquees as well as a place in their audience's memory: the teenage Turner girl, Julia Jean Mildred Frances, for instance, became just Lana.

Or you may decide that two or three examples explained in some detail provide the best support for your topic rather than a series of short examples. In the paragraph that follows, the writer chose to develop two examples to illustrate her point about the unusual dog her family owned when she was a young girl in the late 1970s:

Our family dog Sparky always let us know when he wasn't getting enough attention. For instance, if he thought we were away from home too much, he'd perform his record trick. While we were out, Sparky would push an album out of the record rack and then tap the album cover in just such a way that the record would roll out. Then he would chomp the record! We'd return to find our favorite LP (somehow, always our current favorite) chewed into tiny bits of black vinyl scattered about the room. Another popular Sparky trick was the cat-sit. If the family was peacefully settled on the porch, not playing with him, Sparky would grab the family cat by the ear and drag her over to the steps, whereupon he would sit on top of her until someone paid attention to him. He never hurt the cat; he simply sat on her as one would sit on a fine cushion, with her head poking out under his tail, and a silly grin on his face that said, "See, if you'd play with me, I wouldn't get into such mischief."

You may also find that in some cases, one long, detailed example (called an *extended example*) is more useful than several shorter ones. If you were writing a paragraph urging the traffic department to install a stop sign at a particularly dangerous corner, you probably should cite numerous examples of accidents there. On the other hand, if you were praising a certain kind of local architecture, you might select one representative house and discuss it in detail. In the following paragraph, for instance, the writer might have supported his main point by citing a number of cases in which lives had been saved by seat belts; he chose instead to offer one detailed example, in the form of a personal experience:

> Wearing seat belts can protect people from injury, even in serious accidents. I know because seat belts saved me and my dad two years ago when we were driving to see my grandparents who live in California. Because of the distance, we had to travel late on a rainy, foggy Saturday night. My dad was driving, but what he didn't know was that there was a car a short way behind us driven by a drunk who was following our car's taillights in order to keep himself on the road. About midnight, my dad decided to check the map to make sure we were headed in the right direction, so he signaled, pulled over to the shoulder, and began to stop. Unfortunately for us, the drunk didn't see the signal and moved his car over to the shoulder thinking that the main road must have curved slightly since our car had gone that way. As Dad slowed our car, the other car plowed into us at a speed estimated later by the police as over eighty miles an hour. The car hit us like Babe Ruth's bat hitting a slow pitch; the force of the speeding car slammed us hard into the dashboard but not through the windshield and out onto the rocky shoulder, because, lucky for us, we were wearing our seat belts. The highway patrol, who arrived quickly on the scene, testified later at the other driver's trial that without question my dad and I would have been seriously injured, if not killed, had it not been for our seat belts restraining us in the front seat.

The story of the accident illustrates the writer's claim that seat belts can save lives; without such an example, the writer's statement would be only an unsupported generalization.

In addition to making general statements specific and thus more convincing, good examples can explain and clarify unfamiliar, abstract, or difficult concepts for the reader. For instance, Newton's law of gravity might be more easily understood once it is explained through the simple, familiar example of an apple falling from a tree.

Moreover, clear examples can add vivid details to your prose that hold the reader's attention while you explain your points. A general statement decrying animal abuse, for instance, may be more effective accompanied by several examples detailing the brutal treatment of one particular laboratory's research animals.

The use of good examples is not, however, limited only to exemplification essays. In reality, you will probably use examples in every essay you write. You couldn't, for instance, write an essay classifying kinds of popular teen movies without including examples to help identify your categories. Similarly, you couldn't write an essay defining the characteristics of a good teacher or comparing two schools without a generous use of specific illustration. Examples are essential in essays whose main purpose is evaluation—that is, essays that assert the advantages, benefits, or worth (or, conversely, the disadvantages or negative aspects) of a particular place, person, idea, or thing. An essay recommending your favorite restaurant, for instance, wouldn't be at all convincing without some examples of its delicious dishes.

To illustrate the importance of examples in all patterns of essay development, here are two excerpts from student essays. The first excerpt comes from an essay classifying the Native American eras at Mesa Verde National Park (pages 282–284). In his discussion of a particular time period, the writer uses Balcony House pueblo as an example illustrating the Ancestral Puebloans' skills in building construction.

> The third period lasted until 1300 C.E. and saw the innovation of pueblos, or groups of dwellings, instead of single-family units. Nearly eight hundred dwellings show the large number of people who inhabited the complex, tunneled houses, shops, storage rooms, courtyards, and community centers whose masonry walls, often elaborately decorated, were three and four stories high. At the spacious Balcony House pueblo, for example, an adobe court lies beneath another vaulted roof; on three sides stand two-story houses with balconies that lead from one room to the next. In back of the court is a spring, and along the front side is a low wall that kept the children from falling down the seven-hundred-foot cliff to the canyon floor below. Balcony House pueblo also contains two kivas, circular subterranean ceremonial chambers that show the importance of fellowship and religion to the people of this era.

Another student uses a personal example to help support a point in her essay that contrasts a local food co-op to a big chain grocery store. By using her friend's experience as an example, the writer shows the reader how a co-op can assist local producers in the community:

> Direct selling offers two advantages for producers: they get a better price for their wares than by selling them through wholesalers, and at the same time they establish an independent reputation for their business, which can be immensely valuable to their success later on. In Fort Collins, for example, Luna tofu (bean curd) stands out as an excellent illustration of this kind of mutual support. Several years ago my friend Carol Jones began making tofu in small batches to sell to the co-op as a way to earn a part-time income as well as to contribute to the co-op. Her enterprise has now grown so well that last year her husband quit his job to go into business with her full time. She currently sells to distributors and independent stores from here to Denver; even Lane Grocer, which earlier would not consider selling her tofu even on a trial basis, is now thinking about changing its policy.

Learning to support, explain, or clarify your assertions by clear, thoughtful examples will help you develop virtually every piece of writing you are assigned, both in school and on the job. Development by example is the most widely used of all the expository strategies and by far the most important.

Developing Your Essay

An essay developed by example is one of the easiest to organize. In most cases, your first paragraph will present your thesis; each body paragraph will contain a topic sentence and as many effectively arranged examples as necessary to explain or support each major point; your last paragraph will conclude your essay in some appropriate way. Although the general organization is fairly simple, you should revise the examples in your rough draft by considering the following suggestions.

Make sure your examples are relevant. Each specific example should support, clarify, or explain the general statement it illustrates; each example should provide readers with additional insight into the subject under discussion. Keep the purpose of your paragraphs in mind: don't wander off into an analysis of the causes of theft on your campus if you are only supposed to show various examples of it. Keep your audience in mind, too: which examples will provide the kinds of information that your particular readers need to understand your point?

Choose your examples carefully. To persuade your readers to accept your opinion, you should select those examples that are the strongest and most convincing. Let's say you were writing a research paper exposing a government agency's wastefulness. To illustrate your claim, you would select those cases that most obviously show gross or ridiculous expenditures rather than asking your readers to consider some unnecessary but minor expenses. And you would try to select cases that represent recent or current examples of wastefulness rather than discussing expenditures too dated to be persuasive. In other words, when you have a number of examples to choose from, evaluate them and then select the best ones to support your point.

Use enough examples to make your point clearly and persuasively. Put yourself in your reader's place: Would you be convinced with three brief examples? Five? One extended example? Two? Use your own judgment, but be careful to support or explain your major points adequately. It's better to risk over-explaining than to leave your reader confused or unconvinced.

Problems to Avoid

Avoid the use of examples that lack clear, specific details. Too often, novice writers present a sufficient number of relevant, well-chosen examples, but the illustrations themselves are too general, vague, or brief to be helpful. Examples should be clear, specific, and adequately detailed so that the reader receives the full persuasive impact of each one. For instance, in an essay claiming that junior high football has become too violent, don't merely say, "Too many players were hurt last year." Such a statement only hints; it lacks enough development to be fully effective. Go into more detail by giving actual examples of jammed fingers, wrenched backs, fractured legs, crushed kneecaps, and broken dreams. Present these examples in specific, vivid language; once your readers begin to "see" that field covered with blood and bruised bodies, you'll have less trouble convincing them that your point of view is accurate. (◆ For more help incorporating specific details into your paragraph development, review pages 61–65 in Chapter 3 and pages 166–168 in Chapter 7.)

Work to ensure coherence between your examples. The reader should never sense an interruption in the flow of thought from one example to the next in paragraphs containing multiple examples. Each body paragraph of this kind should be more than a topic sentence and a choppy list of examples. You should first arrange the examples in an order that best explains the major point presented by your topic sentence; then carefully check to make sure each example is smoothly connected in thought to the statements preceding and following it. You can avoid a listing effect by using transitional devices where necessary to ensure easy movement from example to example and from point to point. A few common transitional words often found in essays of example include "for instance," "for example," "to illustrate," "another," and "in addition." (◆ For a list of other transitional words and additional help on writing coherent paragraphs, review pages 70–76 and pages 79–80.)

Practicing What You've Learned

A. To practice developing examples that will strengthen your essay, try this activity. Select an important principle by which you live your life. It could be anything that informs your decision-making processes. It could be as simple as "waste not, want not." Next, think about what that principle really means. How would you explain it to someone else? In other words, how would you elaborate on the idea to make it clear to a listener or reader? Now begin to quickly list concise examples of that principle in action. When have you seen it proven true in your own life? What about in the lives of others? Finally, select the two or three examples that you feel best illustrate the truth of this principle and work to develop those illustrations into detailed extended examples.

B. *Collaborative Activity*: Pair off with a classmate and share the examples created in the previous activity. Evaluate each other's selected examples, taking into consideration relevance and level of detail. Provide evaluative feedback as needed. Encourage your partner to prioritize your examples based on relevance, appropriateness, and interest level.

Essay Topics

Consider one of the following eighteen general statements as a prompt to help you discover a focused essay topic of your own design, or choose one of the two more specific assignments, numbers 19 and 20. ◆ For additional ideas, turn to the "Suggestions for Writing" section following the professional essay (page 215); the quotations in the Assignment on pages 45–47 may also spark topics.

1. Failure is a better teacher than success.

2. First impressions are often the best/worst means of judging people.

3. Product X (e.g., smartphone, bicycle, e-reader, backpack) is the best choice in its field for college students.

4. Time spent on social networking sites interferes with/enhances good interpersonal skills.

5. The willingness to undertake adventure is a necessary part of a satisfying existence.

6. Complaining can produce unforeseen results.

7. Sometimes it's smart to ignore conventional wisdom.

8. Failure to keep my mouth shut (or some other bad habit) leads me into trouble.

9. Participation in (a sport, club, hobby, event) teaches valuable lessons.

10. Modern technology can produce more inconvenience than convenience.

11. Extensive research leads to more informed decision making and better results.

12. Moving frequently has its advantages (or disadvantages).

13. Good deeds can backfire (or make a wonderful difference).

14. Many required courses are/are not relevant to a student's education.

15. My hometown has much/little to offer young people.

16. One important event can change the course of a life.

17. Effective time management techniques can improve the first-year experience of incoming college students.

18. Working a job teaches valuable lessons not learned in school.

19. *Collaborative Activity:* With two classmates, brainstorm on the topic of time-management tips for college students. From your discussion, select one piece of good advice, and then choose at least two examples that most effectively show the benefit of your recommendation. Together, draft a one-page mini-essay presenting your suggestion to a group of incoming students.

20. To encourage people to use their products or services, companies often offer advertisements containing examples of satisfied customers or clients. Analyze the

continued on next page

ad that follows plus one of your own choosing that is also developed by examples. As you look at each ad, consider: How and why are the examples used? Are the examples well chosen for the particular target audience? Are there too many or too few? Overall, what part does the use of example play in the success of the ad? (Hint: In your search for other ads using examples, you might turn to pages 332–343 in this text for some possible choices.)

JACQUELINE GOLSON, CERVICAL CANCER

LUIS RIVERA, BRAIN CANCER

PATTY HILL, PANCREATIC CANCER

SANDY PIERCE, MELANOMA

Cancer strikes indiscriminately. When it does, it's critical to choose the best team possible to help you in your battle. These people were once faced with just such decisions. They didn't ask for cancer. But they did ask lots of questions. And in doing so, they chose the nation's number-one rated cancer hospital as their ally. It's a decision they'll celebrate for the rest of their lives.

THE UNIVERSITY OF TEXAS
MD ANDERSON
CANCER CENTER
Making Cancer History®

WHEN YOU'RE READY TO FIGHT, CALL 1-800-392-1611 OR VISIT WWW.MDANDERSON.ORG. RATED THE NUMBER-ONE CANCER HOSPITAL IN AMERICA BY *U.S. NEWS & WORLD REPORT.*

Courtesy of M.D. Anderson Cancer Center

A Topic Proposal for Your Essay

Selecting the right subject matter is important to every writer. To help you clarify your ideas and strengthen your commitment to your topic, here is a proposal sheet that asks you to describe some of your preliminary ideas about your subject before you begin drafting. Although your ideas may change as you draft (they will almost certainly become more refined), thinking through your choice of topic now may help you avoid several false starts.

1. In a few words, identify the subject of your essay as you have narrowed and focused it for this assignment. Write a rough statement of your opinion or attitude toward this topic.

2. Why are you interested in this topic? Do you have a personal or professional connection to the subject? State at least one reason for your choice of topic.

3. Is this a significant topic of interest to others? Why? Who specifically might find it interesting, informative, or entertaining?

4. Describe in one or two sentences the primary effect you would like to have on your audience. After they read your essay, what do you want your audience to think, feel, or do? (In other words, what is your *purpose* in writing this essay?)

5. Writers use examples to explain and clarify their ideas. Briefly list two or three examples you might develop in your essay to support discussion of your chosen topic.

6. What difficulties, if any, might this topic present during your drafting? For example, do you know enough about this topic to illustrate it with specific rather than vague examples? Might the topic still be too broad or unfocused for this assignment? Revise your topic now or make notes for an appropriate plan of action to resolve any difficulties you foresee.

Once you have chosen your topic, take a moment to read through Figure 9.1 (page 202) to remind yourself of key questions you should be asking at each stage of the writing process for your exemplification essay.

Sample Student Essay

Study the use of specific examples in the brief student essay that follows. If the writer were to revise this essay, where might he add more examples or details? How might he strengthen the introduction or conclusion to the essay?

If You Want to Get to Know a New Place, Go For a Run

Introduction: An anecdote that serves as a catchy lead-in

1   Imagine this scene: I'm in a new town, on a new campus, and I don't know anyone. Everything feels strange and foreign—the food seems weird, I've gotten lost twice already, and I miss home. All I want to do is curl up on the bed and not leave the dorm room where I've been staying for orientation. But instead, a little voice pipes in, and somehow I find myself back out on those unknown campus streets. I lace up my running shoes and hit the pavement, and gradually, my mood lifts. I notice shop fronts and food stands I make a mental note to revisit; the runner's high kicks in, and by the end, I don't feel quite as lost. The benefits of jogging in a new place provide a closer look at new surroundings, a positive feeling associated with exercise, and a familiar routine in an unfamiliar setting.

Thesis

Essay map

Paragraphs in the sample student essays are numbered for ease of discussion; do not number your own paragraphs.

2   The act of running somewhere new familiarizes the unfamiliar. On that college campus, for example, the first time I ran what would soon become "my" daily course, I felt uncertain about where I would end up and how I would get back. But the next time, I recognized the big old houses and stream running by the road, and with that recognition, I grew more confidence. This process allowed me to better orient myself to the new town where I lived, and in so doing, get to know my new home.

3   One of the most important benefits of running through a new place is the closer look you get from the ground. Tourists often ride buses or take taxis in new cities, hopping from one crowded attraction to the next. But there's more to a new city than the popular sites. When I was visiting my friend, who had just moved into her first off-campus apartment, we went out on a run, and we had time to see the neighborhoods more directly, and feel the streets beneath our feet. We noticed things off the beaten track we normally wouldn't have caught—like the abandoned factory on the side of the road, for example, because we needed to have landmarks so we could remember our way back. In addition, we could people-watch while we jogged: strollers, dog-walkers, other runners all passed by. My friend acclimated to her new part of town, and I got a closer glimpse of how it feels to actually live there, not just visit.

4   A bonus of taking in new scenery while running is the physical exercise you get. Research has shown cardio activity releases positive hormones and overall feelings of well-being. But a gym workout means you're stuck inside. When I started my new summer job, I was exhausted at the end of every work day. But I forced myself, when work was finished, to head into the park across the street with my coworker for a run, where we bonded while burning calories. Running provided us with the energy that I sorely needed after a long day at work, and it made us happy to discover the ins and outs of our office's surrounding environs.

Topic sentence 1: Running somewhere new familiarizes the unfamiliar

Two examples:
1. The first run
2. The second run

Topic sentence 2: Running somewhere new allows for a closer look at ground level

One example: Going for a run with a friend in new neighborhood

Topic sentence 3: Running is good physical exercise

Example: Going for a run after work with a coworker

Topic sentence 4: In a new location, getting lost can be a surprising adventure

5   Unlike my regular route, where I always do the same course over and over, in a new location, getting lost can be a surprising adventure. For example, on a trip to visit my grandparents, who were staying at a lake house, I found myself on a run lost in the woods, with darkness approaching. I hadn't seen another human in over an hour. I was filled with fear, but also deeply struck by the beautiful landscape around me—the thicket of trees and the silver lake somewhere beyond my sight range. I was forced to try and retrace my steps, and eventually stumbled back to the road and found my way back. The "lost" part of my run ended up being my favorite part— the quiet forest, the untouched trails—it felt like my secret garden.

Example: A trail run at the grandparents' lake house

Conclusion: Summary of the benefits

6   In conclusion, going running in a new place offers multiple benefits for better understanding the surroundings, and, even more importantly, better understanding ourselves.

PROFESSIONAL ESSAY*

So What's So Bad about Being So-So?

Lisa Wilson Strick

Lisa Wilson Strick is a freelance writer who publishes in a variety of magazines, frequently on the subjects of family and education. She is co-author of *Learning Disabilities: A to Z: A Complete Guide to Learning Disabilities from Preschool to Adulthood* (2010). This essay first appeared in *Woman's Day* in 1984.

Pre-reading Thoughts: As a participant in your favorite sport, game, or other recreational activity, does strong competition make you a better or worse player? Why?

1   The other afternoon I was playing the piano when my seven-year-old walked in. He stopped and listened awhile, then said: "Gee, Mom, you don't play that thing very well, do you?"

2   No, I don't. I am a piano lesson dropout. The fine points of fingering totally escape me. I play everything at half-speed, with many errant notes. My performance would make any serious music student wince, but I don't care. I've enjoyed playing the piano badly for years.

---

* ◆ To help you read this essay analytically, review pages 183–186.

3   I also enjoy singing badly and drawing badly. (I used to enjoy sewing badly, but I've been doing that so long that I finally got pretty good at it.) I'm not ashamed of my incompetence in these areas. I do one or two other things well and that should be enough for anybody. But it gets boring doing the same things over and over. Every now and then it's fun to try something new.

4   Unfortunately, doing things badly has gone out of style. It used to be a mark of class if a lady or a gentleman sang a little, painted a little, played the violin a little. You didn't have to be *good* at it; the point was to be fortunate enough to have the leisure time for such pursuits. But in today's competitive world we have to be "experts"—even in our hobbies. You can't tone up your body by pulling on your sneakers and slogging around the block a couple of times anymore. Why? Because you'll be laughed off the street by the "serious" runners—the ones who log twenty-plus miles a week in their headbands, sixty-dollar running suits and fancy shoes. The shoes are really a big deal. If you say you're thinking about taking up almost any sport, the first thing the aficionados will ask is what you plan to do about shoes. Leather or canvas? What type of soles? Which brand? This is not the time to mention that the gym shoes you wore in high school are still in pretty good shape. As far as sports enthusiasts are concerned, if you don't have the latest shoes you are hopelessly committed to mediocrity.

5   The runners aren't nearly so snobbish as the dance freaks, however. In case you didn't know, "going dancing" no longer means putting on a pretty dress and doing a few turns around the ballroom with your favorite man on Saturday night. "Dancing" means squeezing into tights and a leotard and leg warmers, then sweating through six hours of warm-ups and five hours of ballet and four hours of jazz classes. Every week. Never tell anyone that you "like to dance" unless this is the sort of activity you enjoy. (At least the costume isn't so costly, as dancers seem to be cultivating a riches-to-rags look lately.)

6   We used to do these things for fun or simply to relax. Now the competition you face in your hobbies is likely to be worse than anything you run into on the job. "Oh, you've taken up knitting," a friend recently said to me. "Let me show you the adorable cable-knit, popcorn-stitched cardigan with twelve tiny reindeer prancing across the yoke that I made for my daughter. I dyed the yarn myself." Now why did she have to go and do that? I was getting a kick out of watching my yellow stockinette muffler grow a couple of inches a week up till then. And all I wanted was something to keep my hands busy while I watched television anyway.

7   Have you noticed what this is doing to our children? "We don't want that dodo on our soccer team," I overheard a ten-year-old sneer the other day. "He doesn't know a goal kick from a head shot." As it happens, the boy was talking about my son, who did not—like some of his friends—start soccer instruction at age three (along with preschool diving, creative writing and Suzuki clarinet). I'm sorry, Son, I guess I blew it. In *my* day when we played softball on the corner lot, we expected to give a little instruction to the younger kids who didn't know how. It didn't matter if they were terrible; we weren't out to slaughter the other team. Sometimes we didn't even keep score. To us, sports were just a way of having a *good time*. Of course we didn't have some of the nifty things kids have today—such as matching uniforms and professional coaches. All we had was a bunch of kids of various ages who enjoyed each other's company.

8   I don't think kids have as much fun as they used to. Competition keeps getting in the way. The daughter of a neighbor is a nervous wreck worrying about getting into the *best*

gymnastics school. "I was a late starter," she told me, "and I only get to practice five or six hours a week, so my technique may not be up to their standards." The child is nine. She doesn't want to *be* a gymnast when she grows up; she wants to be a nurse. I asked what she likes to do for fun in her free time. She seemed to think it was an odd question. "Well, I don't actually *have* a lot of free time," she said. "I mean homework and gymnastics and flute lessons kind of eat it all up. I have flute lessons three times a week now, so I have a good shot at getting into the all-state orchestra."

9   Ambition, drive and the desire to excel are all admirable within limits, but I don't know where the limits are anymore. I know a woman who has always wanted to learn a foreign language. For years she has complained that she hasn't the time to study one. I've pointed out that an evening course in French or Italian would take only a couple of hours a week, but she keeps putting it off. I suspect that what she hasn't got the time for is to become completely fluent within the year—and that any lesser level of accomplishment would embarrass her. Instead she spends her evenings watching reruns on television and tidying up her closets—occupations at which no particular expertise is expected.

10   I know others who are avoiding activities they might enjoy because they lack the time or the energy to tackle them "seriously." It strikes me as so silly. We are talking about *recreation*. I have nothing against self-improvement. But when I hear a teenager muttering "practice makes perfect" as he grimly makes his four-hundred-and-twenty-seventh try at hooking the basketball into the net left-handed, I wonder if some of us aren't improving ourselves right into the loony bin.

11   I think it's time we put a stop to all this. For sanity's sake, each of us should vow to take up something new this week—and to make sure we never master it completely. Sing along with grand opera. Make peculiar-looking objects out of clay. I can tell you from experience that fallen soufflés still taste pretty good. The point is to enjoy being a beginner again; to rediscover the joy of creative fooling around. If you find it difficult, ask any two-year-old to teach you. Two-year-olds have a gift for tackling the impossible with zest; repeated failure hardly discourages them at all.

12   As for me, I'm getting a little out of shape so I'm looking into tennis. A lot of people I know enjoy it, and it doesn't look too hard. Given a couple of lessons I should be stumbling gracelessly around the court and playing badly in no time at all.

QUESTIONS ON CONTENT, STRUCTURE, AND STYLE

1. Why does Strick begin her essay with the comment from her son and the list of activities she does badly?

2. What is Strick's thesis? Is it specifically stated or clearly implied?

3. What examples does Strick offer to illustrate her belief that we no longer take up hobbies for fun? Are there enough well-chosen examples to make her position clear?

4. What is the effect, according to Strick, of too much competition on kids? In what ways does she show this effect?

5. Does Strick use enough details in her examples to make them clear, vivid, and persuasive? Point out some of her details to support your answer.

6. What does Strick gain by using dialogue in some of her examples?

7. What solution to the problem does Strick offer? How does she clarify her suggestion?

8. Characterize the tone of Strick's essay. Is it appropriate for her purpose and for her intended audience? Why, or why not?

9. Evaluate Strick's conclusion. Does it effectively wrap up the essay?

10. Do you agree or disagree with Strick? What examples could you offer to support your position?

VOCABULARY*

errant (2)

aficionados (4)

fluent (9)

incompetence (3)

mediocrity (4)

zest (11)

SUGGESTIONS FOR WRITING

Try using Lisa Strick's essay "So What's So Bad about Being So-So?" as a stepping-stone, moving from one or more of her ideas to a subject for your own essay. For instance, you might write an essay based on your personal experience that illustrates or challenges Strick's view that competition is taking all the fun out of recreation. Or perhaps Strick's advice urging her readers to undertake new activities might lead you to an essay about your best or worst "beginner" experience. Look through Strick's essay once more to find other springboard ideas for *your* writing.

A Revision Worksheet

As you write your rough drafts, consult Chapter 5 for guidance through the revision process. In addition, here are a few questions to ask yourself as you revise your example essay:

1. Is the essay's thesis clear to the reader?

2. Do the topic sentences support the thesis?

3. Does each body paragraph contain examples that effectively illustrate the claim of the topic sentence rather than offering mere generalities?

4. Are there enough well-chosen examples to make each point clear and convincing?

5. Is each example developed in enough specific detail? Where could more details be added? More precise language?

6. If a paragraph contains multiple examples, are they arranged in the most effective order, with a smooth transition from one to another?

7. If a paragraph contains an extended example, does the discussion flow logically and with coherence?

Collaborative Activity: After you've revised your essay extensively, exchange rough drafts with a classmate and answer these questions for each other, making specific suggestions for improvement wherever appropriate. (◆ For advice on productive participation in classroom workshops, see pages 121–123.)

---

*Numbers in parentheses following vocabulary words refer to paragraphs in the essay.

Using Strategies and Sources

The following assignments ask you to not only incorporate what you've learned in this chapter regarding exemplification, but also to employ other strategies of development and to incorporate secondary sources into your response.

1. In a brief exemplification essay, explore the old adage that "if there is time enough to do it twice, there's time enough to do it right." Specifically, use example stories to support the truth of this old saying. Make sure to employ the techniques of good narration for each of these anecdotes.

2. Consider your favorite painting, sculpture, song, movie, or any other favorite piece of art. Next, in a brief example essay, explain to your audience why this piece is your favorite. Using narration and detailed description, provide an account of your first encounter with this piece and examples of the criteria by which you have established this work as your favorite.

3. Think about the use of technology as a teaching tool in your educational experience. Virtually every college course now requires you to use a computer in some fashion, and classroom experiences are often enriched through the use of presentation software, audio/video segments, and even simulators. Much debate has occurred regarding the benefits and liabilities of such technology. Supporters trumpet technology's ability to provide cash-strapped programs and institutions with affordable access to world-class digital resources, while detractors cite the "dumbing down" influence of PowerPoint and the screen-induced shortening of the average attention span. Write an exemplification essay in which you assert that technology either improves or weakens the educational process. Conduct research to incorporate information from credible secondary sources in support of your claim. (◆ See Chapter 19 for help with conducting research and evaluating the sources you find.)

Chapter 10

Process Analysis

You may recall from the discussion in Chapter 9 that expository writing refers to prose whose primary purpose is giving information. As earlier noted, there are many different strategies for accomplishing this purpose. One such strategy is process analysis; process analysis identifies and explains what steps must be taken to complete an operation or procedure. There are two kinds of process analysis essays: directional and informative. Following a writing process like that represented in Figure 10.1 will help you develop effective process analysis essays.

Types of Process Analysis Essays

A *directional process* tells the reader how to do or make something. In simple words, it gives directions. You are more familiar with directional process than you might think. For example, when you tell friends how to find your house, you're asking them to follow a directional process. When you use a computer, you can learn how to transfer files or download attachments or any one of hundreds of other options by following step-by-step directions often found in a "Help" menu. The most widely read books in American libraries fall into the how-to-do-it (or how-to-fix-it) category: how to wire a house, how to repair a car, how to play winning poker, how to save more money, and so forth. And almost every home contains at least one cookbook full of recipes providing directions for preparing various dishes. (Even Part One of this text is, in detailed fashion, a directional process telling how to write a short essay, beginning with the selection of a topic and concluding with advice on revision.)

An *informative process* tells the reader how something is or was made or done or how something works. Informative process differs from directional process in that it is not designed primarily to tell people how to do it; instead, it describes the steps by which someone other than the reader does or makes something (or how something was made or done in the past). For example, an informative process essay might describe how scientists discovered the polio vaccine, how a bill passes through Congress, how chewing gum is made, how contact lenses were invented, or how an engine propels a jet. In other words, this type of essay gives information on processes that are not intended to be—or cannot be—duplicated by the individual reader.

Figure 10.1 VISUALIZING THE PROCESS: PROCESS ANALYSIS

Prewriting

Identify possible subjects by considering the following questions:

- Do you want to tell your readers how to do something (directional process) or explain how something works (informative process)?
- How well do you understand the steps in the process you've selected?
- Is the process you've selected simple and short enough to describe in detail?
- Are you professionally or personally interested in the topic?

Drafting

Determine the elements of your process essay by asking the following questions:

- What is the audience's knowledge level?
- What equipment or special terms will need to be described or defined for the audience?
- What steps need to be included in order to give the readers a clear understanding of the process?
- Is any additional research needed to accurately present the steps in the process?

Revising

Carefully review the content and organization of your essay by asking the following questions:

- Does your essay begin with a clear thesis?
- Do the steps follow a logical order?
- Is each step clearly, sufficiently, and accurately described or explained?
- If writing a directional process essay, do you provide warnings to help readers avoid missteps? Does it provide descriptions of errors and how to correct them?

Editing/Proofreading

Consider the sentence-level issues of your essay by asking the following questions:

- Did you use transitions between your steps to avoid creating a mechanical list?
- Have you reviewed your sentences for spelling, grammar, and punctuation errors?
- Is your paper formatted according to assignment guidelines?

Developing Your Essay

Of all the expository essays, students usually agree that the process paper is the easiest to organize, mainly because its material is most often presented in a logical, chronological (time-ordered) sequence. To prepare a well-written process essay, you should remember the following advice:

Select an appropriate subject. First, make sure you know your subject thoroughly; one fuzzy step could wreck your entire process. Second, choose a process that is simple and short enough to describe in detail. In a 500- to 800-word essay, for instance, it's better to describe how to build a ship in a bottle than how to construct a life-size replica of Noah's Ark. On the other hand, don't choose a process so simpleminded, mundane, or mechanical that it insults your readers' intelligence or bores them silly ("How to Boil Water"). Be sensitive to the needs, experience, and knowledge of the audience you wish to address; an essay offering advice for purchasing a bicycle to parents buying a first bike for a child would differ in significant ways from an essay directed at a skilled adult rider.

Describe any necessary equipment and define special terms. In some process essays, you will need to indicate what equipment, ingredients, or tools are required. Such information is often provided in a paragraph following the thesis, before the process itself is described; in other cases, the explanation of proper equipment is presented as the need arises in each step of the process. As the writer, you must decide which method is best for your subject. The same is true for any terms that need defining. Don't lose your reader by using terms only you, the specialist, can comprehend. Always remember that you're trying to tell people about a process they don't know or understand.

Include all the necessary steps in a logical order. Obviously, if someone wanted to know how to bake bread, you wouldn't begin with "Put the prepared dough in the oven." Start at the beginning and carefully follow through, step by step, until the process is completed. In many "how to do or make" essays, the subject matter will necessitate a strict adherence to a chronological order to ensure that the proper result is achieved; think, for example, of a magic trick whose progress must be carried out precisely from A to B to C. In other essays, you may have to choose the most effective order of the information you present. In an essay offering college students a plan for creating a better diet, some of the steps might be accomplished at the same time or in a slightly different order without sabotaging the process, so you must select the best organization. What is important, in any kind of process essay, is that your readers see a logical progression of thought, not just pieces of information in a random or confusing order.

Don't omit any necessary steps or directions, no matter how insignificant or obvious they might seem to you, the expert. Without complete instructions, for example, the baker mentioned previously might end up with a gob of sticky dough rather than a crusty loaf of bread—simply because the directions didn't say to pre-heat the oven to a certain temperature.

Explain each step clearly, sufficiently, and accurately. If you've ever tried to assemble a child's toy or a piece of furniture, you probably already know how frustrating—and infuriating—it is to work from vague, inadequate directions. Save your readers from tears and tantrums by describing each step in your process as clearly as possible. Use enough specific details to distinguish one step from another. As the readers finish each step, they should know how the subject matter is supposed to look, feel, smell, taste, or sound—whatever is appropriate—at that stage of the process. You might also explain why a particular step is necessary ("Cutting back the young avocado stem is necessary to prevent a spindly plant"; "Senator Snort then had to win over the chair of the Arms Committee to be sure his bill would go to the Senate floor for a vote"). In some cases, especially in directional processes, it's helpful to give warnings ("When you begin tightrope walking, the condition of your shoes is critical; make sure the soles are not uneven or slick") or descriptions of errors and how to rectify them ("If you pass a white church, you've gone a block too far, so turn right at the church and circle back on Candle Lane"; "If the sauce appears thin, add one teaspoon more of cornstarch to thicken the gravy").

Organize your steps effectively. If you have a few big steps in your process, you might devote a paragraph to each one. On the other hand, if you have many small steps, you might organize them into several manageable units. For example, in the essay "How to Prepare Fresh Fish," the list of small steps on the left has been grouped into three larger units, each of which becomes a body paragraph:

1. scaling	I. Cleaning
2. beheading	A. scaling
3. gutting	B. beheading
4. washing	C. gutting
5. seasoning	II. Cooking
6. breading	A. washing
7. frying	B. seasoning
8. draining	C. breading
9. portioning	D. frying
10. garnishing	III. Serving
	A. draining
	B. portioning
	C. garnishing

In addition, don't forget to use enough transitional devices between steps to avoid the effect of a mechanical list. Some frequently used linking words in process essays include the following:

next	first, second, third, etc.
then	at this point
now	following
to begin	when
finally	at last
before	afterward

Vary your transitional words sufficiently so that your steps are not linked by a monotonous repetition of "and then" or "next."

Problems to Avoid

Don't forget to include a thesis. You already know, of course, that every essay needs a thesis, but the advice bears repeating here because for some reason some writers often omit this statement in their process essays. Your thesis might be (1) your reason for presenting this process—why you feel it's important or necessary for the readers to know it ("Because rescue squads often arrive too late, every adult should know how to administer CPR to accident victims") or (2) an assertion about the nature of the process itself ("Needlepoint is a simple, restful, fun hobby for both men and women"). Here are some other subjects and sample theses:

- Donating blood is not the painful process one might suspect.
- The raid on Pearl Harbor wasn't altogether unexpected.
- Returning to school as an older-than-average student isn't as difficult as it may look.
- Sponsoring a five-mile run can be a fun way for your club or student organization to raise money for local charities.
- Challenging an undeserved speeding ticket can be a time-consuming, energy-draining, but financially rewarding endeavor.
- The series of escalating demonstrations outside the White House influenced the 1920 passage of the Nineteenth Amendment, giving American women the right to vote.

Presenting a thesis and referring to it appropriately gives your essay unity and coherence, as well as ensuring against a monotonous list of steps.

Pay special attention to your conclusion. Don't allow your essay to grind to an abrupt halt after the final step. You might conclude the essay by telling the significance of the completed process or by explaining other uses it may have. Or, if it is appropriate, finish your essay with an amusing story or emphatic comment. However you conclude, leave the reader with a feeling of satisfaction, with a sense of having completed an interesting procedure. (◆ For more information on writing good conclusions, see pages 88–91.)

Practicing What You've Learned

A. To practice selecting a manageable topic for your process essay, try this activity. Brainstorm a list of five processes about which you know a significant amount of information. The list could include both directional and informative processes. Next, consider the major

continued on next page

steps involved in the completion of each of these processes. Do you know all of the steps? Are there any steps about which you're a little fuzzy? Now, create a brief outline of the major steps for each of these processes. Is your outline comprehensive? Will it provide a reader with a clear overview of the entire process?

B. *Collaborative Activity:* Pair off with a classmate and exchange the outlined list of processes that you created in Exercise A. Review each other's outlines for clarity and completion. Do all of the steps make sense to you? If the outline is for a directional process, would you feel confident about carrying out the outlined process? If the outline is for an informative process, do you now possess a clear understanding of how the process works? Indicate to your partner any potential points of confusion and any lingering questions you may have. Finally, provide feedback to your partner about which process is most interesting and why.

Essay Topics

Here are suggested topics for both directional and informative process essays. Some of the topics may be used in humorous essays, such as "How to Flunk a Test," "How to Remain a Bench Warmer," or "How to Say Nothing in Eight Hundred Words." ◆ For additional ideas, turn to the "Suggestions for Writing" sections following the professional essays (page 232 and page 235).

1. How you arrived at a major decision or solved an important problem

2. How to survive the first week of college

3. How to begin a collection or hobby, acquire a skill, or achieve a certification

4. How to select the best computer, smartphone, media player, camera, game console, or other product for your specific needs

5. How a particular scientific process works or occurs

6. How to manage stress, stage fright, homesickness, or an irrational fear

7. How something in nature works or was formed

8. How you learned to drive (or mastered some other complex activity)

9. How a piece of equipment, a machine, or a product works

10. How you made the decision to attend the college in which you're currently enrolled

11. How to lose weight or increase muscle mass

12. How to stop smoking (or break some other bad habit)

13. How to select a car (new or used), house, apartment, roommate

14. How to earn money quickly or easily (and legally)

continued on next page

15. How a famous invention or discovery occurred

16. How to lodge a complaint and win

17. How to succeed or fail in a job or class (or in some other important endeavor)

18. How to build or repair a household item or create something online (e.g., blog, Web site, social media page)

19. How to plan the perfect party, holiday, birthday, or road trip

20. How a historical event occurred or an important law was passed (e.g., Rosa Parks's arrest; the 1773 Boston Tea Party; the passage of Title IX, ensuring equal athletic opportunities for female students)

Rosa Parks, whose refusal to give up her seat in Montgomery, Alabama in 1955, helped to ignite the Civil Rights Movement.

A Topic Proposal for Your Essay

Selecting the right subject matter is important to every writer. To help you clarify your ideas and strengthen your commitment to your topic, here is a proposal sheet that asks you to describe some of your preliminary ideas about your subject before you begin drafting. Although your ideas may change as you write (they will almost certainly become more refined), thinking through your choice of topic now may help you avoid several false starts.

1. What process will you explain in your essay? Is it a directional or an informative process? Can you address the complexity of this process in a short essay?

2. Why did you select this topic? Are you personally or professionally interested in this process? Cite at least one reason for your choice.

3. Why do you think this topic would be of interest to others? Who might find it especially informative or enjoyable?

4. Describe in one or two sentences the ideal response from your readers. What would you like them to do or know after reading about your topic?

5. List at least three of the larger steps or stages in the process.

6. What difficulties might this topic present during your drafting? Will this topic require any additional research on your part?

Once you have chosen your topic, take a moment to read through Figure 10.1 (page 218) to remind yourself of key questions you should be asking at each stage of the writing process for your process analysis essay.

Sample Student Essay

The following essay is a directional process telling readers how to spend seven days tracking the money that they spend and taking steps to spend as little money as possible. To make the instructions clear and enjoyable, the writer described six steps and offered many specific examples, details, and warnings. Of particular note is the essay's organization. Though this essay's steps could be rearranged without impacting the process's outcome, the author has been careful to include transitions that establish a logical progression through the essay's steps and help to avoid reader confusion.

An Experiment in Spending Less

Introduction: The author starts with an appeal to a common experience

1   For most of us, cash (and credit) is spent without much thinking about it: a granola bar one afternoon between classes, a cheap umbrella on a rainy day when you forgot yours at home, breakfast with a friend you've been wanting to catch up with. Sometimes, it feels like it would be just as useful to drop your cash on the bank floor right after you take it out.

Introduction continued

Thesis is implied and in the form of a question

2   But what would happen if, for seven days, you focused on consciously not spending money unconsciously? You would certainly see where your cash was mysteriously disappearing to. Would you have to stay home, miserable, while your friends had more fun? No! With a little planning and help from those who often help you spend it, purposefully suspending your cash flow might be easier than you think. It might even be fun.

Step one: Choose a week that holds the greatest potential for success

3   The first and perhaps most important step to having fun without your money is to choose a week that will give you the greatest chance of success. Try to avoid weeks where friends or family are visiting or a birthday is happening. But don't worry if it's rent week or when your car payment is due; fixed expenses can't be ignored even for this experiment. But think about what can be skipped or delayed for one week. Do you *need* to refill your car with gas? Could you walk instead, or take a free shuttle to campus, or bike? Know your limits. If driving takes twenty minutes and walking takes seventy, you'll set yourself up to fail. The goal is stick to your plan,

not make yourself crazy. Remember, this is a seven-day experiment, not your last week on Earth. Next week, you can get a cup of coffee, go out with a friend, buy a new shirt. Everything will still be there when the week is out.

4   Having fun with or without money is easier with friends, so your next move is to think of your most creative, positive, and perhaps competitive people you know and ask them to join you in your experiment. This can be someone who lives near you, or someone you can check in with over phone or e-mail. Don't be afraid to talk up your experiment; you might be surprised who is up for the challenge. You can work with your friend to come up with a list of activities together, or ask each other to come up with something small to teach each other: how to cook the perfect pot of rice, build a simple Web site, or juggle. It should be something you can do together for a few hours.

5   Next, spend a few hours looking through your closets, cabinets, and e-mails. Getting through your chosen week will be about relying on what you already have, from food to activities. On the school meal plan? That's your three meals a day (and maybe take a banana back with you from breakfast). Maybe a friend offered to take you out for lunch or a drink, and you can ask them to do that this week. If you find a big bag of rice in the back of your cupboard, look up different recipes you can make with it. If you already belong to a gym or have paid for a movie service, get the most out of it this week by planning an extra gym day or an afternoon watching two films you've never seen before.

6   If you know that being out is what makes you spend money, then you'll likely want to stay home. But remember, the point of the experiment is to still have fun, so your next planning task is to find out what's going on for free where you live. Check that bulletin board at the coffee shop, events at the library, the parks department, fliers on lampposts. Be adventurous. If something sounds even sort

Note the author's use of transitional words like "first" and "next"

Step two: Ask friends to join in the experiment

Step three: Take stock of and use what you already have

Step four: Find out what is going on for free where you live

of interesting, go! Remember, it's free, and you have nothing to lose. Depending on the season and where you live, you'd be surprised to find what free activities take place over one week: nature walks in parks, stargazing at the campus telescope, Wii bowling at the library. If you love cats, maybe go to an animal shelter and visit with them. This is also a good week to teach yourself something new or get back into an old habit. Did you used to take a lot of photographs? Plan an afternoon exploring with your camera. Have you always wanted to learn how to bake a pie? Make a perfect paper airplane? The library is full of non-fiction and how-to books. Spend the week reading everything you can about baking a pie; save the baking for next week, unless you have the ingredients on hand.

Step five: Consider your spending triggers

7   Don't forget to consider your spending triggers, and make plans around them. If certain nights, like Fridays, are ones when you are usually too tired to cook and end up eating out, anticipate how you'll avoid that—have you found an event with free food? Cooking something on Thursday you'd love to eat the leftovers of on Friday? If someone asks you to do something that you know involves spending money, ask them to reschedule to the next week or to come over for a potluck meal instead. When you do go out, consider filling your wallet with just what you need for the day ahead: your identification, a public transportation pass, and one emergency item: a small amount of cash, or a credit card you really don't want to have to use. Make it hard for yourself. If your home is within a quick trip of your school or work, consider leaving this last item at home all together: nothing like walking fifteen minutes each way to get cash to buy a cookie to cure you wanting to buy a cookie.

Step six: Take care of emergencies as they arise

8   Of course, emergencies can and will happen: your dog gets sick, your car battery dies, your lunch gets stolen by a squirrel with only twenty minutes before your next class. Take care of what you need to, but don't let it be a slippery slope to going off-plan. Instead, let it be a reminder that having money to spare when you really need

it (like when your dog has swallowed half a tennis ball and needs emergency surgery) is a bonus of saving money when you don't need to spend it.

9   At the end of seven days, reflect on your week and your wallet. If your goal is savings, maybe keep a record of what you're *not* spending: noticing the times when you would have pulled out your wallet but didn't. If your goal is finding out other ways to keep yourself busy, reflect on something you've learned in your week: who shows free movies, or how long it's been since you've been swimming. What would you do again? What did you miss? Maybe you found eating in on Friday night torture but walking to school a great way to clear your mind before class. Try and carry one of your free habits forward. If you've done the experiment with a buddy, check in with them. Over all that leftover food from the big pot of rice you made that week. Or a pizza out. Your choice. We won't judge.

Conclusion: Evaluate the results of the experiment

The author poses questions to encourage the reader's reflection

Professional Essays

Because there are two kinds of process essays, informative and directional, this section presents two professional essays so that each type is illustrated.

I. THE INFORMATIVE PROCESS ESSAY*
To Bid the World Farewell

Jessica Mitford

As an investigative reporter, Jessica Mitford wrote many articles and books, including *Kind and Unusual Punishment: The Prison Business* (1973), *A Fine Old Conflict* (1977), *Poison Penmanship* (1979), and *The American Way of Birth* (1992). This essay is from her best-selling book *The American Way of Death* (1963), which Mitford began revising before she died in 1996. *The American Way of Death Revisited* was completed by her husband Robert Trehaft and published in 1998.

---

* ◆ To help you read this essay analytically, review pages 183–186.

Pre-reading Thoughts: Investigative reporting can reveal disturbing details. Have you ever read a journalistic investigation, or perhaps watched a documentary, that changed your mind about a product, activity, or person?

1   Embalming is indeed a most extraordinary procedure, and one must wonder at the docility of Americans who each year pay hundreds of millions of dollars for its perpetuation, blissfully ignorant of what it is all about, what is done, how it is done. Not one in ten thousand has any idea of what actually takes place. Books on the subject are extremely hard to come by. They are not to be found in most libraries or bookshops.

2   In an era when huge television audiences watch surgical operations in the comfort of their living rooms, when, thanks to the animated cartoon, the geography of the digestive system has become familiar territory even to the nursery school set, and in a land where the satisfaction of curiosity about almost all matters is a national pastime, the secrecy surrounding embalming can, surely, hardly be attributed to the inherent gruesomeness of the subject. Custom in this regard has within this century suffered a complete reversal. In the early days of American embalming, when it was performed in the home of the deceased, it was almost mandatory for some relative to stay by the embalmer's side and witness the procedure. Today, family members who might wish to be in attendance would certainly be dissuaded by the funeral director. All others, except apprentices, are excluded by law from the preparation room.

3   A close look at what does actually take place may explain in large measure the undertaker's intractable reticence concerning a procedure that has become his major *raison d'être*. Is it possible he fears that public information about embalming might lead patrons to wonder if they really want this service? If the funeral men are loath to discuss the subject outside the trade, the reader may, understandably, be equally loath to go on reading at this point. For those who have the stomach for it, let us part the formaldehyde curtain. . . .

4   The body is first laid out in the undertaker's morgue—or rather, Mr. Jones is reposing in the preparation room—to be readied to bid the world farewell.

5   The preparation room in any of the better funeral establishments has the tiled and sterile look of a surgery, and indeed the embalmer-restorative artist who does his chores there is beginning to adopt the term "dermasurgeon" (appropriately corrupted by some mortician-writers as "demisurgeon") to describe his calling. His equipment, consisting of scalpels, scissors, augers, forceps, clamps, needles, pumps, tubes, bowls and basins, is crudely imitative of the surgeon's as is his technique, acquired in a nine- or twelve-month post-high-school course in an embalming school. He is supplied by an advanced chemical industry with a bewildering array of fluids, sprays, pastes, oils, powders, creams, to fix or soften tissue, shrink or distend it as needed, dry it here, restore the moisture there. There are cosmetics, waxes and paints to fill and cover features, even plaster of Paris to replace entire limbs. There are ingenious aids to prop and stabilize the cadaver: a Vari-Pose Head Rest, the Edwards Arm and Hand Positioner, the Repose Block (to support the shoulders during the embalming), and the Throop Foot Positioner, which resembles an old-fashioned stocks.

6   Mr. John H. Eckels, president of the Eckels College of Mortuary Science, thus describes the first part of the embalming procedure: "In the hands of a skilled practitioner, this

work may be done in a comparatively short time and without mutilating the body other than by slight incision—so slight that it scarcely would cause serious inconvenience if made upon a living person. It is necessary to remove the blood, and doing this not only helps in the disinfecting, but removes the principal cause of disfigurement due to discoloration."

7   Another textbook discusses the all-important time element: "The earlier this is done, the better, for every hour that elapses between death and embalming will add to the problems and complications encountered. . . ." Just how soon should one get going on the embalming? The author tells us, "On the basis of such scanty information made available to this profession through its rudimentary and haphazard system of technical research, we must conclude that the best results are to be obtained if the subject is embalmed before life is completely extinct—that is, before cellular death has occurred. In the average case, this would mean within an hour after somatic death." For those who feel that there is something a little rudimentary, not to say haphazard, about this advice, a comforting thought is offered by another writer. Speaking of fears entertained in early days of premature burial, he points out, "One of the effects of embalming by chemical injection, however, has been to dispel fears of live burial." How true; once the blood is removed, chances of live burial are indeed remote.

8   To return to Mr. Jones, the blood is drained out through the veins and replaced by embalming fluid pumped in through the arteries. As noted in *The Principles and Practices of Embalming*, "every operator has a favorite injection and drainage point—a fact which becomes a handicap only if he fails or refuses to forsake his favorites when conditions demand it." Typical favorites are the carotid artery, femoral artery, jugular vein, subclavian vein. There are various choices of embalming fluid. If Flextone is used, it will produce a "mild flexible rigidity. The skin retains a velvety softness, the tissues are rubbery and pliable. Ideal for women and children." It may be blended with B. and G. Products Company's Lyf-Lyk tint, which is guaranteed to reproduce "nature's own skin texture . . . the velvety appearance of living tissue." Suntone comes in three separate tints: Suntan; Special Cosmetic Tint, a pink shade "especially indicated for young female subjects"; and Regular Cosmetic Tint, moderately pink.

9   About three to six gallons of a dyed and perfumed solution of formaldehyde, glycerin, borax, phenol, alcohol and water is soon circulating through Mr. Jones, whose mouth has been sewn together with a "needle directed upward between the upper lip and gum and brought out through the left nostril," with the corners raised slightly "for a more pleasant expression." If he should be bucktoothed, his teeth are cleaned with Bon Ami and coated with colorless nail polish. His eyes, meanwhile, are closed with flesh-tinted eye caps and eye cement.

10   The next step is to have at Mr. Jones with a thing called a trocar. This is a long, hollow needle attached to a tube. It is jabbed into the abdomen, poked around the entrails and chest cavity, the contents of which are pumped out and replaced with "cavity fluid." This done, and the hole in the abdomen sewn up, Mr. Jones' face is heavily creamed (to protect the skin from burns which may be caused by leakage of the chemicals), and he is covered with a sheet and left unmolested for a while. But not for long—there is more, much more, in store for him. He has been embalmed, but not yet restored, and the best time to start the restorative work is eight to ten hours after embalming, when the tissues have become firm and dry.

11   The object of all this attention to the corpse, it must be remembered, is to make it presentable for viewing in an attitude of healthy repose. "Our customs require the presentation of our dead in the semblance of normality . . . unmarred by the ravages of illness, disease or mutilation," says Mr. J. Sheridan Mayer in his *Restorative Art*. This is rather a large order since few people die in the full bloom of health, unravaged by illness and unmarked by some disfigurement. The funeral industry is equal to the challenge: "In some cases the gruesome appearance of a mutilated or disease-ridden subject may be quite discouraging. The task of restoration may seem impossible and shake the confidence of the embalmer. This is the time for intestinal fortitude and determination. Once the formative work is begun and affected tissues are cleaned or removed, all doubts of success vanish. It is surprising and gratifying to discover the results which may be obtained."

12   The embalmer, having allowed an appropriate interval to elapse, returns to the attack, but now he brings into play the skill and equipment of sculptor and cosmetician. Is a hand missing? Casting one in plaster of Paris is a simple matter. "For replacement purposes, only a cast of the back of the hand is necessary; this is within the ability of the average operator and is quite adequate." If a lip or two, a nose or an ear should be missing, the embalmer has at hand a variety of restorative waxes with which to model replacements. Pores and skin texture are simulated by stippling with a little brush, and over this cosmetics are laid on. Head off? Decapitation cases are rather routinely handled. Ragged edges are trimmed, and head joined to torso with a series of splints, wires and sutures. It is a good idea to have a little something at the neck—a scarf or high collar—when time for viewing comes. Swollen mouth? Cut out tissue as needed from inside the lips. If too much is removed, the surface contour can easily be restored by padding with cotton. Swollen necks and cheeks are reduced by removing tissue through vertical incisions made down each side of the neck. "When the deceased is casketed, the pillow will hide the suture incisions . . . as an extra precaution against leakage, the suture may be painted with liquid sealer."

13   The opposite condition is more likely to present itself—that of emaciation. His hypodermic syringe now loaded with massage cream, the embalmer seeks out and fills the hollowed and sunken areas by injection. In this procedure the backs of the hands and fingers and the under-chin area should not be neglected.

14   Positioning the lips is a problem that recurrently challenges the ingenuity of the embalmer. Closed too tightly, they tend to give a stern, even disapproving expression. Ideally, embalmers feel, the lips should give the impression of being ever so slightly parted, the upper lip protruding slightly for a more youthful appearance. This takes some engineering, however, as the lips tend to drift apart. Lip drift can sometimes be remedied by pushing one or two straight pins through the inner margin of the lower lip and then inserting them between the two front teeth. If Mr. Jones happens to have no teeth, the pins can just as easily be anchored in his Armstrong Face Former and Denture Replacer. Another method to maintain lip closure is to dislocate the lower jaw, which is then held in its new position by a wire run through holes which have been drilled through the upper and lower jaws at the midline. As the French are fond of saying, *il faut souffrir pour être belle.**

15   If Mr. Jones has died of jaundice, the embalming fluid will very likely turn him green. Does this deter the embalmer? Not if he has intestinal fortitude. Masking pastes and cosmetics are heavily laid on, burial garments and casket interiors are color-correlated

---

* "One must suffer to be beautiful."

with particular care, and Jones is displayed beneath rose-colored lights. Friends will say, "How *well* he looks." Death by carbon monoxide, on the other hand, can be rather a good thing from the embalmer's viewpoint: "One advantage is the fact that this type of discoloration is an exaggerated form of a natural pink coloration." This is nice because the healthy glow is already present and needs but little attention.

16   The patching and filling completed, Mr. Jones is now shaved, washed and dressed. Cream-based cosmetic, available in pink, flesh, suntan, brunette and blond, is applied to his hands and face, his hair is shampooed and combed (and, in the case of Mrs. Jones, set), his hands manicured. For the horny-handed son of toil special care must be taken; cream should be applied to remove ingrained grime, and the nails cleaned. "If he were not in the habit of having them manicured in life, trimming and shaping is advised for better appearance—never questioned by kin."

17   Jones is now ready for casketing (this is the present participle of the verb "to casket"). In this operation his right shoulder should be depressed slightly "to turn the body a bit to the right and soften the appearance of lying flat on the back." Positioning the hands is a matter of importance, and special rubber positioning blocks may be used. The hands should be cupped slightly for a more lifelike, relaxed appearance. Proper placement of the body requires a delicate sense of balance. It should lie as high as possible in the casket, yet not so high that the lid, when lowered, will hit the nose. On the other hand, we are cautioned, placing the body too low "creates the impression that the body is in a box."

18   Jones is next wheeled into the appointed slumber room where a few last touches may be added—his favorite pipe placed in his hand or, if he was a great reader, a book propped into position. (In the case of little Master Jones a Teddy bear may be clutched.) Here he will hold open house for a few days, visiting hours 10 A.M. to 9 P.M.

QUESTIONS ON CONTENT, STRUCTURE, AND STYLE

1. By studying the first three paragraphs, summarize both Mitford's reason for explaining the embalming process and her attitude toward undertakers who wish to keep their patrons uninformed about this procedure.

2. Does Mitford use enough specific details to help you visualize each step as it occurs? Point out examples of details that create vivid descriptions by appealing to your sense of sight, smell, or touch.

3. How does the technique of using the hypothetical "Mr. Jones" make the explanation of the process more effective? Why didn't Mitford simply refer to "the corpse" or "a body" throughout her essay?

4. What is Mitford's general attitude toward this procedure? The overall tone of the essay? Study Mitford's choice of words and then identify the tone in each of the following passages:

   • "The next step is to have at Mr. Jones with a thing called a trocar." (10)*

   • "The embalmer, having allowed an appropriate interval to elapse, returns to the attack. . . ." (12)

---

* Numbers in parentheses following quoted material in the questions above and the vocabulary words on the next page refer to paragraphs in the essay.

- "Friends will say, 'How *well* he looks.'" (15)
- "On the other hand, we are cautioned, placing the body too low 'creates the impression that the body is in a box.'" (17)
- "Here he will hold open house for a few days, visiting hours 10 A.M. to 9 P.M." (18)

What other words and passages reveal Mitford's attitude and tone?

5. Why does Mitford repeatedly quote various undertakers and textbooks on the embalming and restorative process ("'needle directed upward between the upper lip and gum and brought out through the left nostril'")? Why is the quotation in paragraph 7 that begins "'On the basis of such scanty information made available to this profession through its rudimentary and haphazard system of technical research'" particularly effective in emphasizing Mitford's attitude toward the funeral industry?

6. What does Mitford gain by quoting euphemisms used by the funeral business, such as "dermasurgeon," "Repose Block," and "slumber room"?

7. What are the connotations of the words "poked," "jabbed," and "left unmolested" in paragraph 10? What effect is Mitford trying to produce with the series of questions (such as "Head off?") in paragraph 12?

8. Does this process flow smoothly from step to step? Identify several transitional devices connecting the paragraphs.

9. Evaluate Mitford's last sentence. Does it successfully sum up the author's attitude and conclude the essay?

10. By supplying information about the embalming process, did Mitford change your attitude toward this procedure or toward the funeral industry? Are there advantages Mitford fails to mention?

VOCABULARY

docility (1)	*raison d'être* (3)	pliable (8)
perpetuation (1)	ingenious (5)	semblance (11)
inherent (2)	cadaver (5)	ravages (11)
mandatory (2)	somatic (7)	stippling (12)
intractable (3)	rudimentary (7)	emaciation (13)
reticence (3)	dispel (7)	

SUGGESTIONS FOR WRITING

Try using Jessica Mitford's "To Bid the World Farewell" as a stepping-stone to your own writing. Mitford's graphic details and disparaging tone upset some readers who feel funerals are important for the living. If you agree, consider writing an essay that challenges Mitford's position. Or adopt Mitford's role as an investigative reporter exposing a controversial process. For example, how is toxic waste disposed of at the student health center? Dangerous chemicals from science labs? What happens to unclaimed animals at your local shelter? Or try a more lighthearted investigation: Just how do they obtain that mystery meat served in the student center cafeteria? Use Mitford's vivid essay as a guide as you present your discoveries.

II. THE DIRECTIONAL PROCESS ESSAY*

Preparing for the Job Interview: Know Thyself

Katy Piotrowski

Katy Piotrowski, M.Ed., is the owner of Career Solutions Group, through which she provides career and job-search support, and the author of five books in the Career Cowards Guide series. Her essay, which originally appeared in 2005 in her "On the Job" column for the Fort Collins, Colorado, *Coloradoan* newspaper, has been slightly revised for this text.

> **Pre-reading Thoughts:** Have you ever successfully interviewed for a job or for a position in a school or community organization? What factors contributed to your effective interview?

1   "I have a job interview this afternoon!" Shawn told me. "Are you ready for it?" I asked. "I'm not sure," she confessed. So, drawing on my work as a career-search consultant, I helped her through an interview-readiness procedure, a quick, six-step process that can successfully prepare almost anyone for a job interview.

2   First, I asked, can you identify the top two or three responsibilities of the job? Shawn hesitated, so I asked her to reread the position description and tell me which parts or key words stood out most. "Evaluating the effectiveness of health-care programs" and "coordinating information exchange in the hospital," she determined. With the key responsibilities in mind, we were ready for the next step. For each of the primary responsibilities, can you describe at least three examples from your past that demonstrate your expertise in those areas? Shawn had one example ready to share, but she needed more. "Tell me about a time when you evaluated the effectiveness of health-care or coordinated information among people or agencies," I prompted her. Within minutes, she'd created a longer list of examples.

3   Moving on, I asked Shawn to think of other experiences in her professional background that would show her as an attractive candidate for this job. Shawn's responses were unfocused, so I taught her a simple three-step STAR process for answering a number of interview questions: 1) describe the **s**ituation or **t**asks, 2) talk about the **a**ctions you took, 3) finish with the **r**esults of your efforts. Try to frame your answers concisely but in a compelling way, using action verbs that show leadership, such as "designed," "coordinated," "implemented," "created," and "managed," when such words are appropriate. Shawn practiced the process, and soon her answers were much more effective.

4   In addition to questions about specific qualifications, interviewers often ask general questions designed to reveal a candidate's "fit" as an employee in their business. "Tell me a little about yourself" is a common request; it may even come at the beginning of an interview when you are the most nervous, so it helps to have some prepared (though not stiffly memorized) thoughts. Shawn's response included highlights of her work history, information about her education, and a statement about why she was excited about the job opening. Variations on this line of questioning might include "As a worker in this field, what is your greatest strength? Biggest weakness?" or "How have you handled a difficult situation?" Shawn had impressive responses to these kinds of questions; she just needed to practice them several more times.

---

* ◆ To help you read this essay analytically, review pages 183-186.

5   As well as presenting themselves to companies, interviewees also need to know something about the companies to which they are applying. Whether you are asked directly or not, it's important to be acquainted with the goals, products, and services of your prospective employer. A quick online search may lead you to a company Web page and any recent publicity. Knowing current information about your prospective employer may better help you respond to questions such as "What knowledge or skills can you bring to our company?" with specific answers that happily fit their needs.

6   Often interviewers' final question may be "Do you have any questions for us?" so the last step in your preparation process calls for thinking of at least one good response. You might ask about the ways this position fits into the larger organization or the company's future plans or ask for more details about the advertised position. You might ask them to describe the most successful employees they've ever hired for this job. (At this time, you probably do not want to negotiate salary, especially if you are an entry-level applicant.) If it seems appropriate, you may also ask how you should proceed: would they prefer for you to contact them or to wait for their response? Is there any other information you can provide that would be helpful in furthering your application for this job? (Don't forget, I reminded Shawn, at the close of your meeting, to thank the interviewers for their time.)

7   Within an hour, following these few steps, Shawn was much more prepared for her interview. Though few people can be totally relaxed during an interview, she was calmed with the knowledge that she was ready to effectively give meaningful responses to a variety of questions. And, yes, she *did* get the job.

QUESTIONS ON CONTENT, STRUCTURE, AND STYLE

1. What process is explained in this essay? What is Piotrowski's main purpose?

2. Although Piotrowski describes her conversation with Shawn, why may this article be considered a directional process essay for its readers?

3. What are the primary steps in this process?

4. Piotrowski uses an actual job applicant, Shawn, to show how the interview-preparation process works. What benefits for the reader does this choice of organization present?

5. Consider ways in which Piotrowski explains each step of the process. How does she clarify her advice by using examples?

6. Cite some ways Piotrowski moves her reader from one step in the preparation process to the next. What transitional words or phrases help guide the reader through the steps?

7. Effective writers of process essays often offer warnings or point out what not to do. Where does Piotrowski use this technique?

8. In paragraph 3, how does Piotrowski use an *acronym* (a word formed from the first letters or parts of other words) to explain her advice?

9. Describe Piotrowski's tone or "voice" in this essay. Is it appropriate and effective? Cite some examples of her language to support your answer.

10. Evaluate Piotrowski's conclusion. How does it wrap up the essay? In particular, what is the effect of the last sentence?

VOCABULARY

expertise (2)

implemented (3)

prospective (5)

SUGGESTIONS FOR WRITING

Try using Piotrowski's essay as a stepping-stone to your own writing. Think of a job that you would like to have soon, perhaps this summer or after you finish your education. Following Piotrowski's procedure for interview preparation, write an essay showing why you are the best candidate for the position. Keep this essay for later use when you face a real interview or for help designing a résumé. (Or, if you prefer, try writing a lighthearted, tongue-in-cheek process essay that makes a serious point by humorously advising readers what *not* to do in the workplace: how not to impress your boss, how not to cooperate with your co-workers, how not to get a raise, and so on.)

A Revision Worksheet

As you write your rough drafts, consult Chapter 5 for guidance through the revision process. In addition, here are a few questions to ask yourself as you revise your process essay:

1. Is the essay's purpose clear to the reader?

2. Has the need for any special equipment been noted and explained adequately? Are all terms unfamiliar to the reader defined clearly?

3. Does the essay include all the steps (and warnings, if appropriate) necessary to understanding the process?

4. Is each step described in enough detail to make it understandable to all readers? Where could more detail be effectively added?

5. Are all the steps in the process presented in an easy-to-follow, logical order, with smooth transitions between steps or stages?

6. Are there any steps that might be combined in a paragraph describing a stage in the process?

7. Does the essay have a pleasing conclusion?

Collaborative Activity: After you've revised your essay extensively, exchange rough drafts with a classmate and answer the preceding questions for each other, making specific suggestions for improvement wherever appropriate. (◆ For advice on productive participation in classroom workshops, see pages 121–123.)

Using Strategies and Sources

The following assignments ask you to not only incorporate what you've learned in this chapter regarding process analysis, but also to employ other strategies of development and to incorporate secondary sources into your responses.

1. In a brief directional process essay, advise your readers on the best way to select a mentor or best friend. Use exemplification to illustrate the different steps of your process with personal examples from your own experiences.

2. Consider the different businesses in your hometown or the town where you're attending college and select one of these to be the subject of a process analysis essay. Every business is involved in a process of some type, from the manufacturing of some commodity or service to the retail sales of these commodities and services. Such businesses in your town could range from a major local factory to a "mom-and-pop" corner store. In a brief essay, provide your audience with an overview of how this business works, an informative process. Conduct research using credible sources to gain a working understanding of the steps in the business's manufacturing or sales process. (◆ See Chapter 19 for help with conducting research and evaluating the sources you find.) Remember to consider what your audience is likely to know or not know as you write your essay.

3. Carefully consider your dominant personality traits. Which is your favorite? Which is your least favorite? Pick one or the other to be the subject of an informative process essay. Explore the process by which that trait became dominant in your personality. Use exemplification, narration, and/or description to elaborate on each of the steps in the process that you outline for your readers.

Chapter 11

Comparison and Contrast

Every day you exercise the mental process of comparison and contrast. When you get up in the morning, for instance, you may contrast two choices of clothing—a short-sleeved shirt versus a long-sleeved one—and then make your decision after hearing the weather forecast. Or you may contrast and choose between Sugar-Coated Plastic Pops and Organic Millet Kernels for breakfast, between the health advantages of walking to campus and the speed afforded by your car or bicycle. Once on campus, preparing to register, you may first compare both professors and courses; similarly, you probably compared the school you attend now to others before you made your choice. In short, you frequently use the process of comparison and contrast to come to a decision or make a judgment about two or more objects, persons, ideas, or feelings.

When you write a comparison or contrast essay, you are engaging in yet another form of expository writing. Remember that the purpose of such writing is to provide information to your reader, and a comparison or contrast essay is no different. In this type of essay, the information you provide typically focuses on the similarities (examined through a *comparison*) and/or differences (examined through a *contrast*) between two items, ideas, people, etc. As a writer, you may choose to compare two subjects, contrast two subjects, or examine both similarities and differences. Your opinion about the two elements* in question becomes your thesis statement; the body of the paper then shows why you arrived at that opinion. For example, if your thesis states that Mom's Kum-On-Back Hamburger Haven is preferable to McPhony's Mystery Burger Stand, your body paragraphs might contrast the two restaurants in terms of food, service, and atmosphere, revealing the superiority of Mom's on all three counts. Following a writing process like that represented in Figure 11.1 will help you develop effective comparison or contrast essays.

Developing Your Essay

There are two principal patterns of organization for comparison or contrast essays. For most short papers, you should choose one of the patterns and stick with it throughout the essay. Later, if you are assigned a longer essay, you may want to mix the patterns for variety as some professional writers do, but do so only if you can maintain clarity and logical organization.

---

* It is possible to compare or contrast more than two elements. But until you feel confident about the organizational patterns for this kind of essay, you should probably stay with the simpler format.

Figure 11.1 VISUALIZING THE PROCESS: COMPARISON AND CONTRAST

Prewriting

Identify possible subjects by considering the following questions:

- In what two subjects do you have an interest? About which two subjects do you have sufficient knowledge to write a comparison and contrast paper?
- In what ways are these subjects similar and different?
- What would the purpose of your comparison or contrast be? What's the answer to the "so what" question?
- Why would people find this comparison and contrast interesting?

Drafting

Determine the organization and content of your essay by asking the following questions:

- Which pattern of development works best for your chosen topic: point by point or block?
- Is an overall picture of each subject desirable? If so, use the block pattern.
- Do you plan to argue for the superiority of one subject over the other? If so, use the point by point pattern.

Revising

Carefully review your thesis and the supporting details you use by asking the following questions:

- Did you provide your reader with an answer to the "so what" question?
- Does your comparison and contrast serve to make a larger point of interest to your readers?
- Does your draft establish why your readers need to know the information you've provided?
- Does your draft consistently follow a logical pattern of organization?

Editing/Proofreading

Consider the sentence-level issues of your essay by asking the following questions:

- Did you use good transitions to avoid a choppy seesaw effect?
- Do you incorporate vividly detailed examples to help your readers "see" the similarities and differences between your subjects?
- Have you reviewed your sentences for spelling, grammar, and punctuation errors?
- Is your paper formatted according to the assignment guidelines?

Pattern One: Point-by-Point

This method of organization calls for body paragraphs that compare or contrast the two subjects first on point one, then on point two, then point three, and so on. Study the following example:

Thesis: Mom's Hamburger Haven is a better family restaurant than McPhony's because of its superior food, service, and atmosphere.

Point 1:   Food
    A. Mom's
    B. McPhony's

Point 2:   Service
    A. Mom's
    B. McPhony's

Point 3:   Atmosphere
    A. Mom's
    B. McPhony's

Conclusion

If you select this pattern of organization, you must make a smooth transition from subject "A" to subject "B" in each discussion to avoid a choppy seesaw effect. Be consistent: present the same subject first in each discussion of a major point. In the essay just outlined, for instance, Mom's is always introduced before McPhony's.

Pattern Two: The Block

This method of organization presents body paragraphs in which the writer first discusses subject "A" on points one, two, three, and so on, and then discusses subject "B" on the same points. The following model illustrates this Block Pattern:

Thesis: Mom's Hamburger Haven is a better family restaurant than McPhony's because of its superior food, service, and atmosphere.

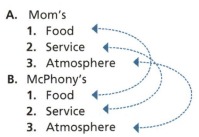

    A. Mom's
      1. Food
      2. Service
      3. Atmosphere
    B. McPhony's
      1. Food
      2. Service
      3. Atmosphere

Conclusion

If you use the Block Pattern, you should discuss the three points—food, service, atmosphere—in the same order for each subject. In addition, you must include in your discussion of subject "B" specific references to the points you made earlier about subject "A" (see outline). In other words, because your statements about Mom's superior food may be several pages away by the time your comments on McPhony's food appear, the readers may not remember precisely what you said. Gently, unobtrusively, remind them with a specific reference to the earlier discussion. For instance, you might begin your paragraph on McPhony's service like this: "Unlike the friendly, attentive help at Mom's, service at McPhony's features grouchy employees who wait on you as if they consider your presence an intrusion on their privacy." The discussion of atmosphere might begin, "McPhony's atmosphere is as cold, sterile, and plastic as its decor, in contrast to the warm, homey feeling that pervades Mom's." Without such connecting phrases, what should be one unified essay will look more like two distinct mini-essays, forcing readers to do your job of comparing or contrasting for themselves.

Which Pattern Should You Use?

As you prepare to compose your first draft, you might ask yourself, "Which pattern of organization should I choose—Point-by-Point or Block?" Indeed, this is not your simple "paper or plastic" supermarket choice. It's an important question—to which there is no single, easy answer.

For most writers, choosing the appropriate pattern of organization involves thinking time in the prewriting stage, before beginning a draft. Many times, your essay's subject matter itself will suggest the most effective method of development. The Block Pattern might be the better choice when a complete, overall picture of each subject is desirable. For example, you might decide that your "then-and-now" essay (your disastrous first day at a new job contrasted with your success at that job today) would be easier for your readers to understand if your description of "then" (your first day) was presented in its entirety, followed by the contrasting discussion of "now" (current success). Later in this section, you will see that Mark Twain chose this method in his essay "Two Ways of Viewing the River" to contrast his early and later impressions of the Mississippi.

On the other hand, your essay topic might best be discussed by presenting a number of distinct points for the reader to consider one by one. Essays that evaluate, that argue the superiority or advantage of one thing over another ("A cat is a better pet for students than a dog because . . ."), often lend themselves to the Point-by-Point Pattern because each of the writer's claims may be clearly supported by the side-by-side details. "When It's Time to Study, Get Out Of Your Pajamas," a student essay in this chapter (see page 246), employs this method to make the case that students can be more productive when working in public than when working at home.

However, none of the preceding advice always holds true. There are no hard-and-fast rules governing this rhetorical choice. Each writer must decide which method of organization works best in any particular comparison/contrast essay. Before drafting begins, therefore, writers are wise to sketch out an informal outline or rough plan using one method and then the other to see which is more effective for their topic, their purpose, and their audience. By spending time in the prewriting stage "auditioning" each method of development, you may spare yourself the frustration of writing an entire draft whose organization doesn't work well for your topic.

Problems to Avoid

The single most serious error is the "so-what" thesis. Writers of comparison and contrast essays often wish to convince their readers that something—a restaurant, a movie, a product—is better (or worse) than something else: "Mom's Haven is a better place to eat than McPhony's." But not all comparison or contrast essays assert the absolute superiority or inferiority of their subjects. Sometimes writers simply want to point out the similarities or differences in two or more people, places, or objects, and that's fine, too—*as long as the writer avoids the "so-what" thesis problem.*

Too often, novice writers will present thesis statements such as "My sister and I are very different" or "Having a blended family with two stepbrothers and a stepsister has advantages and disadvantages for me." To such theses, readers can only respond, "So what? Who cares?" There are many similarities and differences (or advantages and disadvantages) between countless numbers of things—but why should your readers care about those described in your essay? Comparing or contrasting for no apparent reason is a waste of the readers' valuable time; instead, find a purpose that will draw in your audience. You may indeed wish to write an essay contrasting the pros and cons of your blended family, but do it in a way that has a universal appeal or application. For instance, you might revise your thesis to say something like "Although a blended family often does experience petty jealousies and juvenile bickering, the benefits of having stepsiblings as live-in friends far outweigh the problems," and then use your family to show the advantages and disadvantages. In this way, your readers realize they will learn something about the blended family, a common phenomenon today, as well as learning some information about you and your particular family.

Another way to avoid the "so-what" problem is to direct your thesis to a particular audience. For instance, you might say that "Although Stella's Sweatateria and the Fitness Fanatics Gym are similar in their low student-membership prices and excellent instructors, Stella's is the place to go for those seeking a variety of exercise classes rather than hard-core bodybuilding machines." Or your thesis may wish to show a particular relationship between two subjects. Instead of writing "There are many similarities between the movie *Riot of the Killer Snails* and Mary Sheeley's novel *Salt on the Sidewalk*," write "The many similarities in character and plot (the monster, the scientist, and vegetable garden scene) clearly suggest that the movie director was greatly influenced by—if not actually guilty of stealing—parts of Mary Sheeley's novel."

In other words, tell your readers your point and then use comparison or contrast to support that idea; don't just compare or contrast items in a vacuum. Ask yourself, "What is the significant point I want my readers to learn or understand from reading this comparison/contrast essay? Why do they need to know this?"

Describe your subjects clearly and distinctly. To comprehend a difference or a similarity between two things, the reader must first be able to "see" them as you do. Consequently, you should use as many vivid examples and details as possible to describe both your subjects. Beware a tendency to over elaborate on one subject and then grossly skimp on the other, an especially easy trap to fall into in an essay that asserts "X" is preferable to "Y." By giving each side a reasonable treatment, you will do a better job of convincing your reader that you know both sides and have made a valid judgment.

Avoid a choppy essay. Whether you organize your essay by the Point-by-Point Pattern or the Block Pattern, you need to use enough transitional devices to ensure a smooth flow from one subject to another and from one point to the next. Without transitions, your essay may assume the distracting movement of a Ping-Pong game, as you switch back and forth between discussions of your two subjects. Listed here are some appropriate words to link your points:

Comparison	Contrast
also	however
similarly	on the contrary
too	on the other hand
both	in contrast
like	although
not only . . . but also	unlike
have in common	though
share the same	instead of
in the same manner	but

(◆ For a review of other transitional devices, see pages 72–76.)

Practicing What You've Learned

A. To practice developing ideas for an essay of comparison or contrast, try this activity: begin by thinking of several different pairs of elements that interest you: two teachers, two sitcoms, two of your favorite novels, two pets, two of your best friends, two of your worst enemies, etc. Now, for each of the pairs you've listed, brainstorm a short list of points of comparison or contrast. What are the most interesting similarities or differences for each of these pairs? Finally, determine the organizational pattern that works most effectively for each of these pairs. Is it the Point-by-Point or the Block Pattern? Create a rough outline for each of these pairs using the chosen pattern.

B. *Collaborative Activity:* To get useful feedback on Exercise A, pair off with a classmate and exchange the work you just completed. As you review each other's work, evaluate the points of comparison and contrast for audience appeal and interest. Also consider the author's selected pattern of organization. Does it work? Would the other pattern work more effectively? Finally, consider the "so what" question. Why would you want to know about the outlined comparisons that your partner has created? Provide feedback to your classmate on these questions and any follow up with any other insights you might be able to offer.

Essay Topics

Here are some topics that may be compared or contrasted. Remember to narrow your subject, formulate a thesis that presents a clear point, and follow one of the two organizational patterns discussed on pages 239–240. ◆ For additional ideas, turn to the "Suggestions for Writing" sections following the professional essays (page 254 and page 256).

1. An expectation and its reality

2. A memory of a person or place and a more recent encounter (or a first impression and a later point of view)

3. Two music festivals in your region

4. A classic car and a more recent model that revives the classic name

5. Coverage of the same story by two newspapers or magazines (the *National Enquirer* and the *Dallas Morning News*, for example, or *Time* and *Newsweek*)

6. An original song by an artist and a cover of the same tune by another band of a different genre

7. Two essays or pieces of literature with similar themes but different styles

8. Two kinds of classes (online and on campus; lecture and lab; high school and college, etc.)

9. Two pieces of technology or two pieces of sports equipment (or an older and newer version of a product)

10. Two paintings/photographs/posters (You might select any of the many images in this text; a list of the artworks follows the Detailed Table of Contents. You could choose two portraits or a portrait and a self-portrait [for example, *Migrant Mother* or *Repose*]; two landscapes [*Early Snow, Starry Night*, or *Moonrise, Hernandez, New Mexico*]; two scenes of action [*The Third of May* or *Tornado over Kansas*]; or two pictures with contrasting themes, styles, or media or two that share certain themes or techniques [the surrealism of *The Persistence of Memory* or *Birthday*, for example]. ◆ For help writing about artworks, see the MindTap® Online Chapter: "Writing about Visual Arts.")

11. Two amusement parks or other entertainment venues such as concert halls, bars, or dance clubs

12. Two places you've lived or visited or two schools you've attended

13. Two instructors or coaches whose teaching styles are effective but different

14. Two movies; a book and its movie adaptation; a movie and its sequel; an older movie and its remake (◆ For help writing about film, see the MindTap® Online Chapter: "Writing about Film.")

continued on next page

15. Two jobs, bosses, or employers (or your current job and your dream job)

16. Two of your closest friends who are special to you in different ways

17. An opinion you held before coming to college that has changed

18. Your attitude toward a social custom or political belief and your parents' (or grandparents') attitude toward that belief or custom

19. *Collaborative Activity:* Interview a classmate who grew up in a different town, state, or country. In comparison to your own experience, what are some important similarities or differences? Advantages/disadvantages? Given a choice between the two places, in which area would you relocate today and why?

20. Compare or contrast two advertisements that are themselves developed by comparison/contrast or analogy. (Consider, for example, the ad shown here. What is its purpose and who is its target audience? How does the ad incorporate the strategy of contrast to sell its product? What other appeals are used? Is this ad effective? Why or why not?)

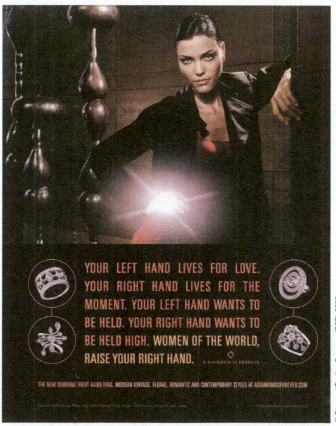

A Topic Proposal for Your Essay

Selecting the right subject matter is important to every writer. To help you clarify your ideas and strengthen your commitment to your topic, here is a proposal sheet that asks you to describe some of your preliminary ideas about your subject before you begin drafting. Although your ideas may change as you write (they will almost certainly become more refined), thinking through your choice of topic now may help you avoid several false starts.

1. What two subjects will your essay discuss? In what ways are these subjects similar? Different?

2. Do you plan to compare or contrast your two subjects?

3. Write one or two sentences describing your attitude toward these two subjects. Are you stating a preference for one or are you making some other significant point? In other words, what is the purpose of this essay?

4. Why would other people find this topic interesting and important? Would a particular group of people be more affected by your topic than others? Are you avoiding the "so-what" thesis problem?

5. List three or four points of comparison or contrast that you might include in this essay.

6. What difficulties might this topic present during your drafting? For example, would your topic be best explained using the Block or Point-by-Point Pattern?

Once you have chosen your topic, take a moment to read through Figure 11.1 (page 238) to remind yourself of key questions you should be asking at each stage of the writing process for your comparison/contrast essay.

Sample Student Essay

Because there are two popular ways to develop comparison/contrast essays, this section offers two student essays so that each pattern is illustrated.

I. The Point-by-Point Pattern

The author of the following comparison/contrast paper selected the point-by-point method of organization. Throughout the essay, she contends that it is easier to be more productive when working in public than when working at home. Her different points of comparison include the mindset that each location produces, the impact of the people around you, and the relative duration of breaks. As you read, note the author's use of concrete details and examples to support her comparative analysis. How successfully does the author communicate her point? Did the essay cause you to reconsider your own study habits? How does this essay cause you to reflect on your own writing?

When It's Time to Study, Get Out of Your Pajamas

Attention getter

1   On the surface, home seems like the best place to get work done: you don't have to get out of your pajamas, and everything you need is right there, from textbooks to snacks to a bathroom you don't have to wait in line for. You don't have to worry about traveling to a good study spot or finding a good seat when you get there. But

Thesis

when you compare working at home with working in a public place, the increased organization and focus that you need to work in public makes up for the inconvenience of taking your work with you.

Point 1: Mindset— working and studying mode vs. hanging out at home mode

2   The first advantage of working in public is going from hanging out at home mode to working and studying mode. Putting effort into getting ready to go—getting dressed, organizing your materials, the travel time to where you're going—is like getting your study game face on. Though many people are most comfortable studying in cozy clothes, pajamas get you ready for sleeping and eating pancakes. Showering, putting on fresh clothes and a pair of shoes gets you ready for facing your to-do list. A better-organized study session is also a more effective one. At home, if you need something, such as a book or highlighter, you can always stop

Examples of being in working and studying mode

what you're doing and get it, no matter what room it's in. But interrupting your work flow to find something that should already be close by is both a waste of time and an easy way to get distracted. It's better to consider exactly which supplies and materials you need to get your work done before you begin and to put everything in one bag to take with you. There is also the advantage of not being surrounded by lots of other things you might like to do—dishes, other work that's due later, the marble collection you've been meaning to organize—and being in a place where you can only interact with what you need to get done.

Point 2: Surrounding people— respectful quiet strangers vs. talkative friends and family

3   Of course, once you've made your way to your destination— maybe it's a favorite coffee shop, or a quiet floor of the library— you are going to be surrounded by lots of other people, more than you're likely to have around you at home. Luckily, strangers will be much more respectful of your boundaries than a roommate or family member who might only see your unfinished chores or the

conversation they've been meaning to have with you once you're both home. It's much harder to say no to people you know than to strangers. No one in the coffee shop will ask you to do anything other than maybe move your books off a chair or watch their laptop while they use the bathroom. Second of all, there's a good chance all these other people share the same goal of working quietly and making the most of their time. Your roommates, on the other hand, might have plans to binge-watch a TV series you haven't caught up on or get ready for a night out. Besides being distracted by the noise, it can be frustrating to be around others who can focus on fun when you need to get work done. Even if you live alone, studying in public, surrounding yourself with others who have the same goals of getting work done can make you feel less lonely than you might if you study at home alone. It might even be motivating.

Example of distracting roommates

4   Wherever you work, you will need to take breaks, and a public place is more likely to provide you with shorter ones. At a coffee shop, you can reward yourself for getting through a chapter by buying yourself a treat. If you need a longer break, you can walk from one end of the library to the other or find a friend studying nearby to have lunch with before you both return to work. At home, a break is more likely to involve a household chore, which might lead to another household chore, like the way watching one episode of that half-hour show will lead you to watch the next four of them. Even though it might cost you a little bit of money, the study breaks you take in public are less likely to be as distracting as the ones you would take at home.

Point 3: Duration of breaks— short breaks vs. time- consuming breaks

Example of how watching TV or doing chores can become absorbing

5   There's a big advantage to learning to study anywhere, of course. But the focus and organization required to work in public encourages you to be a more efficient and attentive worker. Even if you factor in commuting time, working at home can be a bigger waste of time in the end. The efforts you put into leaving your house and committing to getting work accomplished will show in the work itself. So, the next time you're up against an important school project, consider leaving your home to best focus on your work.

Conclusion: Summary of the advantages of working or studying in a public place

II. The Block Pattern

After thinking through both methods of development, a second student writer chose the Block Pattern to contrast two kinds of pizza. He felt it was more effective to give his readers a complete sense of his favorite pizza, Chicago-style, with its superior taste, fullness factor, and visual appeal, instead of addressing each point of the contrast separately, as did the first student writer in this section. Do you agree with his choice of organizational method? Why or why not? Note, too, the ways in which this writer tries to avoid the "split essay" problem by making clear connections between his personal favorite, Chicago-style pizza, and New York-style pizza in the second half of the essay.

More Than Just the Crust: New York- and Chicago-Style Pizza

Introduction of topic: New York-style pizza vs. Chicago-style pizza

1   For pizza fans, few topics are as hotly debated as New York-style versus Chicago-style pizza. Both of these styles of pizza are well-known and available outside of their respective cities, thanks to food chains such as Uno Chicago Grill and Sbarro. For people everywhere, emotions can run high when discussing this important topic; I know of a relationship that almost ended because both parties were so fired up about which side was right. After going on a

Attention-getting anecdotes

rant about deep-dish pizza, aka traditional Chicago-style pizza, even proud New Yorker Jon Stewart, former host of *The Daily Show*, had to retract his previous trash talk when he tried some Chicago-style on the show. On air and for the record, he admitted that the

Thesis and essay map

Chicago-style was very good. And with good reason! For the tastiness, the fullness-factor and the visual effect, Chicago-style pizza is the true winner of this contest.

Block A: Chicago-style pizza

2   In terms of deliciousness, Chicago-style has no equal. Let's examine the layers of flavor. The deep-dish crust is the star of the show. It's buttery, flaky, and, because it's baked in a pan and lightly oiled for a fried-effect, the crust almost tastes like cake. Because the pizza is cooked in a pan, the crust has a deep surface area and high edges. In Chicago-style pizza, the cheese comes *before* the tomato sauce, and the mozzarella is creamy and white and snaps back when you slice it. Then come toppings: fresh veggies

or spicy meats (another Chicago specialty)—meld with the cheese and crust, creating thick layers of deliciousness, almost like a really yummy casserole. Finally, the sauce goes *on top*—and Chicago-style doesn't cheat with the thin tomato sauce you can get from a jar. No—real crushed tomatoes round out the dish with a dusting of parm. Baked together, the flavors commingle and complement each other for the perfect all-around pizza. The ingredients offer layers of flavor that are a proud tradition and also fresh and veggie-forward.

Point 1: Superior flavor (crust, cheese, sauce, toppings)

3   But it's not only the taste that matters. Chicago-style pizza is also a more filling and attractive meal. Because of its thick crust and layers of goodness, this is not the kind of dish you can eat with your hands: you need a knife and fork. It has the weight and fullness of a family dinner at Grandma's house, not just an on-the-go snack. Baked for 45 minutes in the oven, the layers have had time to come together. Because of the deep dish with the tall edges, the crust can hold a significant portion of toppings, cheese, and sauce. Moreover, visually, the pie is pleasing when it arrives at the table in its pan with its silver lifter (again, almost like a baked cake). Because the crust is often baked with cornmeal or semolina, it has a yellowy color, reminiscent of corn bread. The pizza is substantively filling and also gourmet-looking; pleasing to the eye and the belly.

Point 2: Fullness factor (thick crust, portion size)

Point 3: Visual appeal (silver lifter, yellow crust)

4   By contrast, while also tasty, New York-style pizza simply does not match up overall. The crust is flat and flavorless, often discarded once you finish the cheese-and-sauce portion of the slice. Unlike Chicago-style deep-dish crusts, in New York-style slices, the crust is almost an afterthought. Also, the sauce is thin and liquidy, hardly reminiscent of fresh tomatoes, barely visible under the cheese. The cheese itself is melted but oily—you often need napkins to take off the excess grease. Toppings overwhelm the mix—sticking up on top of the cheese where they often dry out and lose flavor.

Block B: New York-style pizza

Point 1: Inferior flavor (flat crust, thin sauce, oily cheese)

Point 2:
Insubstantial
serving
(soggy slice,
eat with your
hands)

5   As far as the fullness-factor, too, unlike the real-meal effect of tucking into a Chicago-style pie with a knife and fork, a New York-style pizza slice is something you could fold over and eat with your hands while walking around the block. The crust doesn't hold the same amount of toppings, cheese, and sauce, and too many veggies often weigh it down and make it soggy. You can cut a New York slice with a roller, unlike the weighty lift of the Chicago piece,

Point 3:
Visually
unappealing

and the result is that a New York slice feels insubstantial. You need more of it to feel full, and the visual effect is not as pleasing as the brightly-colored Chicago reds and yellows.

6   While it will always be enjoyable to debate a good rivalry, in this matter, the choice is clear. Although New York-style pizza is tasty in

Conclusion:
Chicago-style
is the clear
winner

its own right, Chicago-style, in the end, creates a more filling, flavorful, and memorable all-around meal. I bet deep down, even Jon Stewart would agree.

Professional Essays

Because there are two common ways to develop comparison/contrast essays, this section offers two professional essays so that each pattern is illustrated.

I. THE POINT-BY-POINT PATTERN*

Grant and Lee: A Study in Contrasts

Bruce Catton

Bruce Catton, an authority on the Civil War, won both the Pulitzer Prize for historical work and the National Book Award in 1954. He wrote numerous books, including *Mr. Lincoln's Army* (1951), *A Stillness at Appomattox* (1953), *Never Call Retreat* (1966), and *Gettysburg: The Final Fury* (1974). This classic essay is from *The American Story* (1956), a collection of essays by noted historians. In 1977, the year before he died, Catton was awarded the Presidential Medal of Freedom, the nation's highest civil honor.

---

* ◆ To help you read this essay analytically, review pages 183–186.

Pre-reading Thoughts: Consider the most important character traits of two people you admire. Do these two people have similar backgrounds, strengths, or goals? Do they share common values or virtues?

1   When Ulysses S. Grant and Robert E. Lee met in the parlor of a modest house at Appomattox Court House, Virginia, on April 9, 1865, to work out the terms for the surrender of Lee's Army of Northern Virginia, a great chapter in American life came to a close, and a great new chapter began.

2   These men were bringing the Civil War to its virtual finish. To be sure, other armies had yet to surrender, and for a few days the fugitive Confederate government would struggle desperately and vainly, trying to find some way to go on living now that its chief support was gone. But in effect it was all over when Grant and Lee signed the papers. And the little room where they wrote out the terms was the scene of one of the poignant, dramatic contrasts in American history.

3   They were two strong men, these oddly different generals, and they represented the strengths of two conflicting currents that, through them, had come into final collision.

4   Back of Robert E. Lee was the notion that the old aristocratic concept might somehow survive and be dominant in American life.

5   Lee was tidewater Virginia, and in his background were family, culture, and tradition . . . the age of chivalry transplanted to a New World which was making its own legends and its own myths. He embodied a way of life that had come down through the age of knighthood and the English country squire. America was a land that was beginning all over again, dedicated to nothing much more complicated than the rather hazy belief that all men had equal rights, and should have an equal chance in the world. In such a land Lee stood for the feeling that it was somehow of advantage to human society to have a pronounced inequality in the social structure. There should be a leisure class, backed by ownership of land; in turn, society itself should be keyed to the land as the chief source of wealth and influence. It would bring forth (according to this ideal) a class of men with a strong sense of obligation to the community; men who lived not to gain advantage for themselves, but to meet the solemn obligations which had been laid on them by the very fact that they were privileged. From them the country would get its leadership; to them it could look for the higher values—of thought, of conduct, of personal deportment—to give it strength and virtue.

6   Lee embodied the noblest elements of this aristocratic ideal. Through him, the landed nobility justified itself. For four years, the Southern states had fought a desperate war to uphold the ideals for which Lee stood. In the end, it almost seemed as if the Confederacy fought for Lee; as if he himself was the Confederacy . . . the best thing that the way of life for which the Confederacy stood could ever have to offer. He had passed into legend before Appomattox. Thousands of tired, underfed, poorly clothed Confederate soldiers, long-since past the simple enthusiasm of the early days of the struggle, somehow considered Lee the symbol of everything for which they had been willing to die. But they could not quite put this feeling into words. If the Lost Cause, sanctified by so much heroism and so many deaths, had a living justification, its justification was General Lee.

7   Grant, the son of a tanner on the Western frontier, was everything Lee was not. He had come up the hard way, and embodied nothing in particular except the eternal toughness and sinewy fiber of the men who grew up beyond the mountains. He was one of a body of men who owed reverence and obeisance to no one, who were self-reliant to a fault, who cared hardly anything for the past but who had a sharp eye for the future.

8   These frontier men were the precise opposites of the tidewater aristocrats. Back of them, in the great surge that had taken people over the Alleghenies and into the opening Western country, there was a deep, implicit dissatisfaction with a past that had settled into grooves. They stood for democracy, not from any reasoned conclusion about the proper ordering of human society, but simply because they had grown up in the middle of democracy and knew how it worked. Their society might have privileges, but they would be privileges each man had won for himself. Forms and patterns meant nothing. No man was born to anything, except perhaps to a chance to show how far he could rise. Life was competition.

9   Yet along with this feeling had come a deep sense of belonging to a national community. The Westerner who developed a farm, opened a shop, or set up in business as a trader could hope to prosper only as his own community prospered—and his community ran from the Atlantic to the Pacific and from Canada down to Mexico. If the land was settled, with towns and highways and accessible markets, he could better himself. He saw his fate in terms of the nation's own destiny. As its horizons expanded, so did his. He had, in other words, an acute dollars-and-cents stake in the continued growth and development of his country.

10   And that, perhaps, is where the contrast between Grant and Lee becomes most striking. The Virginia aristocrat, inevitably, saw himself in relation to his own region. He lived in a static society which could endure almost anything except change. Instinctively, his first loyalty would go to the locality in which that society existed. He would fight to the limit of endurance to defend it, because in defending it he was defending everything that gave his own life its deepest meaning.

11   The Westerner, on the other hand, would fight with an equal tenacity for the broader concept of society. He fought so because everything he lived by was tied to growth, expansion, and a constantly widening horizon. What he lived by would survive or fall with the nation itself. He could not possibly stand by unmoved in the face of an attempt to destroy the Union. He would combat it with everything he had, because he could only see it as an effort to cut the ground out from under his feet.

12   So Grant and Lee were in complete contrast, representing two diametrically opposed elements in American life. Grant was the modern man emerging; beyond him, ready to come on the stage, was the great age of steel and machinery, of crowded cities and a restless, burgeoning vitality. Lee might have ridden down from the old age of chivalry, lance in hand, silken banner fluttering over his head. Each man was the perfect champion of his cause, drawing both his strengths and his weaknesses from the people he led.

13   Yet it was not all contrast, after all. Different as they were—in background, in personality, in underlying aspiration—these two great soldiers had much in common. Under everything else, they were marvelous fighters. Furthermore, their fighting qualities were really very much alike.

14   Each man had, to begin with, the great virtue of utter tenacity and fidelity. Grant fought his way down the Mississippi Valley in spite of acute personal discouragement and profound military handicaps. Lee hung on in the trenches at Petersburg after hope itself had died. In each man there was an indomitable quality . . . the born fighter's refusal to give up as long as he can still remain on his feet and lift his two fists.

15   Daring and resourcefulness they had, too; the ability to think faster and move faster than the enemy. These were the qualities which gave Lee the dazzling campaigns of Second Manassas and Chancellorsville and won Vicksburg for Grant.

16   Lastly, and perhaps greatest of all, there was the ability, at the end, to turn quickly from war to peace once the fighting was over. Out of the way these two men behaved at Appomattox came the possibility of a peace of reconciliation. It was a possibility not wholly realized, in the years to come, but which did, in the end, help the two sections to become one nation again . . . after a war whose bitterness might have seemed to make such a reunion wholly impossible. No part of either man's life became him more than the part he played in their brief meeting in the McLean house at Appomattox. Their behavior there put all succeeding generations of Americans in their debt. Two great Americans, Grant and Lee—very different, yet under everything very much alike. Their encounter at Appomattox was one of the great moments of American history.

QUESTIONS ON CONTENT, STYLE, AND STRUCTURE

1. What is Catton's thesis?

2. According to Catton, how did Lee view society? What "ideal" did he embody? Why do you think Catton avoided mentioning slavery in this description?

3. Who did Grant represent? How did they view the country's social structure?

4. After carefully studying paragraphs 4 through 16, describe the pattern of organization Catton uses to present his discussion.

5. What new means of development begins in paragraph 13?

6. How does Catton avoid the choppy seesaw effect as he compares and contrasts his subjects? Point out ways in which Catton makes a smooth transition from point to point.

7. Evaluate Catton's ability to write unified, coherent paragraphs with clearly stated topic sentences. Are his paragraphs adequately developed with enough specific detail? Cite evidence to support your answer.

8. What is the advantage or disadvantage of having only one sentence in paragraph 3? In paragraph 4?

9. What is Catton's opinion of these men? Select words and passages to support your answer. How does Catton's attitude affect the tone of this essay? Is his tone appropriate? Why or why not?

10. Instead of including a separate paragraph, Catton presents his concluding remarks in paragraph 16, in which he discusses his last major point about Grant and Lee. Many essays lacking concluding paragraphs end too abruptly or merely trail off; how does Catton avoid these weaknesses?

VOCABULARY*

chivalry (5)	tenacity (11)	indomitable (14)
deportment (5)	diametrically (12)	reconciliation (16)
embodied (6)	burgeoning (12)	

SUGGESTIONS FOR WRITING

Try using Bruce Catton's "Grant and Lee: A Study in Contrasts" as a stepping-stone to your writing. Comparing public figures is a familiar activity. People often discuss the styles and merits of various politicians, writers, business leaders, humanitarians, sports celebrities, and media stars. Write your own essay about two public figures who interest you. Similar or different, these people may have lived in the same times (Winston Churchill and Franklin D. Roosevelt, Ernest Hemingway and F. Scott Fitzgerald, Babe Didrikson Zaharias and Babe Ruth), or you might choose two people from different eras (Clara Barton and Mother Teresa, Mozart and Madonna, Susan B. Anthony and Cesar Chavez, Harriet Tubman and Martin Luther King, Jr.). The possibilities are endless and thought-provoking; use your essay to make an interesting specific point about the fascinating (and perhaps heretofore unrecognized) differences/similarities between the people you choose.

II. THE BLOCK PATTERN**

Two Ways of Viewing the River

Samuel Clemens

Samuel Clemens, whose pen name was Mark Twain, is regarded as one of America's most outstanding writers. Well known for his humorous stories and books, Twain was also a pioneer of fictional realism and local color. His most famous novel, *Adventures of Huckleberry Finn* (1884), is often hailed as a masterpiece. This selection is from the autobiographical book *Life on the Mississippi* (1883), which recounts Clemens' job as a riverboat pilot.

> **Pre-reading Thoughts:** Have you ever revisited a place and discovered that your perception of it had greatly changed over time? What might have caused this change? Did the place itself change—or did you?

1   Now when I had mastered the language of this water and had come to know every trifling feature that bordered the great river as familiarly as I knew the letters of the alphabet, I had made a valuable acquisition. But I had lost something, too. I had lost something which could never be restored to me while I lived. All the grace, the beauty, the poetry, had gone out of the majestic river! I still kept in mind a certain wonderful sunset which I witnessed when steamboating was new to me. A broad expanse of the river was turned to blood; in the middle distance the red hue brightened into gold, through which a solitary log came floating, black and conspicuous; in one place a long, slanting mark lay sparkling upon the water; in another the surface was broken by boiling,

---

*Numbers in parentheses following the vocabulary words refer to paragraphs in the essay.

** ◆ To help you read this essay analytically, review pages 183–186.

tumbling rings, that were as many-tinted as an opal; where the ruddy flush was faintest, was a smooth spot that was covered with graceful circles and radiating lines, ever so delicately traced; the shore on our left was densely wooded and the somber shadow that fell from this forest was broken in one place by a long, ruffled trail that shone like silver; and high above the forest wall a clean-stemmed dead tree waved a single leafy bough that glowed like a flame in the unobstructed splendor that was flowing from the sun. There were graceful curves, reflected images, woody heights, soft distances, and over the whole scene, far and near, the dissolving lights drifted steadily, enriching it every passing moment with new marvels of coloring.

2   I stood like one bewitched. I drank it in, in a speechless rapture. The world was new to me and I had never seen anything like this at home. But as I have said, a day came when I began to cease from noting the glories and the charms which the moon and the sun and the twilight wrought upon the river's face; another day came when I ceased altogether to note them. Then, if that sunset scene had been repeated, I should have looked upon it without rapture, and should have commented upon it inwardly after this fashion: "This sun means that we are going to have wind tomorrow; that floating log means that the river is rising, small thanks to it; that slanting mark on the water refers to a bluff reef which is going to kill somebody's steamboat one of these nights, if it keeps on stretching out like that; those tumbling 'boils' show a dissolving bar and a changing channel there; the lines and circles in the slick water over yonder are a warning that that troublesome place is shoaling up dangerously; that silver streak in the shadow of the forest is the 'break' from a new snag and he has located himself in the very best place he could have found to fish for steamboats; that tall dead tree, with a single living branch, is not going to last long, and then how is a body ever going to get through this blind place at night without the friendly old landmark?"

3   No, the romance and beauty were all gone from the river. All the value any feature of it had for me now was the amount of usefulness it could furnish toward compassing the safe piloting of a steamboat. Since those days, I have pitied doctors from my heart. What does the lovely flush in a beauty's cheek mean to a doctor but a "break" that ripples above some deadly disease? Are not all her visible charms sown thick with what are to him the signs and symbols of hidden decay? Does he ever see her beauty at all, or doesn't he simply view her professionally and comment upon her unwholesome condition all to himself? And doesn't he sometimes wonder whether he has gained most or lost most by learning his trade?

QUESTIONS ON CONTENT, STRUCTURE, AND STYLE

1. What is Clemens contrasting in this essay? Identify his thesis.
2. What organizational pattern does he choose? Why is this an appropriate choice for his purpose?
3. How does Clemens make a smooth transition to his later view of the river?
4. Why does Clemens refer to doctors in paragraph 3?
5. What is the purpose of the questions in paragraph 3? Why is the last question especially important?
6. Characterize the language Clemens uses in his description in paragraph 1. Is his diction appropriate?
7. Point out several examples of similes in paragraph 1. What do they add to the description of the sunset?

8. How does the language in the description in paragraph 2 differ from the diction in paragraph 1? What view of the river is emphasized there?

9. Identify an example of personification in paragraph 2. Why did Clemens add it to his description?

10. Describe the tone of this essay. Does it ever shift?

VOCABULARY

trifling (1)   ruddy (1)

acquisition (1)   wrought (2)

conspicuous (1)   compassing (3)

SUGGESTIONS FOR WRITING

Try using Samuel Clemens' "Two Ways of Viewing the River" as a stepping-stone to your own writing. Consider, as Clemens did, writing about a subject before and after you experienced it from a more technically informed point of view. Did your appreciation of your grandmother's quilt increase after you realized how much skill went into making it? Did a starry night have a different appeal after your astronomy course? Did your admiration of a story or poem diminish or increase after you studied its craft? Clemens felt that a certain loss came with his expertise, but was this the case in your experience?

A Revision Worksheet

As you write your rough drafts, consult Chapter 5 for guidance through the revision process. In addition, here are a few questions to ask yourself as you revise your comparison/contrast essay:

1. Does the essay contain a thesis that makes a significant point instead of a "so-what" thesis?

2. Is the material organized into the best pattern for the subject matter?

3. If the essay is developed by the Point-by-Point Pattern, are there enough transitional words used to avoid the seesaw effect?

4. If the essay is developed by the Block Pattern, are there enough transitional devices and references connecting the two subjects to avoid the split-essay problem?

5. Are the points of comparison/contrast presented in a logical, consistent order that the reader can follow easily?

6. Are both subjects given a reasonably balanced treatment?

7. Are both subjects developed in enough specific detail so that the reader clearly understands the comparison or contrast? Where might more detail be added?

continued on next page

Collaborative Activity: After you've revised your essay extensively, exchange rough drafts with a classmate and answer these questions for each other, making specific suggestions for improvement wherever appropriate. (◆ For advice on productive participation in classroom workshops, see pages 121–123.)

A Special Kind of Comparison: The Analogy

In the past few pages of this text, you've learned about essays developed by comparison/contrast, which generally point out similarities and differences between two things with enough common ground to merit meaningful discussion (two apartments, two computers, a book and its movie adaptation, etc.). In comparison/contrast essays, two subjects ("X" and "Y") are explained to make a point. An *analogy* is slightly different: it is a comparison that uses one thing ("X") only to clarify or argue a second thing ("Y"). In an analogy, one element is the main focus of attention.

You've probably heard several colorful analogies this week. Perhaps a friend who holds a hectic, dead-end job has tried to explain life at that moment by comparing herself to a crazed gerbil on a cage treadmill—always running, getting nowhere, feeling trapped in a never-changing environment. Or perhaps your science teacher explained the behavior of cancer cells by comparing them in several ways to an invading army on a destructive mission. If you read the Preface to this text, you were asked to see your writing instructor as a coach who helps you practice your skills, gives constructive criticism, and encourages your successes. Analogies are plentiful in our conversations and in both our reading and writing.

Writers often find analogies useful in three ways:

1. **To clarify and explain:** Most often writers use analogies to clarify an abstract, unfamiliar, or complex element by comparing it to something that is familiar to the reader—often something that is more concrete or easier to understand. For example, raising children has often been compared to nourishing baby birds, with parents feeding and nurturing but ultimately nudging offspring out of the nest. A relationship might be explained as having grown from a seed that eventually blossomed into a flower (or a weed!). Popular novelist Stephen King has used a roller coaster analogy to explain some people's enjoyment of horror movies.

   Frequently, scientific and medical topics profit from analogies that a general audience of readers can more readily understand. A technical discussion of the human eye, for instance, might be explained using the analogy of a camera lens; photosynthesis might be compared to the process of baking bread. One biology teacher explains the semi-permeability of a cell membrane with a football analogy: the offensive line wants to let out the running back with the ball but keep the defensive line in. In short, analogies can make new or difficult material easier to grasp.

2. **To argue and persuade:** Writers often use analogies to try to convince their audience that what is true about "X" would also be true about "Y" because the two elements have so many important similarities. For example, someone against new

anti-drug laws might argue that they are similar to those passed under Prohibition, the banning of alcohol in the 1930s, and thus the drug laws are doomed to failure. Or perhaps a NASA official might argue for more money for space exploration by comparing trips into outer space with those expeditions to the New World by explorers such as Columbus. How convincing an analogy is depends to a large extent on how similar the two elements appear to be. Remember, however, that analogies by themselves cannot *prove* anything; they can merely suggest similarities between two cases or things.

3. **To dramatize or capture an image:** Writers (and speakers) often use analogies because they wish their audience to remember a particular point or to see something in a new way. Using a vivid analogy—sometimes referred to as an extended metaphor or simile—can effectively impress an image upon the reader's or listener's mind ("Using crack is like burning down your own house. And the insurance policy ran out a long time ago . . ."). Analogies can be enjoyable too for their sheer inventiveness and their colorful language. Perhaps one of the most well-known analogies in American literature is Thoreau's description, in *Walden*, of a battle between two ant colonies, with the tiny creatures drawn as rival warriors fighting to the death in classical epic style. Analogies may even be used for comic effect in appropriate situations (moving into your basement apartment in sweltering August heat as analogous to a trip to the Underworld, for instance). Fresh, creative analogies can delight your readers and hold their attention.

Although analogies can be helpful and memorable, they can also present problems if they are trite, unclear, or illogical. Analogies can be especially harmful to a writer's credibility in an argument if readers don't see enough logical similarities to make the comparison convincing. Some faulty analogies may seem acceptable on first glance but fall apart when the details of the comparison are considered closely. For example, perhaps you have seen a bumper sticker that reads "Giving money and power to the government is like giving whisky and car keys to teenage boys." Are the two situations really alike? Do government agencies/officials and adolescents share many similarities in maturity, experience, and goals? Does financial support have the same effect as alcohol? If too many points of comparison are weak, readers will not find the analogy persuasive. Or perhaps you have read that "America is like a lifeboat already full of people; letting in more immigrants will cause the boat to sink." If readers do not accept the major premise—that America, a country with many renewable resources, closely resembles a lifeboat, a confined space with unchanging dimensions—they are likely to reject the argument.

Also be wary of those writers who try to substitute an analogy in place of any other kind of evidence to support their points in an argument, and be especially suspicious of those using analogies as "scare tactics" ("This proposed legislation is just like laws passed in Nazi Germany"). As a writer, use only those analogies that will help your reader understand, remember, or accept your ideas; as a reader, always protect yourself by questioning the validity of the analogy offered to you. (◆ For more on *faulty analogy* as a logical fallacy, see page 319.)

To illustrate use of analogy, here are three examples from professional writers. In each case, what was the writer's purpose? How is "X" used to clarify or argue for "Y"? Which of these analogies do you find the most effective, and why?

A good lab course is an exercise in *doing* science. As such it differs totally in mission from a good lecture course where the object is learning *about* science. In the same way that one can gain vastly greater insight into music by learning to play an instrument, one can experience the doing of science only by going into the lab and trying one's hand at measurement.

—*Miles Pickering, "Are Lab Courses a Waste of Time?"*

For a long time now, since the beginning, in fact, men and women have been sparring and dancing around with each other, each pair trying to get it together and boogie to the tune called Life. For some people, it was always a glide, filled with grace and ease. For most of us, it is a stumble and a struggle, always trying to figure out the next step, until we find a partner whose inconsistencies seem to fit with ours, and the two of us fit into some kind of rhythm. Some couples wind up struggling and pulling at cross purposes; and of course, some people never get out on the floor, just stand alone in the corners, looking hard at the dancers.

—*Jay Molishever, "Changing Expectations of Marriage"*

One afternoon while we were there at that lake a thunderstorm came up. It was like the revival of an old melodrama that I had seen long ago with childish awe. The second-act climax of the drama of the electrical disturbance over a lake in America had not changed in any important respect. This was the big scene, still the big scene. The whole thing was so familiar, the first feeling of oppression and heat and a general air around camp of not wanting to go very far away. In midafternoon (it was all the same) a curious darkening of the sky, and a lull in everything that had made life tick; and then the way the boats suddenly swung the other way at their moorings with the coming of a breeze out of the new quarter, and the premonitory rumble. Then the kettle drum, then the snare, then the bass drum and cymbals, then crackling light against the dark. . . . Afterward the calm, the rain steadily rustling in the calm lake, the return of light and hope and spirits, and the campers running out in joy.

—*E. B. White, "Once More to the Lake"*

Analogies come in a variety of lengths, from several sentences to an entire essay, depending upon the writer's purpose. As you practice your writing in this composition class, you may find that incorporating an analogy into one of your essays is an effective way to explain, emphasize, or help support an idea.

Using Strategies and Sources

The following assignments ask you to not only incorporate what you've learned in this chapter regarding comparison and contrast but also to employ other strategies of development and to incorporate secondary sources into your response.

1. Consider two different career paths that you might choose to pursue. You could choose two careers that are related somehow to jobs you have held, or you could choose two career paths that are completely different from any work experiences you have had up until now. For which of the two careers are you best suited? Which of the two best meets your goals and aspirations? Write a brief essay of comparison and/or contrast in which you analyze the two career paths and reach a decision based on what you discover. Make sure to use the strategy of exemplification to support your examination of the differences between the two careers.

2. Using vivid, detailed description and compelling narrative to support your discussion, write a brief essay that compares and contrasts two of your most formative life experiences. In what ways were these experiences similar and/or different? Remember to answer the "so what" question. What larger lesson can you offer your reader based on your analysis of those experiences?

3. Explore the processes by which two different products are created, one by organic means and one by non-organic means. Write an essay that compares and contrasts these two processes and offers conclusions about which process is superior and why. Conduct research to incorporate information from credible secondary sources to support your comparison and contrast. (◆ See Chapter 19 for help with conducting research and evaluating the sources you find.)

Chapter 12

Definition

Frequently in conversation we must stop to ask, "What do you mean by that?" because in some cases our failure to comprehend just one particular term may lead to total misunderstanding. Suppose, for example, in a discussion with a friend, you refer to a new law as a piece of "liberal legislation"; if you and your friend do not share the same definition of "liberal," your remark may be completely misinterpreted. Here's another example: if you tell your grandparents that you are "headed for the man-cave for some plasma and tweets," will they think you are going for a blood transfusion and bird watching in a natural area or that you are headed to the basement rec room for TV and text messaging? In other words, a clear understanding of terms or ideas is often essential to meaningful communication.

Sometimes a dictionary definition or a one- or two-sentence explanation is all a term needs (Hemingway, for example, once defined courage as "grace under pressure"). And sometimes a brief, humorous definition can cut right to the heart of the matter (e.g., Destinesia: wandering into a room and forgetting what you came for).*

Frequently, however, you will find it necessary to provide an *extended definition*—that is, a longer, more detailed explanation that thoroughly defines the subject. Such a definition is yet another strategy of expository prose, writing whose primary purpose is giving information. Expository essays of extended definitions are quite common; think, for instance, of articles you've seen on gender-fluidity and being transgender, bigender, or agender that define gender identity in a variety of ways. Other published works have grappled with defining complex concepts such as free speech, animal rights and privacy rights, as well as addressing recent trends and issues such as distracted driving, the boomerang generation, and online sockpuppets. When writing your own extended definition, following a process like that represented in Figure 12.1 will help you develop an effective essay.

---

* Even graffiti employ definition. One bathroom wall favorite: "Death is Nature's way of telling you to slow down." Another, obviously written by an English major: "A double negative is a no-no."

Figure 12.1 VISUALIZING THE PROCESS: DEFINITION

Prewriting

Identify possible subjects by considering the following questions:

- In what topics do you have sufficient interest to generate an extended definition essay?
- About what topics do you have sufficient knowledge to create such an essay? Will additional research be required?
- What is your reason for creating your extended definition? Your essay is only as strong as your sense of purpose.
- Do you intend to provide an objective or subjective definition?

Drafting

Determine the purpose and content of your essay by asking the following questions:

- What's the best way to introduce your subject? By confronting the misuse of your term? By addressing the confusion surrounding the clear understanding of your term?
- Have you analyzed your audience fully to discover gaps in understanding?
- What steps can you take to ensure clarity for your reader?
- Which rhetorical strategies will be most effective in helping present your definition?
- What do you hope the reader will gain from your definition?

Revising

Carefully review your thesis and the supporting details you use by asking the following questions:

- Have you provided a complete definition?
- Have you avoided a trite introduction, such as using the dictionary definition?
- Is your definition circular or does it actually define your term?
- Have you used enough strategies to provide a clear definition?

Editing/Proofreading

Consider the sentence-level issues of your essay by asking the following questions:

- Do you use specific details to avoid vagueness and generalities?
- Have you reviewed your sentences for spelling, grammar, and punctuation errors?
- Is your paper formatted according to the assignment guidelines?

Why Do We Define?

Essays of extended definition are usually written for one or more of the following reasons:

1. To clarify an abstract term or concept ("hero," "success," "friendship," "loyalty")

2. To provide a personal interpretation of a term that the writer feels is vague, controversial, misused, or misunderstood ("feminist," "meme," "eco-terrorist," "multiculturalism")

3. To explain a new or unusual term or phrase found in popular culture, slang, or dialect, or within a particular geographic area, age set, or cultural group ("Twittersphere," "slactivism," "helicopter parent," "lagniappe," "binge-watching")

4. To make understandable the language or technical terms of a particular field of study, a profession, or an industry ("deconstruction," "identity spoofing," "retinitis pigmentosa," "subprime mortgage")

5. To offer information about a term or an idea to a particular interested audience (antique collectors learning about "Depression glass," movie buffs understanding "film noir," home decorators exploring "Feng Shui")

6. To inform and entertain by presenting the colorful history, uses, effects, or examples of a word, expression, concept, group, or group activity ("comfort food," "Zydeco music," "urban legends," "Kwanzaa," "power yoga")

Discussions of many nationwide issues often contain confusing or controversial terms. Hearing about the state of American finances, you might wish for a clearer understanding of words such as "recession," "bailout," or "toxic assets." Ecological proposals often talk about "sustainability" and "green" choices. Following the events of September 11, 2001, the definitions of many words were widely debated. Who is a "terrorist"? What is the difference between an "enemy combatant," a "detainee," and a "political prisoner"? Is it "patriotic" to oppose military actions of one's country? Today we need to understand specific meanings of language before we can make intelligent decisions or take appropriate actions.

Developing Your Essay

Here are four suggestions to help you prepare your essay of extended definition.

Know your purpose. Sometimes we need to define a term as clearly and objectively as possible. As a laboratory assistant, for instance, you might need to explain a technical measuring instrument to a group of new students. At other times, however, we may wish to persuade as well as inform our readers. People's interpretations of words, especially abstract or controversial terms, can, and often do, differ greatly depending on their point of view. After all, one person's protest march can be another person's street riot. Consequently, before you begin writing, decide on your purpose. If your readers need objective information only, make your definition as unbiased as you can; if your goal is to convince them that your point of view is the right or best one, you may adopt a variety of persuasive techniques as well as subjective (or even humorous) language. For example, readers of a paper entitled "The Joys of Catching Bronco-mania" should quickly realize they are not getting an objective medical analysis of Colorado football fever.

Give your readers a reason to read. One way to introduce your subject is to explain the previous use, misuse, or misunderstanding of the term; then present your new or better interpretation of the term or concept. An introduction and thesis defining a new word in popular usage might state, "Although people who suffer from weak immune systems might suddenly fear breathing the same air as someone suffering from affluenza, they needn't worry. 'Affluenza' isn't germ-laden; it's simply a colorful term describing the out-of-control consumerism spreading like an epidemic through America today." Or consider this introduction and thesis aimed at a word the writer feels is unclear to many readers: "When the credits roll at the end of a movie, much of the audience may be perplexed to see the job of 'best boy' listed. No, the 'best boy' isn't the nicest kid on the set—he (or she) is, in fact, the key electrician's first assistant, who helps arrange the lights for the movie's director of photography."

Keep your audience in mind to anticipate and avoid problems of clarity. Because you are trying to present a new or improved definition, you must strive above all for clarity. Ask yourself, "Who is my intended audience? What terms or parts of my definition are strange to them?" You don't help your audience, for example, by defining one campus slang expression in terms of other bits of unfamiliar slang. If, in other words, you discuss "mouse potatoes" as "Google bombers," you may be confusing some readers more than you are informing them. If your assignment doesn't specify a particular audience, you may find it useful to imagine one. You might pretend, for instance, that you're defining current campus slang for your parents, clarifying a local expression for a foreign visitor, or explaining a computer innovation to a technophobic friend. Remember that your definition is effective only if your explanation is clear, not just to you but to those unfamiliar with or confused about the term or concept under discussion.

Use as many strategies as necessary to clarify your definition. Depending on your subject, you may use any number of the following methods in your essay to define your term:

1. Describe the parts or distinguishing characteristics.*
2. Offer some examples.
3. Compare to or contrast with similar terms.
4. Explain an operation or a process.
5. State some familiar synonyms.
6. Define by negation (that is, tell what the term doesn't mean).
7. Present the history or trace its development or changes from the original linguistical meaning.

---

* With some topics, it may also be useful to describe the genus, class, or species to which the subject belongs.

8. Discuss causes or effects.

9. Identify times/places of use or appearance.

10. Associate it with recognizable people, places, or ideas.

To illustrate some of the methods suggested here, let's suppose you want to write an extended definition of "crossover" country music. You might choose several of these methods:

- Describe the parts: lyrics, musical sound, instruments, typical subject matter.
- Compare to or contrast with other kinds of music, such as traditional country music, pop, and rockabilly.
- Give some examples of famous "crossover" country songs and artists.
- Trace its historical development from traditional country music to the present.

In the paper on "crossover" country music or in any definition essay, you should, of course, use only those methods that will best define your term. Never include methods purely for the sake of exhibiting a variety of techniques. You, the writer, must decide which method or methods work best, which should receive the most emphasis, and in which order the chosen methods of definition should appear.

Problems to Avoid

Here is a list of "don'ts" for the writer of extended definition essays.

Don't present an incomplete definition. An inadequate definition is often the result of choosing a subject too broad or complex for your essay. You probably can't, for instance, do a good job of defining "twentieth-century modern art" in all its varieties in a short essay; you might, however, introduce your reader to some specific school of modern art, such as Cubism or Surrealism. Always narrow your subject to a manageable size and then define it as thoroughly as possible.

Don't begin by quoting Webster. If you must include a standard definition of your term, try to find a unique way of blending it into your discussion, perhaps as a point of contrast to your explanation of a word's new or expanded meaning. Dictionary definitions are generally so overused as opening sentences that they can drive composition teachers to seek more interesting jobs, such as measuring spaghetti in a pasta factory. Don't bore your audience to death; it's a terrible way to go.

Don't define vaguely or by using generalities. As always, use specific, vivid details to explain your subject. If, for example, you define a shamrock as "a green plant with three leaves," you have also described hundreds of other plants, including poison ivy. Consequently, you must select details that will make your subject distinct from any other. Including concrete examples is frequently useful in any essay but especially so when you are defining an abstract term, such as "pride," "patriotism," or "prejudice." To make your definition both interesting and clear, always add as many precise details as possible. (◆ For a review of using specific, colorful language, see pages 132, 146–147, and 166–170.)

Don't offer circular definitions. To define a poet as "one who writes poetry" or the American Dream as "the dream most Americans hold dear" is about as helpful as a doctor telling a patient, "Your illness is primarily a lack of good health." Explain your subject; don't just rename it.

Practicing What You've Learned

A. To practice developing definitions of various terms and concepts, try this activity. Consider different ways in which you have been labeled throughout your life. Perhaps you have been called a "jock" or a "nerd." You might have been or still be a "band geek" or a "hipster." Take a few moments to select one or two of these labels that you feel have been misunderstood. Next, brainstorm a list of characteristics that more accurately defines that label or type. Remember to use a variety of strategies if appropriate, such as description, comparison and contrast, exemplification, etc.

B. *Collaborative Activity:* To get feedback on what you've written in Exercise A, partner with a classmate and exchange your lists. Review the defining characteristics in your partner's list. Which characteristics are the most interesting to you and why? What strategies work most effectively in your partner's definition? Provide feedback regarding the effectiveness of the list and offer suggestions for additional defining characteristics and strategies that might strengthen your classmate's definition.

Essay Topics

Here are several suggestions for terms or concepts whose meanings might be unclear to a particular audience. Narrow any topic that seems too broad for your assignment, and decide before writing whether your definition will be objective or subjective, as appropriate for your purpose and readers. (Student writers, by the way, often note that abstract concepts are harder to define than the more concrete subjects, so proceed at your own risk, and remember to use plenty of specific detail in your essay.) ◆ For additional ideas, turn to the "Suggestions for Writing" section following the professional essay (page 274).

1. A current slang, campus, local, or popular culture expression

2. A term from your field of study

3. A slob (or some other annoying kind of roommate, friend, relative, or coworker)

4. An eldest, middle, or youngest child

5. A good/bad teacher, clerk, coach, friend, date, or spouse

6. Heroism or cowardice

continued on next page

7. Your favorite movie genre

8. A kind of music, painting, architecture, or dance

9. Cyberbullying (or some other form of social harassment)

10. A current fad or style or one from the past

11. A social group to which you belong or to which you aspire

12. A family or hometown expression

13. A good/bad restaurant, store, movie theater, nightspot, class

14. A winner

15. Prejudice or discrimination

16. An important historical movement or group

17. Good parenting

18. A term from a hobby or sport

19. Patriotism

20. Select a painting or photograph in which you think the artist offers a visual definition of the subject matter (e.g., heroism, sorrow, mortality, prosperity). Explain this definition by examining the artist's choice and arrangement of details in the picture. For example, study George Tooker's painting *The Subway*. What aspect of urban life is represented here? What parts of the picture illustrate and clarify this point of view? Or consider another picture in this text (see the list of artworks that follows the Detailed Table of Contents).

The *Subway*, 1950, by George Tooker
George Tooker, 1920-2011, *The Subway*, 1950. Egg tempera on composition board: 18 1/8 x 36 1/8 in. (46.04 x 91.76 cm). Whitney Museum of American Art, New York; Purchase, with funds from the Juliana Force Purchase Award 50.23

DC Moore Gallery/Whitney Museum of American Art

A Topic Proposal for Your Essay

Selecting the right subject matter is important to every writer. To help you clarify your ideas and strengthen your commitment to your topic, here is a proposal sheet that asks you to describe some of your ideas about your subject before you begin drafting. Although your ideas may change as you write (they will almost certainly become more refined), thinking through your topic now may help you avoid several false starts.

1. What subject will your essay define? Will you define this subject objectively or subjectively? Why?

2. Why are you interested in this topic? Do you have a personal or professional connection to the subject? State at least one reason for your choice of topic.

3. Is this a significant topic of interest to others? Why? Who specifically might find it interesting, informative, or entertaining?

4. Is your subject a controversial, ambiguous, or new term? What will readers gain by understanding this term as defined from your point of view?

5. Writers use a variety of techniques to define terms. At this point, list at least two techniques you think you might use to help readers understand your topic.

6. What difficulties, if any, can you foresee during the drafting of this essay? For example, do you need to do any additional reading or interviewing to collect information for your definition?

Once you have chosen your topic, take a moment to read through Figure 12.1 (page 262) to remind yourself of key questions you should be asking at each stage of the writing process for your definition essay.

Sample Student Essay

A student with an interest in running wrote the following essay defining "runner's high." Note that he uses several methods to define his subject, one that is difficult to explain to those who have not experienced it firsthand.

Introduction: An example and a general definition of the term

Blind Paces

1   After running the Mile-Hi ten-kilometer race in my hometown, I spoke with several of the leading runners about their experiences in the race. While most of them agreed that the course, which passed through a beautifully wooded yet overly hilly country area, was difficult, they also agreed that it was one of the best races of their running

careers. They could not, however, explain why it was such a wonderful race but could rather only mumble something about the tall trees, cool air, and sandy path. When pressed, most of them didn't even remember specific details about the course, except the start and finish, and ended their descriptions with a blank—but contented—stare. This self-satisfied, yet almost indescribable, feeling is often the result of an experienced runner running, a feeling often called, because of its similarities to other euphoric experiences, "runner's high."

2   Because this experience is seemingly impossible to define, perhaps a description of what runner's high is not might, by contrast, lead to a better understanding of what it is. I clearly remember—about five years ago—when I first took up running. My first day, I donned my tennis shorts, ragged T-shirt, and white discount-store tennis shoes somewhat ashamedly, knowing that they were symbolic of my novice status. I plodded around my block—just over a half mile—in a little more than four minutes, feeling and regretting every painful step. My shins and thighs revolted at every jarring move, and my lungs wheezed uncontrollably, gasping for air, yet denied that basic necessity. Worst of all, I was conscious of every aspect of my existence—from the swinging of my arms to the slap of my feet on the road, and from the sweat dripping into my eyes and ears and mouth, to the frantic inhaling and exhaling of my lungs. I kept my eyes carefully peeled on the horizon or the next turn in the road, judging how far away it was, how long it would take me to get there, and how much torture was left before I reached home. These first few runs were, of course, the worst—as far from any euphoria or "high" as possible. They did, however, slowly become easier as my body became accustomed to running.

Definition by negation, contrast

3   After a few months, in fact, I felt serious enough about this new pursuit to invest in a pair of real running shoes and shorts. Admittedly, these changes added to the comfort of my endeavor, but it wasn't

Personal
example

until two full years later that the biggest change occurred—and I experienced my first real "high." It was a fall day. The air was a cool sixty-five degrees, the sun was shining intently, the sky was a clear, crisp blue, and a few dead leaves were scattered across the browning lawn. I stepped out onto the road and headed north towards a nearby park for my routine jog. The next thing I remember, however, was not my run through the park, but rather my return, some forty-two minutes and six miles later, to my house. I woke, as if out of a

Effects of the
"high"

dream, just as I slowed to a walk, cooling down from my run. The only memory I had of my run was a feeling of floating on air—as if my real self were somewhere above and detached from my body, looking down on my physical self as it went through its blind paces. At first, I felt scared—what if I had run out in front of a car? Would I have even known it? I felt as if I had been asleep or out of control, that my brain had, in some real sense, been turned off.

4   Now, after five years of running and hundreds of such mystical experiences, I realize that I had never lost control while in this euphoric state—and that my brain hadn't been turned off, or, at least, not completely. But what does happen is hard to prove. George Sheehan, in a column for *Runner's World*, suggests that "altered states," such as runner's high, result from the loss of conscious control, from the

Possible
causes of the
feeling: Two
authorities

temporary cessation of left-brain messages and the dominance of right-brain activity (the left hemisphere being the seat of reason and rationality; the right, of emotions and inherited archetypal feelings) (14). Another explanation comes from Dr. Jerry Lynch, who argues, in his book *The Total Runner*, that the "high" results from the secretion of natural opiates, called beta endorphins, in the brain (213). My own explanation draws on both these medical explanations and is perhaps

The writer's
explanation

slightly more mystical. It's just possible that indeed natural opiates do go to work and consequently our brains lose track of the ins and outs of everyday activities—of jobs and classes and responsibilities. And because of this relaxed, drugged state, we are able to reach down into something more fundamental, something that ties us not only to each other but to all creation, here and gone. We rejoin nature, rediscovering the thread that links us to the universe.

5   My explanation is, of course, unscientific and therefore suspect. But I found myself, that day of the Mile-Hi Ten K run, eagerly trying to discuss my experience with the other runners: I wanted desperately to discover where I had been and what I had been doing during the race for which I received my first trophy. I didn't discover the answer from my fellow runners that day, but it didn't matter. I'm still running and still feeling the glow—whatever it is.

Conclusion: An incomplete understanding doesn't hamper enjoyment

Works Cited

Lynch, Jerry. *The Total Runner: A Complete Mind-Body Guide to Optimal Performance*. Prentice Hall, 1987, p. 213.

Sheehan, George. "Altered States." *Runner's World*, vol. 23, no. 8, Aug. 1988, p. 14.

In a formal research paper, the "Works Cited" list appears on a separate page.

The Munchausen Mystery

Don R. Lipsitt

As a clinical professor of psychiatry at Harvard Medical School, Don R. Lipsitt has written over one hundred articles on mental health and coedited five books, including *Hypochondriasis: Modern Perspectives on an Ancient Malady* (2001) and the *Handbook of Studies on General Hospital Psychiatry* (1991). In 2001 he was awarded a Lifetime Achievement Award from the Association of Academic Psychiatry. He published this article in *Psychology Today* in 1983.

Pre-reading Thoughts: Recall the last time someone clearly explained a new concept to you, perhaps in a class, at work, or during recreation. By what means was this subject defined and clarified for you—examples, description, comparisons, analysis of parts, or other techniques?

* ◆ To help you read this essay analytically, review pages 183–186.

1   In Thomas Mann's *Confessions of Felix Krull, Confidence Man*, young Felix fabricates an illness and convinces both his mother and the family doctor that he is sick. Felix describes the intense pleasure that his performance brings him. "I was delirious with the alternate tension and relaxation necessary to give reality, in my own eyes and others, to a condition that did not exist."

2   I estimate that in any given year in the United States, every general hospital with 100 or more beds admits an average of two patients who deliberately mimic symptoms of disease so convincingly that they deceive reasonably competent physicians. The patients' ages range from 11 to 60, but most are men in their 20s and 30s. Often these strange imposters wander from hospital to hospital, but even if we count only one patient per hospital, we are left with the staggering figure of approximately 4,000 people each year who devote their energies to fooling medical practitioners. If each incurs a cost of $1,000 to $10,000—bills that are not unusual, and that are rarely paid—the annual drain on health services alone is between $4 million and $40 million.

3   What do these people hope to gain? Nothing more, experience and research suggest, than the opportunity to assume the role of patient—in some cases, all the way to the operating table.

4   Unlike hypochondriacs, who really believe that they are ill, these people intentionally use varied and often sophisticated deceptions to duplicate medical problems. These deceptions include: blood "spit up" from a rubber pouch concealed in the mouth; genital bleeding deliberately caused by sharp objects; hypoglycemia (low blood sugar) induced by insulin injections; and skin infections or abscesses caused by injecting oneself with feces, sputum, or laboratory cultures of bacteria. A patient who called himself "the Duncan Hines of American hospitals" logged about 400 admissions in 25 years. Another patient, dubbed the "Indiana cyclone," was hospitalized in at least 12 states and two countries. The dramatic fabrication and extensive wandering often observed in such individuals prompted the late British physician Richard Asher in 1951 to label their "condition" the Munchausen Syndrome, after a flamboyant 18th-century teller of tall tales fictionalized in *The Adventures of Baron von Munchausen*, by Rudolph Erich Raspe. But as Asher himself came to realize, the name is somewhat misleading. While stories of the Baron's escapades are always palpably absurd, the accounts of patients whose condition bears his name are generally quite feasible. "Indeed," says Asher, "it is the credibility of their stories that makes these patients such a perpetual and tedious problem."

5   For obvious reasons, Munchausen patients have been difficult to study—they usually flee once their fictions are exposed. But research to this point provides a minimal portrait. In addition to being primarily men in their 20s and 30s, most have high IQs (as their imaginative inventions indicate), often abuse but are not necessarily addicted to drugs, come from a background in which a doctor was an important figure, are employed in health care, and are productive citizens between episodes.

6   What produces their medical madness? There are three main explanations:

7   The psychoanalytic interpretation draws attention to the unconscious. The Munchausen patient, by feigning illness, presents himself simultaneously as victim and victimizer, and compulsively re-enacts unresolved conflicts: The weak child/patient is challenging and even defying the strong father/surgeon. Paradoxically, the weak

patient controls the surgeon/parent—and risks death!—by "making" the doctor perform needless surgery. The psychoanalytic view also sees in the syndrome an attempt to continue into adulthood the game of "doctor," which characterizes a phase of childhood development.

8   A second explanation locates the source of Munchausen behavior in a personality trait known as borderline character disorder. According to Otto Kernberg, a psychoanalyst at Cornell who has most fully researched this trait, the core problems are untamed (often unconscious) rage and chronic feelings of boredom, two emotions that work against each other. The Munchausen character, for example, presents himself as a "sick" patient, a condition that should appeal to a dedicated physician—yet no accepting relationship can grow between a deceptive patient and a suspecting physician who is alternately idealized and despised.

9   The third explanation looks to excessive stress as the trigger that starts Munchausen patients on their medical odyssey. Many of them began their "wandering" and symptom mimicry in response to cumulative major disappointments, losses, or damage to self-image. One patient first sought surgery for questionable persistent stomach pains after being jilted by a medical-student lover, beginning a long string of lies and hospitalizations.

10   We are beginning to identify the reasons for the behavior of Munchausen patients, but we are still far from knowing how to free them of their remarkably creative compulsion for self-destructive behavior.

QUESTIONS ON CONTENT, STRUCTURE, AND STYLE

1. Why does Lipsitt begin his essay with reference to Thomas Mann's character in *Confessions of Felix Krull, Confidence Man*?

2. What effect does the essay's title have on readers? Why didn't Lipsitt simply call this essay "Munchausen Syndrome"?

3. Why does Lipsitt feel this syndrome is important to understand? How does this problem affect the health-care system?

4. Why explain the origin of the syndrome's name?

5. Why does Lipsitt use specific examples of "deceptions" to develop his extended definition?

6. Similarly, why does Lipsitt offer examples of actual patients? Would additional examples be helpful?

7. How does Lipsitt use contrast as a technique of definition in paragraph 4?

8. What other strategy of definition does Lipsitt employ in paragraphs 6–9? Why might readers interested in understanding this syndrome want such discussion?

9. Evaluate the essay's conclusion. Is it an effective choice for this essay?

10. After reading Lipsitt's descriptive details, examples, and analysis, do you feel you now have a general understanding of a new term? If the writer were to expand his definition, what might he add to make your understanding even more complete? More statistics? Case studies? Testimony from doctors or patients themselves?

VOCABULARY*

fabricates (1)

mimic (2)

incurs (2)

hypochondriacs (4)

sputum (4)

palpably (4)

feasible (4)

psychoanalytic (7)

paradoxically (7)

odyssey (9)

SUGGESTIONS FOR WRITING

Try using Don Lipsitt's "The Munchausen Mystery" as a stepping-stone to your essay. Select a puzzling or "mysterious" subject from a field of study (e.g., black holes in space) or from an interest you have explored (or would like to explore). Write an extended definition, as Lipsitt did, that explains this mystery for your readers. As appropriate, include information about its characteristics, parts, history, possible causes, effects, solutions, benefits, or dangers. Or investigate a well-known mystery, such as Stonehenge, the Bermuda Triangle, the Nazca path drawings, the Marfa lights, King Tut's "curse," Bigfoot, the Easter Island statues, or perhaps even a famous local ghost. Remember that your essay should offer in-depth explanation, not just general description.

A Revision Worksheet

As you write your rough drafts, consult Chapter 5 for guidance through the revision process. In addition, here are a few questions to ask yourself as you revise your extended definition essay:

1. Is the subject narrowed to manageable size, and is the purpose of the definition clear to the readers?

2. If the definition is objective, is the language as neutral as possible?

3. If the definition is subjective, is the point of view obvious to the readers?

4. Are all the words and parts of the definition itself clear to the essay's particular audience?

5. Are there enough explanatory methods (examples, descriptions, history, causes, effects, etc.) used to make the definition clear and informative?

6. Have the various methods been organized and ordered in an effective way?

7. Does the essay contain enough specific details to make the definition clear and distinct rather than vague or circular? Where could additional details be added?

Collaborative Activity: After you've revised your essay extensively, exchange rough drafts with a classmate and answer these questions for each other, making specific suggestions for improvement wherever appropriate. (◆ For advice on productive participation in classroom workshops, see pages 121–123.)

---

*Numbers in parentheses following the vocabulary words refer to paragraphs in the essay.

Using Strategies and Sources

The following assignments ask you to not only incorporate what you've learned in this chapter regarding definition but also to employ other strategies of development and to incorporate secondary sources into your response.

1. In a brief definition essay, explore your interpretation of the meaning of an abstract concept like heroism, righteous anger, privacy, etc. Use the strategy of comparison or contrast to support your definition by also explaining what the concept is not.

2. Thoughtfully consider your favorite genre, subgenre, or style of music. In an essay of extended definition, thoroughly explain that genre to your reader. You might discuss the characteristics and history of the genre, as well as notable artists from that genre. Use a variety of strategies such as exemplification, comparison or contrast, narration, and others to convey to your reader what that genre is and what it is not. Support for such a definition could include examples of specific artists and albums, live concert experiences, or analysis of lyrics and musical themes.

3. In recent years, there has been growing resistance to the idea of GMOs or Genetically Modified Organisms. Write an extended definition essay in which you define GMOs, including potential benefits and hazards in your exploration, before offering the reader a recommendation for or against the consumption of such products. Incorporate supporting information from credible secondary sources. (◆ See Chapter 19 for help with conducting research and evaluating the sources you find.)

Chapter 13

Division and Classification

To make large or complex subjects easier to comprehend, we frequently apply the principles of *division* or *classification*. Following a writing process like that represented in Figure 13.1 will help you develop an effective division or classification essay.

Division

Division is the act of separating something into its component parts so that it may be better understood or used by the reader. For example, consider a complex subject such as the national budget. Perhaps you have seen a picture on television or in the newspaper of the budget represented by a circle or a pie that has been divided into parts and labeled: a certain percentage or "slice" of the budget designated for military spending, another slice for social services, another for education, and so on. By studying the budget after it has been divided into its parts, taxpayers may have a better sense of how their money is being spent.

As a student, you see division in action in many of your college courses. A literature teacher, for instance, might approach a particular drama by dividing its plot into stages such as exposition, rising action, climax, falling action, and dénouement. Or your chemistry lab instructor may ask you to break down a substance into its components to learn how the parts interact to form the chemical compound. Even this textbook is divided into chapters to make it easier for you to use. When you think of *division*, then, think of dividing, separating, or breaking down one subject (often a large or complex or unfamiliar one) into its parts to help people understand it more easily.

Classification

While the principle of division calls for separating one thing into its parts, *classification* systematically groups a number of things into categories to make the information easier to grasp. Without some sort of imposed system of order, a body of information can be a jumble of facts and figures. For example, at some point you may have turned to the classified ads in a print newspaper or to an online site such as Craigslist. If the ads were not classified into categories such as "houses to rent," "cars for sale," and "jobs," you

Figure 13.1 VISUALIZING THE PROCESS: DIVISION AND CLASSIFICATION

Prewriting

Identify possible subjects by considering the following questions:

- In what topics are you interested and about which do you have significant knowledge? How much research will you need to do?
- Why would your audience be interested in this topic?
- For your potential topics, would you write an essay of classification or division?
- What principle of classification or division would you use? Why would this be a useful way to look at your potential topic?

Drafting

Determine the development and content of your essay by asking the following questions:

- Have you devoted at least one body paragraph to each of your parts or categories?
- How will you make the purpose of your division or classification clear to your audience?
- What methods of develop can you use to fully develop your different categories?
- What is the best number of categories for your discussion?

Revising

Carefully review your thesis and the supporting details you use by asking the following questions:

- Is your essay's purpose clear to your reader?
- Does your essay maintain the principle of classification or division consistently throughout?
- Have all the parts of your subject been accounted for in your systematic classification or division?
- Are your categories distinct, with no overlap between them?
- Is your essay organized logically?

Editing/Proofreading

Consider the sentence-level issues of your essay by asking the following questions:

- Have you provided enough specific detail for each of your categories?
- Do you include strong transitions to carry your essay from your discussion of one category to the next?
- Have you reviewed your sentences for spelling, grammar, and punctuation errors?
- Is your paper formatted according to the assignment guidelines?

would have to search through numerous ads to find the service, opportunity, or item you needed.

Classification occurs everywhere around you. As a student, you may be classified as a freshman, sophomore, junior, or senior; you may also be classified by your major. If you vote, you may be categorized as a Democrat, Republican, Independent, Socialist, or something else; if you attend religious services, you may be classified as Baptist, Methodist, Catholic, Jewish, and so on. The books you buy may be grouped and shelved by the bookstore into "mysteries," "Westerns," "biographies," "science fiction," and other categories; the movies you see have already been typed as "G," "PG," "PG-13," "R," or "NC-17." Professionals classify almost every kind of knowledge: ornithologists classify birds; etymologists classify words by origins; botanists classify plants; zoologists classify animals.

Remember that *classification* differs from division in that it sorts and organizes *many* things into appropriate groups, types, kinds, or categories. *Division* begins with *one* thing and separates it into its parts.

Developing Your Essay

Classification or division is yet another strategy of expository writing, whereby a writer creates a prose text to convey information to an audience. A classification or division paper is generally easy to develop. Each part or category is identified and described in a major part of the body of the essay. Frequently, one body paragraph will be devoted to each category. Here are three additional hints for writing your essay:

Select one principle of classification or division and stick to it. If you are classifying students by major, for instance, don't suddenly switch to classification by college: French, economics, psychology, *arts and sciences*, math, and chemistry. A similar error occurs in this classification of dogs by breeds because it includes a physical characteristic: spaniels, terriers, *long-haired*, hounds, and retrievers. Decide on what basis of division you will classify or divide your subject and then be consistent throughout your essay.

Make the purpose of your division or classification clear to your audience. Don't just announce that "There are four kinds of 'X'" or that "'Z' has three important parts." Why does your particular audience need this information? Consider these sample thesis statements:

- By recognizing the three kinds of poisonous snakes in this area, campers and backpackers may be able to take the proper medical steps if they are bitten.
- Knowing the four types of spinning reels will help those new to mullet fishing purchase the equipment best suited to their needs.
- Although karate has become a popular form of exercise as well as of self-defense, few people know what the ascending levels of achievement—or "belts" as they are called—actually stand for.

Organize your material for a particular purpose and then explain to your readers what that purpose is.

Account for all the parts in your division or classification. Don't, for instance, claim to classify all the evergreen trees native to your hometown and then leave out one or more species. For a short essay, narrow your ruling principle rather than omit categories. You couldn't, for instance, classify all the architectural styles in the United States in a short paper, but you might discuss the major styles on your campus. In the same manner, the enormous task of classifying all types of mental illness might be narrowed to the most common forms of childhood schizophrenia. However you narrow your topic, remember that in a formal classification, all the parts must be accounted for.

Like most rules, the preceding one has an exception. If your instructor permits, you can also write a satirical or humorous classification. In this sort of essay, you make up your own categories as well as your thesis. One writer, for example, recently wrote about the kinds of moviegoers who spoil the show for everyone else, such as "the babbling idiot," "the texting screen-flasher," and "the wandering dawdler." Another female student described blind dates to avoid, including "Mr. Neanderthal," "Timothy Timid," "Red, the Raging Rebel," and "Frat-Rat Freddie," among others. Still another student classified the various kinds of people who frequent the school library at 2 A.M. In this kind of informal essay, in which you're making a humorous or satirical point about your subject, your classification should be more than random silliness. Effective humor should ultimately make good sense, not nonsense.

Problems to Avoid

Avoid underdeveloped categories. A classification or division essay is not a mechanical list; each category should contain enough specific details to make it clearly recognizable and interesting. To present each category or part, you may draw on the methods of development you already know, such as example, comparison and contrast, and definition. Try to use the same techniques in each category so that no one category or part of your essay seems underdeveloped or unclear.

Avoid indistinct categories. Each category should be a separate unit; there should be no overlap among categories. For example, in a classification of shirts by fabric, the inclusion of flannel with silk, nylon, and cotton is an overlap because flannel is a kind of cotton. Similarly, in a classification of soft drinks by flavor, to include sugar-free with cola, root beer, orange, grape, and so on, is misleading because sugar-free drinks come in many different flavors. In other words, make each category unique.

Avoid too few or too many categories. A classification essay should have at least three categories, avoiding the either-or dichotomy. On the other hand, too many categories give a short essay the appearance of a list rather than a discussion. Whatever the number, don't forget to use transitional devices for easy movement from category to category.

Practicing What You've Learned

A. To practice dividing a whole into parts or classifying many into categories, try the following activity. Spend a few minutes thinking about the people that visit a place you frequently spend time: your college's student center, your place of employment, your favorite bar or hangout, your church, etc. Think about the different types or categories of people that you encounter there. Now, jot down the different ways you could classify these people. What principles of classification emerge from your thoughts? Race? Socioeconomic status? Clothing styles? Attitudes? What are some humorous ways of classifying these people? What are more serious ways of doing so? Consider also the reasons you might offer for such a classification. What point might you make by creating such a classification?

B. *Collaborative Activity*: Practice giving and receiving feedback on your ideas by pairing up with a classmate and trading the work you produced in Exercise A. As you review your classmate's work, consider which of these classifying principles you find most compelling and why. Look carefully at the groups or classifications that your classmate has produced under each principle. Do the groups account for everyone? Are there groups that are omitted? Are the groups organized according to one singular principle of classification? Offer your classmate such feedback on his or her work and supply any additional insights you might have.

Essay Topics

Narrow and focus your subject by selecting an appropriate principle of division or classification. Some of the following suggestions may be appropriate for humorous essays ("The Three Best Breeds of Cats for Antisocial People"). ◆ For additional ideas, see the "Suggestions for Writing" section following the professional essays (pages 287 and 289).

1. Attitudes towards a current controversy

2. Theories explaining "X" (e.g., disappearance of dinosaurs, climate change in Antarctica)

3. Chronic moochers, dangerous drivers, annoying cell phone users, or some other irritating group

4. Types of professional athletes

5. Reasons people participate in some activity (or excuses for not participating)

6. Summer or part-time jobs on campus

7. Customers at your work or at a business you frequent

continued on next page

8. Kinds of students on your campus

9. Specializations in your field of study

10. Different types of romance novels, science fiction novels, Western novels, etc.

11. Myths or common misperceptions about a person, place, or thing

12. Residents of your hometown

13. Popular kinds of movies, music, or video games (or types within a larger category: kinds of teen vampire-movies or varieties of heavy-metal music)

14. Vacations or Spring Break trips

15. Most common distractions interfering with composition students' vows to revise their essays one more time

16. Different types of "good" teachers or "bad" teachers

17. Bosses or co-workers to avoid or cultivate

18. Kinds of tools or equipment for a particular task in your field of study

19. Diets, exercise, or stress-reduction programs (or their participants)

20. Amateur athletes, coaches, or sports fans (including those you hope aren't sitting next to you at an athletic event)

Wisconsin Cheeseheads cheer on the Green Bay Packers.

A Topic Proposal for Your Essay

Selecting the right subject matter is important to every writer. To help you clarify your ideas and strengthen your commitment to your topic, here is a proposal sheet that asks you to describe some of your preliminary ideas about your subject before you begin drafting. Although your ideas may change as you write (they will almost certainly become more refined), thinking through your choice of topic now may help you avoid several false starts.

1. What is the subject of your essay? Will you write an essay of classification or division?

2. What principle of classification or division will you use? Why is this a useful or informative principle for your particular topic and readers?

3. Why are you interested in this topic? Do you have a personal or professional connection to the subject? State at least one reason for your choice of topic.

4. Is this a significant topic of interest to others? Why? Who specifically might find it interesting, informative, or entertaining?

5. List at least three categories you are considering for development in your essay.

6. What difficulties, if any, might arise from this topic during the drafting of your essay? For example, do you know enough about your topic to offer details that will make each of your categories clear and distinct to your readers?

Once you have chosen your topic, take a moment to read through Figure 13.1 (page 277) to remind yourself of key questions you should be asking at each stage of the writing process for your division or classification essay.

Sample Student Essay

In the following essay, the student writer divided the Mesa Verde Native American Era into three time periods that correspond to changes in the people's domestic skills, crafts, and housing. Note the writer's use of description and examples to help the reader distinguish one time period from another.

The Native American Era at Mesa Verde

1   Visiting Mesa Verde National Park is a trip back in time to two and a half centuries before Columbus.[1] The park, located in southwestern Colorado, is the setting of a silent stone city, ten ruins built into protective seven-hundred-foot cliffs that housed hundreds of people from the pre-Columbian era to the end of the thirteenth century. Visitors to the park often enjoy its architecture and history more if they know a little about the various people who lived there. The Native American Era may be divided into three time periods that show growing sophistication in such activities as crafts, hunting, trade, and housing: Basket Maker (1–450 C.E.), Modified Basket Maker (450–750 C.E.), and Pueblo (750–1300 C.E.).

2   The earliest Mesa Verdeans, the Basket Makers, whose ancestors had been nomads, sought shelter from the dry plains in the cliff caves and became farmers. During growing seasons they climbed up toeholds cut in the cliffs and grew beans and squash on the green

Introduction: Establishing a reason for knowing the classification

Principle of division of the Native American Era

Time period one: Early cliff life

[1] Last summer I worked at Mesa Verde as a student-guide for the Parks Service; the information in this paper is based on the tour I gave three times a week to hundreds of visitors to the park.

mesa above. Settling down also meant more time for crafts. They didn't make pottery yet but instead wove intricate baskets that held water. Instead of depending on raw meats and vegetables, they could now cook food in these baskets by dropping heated rocks into the water. Because the Basket Makers hadn't discovered the bow and arrow yet, they had to rely on the inaccurate spear, which meant little fresh meat and few animal skins. Consequently, they wore little clothing but liked bone, seed, and stone ornaments.

3   The second period, 450–750 C.E., saw the invention of pottery, the bow and arrow, and houses. Pottery was apparently learned from other tribes. From crude clay baked in the sun, the Mesa Verdeans advanced to clay mixed with straw and sand and baked in kilns. Paints were concocted from plants and minerals, and the tribe produced a variety of beautifully decorated mugs, bowls, jars, pitchers, and canteens. Such pots meant that water could be stored for longer periods, and perhaps a water supply encouraged more trade with neighboring tribes. These Mesa Verdeans also acquired the bow and arrow, a weapon that improved their hunting skills, and enlarged their wardrobes to include animal skins and feather blankets. Their individual living quarters, called pithouses, consisted of twenty-foot-wide holes in the ground with log, grasses, and earthen framework over them.

Time period two: New crafts, trade, and housing

4   The third period lasted until 1300 C.E. and saw the innovation of pueblos, or groups of dwellings, instead of single-family units. Nearly eight hundred dwellings show the large number of people who inhabited the complex tunneled houses, shops, storage rooms, courtyards, and community centers whose masonry walls, often elaborately decorated, were three and four stories high. At the spacious Balcony House pueblo, for example, an adobe court lies beneath another vaulted roof; on three sides stand two-story houses with balconies that lead from one room to the next. In back of the court is a spring, and along the front side is a low wall that

Time period three: Expanded community living and trade

kept the children from falling down the seven-hundred-foot cliff to the canyon floor below. Balcony House pueblo also contains two kivas, circular subterranean ceremonial chambers that show the importance of fellowship and religion to the people of this era. During this period the Mesa Verdeans were still farmers and potters, but cotton cloth and other nonnative products found at the ruins suggest a healthy trade with the south. But despite the trade goods, sophisticated pottery, and such innovations in clothing as the "disposable" juniper-bark diapers of babies, life was still simple; the Mesa Verdeans had no system of writing, no wheel, and no metal.

5   Near the end of the thirteenth century, the cliff dwellings became ghost towns. Archaeologists don't know for certain why the Mesa Verdeans left their elaborate homes, but they speculate that a drought that lasted some twenty years may have driven them south into New Mexico and Arizona, where strikingly similar crafts and tools have been found. Regardless of their reason for leaving, they left an amazing architectural and cultural legacy. Learning about the people who lived in Mesa Verde centuries ago provides an even deeper appreciation of the cliff palaces that awe thousands of national park visitors every year.

Conclusion: The importance of understanding Mesa Verde's people

---

PROFESSIONAL ESSAY: CLASSIFICATION*

The Plot Against People

Russell Baker

Russell Baker was a journalist and social commentator for over forty years before his retirement in 2004. His "Observer" columns, written for the *New York Times* and syndicated throughout the country, won him both the George Polk Award for Distinguished Commentary and a Pulitzer Prize for journalism. He has published numerous books, including *Growing Up* (1982), an autobiography that won him a second Pulitzer Prize; *The Good Times* (1989); and *Looking Back* (2002). This often-reprinted essay originally appeared in the *New York Times* in 1968.

---

* ◆ To help you read this essay analytically, review pages 183–186.

Pre-reading Thoughts: What one possession or piece of technology in your life causes the most frustration for you? How do you successfully triumph over this misery?

1   Inanimate objects are classified into three major categories—those that don't work, those that break down and those that get lost.

2   The goal of all inanimate objects is to resist man and ultimately to defeat him, and the three major classifications are based on the method each object uses to achieve its purpose. As a general rule, any object capable of breaking down at the moment when it is most needed will do so. The automobile is typical of the category.

3   With the cunning typical of its breed, the automobile never breaks down while entering a filling station with a large staff of idle mechanics. It waits until it reaches a downtown intersection in the middle of the rush hour, or until it is fully loaded with family and luggage on the Ohio Turnpike.

4   Thus it creates maximum misery, inconvenience, frustration and irritability among its human cargo, thereby reducing its owner's life span.

5   Washing machines, garbage disposals, lawn mowers, light bulbs, automatic laundry dryers, water pipes, furnaces, electrical fuses, television tubes, hose nozzles, tape recorders, slide projectors—all are in league with the automobile to take their turn at breaking down whenever life threatens to flow smoothly for their human enemies.

6   Many inanimate objects, of course, find it extremely difficult to break down. Pliers, for example, and gloves and keys are almost totally incapable of breaking down. Therefore, they have had to evolve a different technique for resisting man.

7   They get lost. Science has still not solved the mystery of how they do it, and no man has ever caught one of them in the act of getting lost. The most plausible theory is that they have developed a secret method of locomotion which they are able to conceal the instant a human eye falls upon them.

8   It is not uncommon for a pair of pliers to climb all the way from the cellar to the attic in its single-minded determination to raise its owner's blood pressure. Keys have been known to burrow three feet under mattresses. Women's purses, despite their great weight, frequently travel through six or seven rooms to find hiding space under a couch.

9   Scientists have been struck by the fact that things that break down virtually never get lost, while things that get lost hardly ever break down.

10   A furnace, for example, will invariably break down at the depth of the first winter cold wave, but it will never get lost. A woman's purse, which after all does have some inherent capacity for breaking down, hardly ever does; it almost invariably chooses to get lost.

11   Some persons believe this constitutes evidence that inanimate objects are not entirely hostile to man, and that a negotiated peace is possible. After all, they point out, a furnace could infuriate a man even more thoroughly by getting lost than by breaking down, just as a glove could upset him far more by breaking down than by getting lost.

12   Not everyone agrees, however, that this indicates a conciliatory attitude among inanimate objects. Many say it merely proves that furnaces, gloves and pliers are incredibly stupid.

13   The third class of objects—those that don't work—is the most curious of all. These include such objects as barometers, car clocks, cigarette lighters, flashlights and toy-train locomotives. It is inaccurate, of course, to say that they never work. They work

once, usually for the first few hours after being brought home, and then quit. Thereafter, they never work again.

14   In fact, it is widely assumed that they are built for the purpose of not working. Some people have reached advanced ages without ever seeing some of these objects—barometers, for example—in working order.

15   Science is utterly baffled by the entire category. There are many theories about it. The most interesting holds that the things that don't work have attained the highest state possible for an inanimate object, the state to which things that break down and things that get lost can still only aspire.

16   They have truly defeated man by conditioning him never to expect anything of them, and in return they have given man the only peace he receives from inanimate society. He does not expect his barometer to work, his electric locomotive to run, his cigarette lighter to light or his flashlight to illuminate, and when they don't, it does not raise his blood pressure.

17   He cannot attain that peace with furnaces and keys and cars and women's purses as long as he demands that they work for their keep.

QUESTIONS ON CONTENT, STRUCTURE, AND STYLE

1. What is Baker's purpose in writing this classification? What reaction do you think Baker wants to evoke from his newspaper audience?

2. Where is Baker's thesis statement? Would his essay be more effective if his thesis were preceded by a fully developed lead-in? Why, or why not?

3. Identify Baker's categories and principle of classification. What do these categories have in common?

4. Why does Baker give examples of items that belong to each category? Does this strengthen his essay? Why or why not?

5. Of the categories of inanimate objects discussed in the essay, which one is most effectively developed? List some examples of details.

6. Consider Baker's use of personification as he talks about inanimate objects. Give some examples of descriptions that give human qualities to these items. What effect does this have on tone and style?

7. How does Baker's word choice affect his tone? What does Baker's title contribute to his tone?

8. How does publication in a newspaper affect Baker's paragraphing style? How might paragraphs 7 and 8, for example, appear in essay format?

9. If Baker were to revise his article today, how might he change his word choice in paragraphs 2, 7, 11, 16, and 17 to make his language more gender inclusive?

10. Evaluate Baker's conclusion. Is it effective or too abrupt?

VOCABULARY*

inanimate (1)	locomotion (7)	constitutes (11)
cunning (3)	virtually (9)	conciliatory (12)
evolve (6)	inherent (10)	barometer (13)

———————————

*Numbers in parentheses following the vocabulary words refer to paragraphs in the essay.

SUGGESTIONS FOR WRITING

Try using Russell Baker's "The Plot Against People" as a stepping-stone to your writing. To parallel Baker's criticisms of objects that inflict misery, think about kinds of people or forces that you feel are secretly conspiring to destroy your peace of mind. Consider, for example, kinds of crazed drivers who are contributing to road rage today. Annoying telephone solicitors? Obnoxious wait-staffers or clerks? Grocery shoppers in the checkout line in front of you? Or consider the kinds of rules that govern your life. Inane parking regulations that ensure you will never find a space anywhere near campus? Financial-aid red tape only an accounting genius could cut through? Your essay might be humorous, like Baker's, or quite serious, as you expose still another "plot" against humankind.

PROFESSIONAL ESSAY: DIVISION*
What Is REALLY in a Hot Dog?

This 2008 article was written by the staff of SixWise, a Web site focused on family, career, and home safety advice. The mission of SixWise.com, and its newsletter, is to help its readers "be safe, live longer, and prosper."

> **Pre-reading Thoughts:** Have you ever looked closely at the ingredients or the nutritional facts listed on a food or personal-use item and consequently rejected that product? In general, how important are healthful ingredients in your choice of favorite foods?

1   Now that baseball season is wrapping up, and you've likely eaten your share of ballpark dogs (9 percent of all hot dogs purchased are bought at baseball stadiums, after all), it's the perfect time to delve into what's really in one of America's favorite foods: the hot dog. It's the subject of many urban legends, the object of many grade-schoolers' double dares: do hot dogs contain pig snouts and chicken feathers, or are they really made from high-quality meat?

2   The debate certainly hasn't put a damper on Americans' enthusiasm for the food. The U.S. population consumes about 20 billion hot dogs a year, according to the National Hot Dog and Sausage Council. That works out to about 70 hot dogs per person, per year. And, an estimated 95 percent of U.S. homes serve hot dogs at one meal or another. Wondering how many hot dogs are sold each year? In 2005, retail stores sold 764 million packages of hot dogs (not including Wal-Mart), which adds up to more than $1.5 billion in retail sales.

What's in a Hot Dog?

3   On to the million-dollar question: what are hot dogs made of? According to the National Hot Dog and Sausage Council:

> All hot dogs are cured and cooked sausages that consist of mainly pork, beef, chicken and turkey or a combination of meat and poultry. Meats used in hot dogs come from the muscle of the animal and looks much like what you buy in the

_____

* ◆ To help you read this essay analytically, review pages 183–186.

grocer's case. Other ingredients include water, curing agents and spices, such as garlic, salt, sugar, ground mustard, nutmeg, coriander and white pepper.

However, there are a couple of caveats. "Variety meats," which include things like liver, kidneys and hearts, may be used in processed meats like hot dogs, but the U.S. Department of Agriculture requires that they be disclosed in the ingredient label as "with variety meats" or "with meat by-products." Further, watch out for statements like "made with mechanically separated meats (MSM)." Mechanically separated meat is "a paste-like and batter-like meat product produced by forcing bones, with attached edible meat, under high pressure through a sieve or similar device to separate the bone from the edible meat tissue," according to the U.S. Food Safety and Inspection Service (FSIS).

4   Although the FSIS maintains that MSM are safe to eat, mechanically separated beef is no longer allowed in hot dogs or other processed meats (as of 2004) because of fears of mad cow disease. Hot dogs can contain no more than 20 percent mechanically separated pork, and any amount of mechanically separated chicken or turkey. So if you're looking for the purest franks, pick those that are labeled "all beef," "all pork," or "all chicken, turkey, etc." Franks labeled in this way must be made with meat from a single species and do not include by-products. (But check the label anyway, just to be sure. Turkey and chicken franks, for instance, can include turkey or chicken meat and turkey or chicken skin and fat in proportion to a turkey or chicken carcass.)

Are Hot Dogs Unhealthy?

5   Eating lots of processed meats like hot dogs has been linked to an increased risk of cancer. Part of that risk is probably due to the additives used in the meats, namely sodium nitrite and MSG. Sodium nitrite (or sodium nitrate) is used as a preservative, coloring and flavoring in hot dogs (and other processed meats), and studies have found it can lead to the formation of cancer-causing chemicals called nitrosamines. MSG, a flavor enhancer used in hot dogs and many other processed foods, has been labeled as an "excitotoxin," which, according to Dr. Russell Blaylock, an author and neurosurgeon, are "a group of excitatory amino acids that can cause sensitive neurons to die."

6   If you love hot dogs and are looking for a healthier alternative, opt for nitrate-free, organic varieties (available in health food stores and increasingly in regular supermarkets) that contain all meat, no by-products and no artificial flavors, colors or preservatives.

QUESTIONS ON CONTENT, STRUCTURE, AND STYLE

1. How does this article illustrate division rather than classification?
2. What is the main purpose of this article? What kinds of readers might be especially interested in this topic?
3. Why include the figures on hot dog consumption and sales?
4. In terms of organization, why did the staff writers begin with a statement from the National Hot Dog and Sausage Council?
5. What is gained by quoting directly from such organizations as the US Department of Agriculture and the US Food Safety and Inspection Service?
6. What warnings about hot dog variety are presented through use of description, definition, and examples? Were any of the details surprising to you?

7. Paragraph 5 offers several claims about the links of hot dogs to cancer. How might these claims be better supported?

8. Why is Dr. Blaylock's testimony included in the paragraph?

9. Would you consider this article an objective or subjective treatment of its subject? What choices are the writers advocating?

10. Did this article successfully persuade you to follow the advice given in its conclusion? Why or why not?

VOCABULARY

delve (1)   caveats (3)

snouts (1)   sieve (3)

damper (2)   carcass (4)

SUGGESTIONS FOR WRITING

Use the article "What Is REALLY in a Hot Dog?" as a stepping-stone to your own essay. As a consumer, what other products would you like to know more about? What ingredients, for example, go into your favorite snack food? Soft drink? Energy bar? Chewing gum? Or nutritionally analyze a popular fast-food dinner: How healthful is a Happy Meal? What is the meat-filler "pink slime"? Or consider a household product. What's really in our deodorants, cosmetics, hair products, or mouthwash? Are your choices of detergents or other cleaners more toxic than "green"? Write an essay that not only gives information but also influences your readers to buy or reject the product. (◆ Consult Chapter 19 if you need help researching your topic.)

A Revision Worksheet

As you write your rough drafts, consult Chapter 5 for guidance through the revision process. In addition, here are a few questions to ask yourself as you revise your classification essay:

1. Is the purpose of the essay clear to the reader?

2. Is the principle of classification or division maintained consistently throughout the essay?

3. If the essay presents a formal division or classification, has the subject been narrowed so that all the parts are accounted for?

4. If the essay presents an informal or humorous division or classification, does the paper nevertheless make a significant or entertaining point?

5. Is each category developed with enough specific detail? Where might more details be effectively added?

6. Is each class distinct, with no overlap among categories?

continued on next page

7. Is the essay organized logically and coherently with smooth transitions between the discussions of the categories?

Collaborative Activity: After you've revised your essay extensively, you might exchange rough drafts with a classmate and answer these questions for each other, making specific suggestions for improvement wherever appropriate. (◆ For advice on productive participation in classroom workshops, see pages 121–123.)

Using Strategies and Sources

The following assignments ask you to not only incorporate what you've learned in this chapter regarding classification and division, but also to employ other strategies of development and to incorporate secondary sources into your response.

1. Athletes are frequently known for their attitudes, good or bad. Think about the different professional or amateur athletes you have known or read about during your lifetime. How could you categorize these athletes according to their attitudes? What sort of classifying principle might you use? Write an essay of classification in which you explore these different categories, offering examples as support for each category.

2. Writer Judith Viorst describes her relationships with others in an essay entitled "Friends, Good Friends, and Such Good Friends." In this essay, Viorst categorizes her friends based on their level of intimacy, creating such categories as "convenience friends," "special-interest friends," and "historical friends." Using a variety of expository strategies such as exemplification, narration, description, and comparison or contrast, write an essay in which you classify your friends into at least three discrete groups. Make sure that your organizing principle is consistent and accounts for all of your friends in some way.

3. Consider the many genres that exist in music, film, and literature. Select your favorite genre in one of those mediums and devise a dividing principle that will allow you to write a brief paper explaining to an audience the different styles or types that make up the genre as a whole. Be sure to incorporate supporting information from credible secondary sources. (◆ See Chapter 19 for help with conducting research and evaluating the sources you find.)

Chapter 14

Causal Analysis

ausal analysis explains the cause-and-effect relationship between two (or more) elements. When you discuss the condition producing something, you are analyzing *cause*; when you discuss the result produced by something, you are analyzing *effect*. To find examples of causal analysis, you need only look around you. If your car stops running on the way to class, for example, you may discover that the cause was an empty gas tank. On campus, in your history class, you may study the causes of the Civil War; in your economics class, the effects of teenage spending on the cosmetics market; and in your biology class, both the causes and effects of heart disease. Over dinner, you may discuss the effects of some crisis in the Middle East on American foreign policy, and as you drift to sleep, you may ponder the effects of your studying—or *not* studying—for your math test tomorrow.

To express it most simply, *cause* asks:

- why did "X" happen?
- or why does "X" happen?
- or why will "X" happen?

Effect, on the other hand, asks:

- what did "Y" produce?
- or what does "Y" produce?
- or what will "Y" produce?

Causal analysis is another powerful strategy of expository writing, whose primary purpose is to provide your reader with information on your chosen topic. Some essays of causal analysis focus primarily on the cause(s) of something; others mainly analyze the effect(s); still others discuss both causes and effects. If, for example, you wanted to concentrate on the major causes of the Wall Street crash of 1929, you might begin by briefly describing the effects of the crash on the economy, then devote your thesis and the rest of your essay to analyzing the major causes, perhaps allotting one major section (or one paragraph, depending on the complexity of the reasons) to each cause. Conversely, an effect paper might briefly note the causes of the crash and then detail the most important effects. An essay covering both the causes and effects of something often demands a longer paper so that each part will be clear. (Your assignment will frequently indicate

Figure 14.1 VISUALIZING THE PROCESS: CAUSAL ANALYSIS

Prewriting

Identify possible subjects by considering the following questions:

- What will the purpose of your causal analysis be?
- Do you want to emphasize causes or effects?
- In what topics do you have sufficient interest and knowledge to create an essay?
- Why might your topic be of interest to others?

Drafting

Determine the approach and organization of your essay by asking the following questions:

- How can you word your thesis to make it reasonable rather than dogmatic or overly broad?
- What are the major causes or effects that you want to include in your discussion, avoiding minor or remote ones?
- What organization will work best for your essay?
- How will you "show" the reader the connections between cause and effect?
- What should you include in your analysis to avoid the pitfalls of faulty logic?

Revising

Carefully review your thesis, organization, and the supporting details you use by asking the following questions:

- Is your thesis limited to a reasonable claim that you adequately support in the essay?
- Does your essay focus on the most important causes or effects, or both?
- Does your essay include enough evidence to support the connections you make between causes and effects?

    Have you avoided the problems of oversimplification, circular logic, and the *post hoc* fallacy?

Editing/Proofreading

Consider the sentence-level issues of your essay by asking the following questions:

- Do you include enough specific detail to "show" the reader how or why relationships exist, rather than simply naming and describing them?
- Have you reviewed your sentences for spelling, grammar, and punctuation errors?
- Is your paper formatted according to the assignment guidelines?

which kind of causal analysis to write. However, if the choice is yours, let your interest in the subject be your guide.) Following a writing process like that represented in Figure 14.1 will help you develop an effective causal analysis essay.

Developing Your Essay

Whether you are writing an essay that primarily discusses either causes or effects, or one that focuses on both, you should follow these rules:

Present a reasonable thesis statement. If your thesis makes dogmatic, unsupportable claims ("This national health care plan will lead to a complete collapse of quality medical treatment") or overly broad assertions ("Peer pressure causes alcoholism among students"), you won't convince your reader. Limit or qualify your thesis whenever necessary by using such phrases as "may be," "a contributing factor," "one of the main reasons," "two important factors," and so on ("Peer pressure is *one of the major causes* of alcoholism among students").

Limit your essay to a discussion of recent, major causes or effects. In a short paper you generally don't have space to discuss minor or remote causes or effects. If, for example, you analyzed your car wreck, you might decide that the three major causes were defective brakes, a hidden yield sign, and bad weather. A minor, or remote, cause might include being slightly tired because of less-than-usual sleep, less sleep because of staying out late the night before, staying out late because of an out-of-town visitor, and so on— back to the womb. In some cases, you may want to mention a few of the indirect causes or effects, but do be reasonable. Concentrate on the most immediate, most important factors. Often, a writer of a 500- to 800-word essay will discuss no more than two, three, or four major causes or effects of something; trying to cover more of either frequently results in an underdeveloped essay that is not convincing.

Organize your essay clearly. Organization of your causal analysis essay will vary, of course, depending on whether you are focusing on the causes of something or the effects, or both. To avoid becoming tangled in causes and effects, you might try sketching out a drawing of your thesis and essay map before you begin your first draft. Here, for instance, are a couple of sketches for essays you might write on your recent traffic accident:

Thesis Emphasizing the Causes:

Cause (defective brakes)
Cause (hidden yield sign)   produced   Effect (my car wreck)
Cause (bad weather)

Thesis Emphasizing the Effects:

                                                 Effect (doctor bills)
Cause (my car wreck)   produced   Effect (loss of car)
                                                 Effect (higher insurance rates)

Sometimes you may discover that you can't isolate "the three main causes/effects of 'X'"; some essays do, in fact, demand a narrative explaining a chain reaction of causes and effects. For example, a paper on the rebellion of the American colonies might show how one unjust British law or restriction after another led to the war for independence. In this kind of causal analysis essay, be careful to limit your subject so that you'll have the space necessary to show your readers how each step in the chain led to the next. Here's a sketch of a slightly different car-wreck paper presented in a narrative or chain-reaction format:

Cause ——————→ 1st Effect —causes→ 2nd Effect —causes→ 3rd Effect
(bad weather)   (wet brakes)   (car wreck)   (doctor bills)

Sometimes your subject matter will suggest the plan for organizing your causal analysis paper; often, however, you'll have to devote some of your prewriting time to deciding,

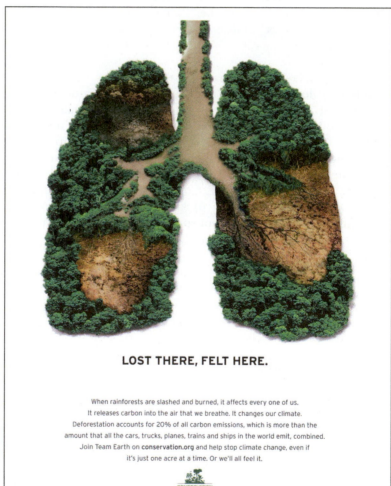

LOST THERE, FELT HERE.

When rainforests are slashed and burned, it affects every one of us.
It releases carbon into the air that we breathe. It changes our climate.
Deforestation accounts for 20% of all carbon emissions, which is more than the
amount that all the cars, trucks, planes, trains and ships in the world emit, combined.
Join Team Earth on **conservation.org** and help stop climate change, even if
it's just one acre at a time. Or we'll all feel it.

CONSERVATION
INTERNATIONAL

Advertisements often use short bursts of causal analysis to persuade their viewers to take action. What is the cause-effect relationship presented here, and do you find it effective?

Courtesy of Conservation International

first, whether you want to emphasize causes or effects and, then, in what arrangement you will present your analysis.

Convince your reader that a causal relationship exists by showing how the relationship works. Let's suppose you are writing an essay in which you want to discuss the three major changes you've undergone since coming to college. Don't just state the changes and describe them; your job is to show the reader how college has *brought about* these changes. If, for instance, your study habits have improved, you must show the reader how the academic demands of your college courses caused you to change your habits; a simple description of your new study techniques is not enough. Remember that a causal analysis essay should stress *how* (and often *why*) "X" caused "Y," rather than merely describing "Y" as it now exists.

Problems to Avoid

Don't oversimplify. Most complex subjects have more than one cause (or effect), so make your analysis as complete and objective as you can, especially when dealing with your own problems or beliefs. For example, was that car wreck really caused only by the bad weather—or also because of your carelessness? Did your friend do poorly in astronomy class only because the instructor didn't like her? Before judging a situation too quickly, investigate your own biases. Then provide a thoughtful, thorough analysis, effectively organized to convince your readers of the validity of your viewpoint.

Avoid the *post hoc* fallacy. This error in logic (from the Latin phrase *post hoc, ergo propter hoc*, meaning "after this, therefore because of this") results when we mistake a temporal connection for a causal relationship—or in other words, when we assume that because one event follows another in time, the first event caused the second. Most of our superstitions are *post hoc* fallacies; we now realize that bad luck after walking under a ladder is a matter of coincidence, not cause and effect. The *post hoc* fallacy provided the basis for a rather popular joke in the early debates over decriminalizing marijuana. Those against argued that marijuana led to heroin because most users of the hard drug had first smoked the weed. The proponents retorted that milk, then, was the real culprit, because both marijuana and heroin users had drunk milk as babies. The point is this: in any causal analysis, you must be able to offer proof or reasoned logic to show that one event *caused* another, not just that it preceded it in time.

Avoid circular logic. Often causal essays seem to chase their own tails when they include such circular statements such as, "There aren't enough parking spaces for students on campus because there are too many cars." Such a statement merely presents a second half that restates what is already implied in the first half. A revision might say, "There aren't enough parking spaces for students on campus because the parking permits are not distributed fairly." This kind of assertion can be argued specifically and effectively; the other is a dead end.

Important reminder: Many essays developed by causal analysis draw on personal experience; others, however, need research material to provide explanation, evidence, or background. For example, an essay analyzing the effects of an historical event (e.g., Lincoln's assassination) would need to provide readers with some facts about the event itself. Remember that any borrowed information (quoted directly or paraphrased) appearing in your essay—including ideas, statistics, or quotations—must be properly attributed to its source. ◆ To understand how to thoughtfully choose, incorporate, and document research material in your essay, consult Chapters 19 and 20 in this text.

Practicing What You've Learned

A. To gain some practice in developing cause and effect, try this activity. Think about your current status as a student in college. What led you to this point? Why are you enrolled? What influences played a part in that decision? Make a list of these causes. Now think about where you hope to go from here. What is your plan? What major(s) are you interested in? What career field do you hope to enter? In other words, make a list of the effects that you hope will result from your enrollment and pursuit of a degree. Some of the effects may be unintended and negative. Some may be unclear at this stage of the game. Try to be concrete in your lists of causes and potential effects.

B. *Collaborative Activity:* In order to receive feedback on the lists you've prepared, pair up with a classmate and exchange the work you completed in Exercise A. Carefully review what your partner has written. Do any of the causes seem unreasonable or exhibit *post hoc* fallacy or circular logic? (◆ For more on fallacies, see pages 316–319.) Is any part of either list oversimplified? What thesis might your classmate use to begin an essay based on such lists? Provide constructive feedback on your partner's work along with any additional insights you might have.

Essay Topics

The following subjects may be developed into essays emphasizing cause or effect, or both. ◆ For additional ideas, turn to the "Suggestions for Writing" section following the professional essay (page 304).

1. Your enrollment in college

2. A change of mind about some important issue or belief

continued on next page

3. An accident, a misadventure, a lucky break, or an unexpected turn of good fortune

4. A family tradition

5. A move, a trip, or an experience in a different country or culture

6. The best gift you ever received or ownership of a particular possession

7. A radical change in your behavior or appearance

8. A hobby, sport, or class

9. The best (or worst) advice you ever gave, followed, or rejected

10. An important decision or choice

11. An act of heroism or sacrifice (your own or someone else's)

12. An important idea, event, or discovery in your field of study

13. Your experience in your first job

14. A currently popular kind of entertainment (e.g., social media sites, reality shows, superhero movies, zombie stories, graphic novels)

15. A disappointment or a success

16. Bullying, racism, sexism, or some other kind of discrimination or prejudice

17. An influential person (teacher, coach, friend, etc.)

18. A political action (campus, local, state, national), historical event, or social movement

19. A popular cultural trend (current or emerging uses of social media such as Facebook, Snapchat, and Instagram; clothing or hair styles; food trends, etc.)

20. A piece of visual art promoting a particular cause or point of view (Consider, for example, the famous image of Rosie the Riveter, who first appeared on a poster sponsored by the War Production Committee during World War II [see next page]. Considering the gender roles of the time, why was such a poster needed? What effects was this image designed to have on both its male and female viewers? What specific elements in this picture produce these effects? What effect does this image have on viewers today? If you prefer, select another visual image reproduced in this text for analysis of its effects on the viewer, a famous photograph such as *Migrant Mother* [page 364] or perhaps one of the advertisements in Chapter 15 or in other chapters in this book. A list of all the artworks and ads in this text follows the Detailed Table of Contents. ◆ For help writing about art, see the MindTap® Online Chapter: "Writing about Visual Arts.")

continued on next page

The poster *Rosie the Riveter*, by graphic artist J. Howard Miller, was created in 1943 as part of a government campaign to encourage women to enter the factory workforce during World War II.

A Topic Proposal for Your Essay

Selecting the right subject matter is important to every writer. To help you clarify your ideas and strengthen your commitment to your topic, here is a proposal sheet that asks you to describe some of your preliminary ideas about your subject before you begin drafting. Although your ideas may change as you write (they will almost certainly become more refined), thinking through your choice of topic now may help you avoid several false starts.

1. What is the subject and purpose of your causal analysis essay? Is this subject appropriately narrowed and focused for a discussion of major causes or effects?

2. Will you develop your essay to emphasize primarily the effects or the causes of your topic? Or is a causal chain the most appropriate method of development?

3. Why are you interested in this topic? Do you have a personal or professional connection to the subject? State at least one reason for your choice of topic.

4. Is this a significant topic of interest to others? Why? Who specifically might find it interesting, informative, or entertaining?

5. List at least two major causes or effects that you might develop in the discussion of your topic.

6. What difficulties, if any, might arise during your drafting on this topic? For example, how might you convince a skeptical reader that your causal relationship is not merely a temporal one?

Once you have chosen your topic, take a moment to read through Figure 14.1 (page 292) to remind yourself of key questions you should be asking at each stage of the writing process for your causal analysis essay.

Sample Student Essay

In the following essay, a student explains why working in a local motel damaged her self-esteem, despite her attempts to do a good job. Note that the writer uses many vivid examples and specific details to show the reader how she was treated and, consequently, how such treatment made her feel.

It's Simply Not Worth It

1   It's hard to find a job these days, and with our county's unemployment rate reaching as high as seven percent, most people feel obligated to "take what they can get." But after working as a maid at a local motel for almost a year and a half, I decided no job is worth keeping if it causes a person to doubt his or her worth. My hard work rarely received recognition or appreciation, I was underpaid, and I was required to perform some of the most disgusting cleaning tasks imaginable. These factors caused me to devalue myself as a person and ultimately motivated me to return to school in hope of regaining my self-respect.

2   It may be obvious to say, but I believe that when a maid's hours of meticulous cleaning are met only with harsh words and complaints, she begins to lose her sense of self-esteem. I recall the care I took in making the motel's beds, imagining them as globs of clay and molding them into impeccable pieces of art. I would teeter from

Introduction: Her job as a motel maid

Thesis: No appreciation, low pay, disgusting tasks (causes) produce damaged self-esteem and action (effects)

Cause one:
Lack of
appreciation

one side of a bed to the other, over and over again, until I smoothed out every intruding wrinkle or tuck. And the mirrors—I would vigorously massage the glass, erasing any toothpaste splotches or oil smudges that might draw my customer's disapproval. I would scrutinize the mirror first from the left side, then I'd move to the right side, once more to the left until every possible angle ensured an unclouded reflection. And so my efforts went, room after room. But, without fail, each day more than one customer would approach me, not with praise for my tidy beds or spotless mirrors, but with nitpicking complaints that undermined my efforts: "Young lady, I just checked into room 143 and it only has one ashtray. Surely for $69.95 a night you people can afford more ashtrays in the rooms."

3   If it wasn't a guest complaining about ashtrays, it was an impatient customer demanding extra towels or a fussy stay-over insisting his room be cleaned by the time he returned from breakfast at 8:00 A.M. "Can't you come to work early to do it?" he would urge thoughtlessly. Day after day, my spotless rooms went unnoticed, with no spoken rewards for my efforts from either guests or management. Eventually, the ruthless complaints and thankless work began wearing me down. In my mind, I became a servant undeserving of gratitude.

Cause two:
Low pay

4   The lack of spoken rewards was compounded by the lack of financial rewards. The $7.30/hour appraisal of my worth was simply not enough to support my financial needs or my self-esteem. The measly $3.65 I earned for cleaning one room took a lot of rooms to add up, and by the end of the month I was barely able to pay my bills and buy some food. (My mainstay became ninety-two cent, generic macaroni and cheese dinners.) Because the flow of travelers kept the motel full for only a few months of the year, during some weeks I could only work half time, making a mere $584.00 a month. As a result, one month I was forced to request an extension on my rent payment. Unsympathetically, my landlord threatened to evict me if I didn't pay. Embarrassed, yet desperate, I went to a friend and

borrowed money. I felt uneasy and awkward and regretted having to beg a friend for money. I felt like a mooch and a bum; I felt degraded. And the constant reminder from management that there were hundreds of people standing in unemployment lines who would be more than willing to work for minimum wage only aided in demeaning me further.

5   In addition to the thankless work and the inadequate salary, I was required to clean some of the most sickening messes. Frequently, conventions for high school clubs booked the motel. Once I opened the door of a conventioneer's room one morning and almost gagged at the odor. I immediately beheld a trail of vomit that began at the bedside and ended just short of the bathroom door. At that moment I cursed the inventor of shag carpet, for I knew it would take hours to comb this mess out of the fibers. On another day I spent thirty minutes dislodging the bed linen from the toilet where it had been stuffed. And I spent what seemed like hours removing from one of my spotless mirrors the lipstick-drawn message that read, "Yorktown Tigers are number one." But these inconsiderate acts were relaying another message, a message I took personally: "Lady, you're not worth the consideration—you're a maid and you're not worth respecting."

Cause three: Repulsive duties

6   I've never been afraid to work hard or do jobs that weren't particularly "fun." But the line must be drawn when a person's view of herself becomes clouded with feelings of worthlessness. The thankless efforts, the inadequate wage, and the disgusting work were just parts of a total message that degraded my character and caused me to question my worth. Therefore, I felt compelled to leave this demeaning job in search of a way to rebuild my self-confidence. Returning to school has done just that for me. As my teachers and fellow students take time to listen to my ideas and compliment my responses, I feel once again like a vital, valued, and worthwhile person. I feel human once more.

Conclusion: Review of the problem and a brief explanation of the solution she chose

PROFESSIONAL ESSAY*

Why Are Young People Ditching Cars for Smartphones?

Jordan Weissmann

Jordan Weissmann, B.S.J., is currently the senior business and economics correspondent for *Slate* magazine. The essay "Why Are Young People Ditching Cars for Smartphones?" published in *The Atlantic* in 2012, traces cultural and economic causes to explain a decline in car sales and driving among younger Americans. Weissmann posits that the shift from physical to digital locomotion has both practical and philosophical roots and he frames this national trend within a broader global context.

> **Pre-reading Thoughts:** Consider your use of personal electronic devices (laptops, phones, tablets, etc.). How has your reliance on these devices decreased the amount of time you interact with others in person? How has it changed your travel habits?

1   Youth culture was once car culture. Teens cruised their Thunderbirds to the local drive-in, Springsteen fantasized about racing down Thunder Road, and Ferris Bueller** staged a jailbreak from the 'burbs in a red Ferrari. Cars were Friday night. Cars were Hollywood.

2   Yet these days, they can't even compete with an iPhone—or so car makers, and the people who analyze them for a living, seem to fear. As *Bloomberg* reported [in August 2012], many in the auto industry "are concerned that financially pressed young people who connect online instead of in person could hold down peak demand by 2 million units each year." In other words, Generation Y may be happy to give up their wheels as long as they have the web. And in the long term, that could mean Americans will buy just 15 million cars and trucks each year, instead of around 17 million.

3   "A car is a symbol of freedom," one consumer researcher told *Bloomberg.* "But unlike previous years, there are many different ways that a Gen Y person can capture that freedom."

4   Young adults are in fact buying fewer cars and trucks today than in the past. According to CNW Marketing Research, Americans between the ages of 21 to 34 purchased just 27 percent of new cars in 2010, down from 38 percent in 1985. Bloomberg quotes the industry analysts at R.L. Polk & Co., who say that "the rate of U.S. auto sales to 18–34-year-old buyers declined to 11 percent in April 2012, down from 17 percent for the same age group in April 2007, before the recession."

5   Is it really reasonable to blame that drop on Gen Y's love of tech? No, not entirely. But it is fair to think that our preoccupation with smartphones and laptops might be contributing to the fall. Here's why.

6   First, Gen Y is strapped for cash. Badly. Thanks to the recession and slow recovery, it's been slammed with high rates of joblessness. Even college graduates, who have better prospects than most, are still collectively underemployed and staggering around beneath the weight of unprecedented student debt. In the scheme of a young person's budget, a $12,000 Kia and a $2,000 Macbook Pro both count as major life purchase.

---

* ◆ To help you read this essay analytically, review pages 183–186.

** Ferris Bueller is a character in the 1986 movie *Ferris Bueller's Day Off.*

Given the centrality of the web to everybody's personal and professional lives, the computer (or heck, even a phone) may be the higher priority.

7   Second, young Americans aren't simply turning their back on buying cars. They're also turning their backs on driving. The percentage of teens and twenty-somethings with licenses has dropped dramatically over the past thirty years, which may be the sign that Gen Y's indifference towards autos is a cultural shift as much as an economic one. Of course, we don't know precisely why the young are driving less. Urbanites may be embracing mass transit, biking, and car sharing services like Zipcar. Other young people may be gravitating towards walkable suburbs, where cars are often optional. But it's not far fetched to think that the ability to connect with friends and family, shop, and entertain ourselves online has contributed to the trend.

8   Finally, this all might be part of a global pattern. Michael Sivak and Brandon Schoettle of the University of Michigan Transportation Research Institute have found that the fraction of teen drivers tends to fall as a country's level of Internet access increases. There's also vivid, albeit anecdotal, evidence from Japan, where in 2008, the *Wall Street Journal* reported that the country's tech-obsessed youth had all but forgotten about cars:

> Reasons [for the drop in sales] include higher gasoline prices and Japan's graying population. But even more worrying to auto makers are signs that the downturn is part of a deeper generational shift among young Japanese consumers. Unlike their parents' generation, which viewed cars as the passport to freedom and higher social status, the Internet-connected Japanese youths today look to cars with indifference, according to market research by the Japan Automobile Manufacturers Association and Nissan. Having grown up with the Internet, they no longer depend on a car for shopping, entertainment and socializing and prefer to spend their money in other ways.*

9   Sound familiar? As youth culture becomes tech culture, it may be that cars just tend to get pushed out of the way. No matter where you are in the world.

QUESTIONS ON CONTENT, STRUCTURE, AND STYLE

1. What cause-effect relationship is presented in this essay? Does this essay focus primarily on causes or effects?

2. What are some of the significant causes Weissmann outlines in his essay?

3. What strategy does Weissmann use to start his essay and why? How is this strategy continued throughout the essay?

4. In paragraph 1, what concrete examples does Weissmann offer? What impact do these examples have on the reader and the reader's interest?

5. What specific secondary sources does Weissmann use to support his points? What kind of information does he pull from these sources? How does this information work to support his argument?

6. Weissmann uses colloquial language throughout ("strapped for cash," "or heck, even a phone," etc.). What impact does this conversational tone have on the reader?

---

* Murphy, John. "Japan's Young Won't Rally Round the Car." *The Wall Street Journal,* 29 Feb. 2008, www.wsj.com/articles/SB120422248421700325.

7. Weissmann links the United States trend to a larger global decline. How does this connection enhance his argument?

8. Evaluate the author's use of direct quotations. What do they add to the essay?

9. Evaluate Weissmann's conclusion. How does his use of a question shape the reader's response?

10. Overall, how effective is Weissmann's essay? How would compare this essay's effectiveness to that of the student essay in this chapter?

VOCABULARY

Generation Y (2)	recession (4)	tech (5)	far fetched (7)
preoccupation (5)	slammed (6)	underemployed (6)	downturn (9)
unprecedented (6)	centrality (6)	urbanites (7)	

SUGGESTIONS FOR WRITING

Use Jordan Weissmann's essay "Why Are Young People Ditching Cars for Smartphones?" as a stepping-stone to your essay. If you own a cellphone or Internet-connected tablet or laptop, think of how it has affected you in specific ways that have changed your lifestyle, recreation, and work habits. Perhaps you have noticed an increase in productivity. Perhaps you now feel more isolated despite increased virtual connectivity. Consider the impact of such devices on you, your family, and your friends. To help your readers understand the cause-effect relationship you're presenting, be sure to include enough logical explanation and vivid details to show clearly how "X" caused "Y."

A Revision Worksheet

As you write your rough drafts, consult Chapter 5 for guidance through the revision process. In addition, here are a few questions to ask yourself as you revise your causal analysis essay:

1. Is the thesis limited to a reasonable claim that can be supported in the essay?

2. Is the organization clear and consistent so that the reader can understand the purpose of the analysis?

3. Does the essay focus on the most important causes or effects, or both?

4. If the essay has a narrative form, is each step in the chain reaction clearly connected to the next?

5. Does the essay convincingly show the reader *how* or *why* relationships between the causes and effects exist, instead of merely naming and describing them?

6. Does the essay provide enough evidence to show the connections between causes and effects? Where could additional details be added to make the relationships clearer?

continued on next page

7. Has the essay avoided the problems of oversimplification, circular logic, and the *post hoc* fallacy?

Collaborative Activity: After you've revised your essay extensively, exchange rough drafts with a classmate and answer these questions for each other, making specific suggestions for improvement wherever appropriate. (◆ For advice on productive participation in classroom workshops, see pages 121–123.)

Using Strategies and Sources

The following assignments ask you to not only incorporate what you've learned in this chapter regarding cause and effect, but also to employ other strategies of development and to incorporate secondary sources into your response.

1. Think about the popularity of a current television show or series. To what do you attribute the show's popularity? Create a cause and effect essay that answers this question. Make sure to avoid logical fallacies in your argument and to use concrete, vivid examples in support of your claims. (◆ To learn more about logical fallacies, see pages 316–319 in Chapter 15.)

2. Occasionally, decisions are made that have unintended, negative results. Take a moment to think of a policy instituted at your college or by your local town or city government that has created such results. In a cause and effect essay, examine this decision and the results, using exemplification, narration, description, or any other expository strategy as appropriate. Imagine that your audience is a college campus administrator or a local government official, and you are trying to convince him or her that such a policy should be reconsidered.

3. Consider a major commercial success (Disney, Nike, Apple) or a major business or product failure (Sharper Image, Enron, New Coke). You could also choose the success or failure of a local business or industry in your hometown or the town in which you attend college. What factors led to the success or failure of these businesses? What was the impact of the company's demise or its expansion? Choose either of these questions to address in a brief cause and effect essay that incorporates supporting information from credible secondary sources. (◆ See Chapter 19 for help with conducting research and evaluating the sources you find.)

Chapter 15

Argumentation

Almost without exception, each of us, every day, argues for or against something with somebody. The discussions may be short and friendly ("Let's go to this restaurant rather than that one") or long and complex ("Mandatory motorcycle helmets are an intrusion on civil rights"). Because we do argue our viewpoints so often, most of us realized long ago that shifting into high whine does not always get us what we want. On the contrary, we've learned that we usually have a much better chance at winning a dispute or having our plan adopted or changing someone's mind if we present our side of an issue in a calm, logical fashion, giving sound reasons for our position. This approach is just what a good argumentative essay does: it presents logical reasoning and solid evidence that will persuade your readers to accept your point of view.

Some essays are *position arguments* that declare the best solution to a problem ("Raising the drinking age will decrease traffic accidents") or argue a certain way of looking at an issue ("Rap music degrades women"). Other essays are *proposal arguments* that urge adoption of a specific proposal or plan of action ("Voters should pass ordinance 10 to fund the new ice rink"). Whatever your purpose, your argumentative essay should be composed of a clear thesis and body paragraphs that offer enough sensible reasons and persuasive evidence to convince your readers to agree with you. Following a writing process like that represented in Figure 15.1 will help you develop an effective argumentative essay.

Developing Your Essay

Here are some suggestions for developing and organizing an effective argumentative essay:

Choose an appropriate topic. Selecting a good topic for any essay is important. Choosing a focused, appropriate topic for your argument essay will save you enormous amounts of time and energy even before you begin prewriting. Some subjects are simply too large and complex to be adequately treated in a three-to-five-page argumentative essay; selecting such a subject might produce a rough draft of generalities that will not be persuasive. If you have an interest in a subject that is too general or complex for the length of your assignment, try to find a more focused, specific issue within it to argue.

Figure 15.1 VISUALIZING THE PROCESS: ARGUMENTATION

Prewriting

Identify possible subjects by considering the following questions:

- About what topics do you have strong opinions?
- Are any of these topics of interest to others? What might your audience think of these topics?
- Which of these topics can be properly covered in an essay of the length you've been assigned?
- About which topics do you have solid knowledge? What additional research might be required?

Drafting

Determine the effect you hope your essay will have on your audience by asking the following questions:

- What are the main arguments and evidence you want to use in support of your thesis?
- What opposing arguments do you need to take into consideration?
- Are your main points soundly reasoned, avoiding common logical fallacies?
- How are your opinions shaping your argument?
- What is the strongest organization pattern for your essay?

Revising

Carefully review your thesis and the supporting details you use by asking the following questions:

- Is your thesis clearly stated and appropriate to the assigned length of your assignment?
- How persuasive are your main arguments in support of your thesis?
- Does your essay follow an organized pattern that eliminates repetition and confusion?
- Have you included sufficient supporting evidence for your main arguments?

Editing/Proofreading

Consider the sentence-level issues of your essay by asking the following questions:

- Have you used any specialized language that may require further clarification for your readers?
- Have you reviewed your sentences for spelling, grammar, and punctuation errors?
- Is your paper formatted according to the assignment guidelines?

For example, the large, controversial (and rather overdone) subject "capital punishment" might be narrowed and focused to a paper advocating time limits for the death-row appeal process or required use of DNA testing. A general opinion on "unfair college grading" might become a more interesting persuasive essay in which the writer takes a stand on the use of pluses and minuses (A–, B+, B–, etc.) on transcript grades. Your general annoyance with smokers might move from "All smoking should be outlawed forever" to an essay focused on the controversial use of e-cigarettes in smoke-free venues. The complex subject of gun control might be narrowed into an essay arguing support for or against new laws regarding concealed weapons on campuses or in national parks. In other words, while we certainly do debate large issues in our lives, in a short piece of writing it may be more effective, and often more interesting, to choose a focused topic that will allow for more depth in the arguments. You must ultimately decide whether your choice of subject is appropriate for your assignment, but taking a close, second look at your choice now may save you frustration later.

Explore the possibilities . . . and your opinions. Perhaps you have an interesting subject in mind for your argumentative essay, but you don't yet have a definite opinion on the controversy. Use this opportunity to explore the subject! Do some research; talk to appropriate people; investigate the issues. By discovering your own position, you can address others who may be similarly uncertain about the subject.

Many times, however, you may want to argue for a belief or position you already hold. But before you proceed, take some time to consider the basis of your strong feelings. Not surprisingly, we humans have been known, on various occasions, to spout opinions we can't always effectively support when challenged to do so. Sometimes we hold an opinion simply because on the surface it seems to make good sense to us or because it fits comfortably with our other social, ethical, or political beliefs. Or we may have inherited some of our beliefs from our families or friends, or perhaps we borrowed ideas from well-known people we admire. In some cases, we may have held an opinion for so long that we can't remember why we adopted it in the first place. We may also have a purely sentimental or emotional attachment to some idea or position. Whatever the origins of our beliefs, we need to examine the real reasons for thinking what we do before we can effectively convince others.

If you have a strong opinion you want to write about, try jotting down a list of the reasons or points that support your position. Then study the list—are your points logical and persuasive? Which aren't, and why not? After this bit of prewriting, you may discover that although you believe something strongly, you really don't have the kinds of factual evidence or reasoned arguments you need to support your opinion. In some cases, depending on your topic, you may wish to talk to others who share your position or you may decide to research your subject (◆ for help with research or interviewing, see Chapter 19); in other cases, you may just need to think longer and harder about your topic and your reasons for maintaining your attitude toward it. Keep an open mind; your exploration may lead you to a surprising new position. (Remember the words of humorist F. G. Burgess: "If in the last few years you haven't discarded a major opinion or acquired a new one, check your pulse. You may be dead.") But with or without formal research, the better you know your subject, the more confident you will be about writing your argumentative essay.

Anticipate opposing views. An argument assumes that there is more than one side to an issue. To be convincing, you must be aware of your opposition's views on the subject and then organize your essay to answer or counter those views. If you don't have a good sense of the opposition's arguments, you can't effectively persuade your readers to dismiss their objections and see matters your way. Therefore, before you begin your first rough draft, write down all the opposing views you can think of and an answer to each of them so that you will know your subject thoroughly. If you are unfamiliar with the major objections to your position, now is the time to investigate your subject further. (For the sake of clarity throughout this chapter, your act of responding to those arguments against your position will be called *refuting the opposition*; "to refute" means "to prove false or wrong," and that's what you will try to do to some of the arguments of those who disagree with you.)

Know and remember your audience. Although it's important to think about your readers' needs and expectations whenever you write, it is essential to consider carefully the audience of your argumentative essay both before and as you write your rough drafts. Because you are trying to persuade people to adopt some new point of view or perhaps to take some action, you need to decide what kinds of supporting evidence will be most convincing to your particular readers. Try to analyze your audience by asking yourself a series of questions. What do they already know about your topic? What information or terms do they need to know to understand your point of view? What biases might they already have for or against your position? What special concerns might your readers have that influence their receptiveness? ◆ To be convincing, you should consider these questions and others by carefully reviewing the discussion of audience on pages 20–23 *before* you begin your drafts.

Decide which points of argument to include. Once you have a good sense of your audience, your own position, and your opposition's strongest arguments, try making a Pro-and-Con Sheet to help you sort out which points you will discuss in your essay.

Let's suppose you want to write an editorial on the importance of healthy nutrition to you and your classmates at your school. Should all campus food outlets be required to provide consumers with nutritional information about the food they serve? After reviewing the evidence on both sides, you have decided to argue that all your school's food service outlets should provide calorie labels for the food they sell to allow students to make informed nutritional choices. To begin planning your essay, you list all the pro-and-con arguments you can think of concerning the debate.

My Side: For the posting of nutritional information

1. Students often struggle with good decision-making when they first go off to college.
2. Consumers have the right to know what they are consuming.
3. The U.S. government says it is important to post this information.
4. The FDA calorie labeling rules apply to many of the chain eateries on campus.
5. Many students prefer the traditional cafeteria, which is exempted from the FDA rules.
6. The cafeteria could be serving anything since they don't have to post such information.

7. The FDA's guidelines aren't too rigid or hard to follow.

8. Trans fat may be in the cafeteria's food.

9. The cafeteria charges too much for what it offers.

My Opposition's Side: Against the posting of nutritional information

1. The FDA guidelines aren't intended for independent cafeterias.

2. Cafeterias aren't "chain" businesses.

3. The FDA guidelines are too stringent for individual food operators to follow.

4. The financial burden of researching and accurately posting nutritional information is too great.

5. Cafeterias don't offer packaged meals; instead, they offer a customized approach that makes calorie labeling impossible.

6. Students don't really pay attention to nutritional information anyway.

7. Traditional cafeterias already struggle to compete with the chain eateries that have been allowed on many college campuses.

After making your Pro-and-Con Sheet, look over the list and decide which of your strongest points you want to argue in your paper and also which of your opposition's claims you want to refute. At this point you may also see some arguments on your list that might be combined and some that might be deleted because they're irrelevant or unconvincing. (Be careful not to select more arguments or counter-arguments to discuss than the length of your writing assignment will allow. It's far better to present a persuasive analysis of a few points than it is to give an underdeveloped, shallow treatment of a host of reasons.)

Let's say you want to cover the following points in your essay:

- The federal government has officially recognized the need for posted nutritional information. (combination of 2 and 3)

- Federal guidelines are reasonable, flexible, and fair. (4 and 7)

- On our campus, some food outlets, including many in the student center, are part of national chains that are required to follow the new rules. (5 and 6)

Your assignment calls for an essay of 750 to 1,000 words, so you figure you'll only have space to refute your opposition's strongest claim. You decide to refute this claim:

- "Customized" food service provided by college cafeterias is too complex to allow for accurate calorie labeling. (3 and 5)

The next step is to formulate a working thesis. At this stage, you may find it helpful to put your working thesis in an "although-because" statement so you can clearly see both your opposition's arguments and your own. An "although-because" thesis for the note-taking essay might look something like this:

Although many campus food service operators maintain that being required to post nutritional information would be too difficult, such "customized" food service providers should be required to do so since the government acknowledges the importance of providing such information, the FDA guidelines for posting are reasonable and flexible, and most of the other campus "chain" eateries are already complying with this government directive.

Frequently, your "although-because" statement will be too long and awkward to use in the later drafts of your essay. But for now, it can serve as a guide, allowing you to see your overall position before the writing of the first draft begins. (◆ To practice compiling a Pro-Con Sheet and writing an "although-because" working thesis, turn to the exercise on pages 320–321.)

Organize your essay clearly. Although there is no set model of organization for argumentative essays, here are some common patterns that you might use or that you might combine in some effective way.

Important note: For the sake of simplicity, the first two outlines present two of the writer's points and two opposing ideas. Naturally, your essay may contain any number of points and refuted points, depending on the complexity of your subject and the assigned length of your essay.

In Pattern A, you devote the first few body paragraphs to arguing points on your side and then turn to refuting or answering the opposition's claims.

Pattern A: Thesis
Body paragraph 1: you present your first point and its supporting evidence
Body paragraph 2: you present your second point and its supporting evidence
Body paragraph 3: you refute your opposition's first point
Body paragraph 4: you refute your opposition's second point
Conclusion

Sometimes you may wish to clear away the opposition's claims before you present the arguments for your side. To do so, you might select Pattern B:

Pattern B: Thesis
Body paragraph 1: you refute your opposition's first point
Body paragraph 2: you refute your opposition's second point
Body paragraph 3: you present your first point and its supporting evidence
Body paragraph 4: you present your second point and its supporting evidence
Conclusion

In some cases, you may find that the main arguments you want to present are the very same ones that will refute or answer your opposition's primary claims. If so, try Pattern C, which allows each of your argumentative points to refute one of your opposition's claims in the same paragraph:

Pattern C: Thesis
Body paragraph 1: you present your first point and its supporting evidence, which also refutes one of your opposition's claims

Body paragraph 2: you present a second point and its supporting evidence, which also refutes a second opposition claim

Body paragraph 3: you present a third point and its supporting evidence, which also refutes a third opposition claim

Conclusion

Now you might be thinking, "What if my position on a topic as yet has no opposition?" Remember that almost all issues have more than one side, so try to anticipate objections and then answer them. For example, you might first present a thesis that calls for a new traffic signal at a dangerous intersection in your town, and then address hypothetical counter-arguments such as "The City Council may say that a stoplight at Lemay and Columbia will cost too much, but the cost in lives will be much greater" or "Commuters may complain that a traffic light there will slow the continuous flow of north-south traffic, but it is precisely the uninterrupted nature of this road that encourages motorists to speed." By answering hypothetical objections, you impress your readers by showing them you've thought through your position thoroughly before you asked them to consider your point of view.

You might also be thinking, "What if my opposition actually has a valid objection, a legitimate point of criticism? Should I ignore it?" Hoping that an obviously strong opposing point will just go away is like hoping the IRS will cancel income taxes this year—a nice thought but hardly likely. Don't ignore your opposition's good point; instead, acknowledge it, but then go on quickly to show your readers why that reason, though valid, isn't compelling enough by itself to motivate people to adopt your opposition's entire position. Or you might concede that one point while simultaneously showing why your position isn't really in conflict with that criticism, but rather with other, more important, parts of your opponent's viewpoint. By admitting that you see some validity in your opposition's argument, you can again show your readers that you are both fair-minded and informed about all aspects of the controversy.

If you are feeling confident about your ability to organize an argumentative essay, you might try some combination of patterns, if your material allows such a treatment. For example, you might have a strong point to argue, another point that simultaneously answers one of your opposition's strongest claims, and another opposition point you want to refute. Your essay organization might look like this:

Combination: Thesis

Body paragraph 1: a point for your side

Body paragraph 2: one of your points, which also refutes an opposition claim

Body paragraph 3: your refutation of another opposition claim

Conclusion

In other words, you can organize your essay in a variety of ways as long as your paper is logical and clear. Study your Pro-and-Con Sheet and then decide which organization best presents the arguments and counter-arguments you want to include. Try sketching out your essay following each of the patterns; look carefully to see which pattern (or variation of one of the patterns) seems to put forward your particular material most persuasively, with the least repetition or confusion. Sometimes your essay's material will clearly fall into a particular pattern of organization, so your choice will be easy. More often, however, you will have to arrange and rearrange your ideas and counter-arguments until you see the best approach. Don't be discouraged if you decide to change patterns after you've begun a rough draft; what matters is finding the most effective way to persuade the reader to your side.

If no organizational pattern seems to fit at first, ask yourself which of your points or counter-arguments is the strongest or most important. Try putting that point in one of the two most emphatic places: either first or last. Sometimes your most important discussion will lead the way to your other points and, consequently, should be introduced first; perhaps more often, effective writers and speakers build up to their strongest point, presenting it last as the climax of their argument. Again, the choice depends on your material itself, though it's rare that you would want to bury your strongest point in the middle of your essay.

Now let's return to the essay on posting nutritional information first discussed on page 309. After selecting the most important arguments and counter-arguments (pages 309–310), let's say that you decide that your main point concerns the ability of students to make informed health choices. Since your opposition claims that providing nutritional information is too complex, you see that you can make your main point as you refute theirs. But you also wish to include a couple of other points for your side. After trying several patterns, you decide to put the "too complex" rebuttal last for emphasis and present your other points first. Consequently, Pattern A best fits your plan. A sketch outline might look like this:

- **Revised working thesis and essay map:** The new 2014 FDA calorie labeling rules should be applied to all campus food establishments. The FDA ruling indicates that this nutritional information is important for people to know, and the FDA guidelines are fair and not too rigid. If our campus's chain eateries are already following these rules, then posting calorie labels in the cafeteria will allow students to make more informed nutrition decisions all over campus.

- **Body paragraph 1 (a first point for the writer's side):** The federal government has officially recognized the need for posted nutritional information.

- **Body paragraph 2 (another point for the writer's side):** The FDA's federal guidelines are reasonable, flexible, and fair.

- **Body paragraph 3 (another point for the writer's side):** On our campus, some food outlets, including many in the student center, are part of national chains that are required to follow the new rules.

- **Body paragraph 4 (rebuttal of the opposition's strongest claim):** The cafeteria claims that "customized" food service would be too complex to accurately label calories, but better labeling would reveal the calorie content of each individual ingredient, allowing students to make better choices about what to put on their plates.

Once you have a general notion of where your essay is going, plan to spend some more time thinking about ways to make each of your points clear, logical, and persuasive to your particular audience.

Argue your ideas logically. To convince your readers, you must provide sufficient reasons for your position. You must give more than mere opinion—you must offer logical arguments to back up your assertions. Some of the possible ways of supporting your ideas should already be familiar to you from writing expository essays; listed here are several methods and illustrations:

1. **Give examples (real or hypothetical):** "Many of my friends on campus report a weight gain of about fifteen pounds during their first year at school." Also: "The Subway sandwich shop in the Grayson Center, for example, is part of a chain with more than twenty locations, so the menu at its store will be required to include the new calorie labels by the end of 2015."

2. **Present a comparison or contrast:** "On our campus, some food outlets, including many in the student center, are part of national chains that are required to follow the new rules. Our campus dining services and other local food outlets would not fall under the new FDA guidelines. Because they are not part of a national chain, and have fewer than twenty locations, these places, where many of my friends eat one or more meals daily, will not be required to post calorie contents for their menu items."

3. **Show a cause-and-effect relationship:** "Information by itself, of course, will not solve the obesity crisis, but without detailed knowledge about the contents of various menu items, how can we make good choices about what to eat?"

4. **Provide statistical evidence:** "A recent article on the topic of food labeling states that more than one third of American adults today are obese."

The well-thought-out arguments you choose to support your case may be called *logical appeals* because they appeal to, and depend on, your readers' ability to reason and to recognize good sense when they see it. But there is another kind of appeal often used today: the *emotional appeal.*

Emotional appeals are designed to persuade people by playing on their feelings rather than appealing to their intellect. Rather than using thoughtful, logical reasoning to support their claims, writers and speakers using *only* emotional appeals often try to accomplish their goals by distracting or misleading their audiences. Frequently, emotional appeals are characterized by language that plays on people's fears, material desires, prejudices, or sympathies; such language often triggers highly favorable or unfavorable responses to a subject. For instance, emotional appeals are used constantly in advertising, where feel-good images, music, and slogans ("I'm Lovin' It"; "The Heartbeat of America Is Today's Chevy Truck") are designed to sway potential customers to a product without their thinking about it too much. Some politicians also rely heavily on emotional appeals, often using scare tactics to disguise a situation or to lead people away from questioning the logic of a particular issue.

But in some cases, emotional appeals can be used for legitimate purposes. Good writers should always be aware of their audience's needs, values, and states of mind, and they may be more persuasive on occasion if they can frame their arguments in ways that appeal to both their readers' logic and their emotions. For example, when Martin Luther King, Jr., delivered his famous "I Have a Dream" speech to the crowds gathered in Washington, D.C., in 1963 and described his vision of little children of different races walking hand in hand, being judged not "by the color of their skin but by the content of their character," he certainly spoke with passion that was aimed at the hearts of his listeners. But King was not using an emotional appeal to keep his audience from thinking about his message; on the contrary, he presented powerful emotional images that he hoped would inspire people to act on what they already thought and felt, their deepest convictions about equality and justice.

Appeals to emotions are tricky: you can use them effectively in conjunction with appeals to logic and with solid evidence, but only if you use them ethically. Too many appeals to the emotions are also overwhelming; readers tire quickly from excessive tugs on the heartstrings. To prevent your readers from suspecting deception or feeling manipulated, support your assertions with as many logical arguments as you can muster, and use emotional appeals only when they legitimately advance your cause.

Offer evidence that effectively supports your claims. In addition to presenting thoughtful, logical reasoning, you may wish to incorporate a variety of convincing evidence to persuade your readers to your side. Your essay might profit from including, where appropriate, some of the following kinds of supporting evidence:

- Personal experiences
- The experiences or testimony of others whose opinions are pertinent to the topic
- Factual information you've gathered from research
- Statistics from current, reliable sources
- Hypothetical examples
- Testimony from authorities and experts
- Charts, graphs, or diagrams

You'll need to spend quite a bit of your prewriting time thinking about the best kinds of evidence to support your case. Remember that not all personal experiences or research materials are persuasive. For instance, the experiences we've had (or that our friends have had) may not be representative of a universal experience and consequently may lead to unconvincing generalizations. Even testimony from an authority may not be convincing if the person is not speaking on a topic from his or her field of expertise; famous football players, for instance, don't necessarily know any more about underwear or soft drinks than anyone else. Always put yourself in the skeptical reader's place and ask, "Does this point convince me? If not, why not?" (◆ For more information on incorporating research material into your essays, see Chapter 19. For more advice on the selection of evidence, see the section on critical thinking in Chapter 5.)

Find the appropriate tone. Sometimes when we argue, it's easy to get carried away. Remember that your goal is to persuade and perhaps change your readers, not alienate them. Instead of laying on insults or sarcasm, present your ideas in a moderate let-us-reason-together spirit. Such a tone will persuade your readers that you are sincere in your attempts to argue as truthfully and fairly as possible. If your readers do not respect you as a reasonable person, they certainly won't be swayed to your side of an issue. Don't preach or pontificate either; no one likes—or respects—a writer with a superior attitude. Write in your natural "voice"; don't adopt a pseudo-intellectual tone. In short, to argue effectively you should sound logical, sincere, and informed. (◆ For additional comments on tone, review pages 161–164.)

Consider using Rogerian techniques, if they are appropriate. In some cases, especially those involving tense situations or highly sensitive issues, you may wish to incorporate some techniques of the noted psychologist Carl Rogers, who developed a procedure for presenting what he called the nonthreatening argument. Rogers believed that people involved in a debate should strive for clear, honest communication so that the problem under discussion could be resolved. Instead of going on the defensive and trying to "win" the argument, each side should try to recognize common ground and then develop a solution that will address the needs of both parties.

A Rogerian argument uses these techniques:

1. A clear, objective statement of the problem or issue

2. A clear, objective summary of the opposition's position that shows you understand its point of view and goals

3. A clear, objective summary of your point of view, stated in nonthreatening language

4. A discussion that emphasizes the beliefs, values, and goals that you and your opposition have in common

5. A description of any of your points that you are willing to concede or compromise

6. An explanation of a plan or proposed solution that meets the needs of both sides

By showing your opposition that you thoroughly understand its position and that you are sincerely trying to effect a solution that is in everyone's—not just your—best interests, you may succeed in some situations that might otherwise be hopeless because of their highly emotional nature. Remember, too, that you can use some of these Rogerian techniques in any kind of argument paper you are writing, if you think they would be effective.

Problems to Avoid

Writers of argumentative essays must appear logical or their readers will reject their point of view. Here is a short list of some of the most common *logical fallacies*—that is, errors in reasoning. Check your rough drafts carefully to avoid these problems.

Students sometimes ask, "If a logical fallacy works, why not use it? Isn't all fair in love, war, and argumentative essays?" The honest answer is maybe. It's quite true that speakers and writers do use faulty logic and irrational emotional appeals to persuade people every day (one needs only to look at television or a newspaper to see example after example). But the cost of the risk is high: if you do try to slide one by your readers and they see through your trick, you will lose your credibility instantly. On the whole, it's far more effective to use logical reasoning and strong evidence to convince your readers to accept your point of view.

Common Logical Fallacies

Hasty generalization: The writer bases the argument on insufficient or unrepresentative evidence. Suppose, for example, you have owned two poodles and they have both bitten you. If you declare that all poodles are vicious dogs, you are making a hasty generalization. There are, of course, thousands of poodles who have not attacked anyone. Similarly, you're in error if you interview only campus athletes and then declare, "University students favor a new stadium." What about the opinions of the students who aren't athletes? In other words, when the generalization is drawn from a sample that is too small or select, your conclusion isn't valid.

Non sequitur ("it doesn't follow"): The writer's conclusion is not necessarily a logical result of the facts. An example of a *non sequitur* occurs when you conclude, "Professor Smith is a famous chemist, so he will be a brilliant chemistry teacher." As you may have realized by now, the fact that someone knows a subject well does not automatically mean that he or she can communicate the information clearly in a classroom; hence, the conclusion is not necessarily valid.

Begging the question: The writer presents as truth what is not yet proven by the argument. For example, in the statement "All useless laws such as Reform Bill 13 should be repealed," the writer has already pronounced the bill useless without assuming responsibility for proving that accusation. Similarly, the statement "Professor Austin, one of the many instructors on our campus using their classrooms solely for preaching their political ideas, should be fired" begs the question (that is, tries like a beggar to get something for nothing from the reader) because the writer gives no evidence for what must first be argued, not merely asserted—that there are in fact professors on that particular campus using class time solely for spreading their political beliefs.

Red herring: The writer introduces an irrelevant point to divert the readers' attention from the main issue. This term originates from the old tactic used by escaped prisoners of dragging a smoked herring, a strong-smelling fish, across their trail to confuse tracking dogs by making them follow the wrong scent. For example, roommate A might be criticizing roommate B for his repeated failure to do the dishes when it was his turn. To escape facing the charges, roommate B brings up times in the past when the other roommate failed to repay some money he borrowed. Although roommate A may indeed have a problem with remembering his debts, that discussion isn't relevant to the original argument about sharing the responsibility for the dishes. (By the way, you might have run across a well-known newspaper photograph of a California environmentalist group demonstrating for more protection of dolphins, whales, and other marine life; look closely to see, over in the left corner, almost hidden by the host of placards and banners, a fellow slyly holding up a sign that reads "Save the Red Herring!" Now, who says rhetoricians don't have a good sense of humor?)

Post hoc, ergo propter hoc. See page 295.

Argument *ad hominem* ("to the man"): The writer attacks the opponent's character rather than the opponent's argument. The statement "Dr. Bloom can't be a competent marriage counselor because she's been divorced" may not be valid. Bloom's advice to her clients may be excellent regardless of her own marital status.

Faulty use of authority: The writer relies on "authorities" who are not convincing sources. Although someone may be well known in a particular field, he or she may not be qualified to testify in a different area. A baseball player in an ad for laser surgery may stress his need for correct vision, but he may be no more knowledgeable about eye care than anyone else on the street. In other words, name recognition is not enough. For their testimony to count with readers, authorities must have expertise, credentials, or relevant experience in the area under discussion. (◆ See also pages 315, 414–417, and "transfer of virtue" in the discussion of "bandwagon appeal" on page 318.)

Argument *ad populum* ("to the people"): The writer evades the issues by appealing to readers' emotional reactions to certain subjects. For example, instead of arguing the facts of an issue, a writer might play on the readers' negative response to such words as "socialism," "terrorist," or "radical," and their positive response to words like "God," "country," "liberty," or "patriotic." In the statement "If you are a true American, you will vote against the referendum on flag burning," the writer avoids any discussion of the merits or weaknesses of the bill and merely substitutes an emotional appeal. Other popular "virtue words" include "duty," "common sense," "courage," and "healthy." (Advertisers, of course, also play on consumers' emotions by filling their ads with pictures of babies, animals, status objects, and sexually attractive men and women.)

Circular thinking. See page 295.

Either/Or: The writer tries to convince readers that there are only two sides to an issue—one right, one wrong. The statement "If you don't go to war against Iceland, you don't love your country" is irrational because it doesn't consider the other possibilities, such as patriotic people's right to oppose war as an expression of love for their country. A classic example of this sort of oversimplification was illustrated in the 1960s bumper sticker that was popular during the debate over the Vietnam War: "America: Love It or Leave It." Obviously, there are other choices ("Change It or Lose It," for instance, to quote another either/or bumper sticker of that era).

Hypostatization: The writer uses an abstract concept as if it were a concrete reality. Always be suspicious of a writer who frequently relies on statements beginning "History has always taught us . . ." or "Science has proven . . ." or "Research shows . . ." The implication in each case is that history or science (or any other discipline) has only one voice, one opinion. On the contrary, "history" is written by a multitude of historians who hold a variety of opinions; doctors and scientists also frequently disagree. Instead of generalizing about a particular field, quote a respected authority or simply qualify your statement by referring to "many" or "some" scientists, historians, or other professionals.

Bandwagon appeal: The writer tries to validate a point by intimating that "everyone else believes in this." Such a tactic evades discussion of the issue itself. Advertising often uses this technique: "Everyone who demands real taste smokes Phooey cigarettes"; "Discriminating women use Smacky-Mouth lipstick." (The ultimate in "bandwagon" humor may have appeared on a recent Colorado bumper sticker: "Eat lamb—could 1000s of coyotes be wrong?") A variation of the "bandwagon" fallacy is sometimes referred to as "transfer of virtue," the sharing of light from someone else's sparkle. Advertisers often use this technique by paying attractive models or media stars to endorse their product. The underlying premise is this:

Popular/beautiful/"cool"/rich people use/buy/wear "X"; if you use "X," you too will be popular/beautiful/etc.

Intelligent readers and consumers know, of course, to suspect such doubtful causal relationships.

Straw man: The writer selects the opposition's weakest or most insignificant point to argue against, to divert the readers' attention from the real issues. Instead of addressing the opposition's best arguments and defeating them, the writer "sets up a straw man"—that is, the writer picks out a trivial (or irrelevant) argument against his or her own position and easily knocks it down, just as one might easily push over a figure made of straw. Perhaps the most famous example of the "straw man" occurred in 1952 when, during his vice-presidential campaign, Richard Nixon was accused of misappropriating campaign funds for his personal use. Addressing the nation on television, Nixon described how his six-year-old daughter, Tricia, had received a little cocker spaniel named Checkers from a Texas supporter. Nixon went on about how much his children loved the dog and how, regardless of what anyone thought, by gosh, he was going to keep that cute dog for little Tricia. Of course, no one was asking Nixon to return the dog; they were asking about the $18,000 in missing campaign funds. But Nixon's canine gift was much easier for him to defend, and the "Checkers" speech is now famous as one of the most notorious "straw man" diversions.

Faulty analogy: The writer uses an extended comparison as proof of a point. Look closely at all extended comparisons and metaphors to see if the two things being compared are really similar. For example, in a recent editorial, a woman protested new laws requiring parents to use car seats for small children, arguing that if the state could require the seats, they could just as easily require mothers to breast-feed instead of using formula. Are the two situations alike? Car accidents are the leading cause of death of children under four; is formula deadly? Or perhaps you've read that putting teenagers in sex education classes is like taking an alcoholic to a bar. Is it? Is stem cell research the same as Nazi medical experiments on prisoners, as the leader of a family-outreach group has claimed? If readers don't see a close similarity, the analogy may not be persuasive. Moreover, remember that even though a compelling analogy may suggest similarities, it alone cannot *prove* anything. (◆ For more discussion of analogy, see pages 257–259.)

Quick fix: The writer leans too heavily on catchy phrases or empty slogans. A clever turn of phrase may grab one's attention, but it may lose its persuasiveness when scrutinized closely. For instance, a banner at a recent rally to protest a piece of anti-gun legislation read, "When guns are outlawed, only outlaws will have guns." Although the sentence had nice balance, it oversimplified the issue. The legislation in question was not trying to outlaw all guns, just the sale of the infamous Saturday Night Specials, most often used in crimes and domestic violence; the sale of guns for sport, such as hunting rifles, would remain legal. Other slogans sound good but are simply irrelevant: a particular soft drink, for example, may be "the real thing," but what drink isn't? The advertising slogan "The XYZ truck runs deep" means what, exactly? Look closely at clever lines substituted for reasoned argument; always demand clear terms and logical explanations.*

---

*Sometimes advertisers get more for their slogans than they bargained for. According to one news source, a popular soft-drink company had to spend millions to revise its slogan after introducing its product into parts of China. Apparently the slogan "Come alive! Join the Blah-Blah-Cola Generation!" translated into some dialects as "Blah-Blah Cola Brings Your Ancestors Back from the Dead!"

Practicing What You've Learned

A. Imagine that you are writing an argumentative essay addressing the controversial question "Should home-schooled students be allowed to play on public school athletic teams?" You have investigated the topic and have noted the variety of opinions listed here. Arrange the statements into two lists: a "Pro" list (those statements that argue for allowing home schoolers to play) and a "Con" list (those statements that are against allowing home schoolers to play). Cross off any inappropriate or illogical statements you find; combine any opinions that overlap.

1. Parents of home schoolers pay the same taxes as public school parents.

2. Public school kids must meet grade requirements to be eligible.

3. School rules prohibit non-enrolled youth on campus.

4. Home schoolers shouldn't get the benefits of a school they've rejected.

5. Public school kids are bad influences on home schoolers.

6. Home schoolers need the social interaction.

7. Public school teams can always use more good athletes.

8. More students will overburden athletic facilities.

9. Home schoolers miss their public school friends, and vice versa.

10. Ten states allow home schoolers to play on teams.

11. Home schoolers will displace public school students on teams.

12. Public school students have to meet attendance rules to be eligible.

13. Athletic competition is good for everybody.

14. Home schoolers often have controversial political beliefs that will cause fights.

15. Team members need to share the same community on a daily basis.

16. Home schoolers aren't as invested in school pride.

Once you have your two lists, decide your own position on this topic. Then select two points you might use to argue your position and one opposing criticism you might refute. Put your working thesis into an "although-because" format, as explained on pages 310–311. Compare your choices to those of your classmates.

B. Errors in reasoning can cause your reader to doubt your credibility. In the following mock essay, for example, the writer includes a variety of fallacies that undermine his argument; see if you can identify all his errors.

continued on next page

Ban Those Books!

1   A serious problem faces America today, a problem of such grave importance that our very existence as a nation is threatened. We must either cleanse our schools of evil-minded books, or we must reconcile ourselves to seeing our children become welfare moochers and homeless bums.

2   History has shown time and time again that placement of immoral books in our schools is part of an insidious plot designed to weaken the moral fiber of our youth from coast to coast. In Wettuckett, Ohio, for example, the year after books by Mark Twain, such as *Tom Sawyer* and *Huckleberry Finn*, were introduced into the school library by liberal free-thinkers and radicals, the number of students cutting classes rose by six percent. And in that same year, the number of high school seniors going on to college dropped from thirty to twenty-two.

3   The reason for this could be either a natural decline in intelligence and morals or the influence of those dirty books that teach our beloved children disrespect and irresponsibility. Since there is no evidence to suggest a natural decline, the conclusion is inescapable: once our children read about Twain's characters skipping school and running away from home, they had to do likewise. If they hadn't read about such undesirable characters as Huckleberry Finn, our innocent children would never have behaved in those ways.

4   Now, I am a simple man, a plain old farm boy—the pseudo-intellectuals call me redneck just like they call you folks. But I can assure you that, redneck or not, I've got the guts to fight moral decay everywhere I find it, and I urge you to do the same. For this reason I want all you good folks to come to the ban-the-books rally this Friday so we can talk it over. I promise you all your right-thinking neighbors will be there.

Assignment

Collaborative Activity: Out of class, search for one of the following:

1. An example of an advertisement that illustrates one or more of the fallacies or appeals discussed on pages 316–319;

2. An example of illogical or fallacious reasoning in a piece of writing (you might try looking at the editorial page or "Letters to the Editor" section of your local or campus newspaper);

3. An example of a logical, persuasive point in a piece of writing.

Be prepared to explain your analysis of your sample, but do not write any sort of identifying label or evaluation on the sample itself. Bring your ad or piece of writing to class and exchange it with that of a classmate. After ten minutes, compare notes. Do you and your classmate agree on the evaluation of each sample? Why or why not?

Essay Topics

Write a convincing argument attacking or defending one of the following statements, or use them to help you think of your own topic. Remember to narrow and focus the topic as necessary. (◆ Note that essays on some of the topics presented here might profit from research material; see Chapter 19 for help.) For additional ideas, see the "Suggestions for Writing" section following the professional essays (page 330).

1. Students should/should not work throughout high school.

2. Drivers' use of cell phones while vehicles are in motion should/should not be prohibited.

3. A controversial ordinance in your hometown should/should not be repealed.

4. Academically qualified children of undocumented immigrants should/should not be allowed to apply for in-state tuition at public universities.

5. Violent video games should/should not be available for purchase by anyone under age eighteen.

6. Universities should/should not allow students or faculty to carry concealed handguns on campus.

7. A school voucher system should/should not be used in this state.

8. Students who do poorly in their academic courses should/should not be allowed to participate in athletic programs.

9. All colleges should/should not adopt a smoke-free campus policy.

10. The first two years of college should/should not be provided free of charge to all American citizens.

11. Plastic shopping bags should/should not be legally banned from grocery and other retail stores.

12. Sodas and high-sugar foods should/should not be sold in public school vending machines.

13. Public school districts should/should not be allowed to sell advertising inside or outside of school buses.

14. Americans should/should not be required to perform a year of public service or military service after high school graduation.

15. Public school students should/should not be required to wear uniforms.

16. Employers should/should not be allowed to require job applicants to take a personality test.

continued on next page

17. Controversial names or symbols of athletic teams ("Redskins," the Confederate flag, the tomahawk chop) should/should not be changed.

18. A law prohibiting demonstrations close to military or other funerals (or some other controversial law, bill, or policy) should/should not be passed.

19. Individuals under age fourteen charged with felonies should/should not be tried as adults.

20. Advertising for "Product X" rarely/often relies on use of emotional appeals and faulty logic. (Focus on one kind of product—cars, cosmetics, computers, soft drinks, cell phones, etc.—or on one especially popular brand, and collect a number of its ads to analyze. What does your analysis reveal about the major ways the product is advertised to its target audience? Do the ads appeal to consumers' reason or do they employ logical fallacies? Some combination? Which ads are more effective and why? If it's helpful, consider the appeals of ads reprinted in this text. A complete list of ads follows the Detailed Table of Contents.)

A Topic Proposal for Your Essay

Selecting the right subject matter is important to every writer. To help you clarify your ideas and strengthen your commitment to your topic, here is a proposal sheet that asks you to describe some of your preliminary ideas about your subject before you begin drafting. Although your ideas may change as you write (they will almost certainly become more refined), thinking through your choice of topic now may help you avoid several false starts.

1. What is the subject of your argumentative essay? Write a rough statement of your opinion on this subject.

2. Why are you interested in this topic? Is it important to your personal, civic, or professional life? State at least one reason for your choice of topic.

3. Is this a significant topic of interest to others? Why? Is there a particular audience you would like to address?

4. At this point, can you list at least two reasons that support your opinion of your topic?

5. Who opposes your opinion? Can you state clearly at least one of your opposition's major criticisms of your position?

6. What difficulties, if any, might arise during drafting? For example, might you need to collect any additional evidence through reading, research, or interviewing to support your points or to refute your opposition?

Once you have chosen your topic, take a moment to read through Figure 15.1 (page 307) to remind yourself of key questions you should be asking at each stage of the writing process for your argumentative essay.

Sample Student Essay

In the following student essay, you can see many of the strategies outlined in this chapter. The author most closely follows Pattern A with its presentation of the author's points followed by a rebuttal of the opposition's arguments. As you read this essay, note throughout the author's strong use of facts and examples to support her points. Note, too, the wide variety of rhetorical strategies that the author uses to assemble a convincing argument. Does the author convince you of her argument? What parts were most convincing? Which parts needed further support? What does this essay help you realize about your own writing?

Alonso 1

Lucia Alonso

Professor Montieth

Rhetoric 103

15 Mar. 2015

Better Information Equals Healthier Eating

Introduction: Uses a common phrase to catch the reader's attention

1   In conversations about food and the options available to students on our campus, the topic of the dreaded "freshmen fifteen" is bound to arise. While the term itself may be politically incorrect, the problem is real. Many of my friends on campus report a weight gain of about fifteen pounds during their first year at school. While some of this gain may be the result of stress or bad self-discipline when living away from home, a lack of reliable nutrition information plays a major role. Students who want to make healthy choices about what to eat simply do not have enough information. Campus dining services and other food vendors on campus should offer improved nutritional labeling to help students make healthy **Thesis** choices about what they eat. As I will argue, the new 2014 FDA calorie labeling rules should also be applied to all campus food establishments.

Alonso 2

2   A recent article on the topic of food labeling states that more than one third of American adults today are obese ("Calorie Labeling"). By addressing the ongoing obesity crisis, as the article states, "the Obama administration has done America a favor" by creating new calorie labeling rules that require restaurant chains and other outlets to post information about the calories in each item they sell (par. 4). Information by itself, of course, will not solve the obesity crisis, but without detailed knowledge about the contents of various menu items, how can we make good choices about what to eat? The new federal calorie labeling rules are an outgrowth of the Affordable Care Act, and they are scheduled to take effect in November 2015.

> A point for the writer's position: The federal government has officially recognized the need for posted nutritional information

3   The FDA web site provides additional details to help us understand what the new calorie labeling guidelines cover (United States). The labeling rules apply to restaurants and retail food establishments that are part of a chain with twenty or more locations. The rule requires these outlets to "clearly and conspicuously display calorie information for standard menu items," either next to the item name or price on the menu. As the FDA explains, seasonal items, temporary menu options (like daily specials), and condiments would be exempt from the labeling rule. The labeling is based on a daily calorie intake of 2,000 calories, and the rules were developed in consideration of over 1,100 comments from consumers and industry representatives (United States, par. 5). Any way you look at it, these new guidelines are reasonable, flexible, and fair.

> Another point for the writer's position: Federal guidelines are reasonable, flexible, and fair

4   On our campus, some food outlets, including many in the student center, are part of national chains that are required to follow the new rules. The Subway sandwich shop in the Grayson Center, for example, is part of a chain with more than twenty locations, so the menu at its store will be required to include the new calorie labels by

> A third point for the writer's position: Campus food outlets that are chains will have to post nutritional info by the end of 2015

Alonso 3

the end of 2015. Subway has long been known for its healthy eating campaign, including the famous "Jared" advertisements featuring the many healthy, low-fat options on its menu. Subway, like many of today's fast-food companies, understands the importance of dietary information and healthy eating, and has cashed in on America's healthy eating trend as part of its marketing campaigns for years.

5   Our campus dining services and other local outlets would not fall under the new FDA guidelines. Because they are not part of a national chain, and have fewer than twenty locations, these places, where many of my friends eat one or more meals daily, will not be required to post calorie contents for their menu items. Should we be left in the dark about how many calories we are eating? While the guidelines may not legally require calorie labeling, dining services should voluntarily follow the new rules. Posting the calorie count for students to see will help promote healthier habits in student eating. Dining services has an opportunity to join the national campaign against obesity, and to become part of the current trend toward healthy eating. The success of chains like Subway and Chipotle shows that healthy, low-calorie foods—and visible labeling—can be profitable and popular too.

6   Why would any food business object to the new guidelines? As a spokesperson for the Food Marketing Institute argues, supermarkets and other food retailers "are in the business of customization" (Sarasin, par. 2). Thus, "the rule applies a formula that may fit chain restaurants but was not designed for the complexities of supermarkets" (par. 8). So, in this argument, a salad bar, cafeteria line, or other "customized" food service would be too complex to accurately label calories. While it is true that individuals could assemble a custom meal from the salad or sandwich bar in the student center, better labeling would reveal the calorie counts for each individual ingredient.

The author returns to her thesis as outlined in the introduction.

Presentation and rebuttal of the opposition's claim that "customized" food service is too complex to provide accurate nutritional information

Anzai 4

These labels would help students make better choices about piling a heap of high-calorie ranch dressing on a healthy spinach salad.

7   Better calorie labeling is not just about obesity—it's about overall health and building a pattern of smart eating. Heart disease, diabetes, and other ailments are all related to calorie intake and diet. As college students, we are trying to be better educated so we can make better decisions in all aspects of our lives. Even though the new national food labeling guidelines do not legally require them to, campus food services should join the moment to promote healthy eating through better nutritional information. Providing students with the most complete information about daily food choices is one way the campus dining services can help.

Conclusion: Restatement of thesis and appeals to both logic and ethics

---

Anzai 5

Works Cited

"Calorie Labeling You Can Count On." Editorial. *USA Today*, Gannett Satellite Information Network, 1 Dec. 2014, www.usatoday.com/story/opinion/2014/12/01/food-labeling-calories-obama-fda-editorials-debates/19756291/.

Sarasin, Leslie G. "Don't Include Grocery Stores." *USA Today*, Gannett Satellite Information Network, 1 Dec. 2014, www.usatoday.com/story/opinion/2014/12/01/fda-nutrition-food-marketing-institute-editorials-debates/19756553/.

United States, Dept. of Health and Human Services. "FDA Finalizes Menu and Vending Machine Calorie Labeling Rules." *FDA.gov*, U.S. Food and Drug Administration, 25 Nov. 2014, www.fda.gov/NewsEvents/Newsroom/PressAnnouncements/ucm423952.htm.

PROFESSIONAL ESSAYS*

The following essays on mandatory voting in the United States first appeared together in *USA Today* on April 5, 2015. The first essay represents the view of *USA Today's* editorial board; and the second essay is an "opposing view" piece written by Thomas E. Mann, a senior fellow at the Brookings Institution and a scholar at the University of California, Berkeley. Although you may already have an opinion on this controversial issue, try to objectively analyze the strengths and weaknesses of each essay. Which points are the most and least persuasive, and why?

Editor's note: The *USA Today* essay references events of August 9, 2014, when Michael Brown, an unarmed 18-year-old black male, was shot and killed by a white male police officer in Ferguson, Missouri. When a grand jury failed to indict the officer and the Justice Department released a report documenting long-standing racial discrimination in the Ferguson police department and court system, protests erupted in Ferguson and throughout the country.

Pre-reading Thoughts: Have you ever participated in an election process? Perhaps you voted in the most recent congressional election or you campaigned to elect a friend as president of the Student Government Association. How did that turn out? Did your candidate win? How did your candidate's win or loss impact your feelings about your vote and the election process?

Mandatory Voting Won't Cure Dismal Turnout

The Editorial Board of USA Today

1   Voter turnout in U.S. elections hardly inspires pride. The nation lags far behind most modern democracies in the percentage of its citizens who go to the polls. Even in presidential elections, only about 60% of voters show up; turnout for midterm elections is far lower — just 36% last fall.

2   Policymakers have tried for years to come up with ways to increase those numbers — early voting, same-day registration and voting by mail — but the impact has been small. President Obama provoked controversy last month when he mused about requiring Americans to vote, as is done in Australia and several other countries. The president was responding to a question about how to offset the effect of big money in politics. "That would counteract money more than anything," the president said.

3   In Australia, 90% of eligible voters go to the polls despite minimal enforcement. Registered voters who fail to vote get a form letter asking why; almost any excuse will do to get someone off the hook. Those with no valid excuse face a fine of about $20, which can escalate if someone refuses to pay, though that is rare.

4   But the idea is a non-starter in the defiantly individualistic U.S., for good reason: A nation predicated on personal freedom rightly forces its citizens to do only a very few things — pay taxes, serve on juries, educate children, be drafted and serve in some wars, and lately, buy health insurance.

---

* ◆ For help reading these essays analytically, review pages 183–186.

5 There's a compelling reason for each of those, but not to require people to vote. Low turnout, troubling as it is, doesn't pose an existential threat in a nation that has succeeded despite it, nor would forcing disinterested voters to the polls have much value.

6 If there is an exception, it's in local elections, for which turnout is generally dismal despite the high impact of local government.

7 Ferguson, Mo., is a prominent example. After a white police officer shot and killed an unarmed black teenager last summer, igniting angry protests, it came to light that the voter turnout in Ferguson's local elections is about 12%, which explains why a city that is two-thirds black has only one black city council member and a nearly all-white police force.

8 Ferguson's voters go to the polls again Tuesday with a chance to elect as many as three black council members, but turnout remains in doubt.

9 Instead of forcing people to vote, though, government should be educating them — particularly as children — about the power of democratic choice, and it should be removing obstacles that make it hard for interested voters to cast a ballot, especially would-be voters whose long working days make voting difficult.

10 Lately, though, politicians have been doing the opposite. Ostensibly to save money and combat fraud, state officials, almost exclusively Republicans, have been pursuing a thinly veiled campaign to make voting harder. Methods include cutting back on early voting and instituting voter ID laws while making it difficult for many voters to get the required ID. Those most likely to be deterred are lower-income people, minorities and younger voters who tend not to vote Republican.

11 The last thing a nation with a turnout problem needs are policies that make it harder to vote. Deliberately keeping people away from the polls is just as bad as forcing them to go.

Required Voting Yields Benefits

Thomas E. Mann

1 Mandatory voting seems downright un-American. We rightly value our individual freedom and don't like to be told what to do by a paternalistic government. Indeed, the cynics amongst us resonate to the old line against voting at all: "It only encourages them."

2 But American federal, state and local governments tell us what to do and not do all the time. Paying taxes—the price of a civilized society—is compulsory. Abiding by traffic regulations restricts our freedom but helps secure our physical safety and that of our fellow citizens. Though now replaced by an all-volunteer army, conscription has been used throughout our history to secure the military personnel needed to defeat our enemies and secure our liberty. In every case, it comes down to the costs of public requirements of citizens relative to their benefits.

3 Several factors motivate an interest in mandatory voting today: Low turnout, especially in midterm and primary elections, contributes to extreme partisan polarization; modern campaigns reinforce non-negotiable demands by focusing disproportionately on mobilizing (or demobilizing) the base; and politicians have little incentive to respond to those who are not reliable voters. Near universal voting is not a certain remedy for these maladies, but it just might create a virtuous cycle that improves our public life.

4   Dozens of countries have some form of mandatory voting. Our sister democracy, Australia, has had a particularly positive experience with it and could serve as a model for us. It requires mandatory attendance at the polls (voting for "none of the above" remains an option), with a very modest fine and liberal excuse policy for not voting. Think of it as a "nudge" rather than a punitive command. Newly eligible voters are enrolled on the registration lists and civic education programs in the schools prepare them for their responsibilities as citizens; parties and candidates go looking for their support.

It's not hard to imagine new generations of American citizens benefiting from similar developments and taking their responsibility to vote in stride.

QUESTIONS ON CONTENT, STRUCTURE, AND STYLE

1. Evaluate the introduction of the *USA Today's* essay? Does it effectively draw the reader into the essay? What is the purpose of the statistics that are included in the introduction?

2. What is the opinion of the *USA Today* editorial board regarding mandatory voting? What are the essay's main points in support of this stance?

3. For what rhetorical purpose does the editorial board include the example of Ferguson, Missouri? How does this example function as support for the essay's argument?

4. How does the *USA Today* essay address opposing viewpoints?

5. What alternative solutions to mandatory voting does the editorial board suggest in its essay?

6. Evaluate the introduction to Thomas Mann's essay. Does it effectively draw the reader into his essay? What is the purpose of the sentence "It only encourages them"?

7. What is Mann's opinion about mandatory voting? What are the main points he makes in support of this stance?

8. Why do both essays cite Australia as an example? How do the two essays use this example to make different points?

9. How does Mann address opposing viewpoints in his essay?

10. What does Mann suggest are the benefits of mandatory voting? What support does he offer for these benefits?

VOCABULARY

USA Today's essay:

mused (2)

non-starter (4)

individualistic (4)

predicated (4)

existential (5)

democratic (9)

ostensibly (10)

deterred (10)

deliberately (11)

Mann's essay:

mandatory (1)

paternalistic (1)

resonate (1)

compulsory (2)

conscription (2)

partisan (3)

polarization (3)

disproportionately (3)

punitive (4)

REP. ALBERTO GUTMAN: Florida Legislator, Businessman, Husband, Member of the National Rifle Association.

"Being from a country that was once a democracy and turned communist, I really feel I know what the right to bear arms is all about. In Cuba, where I was born, the first thing the communist government did was take away everybody's firearms, leaving them defenseless and intimidated with fear. That's why our constitutional right to bear arms is so important to our country's survival.

"As a legislator I have to deal with reality. And the reality is that gun control does not work. It actually eliminates the rights of the law-abiding citizen, not the criminal. Criminals will always have guns, and they won't follow gun control laws anyway. I would like to see tougher laws on criminals as opposed to tougher laws on legitimate gun owners. We need to attack the problem of crime at its roots, instead of blaming crime on gun ownership and citizens who use them lawfully.

"It's a big responsibility that we face retaining the right to bear arms. That's why I joined the NRA. The NRA is instrumental in protecting these freedoms. It helps train and educate people, supporting legislation that benefits not only those who bear arms but all citizens of the United States. The NRA helps keep America free." **I'm the NRA.**

The NRA's lobbying organization, the Institute for Legislative Action, is the nation's largest and most influential protector of the constitutional right to keep and bear arms. At every level of government and through local grassroots efforts, the Institute guards against infringement upon the freedoms of law-abiding gun owners. If you would like to join the NRA or want more information about our programs and benefits, write J. Warren Cassidy, Executive Vice President, P.O. Box 37484, Dept. AG-15, Washington, D.C. 20013.

Paid for by the members of the National Rifle Association of America. Copyright 1986.

National Rifle Association advertisement featuring Representative Alberto Gutman

SUGGESTIONS FOR WRITING

Use the essays by *USA Today's* editorial board and Thomas E. Mann as a stepping stone to your essay. Using your answers to the questions following the essays and your personal experiences, write an editorial for your school or local newspaper arguing your position on mandatory voting. You may wish to research the subject further, checking the voter turnout rates in your area or region. Or perhaps you might explore other controversial voting-related topics, such as voter drives, voting restrictions, etc. (◆ If you wish to incorporate research material into your essay, see Chapter 19 for help.)

Analyzing Advertisements

Because they are designed to be persuasive, advertisements use a variety of logical and emotional appeals. Ads might be considered arguments in brief form, as they frequently try to convince the public to buy a product, take an action, vote for or against something, join a group, or change an attitude or a behavior. By analyzing the ads that follow, you can practice identifying a variety of persuasive appeals and evaluating their effectiveness. After discussing these ads, apply what you've learned about logical appeals, target audiences, and choice of language to your argumentative essay.*

Divergent Viewpoints: Gun Ownership in America

The four advertisements that follow address the controversial subject of gun ownership. The first ad (page 332) is one of a series published by the National Rifle Association (NRA) to tell the public about its organization and its interpretation of the Second Amendment; other ads in this series have featured author Tom Clancy and basketball legend Karl Malone. The controlarms.org ad (page 333) urges the reader to consider the ease with which guns are obtained. This ad features an easily recognizable visual of a banana-shaped gun to make its point. The CeaseFirePA.org ad (page 334) uses statistics and also makes an appeal to pathos in its presentation of a visual that links a revolver with a child at play. This ad urges the reader to consider the high cost of gun violence to America's children. Finally, the Evolve Together ad (page 335) takes a humorous approach to the issue of gun safety and responsible gun ownership. Analyze the appeals used in each advertisement. Which methods of persuasion do you think are the most effective and why? Do you find any of the logical fallacies previously described in this chapter?

---

* ◆ For additional practice analyzing the arguments and appeals of other advertisements that appear in this text, see the list of advertisements that follows the Detailed Table of Contents.

controlarms.org advertisement

CeaseFirePA.org advertisement
("In America, gun violence sets its sights on kids every 30 minutes. Take a stand at CeasefirePA.org.")

Evolve Together advertisement ("If they find it, they'll play with it. Always lock up your guns.")

Competing Products: Sources of Energy

The advertisement by the Metropolitan Energy Council (on page 337) argues for the use of oil to provide heating. What arguments are offered? What emotional appeals does this ad incorporate? To whom are these appeals directed? How does the next ad for Xcel Energy, a large Midwestern and Western natural gas utility company (on page 338), try to respond to some of the first ad's arguments against using gas heat? Why might Xcel run a newspaper advertisement that appears to be primarily a public safety announcement?

The third advertisement (page 339) is part of a series sponsored by the U.S. Council for Energy Awareness to promote the building of more nuclear energy plants. How does it argue against both oil and gas? What emotional appeals do you see in this ad?

Considering both the language and the visual appeals of all three advertisements, which ad do you find the most persuasive, and why?

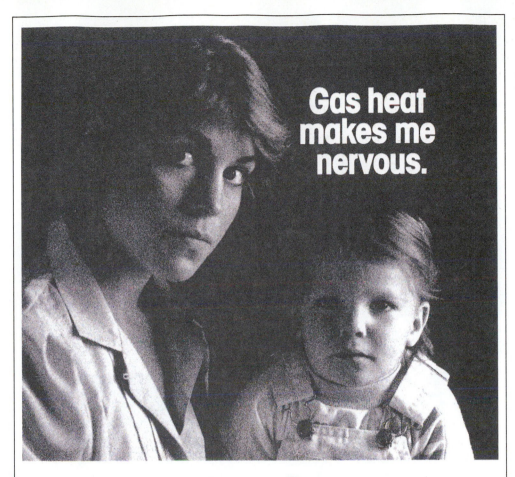

Metropolitan Energy Council advertisement

"WE COULD MAKE NATURAL GAS SMELL LIKE LILACS OR BACON COOKING IN THE MORNING. BUT THAT WOULDN'T GET YOU OUT OF THE HOUSE."

"Natural gas is naturally odorless. So we mix a harmless chemical in with it that smells like sulfur or rotten eggs. If you ever smell that in your house, you could well have a dangerous gas leak. That's when you have to get everyone out of the house immediately, get to a neighbor's house, and call 1-800-895-2999 to get one of our inspectors over. In an emergency, call 911 first. Most people don't know this either, but if you suspect you have a leak, you should NEVER turn lights or appliances on or off. And NEVER use your phone or cell phone in a house that may be filling with gas. The spark from a switch or phone could cause an explosion. By the same token, don't be lighting a match or opening windows. Just get out of there. Then make that call for help. Remember: Stay away. Stay alive."

Timio, Lead Welder

For more safety tips, visit our website at www.xcelenergy.com.

Xcel Energy

Every time you flip a switch or turn a dial, you tap into the energy of over 12,000 people working to make your life better. Xcel Energy. You get all of our energy.

Xcel Energy advertisement

SOME ARGUMENTS FOR NUCLEAR ENERGY ARE SMALLER THAN OTHERS.

Around the nuclear electric plant on Florida's Hutchinson Island, endangered wildlife have a safe haven. The baby sea turtles hatching on nearby beaches are more evidence of the truth about nuclear energy: it peacefully coexists with the environment.

America's 110 operating nuclear plants don't pollute the air, because they don't burn anything to generate electricity. Nor do they eat up valuable natural resources such as oil and natural gas.

Still, more plants are needed—to help satisfy the nation's growing need for electricity without sacrificing the quality of our environment. For a free booklet on nuclear energy, write to the U.S. Council for Energy Awareness, P.O. Box 66080, Dept. TR01, Washington, D.C. 20035.

NUCLEAR ENERGY MEANS CLEANER AIR.

© 1992 USCEA

As seen in April 1992 issues of The Washington Post, FORTUNE, and National Journal; May 1992 issues of TIME, Newsweek, Washington Post National Weekly and Congressional Quarterly; June 1992 issues of National Geographic, Smithsonian, New Choices and Christian Science Monitor; July 1992 issue of Forbes; August 1992 issue of World Monitor; September 1992 issue of Ladies' Home Journal and Natural History; October 1992 issues of Good Housekeeping, Atlantic and American Heritage; and November 1992 issue of Reader's Digest.

U.S. Council for Energy Awareness advertisement

Popular Appeals: Spending Our Money

How do all three of the following advertisements employ variations of the "bandwagon" or "transfer of virtue" appeal, discussed on page 318?

In the Timberland ad, what sort of company identity is created with the large text and the image of the boot crushing the bottle? Why does Timberland try to connect their brand identity with concern for environmental conservation? What message does the company hope potential buyers will associate with purchase of its products? To what kind of person might this ad appeal?

The TAG Heuer watch ad (page 342) may appeal to a different audience in its use of tennis star Maria Sharapova. This ad is just one in a series that incorporates endorsements by successful athletes, movie stars, and celebrities. Given Sharapova's celebrity status, personal attractiveness, and professional reputation for toughness, what is the appeal of the ad's tag line: "Don't Crack Under Pressure"? What connection between the consumer and Sharapova does the watch company wish to establish? To whom is this ad primarily directed, and is the ad effective? Why or why not?

The third ad (page 343) is sponsored by People for the Ethical Treatment of Animals (PETA). PETA is well known for its use of celebrity endorsements by actors, musicians, and athletes; however, this PETA ad departs from the organization's usual practice. This ad uses the image of a smoking baby to argue its cause. Though not explicitly about purchasing a specific product like the TAG Heuer and Timberland ads, this PETA ad also attempts to influence the way that people spend their money. What comparison or analogy (X is like Y) does the ad hope to promote in the reader's mind? What other types of appeals are present in the ad? Do you find this ad's argument logical and persuasive? Why or why not? (◆ If it's helpful, review the discussions of analogies on pages 257–259 and 319.)

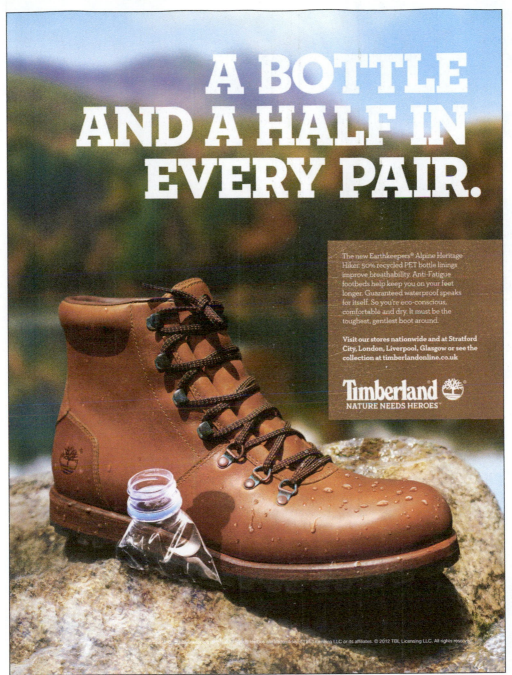

Timberland® Earthkeepers Alpine Heritage Hiker boot advertisement

TAG Heuer® Carrera watch advertisement featuring Maria Sharapova

Courtesy of Advertising Archives

People for the Ethical Treatment of Animals (PETA) "Go vegan!" billboard advertisement

Practicing What You've Learned

Continue practicing your critical thinking skills by analyzing the 1920s advertisement that appears here. Who was the likely target audience in terms of gender, age, socioeconomic group, and marital status? Why might this ad have appealed to its audience at that time in our country? After analyzing this ad, compare it to an advertisement for one of today's cars, SUVs, or trucks. Has the audience changed? What kinds of arguments, appeals, and language are employed to sell the vehicle in the current ad? In what ways do you find the two ads similar and different in their persuasive techniques?

Butler / CORBIS

A Revision Worksheet

As you write your rough drafts, consult Chapter 5 for guidance through the revision process. In addition, here are a few questions to ask yourself as you revise your argumentative essay:

1. Does this essay present a clear thesis limited to fit the assigned length of this paper?

2. Does this essay contain a number of strong, persuasive points in support of its thesis?

continued on next page

3. Is the essay organized in an easy-to-follow pattern that avoids repetition or confusion?

4. Does the essay present enough supporting evidence to make each of its points convincing? Where could additional examples, factual information, testimony, or other kinds of supporting material be added to make the arguments even more effective?

5. Will all the supporting evidence be clear to the essay's particular audience? Do any terms or examples need additional explanation or special definition?

6. Has at least one major opposing argument been addressed?

7. Does the essay avoid any logical fallacies or problems in tone?

Collaborative Activity: After you've revised your essay extensively, exchange rough drafts with a classmate and answer these questions for each other, making specific suggestions for improvement wherever appropriate. (◆ For advice on productive participation in classroom workshops, see pages 121–123.)

Using Strategies and Sources

The following assignments ask you to not only incorporate what you've learned in this chapter regarding argumentation but also to employ other strategies of development and to incorporate secondary sources into your response.

1. Frequently, a contemporary musical act will chart a popular hit with the remake or "cover" of an older song. Write an essay in which you argue for or against the superiority of the tune's original version over the "cover" version. Is the "authenticity" of one version greater than that of the other? If the versions are of different musical genres, is one genre better suited to the song's lyrics than the other? Consider the quality of the vocals, the production values, and the instrumentation. Though you will obviously have an opinion about one version or the other, be sure to support this opinion with reasoned, well-supported arguments. Be sure to use the strategies of comparison/contrast, description, and other strategies as appropriate.

2. Investigate your college's current recycling practices (or lack thereof). Write an argumentative essay proposing changes to these current practices. You may want to advocate for adopting greater recycling efforts or for stopping some recycling practices in favor of implementing others or for some other position. Remember to address arguments that people (students, college administrators, college staff) might raise opposing changes to current recycling practices. Use credible secondary sources on recycling's costs and benefits to provide convincing support for your argument. (◆ See Chapter 19 for help with conducting research and evaluating the sources you find.)

3. Lord Acton, a British historian, is credited with the following adage: "Power tends to corrupt, and absolute power corrupts absolutely. Great men are almost always bad men." Though Acton refers to "men," the debatable veracity of this modern-day proverb is not gender-specific. Consider specific examples of great men and women of history, both famous and infamous. How many of these examples support Acton's assertion? How many refute it? Write a researched essay in which you argue either for or against the truth of Acton's adage, using 2–3 detailed concrete examples to support your argument. Make sure to use credible secondary sources to support your claims. (◆ See Chapter 19 for help with conducting research and evaluating the sources you find.)

Chapter 16

Description

The writer of description creates a word-picture of people, places, objects, and emotions, using a careful selection of details to make an impression on the reader. If you have already written expository or argumentative essays in your composition course, you almost certainly have written some descriptive prose. Nearly every essay, after all, calls for some kind of description; for example, in the student comparison/contrast essay (pages 248–250) the writer describes two kinds of pizza; in the professional process essay (pages 227–231) the writer describes the embalming procedure in great detail. To help you write better description in your other essays, however, you may want to practice writing descriptive paragraphs or a short descriptive essay. Following a writing process like that represented in Figure 16.1 will help you develop an effective descriptive essay.

How to Write Effective Description

When descriptive prose is called for in your writing, consider these four basic suggestions.

Recognize your purpose. Description is not free-floating; it appears in your writing for a particular reason: to help you inform, clarify, persuade, or create a mood. In some essays you will want your description as *objective*—without personal impressions—as you can make it; for example, you might describe a scientific experiment or a business transaction in straight factual detail. Other times, however, you will want to convey a particular attitude toward your subject; this approach to description is called *subjective* or *impressionistic*. Note the differences between the following two descriptions of a tall, thin boy: the objective writer sticks to the facts by saying, "The eighteen-year-old boy was 6'1" and weighed 155 pounds," whereas the subjective writer gives an impressionistic description: "The young boy was as tall and scrawny as a birch tree in winter." Before you begin describing anything, you must first decide your purpose and whether it calls for objective or subjective reporting.

Describe clearly, using specific details. To make any description clear to your reader, you must include a sufficient number of details that are specific rather than fuzzy or vague. If, for example, your family dog were missing, you wouldn't call the animal shelter

Figure 16.1 VISUALIZING THE PROCESS: DESCRIPTION

Prewriting

Identify possible subjects by considering the following questions:

- About what topics do you have both interest and knowledge sufficient for a brief essay?
- Do you want to provide an objective or subjective description to your readers?
- What might your reader's interest level be in the topics you've selected?
- What will the main purpose of your description be?

Drafting

Determine the organization and content of your essay by asking the following questions:

- How can you return periodically to your essay's purpose throughout your description to keep it at the forefront of your reader's mind?
- Where can you include specific sensory details to ensure that your descriptions are clear and powerful?
- Are the details you're including relevant to the dominant impression you're trying to create for your readers?
- What pattern of organization makes the most sense for the impression you're trying to create in the reader's mind?

Revising

Carefully review your thesis and the supporting details you use by asking the following questions:

- Is your descriptive purpose obvious to the reader?
- Has your description provided enough specific details to create a concrete image in your reader's mind?
- Does your description follow a logical pattern of organization?
- If you've written an objective description, is your language as neutral as possible? If you've created a subjective description, is your approach consistent throughout?

Editing/Proofreading

Consider the sentence-level issues of your essay by asking the following questions:

- Where might you add sensory details and figurative language to enhance the reader's mental image of your subject matter?
- Have you reviewed your sentences for spelling, grammar, and punctuation errors?
- Is your paper formatted according to the assignment guidelines?

to ask if they'd seen a "big brown dog with a short tail"—naturally, you'd mention every distinguishing detail about your pet you could think of: size, color, breed, cut of ears, and special markings. Similarly, if your car had been stolen, you'd give the police as clear and as complete a description of your vehicle as possible. Look at the following sentence. Does it clearly identify a vaulting horse?

> A vaulting horse is a thing usually found in gyms that has four legs and a beam and is used by gymnasts making jumps.

If you didn't already know what a vaulting horse was, you might have trouble picking it out in a gymnasium crowded with equipment. A description with additional details would help you locate it:

> A vaulting horse is a piece of equipment used by gymnasts during competition to help propel them into the air when they perform any of a variety of leaps known as vaults. The gymnasts usually approach the vaulting horse from a running start and then place their hands on the horse for support or for a push off as they perform their vaults. The horse itself resembles a carpenter's sawhorse, but the main beam is made of padded leather rather than wood. The rectangular beam is approximately 5 feet, 3 inches long and $13\frac{1}{2}$ inches wide. Supported by four legs usually made of steel, the padded leather beam is approximately 4 feet, $\frac{1}{2}$ inch above the floor in men's competitions and 3 feet, 7 inches in women's competitions. The padded leather beam has two white lines marking off three sections on top: the croup, the saddle, and the neck. The two end sections—the croup and the neck—are each $15\frac{1}{2}$ inches long. Gymnasts place their hands on the neck or croup, depending on the type of vault they are attempting.

Moreover, the reader cannot imagine your subject clearly if your description is couched in vague generalities. The following sentence, for example, presents only a hazy picture:

> Larry is a sloppy dresser.

Revised, the picture is now sharply in focus:

> Larry wears dirty, baggy pants, shirts too small to stay tucked in, socks that fail to match his pants or each other, and a stained coat the Salvation Army rejected as a donation.

Specific details can turn cloudy prose into crisp, clear images that can be reproduced in the mind like photographs.

Select only appropriate details. In any description, the choice of details depends largely on the writer's purpose and audience. However, many descriptions—especially the more subjective ones—will present a *dominant impression*; that is, the writer selects primarily those details that communicate a particular mood or feeling to the reader. The dominant impression is the controlling focus of a description; for example, if you wrote a description of your grandmother to show her thoughtfulness, you would select only those details that convey an impression of a sweet, kindly old lady. Here are two brief descriptions illustrating the concept of dominant impression. The first writer tries to create a mood of mystery:

> Down a black winding road stands the abandoned old mansion, silhouetted against the cloud-shrouded moon, creaking and moaning in the wet, chill wind.

The second writer tries to present a feeling of joy and innocence.

> A dozen kites filled the spring air, and around the bright picnic tables spread with hot dogs, hamburgers, and slices of watermelon, Tom and Annie played away the warm April day.

In the description of the deserted mansion, the writer would have violated the impression of mystery had the sentence read,

> Down the black winding road stands the abandoned old mansion, surrounded by bright, multicolored tulips in early bloom.

Including the cheerful flowers as a detail in the description destroys the dominant mood of bleakness and mystery. Similarly, the second example would be spoiled had the writer ended it this way:

> Tom and Annie played away the warm April day until Tom got so sunburned he became ill and had to go home.

Therefore, remember to select only those details that advance your descriptive purpose. Omit any details you consider unimportant or distracting.

See if you can determine the dominant impression of each of the following descriptions:

> The wind had curled up to sleep in the distant mountains. Leaves hung limp and motionless from the silent trees, while birds perched on the branches like little statues. As I sat on the edge of the clearing, holding my breath, I could hear a squirrel scampering through the underbrush. Somewhere far away a dog barked twice, and then the woods were hushed once more.

> This poor thing has seen better days, but one should expect the sofa in a fraternity house den to be well worn. The large, plump, brown corduroy pillows strewn lazily on the floor and propped comfortably against the threadbare arms bear the pencil-point scars of frustrated students and foam-bleeding cuts of multiple pillow wars. No fewer than four pairs of rotting Nikes stand twenty-four-hour guard at the corners of its carefully mended frame. Obviously the relaxed, inviting appearance masks the permanent odors of cheap cigars from Thursday night poker parties; at least two or three guests each weekend sift through the popcorn kernels and Doritos crumbs, sprawl face down, and pass out for a nap. However, frequent inhabitants have learned to avoid the brown stains courtesy of the house pup and the red fruit punch designs of the chapter klutz. Habitually, they strategically lunge over the back of the sofa to an unsoiled area easily identifiable in flight by the large depression left by previous regulars. The quiet *hmmph* of the cushions and harmonious squeal of the

exhausted springs signal a perfect landing and utter a warm greeting from an old and faithful friend.

Make your descriptions vivid. By using clear, precise words, you can improve any kind of writing. ◆ Chapters 7 (on words) and 6 (on sentences) offer a variety of tips on clarifying your prose style. In addition to the advice given there, here are two other ways to enliven your descriptions, particularly those that call for a subjective approach.

Use sensory details. If it's appropriate, try using images that appeal to your readers' five senses. If, for example, you are describing your broken leg and the ensuing stay in a hospital, tell your readers how the place smelled, how it looked, what your cast felt like, how your pills tasted, and what noises you heard. Here are some specific examples using sensory details:

Sight	The clean white corridors of the hospital resembled the set of a sci-fi movie, with everyone scurrying around in identical starched uniforms.
Hearing	At night, the only sounds I heard were the quiet squeakings of sensible white shoes as the nurses made their rounds.
Smell	The green beans on the hospital cafeteria tray smelled stale and waxy, like crayons.
Touch	The hospital bed sheet felt as rough and heavy as a feed sack.
Taste	Every four hours they gave me an enormous gray pill whose aftertaste reminded me of the stale licorice my great-aunt kept in candy dishes around her house.

By appealing to the readers' senses, you better enable them to imagine the subject you are describing. Joseph Conrad, the famous nineteenth-century novelist, agreed, believing that all art "appeals primarily to the senses, and the artistic aim when expressing itself in written words must also make its appeal through the senses, if its highest desire is to reach the secret spring of responsive emotions." In other words, to make your readers feel, first make them "see."

Use figurative language when appropriate. As you may recall from Chapter 7, figurative language produces images or pictures in the readers' minds, helping them to understand unfamiliar or abstract subjects. Here are some devices you might use to clarify or spice up your prose:

1. Simile: a comparison between two things using the words "like" or "as" (◆ see also pages 176–178)

   Example Seeing exactly the video game he wanted, he snatched it off the shelf as quickly as a starving teenager grabbing pie in a refrigerator full of leftover vegetables.

2. Metaphor: a direct comparison between two things that does not use "like" or "as" (◆ see also pages 176–178)

   Example I was a puppet with my father controlling all the financial strings.

3. Personification: the attribution of human characteristics and emotions to inanimate objects, animals, or abstract ideas

Example   The old teddy bear sat in a corner, dozing serenely before the fireplace.

4. Hyperbole: intentional exaggeration or overstatement for emphasis or humor

Example   The cockroaches in my kitchen had now grown to the size of carry-on luggage.

5. Understatement: intentional representation of a subject as less important than the facts would warrant (◆ see also irony, page 162)

Example   "It was rather a serious evening, you know."—Sir Cosmo Duff Gordon, describing his survival of the sinking of the Titanic

6. Synecdoche: a part of something used to represent the whole

Example   A hundred tired feet hit the dance floor for one last jitterbug. [Here "feet" stand for the dancing couples themselves.]

7. Allusion: a brief reference to real or fictitious people, places, events, or things to produce certain associations in the reader's mind

Example   She proofread her essay again and again, searching for errors with the tenacity of Captain Ahab. [Ahab, the ship captain in the novel *Moby-Dick*, was obsessively devoted to hunting the white whale.]

If you do choose to include figurative language in your descriptions, be sure you are creating the specific image and tone you want to convey. These similes, taken from actual student papers, may have a distracting (and/or humorous) effect:

- She grew on him like she was a colony of E. coli, and he was room-temperature Canadian beef.
- He had a deep, throaty, genuine laugh, like the sound a dog makes just before it throws up.
- He was deeply in love and when she spoke, he heard bells, as if she were a garbage truck backing up.
- Her hair glistened in the rain like nose hair after a sneeze.

And sometimes, as in the following case, a feeble comparison is worse than nothing at all!

The little boat gently drifted across the pond exactly the way a bowling ball wouldn't.

Used sparingly and with careful crafting, however, figures of speech can make your prose enjoyable (as expensive chocolate?) and memorable (as your best weekend ever?). (◆ For more discussion of figurative language, including mixed metaphors, see pages 176–178.)

Problems to Avoid

Keep in mind these three pieces of advice to solve problems that frequently arise in description.

Remember your audience. Sometimes the object of our description is so clear in our minds that we forget that our readers haven't seen it too. Consequently, the description we write turns out to be vague, bland, or skimpy ("The big tree was beautiful"). Ask yourself about your audience: what do they need to know to see this sight as clearly as I do? Then fill in your description with ample, precise details that reveal the best picture possible. Don't forget to define or explain any terms you use that may be puzzling to your audience. (◆ For more advice on clear, vivid language, see pages 166–178.)

Avoid an erratic organization of details. Too often, descriptions are a hodgepodge of details, jotted down randomly. When you write a lengthy description, you should select a plan that will arrange your details in an orderly fashion. Depending on your subject matter and your purpose, you might adopt a plan calling for a description of something from top to bottom, left to right, front to back, and so on. For example, a description of a woman might begin at the head and move to the feet; furniture in a room might be described as your eyes move from one side of the room to another. A second plan for arranging details presents the subject's outstanding characteristics first and then fills in the lesser information; a child's red hair, for example, might be his most striking feature and therefore would be described first. A third plan presents details in the order you see them approaching: dust, then a car, then details about the car, its occupants, and so on. Or you might describe a subject as it unfolds chronologically, as in some kind of process or operation. Regardless of which plan of organization you choose, the reader should feel a sense of order in your description.

Avoid any sudden change in perspective. If, for example, you are describing the White House from the outside, don't suddenly include details that could be seen only from the inside. Similarly, if you are describing a car from a distance, you might be able to tell the car's model, year, and color, but you could hardly describe the upholstery or reveal the mileage. It is, of course, possible for you—or your observer—to approach or move around the subject of your description, but the reader must be aware of this movement. Any shift in point of view must be presented clearly and logically, with no sudden, confusing leaps from a front to a back view, from outside to inside, and so on.

Practicing What You've Learned

A. Choose sensory details (sight, taste, smell, touch, and hearing) and/or figurative language (similes, metaphors, personification, etc.) to vividly describe each of the following in a few sentences. Avoid clichés and Insta-Prose by creating memorable new images (serious or humorous) for your reader.

   1. A dessert

   2. A pair of jeans

continued on next page

3. A pet

4. The floor of a restaurant following a kids' party

5. A sunset

6. February

7. A scene in nature or in the city

8. Your favorite pillow

9. A dentist's office

10. Yourself in either a happy or grouchy mood

B. Describe a confined or small familiar place (your classroom, bedroom, work cubicle, inside of your car, etc.) in a paragraph using language that presents a positive impression; then rewrite your paragraph creating a negative view of the same space. Which details are the most effective in each paragraph, and why?

C. *Collaborative Activity:* Bring a small (palm-sized), inexpensive, unbreakable object from home to class. This might be a household or personal item (such as a fork or a key) or perhaps something from nature (a rock or leaf) or even something left over from your lunch (a piece of fruit or candy). With your classmates, deposit each object in a large bag or cardboard box that your instructor has brought. Join two other students and direct a group representative to choose, without peeking, an object from the bag or box, one item that no one in your group contributed to the collection. Together, practice your objective descriptive skills by composing a detailed, factual picture of this object in a paragraph of at least five sentences. If time permits, write another paragraph describing the same object subjectively, using colorful language to offer a dominant impression. Which description was easier for your group? Be ready to read your paragraphs to the rest of the class.

Assignment

Use the painting reproduced here to practice your descriptive writing skills. Often influenced by his Russian-Jewish heritage, artist Marc Chagall (1887–1985) painted this picture titled *Birthday* in 1915. Describe what you feel is the dominant mood of this picture, pointing out some of the details that communicate that tone to you. Consider the painting's people, setting, colors, and even shapes. In a short descriptive essay, re-create this painting as you see it for someone unfamiliar with the work. To get you started, ponder this: some viewers have questioned whether the male figure is "floating on air" with happiness or is instead an imaginary guest, perhaps even someone deceased. What do *you* think?

continued on next page

Birthday (L'Anniversaire), 1915, by Marc Chagall

(◆ For additional advice and exercises designed to improve descriptive writing skills, see pages 146–149 and 166–169 in Part One of this text.)

Essay Topics

Here are some suggestions for a descriptive paragraph or essay; focus your topic to fit your assignment. Don't forget that every description, whether objective or subjective, has a purpose, and your details should support that purpose. ◆ For additional ideas, see "Suggestions for Writing" on page 363.

1. A favorite painting, photograph, poster, or sculpture (Or choose one of the many artworks in this textbook. A complete list of visual art images follows the Detailed Table of Contents.)

2. A favorite piece of music or song

3. A piece of equipment important to your major, a hobby, or a favorite sport

continued on next page

4. A childhood object you have kept (or wished that you had kept)

5. Your most precious material possession (Consider: after people and pets, what would you save first if you had fifteen minutes to evacuate your home as a fire approached?)

6. Yourself (how you looked at a certain age or on a memorable occasion or in a particular photograph)

7. A product or purchase whose ownership has disappointed you

8. The ugliest/most beautiful place or building on your campus or in town

9. A holiday, celebration, or ritual in your family

10. Your first or worst car or apartment

11. Your favorite vacation destination

12. A common object with uncommon beauty

13. A poster for a movie, concert, or campus event or an album cover by a favorite band

14. Your favorite pet

15. One brief but unforgettable moment

16. An event, element, or creature in nature

17. A shopping mall, student cafeteria, or other crowded public place that you frequent

18. The inside of your refrigerator, your closet, or some other equally loathsome place in your home

19. A treasure from a personal collection or a family heirloom

20. A Special Place (Perhaps your place offers you solitude, beauty, or renewed energy. The scene shown here was painted over a half-dozen different ways by nineteenth-century artist Claude Monet, who loved this tranquil lily pond near his farmhouse in France. Re-create your special place for your readers by choosing the right descriptive words, just as Monet did with each brushstroke of color.)

The Water-Lily Pond, 1899, by Claude Monet

SuperStock / SuperStock

A Topic Proposal for Your Essay

Selecting the right subject matter is important to every writer. To help you clarify your ideas and strengthen your commitment to your topic, here is a proposal sheet that asks you to describe some of your preliminary ideas about your subject before you begin drafting. Although your ideas may change as you write (they will almost certainly become more refined), thinking through your choice of topic now may help you avoid several false starts.

1. What subject will your essay describe? Will you describe this subject objectively or subjectively? Why?

2. Why are you interested in this topic? Do you have a personal or professional connection to the subject? State at least one reason for your choice of topic.

3. Is this a significant topic of interest to others? Why? Who specifically might find it interesting, informative, or entertaining?

4. What is the main purpose of your description? In one or two sentences, describe the major effect you'd like your descriptive essay to have on your readers. What would you like for them to understand or "see" about your subject?

5. List at least three details that you think will help clarify your subject for your readers.

6. What difficulties, if any, might arise during drafting? For example, what organizational strategy might you think about now that would allow you to guide your readers through your description in a coherent way?

Once you have chosen your topic, take a moment to read through Figure 16.1 (page 348) again to remind yourself of key questions you should be asking at each stage of the writing process for your descriptive essay.

Sample Student Essay

In her descriptive essay, this student writer recalls her childhood days at the home of her grandparents to make a point about growing up. Notice that the writer uses both figurative language and contrasting images to help her readers understand her point of view.

Treeclimbing

1   It was Mike's eighteenth birthday and he was having a little bit of a breakdown. "When was the last time you made cloud pictures?" he asked me absently as he stared up at the ceiling before class started. Before I could answer, he continued, "Did you know that by the time you're an adult, you've lost 85 percent of your

Introduction: The conversation that triggers her memory

imagination?" He paused. "I don't want to grow up." Although I doubted the authenticity of his facts, I understood that Mike—the hopeless romantic with his long ponytail, sullen black clothes, and glinting dark eyes—was caught in a Peter Pan complex. He drew those eyes from the ceiling and focused on me: "There are two types of children. Tree children and dirt children. Kids playing will either climb trees or play in the dirt. Tree children are the dreamers—the hopeful, creative dreamers. Dirt children, they just stay on the ground. Stick to the rules." He trailed off, and then picked up again: "I'm a tree child. I want to make cloud pictures and climb trees. And I don't ever want to come down." Mike's story reminded me of my own days as a tree child, and of the inevitable fall from the tree to the ground.

The grandparents' neighborhood remembered in military images and sensory details

2   My childhood was a playground for imagination. Summers were spent surrounded by family at my grandparents' house in Milwaukee, Wisconsin. The rambling Lannonstone bungalow was located on North 46th Street at Burleigh, a short drive from center-city Milwaukee and the historic Schuster's department store. In the winter, all the houses looked alike, rigid and militant, like white-bearded old generals with icicles hanging from their moustaches. One European-styled house after the other lined the streets in strict parallel formation, block after block.

3   But in the summer it was different . . . softer. No subzero winds blew lonely down the back alley. Instead, kids played stickball in it. I had elegant, grass-stained tea parties with a neighborhood girl named Shelly, while my grandfather worked in his thriving vegetable garden among the honeybees, and watched sprouts grow. An ever-present warming smell of yeast filtered down every street as the nearby breweries pumped a constant flow of fresh beer. Above, the summer sky looked like an Easter egg God had dipped in blue dye.

4   Those summer trips to Milwaukee were greatly anticipated events back then. My brother and I itched with repressed energy

throughout the long plane ride from the West Coast. We couldn't wait to see Grandma and Papa. We couldn't wait to see what presents Papa had for us. We couldn't wait to slide down the steep, blue-carpeted staircase on our bottoms, and then on our stomachs. Most of all, we couldn't wait to go down to the basement.

Use of parallel sentences to emphasize anticipation

5   The basement was better than a toy store. Yes, the old-fashioned milk cabinet in the kitchen wall was enchanting, and the laundry chute was fun because it was big enough to throw down Ernie, my stuffed dog companion, so my brother could catch him below in the laundry room, as our voices echoed up and down the chute. But the basement was better than all of these, better even than sliding down those stairs on rug-burned bottoms.

6   It was always deliciously cool down in the basement. Since the house was built in the 1930s, there was no air conditioning. Upstairs, we slept in hot, heavy rooms. My nightgown stuck to the sheets, and I would lie awake, listening to crickets, inhaling the beer-sweet smell of the summer night, hoping for a cool breeze. Nights were forgotten, however, as my brother and I spent hours every day in the basement. There were seven rooms in the basement; some darker rooms I had waited years to explore. There was always a jumbled heap of toys in the middle room, most of which were leftovers from my father's own basement days. It was a child's safe haven; it was a sacred place.

The basement in contrast to other parts of the house

7   The hours spent in the basement were times of a gloriously secure childhood. Empires were created in a day with faded colored building blocks. New territories were annexed when either my brother or I got the courage to venture into one of those Other Rooms—the dark, musty ones without windows—and then scamper back to report of any sightings of monsters or other horrific childhood creatures. In those basement days everything seemed safe and wholesome and secure, with my family surrounding me, protecting me. Like childhood itself, entering the basement was like entering another dimension.

Adventures in the basement

The house
and
neighborhood
years later

8   Last summer I returned to Milwaukee to help my grandparents pack to move into an apartment. I went back at seventeen to find the house—my kingdom—up for sale. I found another cycle coming to a close, and I found myself separated from what I had once known. I looked at the house. It was old; it was crumbling; it needed paint. I looked down the back alley and saw nothing but trash and weeds. I walked to the corner and saw smoke-choked, dirty streets and thick bars in shop windows, nothing more than another worn-out Midwestern factory city. I went back to the house and down to the basement, alone.

The basement
years later

9   It was gray and dark. Dust filtered through a single feeble sunbeam from a cracked window pane. It was empty, except for the overwhelming musty smell. The toys were gone, either packed or thrown away. As I walked in and out of rooms, the quietness filled my ears, but in the back of my head the sounds of childhood laughter and chatter played like an old recording.

10   The dark rooms were filled not with monsters but with remnants of my grandfather's business. A neon sign was propped against the wall in a corner: Ben Strauss Plumbing. Piles of heavy pipes and metal machine parts lay scattered about on shelves. A dusty purple ribbon was thumbtacked to a door. It said SHOOT THE WORKS in white letters. I gently took it down. The ribbon hangs on my door at home now, and out of context it somehow is not quite as awe-inspiring and mystifying as it once was. However, it does serve its purpose, permanently connecting me to my memories.

11   All children are tree children, I believe. The basement used to be my tree, the place I could dream in. That last summer I found myself, much to Mike's disappointment, quite mature, quite adult. Maybe Mike fell from his tree and was bruised. Climbing down from that tree doesn't have to be something to be afraid of. One needn't hide in the tree for fear of touching the ground and forgetting how to

climb back up when necessary. I think there is a way to balance the two extremes. Climb down gracefully as you grow up, and if you fall, don't land in quicksand. I like to think I'm more of a shrubbery child: not so low as to get stuck in the mud and just high enough to look at the sky and make cloud pictures.

Conclusion: A return to the introduction's images and some advice

Pretty Girl

Rick Bragg

An American journalist and writer of nonfiction, Rick Bragg was born in 1959 and raised in north Alabama. Heavily influenced by his family's long tradition of oral storytelling, Bragg's nonfiction novels focus on the dignity of those who grew up poverty-stricken in the hardscrabble areas of the rural South. A long-time journalist, Bragg joined the staff of the *New York Times* in 1994. Covering such stories as the Oklahoma City bombing, Bragg was awarded a Pulitzer Prize in 1996. Subsequently, Bragg has become a much sought-after speaker and reader based on the success of his non-fiction novels, most notably his memoir *All Over But the Shoutin'*. Bragg currently teaches in the journalism program at the University of Alabama.

Pre-reading Thoughts: Think about a time in which you have been involved in what others considered to be a "lost cause," a situation, project, or person that seemed to have little potential for success. How did it turn out? What kind of investment did it require from you? What was the reward for your involvement?

1   Her name was perfect.
2   She came to them in the dead of night, in the cold. She was more than half dead, starved down to bones, her hair completely eaten away by mange. She had been run off from more than one yard when she finally crept into an empty doghouse in the trees beyond my mother's yard. At least she was out of the wind.
3   They found her, my mother and brother, in the daylight of the next day. They could not even tell, at first, she was a dog.
4   "And it broke my heart," my mother said.
5   They did not call the vet because she knew what the vet would do. She was too far gone to save; any fool could see that. My mama lives in the country and has to run off

---

*◆ To help you read this essay analytically, review pages 183–186. For two other professional essays in Part Two that make extensive use of description, see "To Bid the World Farewell" (pages 227–231) and "Two Ways of Viewing the River" (pages 254–255).

two wandering dogs a week, but this time, "I just couldn't. She couldn't even get up." How do you run off a dog that cannot stand?

6   The broke-down dog had stumbled on two people who hate to give up on anything, even a month-old newspaper. They save batteries that have not had a spark of anything in them for a long, long time. My mother keeps pens that stopped writing in 1974. My point is, there is always a little use, a little good, a little life left in anything, and who are they to decide when something is done for good.

7   My brother Mark looked at her, at her tragic face, and named her.

8   "Hey, Pretty Girl," he said.

9   It was like he could see beyond the ruin, or maybe into it. I don't know.

10   Her hips were bad, which was probably why she was discarded in the first place, and her teeth were worn down. Her eyes were clouded. But they fed her, and gave her water, and bathed her in burnt motor oil, the way my people have been curing the mange for generations. They got her looking less atrocious, and then they called the vet.

11   The vet found she had heartworms. She was walking dead, anyway, at her age. It was then I saw her, still a sack of bones. It would be a kindness, I told my mother, to put her down. She nodded her head.

12   A month later I pulled into the driveway to see a beautiful white German shepherd standing watch at the front of the house. It was not a miracle; her ailments did not magically cease. But together, my mother and brother had tended her, and even let her live in the house. She ate people food, and drank buttermilk out of an aluminum pie tin. She was supposed to last, at most, a few weeks or months. She lived three more years—decades, in dog years—following my brother to the garden to watch for snakes and listen for thunder.

13   "I prayed for her," my mother said. "Some people say you ain't supposed to pray for a dog, but . . ." And then after the gift of years, Pretty Girl began to fail, and died. She is buried in the mountain pasture.

14   The hot weather will be on us soon. The garden is already planted. Some things were planted according to science, according to soil and weather. And some things were planted according to lore, the shape of the moon, and more. That is fine with me. There are things we cannot explain, things beyond science, like how a man could name a ravaged and dying dog, and have her rise inside that, somehow, to make it true.

QUESTIONS ON CONTENT, STRUCTURE, AND STYLE

1. Bragg uses an especially abbreviated introduction in his essay. Why do you think he does this? How effectively does this work?

2. What is the thesis of "Pretty Girl"? Is it explicit or implied?

3. Bragg uses dialogue just four times in this essay, relying instead on descriptive language. What impact does his spare use of quotations have on the reader and the narrative? What do the snippets of conversation reveal about the author's mother?

4. How would you characterize the tone of this essay? What emotion does the author attempt to leave you feeling at story's end?

5. Consider Bragg's use of sensory details in this piece. How do they strengthen his overall thesis and main idea?

6. Bragg delays explicitly revealing the subject of his essay, referring to the dog instead with the feminine pronouns "she" and "her" before finally announcing "she was a dog" in paragraph three. What is the purpose of this delay?

7. In paragraph five, Bragg writes that "they did not call the vet because she knew what the vet would do." What does he mean? Why does his mother refuse to take the dog to the vet? How does Bragg use this description of a dog to illustrate a larger point about his mother?

8. What descriptive details does the author use to establish the surprise revealed in paragraph twelve? How does this revelation impact the reader?

9. What contrast does Bragg's description establish between the story's narrator and the narrator's mother and brother? How do their views of the dog differ? How does Bragg use this contrast to set up the story's conclusion?

10. Does Bragg successfully create a portrait of the Pretty Girl in his essay? How might he have improved his description? Where might he have used more vivid or more concrete descriptive language?

VOCABULARY

mange (3)	atrocious (11)
ailments (13)	ravaged (15)

SUGGESTIONS FOR WRITING

1. Try using Rick Bragg's description as a springboard for your own writing. Descriptive detail can be a wonderful tool for bringing to life an important or meaningful person or event from your life. Describe a person who has taught you valuable lessons, perhaps someone who has been a mentor or a relative or friend who you admire for a particular trait. What character traits stand out in your memory? What do you remember physically about this person? How might she or he have been an unlikely mentor or an unexpected source of inspiration in your life? Remember, also, the importance of sensory details, dialogue, and imagery to strong description.

2. Rick Bragg talks about his mother and her affinity for lost causes. Write a description of another mother figure, one whose face is forever identified with the Great Depression (see the *Migrant Mother* photo on the next page). In 1936 photographer Dorothea Lange stopped on a dirt road in California to take a half-dozen pictures of a thirty-two-year-old woman and her children as they huddled in the rain under a lean-to tent. The woman told Lange they had been living off birds the children had killed and that she had just sold the tires off their car to buy food. What is the dominant impression of this picture? What does this person's face (or posture or choice of clothing) say to you about his or her character or style? Use strong description to recreate a mental portrait of this photograph for your reader. Why do you think *Migrant Mother* is considered one of the most affecting photographs of all time?

Library of Congress Prints and Photographs Division

Migrant Mother, 1936, by Dorothea Lange

A Revision Worksheet

As you write your rough drafts, consult Chapter 5 for guidance through the revision process. In addition, here are a few questions to ask yourself as you revise your description:

1. Is the descriptive essay's purpose clear to the reader?

2. Are there enough specific details in the description to make the subject matter distinct to readers who are unfamiliar with the scene, person, or object? Where might more detail be added?

3. Are the details arranged in an order that's easy to follow?

4. If the assignment called for an objective description, are the details as "neutral" as possible?

5. If the assignment called for a subjective description, does the writer's particular attitude come through clearly with a consistent use of well-chosen details or imagery?

6. Could any sensory details or figurative language be added to help the reader "see" the subject matter?

7. Does this essay end with an appropriate conclusion or does description merely stop?

Collaborative Activity: After you've revised your essay extensively, exchange rough drafts with a classmate and answer these questions for each other, making specific suggestions for improvement wherever appropriate. (◆ For advice on productive participation in classroom workshops, see pages 121–123.)

Using Strategies and Sources

The following assignments ask you to not only incorporate what you've learned in this chapter regarding description, but also to employ other strategies of development and to incorporate secondary sources into your response.

1. Consider your two favorite bands, athletes, friends, etc. Then carefully describe the two in an expository that uses the elements of comparison and contrast to strengthen your description.

2. In an expository essay, describe one of America's many famous landmarks. The site you pick could be manmade or naturally occurring. Be sure to use the principles of description and incorporate information from credible secondary sources to further support your description. (◆ See Chapter 19 for help with conducting research and evaluating the sources you find.)

3. In a brief expository essay, describe your favorite childhood tradition. In addition to the strategy of description, you'll likely want to use narration, exemplification, and any other strategy as appropriate.

Chapter 17

Narration

When many people hear the word "narrative," they think of a made-up story. But not all stories are fiction. In this chapter we are not concerned with writing literary short stories—that's a skill to develop in a creative writing class—but rather with nonfiction *expository narratives*, stories that are used to explain or prove a point. We most often use two kinds of these stories:

1. The *extended narrative*—a long episode that by itself illustrates or supports an essay's thesis

2. The *brief narrative*—a shorter incident that is often used in a body paragraph to support or illustrate a particular point in an essay.

Let's suppose, for example, you want to write an essay showing how confusing the registration system is at your school. To illustrate the problems vividly, you might devote your entire essay to the retelling of a friend's seven-hour experience signing up for classes last fall, thus making use of extended narration. Or take another example: in an argumentative essay advocating a new state law prohibiting drivers' use of cell phones in moving vehicles, you might include a brief narrative about a recent wreck to support a paragraph's point about the dangerous distraction of glancing at text messages. Regardless of which type of narrative best fits your purpose, the telling of a story or an incident can be an interesting, persuasive means of informing your readers. Following a writing process like that represented in Figure 17.1 will help you develop an effective narrative essay.

Writing the Effective Narrative Essay

Know your purpose. What are you trying to accomplish by writing this narrative essay? Are you, for example, offering an *objective* retelling of a historical event (the dropping of the atomic bomb) to inform your readers who may not be acquainted with the facts? Or are you presenting a *subjective* narrative, which persuasively tells a story (Susan B. Anthony's 1872 arrest for voting) from a clearly defined point of view? Perhaps your narrative is a personal story whose lesson you wish readers to share. Whatever your choice—an objective, factual retelling or a subjective interpretation—your narrative's purpose should be clear to your readers, who should never reach the end of the story wondering "What was

Figure 17.1 VISUALIZING THE PROCESS: NARRATION

Prewriting

Identify possible subjects by considering the following questions:

- What is your role in the narrative subject you're considering? Do you have enough knowledge and interest to create an essay on this subject?
- What about this topic makes it important enough to you and your audience to warrant treatment in an essay?
- What will the purpose of your narrative essay be? Will you seek to inform or to entertain? Will it be subjective or objective?

Drafting

Determine the effect you hope your essay will have on your audience by asking the following questions:

- How can you present your main point clearly to your reader?
- What is the best way to indicate a logical time sequence in the order of your narrative's events?
- How can you best use dialogue and sensory details to increase authenticity in both character and action?
- How can you limit your narrative's scope to make its size manageable and appropriate?

Revising

Carefully review your thesis and the supporting details you use by asking the following questions:

- Is your narrative purpose clear to the reader?
- How clear is your thesis statement and the narrative's connection to it?
- Does your narrative maintain a logical point of view and an understandable order of action?
- Does your narrative lag or wander in places? Does the pacing maintain reader interest?

Editing/Proofreading

Consider the sentence-level issues of your essay by asking the following questions:

- Have you used sufficient transitions to make your narrative flow smoothly?
- Where might you add additional details to make the narrative more believable?
- Have you reviewed your sentences for spelling, grammar, and punctuation errors?
- Is your paper formatted according to the assignment guidelines?

that all about?" Knowing your purpose will help you select the information and language best suited to meet your audience's needs.

Present your main point clearly. To ensure that readers understand their purpose, many writers first state a thesis claim followed by a narrative that supports it. Sometimes writers begin with their narrative and use their concluding paragraph to state or sum up the point or "lesson" of their story. Still others choose to imply a main point or attitude through the unfolding action and choice of descriptive details. An implied thesis is always riskier than a stated one, so unless you are absolutely convinced that your readers could not possibly fail to see your point, work on finding a smooth way to incorporate a statement of your main idea into your essay.

Follow a logical time sequence. Many narrative essays—and virtually all brief stories used in other kinds of essays—follow a chronological order, presenting actions as they naturally occur in the story. Occasionally, however, a writer will use the flashback technique, which takes the readers back in time to reveal an event that occurred before the present scene of the essay. If you decide to use shifts in time, use transitional phrases or other signals to ensure that your readers don't become confused or lost.

Use sensory details to hold your readers' interest. For example, if the setting plays an important role in your story, describe it in vivid terms so that your readers can imagine the scene easily. Suppose you are pointing out the necessity of life preservers on sailboats by telling the story of how you spent a stormy night in the lake, clinging to a capsized boat. To convince your readers, let them "feel" the stinging rain and the icy current trying to drag you under; let them "see" the black waves and the dark menacing sky; let them "hear" the howling wind and the gradual splitting apart of the boat. Effective narration often depends on effective description, and effective description depends on vivid, specific detail. (◆ For more help on writing description, see Chapter 16; review Chapter 7 for advice on word choice.)

Create authentic characters. Again, the use of detail is crucial. Your readers should be able to visualize the people (or animals) in your narrative clearly; if your important characters are drawn too thinly, or if they seem phony or stereotyped, your readers will not fully grasp the meaning of your story. Show your readers the major characters as you see them by commenting unobtrusively on their appearances, speech, and actions. In addition, a successful narrative may depend on the reader's understanding of people's motives—why they act the way they do in certain situations. A narrative about your hometown's grouchiest miser who suddenly donated a large sum of money to a poor family isn't very believable unless we know the motive behind the action. In other words, let your readers know what is happening to whom by explaining or showing why.

Use dialogue realistically. Writers often use dialogue, their characters' spoken words, to reveal action or personality traits of the speakers. By presenting conversations, writers show rather than tell, often creating emphasis or a more dramatic effect. Dialogue may also help readers identify with or feel closer to the characters or action by creating a sense of "you are there." If your narrative would profit from dialogue, be certain the word choice and the manner of speaking are in keeping with each character's education, background, age, location, and so forth. Don't, for example, put a sophisticated philosophical treatise into the mouth of a ten-year-old boy or the latest campus slang into the speech of a fifty-year-old farmer from Two Egg, Florida. Also, make sure that your dialogue doesn't sound wooden or phony. The right dialogue can help make your story more realistic and interesting, provided that the conversations are essential to the narrative and are not merely padding the plot. (◆ For an example of dialogue in a narrative, read Jada Smith's "Don't Mess With Auntie Jean" on pages 375–378. For help in punctuating dialogue, see pages 586–587 in the Handbook.)

Problems to Avoid

Weak, boring narratives are often the result of problems with subject matter or poor pacing; therefore, you should keep in mind the following advice:

Choose your subject carefully. Many of the best narrative essays come from personal experience or study, and the reason is fairly obvious: it's difficult to write convincingly about something you've never seen or done or read about. You probably couldn't, for instance, write a realistic account of a bullfight unless you'd seen one or at least had studied the subject in great detail. The simplest, easiest, most interesting nonfiction narrative you can write is likely to be about a subject with which you are personally familiar. This doesn't mean that you can't improvise many details, create a hypothetical story to illustrate a point, or recount an event you've learned about through research, as long as you identify the source of your borrowed material. Even so, you still may have more success basing your narrative—real or hypothetical—on something or someone you know well.

Limit your scope. When you wish to use an extended narrative to illustrate a thesis, don't select an event or series of actions whose retelling will be too long or complex for your assignment. In general, it's better to select one episode and flesh it out with many specific details so that your readers can clearly see your point. For instance, you may have had many rewarding experiences during the summer you worked as a lifeguard, but you can't tell them all. Instead, you might focus on one experience that captures the essence of your attitude toward your job—say, the time you saved a child from drowning—and present the story so vividly that the readers can easily understand your point of view.

Don't let your story lag or wander. At some time, you've probably listened to a storyteller who became stuck on some insignificant detail ("Was it Friday or Saturday the letter came? Let's see now . . ."; "Then Joe said to me—no, it was Sally—no, wait, it was . . ."). And you've probably also heard bores who insist on making a short story long by including too many unimportant details or digressions. These mistakes ruin the *pacing* of their stories; in other words, the story's tempo or movement becomes bogged down until the readers are bored witless. To avoid creating a sleeping tonic in word form, dismiss all unessential information and focus your attention—and use of detail—on the important events, people, and places. Skip uneventful periods of time by using such phrases as "A week went by before Mr. Smith called . . ." or "Later that evening, around nine o'clock. . . ." In short, keep the story moving quickly enough to hold the readers' interest. Moreover, use a variety of transitional devices to move the readers from one action to another; don't rely continuously on the "and then . . . and then . . ." method.

Practicing What You've Learned

A. To practice collecting details that will strengthen your narrative, try this activity. Study the painting below, *Tornado Over Kansas*, and then list as many specific, descriptive details about the scene as you can see or imagine. For example, what do details about the setting and the family's appearance reveal about these people and where they live? What unusual noises, colors, and smells might be vividly described? What does each person's facial expression and body language tell you about his or her thoughts at this very moment? What words might be spoken by each person and in what tone of voice?

Now think of a time in which you experienced a narrow escape or conquered a fearful moment—some event in your life that might be retold in an exciting narrative essay. Using the impressions recorded from the painting as a guide to prompt your memory, compile a similar list of vivid, sensory details describing the people, setting, and action at the most dramatic point of your story. Which words or phrases on your list most effectively communicate your experience, and why?

Collection of the Muskegon Museum of Art, Michigan, Hackley Picture Fund Purchase, 1935.4

Tornado Over Kansas (oil on canvas), 1929, by John Steuart Curry

B. *Collaborative Activity:* Think of an important event in your life that you would like known to future generations of your family. Or perhaps there is a story about your ancestors that you want to record so it is not forgotten. Draft some notes

continued on next page

about your story, and then, in class, pair with another student. Take turns telling your stories; as each person talks, the partner should ask for more details. Simple questions such as "What did he look like at that moment?" or "Why was that decision so important?" or "What exactly did you say then?" can help a writer shape and invigorate a narrative. Incorporate any useful new details, descriptions, or dialogue into the final draft of your essay.

Essay Topics

Use one of the following topics to suggest an essay that is developed by narration. Remember that each essay must have a clear purpose. ◆ For additional ideas, see the "Suggestions for Writing" section following the professional essay (page 379); the quotations on pages 45–46 may also spark topics.

1. An experience revealing courage, loyalty, or generosity

2. An event of historical, medical, or scientific importance (◆ See Chapter 19 for help incorporating research material.)

3. An interaction that changed your thinking on a particular subject or informed an important decision

4. Your best/worst holiday, trip, or first day (school, job, camp, etc.)

5. A time that you rendered or received much-needed assistance

6. Your worst accident or brush with danger

7. An unforgettable childhood experience

8. The first time you spent the night away from home

9. A time you gained self-confidence or improved your self-image

10. Your participation in a civic event, social justice activity, or charity (an election campaign, voter registration work, Red Cross blood drive, Habitat for Humanity, etc.), showing how you were informed or changed

11. A meaningful event experienced in another culture or country

Habitat for Humanity volunteers from Mountain View Chinese Baptist Church of Mountain View, California, help construct homes at Musician's Village in the Upper 9th Ward of New Orleans, Louisiana.

continued on next page

12. A triumph over prejudice, anger, or violence

13. A family story (perhaps one about you—for example, how did you get your name?)

14. The hardest or most satisfying work you've ever accomplished

15. The most frightening event you've ever experienced

16. A gain or loss of something or someone important

17. A risk that paid off (or a triumph against the odds)

18. A nonacademic lesson learned at school, on a job, or on a team

19. An episode marking your passage from one stage of your life to another

20. A habit that got you into (or out of) trouble

A Topic Proposal for Your Essay

Selecting the right subject matter is important to every writer. To help you clarify your ideas and strengthen your commitment to your topic, here is a proposal sheet that asks you to describe some of your preliminary ideas about your subject before you begin drafting. Although your ideas may change as you write (they will almost certainly become more refined), thinking through your choice of topic now may help you avoid several false starts.

1. In a sentence or two, briefly state the subject of your narrative. Did you or someone you know participate in this story?

2. Why did you select this narrative? Does it have importance for you personally, academically, or professionally? In some other way? Explain your reason, or purpose, for telling this story.

3. Will others be informed or entertained by this story? Who might be especially interested in hearing your narrative? Why?

4. What is the primary effect you would like your narrative to have on your readers? What would you like them to feel or think about after they read your story? Why?

5. What is the critical moment in your story? At what point, in other words, does the action reach its peak? Summarize this moment in a few descriptive words.

6. What difficulties, if any, might this narrative present as you are drafting? For example, if the story you want to tell is long or complex, how might you focus on the main action and pace it appropriately?

Once you have chosen your topic, take a moment to read through Figure 17.1 again (page 367) to remind yourself of key questions you should be asking at each stage of the writing process for your narration essay.

Sample Student Essay

In this narrative, a student uses a story about a sick but fierce dog to show how she learned a valuable lesson in her job as a veterinarian's assistant. Notice the student's good use of vivid details that make this well-paced story both clear and interesting.

Never Underestimate the Little Things

1   When I went to work as a veterinarian's assistant for Dr. Sam Holt and Dr. Jack Gunn last summer, I was under the false impression that the hardest part of veterinary surgery would be the actual performance of an operation. The small chores demanded before this feat didn't occur to me as being of any importance. As it happened, I had been in the veterinary clinic only a total of four hours before I met a little animal who convinced me that the operation itself was probably the easiest part of treatment. This animal, to whom I owe thanks for so enlightening me, was a chocolate-colored chihuahua of tiny size and immense perversity named Smokey.

Introduction: A misconception

Thesis: Small preliminary details can be as important as the major action

2   Smokey could have very easily passed for some creature from another planet. It wasn't so much his gaunt little frame and overly large head, or his bony paws with nearly saberlike claws, as it was his grossly infected eyes. Those once-shining eyes were now distorted and swollen into grotesque balls of septic, sightless flesh. The only vague similarity they had to what we'd normally think of as the organs of vision was a slightly upraised dot, all that was left of the pupil, in the center of a pink and purply marble. As if that were not enough, Smokey had a temper to match his ugly sight. He also had surprisingly good aim, considering his largely diminished vision, toward any moving object that happened to place itself unwisely before his ever-inquisitive nose; with sudden and wholly vicious intent, he would snap and snarl at whatever blocked the little light that could filter through his swollen and ruptured blood vessels. Truly, in many respects, Smokey was a fearful dog to behold.

Description of the main character: His appearance

His personality

3   Such an appearance and personality did nothing to encourage my already flagging confidence in my capabilities as a vet's assistant. How was I supposed to get that little demon out of his cage? Jack had casually requested that I bring Smokey to the surgery room, but did he really expect me to put my hands into the cage of that devil

The difficulty of moving the dog to the surgery room

dog? I suppose it must have been my anxious expression that saved me, for as I turned uncertainly toward the kennel, Jack chuckled nonchalantly and accompanied me to demonstrate how professionals in his line of work dealt with professionals in Smokey's. He took a small rope about four feet long with a no-choke noose at one end and unlatched Smokey's cage. Then cautiously he reached in and dangled the noose before the dog's snarling jaws. Since Smokey could only barely see what he was biting at, his attacks were directed haphazardly in a semicircle around his body. The tiny area of his cage led to his capture, for during one of Smokey's forward lunges, Jack dropped the noose over his head and moved the struggling creature out onto the floor. The fight had only just begun for Smokey, however, and he braced his feet against the slippery linoleum tiling and forced us to drag him, like a little pull toy on a string, to the surgery.

The difficulty of moving the dog to the table

4   Once Smokey was in the surgery, however, the question that hung before our eyes like a veritable presence was how to get the dog from the floor to the table. Simply picking him up and plopping him down was out of the question. One glance at the quivering little figure emitting ominous and throaty warnings was enough to assure us of that. Realizing that the game was over, Jack grimly handed me the rope and reached for a muzzle. It was a doomed attempt from the start: the closer Jack dangled the tiny leather cup to the dog's nose, the more violent did Smokey's contortions and rage-filled cries become and the more frantic our efforts became to try to keep our feet and fingers clear of the angry jaws. Deciding that a firmer method had to be used, Jack instructed me to raise the rope up high enough so that Smokey would have to stand on his hind legs. This greatly reduced his maneuverability but served to increase his tenacity, for at this the little dog nearly went into paroxysms of frustration and rage. In his struggles, however, Smokey caught his forepaw on his swollen eye, and the blood that had been building

up pressure behind the fragile cornea burst out and dripped to the floor. In the midst of our surprise and the twinge of panic startling the three of us, Jack saw his chance and swiftly muzzled the animal and lifted him to the operating table.

5   Even at that point it wasn't easy to put the now terrified dog to sleep. He fought the local anesthesia and caused Jack to curse as he was forced to give Smokey more of the drug than should have been necessary for such a small beast. After what seemed an eternity, Smokey lay prone on the table, breathing deeply and emitting soft snores and gentle whines. We also breathed deeply in relief, and I relaxed to watch fascinated, while Jack performed a very delicate operation quite smoothly and without mishap.

The difficulty of putting the dog to sleep before the surgery

6   Such was my harrowing induction into the life of a veterinary surgeon. But Smokey did teach me a valuable lesson that has proven its importance to me many times since: wherever animals are concerned, even the smallest detail is important and should never be taken for granted.

Conclusion: The lesson she learned

PROFESSIONAL ESSAY*

Don't Mess With Auntie Jean

Jada F. Smith

Jada F. Smith is a news assistant in the Washington bureau of *The New York Times*. A graduate of Howard University, Smith previously worked for the *PBS NewsHour* and C-SPAN. She is a frequent contributor to the *Times*'s political blogs, "First Draft" and "The Caucus." Smith's news assignments focus on politics, Congress, and the White House. Her essay "Don't Mess with Auntie Jean" first appeared as an op-ed piece in the March 15, 2015 issue of the *Times*'s New York Edition.

Pre-Reading Thoughts: Remember a family story that has been passed down through the generations. How many different ways have you heard the story told? Who was the hero or villain of the story? How has that story shaped your understanding of your family?

---

* ◆ To help you read this essay analytically, review pages 183–186.

1   Everyone in my family has an Auntie Jean story.

2   There was the time my big brother and cousins thought they were calling her bluff about making them walk home from the rec center because they wouldn't stop clowning in the back seat. "Keep talkin'," she said, as she casually pulled into a gas station, reached back and opened the door, then flashed the peace sign as we sped off without them. I could see them in the rearview mirror, jaws almost touching the concrete.

3   Another cousin, Alaric, becomes animated when he recalls announcing his plans to have a girl over for the evening while his mom was out of town. "No you ain't!" Auntie Jean said, dashing his teenage dreams. "Not until you clean this house!" She stood over him for the next hour, puffing on a Newport and watching closely as he scrubbed each tile, fixture and faucet until the girl would be able to check her lipstick in the doorknob.

4   She is our fierce Auntie Jean who doesn't care what others think: the one who will send her bacon back three times if it isn't crispy enough, the one who once hopped out of the car at a red light to dance in the street to Maze's "Happy Feelings."

5   But the most famous story about her isn't cute or funny at all. One day, sometime in the 1960s, she, my mom, their siblings and cousins and a bunch of other kids went down to Airport Road in their hometown, LaGrange, Ga., as part of an organized effort to integrate the local roller rink. They were teenagers and preteens, led by my grandfather, Frank Cox, the Rev. Elijah Jackson and others—and they refused to move when the white owner demanded that they leave.

6   The man seemed so big to them, and he grew angry at their show of defiance. Some say he loomed over them like something that emerged from the backwoods of the county. Others say he was foaming at the mouth with rage.

7   Auntie Jean stood right in his face, staring him down, transfixed by the level of hatred she had seen in his eyes. Her knees were buckling and her hands were shaking, yet she stood and stared. As the story goes, he reached into a drawer and pulled out a revolver, letting off a series of shots into the ceiling above his head, sending everyone running for safety.

8   It took a long time for me to keep a dry eye whenever I heard that story. The civil rights movement wasn't just some historic event or fodder for my middle-school field trip. It was real and part of our immediate past, something that could have killed my mom, my auntie and their siblings. Something as benign and innocent as roller-skating had to be fought for.

9   I traveled home to Houston a couple of months ago when my relatives were gathered there for a holiday. While lounging around my mom's bedroom, I happened upon a scrapbook she made during her senior year of high school. She swore I'd seen it before, but I hadn't. I had never seen pictures of Willie, her high school boyfriend, who looked like one of the Jackson 5. There were also pictures of her with a homecoming sash across her chest, an obituary for the "Ain't No Mountain High Enough" singer Tammi Terrell and a five-year plan written in pink ink.

10   And there was a newspaper clipping with the headline, "Skating Rink Closed; Negroes Turned Away."

11   My heart stopped.

12   I had definitely never seen this before. A piece of my family history was right there for me to touch. That story, one that I'd heard countless times, had helped shape me: I was the daughter and niece of civil-rights heroes who fought for something as

seemingly mundane as the right to roller-skate. Now it was canonized in some obscure newspaper article that my mother had thought to save all those years ago at the age of 18.

13   Excited for a further glimpse into my history, I began to read.

14   "The skating rink on the Airport Road was closed Tuesday night after the owner refused to allow a group of Negroes to skate," it began. "Deputy Mac Smith said between 50 and 60 young Negroes were at the rink when he arrived to answer a call from the owner, O. L. (Tot) Underwood."

15   In bland newspaperese, the article explained that the officer gave Mr. Underwood two options—allow them to skate, or close down for the day. The owner, the article stated, chose the latter: "They were denied admittance and left."

16   It said there was no further disturbance and described everyone as orderly. And that was it. No mention of gunshots. No mention of terrified teenagers. No mention of Auntie Jean in a standoff with the roller rink owner.

17   I was shocked.

18   "Y'all?" I shouted. "This ain't right!"

19   I read it out loud to my mom, my Auntie Caroline, Great-Aunt Betty Ruth and Auntie Jean, who were all sitting around my mother's room with me.

20   "That's a lie," Auntie Caroline said, barely roused. "They sanitized it."

21   Auntie Jean was quiet. She just kept shaking her head.

22   I was shattered.

23   I wanted to believe the article. I write articles just like that for a living. Journalists deal in truth, right? Had my entire family conjured a tall tale and kept it alive my whole life? Was this moment of bravery a gross exaggeration? Somebody had lied.

24   Then I noticed, in that same pink ink my mom had used to write down her teenage thoughts and aspirations, the words "He shot at us!" above the headline.

25   Of course, I thought. History is written by the victors.

26   We don't just share memories because they're funny and make us feel nostalgic. We tell those Auntie Jean stories and Uncle Bus stories and Granddaddy Frank stories because if we don't, someone else surely will. By filling my childhood with those anecdotes, my mom and her siblings had entrusted me with our family record.

27   And that record is foundational, letting me know that I came from people who owned businesses and organized protests, folks who were passionate about their beliefs and courageous enough to not back down even in the face of life-threatening adversity. That family history—told through sometimes hilarious anecdotes, sometimes muddled memories—gave me a sense of pride. If they could accomplish such things, then I could, too.

28   I sat on the bed, staring at the scrapbook in my lap as my mom and aunts went downstairs for poundcake and coffee, talking about something else entirely. They were far more nonchalant about what I had just read than I was. I guess they were used to this kind of thing.

"Don't Mess with Auntie Jean" by Jada F. Smith, March 14, 2015 in The New York Times

He shot at us!

ꙅкating Rink Is Closed; Negroes Turned Away

The skating rink on the Airport Road was closed Tuesday night after the owner refused to allow a group of Negroes to skate.

said Underwood decided to close down.

Rev. Jackson then told Negroes this and instructed them to leave. They filed

A photo of a newspaper clipping from the 1960s that was saved and annotated by the author's mother.

29   Not me. I stayed behind and took a picture of the article, with my mom's notation written above, and uploaded it to Instagram.

30   The story would live on. And it would be the Auntie Jean version.

QUESTIONS ON CONTENT, STRUCTURE, AND STYLE

1. What is the main purpose of Smith's narrative? In what ways does this story shape her understanding of herself and her family?

2. How does Smith create a mental picture of the scene in the roller rink? Which sensory details are particularly effective in helping the reader feel present at the "standoff" between O.L. Underwood and Auntie Jean?

3. Why does Smith begin the essay with a series of humorous anecdotes about her Auntie Jean before beginning the core story of her narrative? What effect does this introduction have on the narrative's impact?

4. The author includes dialogue between her and her relatives. What does this use of dialogue add to the story? What does the dialogue reveal to the reader?

5. How does Smith react when she discovers the old newspaper article in the scrapbook? What realizations prompt her dramatic response?

6. What impact does the inclusion of the picture create? How does the contrast between the printed article and the handwritten comment influence the reader's understanding of the narrative?

7. Smith writes, "History is written by the victors." What does she mean by this? How can this old adage be applied to the story of her Auntie Jean's confrontation in the roller rink?

8. Throughout the story, Smith uses occasional simple sentence constructions for dramatic effect: "My heart stopped," "I was shocked," and "I was shattered." How do these simple, declarative sentences impact the reader? How do they impact the flow of the narrative?

9. How would you describe the author's style in this narrative? What factors lead you to that characterization? How does the author's conversational style impact the reader's understanding and appreciation of the narrative?

10. Overall, how effective is Smith's story about her Auntie Jean and her subsequent discovery of the newspaper article? How do her concluding lines ("The story would live on. And it would be the Auntie Jean version.") impact the reader's empathy towards the narrator?

VOCABULARY

integrate (5)	defiance (6)	transfixed (7)
fodder (8)	benign (8)	mundane (12)
canonized (12)	bland (15)	newspaperese (15)
sanitized (20)	conjured (23)	nostalgic (26)
nonchalant (28)		

SUGGESTIONS FOR WRITING

Try using Jada F. Smith's essay as a stepping-stone to your own writing. You might remember a particular family story that you have always found compelling. What lessons have you drawn from that story throughout your life? How has that story shaped your understanding of your family history and of who you are? You might, instead, remember a time in your life where your desire to stand up for what's right has led to an unsettling confrontation. This story, too, has likely shaped your life in important ways. How has this story contributed to who you are and how you understand yourself and the world about you? Imagine that you are writing to an audience who might profit from hearing your story, such as high school or college students or members of a particular social group or organization facing a similar situation. Consider using sensory details to help your readers understand the people, places, and actions in your narrative.

A Revision Worksheet

As you write your rough drafts, consult Chapter 5 for guidance through the revision process. In addition, here are a few questions to ask yourself as you revise your narrative:

1. Is the narrative essay's purpose clear to the reader?

2. Is the thesis plainly stated or at least clearly implied?

3. Does the narrative convincingly support or illustrate its intended point? If not, how might the story be changed?

4. Does the story maintain a logical point of view and an understandable order of action? Are there enough transitional devices used to give the story a smooth flow?

5. Are the characters, actions, and settings presented in enough vivid detail to make them clear and believable? Where could more detail be effectively added? Would use of dialogue be appropriate?

6. Is the story coherent and well paced, or does it wander or bog down in places because of irrelevant or repetitious details? What might be condensed or cut? Could any bland or wordy description be replaced?

7. Does the essay end in a satisfying way, or does the action stop too abruptly?

Collaborative Activity: After you've revised your essay extensively, you might exchange rough drafts with a classmate and answer these questions for each other, making specific suggestions for improvement wherever appropriate. (◆ For advice on productive participation in classroom workshops, see pages 121–123.)

Using Strategies and Sources

The following assignments ask you to not only incorporate what you've learned in this chapter regarding narration, but also to employ other strategies of development and to incorporate secondary sources into your response.

1. In a narrative essay, relate the story of the single most thrilling moment of your life thus far, defining "thrilling" in any fashion you choose. Be sure to use good description, particularly vivid sensory details, to make the narrative come to life for your readers.

2. Write an expository narrative essay in which you use a personal experience or others' stories to define "heroic." Remember that your definition of the word will be the thesis of your essay. You may want to interview someone who you think is heroic in some way or did something you believe to be heroic, and tell that person's story in your essay. (◆ See Chapter 19 for help with conducting interviews.) Be sure to use well-chosen examples and concrete details throughout.

3. Discover the origins of your hometown. When was it founded? Where did its name come from? Why was the location selected? Who was involved in getting it started? In a narrative essay, recount the early days of your hometown's beginnings. Use credible secondary sources to support your narrative with documented facts.

Chapter 18

Writing Essays Using Multiple Strategies

In Part Two of this text you have been studying essays developed primarily by a single mode or expository strategy. You may have, for example, written essays primarily developed by multiple examples, process analysis, or comparison/contrast. Concentrating on a single strategy in your essays has allowed you to practice, in a focused way, each of the patterns of development most often used in writing tasks. Although practicing each strategy in isolation this way is somewhat artificial, it is the easiest, simplest way to master the common organizational patterns. Consider the parallels to learning almost any skill: before you attempt a complex dive with spins and flips, you first practice each maneuver separately. Having understood and mastered the individual strategies of development, you should feel confident facing any writing situation, including those that would most profit from incorporating multiple strategies to accomplish their goal.

Most essays *do* call upon multiple strategies of development to achieve their purpose, a reality you have probably discovered for yourself as you studied various essays in this text. In fact, you may have found it difficult—or impossible—to avoid combining modes and strategies in your own essays. As noted in the introduction to Part Two, writers virtually always blend strategies, using examples in their comparisons, description in their definitions, causal analysis in their arguments, and so on. Therein is the heart of the matter: the single patterns of development you have been practicing are *thinking* strategies—ways of considering a subject and generating ideas—as well as organizing tools. Successful writers study their tasks and choose the strategies that will most effectively accomplish their purpose.

In addition, some writing tasks, often the longer ones, will clearly profit from combining multiple strategies in distinct ways to thoroughly address the essay's subject, purpose, and audience. Suppose, for example, you are given a problem-solving assignment in a business class: selling the City Council on a plan to build a student housing project in a particular neighborhood. You might call on your writing resources and use multiple strategies to

- Describe the project
- Explain the causes (the need for such a project)
- Argue its strengths; deflect opposing arguments

- Contrast it to other housing options
- Cite similar successful examples in other towns
- Explain its long-term beneficial effects on tenants, neighbors, businesses, etc.

Or perhaps you are investigating disciplinary action taken against a group of high school seniors for decorating their graduation caps and gowns. Your essay might combine strategies by first presenting examples of the controversy, explaining its causes and effects, and then contrasting the opinions of administrators, students, and parents. You might even conclude with a suggested process for avoiding future problems. In other words, many essay assignments—including the widely assigned summary-response paper*—might call for a multistrategy response.

As a writer who now knows how to use a variety of thinking and organizational methods, you can assess any writing situation and select the strategy—or strategies—that will work best for your topic, purpose, and audience.

Choosing the Best Strategies

To help you choose the best means of development for your essay, here is a brief review of the modes and strategies accompanied by some pertinent questions:

1. **Example**: Would real or hypothetical illustrations make my subject more easily understood?

2. **Process**: Would a step-by-step procedural analysis clarify my subject?

3. **Comparison/Contrast**: Would aligning or juxtaposing my subject to something else be helpful?

4. **Definition**: Would my subject profit from an extended explanation of its meaning?

5. **Division/Classification**: Would separating my subject into its component parts or grouping its parts into categories be useful?

6. **Causal Analysis**: Would explaining causes or effects add important information?

7. **Argument**: Would my position be advanced by offering logical reasons and/or addressing objections?

8. **Description**: Would vivid details, sensory images, or figurative language help readers visualize my subject?

9. **Narrative**: Would a story best illustrate some idea or aspect of my subject?

Use these nine questions as prompts to help you generate ideas and select those strategies that best accomplish your purpose.

---

* ◆ For an in-depth look at this popular assignment, see pages 485–490.

Problems to Avoid

Avoid overkill. Being prepared to use any of the writing strategies is akin to carrying many tools in your carpenter's bag. But just because you own many tools doesn't mean you must use all of them in one project; rather, you select only the ones you need for the specific job at hand. If you do decide to use multiple strategies in a particular essay, avoid a hodgepodge of information that runs in too many directions. Sometimes your essay's prescribed length means you cannot present all you know; again, let your main purpose guide you to selection of the best or most important ideas.

Organize logically. If you decide that multiple strategies will work best, you must find an appropriate order and coherent flow for your essay. In the hypothetical problem-solving essay on the housing project mentioned earlier, for instance, the writer must decide whether the long-term effects of the project should be discussed earlier or later in the paper. In the student essay that follows, the writer struggled with the question of discussing kinds of vegetarians before or after giving reasons for adopting vegetarianism. There are no easy answers to such questions—each writer must experiment with outlines and rough drafts to find the most successful arrangement, one that will offer the most effective response to the particular material, the essay's purpose, and the audience's needs. Be patient as you try various ways of combining strategies into a coherent rather than choppy paper.

Practicing What You've Learned

To help you recognize how writers often use multiple strategies in their writing, select one of the professional essays in Chapters 9–14 of this text. Identify at least two strategies at work, explaining their effectiveness and why you think the writer chose to make his or her point in this way.

Sample Student Essay

In the essay that follows, the student writer responds to an assignment that asked her to write about an important belief or distinguishing aspect of her life. The purpose, audience, and development of her essay were left to her; the length was designated as 750 to 1,000 words. As a confirmed vegetarian for well over a decade, she often found herself questioned about her beliefs. After deciding to clarify (and encourage) vegetarianism for an audience of interested but often puzzled fellow students, she developed her essay by drawing on many strategies, including causal analysis, example, classification, contrast, argument, and process analysis. Because she found her early draft too long, the writer edited out an extended narrative telling the story of her own "conversion" to vegetarianism, viewing that section as less central to her essay's main purpose than the other parts.

Pass the Broccoli—Please!

Introduction:
Famous
examples

1   What do Benjamin Franklin, Charles Darwin, Leonardo da Vinci, Percy Bysshe Shelley, Mohandas Gandhi, Albert Einstein, and I have in common? In addition to being great thinkers, of course, we are all vegetarians, people who have rejected the practice of eating animals. Vegetarianism is growing rapidly in America today, but some people continue to see it as a strange choice. If you are thinking of making this decision yourself or are merely curious, taking time to learn about vegetarianism is worthwhile.

Thesis,
purpose,
audience

Contrast to
other parts of
the world

2   In a land where hamburgers, pepperoni pizza, and fried chicken are among our favorite foods, just why do Americans become vegetarians anyway? Worldwide, vegetarianism is often part of religious faith, especially to Buddhists, Hindus, and others whose spiritual beliefs emphasize nonviolence, karma, and reincarnation. But in this country the reasons for becoming vegetarian are more diverse. Some people cite ecological reasons, arguing that vegetarianism is best for our planet because it takes less land and food to raise vegetables and grain than livestock. Others choose vegetarianism because of health reasons. Repeated studies by groups such as the American Heart Association and the American Medical Association show that diets lower in animal fats and higher in fiber decrease the risk of heart disease, cancer, diabetes, hypertension, and osteoporosis.

Causal
analysis:
3 reasons

3   Still other people's ethical beliefs bring them to vegetarianism. These people object to the ways that some animals, such as cows and chickens, are confined and are often fed various chemicals, such as growth hormones, antibiotics, and tranquilizers. They object to the procedures of slaughterhouses. They object to killing animals for consumption or for their decorative body parts (hides, fur, skins, tusks, feathers, etc.) and to their use in science or cosmetic experiments. These vegetarians believe that animals feel fear and pain

and that it is morally wrong for one species to inflict unnecessary suffering on another. I count myself among this group; consequently, my vegetarian choices extend to wearing no leather or fur, and I do not use household or cosmetic products tested on animals.

Personal example

4   Regardless of reasons for our choice, all vegetarians reject eating meat. However, there are actually several kinds of vegetarians, with the majority falling into three categories:

1. Ovo-lacto vegetarians eat milk, cheese, eggs, and honey;
2. Lacto vegetarians do not eat eggs but may keep other dairy products in their diet;
3. Vegans do not eat dairy products or any animal by-products whatsoever.

Classification: Three types

Many people, including myself, begin as ovo-lacto vegetarians but eventually become vegans, considered the most complete or pure type.

5   Perhaps the most common objection to any type of vegetarianism comes from a misconception about deficiencies in the diet, particularly protein. But it is a mistake to think only meat offers us protein. Vegetarians who eat dairy products, grains, vegetables, beans, and nuts receive more than enough nutrients, including protein. In fact, according to the cookbook *The Higher Taste*, cheese, peanuts, and lentils contain more protein per ounce than hamburger, pork, or a porterhouse steak. Many medical experts think that Americans actually eat too much protein, as seen in the revised food pyramid that now calls for an increase in vegetables, fruits, and grains over meat and dairy products. A vegetarian diet will not make someone a limp weakling. Kevin Eubanks, former *Tonight Show* band leader, is, for example, not only a busy musician but also a weightlifter. A former "Mr. Universe," Bill Pearl, is a long-time vegetarian; many other successful athletes include Prince Fielder, Martina Navratilova, Hank Aaron, Billie Jean King, and Edwin Moses. Some

Argument: Refutation, evidence, examples

current members of the Denver Broncos football team, according to their manager, no longer eat red meat at their training table.

6   For those who would like to give vegetarianism a try, here are a few suggestions for getting started:

Process: 4 steps to begin

1. Explore your motives. If you are only becoming a vegetarian to please a friend, for example, you won't stick with it. Be honest with yourself: the reasons behind your choice have a lot to do with your commitment.

2. Read more. The library can provide you with answers to your questions and concerns. There are hundreds of books full of ecological, medical, and ethical arguments for vegetarianism.

(More argument and examples)

3. Eat! Another popular misconception is that vegetarianism means a life of eating tasteless grass; nothing could be less true. Visit a vegetarian restaurant several times to see how many delicious dishes are available. Most grocery stores now carry a variety of vegetarian entrees. Or try one of the many vegetarian cookbooks on the market today. You may be surprised to discover that tofu enchiladas, soy burgers, and stuffed eggplant taste better than you could ever imagine.

4. Start slowly. You don't have to become a vegan overnight if it doesn't feel right. Some people begin by excluding just red meat from their diets. Feeling good as time goes by can direct your choices. Books, such as *The Beginning Vegetarian*, and magazines, such as *Vegetarian Times*, can offer encouragement.

Conclusion: Additional famous examples, witty quotation

7   It's never too late to change your lifestyle. Nobel Prize–winning author Isaac Bashevis Singer became a vegetarian at age fifty-eight. Making this choice now may allow you to live longer and feel better. In fifty years you may be like playwright George Bernard Shaw, who at twenty-five was warned against a vegetarian diet. As a vigorous old man, Shaw wanted to tell all those people they were wrong, but noted he couldn't: "They all passed away years ago"!

PROFESSIONAL ESSAY*

Why Parents Need to Let Their Children Fail

Jessica Lahey

Jessica Lahey is an educator, author, and Vermont Public Radio commentator. Her column, "The Parent-Teacher Conference," appears biweekly in the *New York Times*. Lahey's 2015 book, *The Gift of Failure: How the Best Parents Let Go So Their Children Can Succeed* argues against swooping to our children's rescue at the first sign of an obstacle on the road to independence. Lahey's 2013 article on the consequences that result when overprotective parents pull strings in the classroom first appeared in the *Atlantic*.

> **Pre-reading Thoughts:** Consider the parenting style you experienced as a child. What type of parental figures did you have? (Parental figures include anyone who acted as a parent in your life, whether that was biological parents, extended family, a guardian, or someone else in that capacity.) Were they supportive? Were they absent? What kind of expectations did they have of you? As you read Jessica Lahey's essay, pay close attention to the type of parenting behaviors she cautions against.

1   Thirteen years ago, when I was a relatively new teacher, stumbling around my classroom on wobbly legs, I had to call a student's mother to inform her that I would be initiating disciplinary proceedings against her daughter for plagiarism, and that furthermore, her daughter would receive a zero for the plagiarized paper.

2   "You can't do that. She didn't do anything wrong," the mother informed me, enraged.

3   "But she did. I was able to find entire paragraphs lifted off of web sites," I stammered.

4   "No, I mean *she* didn't do it. I did. *I* wrote her paper."

5   I don't remember what I said in response, but I'm fairly confident I had to take a moment to digest what I had just heard. And what would I do, anyway? Suspend the mother? Keep her in for lunch detention and make her write "I will not write my daughter's papers using articles plagiarized from the Internet" one hundred times on the board? In all fairness, the mother submitted a defense: her daughter had been stressed out, and she did not want her to get sick or overwhelmed.

6   In the end, my student received a zero and I made sure she re-wrote the paper. Herself. Sure, I didn't have the authority to discipline the student's mother, but I have done so many times in my dreams.

7   While I am not sure what the mother gained from the experience, the daughter gained an understanding of consequences, and I gained a war story. I don't even bother with the old reliables anymore: the mother who "helps" a bit too much with the child's math homework, the father who builds the student's science project. Please. Don't waste my time.

8   The stories teachers exchange these days reveal a whole new level of overprotectiveness: parents who raise their children in a state of helplessness and powerlessness, children destined to an anxious adulthood, lacking the emotional resources they will need to cope with inevitable setback and failure.

---

* ◆ For help reading this essay analytically, review pages 183–186.

9   I believed my accumulated compendium of teacher war stories were pretty good—until I read a study out of Queensland University of Technology, by Judith Locke, et. al., a self-described "examination by parenting professionals of the concept of overparenting."

10   Overparenting is characterized in the study as parents' "misguided attempt to improve their child's current and future personal and academic success." In an attempt to understand such behaviors, the authors surveyed psychologists, guidance counselors, and teachers. The authors asked these professionals if they had witnessed examples of overparenting, and left space for descriptions of said examples. While the relatively small sample size and questionable method of subjective self-reporting cast a shadow on the study's statistical significance, the examples cited in the report provide enough ammunition for a year of dinner parties.

11   Some of the examples are the usual fare: a child isn't allowed to go to camp or learn to drive, a parent cuts up a 10 year-old's food or brings separate plates to parties for a 16 year-old because he's a picky eater. Yawn. These barely rank a "Tsk, tsk" among my colleagues. And while I pity those kids, I'm not that worried. They will go out on their own someday and recover from their overprotective childhoods.

12   What worry me most are the examples of overparenting that have the potential to ruin a child's confidence and undermine an education in independence. According to the authors, parents guilty of this kind of overparenting "take their child's perception as truth, regardless of the facts," and are "quick to believe their child over the adult and deny the possibility that their child was at fault or would even do something of that nature."

13   This is what we teachers see most often: what the authors term "high responsiveness and low demandingness" parents." These parents are highly responsive to the perceived needs and issues of their children, and don't give their children the chance to solve their own problems. These parents "rush to school at the whim of a phone call from their child to deliver items such as forgotten lunches, forgotten assignments, forgotten uniforms" and "demand better grades on the final semester reports or threaten withdrawal from school." One study participant described the problem this way:

> I have worked with quite a number of parents who are so overprotective of their children that the children do not learn to take responsibility (and the natural consequences) of their actions. The children may develop a sense of entitlement and the parents then find it difficult to work with the school in a trusting, cooperative and solution focused manner, which would benefit both child and school.

14   *These* are the parents who worry me the most—parents who won't let their child learn. You see, teachers don't just teach reading, writing, and arithmetic. We teach responsibility, organization, manners, restraint, and foresight. These skills may not get assessed on standardized testing, but as children plot their journey into adulthood, they are, by far, the most important life skills I teach.

15   I'm not suggesting that parents place blind trust in their children's teachers; I would never do such a thing myself. But children make mistakes, and when they do, it's vital that parents remember that the educational benefits of consequences are a gift, not a dereliction of duty. Year after year, my "best" students—the ones who are happiest and

successful in their lives—are the students who were allowed to fail, held responsible for missteps, and challenged to be the best people they could be in the face of their mistakes.

16   I'm done fantasizing about ways to make that mom from 13 years ago see the light. That ship has sailed, and I did the best I could for her daughter. Every year, I reassure some parent, "This setback will be the best thing that ever happened to your child," and I've long since accepted that most parents won't believe me. That's fine. I'm patient. The lessons I teach in middle school don't typically pay off for years, and I don't expect thank-you cards.

17   I have learned to enjoy and find satisfaction in these day-to-day lessons, and in the time I get to spend with children in need of an education. But I fantasize about the day I will be trusted to teach my students how to roll with the punches, find their way through the gauntlet of adolescence, and stand firm in the face of the challenges—challenges that have the power to transform today's children into resourceful, competent, and confident adults.

QUESTIONS ON CONTENT, STRUCTURE, AND STYLE

1. Lahey begins her essay with a narrative anecdote from her early days as a teacher. How effective is this anecdote at capturing the reader's attention? Why do you think Lahey chose to begin her argument in this fashion?

2. What is the main purpose of Lahey's essay? What strategies does she employ to achieve that purpose?

3. What types of evidence does the author use in support of her purpose? Which of these types is more effective? Which is less effective?

4. What is the impact of the study that Lahey cites? Does the inclusion of such an outside source bolster her credibility? Does it make her argument more convincing?

5. In paragraph 10, Lahey employs the strategy of definition. How does this definition function within the larger context of the essay? What does it contribute? Should it appear earlier or later in the essay?

6. Lahey uses exemplification frequently in this essay. Identify some of the examples that she uses. Which of these are most effective? What makes them effective? Which are less effective? Why?

7. The author uses a number of quotations in her essay. How does she use these to support her assertions? Which works more effectively for the reader, the short quotations or the longer one? Why?

8. At the beginning of paragraph 16, Lahey again references the anecdote she shared in the introduction to her essay. How does this reference impact the unity of the essay? What does it contribute to the readability of her essay?

9. What does Lahey seem to be asserting in the conclusion of her essay? Is her conclusion effective? How could it be more effective?

10. How effective do you find Lahey's essay overall? Which of her various strategies work well? Which seem weaker? How could it be improved? What would you emulate in your own essay? What would you do differently?

VOCABULARY

plagiarism (1)   subjective (10)   responsiveness (13)

reliables (7)   demandingness (13)   dereliction (15)

compendium (9)   entitlement (13)   gauntlet (17)

SUGGESTIONS FOR WRITING

Try using Lahey's essay as an inspiration for your own work. As her essay makes a case for the negative consequences of overparenting, consider other actions, behaviors, systems, and influences that may have negative consequences for children in modern American society. Are video and online games a positive or negative influence? Is the emphasis on testing in the US education system a possible problem? What impact does the prevalent use of social media as a means of communication, self-presentation, and self-expression have on today's teens and young adults? Write a brief essay in which you develop an argument in support of a position on one of these issues. Remember to use a variety of strategies, just as Lahey does, as evidence to support your argument.

A Revision Worksheet

As you write your rough drafts, consult Chapter 5 for guidance through the revision process. In addition, here are a few questions to ask yourself before and during the early stages of your writing:

1. What is my main purpose in writing this particular essay? Who is my audience?

2. Does my assignment or the subject itself suggest a primary method of development or would combining several strategies be more effective?

3. Have I considered my subject from multiple directions, as suggested by the questions on page 382?

4. Have I selected the best strategies to meet the needs of my particular audience?

5. Would blending strategies help my readers understand my topic and my essay's purpose? Or am I trying to include too many approaches, move in too many directions, resulting in an essay that seems too scattered?

6. Have I considered an effective order for the strategies I've chosen? Do the parts of my essay flow together smoothly?

7. Have I avoided common weaknesses such as vague examples, fuzzy directions, circular definitions, overlapping categories, or logical fallacies, as discussed in the "Problems to Avoid" sections of Chapters 9-17?

Collaborative Activity: After you've revised your essay extensively, exchange rough drafts with a classmate and answer these questions for each other, making specific suggestions for improvement wherever appropriate. (◆ For advice on productive participation in classroom workshops, see pages 121–123.)

Part 3

Special Assignments

The third section of this text addresses several kinds of assignments frequently included in composition classes and in many other college courses. Chapter 19, "Conducting Research and Using Sources," explains ways to conduct formal research on a topic, to evaluate the sources you find, to create an annotated bibliography, and to quote, summarize, and paraphrase sources. Chapter 20, "Documenting Sources," shows you how to create accurate in-text and end-of-text citations for the sources you use, following the MLA and APA documentation style guidelines. Chapter 21, "Classroom Writing: Exams, Timed Essays, and Presentations," confronts the anxiety that writing under pressure may bring by helping you respond quickly but effectively to a variety of assignments, including the widely used summary-response (or reaction) essay. This chapter also contains a section on presentations, with hints suggesting the best ways to write, adapt, and deliver your ideas in a classroom setting. Chapter 22, "Writing about Literature," illustrates several uses of poetry and short stories in the composition classroom and provides some guidelines for both close reading and analytical thinking. Chapter 23, "Writing in the World of Work," presents advice for effective business letters, memos, e-mail messages, and résumés.

Two additional chapters can be found in the online MindTap® edition of this textbook—a "Writing about Visual Arts" chapter offers suggestions for essays analyzing paintings, photographs, and sculptures, and a "Writing about Film" chapter focuses on how to develop thoughtful analyses of movies. Both of these chapters come with accompanying activities in MindTap®.

If you have worked through Parts One and Two of this book, you have already practiced many of the skills demanded by these special assignments. Information in the next several chapters will build on what you already know about good writing.

Chapter 19

Conducting Research and Using Sources

Although the words "research paper" have been known to produce anxiety worse than that caused by the sound of a dentist's drill, you should try to relax. A research paper is similar to the kinds of expository and argumentative essays described in the earlier parts of this book, the difference being the use of documented source material to support, illustrate, or explain your ideas. Research papers still call for thesis statements, logical sequences of paragraphs, well-developed evidence, smooth conclusions—or in other words, all the skills you've been practicing throughout this book. By citing sources in your essays or reports, you show your readers that you have investigated your ideas and found support for them. By using your critical thinking skills to first analyze and then select the most thoughtful research from reliable sources, you demonstrate your own credibility—trustworthiness—as a writer, which in turn gives you the best chance of having others accept your ideas as valid. Last, using sources affords your readers the opportunity to look into your subject further if they so desire, consulting your references for additional information.

The process described in this chapter should help you write a paper using sources thoughtfully, effectively, and ethically. New flowcharts in this chapter highlight key steps in the research process for you. Figure 19.1 (page 394) focuses on what to do when starting work on a research assignment, Figure 19.2 (page 415) summarizes steps for working with sources once you have some in hand, and Figure 19.3 (page 422) highlights strategies for integrating sources into your paper.

Focusing Your Topic

In some cases, you will be assigned your topic, and you will be able to begin your research right away. In other cases, however, you may be encouraged to select your own subject, or you may be given a general subject ("health-care reform," "recycling," "US immigration policies") that you must narrow and then focus into a specific, manageable topic. If the topic is your choice, you need to do some preliminary thinking about what interests you; as in any assignment, you should make the essay a learning experience from which both you and your readers will profit. Therefore, you may want to brainstorm for a while on your general subject before you consult other sources, asking yourself questions about what you already know and don't know. Some of the most interesting papers are argumentative essays in which writers set out to find an answer to a controversy or to

393

Figure 19.1 GETTING STARTED ON YOUR RESEARCH PAPER

Focusing Your Topic

- Consider topics that you find personally interesting.
- Brainstorm before consulting sources.
- Determine your purpose: prove a point, expose, explain, summarize.

Beginning Your Library Research

- Familiarize yourself with library where you'll do your research.
- Ask the librarian for help in getting started.
- Consult research tools: general reference works, library catalogs, databases, the Internet, special collections.

Collecting Primary Research

- Determine whether or not it would be useful to gather your own information.
- Prepare and conduct a personal interview if you have access to an authority on your subject.
- Develop and deliver a questionnaire if you wish to gain wider opinions on your research subject.

Preparing a Working Bibliography

- Maintain a running list of sources you may want to use in your research essay.
- Decide whether you will maintain the list physically or electronically and be consistent.
- Be sure to record all of the required information when you first make the entry in order to avoid last-minute rechecking.

© Cengage Learning 2017

find support for a solution they suspected might work. Other papers, sometimes called "research reports," expose, explain, or summarize a situation or a problem for their audience.

Throughout this chapter, we will track the research and writing process of Gabriela Guerrera, a composition student whose writing assignment called for an investigation of recent developments in computer technology. As a psychology major, Gabriela developed an interest in pervasive computing, a new technology that uses embedded devices to monitor emotions and analyze results. From her psychology class, Gabriela was somewhat familiar with facial expression studies conducted by Paul Ekman, but she became intrigued by more recent uses of Ekman's Facial Action Coding System (FACS). As she began her investigation of pervasive computing, Gabriela was able to think about her topic in terms of some specific *research questions*: How widely is pervasive computing used? Is pervasive computing being used to invade our privacy? How can we be aware of these threats to our privacy? (◆ Gabriela's completed essay with MLA documentation appears on pages 457–465 and with APA documentation on pages 466–476.)

Practicing What You've Learned

1. List three subjects you want to know more about.

2. Which subject would be most interesting for you to do research and write about? Why?

3. Which subject would be most interesting for your audience to read about? Why?

4. Which subject would best lend itself to the assignment you have been given? How?

5. For which of these subjects do you think you would be able to locate the best source material?

6. What do you hope to find out by doing research and writing about this subject?

Beginning Your Library Research

Once you have a general topic (and perhaps have some research questions in mind), your next step is familiarizing yourself with the school or public library where you may do all or part of your research. Most college libraries today have both print and electronic resources to offer researchers, as well as access to the Internet. Your library home page will likely include a catalog of its holdings, a number of selected databases, gateways to other libraries, and other kinds of resources. This system may be accessed from other places on or off campus, which is handy for those times when you cannot be in the library.

Most libraries also have information that will indicate the location of important areas, and almost all have reference librarians who can explain the various kinds of programs and resources available to you. The smartest step you may take is asking a librarian for help before you begin searching. Library staff members may be able to save you enormous amounts of research time by pointing you in just the right direction. Do not be shy about asking the library staff for help at any point during your research!

Once you are familiar with your library, you may find it useful to consult one or more of the following research tools.

General Reference Works

If you need a general overview of your subject, or perhaps some background or historical information, you might begin your library research by consulting an encyclopedia, a collection of biographical entries, or a world fact book, depending on your subject. You might use a comprehensive or specialized dictionary if your search turns up terms that are unfamiliar to you. These and many other library reference guides (in print and online) may also help you find a specific focus for your essay if you feel your topic is still too large or undefined at this point.

Library Catalogs

The library catalog is used as the primary guide to a library's holdings. You can access a library's catalog through the library Web site. Some library catalogs now include database holdings in addition to the library's print and electronic holdings.

Most computer catalogs allow you to look for information by subject, author, and title as well as by keyword(s), by the ISBN (publisher's book number), by the call number, or by a series title (Time-Life books, for example). On-screen prompts will guide you through the process of searching. Because no two library catalog systems are exactly alike, never hesitate to ask a librarian for help if you need it.

Unless you are already familiar with authorities or their works on your topic, you might begin your search by typing in keywords or your general subject. For example, Gabriela began her search by typing in the subject words "affective computing," which produced a listing of four entries related to her topic. One book entitled *Affective Computing* looked particularly promising—especially because Gabriela recognized the author's name from the discussion in her psychology class—so she pulled up the following screen to see more information.

If you find a relevant book, as Gabriela did, look at the catalog record's *Subjects* line to see additional headings ["Human-computer interaction" and "User interfaces

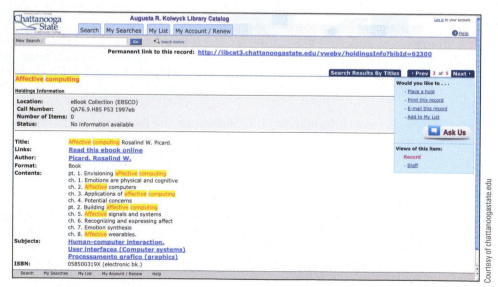

Results of a search for "affective computing" in eBook Collection. Accessed through Chattanooga State Community College's Augusta R. Kolwyck Library.

(Computer systems)"] that may lead you to other useful resources. Often these subject headings are linked to the online catalog, and, by clicking on one, you will be taken to resources related to the topic. For example, when Gabriela clicked on the "Human-computer interaction" subject heading, the library's online catalog provided a listing of more than seventy additional relevant items in the eBook collection. Such a collection, of course, would require extensive evaluation. But the benefits of capitalizing on the library's catalog's search feature are obvious (and sometimes overwhelming). And with a call number for a particular book in hand, a library map will help you find its location on the shelves.

Databases

Most libraries across the country subscribe to a wide variety of information services that lead researchers to appropriate databases for their subjects. After you access your library's Web site, you might find an alphabetically arranged listing of the available databases. A list of this nature is often quite lengthy and not very easily navigated, so many libraries also provide headings (such as those shown in the following list) to organize the options into categories that are more easily searched:

Databases by Subject   Databases by Type
Full-Text Resources   Multidisciplinary Resources

If, indeed, you encounter these options and pursue the "Databases by Subject" link, you might find several headings (e.g., Business, Health, Literature, Music, Science, Social Sciences). Many of these categories may include other subheadings; for example, under "Science" you might find Biology, Chemistry, Environmental Science, and Physics. As you might expect, the organization of Web sites varies from library to library, so when you first visit your library's Web site, devote some time to becoming acquainted with the layout. And, of course, be willing to ask a librarian for assistance.

At your library's Web site, you're likely to find one or more of the popular general databases, including *MasterFILE Premier*, *Academic OneFile*, *General OneFile*, and *InfoTrac Newstand*. Any of these may serve as an excellent starting point for your research. Many college and university libraries subscribe to these databases because they provide access to millions of articles related to an exhaustive range of topics and derived from thousands of publications.

If your library's Web site also provides a listing of specialized categories, look for those that seem most appropriate to your topic. Because many college students write research papers about authors and their literary works, you might find that your library includes "Literature" among its specialized categories. Other categories might include "Science and Technology," "Career Search," "Health," or "Education."

Subscription databases are updated frequently—most on a daily basis—and almost certainly provide you with the most current sources for your research. Do note, however, that because libraries contract and pay a fee for database services, they must restrict most database access to on-campus use or use by particular patrons (for example, enrolled students, faculty, and staff). Know, too, that each database may have its own search method. Always ask a librarian to help if you are struggling with a database search. You may also consult the Help section available in most databases.

As you search your electronic sources, remember that you may have to try a variety of keywords (and their synonyms) to find what you need. Sometimes your keyword search may turn up too few leads—and sometimes you may be overwhelmed with too many matches! To save time and effort, you may be able to broaden or narrow your search by typing in words called *Boolean operators,** as illustrated here:

AND   (pervasive computing AND Affectiva)—narrows your search to those references containing both computing and Affectiva

OR   (pervasive computing OR Affectiva)—broadens search to find items containing either term

NOT   (pervasive computing NOT games)—excludes items irrelevant to your search

Most databases respond to Boolean operators. However, it's always best to consult the searching advice offered by your particular information system.

Unless you are already familiar with authorities or their works on your topic, you might begin your search by typing in keywords or your general subject. Because Gabriela was somewhat familiar with pervasive computing, she knew that Affectiva, Inc. was a leader in the field. With this insight then, Gabriela used the *MasterFILE Premier* database and began her search by typing in the subject words "Affectiva," which produced a listing of nine entries related to the topic. One article entitled "We Know How You Feel" looked particularly promising, so she pulled up the following screen to see more information.

Results of a search for "Affectiva" in *MasterFILE Premier*. Search yielded nine results. Gabriela Guerrera selected "We Know How You Feel," whose information is captured in this screenshot. Accessed through Chattanooga State Community College's Augusta R. Kolwyck Library.

*Named for the nineteenth-century British mathematician and logician George Boole.

As you use the database, capitalize on one of its features that many students often overlook. As she read through the entry for the "We Know How You Feel" article, she noticed a "Subjects" heading that recommended six additional headings and directed her to other useful resources.

Fortunately, the *MasterFILE Premier* database entry for the "We Know How You Feel" article included a full-text version of the article (consisting of almost 8,000 words), but Gabriela found that it appeared on a single "page," making it difficult to include useful specific citations. She suspected that the article might also be available on the *New Yorker*'s Web site, and a quick visit confirmed her suspicion. At the Web site, she found a version of the article in a far more "readable" font size, but pagination was not indicated. Gabriela realized that the *New Yorker* is available in a print version, too, but her school's library no longer subscribes to this (and many other) journals, so the "hard copy" was not readily available. To overcome this problem, Gabriela knew that she could use her library's interlibrary service to secure a copy of the article's print version. And with that in hand a week later, she was able to develop far more specific citations when she incorporated the article in her essay.

Once you have found useful information, remember that libraries have printers available to print out the on-screen data you wish to keep; you may have to pay a small fee for this printing, so it's a good idea to take some cash along, preferably in correct change. (Library users with personal computers or other kinds of technology can avoid this expense by e-mailing data to themselves.) And once again, the very best advice bears repeating: never hesitate to ask your library staff for help.

Special Collections

Your library may contain special collections that will help you research your subject. Some libraries, for example, have extensive collections of government documents or educational materials or newspapers from foreign cities. Other libraries may have invested in manuscripts from famous authors or in a series of works on a particular subject, such as your state's history. Remember, too, that some libraries contain collections of early films, rare recordings, or unique photographs. Consult your librarian or the information sources describing your library's special holdings.

Beginning Your Online Research

You may have access to the Internet through your library, through your school network, or through a personal account with a service provider of your choice. The Internet can offer great research opportunities, but in many cases, it may only supplement—not replace—the information you will need to collect through library sources.

The most effective approach to discovering useful material on the Internet may be through the use of search engines that produce a list of potential electronic documents or Web sites in response to your search. After you type in your keyword(s), the search engine explores its database for word or phrase matches; it then presents you with a list of potential sources, which include the Internet addresses (called URLs—"uniform resource locators"). You may access the sources that seem most promising (often those that appear first on the list), and you may also connect to other material by clicking on any highlighted words (hypertext links) appearing within the text of a particular document.

At this time, the most popular search engine is *Google*, but there are many more worldwide, including *Bing, Yahoo!,* and *Ask*; you might prefer meta-search engines (such as *Mamma* or *Dogpile*), which simultaneously search the Internet's top search engines. Because each search engine pulls its results from a different (but often overlapping) pool of Web pages, and because each one offers distinct "extra features," it pays to try more than one. (If you aren't satisfied with your results, try another set of keywords before moving on.)

Most search engines have their own searching tips; to improve your chances for success, it's well worth the time to read the advice on conducting advanced searches. For example, *Google's* Advanced Search allows you to fill in such fields as "with all of the words," "with the exact phrase," "with at least one of the words," and "without the words." Other options narrow the search by designating certain reading levels, languages, specific dates, or particular kinds of materials. (*Google Scholar*, for example, will search among academic books, journals, theses, and abstracts.)

Most search engines allow use of Boolean operators (see page 398) to narrow or broaden your search. Some allow the use of plus and minus signs to show connected terms or unwanted matches:

affective computing + Rosalind Picard   (find sources containing both affective computing and Rosalind Picard)

affective computing – Rosalind Picard   (find sources containing affective but exclude those that include Rosalind Picard)

Some programs request quotation marks around a key term of multiple words ("Anne Frank"); some are case sensitive (capitalize proper nouns or not?); some use truncation to find various forms of a word ("myth*" will return "mythology" and "mythical"). Other search engines, such as *Ask*, allow users to ask questions in natural language ("Who was Samuel Mudd?"). As technology continues to improve, searching will no doubt become easier, so always take a moment to look at each search engine's current directions.

Here is one more hint for searching the Web: sometimes you can guess the URL you need. Simply fill in the name of a specific company, college, agency, or organization. Do not put spaces between words (usnews.com).

- **Businesses:** <www.nameofcompany.com>
- **Colleges:** <www.nameofcollege.edu>
- **Government agencies:** <www.nameofagency.gov>
- **Organizations:** <www.nameoforganization.org>

You may also consult specialized directories to discover the addresses you need.

Once you find a useful document, you may print it, add the reference to your "bookmarks" or "favorites" list, or copy it to a USB drive or to a home file if you are using your own computer. Whether at the library or at home, always keep a list of your important sites, their addresses, and the date you accessed them. You may need this information for an easy return to a particular document and also for your working bibliography.

To explore other ways to use the Internet for research, check your library's home page, which most likely will offer links to helpful search advice.

Words of Caution for Internet Users: Be Afraid, Be Very Afraid . . .

The Internet offers researchers a wealth of information incredibly fast. However, the Internet poses problems, too. It may offer a great deal of information on your essay topic—but it may not always offer the *best* information, which might be found in a classic text on your library shelf. Background information or historical perspective may not be available; Web site information may be out of date. Moreover, simply finding the specific information you need can be frustrating and time-consuming, especially if your keywords and links don't lead in useful directions. The information superhighway is congested with scores of irrelevant distractions, so beware the wild Web chase.

There is, however, another much more serious problem: *not all material available on the Internet is accurate or reliable.* When an article is printed in a respected journal, for example, readers have assurances that editors have reviewed the information, writers have checked their facts, and authorities have been quoted correctly. However, Web sites may be created by anyone on any subject, from gene splicing to Elvis sightings, without any sort of editorial review. Opinions—wise or crackpot—may be presented as facts; rumors may be presented as reality.*

Because there is no "quality control" of Web sites, writers of research papers must evaluate their sources extremely carefully to avoid gathering unreliable information. For example, as Gabriela Guerrera searched for information about affective computing, she consulted a number of Internet sites that were blogs written by a variety of interested parties. While these blogs frequently contained references to personal interests and experiences, they often contained inaccurate details or rumored stories intermingled with personal interpretations, none of which was helpful to a serious investigation of Gabriela's topic. Gabriela also checked several entries on *Wikipedia*, the popular general Web encyclopedia whose articles may be written or edited by anyone in the world, using a real identity or pseudonym. Although *Wikipedia* strives for information that may be verified and allows readers to demand better documentation (for example, a tag such as "citation needed" may appear after certain claims), Gabriela did in fact find information that contradicted details she was able to confirm in several other published sources. To be trusted as a reliable source of information by her own readers, Gabriela realized that she must always choose the most reliable, accurate sources herself; for that reason, she decided not to use *Wikipedia* as a resource for her essay.**

---

*People sometimes circulate questionable information, stories, or pictures on the Internet as "proof" of their own political, social, or economic views. If you wish to check the validity of a particular message you have received, consider checking Snopes.com, a reference site devoted to killing rumors and exposing hoaxes, as well as identifying urban legends, folklore, and myths. Type in the name or some descriptive words associated with the story or picture you wish to check to see if it has already been identified as fake.

**On her own Web site (anniedillard.com), Pulitzer Prize-winning author Annie Dillard offers this advice: "Please don't use *Wikipedia*. It is unreliable; anyone can post anything, no matter how wrong. . . . The teacher in me says, 'The way to learn about a writer is to read the text. Or texts.'"

Apply your critical thinking skills to your selection of Internet sources by always asking the following questions about each Web site you consider:

- What is the purpose of this Web site? (To inform, persuade, market a product or service, share an interest, entertain?) To whom is this site primarily directed, and why?

- Who is the sponsor, author, or creator of the site? (A business, an educational institution, a nonprofit organization, a government agency, a news bureau, an individual?) Is the sponsor or author known and respected in the particular content area?

- Does the sponsor or author reveal a clear bias or strong opinion? Does such a slant undercut the usefulness of the information?

- When was this site produced? When was it last updated or revised? If links exist, are they still viable? Up to date?

- Is the information accurate? How might the material be cross-checked and verified?

If you have doubts about the accuracy of any material you discover on the Internet, find another authoritative source to validate the information or omit it from your essay. (◆ Following the guidelines on pages 414–417 will help you evaluate *all* your potential research sources; pages 107–109 may also be helpful.)

Practicing What You've Learned

The following assignment is designed to help you determine the general nature and the broad spectrum of results you'll likely gather by using a general search engine. To complete this assignment, use the Web browser and search engine that you prefer.

Type in: **Sistine Chapel**

1. What is the total number of Web results identified by this search?

2. Along with the Web results, are related topics recommended for additional searching? List three related topics that seem most interesting.

3. Take a look through the top fifty items listed in your search results. How many of these Web documents are commercial in some way? For example, they might be advertisements for a tour guide, an airline, or some other product. List three specific examples of commercial sources from your search results.

4. Look again through the top fifty items listed in your search results, this time with a different purpose. How many of these Web documents are from the kind of authoritative or reputable sources that you might want to use in a college research paper? For example, they might be from well-known publications (e.g., Smithsonian) or news organizations (e.g., the BBC) or other respected entities. List three specific examples of reputable sources from your search results.

Conducting Primary Research

To illustrate and support their points, most writers of research papers draw heavily on material found in articles, books, and other library sources. However, researchers sometimes find it useful to gather their own information. Collecting data firsthand is called *primary research* or *original research*, and it is valuable because it provides information not available from other sources.

Students often conduct primary research in a variety of college classes. For example, a chemistry major may gain new knowledge from a lab experiment; an English major may discover original insights reading a work of literature; a political science major may produce thoughtful analysis after studying local election results. In each case, the investigator collects information that was not already in existence.

Although there are many ways to conduct primary research, this section will present suggestions for conducting two strategies composition students may find most helpful: the *interview* and the *questionnaire*.

The Personal Interview

Depending on your choice of topic, you may find all the information you need for your essay by exploring sources through library and online research. However, sometimes you may discover that an authority on your subject lives in your town or works on your campus. In this case, you may wish to conduct a *personal interview* to gather valuable information for your essay.

Preparation is the key word governing a good interview. Here are some suggestions to help you collect useful data in the most effective way possible.

Before You Interview:

1. **Know your purpose.** If you have only a vague notion of why you are talking to the interviewee, you will waste everyone's time as the conversation roams like a lost hiker wandering from one clearing to the next. A close look at your essay's outline or your early drafts should tell you why and how this person might contribute to your research. Be certain that the person you have selected for an interview is, in fact, the best source for the kind of information you are seeking. For example, if you are writing a paper on the campus program that assists students with learning disabilities, you might interview the program's director to obtain expert opinion; on the other hand, if you wish to know some specific ways in which the program has helped its participants, you might interview a student actively involved in the program for his or her personal response.

2. **Make an appointment.** Calling for an interview may make you a bit nervous, but remember that most people like to be asked for their opinions and are usually willing to help students with their research, if their schedules permit. Be sure the interviewee understands who you are, why you are asking for an interview, and approximately how much time you are requesting. Whenever possible, allow the interviewee to select the hour and place most convenient for him or her. Do adjust your schedule to give yourself time after the meeting in case the interview runs long and to allow yourself a few minutes to review and fill in your notes.

3. **Educate yourself.** Before the interview, read about your topic and your interviewee. You want to appear knowledgeable about your subject; you can also save time by skipping questions that have already been answered elsewhere. Busy experts appreciate not having to explain basic information that you could have—and should have—already looked up.

4. **Plan some questions.** Unless you have an excellent memory, it is best to prepare some specific questions to which you can refer during the interview. Some interviewers write each question at the top of an index card, and then use the rest of the card for their notes on the answer. Others use a notebook in which they write a question (or key words) at the top of each page. Try to create questions that are specific, clear, and logically ordered. Avoid "yes/no" questions that don't lead to discussion. If you have a complicated or convoluted issue you want to discuss, try breaking it into a series of simpler questions that can be tackled by the interviewee one at a time.

During the Interview:

5. **Make a good first impression.** Always arrive on time, prepared with pens, paper, or any technology you may need. Some interviewers like to record comments, but you first must secure your interviewee's permission to do so. (Being recorded makes some people uncomfortably self-conscious and hesitant to speak freely, so consider whether the accuracy recording may provide is more important than the spontaneity it may kill.) Always begin by thanking your interviewee for his or her time and briefly say again why you think he or she can provide helpful information to you.

6. **Ask, listen, ask.** Begin asking your prepared questions, but don't rush through them. Listen attentively to your interviewee's answers, and, although it takes practice, try to maintain as much eye contact as possible as you take notes on the answers. Allow the interviewee to do almost all the talking; after all, you are there to collect information, not participate in a debate. Do politely ask for clarification (unfamiliar terms, spelling of names, unclear references, and so on) when you need it.

7. **Be flexible.** Sometimes your interviewee will talk about something fascinating that never occurred to you when you prepared your original list of questions. Be ready to adapt your plan and ask new questions that follow up on unexpected commentary.

8. **"Silence is golden," but . . .** If an interviewee is quiet or hesitates to give the kind of detailed responses you are seeking, you may need to use phrases of this kind to draw out longer or more specific answers:
   - Can you elaborate on that?
   - Tell me more about X.
   - Why did you think that?
   - How did you react to that?

- When did you realize . . . ?
- Why do you believe that?
- What's your reading of that situation?
- Would you explain that for me?

As you ask for more details, try to use a friendly, conversational tone that will put your interviewee at ease.

On the other hand, sometimes interviewees talk too much! They become stuck on one aspect of a topic, going into unnecessary depth, or perhaps they begin to drift off the subject completely. Be courteous but firm in your resolve to redirect the flow of conversation. To get back to your topic, you may need to re-ask the original question, using slightly different words.

9. **Conclude thoughtfully.** At the end of the interview, ask for any additional comments the interviewee would like to offer and for any information (or other sources) he or she thinks you might find useful. Ask the interviewee if you may contact him or her again if you should have another brief question; if such permission is granted, ask for the best means of contact (a telephone number or e-mail address). Give the interviewee your most sincere thanks for his or her time and assistance.

After the Interview:

10. **Review your notes immediately.** Fill in gaps in your notes while your memory is fresh, and write out acronyms or abbreviations whose meanings you might forget in a few days. Make some notes to yourself about using the information in your essay.

Later, if the interview figures prominently in your essay, consider sending your interviewee a copy of your work. Within days of the interview, however, it is ALWAYS polite to send your interviewee a short thank-you note, acknowledging his or her help with your research project.

The Questionnaire

A questionnaire is a series of questions or statements designed to obtain people's opinions about certain ideas, products, issues, activities, or even other people. You have, no doubt, responded to a number of questionnaires yourself: in your school, you may have filled out course evaluation forms; in a store, you may have answered questions about a new product or service; at home, you may have replied to political pollsters or participated in a marketing survey.

Designing effective questionnaires is a complex business. There are, in fact, entire college courses devoted to the analysis and development of polls and surveys, courses often required for marketing majors and political science students. As daunting as composing a questionnaire may sound, student writers often find it useful to conduct small-scale surveys to gain wider opinions on a topic under research. For example, let's assume you've been assigned a paper calling for a specific recommendation to improve a campus service or agency. You have chosen the composition computer lab and, although you have a few ideas of your own, you think it would be valuable to know what other users of the lab would most like to see changed. You design a questionnaire asking lab users to identify their chief areas of concern, and, using that information, you write a persuasive essay calling for a specific change.

Here are some suggestions for designing, administering, and analyzing questionnaires, whose results might prove useful in your research.

Developing the Questionnaire

1. Know your purpose and identify your target audience. Writers of effective questionnaires have a specific goal in mind; articulating that goal clearly in writing will help you create the best survey questions. Ask yourself: what do I most want to know from this particular group of people? Which group of people will give me the information I want? Hint: asking a particular population (computer lab users) to focus on a single issue (computer lab hours) will often produce the most precise responses.

2. Encourage participation. At the top of your questionnaire, briefly state your purpose and your request for response, giving pertinent (but not personal) information. People are more likely to participate if they know who is conducting the survey ("student in English 121"), what you want ("collecting composition students' opinions on . . ."), and how the results will be used ("data for essay whose purpose is . . ."). Some respondents will be naturally sympathetic to a hardworking student; others may need an answer to "what's in this for me?" If it's appropriate, you can appeal to your respondents' sense of the Common Good. In the case of the computer lab survey, for example, respondents might be encouraged to answer the questions if they thought the essay's recommendations would actually go to the lab supervisor, thus creating the possibility of improved service for all.

3. Choose the most effective type of questionnaire for your purpose. There are several kinds of questions or statements you may use to generate information; in a short survey, choose only one or two types to avoid confusing your participants. Common methods include the following:

- *Yes/No* **Answers**
  Example: Do you use the computer lab at least once a week?

  ( ) Yes
  ( ) No

- **Multiple Choice**
  Example: Check one answer. How often do you use the computer lab?

  ( ) Once a week?
  ( ) Twice a week?
  ( ) More than twice a week?

- **Checklist**
  Example: Check all the statements with which you agree.
  ___ The current lab hours of operation are convenient for me.
  ___ The lab should be open on the weekends.
  ___ The lab needs extended evening hours.

- **Rank Order**
  Example: In the following list, identify the issues most important to you by marking the most important as "1" and the least important as "5."
  ___ Hours of operation
  ___ Updated equipment
  ___ Technical assistance available

- **Rating System**
  Example: Rate the following statements as SA (Strongly Agree), A (Agree), D (Disagree), SD (Strongly Disagree), or N (No Opinion).
  ___ The lab should be open on the weekends.
  ___ The lab should be open later at night.
  ___ The lab should have extended hours during final exams.

- **Open-Ended Questions**
  Example: If you could change the lab's hours of operation, what would an ideal schedule look like for you? Why would these hours be better than the current schedule?

Designers of questionnaires should note that although open questions may produce the most interesting answers to read, they are also the most difficult to tally objectively. Multiple-choice questionnaires may be the easiest to score, and their numbers may quickly be converted to percentages.

Once you have decided which method will best retrieve the kind of information you are seeking, clearly state the directions for following that method at the top of your questionnaire, after your statement of purpose. Consider using bold type to emphasize any important words in the instructions.

4. **Watch your language.** It's unfortunately easy to confuse your respondents or "contaminate" your survey with careless use of words or phrases. Avoid problems by remembering the following advice:

- Clarify vague references and avoid abbreviations your participants may not know.

  Unclear   Are you in favor of or opposed to the proposed SB128?

  Better   Are you in favor of or opposed to Colorado Senate Bill 128, which would raise the technology fees at this college by two percent?

- Rewrite any "loaded" questions or leading statements that attempt to shape the respondent's answer.

  Biased   Should the university continue to waste your money on new, overpriced lab equipment?

  Objective   Should the university purchase new lab equipment?

- Ask for one piece of information at a time.

Double question	Are the technical assistants at the lab helpful and friendly? Yes/No
	[Respondents might find the assistants friendly but not particularly helpful, or vice versa, so a single "yes" or a "no" answer would be misleading.]
Better questions	Do you find the technical assistants at the lab helpful? Yes/No
	Do you find the technical assistants in the lab friendly? Yes/No

5. Keep it short, simple, and smooth. People often cooperate with pollsters, but they don't want to be imposed on for too long. After you've drafted a number of potential questions for your survey, cut your list down to the most important ones. Unless you have an overwhelming reason to ignore this advice, limit your questionnaire to a single page. (Some pollsters also advise placing your most important questions first, in case respondents tire of answering and turn in incomplete forms.) Ask your questions in the clearest, most direct way possible to get the most straightforward answers.* Just as you know how to write coherent, smoothly linked paragraphs in your essays, group questions logically to move your respondents' thoughts easily from issue to issue.

Administering the Questionnaire

6. Secure a valid sampling. To get meaningful responses, you must survey the right people, ones with the knowledge or opinions that matter to your research. But at this point you must also ask yourself two other vitally important questions: are the people taking my survey truly representative of my target group as a whole? Does my sample—the number of people contacted—comprise a large enough part of the target group to merit the conclusions I might draw from their comments?

For valid results, first make sure that you are taking a *random sample*; that is, you must ensure that each member of the population has a fair and equal chance of being selected. In a survey on the computer center hours, for example, you would not get an accurate cross-section of opinions if you sampled only the work-study students staffing the lab or your best friends who feel as you do. Similarly, if you sample only a tiny fraction of the students who use the lab, your results will not provide strong support for any broad claims about student opinion. As you prepare to distribute your questionnaire, be sure you will address a significant number of randomly selected people who compose a cross-section of your target group.

---

*Some national pollsters believe that to obtain the most truthful responses, questionnaires should be answered anonymously; others suggest making signatures optional.

7. **Perform a test run.** If time permits, ask several people in your target group to take the survey before you distribute it widely. If the questionnaire has problems or confusing spots, they will surface in time for you to fix them.

8. **Be prepared.** Plan ahead to discover how best to distribute your questionnaires. If you are handing out print copies on school or private property or making online surveys available on school computers, be sure you have permission to do so. If you are placing print questionnaires in a public place for respondents to pick up at their leisure, you'll need a secure drop-box for completed surveys that you can empty frequently. If your respondents are answering by hand, don't forget to provide an extra-large number of pencils or pens as they do "walk off" with great regularity. (For some types of inquiry, you might wish to check with one of several online survey services now available. Some professional services offer free design tools to help you create your own questionnaire, but others charge a fee for their templates, so do consult any Web-based business carefully.)

Totaling and Reporting Results

9. **Analyze your responses.** Depending on your method of surveying, you may simply add up the totals for each answer (in multiple-choice or checklist questionnaires, for example), or you may need to spend some time pondering the nuances of written comments. All returned, completed questionnaires must be included in your analysis. If you wish to convert questionnaire numbers into percentages, divide the number of responses to a particular answer by the total number of questionnaires returned and then multiply that figure by 100 (Example: five responses to one multiple-choice answer out of 25 questionnaires would be 0.20; multiplying 0.20 X 100 = 20%). As you study your results, look for emerging patterns and repeated ideas. What conclusions can you draw based on these responses?

10. **Accurately report your findings.** If you base your essay's assertions, arguments, conclusions, or recommendations on your questionnaire's results, your readers will certainly need a clear understanding of how those results were obtained. To be persuaded that your research is valid, they may wish to know how the questionnaire was designed and why, how many were distributed and completed, how the respondents were chosen, and other such information. Such explanations may appear within the body of your essay or in appropriately marked sections (such as "Purpose and Design," "Results," "Recommendations") or in an appendix; whichever method you choose, always attach a blank sample copy of the questionnaire to your essay.

Conducting research through the distribution of a questionnaire is a challenging but fascinating way to collect information about current unexplored topics. If you have collected data that would be valuable to people on your campus, at your workplace, or in your community, by all means communicate it to them. Your primary research, and your conclusions, could help someone make an important decision.

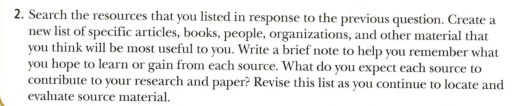

Practicing What You've Learned

1. List the reference books, bibliographies, periodicals, indexes, databases, and other resources that are related to the subject of your research project and are available to you. Add to this list as you make discoveries in the course of your research and writing. Be sure to record all the information you will need for documenting your sources.

2. Search the resources that you listed in response to the previous question. Create a new list of specific articles, books, people, organizations, and other material that you think will be most useful to you. Write a brief note to help you remember what you hope to learn or gain from each source. What do you expect each source to contribute to your research and paper? Revise this list as you continue to locate and evaluate source material.

Preparing a Working Bibliography

As you search for information about your essay topic, keep a list of sources that you may want to use in your essay. This list, called a *working bibliography*, will grow as you discover potential sources, and it may shrink if you delete references that aren't useful. Ultimately, this working bibliography will become the list of references presented at the end of your essay.

There are several ways to record your sources. Some students prefer to compile a list of entries in a research notebook; others keep a working bibliography file on their computer; still others use a computer database. (Potential time-saving hint: some computer programs will format your information in the documentation style required for your essay, which may allow an easy transfer from your file to your paper's APA References or MLA Works Cited page.) However you choose to record your notes, you can avoid last-minute rechecking of your data by always including complete details for each of your sources. Here are some common types of sources and the details that you'll need for a working bibliography entry for each:

Article in a Periodical (Print, Online or Database)

1. Author's full name (if given)
2. Title of the article
3. Title of the journal, magazine, or newspaper
4. Volume and issue number of the journal or magazine
5. Date of publication
6. Page numbers of the article (section and page numbers for newspaper)

7. If found online, then also note the publisher or sponsor of the site, and access information (URL, DOI).*

8. If found in a database, then also note the name of the database, and access information (URL, DOI).

Book (Print, Online, or Database)

1. Author's or editor's full name (and name of translator if given)

2. Complete title, including subtitle if one exists

3. Edition number

4. Volume number if the book is part of a series

5. City of publication and name of publisher

6. Date of publication

7. For a reading or article in an anthology, title and author

8. Page numbers of the information you need

9. Library call number or location of source

10. If found online or in a database, then also note the title of the Web site or database, and access information (URL, DOI).

Other Electronic Sources (Web-only Sources, Blogs, E-mail Messages)

1. Author's full name or name of sponsoring organization

2. Title of document

3. Information about electronic publication (source, such as database or Web site; name of service; date of publication or most recent update)

4. For an e-mail: sender and recipient; date of message

5. For a tweet: *Twitter* sender's name and user name; date and time indicating reader's time zone

6. Access information (URL, DOI)

Interview

1. Interviewee's name and title

2. Interviewee's organization or company, job description, or other information regarding his or her expertise, including pertinent publications, studies, presentations, and so forth

3. Subject of interview

4. Date, place, and method of interview (e.g., in person, by telephone, by e-mail)

---

*Date of access is recommended when an online source has no publication date, is likely to be changed over time (e.g. a wiki), or is likely to be removed. Otherwise, date of access is typically not needed.

Here are notes on four sample entries that might appear in Gabriela Guerrera's working bibliography:

Article in a Periodical (Print)

Khatchadourian, Raffi
"We Know How You Feel"
<u>The New Yorker</u>
19 January 2015
pages 50-59
Location: via interlibrary loan

Book (Print)

Picard, Rosalind W.
<u>Affective Computing</u>
Publisher: MIT Press, 1997
Cambridge, MA
Call Number: QA76.9.H85P53 1997
Location: Chatt State stacks

Article in a Periodical (Online Library Database)

Adee, Sally
"Your Seventh Sense"
New Scientist
2 July 2011
Volume 211   Issue 2819
pages 32-36
MasterFILE Premier Database

Interview

Soutar, Andrew
Professor of Computer Science
University of St. Andrews School of Computer Science
Teaches wide variety of Computer Science courses
Research Interest: Affective Computing
Interview Subject: Future Roles of Affective Computing
Skype Interview: 29 March 2015

Credentials:
—authored (or co-authored) more than three dozen
  textbooks related to the field of Computer Science
—published more than one hundred articles in peer-
  reviewed publications
—Member of the Board of Directors for the British Computer
  Society

Choosing and Evaluating Your Sources

After you have found a number of promising sources, take a closer look at them. The strength and credibility of your research paper will depend directly on the strength and credibility of your sources. In short, a research paper built on shaky, unreliable sources will not convince a thoughtful reader. Even one suspect piece of evidence may lead your reader to wonder about the validity—and integrity—of other parts of your essay.

As you review your potential sources, you must apply your *critical thinking skills.* Remember that critical thinking does not mean scattering negative criticism or hostility everywhere; it refers to the higher-order thinking that allows you to carefully examine and evaluate the validity of observations, experiences, and verbal or written communication. When you analyze the worth of someone's claims, evidence, or methodology presented in potentially useful sources, you may assess elements of accuracy, logic, breadth, depth, relevance, and fairness, among other considerations. (◆ For more discussion of critical thinking skills as applied to your own writing as well as that of others, see pages 106–110 in Chapter 5.)

To help you choose the best print and online sources, ask yourself the following questions as you decide which facts, figures, and testimonies will most effectively support or illustrate your ideas while lending credibility to you as a trustworthy, persuasive writer.

What do I know about the source's author? Does this person have any expertise or particular knowledge about the subject matter? If the author of an article about nuclear fusion is a physics professor at a respected university, her views may be more informed than those of a writer of popular science. Although books and scholarly journals generally cite their author's qualifications, the credentials of journalists and magazine writers may be harder to evaluate. Some kinds of Internet sources, as mentioned earlier, may be highly suspect. In cases in which the background of a writer is unknown, you might examine the writer's use of his or her own sources. Can sources for specific data or opinions be checked or verified? In addition, the objectivity of the author must be considered: some authors are clearly biased and may even stand to gain economically or politically from taking a particular point of view. The president of a tobacco company, for instance, might insist that secondary smoke from the cigarettes of others will not harm nonsmokers, but does he or she have an objective opinion? Try to present evidence only from those authors whose views will sway your intelligent readers.

What do I know about the publisher? Who published your sources? Major, well-known publishing houses can be one indication of a book's credibility. (If you are unfamiliar with a particular publisher, consult a librarian or professor in that field.) Be aware that there are many companies who publish books supporting only a specific viewpoint; similarly, many organizations support Web sites to further their causes. The bias in such sources may limit their usefulness to your research.

For periodicals, consider the nature of the journal, magazine, or newspaper. Who is its intended audience? A highly technical paper on sickle-cell anemia, for example, may be weakened by citing an introductory-level discussion of the disease from a general-readership health magazine; an article from the *Journal of the American Medical Association,* however, may be valuable. Is it a publication known to be fairly objective (the *New York Times*) or does it have a particular cause to support (the *National Sierra Club Bulletin*)? It

Figure 19.2 WORKING WITH SOURCES

Choosing and Evaluating Your Sources

- Apply your critical thinking skills to the potential sources you've selected.
- Consider what you know about the source's author.
- Consider what you know about the source's publisher.
- Review the source for possible bias.
- Evaluate the validity of the source's research.
- Review the currency of the source.

Preparing an Annotated Bibliography

- Annotate your sources to help you remember specific data.
- Write a brief description that contains the basic bibliographic facts and a brief summary of the source's content.
- Review your annotated bibliography for completion and balance of sources.

Taking Notes

- Select a suitable method for your note-taking: index cards, electronic documents, photocopies.
- Remember to include bibliographic information and the specific page numbers or paragraph numbers.
- Take notes in any of the following forms: direct quotations, paraphrase, summary, your own ideas.

© Cengage Learning 2017

is often difficult to determine whether articles are subjected to stringent review before acceptance for publication. Because it indexes peer-reviewed research journals and periodicals, the *Directory of Open Access Journals* (doaj.org) is one resource that can prove helpful in determining a source's credibility. In general, articles published in "open" or nonselective publications should be examined closely for credibility. For example, the newsletter for Mensa—a well-known international society for individuals who have documented IQs in the top 2% of the population—once created a furor when an article appeared recommending the euthanasia of the mentally and physically disabled, the homeless, and other so-called "nonproductive" members of society. The newsletter editor's explanation was that all articles submitted for publication were generally accepted.

Is my research reasonably balanced? Your treatment of your subject—especially if it is a controversial one—should show your readers that you investigated all sides of the issue before reaching a conclusion. If your sources are drawn only from authorities well known for voicing one position, your readers may be skeptical about the quality of your research. For instance, if in a paper arguing against a new gun-control measure, you cite only the opinions voiced by the officers of the National Rifle Association, you may antagonize the reader who wants a thorough analysis of all sides of the question. Do use sources that support your position, but don't limit your research to obviously biased sources.

Are my sources reporting valid research?

Is your source the original researcher, or is he or she reporting someone else's study?* If the information is being reported second-hand, has your source been accurate and clear? Is the original source named or referenced in some way so that the information could be checked?

A thorough researcher might note the names of authorities frequently cited by other writers or researchers and try to obtain the original works by those authorities. This tip was useful for Gabriela Guerrera as she found researcher Rosaline Picard, whose MIT-based research in affective computing was mentioned in a number of magazine articles. Once she obtained a copy of Picard's book, *Affective Computing*, she had additional information to consider for her paper.

Look too at the way information in your source was obtained in the first place. Did the original researchers themselves draw logical conclusions from their evidence? Did they run their study or project in a fair, impartial way? For example, a survey of people whose names were obtained solely from the rolls of one political party will hardly constitute a representative sampling of voters' opinions on an upcoming election.

Moreover, be especially careful with statistics because they can be manipulated quite easily to give a distorted picture. A recent survey, for instance, asked a large sample of people to rate a number of American cities based on questions dealing with quality of life. Pittsburgh—a lovely city to be sure—came out the winner, but only if one agrees that all the questions should be weighted equally; that is, the figures gave Pittsburgh the highest score only if one rates "weather" as equally important as "educational opportunities," "number of crimes," "cultural opportunities," and other factors. In short, always evaluate the quality of your sources' research and the validity of their conclusions before you decide to incorporate their findings into your own paper. (And don't forget Mark Twain's reference to "lies, damned lies, and statistics.")

Are my sources still current?

Although some famous experiments or studies have withstood the years, many topics demand research as current as possible. What was written two years or even two weeks ago may have been disproved or surpassed since, especially in our rapidly changing political world and ever-expanding fields of technology. A paper on the status of the US space program, for example, demands recent sources, and research on tablet computer use in the United States might be severely weakened by the use of a text published as recently as last year for "current" statistics.

If they're appropriate, journals and other periodicals may contain more up-to-date reports than books printed several years ago; library database searches can often provide the most current information. On the other hand, you certainly shouldn't ignore a "classic" study on

---

*Interviews, surveys, studies, and experiments conducted firsthand are referred to as *primary sources*; reports and studies written by someone other than the original researcher are called *secondary sources*.

your subject, especially if it is the one against which all the other studies are measured. A student researching the life of Abraham Lincoln, for instance, might find Carl Sandburg's multivolume biography written over seventy years ago to be just as valuable as more recent works. Be aware, too, that even though Web sites can be continually revised, they are sometimes neglected; always check to see if a "last updated" date has been posted or if the material contains current dates or references.

> ◆ REMEMBER: For more advice to help you think critically about your sources, see pages 106–110 in Chapter 5.

Preparing an Annotated Bibliography

While you are gathering and assessing your sources, you may be asked to compile an annotated bibliography—a description of each important source that includes the basic bibliographic facts as well as a brief summary of each entry's content. After reading multiple articles or books on your subject over a period of days or even weeks, you may discover that the information you've found has begun to blur in your head. Annotating each of your sources will help you remember the specific data in each one so that you can locate the material later in the planning and drafting stages of your writing process.

Here is a sample taken from Gabriela Guerrera's annotated bibliography:

> Khatchadourian, Raffi. "We Know How You Feel." *The New Yorker,* 19 Jan. 2015, pp. 50–59.
>
> This article mentions a variety of methods for gathering data related to emotional communication. The author interviews Rana el Kaliouby, co-founder of Affectiva, Inc., which is a leader in the field of affective computing. The article provides specific information about Affdex, which is Affectiva's "signature software." The author mentions several current uses of this technology and wonders about its future.

Compiling an annotated bibliography will also give you a clear sense of how complete and balanced your sources are in support of your ideas, perhaps revealing gaps in your evidence that need to be filled with additional research data. Later, when your essay is finished, your annotated bibliography might provide a useful reference for any of your readers who are interested in exploring your subject in more depth.

Taking Notes

As you evaluate and select those sources that are both reliable and useful, you will begin taking notes on their information. Most researchers use one or more of the following three methods of note-taking.

1. Some students prefer to make their notes on index cards rather than on notebook paper because a stack of cards may be added to, subtracted from, or shuffled around more easily when it's time to plan the essay. You may find it useful to label each card with a short topic heading that corresponds to a major idea in your

essay. Then, as you read, put pertinent information on its appropriate card. Be sure to identify the source of all your notes. (Hint 1: If you have used bibliography cards, take your notes on cards of different sizes or colors to avoid any confusion; write on only one side of each card so that all your information will be in sight when you draft your essay.)

2. Students with personal computers may prefer to store their notes as computer files because of the easy transfer of quoted material from file to essay draft. (Hint 2: This is a great use for a USB drive.) Always make a hard copy of your notes and back up your files frequently. You may find yourself taking notes by hand on any occasions when you are without your computer (classroom, interview, public speech, etc.), so carry index cards with you and transcribe your notes into your files later.

3. Other students rely on photocopies or printouts of sources, highlighting or under-lining important details. (Hint 3: Print a screen shot of the online source, making certain that the URL is visible and recorded for later reference.)

Whichever note-taking methods you choose, always remember to record bibliographic information and the specific page numbers (in printed sources) or paragraph numbers (in some electronic sources) from which your material is taken. Your notes may be one of the following kinds:

1. **Direct quotations.** When you use material word for word, you must always enclose it in quotation marks and note the precise page number of the quotation, if given.* If the quoted material runs from one printed page onto another, use some sort of signal to yourself, such as a backslash (child/abuse) or arrow ($\rightarrow$ p. 162) at the break so if you use only part of the quoted material in your paper, you will know on which page it appeared. If the quoted material contains odd, archaic, or incorrect spelling, punctuation marks, or grammar, insert the word "sic" in brackets next to the item in question; [*sic*] means "this is the way I found it in the original text," and such a symbol will remind you later that you did not miscopy the quotation. In any case, always double-check to make sure you did copy the material accurately and completely to avoid having to come back to the source as you prepare your essay.

2. **Paraphrase.** You paraphrase when you put into your own words what someone else has written or said. Please note: *paraphrased ideas are borrowed ideas, not your original thoughts, and, consequently, they must be attributed to their owner just as direct quotations are.* If you paraphrase, then also be certain to include an appropriate citation to acknowledge the source from which you "borrowed" the idea.

   To remind yourself that certain information in your notes is paraphrased, always introduce it with some sort of notation, such as a handwritten ℗ or a typed P//. Quotation marks will always tell you what you borrowed directly, but some-times when writers take notes one week and write their first draft a week or two later, they cannot remember if a note was paraphrased or if it was an original

---

*All tables, graphs, and charts that you copy must also be directly attributed to their sources, though you do not enclose graphics in quotation marks.

thought. Writers occasionally plagiarize unintentionally because they erroneously believe that only direct quotations and statistics must be attributed to their proper sources, so make your notes as clear as possible. (◆ For more information on avoiding plagiarism, see pages 424–426.)

3. **Summary.** You may wish to condense a piece of writing so you can offer it as support for your own ideas. Using your own words, you should present in shorter form the writer's thesis and supporting ideas. You may find it helpful to include a few direct quotations in your summary to retain the flavor of the original work. Of course, you will want to tell your readers what you are summarizing and by whom it was written. Remember to make a note (sum:) to yourself to indicate summarized, rather than original, material. Also, be sure to include an appropriate citation to acknowledge the source whose ideas you've summarized. (◆ For more information on writing a summary, see also pages 192–194.)

4. **Your own ideas.** Your notes may also contain your personal comments (judgments, flashes of brilliance, questions, notions of how to use something you've just read, notes to yourself about connections between sources, and so forth) that will aid you in the writing of your paper. In handwritten notes, you might jot these down in a different-colored pen or put them in brackets that you've initialed, so that you will recognize them later as your own responses.

Distinguishing Paraphrase from Summary

Because novice writers sometimes have a hard time understanding the difference between paraphrase and summary, here is an explanation and a sample of each. The original paragraph that appears here was taken from a magazine article describing an important 1984 study that is still frequently cited:

> Another successful approach to the prevention of criminality has been to target very young children in a school setting before problems arise. The Perry Preschool Program, started 22 years ago in a low socioeconomic area of Ypsilanti, Michigan, has offered some of the most solid evidence to date that early intervention through a high-quality preschool program can significantly alter a child's life. A study released this fall tells what happened to 123 disadvantaged children from preschool age to present. The detention and arrest rate for the 58 children who had attended the preschool program was 31 percent, compared to 51 percent for the 65 who did not. Similarly, those in the preschool program were more likely to have graduated from high school, have enrolled in postsecondary education programs and be employed, and less likely to have become pregnant as teenagers.
>
> —from "Arresting Delinquency," Dan Hurley, Psychology Today *March 1985, page 66*

Paraphrase

A *paraphrase* puts the information in the researcher's own words, but it does follow the order of the original text, and it does include the important details:

Quality preschooling for high-risk children may help stop crime before it starts. A 1984 study from the Perry Preschool Program located in a poor area of Ypsilanti, Michigan, showed that of 123 socially and economically disadvantaged children, the 58 who attended preschool had an arrest rate of 31 percent compared to 51 percent for those 65 who did not attend. The adults with preschool experience had also graduated from high school in larger numbers; in addition, more of them had attended postsecondary education programs, were employed, and had avoided teenage pregnancy (Hurley 66).

Summary

A *summary* is generally much shorter than the original; the researcher picks out the key ideas but often omits many of the supporting details:

A 1984 study from the Perry Preschool Program in Michigan suggests that disadvantaged children who attend preschool are less likely to be arrested as adults. They choose more education, have better employment records, and avoid teenage pregnancy more often than those without preschool (Hurley 66).

REMEMBER: Both paraphrased and summarized ideas must be attributed to their sources, even if you do not reproduce exact words or figures.

Practicing What You've Learned

A. Select two of the sources (an article from a print, online, or database periodical; an online or print book; or some other Web publication) that you have identified in the course of doing research for your project, and then analyze their credibility. For the two sources, make notes on or create a list of the outside sources used and cited by the author. What different types of sources are used? How does the author introduce these outside sources and give you (the reader) a sense of the source's validity, credibility, or importance?

B. Select a representative excerpt (a few paragraphs or a few pages) from two of your sources.

1. Does the author use direct quotations or paraphrase or summary most often when mentioning outside sources? If the author seems to prefer direct quotations, do you find the quotes selected to be compelling, convincing, and informative? Would you have elected to paraphrase or summarize instead of quoting? Explain your reasons.

2. If the author seems to prefer to paraphrase or summarize outside sources, then do you agree with the decision? Assuming that the author has accurately represented the sources, are you able to follow the discussion? Did you encounter any difficulties? How might the discussion be improved?

Incorporating Your Source Material

Be aware that a research paper is not a massive collection of direct quotations and paraphrased ideas glued together with a few transitional phrases. It is, instead, an essay in which you offer your thesis and ideas based on and supported by your research. Consequently, you will need to incorporate and blend in your reference material in a variety of smooth, persuasive ways. Here are some suggestions:

Use your sources in a clear, logical way. Make certain that you understand your source material well enough to use it in support of your own thoughts. Once you have selected the best references to use, be as convincing as possible. Ask yourself if you're using enough evidence and if the information you're offering really does clearly support your point. As in any essay, you need to avoid oversimplification, hasty generalizations, *non sequiturs*, and other problems in logic. (◆ For a review of common logical fallacies, see pages 316–319.) Resist the temptation to add quotations, facts, or statistics that are interesting but not really relevant to your paper.

Don't overuse direct quotations. It's best to use a direct quotation *only* when it expresses a point in a far more impressive, emphatic, or concise way than you could say it yourself. Suppose, for instance, you were analyzing the films of a particular director and wanted to include a sample of critical reviews:

> As one movie critic wrote, "This film is really terrible, and people should ignore it" (Dennison 14).

The direct quotation above isn't remarkable and could be easily paraphrased. However, you might be tempted to quote the following line to show your readers an emphatically negative review of this movie:

> As one movie critic wrote, "This film's plot is so idiotic it's clearly intended for people who move their lips not only when they read but also when they watch TV" (Dennison 14).

When you do decide to use direct quotations, don't merely drop them into your prose as if they had fallen from a tall building onto your page. Instead, lead into them smoothly so that they obviously support or clarify what you are saying.

Dropped in	Scientists have been studying the ill effects of nitrites on test animals since 1961. "Nitrites produced malignant tumors in sixty-two percent of the test animals within six months" (Smith 109).
Better	Scientists have been studying the ill effects of nitrites on test animals since 1961. According to Dr. William Smith, head of the Farrell Institute of Research, who conducted the largest experiment thus far, "Nitrites produced malignant tumors in sixty-two percent of the test animals within six months" (109).

Figure 19.3 USING SOURCES IN YOUR PAPER

Incorporating Your Source Material

- Work to incorporate and blend in your reference material.
- Use your sources in a clear, logical way.
- Don't overuse direct quotations.
- When using direct quotations, lead into them smoothly, vary the phrases you use to introduce them, and punctuate them correctly.
- Make sure support or evidence for your ideas and claims is included in the paper.
- Don't let reference material dominate your essay.

Avoiding Plagiarism

- Remember to attribute all borrowed information to its source.
- Be careful of unintentional plagiarism.
- Frame any borrowed information with an introductory phrase and a closing citation.

© Cengage Learning 2017

Vary your sentence pattern when you present your quotations. Here are some sample phrases for introducing quotations:

- In her introduction to *The Great Gatsby*, Professor Wilma Smith points out that Fitzgerald "wrote about himself and produced a narcissistic masterpiece" (5).

- Wilma Smith, author of *Impact*, summarized the situation this way: "Eighty-eight percent of the sales force threatens a walkout" (21).

- "Only the President controls the black box," according to White House Press Secretary Wilma Smith.

- As drama critic Wilma Smith observed last year in the *Saturday Review*, the play was "a rousing failure" (212).

- Perhaps the well-known poet Wilma Smith expressed the idea best when she wrote, "Love is a spider waiting to entangle its victims" (14).

- "Employment figures are down three percent from last year," claimed Senator Wilma Smith, who leads opposition to the tax cut (32).

In other words, don't simply repeat "Wilma Smith said," "John Jones said," "Mary Brown said."

Punctuate your quotations correctly. The proper punctuation will help your reader understand who said what. ◆ For information on the appropriate uses of quotation marks surrounding direct quotations, see pages 586–587 in Part Four. If you are incorporating a long quoted passage into your essay, one that appears as more than four lines in your text, you should present it in block form without quotation marks, as described on page 430. To omit words in a quoted passage, use ellipsis points, explained on page 595.

Make certain support for your assertions or claims is in the paper, not still in your head or back in the original source. As you draw together the information that you've derived from various sources, make certain that you provide appropriate support for your assertions *in your paper*. Do not assume that your reader will be able to read your mind and know what you know. Sometimes after you've read a number of persuasive facts in an article or a book, it's easy to forget that your reader doesn't know your sources as you do now. For instance, the writer of the following paragraph isn't as persuasive as she might be because she hides the support for her controversial point in the reference to the article, forgetting that the reader needs to know what the article actually said:

> An organ transplant from one human to another is becoming a common occurrence, an operation that is generally applauded by everyone as a lifesaving effort. But people are overlooking many of the serious problems that come with the increase in transplant surgery. A study shows that in Asia there may be a risk of traffic in organs on the black market. Figures recorded recently are very disturbing (Wood 35).

For the reader to be persuaded, he or she needs to know what the writer learned from the article: what study? What figures and what exactly do they show? Who has recorded these? Is the source reliable? Instead of offering the necessary support in the essay, the writer merely points to the article as proof. Few readers will take the time to look up the article to find the information they need to understand or believe your point. Here is a revised version of the paragraph above that gives more specific, persuasive details from the source that the writer is using:

> An organ transplant from one human to another is becoming a common occurrence, an operation that is generally applauded by everyone as a lifesaving effort. But people are overlooking many of the serious problems that come with the increase in transplant surgery. One of the most alarming statistics, resulting from a recent investigation sponsored by the United Nations World Health Organization, indicates that black market trafficking of organs has risen significantly in the past decade (Wood 35).

Therefore, when you use source material, always be sure that you have remembered to put your support on the page, *in the essay itself*, for the reader to see. Don't let the essence of your point remain hidden, especially when the claim is controversial.

Don't let reference material dominate your essay. Remember that your reader is interested in *your* thesis and *your* conclusions, not just in a string of references. Use your researched material wisely whenever your statements need clarification, support, or amplification. But don't use quotations, paraphrases, or summarized material at every turn, just to show that you've done your homework.

Avoiding Plagiarism

Unfortunately, most discussions of research must include a brief word about plagiarism. Novice writers often unintentionally plagiarize, as noted before, because they fail to recognize the necessity of attributing paraphrased, summarized, and borrowed ideas to their original owners. And indeed it is sometimes difficult after days of research to know exactly what one has read repeatedly and what one originally thought. Also, there's frequently a thin line between general or common knowledge ("Henry Ford was the father of the automobile industry in America") that does not have to be documented and those ideas and statements that do ("USX reported an operating loss of four million dollars in its last quarter"). As a rule of thumb, ask yourself whether the majority of your readers would recognize the fact or opinion you're expressing or if it's repeatedly found in commonly used sources; if so, you may not need to document it. For example, most people would acknowledge that the Wall Street crash of 1929 ushered in the Great Depression of the 1930s, but the exact number of bank foreclosures in 1933 is not common knowledge and, therefore, needs documenting. Similarly, a well-known quotation from the Bible or Mother Goose or even the Declaration of Independence might pass without documentation, but a line from the vice president's latest speech needs a reference to its source. Remember, too, that much of the material on the Internet is copyrighted. When in doubt, the best choice is to document anything that you feel may be in question.

To help you understand the difference between plagiarism and proper documentation, here is a passage taken from the book *Criminal Investigation*, followed by both incorrect and correct ways of using its information in a paper of your own:

Original   As bicycles have increased in popularity, so has bicycle theft. According to the Web site of the National Bike Registry (www.nationalbikeregistry.com), more than 1.5 million bicycles, worth an estimated $200 million, are stolen each year in the United States. Experienced thieves can steal a locked bike in less than 20 seconds. And while nearly 50 per cent of all stolen bicycles are recovered every year by law enforcement, only 5 per cent are returned to their owners, because most bikes are unregistered.

—*from* Criminal Investigation *(10th edition)*,
Christine Hess Orthmann and Kären M. Hess,
Wadsworth, 2013, page 431

Plagiarized   As more people ride bicycles today, bike theft is on the rise. Over 1.5 million bikes are stolen every year in the United States, at a loss of approximately $200 million. A locked bike can be stolen by a good thief in as little as 20 seconds, and even though police recover almost half of them, only 5 percent of owners ever see their rides again because the bikes are unregistered.

The writer of the preceding paragraph paraphrased the original—changed some words and sentences. But because the writer borrowed the ideas and the statistics without crediting the original source, the passage is plagiarized.

Also plagiarized

Got a nice bicycle? Watch out, as it may become one of the 1.5 million bikes stolen this year alone, with bike theft on the rise (Orthmann and Hess 413). Campus is a prime place for such theft, as I know from personal experience, despite use of a heavy lock and chain. But even if police or campus cops find your bike—and they do recover nearly half of them—you still may not get your transportation back if you are one of the 95 percent who have not registered your bike. You'll join the other U.S. bikers who all together will lose some $200 million this year.

The writer of the preceding paragraph did show the source of the number of stolen bikes, but the rest of the paragraph contains borrowed material that also must be clearly attributed.

Properly documented

This week campus police are holding their annual bicycle registration drive. Unfortunately, too many students ignore this simple procedure—and pay the price. I know I did last year when my new bike was stolen from the rack in front of the chemistry building, despite its heavy lock and chain. I'm not the only one to lose my transportation, of course. According to figures from the National Bike Registry, over 1.2 million bikes are stolen each year, but, more importantly, despite recovery of almost half of them, only 5 percent of owners could claim their recovered bikes through proper registration (Orthmann and Hess 413). Learn from my mistake: it's worth the five-minute hassle of filling out a form. Walk—or ride the bike you want to keep—over to the Student Center any afternoon this week from 2 to 4.

The writer of the preceding paragraph used the properly documented information to support her own point about the value of campus bike registration. She has not tried to pass off any of the facts about national bike loss and recovery as her own, and her readers will know where to find the data should they wish more information.

Although plagiarism is often unintentional, it's your job to be as honest and careful as possible. If you're in doubt about your use of a particular idea, study, statistics or any other kind of borrowed material, consult your instructor for a second opinion.

Here's a suggestion that might help you avoid plagiarizing by accident. When you are drafting your essay and come to a spot in which you want to incorporate the ideas of someone else, think of the borrowed material as if it were in a window.* Always frame the window at the top with some sort of introduction that identifies the author (or source) and frame the window on the bottom with a reference to the location of the material, as illustrated on the following page.

---

*I am indebted to John Clark Pratt, Professor Emeritus of English, Colorado State University, for this useful suggestion. Professor Pratt is the author of *Writing from Scratch: The Essay* (1987), published by Hamilton Press, and the editor of the *Writing from Scratch* series.

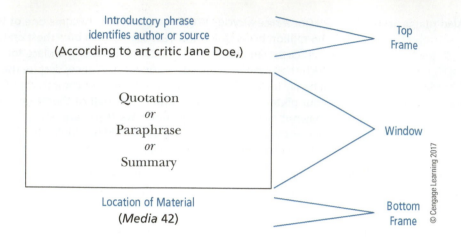

Introductory phrase
identifies author or source
(According to art critic Jane Doe,) — Top Frame

Quotation
or
Paraphrase
or
Summary — Window

Location of Material
(*Media* 42) — Bottom Frame

© Cengage Learning 2017

A sample might look like this:

Introductory phrase identifies author

As humorist Mike McGrady once said about housekeeping, "Any job that requires six hours to do and can be undone in six minutes by one small child carrying a plate of crackers and a Monopoly set—this is not a job that will long capture my interest" (13). — Quotation

Location

In a later draft, you'll probably want to vary your style so that all your borrowed material doesn't appear in exactly the same "window" format (◆ see pages 421–423 for suggestions). But until you acquire the habit of always documenting your sources, you might try using the "window" technique in your early drafts.

Practicing What You've Learned

A. As Gabriella Guerrera investigated the concerns about potentially intrusive uses of affective computing technology, she found the following commentary from one of the leaders in that field. To practice some of the skills you've learned, read the passage and perform the tasks that follow it.

The concerns about privacy and centralized control are not unique to affective computing, nor does affective computing necessarily lead to any of these problems. George Orwell's powerful image of "Big Brother" is largely political, and antithetical to the image of affective computing as a personal technology.

continued on next page

Affective technology places value on human feelings and expression and pays attention to them. Forgive for a moment some [stereotyping], and consider that women, in numerous studies, have proved significantly better at recognizing emotions than men. In this sense, the image of a system that recognizes your emotions may be considered more feminine. Additionally, a system that aims to understand your preferences, to grow and find ways to please you, is reminiscent of someone trying to earn your favor, much like a younger sibling. Within the family metaphor, the closest image of an affective system is not one of a powerful big brother, but of a pleasing little sister.

1. The book from which the passage was taken contains the following information. Select the appropriate data and prepare a working bibliography entry.

   Affective Computing
   MIT Press, publishers
   Boston, Massachusetts
   Copyright 1997
   Author: Rosalind W. Picard
   Passage derived from page 124
   ISBN 0-262-66115-2

2. Paraphrase the first three sentences, showing how you would credit the source of your words in an essay of your own.

3. Practice summarizing the paragraph; do not quote directly from it.

4. Select an idea from the passage to quote directly. Using the "window" technique described on pages 425–426, lead into the quotation with a smooth acknowledgment of its source or authors in the top frame and conclude with the correct location of the material in the bottom frame.

5. Select an idea or take a direct quotation from the passage and use it as support for a point of your own, being careful not to plagiarize the borrowed material.

B. Using library or Web resources, look up a newspaper* from any city and find the issue published on the day of your birth or on some other significant date. Prepare an annotated bibliography entry that includes the source information you need to create a citation for this issue of the newspaper and then summarize an important article that interests you. (Don't forget to acknowledge the source of your summary.)

---

*If the newspaper is not accessible, you might substitute a weekly news magazine, such as *Time* or *Newsweek*.

Assignment

A. To practice searching for and choosing source material, find three recent works on your essay topic available in your library. If you don't have an essay topic yet, pick a subject that interests you, one that is likely to appear in both print and electronic sources (FIFA World Cup competition, hummingbirds, macro photography, scuba certification). If possible, try to find three different kinds of sources, such as a print book, an online periodical (a journal, magazine, or newspaper article), and a government Web site. After you have recorded bibliographic information for each source, locate and evaluate the works. Do all of these sources provide relevant, reliable information? In a few sentences explain why you believe each one would or would not be an appropriate source for your research essay.

B. *Collaborative Activity:* To help you focus your essay topic, engage in a "talk-write" session with another student. Before class, review your research thus far, selecting the most interesting, surprising, or puzzling piece of information you have found. In class, explain your findings to a classmate, and together brainstorm ways this information might be most effectively incorporated into your essay. Take notes on any useful suggestions or unexpected reactions that might help you see a new possibility for the direction of your essay. Also, if time permits, help each other problem-solve any difficulties with a particular research method or source.

Chapter 20

Documenting Sources

Once you begin to write your paper incorporating your source material, you need to know how to show your readers where your material came from. You may have already learned a documentation system in a previous writing class, but because today's researchers and scholars use a number of different documentation styles, it's important that you know which style is appropriate for your current essay. In some cases, your instructors (or the audience for whom you are writing) will designate a particular style; at other times, the choice will be yours.

In this chapter, we will look at two widely used systems—MLA style and APA style—and also briefly review use of the traditional footnote/bibliography format.

MLA Style

Most instructors in the humanities assign the documentation form prescribed by the Modern Language Association of America (MLA). Since 1984, the MLA has recommended a form of documentation that no longer uses traditional footnotes or endnotes to show references.* The current form calls for *parenthetical documentation*, most often consisting of the author's last name and the appropriate page number(s) in parentheses immediately following the source material in your paper. At the end of your discussion, readers may find complete bibliographic information for each source on a Works Cited page, a list of all the sources in your essay.

MLA Citations in Your Essay

Here are some guidelines for using the MLA parenthetical reference form within your paper.

1. If you use a source by one author, place the author's name and page number after the quoted, paraphrased, or summarized material. Note that the parentheses

---

*If you wish a more detailed description of the current MLA form, ask your local bookstore or library for the *MLA Handbook*, 8th ed. (MLA, 2016). The most up-to-date documentation information may be found on the MLA Web site at www.mla.org/style.

go *before* the end punctuation, and there is no punctuation between the author's name and the page number. (Use the author's name and omit the page reference when citing a complete work or a one-page work.)

Example   Although pop art often resembles the comic strip, it owes a debt to such painters as Magritte, Matisse, and de Kooning (Rose 184).

2. If you use a source by one author and give credit to that author by name in your paper, you need only give the page number in the parentheses.

Example   According to art critic Barbara Rose, pop art owes a large debt to such painters as Magritte, Matisse, and de Kooning (184).

3. If you are directly quoting material that extends to more than four print lines, indent the material a half inch from the left margin, double-space, and do not use quotation marks. Do not change the right margin. Note that in this case, the parentheses appear *after* the punctuation that ends the quoted material.

Example

In addition to causing tragedy for others, Crane's characters who are motivated by a desire to appear heroic to their peers may also cause themselves serious trouble. For example, Collins, another Civil War private, almost causes his own death because of his vain desire to act bravely in front of his fellow Union soldiers. (Hall 16)

4. If you are citing more than one work by the same author, include a short title in the parentheses.

Example   Within fifty years, the Inca and Aztec civilizations were defeated and overthrown by outside invaders (Thomas, *Lost Cultures* 198).

5. If you are citing a work by two authors, use both last names and the page number.

Example   Prisons today are overcrowded to the point of emergency; conditions could not be worse, and the state budget for prison reforms is at an all-time low (Smith and Jones 72).

6. For more than two authors, use the last name of the first author plus "et al." (Latin for "and others") and the page number. There is no comma after the author's name.

Example   Casualties of World War II during 1940–45 amounted to more than twenty-five million soldiers and civilians (Blum et al. 779).

7. If you cite a work that has no named author, use the work's title and the page number.

Example   Each year 350,000 Americans will die of a heart attack before reaching a hospital ("First Aid for Heart Attacks" 88).

8. If the work you are citing appears in a series and you are borrowing from more than one volume, include the volume and page number with the author's name. (If you are borrowing from only one volume, you need not include a volume number in the in-text citation.)

Example   On August 28, 1963, King delivered his "I Have a Dream" address to more than 200,000 civil rights supporters in Washington, DC, a speech that added momentum to the passage of the 1964 Civil Rights Act (Lopez 1: 270).

9. If your source is an electronic document, treat it as you would a print source. If you are citing an entire work from an electronic source that has no page, paragraph, or screen numbers, it is preferable to use the name of the author or editor in the text, rather than in a parenthetical reference. If the author's or editor's name is unavailable, use the work's title (shortened or in full).

Example   Cannon College Economics Professor John Thompson argues a different view of the Chinese role in Indonesia's economy.

Some electronic documents include paragraph or screen numbers. When citing these documents, include the appropriate number, preceded by "par." or "pars." for paragraph(s), or "screen." If the paragraphs are not numbered in the original source, however, do not impose your own numbering system.

Example   The Chinese in Indonesia account for only 4% of the population but control 70% of the economy (Thompson, par. 6).

10. If the material you are citing contains a passage quoted from another source, indicate your source for the quotation in the parentheses.

Example   According to George Orwell, "Good writing is like a window-pane" (qtd. in Murray 142).

11. If the work you are citing is a nonprint source with no reference markers, such as an interview, lecture, television show, film, or performance, include in the text the name of the person or the title (e.g., *60 Minutes*) that begins the corresponding entry in the Works Cited list.

Example   In a March 12, 2012, telephone interview, Kate Hall, Chair of the Chipeta Preservation Association, expressed her satisfaction with the progress being made in the negotiations for rebuilding the Red Feather Cafe.

Compiling a Works Cited List: MLA Style

If you are using the MLA format, at the end of your essay do include a Works Cited page—a formal listing of the sources you used in your essay. (If you wish to show all the sources you consulted, but did not cite, add a Works Consulted page.) Arrange the entries alphabetically by the authors' last names; if no name is given, alphabetize the source by the first important word of its title. Double-space each entry, and double-space between entries. If an entry takes more than one line, indent the subsequent lines one-half inch. MLA guidelines indicate one space following end punctuation marks.

The Parts of a Works Cited Entry

The core elements of a works cited entry are **author, title of source, title of container, other contributors, version, number, publisher, publication date,** and **location**. An explanation of each core element will follow. Not every element will be relevant to each entry. Omit those that are not needed.

Below, you'll find a sample MLA entry for an article appearing in an online publication. This sample entry is intended to represent the general format used in MLA entries.*

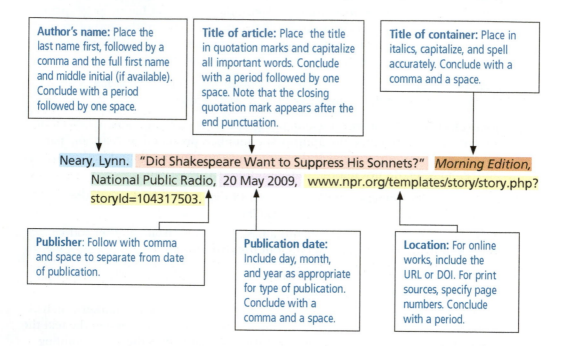

Author's name: Place the last name first, followed by a comma and the full first name and middle initial (if available). Conclude with a period followed by one space.

Title of article: Place the title in quotation marks and capitalize all important words. Conclude with a period followed by one space. Note that the closing quotation mark appears after the end punctuation.

Title of container: Place in italics, capitalize, and spell accurately. Conclude with a comma and a space.

Neary, Lynn. "Did Shakespeare Want to Suppress His Sonnets?" *Morning Edition,* National Public Radio, 20 May 2009, www.npr.org/templates/story/story.php?storyId=104317503.

Publisher: Follow with comma and space to separate from date of publication.

Publication date: Include day, month, and year as appropriate for type of publication. Conclude with a comma and a space.

Location: For online works, include the URL or DOI. For print sources, specify page numbers. Conclude with a period.

Guidelines to MLA Style

Here are some guidelines to help you prepare a Works Cited page according to the MLA Style:

1. Omit business descriptions, such as Incorporated or Company.

2. To cite a university press, use "U" and "P" appropriately (for example, "U of Illinois P" for University of Illinois Press). However, spell out "Press" for commercial publishers.

3. Italicize print titles of books and journals; handwritten titles should be underlined. The titles of articles, essays, and chapters should be enclosed in quotation marks.

---

*To conserve the number of pages in this chapter, sample entries are shown single-spaced. You should double-space the Works Cited entries in your essays.

4. Capitalize the first word, last word, and all important words in a title or subtitle. Do not capitalize the following parts of speech (unless they appear as the first or last word):

- **articles** ("a," "an," "the," as in "Crossing the Bar")

- **prepositions** (e.g., "across," "behind," "at," "of," "up," "down," as in "The Jilting of Granny Weatherall")

- **coordinating conjunctions** ("and," "but," "for," "nor," "or," "so," "yet," as in *Romeo and Juliet*)

- **the "to" in infinitives** ("A Good Man Is Hard to Find")

The Core Elements

You may need to cite a wide variety of source types, from essays in a print textbook to online journal articles to podcasts. The primary goal of responsible documentation is that a works cited entry should be *useful to readers*. An effective entry helps your readers locate its source by citing simple traits (like author, title, and location) shared by most sources.

These traits are referred to as the nine *core elements*, and every source contains some combination (but not necessarily all) of them. Here is an overview of these elements. The sections that follow will examine how to identify and format these elements for specific source types.

1. Author.

The person or people who wrote or otherwise created the source—or whose work on the source you are choosing to emphasize. This could mean an author, an editor, a director, a composer, a performer, or a narrator. It will usually be a full name but could also be a pseudonym such as a Twitter handle.

- **One author:** Davis, Bertram H.
- **Two authors:** McDonough, James Lee, and Thomas L. Connelly.
- **Three or more authors:** Guerin, Wilfred L., et al.

2. Title of source.

The title of the specific source you are citing. This could be a whole book or a short poem within it, if your focus is on that poem. This could be a specific blog entry or an entire album. Shorter works or works that are part of a larger whole usually use quotation marks, while longer or stand-alone works are set in italics.

- **Article:** "We Know How You Feel."
- **Television episode:** "Lost in Translation."
- **Play:** *The Tragedy of Hamlet, Prince of Denmark.*
- **Book:** *Five Tragic Hours: The Battle of Franklin.*

3. Title of container,

The title of a larger source containing the source you are citing. When you are citing an essay within a book, the container is the book. For an episode of a television show, the container is the series title. An article's container is the title of the periodical or Web site where it appeared. Italicize most container titles.

- **Book:** *Compact Literature: Reading, Reacting, Writing,*
- **Television show:** *NCIS,*
- **Website:** *The Toast,*

4. Other contributors,

Noteworthy contributors to the work not listed in element 1. These may include editors, translators, performers, etc. Introduce each name (or set of names) with a description of the role played. If listed after element 2, capitalize the description; if listed after element 3, do not.

- edited by Laurie G. Kirszner and Stephen R. Mandell,
- conducted by Laurie Redmer Minner,
- Translated by Marilyn Sode Smith,

5. Version,

Description of a source that appears in more than one version. This element appears most frequently for books that appear in multiple editions. Note that while most books' editions are numbered, some are indicated merely by a descriptor such as "revised" or "expanded." The element may also apply to the "director's cut" of a film or a version of software.

- director's cut,
- 15th ed.,
- updated ed.,

6. Number,

Number that indicates a source's place in a sequence. This could refer to the volume number of a book that appears in multiple volumes, to the volume and issue numbers of a journal, or to the season and episode numbers of a television show.

- **Television episode:** season 2, episode 1,
- **Book:** Vol. 6,
- **Journal Article:** vol. 119, no. 3,

7. Publisher,

Organization that delivers the source to the public. Publishers should be listed for books, films, television shows, and most Web sites, but *not* for periodicals, works published directly by their authors or editors, Web sites for which the publisher's name is the same as the title, or Web sites that do not produce the works they house (such as *YouTube* or *WordPress*).

- Oxford UP,
- Houghton Mifflin,
- Lucasfilm,

8. Publication date,

When the source was made available to the public. This could mean when a work was published or republished in print or online, or when it was released in theaters or on iTunes, broadcast on television, or performed live. It might be a year, a month, a specific date, or even a specific time.

- 2014,
- Spring 2016,
- 24 Mar. 2015,
- 10 Jan. 2016, 9:30 p.m.,

9. Location.

Where to find the specific source. For a print source, specify location by a page number or page range. For an online source, provide a URL or DOI. (If a DOI is available, you should cite it in preference to a URL.) This is also the place to record the location of a live performance, the disc number of work in a DVD set, or another identifier specific to its source type.

- pp. 30–36.
- www.cnn.com/2008/HEALTH/11/27/ep.avoid.germs.traveling/index. html?iref=newssearch.
- doi:10.1002/cplx.21590.
- Sheraton Hotel, New Orleans.

Remember that not all sources contain all of the nine core elements, and some of them contain additional or optional elements, which you'll learn about in the sections that follow.

Optional Elements

- **Date of original publication.** This may be useful by providing your reader with historical context and showing where the work stands in relation to other published works. The date of original publication is listed after the title of the source and followed by a period. In the example below, note the date of original publication (1873) and the date of the reprinted work (1978).

  Thaxter, Celia. *Among the Isles of Shoals.* 1873. Edited by Leslie Dunn, Heritage Books, 1978.

- **City of publication.** While the city of publication is no longer a standard element of MLA citation, it can occasionally be of use to your readers. A publisher with offices in more than one country may release more than one version of a book—for instance, a British version and an American version, using different spelling and vocabulary. In this case, listing the city of publication will help readers identify the source. The city of publication is listed before the publisher and followed by a comma.

  Rowling, J.K. *Harry Potter and the Philosopher's Stone.* London, Bloomsbury, 1997.

- **Date of access.** The date of access can be important when an online source has no publication date, is likely to be changed over time (such as a wiki entry), or is likely to be removed (e.g., a television episode temporarily available through a service such as *Hulu*). The date of access is listed at the end of an entry, in the format "Accessed 29 March 2016."

- **Series name.** If a book is part of a named series, it may be significant for your readers to understand that context. After the location, include the series name and the series number (if any) followed by a period.

Vance, John A. *Joseph and Thomas Warton.* Edited by Sarah Smith, Twayne-Hall,1983. Twayne English Authors Ser. 380.

- **Other optional elements.** Other useful elements could include a work's prior publication history or a description of its type when that type might be unexpected (e.g., lecture, transcript). A particular works cited entry may benefit from another element not discussed here. You must use your judgment in determining which information would be useful to your readers.

Containers within Containers

Some sources are housed in containers within larger containers. For instance, if you cite an article (source) from a journal (container #1) that you accessed through a service like *ProQuest* (container #2), or if you discuss an episode (source) of a television show (container #1) that you accessed on a service like *Netflix* (container #2), then you must include information about that larger container. This will help readers retrace your steps.

To create a works cited entry for a source found in a container within a container, do the following:

- List core elements 1 (author) and 2 (title of source).
- List core elements 3-9 for the first container.
- List core elements 3-9 for the second container.

In the following example, a writer has identified and ordered source information for a television episode using the core elements. She used this process to create a works cited entry.

SOURCE

1.	Author.	Dan Nowak.
2.	Title of source.	"Unraveling."

CONTAINER 1

3.	Title of container,	*The Killing,*
4.	Other contributors,	directed by Lodge Kerrigan,
5.	Version,	
6.	Number,	season 4, episode 2,
7.	Publisher,	AMC,
8.	Publication date,	1 Aug. 2014.
9.	Location.	

CONTAINER 2

3.	Title of container,	*Netflix,*
4.	Other contributors,	
5.	Version,	
6.	Number,	
7.	Publisher,	
8.	Publication date,	
9.	Location.	www.netflix.com/watch/70306003.

WORKS CITED ENTRY

Dan Nowak. "Unraveling." *The Killing,* directed by Lodge Kerrigan, season 4, episode 2, AMC, 1 Aug. 2014. *Netflix,* www.netflix.com/watch/70306003.

Citations Beyond the Research Paper

Your work throughout college may take other forms than the research paper. Here are some guidelines to citing your sources in other formats. Though there may be more than one correct way to document sources, your goal is always to provide information that is useful to your readers, enabling them to find the sources that underlie your work.

- **Video.** In a video, you can give a brief identification of a source as a text overlay at the bottom of the screen, before including full documentation in your closing credits. For example, the overlay might give the name of an interview subject or the director and title of a video clip.

- **Web projects.** In an interactive Web project, you can link any citation of online materials directly to their original sources. It is recommended that you still include a works cited list at the end of your project.

- **Slide-based presentation.** When making a presentation using software such as *PowerPoint* or *Keynote,* you can give a shortened citation on each slide to identify any borrowed material. Then you can include a complete works cited list on the concluding slide. To ensure the audience has further access to your works cited list, you might provide a printed handout or the URL link to an online posting.

Practice Template for MLA Entries

1. Author.
2. Title of source.

CONTAINER 1

3. Title of container,
4. Other contributors,
5. Version,
6. Number,
7. Publisher,
8. Publication date,
9. Location.

CONTAINER 2

3. Title of container,
4. Other contributors,
5. Version,
6. Number,
7. Publisher,
8. Publication date,
9. Location.

Index of MLA Works Cited Entries

Sample Works Cited Entries: MLA Style

Books

- **A work with one author**

  Davis, Bertram H. *A Proof of Eminence: The Life of Sir John Hawkins*. Indiana UP, 1973.

  Dickens, Charles. *The Adventures of Oliver Twist*. Chapman and Hall, 1858. *Hathi Trust Digital Library*, babel.hathitrust.org/cgi/pt?id=hvd. hwl48g;view=1up;seq=13.

- **Two works by the same author**

    Davis, Bertram H. *A Proof of Eminence: The Life of Sir John Hawkins*. Indiana UP,
    1973.

    ---. *Thomas Percy: A Scholar-Cleric in the Age of Johnson*. U of Pennsylvania P,
    1989.

    Include the author's name in only the first entry. In each subsequent entry,
    type three hyphens followed by a period. The three hyphens stand for exactly
    the same name as in the preceding entry. The hyphens do not represent any
    role other than author (for example, a comma and "editor." are added after
    the hyphens to indicate the role as editor). Such a label (e.g., "director.," "edi-
    tor.," or "translator.") does not affect the order in which the entries appear. For
    works listed under the same name, alphabetize them by title.

- **A work with two authors**

    McDonough, James Lee, and Thomas L. Connelly. *Five Tragic Hours: The Battle of
    Franklin*. U of Tennessee P, 1983.

    Note that only the name of the first author is inverted.

- **A work with more than two authors**

    Guerin, Wilfred L., et al. *A Handbook of Critical Approaches to Literature*. 5th ed.,
    Oxford UP, 2004.

    The phrase "et al." means "and others."

- **A work with author and additional contributor**

    Chaucer, Geoffrey. *The Tales of Canterbury*. Edited by Robert Pratt, Houghton
    Mifflin, 1974.

    Zamora, Martha. *Frida Kahlo: The Brush of Anguish*. Translated by Marilyn Sode
    Smith, Chronicle Books, 1990.

    The editor and translator are included in the "Other contributors" element of
    the entries.

- **A work with corporate authorship**

    National Fire Safety Council. *Stopping Arson before It Starts*. Edmondson, 1992.

    Omit any initial article ("A," "An," "The") in the name of a corporate author,
    and do not abbreviate its name. When the author and the publisher are the
    same organization, omit the author element and list the organization as the
    publisher.

- **A selection or chapter from an anthology or a collection with an editor**

    O'Connor, Flannery. "A Good Man Is Hard to Find." *Compact Literature: Reading,
    Reacting, Writing,* edited by Laurie G. Kirszner and Stephen R. Mandell, 9th ed.,
    Wadsworth Publishing, 2016, pp. 367–78.

    Following the date of publication and comma, include the page numbers on
    which the work appears.

- **One volume of a multivolume work**

    Delaney, John J., editor. *Encyclopedia of Saints*. Vol. 4, Doubleday, 1998.

- **A work in more than one volume**

    Piepkorn, Arthur C. *Profiles in Belief: The Religious Bodies of the United States and Canada.* Harper & Row, 1976–78. 2 vols.

    If the volumes were published over a period of years, give the inclusive dates after the publisher's name.

- **An introduction, preface, foreword, or afterword**

    Soloman, Barbara H. Introduction. *Herland,* by Charlotte Perkins Gilman, Penguin, 1992, pp. xi–xxxi.

    Begin the citation with the name of the writer of the section you are citing; then identify the section but do not italicize or use quotation marks around the word. Next, give the name of the container book and the name of its author, preceded by the word "by."

Periodicals (Magazines, Journals, Newspapers)

Scholarly and professional journals require volume and issue numbers; magazines and newspapers for general readers do not.

If an article is not printed on consecutive pages (for example, if the article begins on page 51, runs through page 55, resumes on page 112, and concludes on page 113), use the first page number and a plus sign with no space between them.

Except for May, June, and July, the months of the year are abbreviated. Use the first three letters for all other months (e.g., Jan., Feb., Mar.) except September (Sept.).

- **A signed article in a magazine published every week or every two weeks**

    Khatchadourian, Raffi. "We Know How You Feel." *The New Yorker,* 19 Jan. 2015, pp. 50–59.

    Carter, Stephen. "Stephen Carter: My Lai Revisited after Afghanistan Massacre." *Newsweek,* 19 Mar. 2012, www.newsweek.com/stephen-carter-my-lai-revisited-after-afghanistan-massacre-63725.

- **An unsigned article in a magazine published every week or every two weeks**

    "Exit Ramp Poses Difficulty for Local Residents." *East Hamilton Weekly,* 16 Mar. 2009, pp. 42–44.

    "10 Things You Didn't Know about Abraham Lincoln." *U.S. News & World Report,* 10 Feb. 2009, www.usnews.com/news/history/articles/2009/02/10/10-things-you-didnt-know-about-abraham-lincoln.

    Because this title begins with a numeral, the article should be alphabetized as if the numeral were spelled out ("Ten Things You Didn't Know about Abraham Lincoln").

- **An article in a magazine published every month or every two months**

    Lawler, Andrew. "A Mystery Fit for a Pharaoh." *Smithsonian,* July 2006, pp. 64–69.

    Lawler, Andrew. "A Mystery Fit for a Pharaoh." *Smithsonian,* July 2006, www.smithsonianmag.com/history/a-mystery-fit-for-a-pharaoh-122192274/?no-ist.

- **A review in a magazine published every month or every two months**

    Rodwan, John. "The Great Migration." Review of *The Warmth of Other Suns,* by Isabel Wilkerson, *The American Interest,* Sept./Oct. 2011, pp. 95–99.

- **A signed article in a scholarly journal**

  Fetters, Allison. "Intrigue in Shakespeare's Sonnets." *Midlothian Review*, vol. 28,
  no. 3, 2009, pp. 17–27.

  Shapiro, Stephen. "Intellectual Labor Power, Cultural Capital, and the
  Value of Prestige." *South Atlantic Quarterly,* vol. 108, no. 2, 2009, doi:
  10.1215/00382876-2008-032.

- **A signed article in a newspaper**

  Brooks, Jennifer. "Belmont to Stop Selling Bottled Water at School." *The Tennessean*
  [Nashville], 22 Apr. 2009, pp. 1B+.

  Lubell, Sam. "Of the Sea and Air and Sky." *The New York Times*, 26 Nov. 2008,
  www.nytimes.com/2008/11/27/garden/27california.html?_r=0.

  When it is not a part of a locally published newspaper's title, add the city name
  in brackets after the title. Note that section designation and page number are
  often combined (B1 or 1B); record the page numbers exactly as they appear.

- **An unsigned article in a newspaper**

  "Workforce Center Offers Youth Activities." *The Denver Post,* 28 Mar. 2012, p. B1.

- **A signed editorial in a newspaper**

  Ball, George. "We Can't Spring Forward Fast Enough to Catch Nature." Editorial. *The
  Atlanta Journal-Constitution,* 15 Apr. 2009, p. A11.

- **An unsigned editorial in a newspaper**

  "Environmental Rules at Risk." Editorial. *Chattanooga Times Free Press,* 30 Apr. 2009,
  p. B6.

  "As Fire Spread, So Did the Confusion." Editorial. *The Denver Post*, 5 Apr. 2012,
  www.denverpost.com/opinion/ci_20327457/editorial-fire-spread-so-did-confusion.

- **A review in a newspaper**

  Lozada, Carlos. "Reggie Love on Life as Obama's `Chief of Stuff.'" Review of *Power
  Forward: My Presidential Education,* by Reggie Love, *The Washington Post*,
  29 Jan, 2015, www.washingtonpost.com/news/book-party/wp/2015/01/29/
  reggie-love-on-life-as-obamas-chief-of-stuff.

- **A letter to the newspaper**

  Byrd, Charles. Letter. *The Gazette* [Denver], 10 Jan. 2012, p. A10.

- **An article in a periodical publication in an online database**

  Webb, Allen. "Digital Texts and the New Literacies." *The English Journal,* vol. 97,
  no. 1, Sept. 2007, pp. 83–88. *JSTOR*, doi: 10.2307/30047213.

Electronic Sources

Beyond Books and Periodicals

The purpose of a citation for an electronic source is the same as that for printed matter:
identification of the source and the best way to locate it. All citations basically name the

author and the work and identify publication information. Citations for various types of electronic sources, however, must also include different kinds of additional information to help researchers locate the sources in the easiest way.

It's important to remember, too, that forms of electronic sources continue to change rapidly. As technology expands, new ways of documenting electronic sources must also be created. The problem is further complicated by the fact that some sources will not supply all the information you might like to include in your citation. In these cases, you simply have to do the best you can by citing what is available.

Before looking at the sample citations given here, you should be familiar with the following information regarding addresses and reference markers in online sources. If you include the URL, place it as the location element. Copy the full URL as seen in a Web browser, but omit *http://* or *https://*. Conclude with a period. If you must divide a URL at the end of a line, break it only after a slash mark. Do not use a hyphen at the break, as this will distort the address. URLs are often long and easy to misread, so take extra time to ensure that you are copying them correctly. Do not use a URL shortening service such as bit.ly.

Important note: Many online databases and some online library catalogs now include a persistent link or URL to their records; use this link in your citations for online works. Whenever it is available, use a DOI (preceded by "doi:") rather than a URL.

- **An article in a nonperiodical online publication**

    Some works on the Web are classified as "nonperiodical publications" because they are not released on a regular schedule (i.e., weekly or monthly). Also within this group are Web sites sponsored by newspapers and magazines, which can post updated revisions after the original print version as well as reporters' blogs written only for the Web site.

    Cohen, Elizabeth. "Five Ways to Avoid Germs While Traveling." *CNN.com*, Cable News Network, 27 Nov. 2008, www.cnn.com/2008/HEALTH/11/27/ ep.avoid.germs.traveling/index.html?iref=newssearch.

    Neary, Lynn. "Did Shakespeare Want to Suppress His Sonnets?" *Morning Edition*, National Public Radio, 20 May 2009, www.npr.org/templates/story/story.php? storyId=104317503.

- **An online government document**

    Ellis, Donna, et al., editors. *Ralph Ellison Papers, 1890–2005*. Lib. of Cong., Aug. 2011, lccn.loc.gov/mm96083111.

    Because a wide variety of government agencies issue publications, citing them can become complicated. For specific information, consult the *MLA Handbook*.

- **A personal or professional Web site**

    In citing Web sites, begin with the name of the person who created the site, if appropriate. If no name is given, begin with the title of the work (italicized if the work is independent; in quotation marks if the work is part of a larger work). Next, provide the title of the overall Web site (italicized), if it is different from the title of the work.

"Humanities and Fine Arts." *Chattanooga State Community College*, www.chattanoogastate.edu/humanities-fine-arts. Accessed 16 Feb. 2016.

Hollmichel, Stefanie. *So Many Books*. 2003–16, somanybooksblog.com.

- **An e-mail communication**

   Begin with the writer's name, followed by the title from the subject line, enclosed in quotation marks with its capitalization standardized. Follow this with the recipient and date of message.

   Carroll, Jean. "Family Celebration." Received by Leti Carpenter, 12 Feb. 2015.

- **A podcast (online audio recording)**

   Fogarty, Mignon. "Parallel Structure: Patterns Are Pleasing." *Grammar Girl's Quick and Dirty Tips for Better Writing*, episode 463, 24 Apr. 2015, www.quickanddirtytips.com/education/grammar/ parallel-structure-patterns-are-pleasing.

- **An online posting on a blog, discussion board, etc.**

   Kastrenakes, Jacob. "NASA's Seemingly Impossible Space Engine Looks More Possible After Latest Test." *The Verge*, Vox Media, 30 Apr. 2015, www.theverge.com/ 2015/4/30/8521691/nasa-seemingly-impossible-space-drive-test-succeeds.

- **A Tweet**

   Begin with the Twitter user name and the message within quotation marks (without change in punctuation or capitalization). Follow with *Twitter* (in italics), both the date and time (reflecting the reader's time zone), and the location.

   @persiankiwi. "We have report of large street battles in east & west of Tehran now - #Iranelection." *Twitter*, 23 June 2009, 11:15 a.m., twitter.com/persiankiwi/ status/2298106072.

Other Sources

Encyclopedias, Pamphlets, Dissertations

- **A signed article in an encyclopedia (full reference)**

   Collins, Dean R. "Light Amplifier." *McGraw-Hill Encyclopedia of Science and Technology*. Edited by Justin Thyme, McGraw-Hill, 1997. 3 vols.

   Use full publication information for reference works, such as encyclopedias and dictionaries, unless they are familiar and often revised. Volume and page numbers are not needed if the information is in alphabetical order. Another optional element is information about the total number of volumes in a multivolume work, placed at the end of the entry.

- **An unsigned article in a well-known encyclopedia**

   "Sailfish." *Encyclopedia Britannica*, 15th ed., 2010.

- **A pamphlet**

   Young, Leslie. *Baby Care Essentials for the New Mother*. Hall, 2012.

   Atlanta Builders Association. *Have Confidence in Your Builder*. Brown, 2009.

- **A government document**

  United States, National Institute on Drug Abuse. *Drug Abuse Prevention*. Government Printing Office, 2008.

- **An unpublished dissertation or thesis**

  Harmon, Gail A. "Poor Writing Skills at the College Level: A Program for Correction." U of Colorado, 2012. Dissertation.

Films, Television, Radio, Performances, Recordings

If you are referring to the contribution of a particular person associated with the performance, put that person's name first.

- **A film**

  Angelina Jolie, director. *Unbroken*. Performance by Jack O'Connell and Takamasa Ishihara, Universal, 2014.

- **A television or radio show**

  Antiques Roadshow. PBS, 1997–2016.

  "Lost in Translation." *NCIS*, directed by Tony Wharmby, performance by Mark Harmon, Michael Weatherly, Pauley Perrett, Sean Murray, Emily Wickersham, Rocky Carroll, Brian Dietzen, and David McCallum, season 12, episode 21, CBS, 14 Feb. 2015.

  Weeks, Linton. "Lincoln's Private Side: Friend, Poet, Jokester." *All Things Considered*, National Public Radio, 14 Apr. 2015.

  Yost, Peter, director. "Invisible Universe Revealed." *NOVA*, narrated by Jay O. Sanders, PBS, 22 Apr. 2015.

- **Performance (plays, concerts, ballets, operas)**

  Messiah. By George Frideric Handel, conducted by Laurie Redmer Minner, performance by Julie Penner, Martha Boutwell, Michael Kull, and Brett Hyberger, 1 Apr. 2009, Collegedale Church of Seventh-day Adventists, Collegedale, TN.

  Hassevoort, Darrin, conductor. "Rhapsody in Blue." By George Gershwin, performance by Alan Nichols, 17 May 2015, Chattanooga Symphony Orchestra, Tivoli Theatre, Chattanooga.

- **A sound recording**

  Celtic Woman. *The Greatest Journey: Essential Collection*. Performance by Chloe Agnew, Orla Fallon, Lynn Hilary, Lisa Kelly, Meav Ni Mhaolchatha, Mairead Nesbitt, and Alex Sharpe, Manhattan Records, 2008.

  You may cite an entire sound recording (with its title italicized) or a specific song (with its title in quotation marks).

Letters, Lectures, and Speeches

- **An unpublished letter, archived**

  Steinbeck, John. Letter to Elizabeth R. Otis. 11 Nov. 1944, Steinbeck Collection, Stanford U Lib., Stanford.

- **A lecture, speech, or other oral presentation**

    Dippity, Sarah N. "The Importance of Prewriting." CLASS Convention, 15 Feb. 2015,
    President Hotel, Colorado Springs. Keynote speech.

    Start with the speaker's name and, if known, the title of the presentation (in quotation marks). Conclude with the delivery format (e.g., Address, Lecture, Reading), neither italicized nor in quotation marks.

Interviews

- **A broadcast or published interview**

    Cardillo, Kenneth. "Increasing Humanities Offerings." Interview by Tim Dills,
    Chattanooga Times Free Press, 23 Apr. 2015, p. D3.

    Cite the person interviewed first and the title of the interview, if any. Use the word "Interview" (neither italicized nor in quotation marks) if the interview has no title. The interviewer's name may be added if relevant.

- **A personal interview**

    Payne, Linda. Telephone interview. 13 Apr. 2015.

    Give the name of the person interviewed, the kind of interview, and the date.

Visual Arts (Paintings, Sculptures, Photographs)

Green, Jon. *Alaskan Landscape.* 1972, Indianapolis Museum of Art, Indianapolis.

State the artist's name, the name of the work, its date of completion (use N.d. if the year is unknown). Identify both the institution (or private collection) that houses the work and the city in which it is located.

Advertisements

Klondike. Advertisement. *Better Homes and Gardens,* May 2015, p. 21.
Universal Studios Florida. Advertisement. WRCB, 30 Apr. 2015.

Practicing What You've Learned

Collaborative Activity: Increase your understanding of documentation styles and practice your editing skills by exchanging your MLA Works Cited page with a classmate. Using the sample entries on the appropriate pages of this chapter, check the accuracy of the forms on the page. Circle any errors you see, but do not correct the problems. Use both the feedback you give and receive as encouragement to proofread your own documentation carefully several more times.

APA Style

The American Psychological Association (APA) recommends a documentation style for research papers in the behavioral and social sciences.* Your instructors in psychology and sociology classes, for example, may prefer that you use the APA form when you write essays for them.

If you are using APA style in an academic paper, put your work's title, your name, the school's name and the department, the instructor's name, the course name and section number, and the assignment due date on a title page, numbered as page 1. If required by your instructor, you would, on page 2, include an *abstract*, a short summary of your research, which can state your reason for undertaking this topic, your research methods, and your findings and conclusions. The essay itself begins on page 2, or if you have included an abstract, on page 3. Include the page number in the top right corner of each page, and if your instructor requires it, include a shortened version (maximum 50 characters) of the essay's title in uppercase letters in the top left corner of all pages. Some papers using APA style also include headings to identify major sections ("Methods," "Results") or key points in the discussion.

APA style also includes guidelines for bias-free language. By using language free of bias, writers ensure that their treatment of groups and individuals is fair. Avoid use of any language that demeans or discriminates, and strive to use accurate, inclusive language at all times. To do this, describe people and groups with an appropriate level of specificity and be sensitive to labels. For example, specify age by saying "groups of adolescents aged 15–17," rather than "groups of teenagers," and be specific and avoid a biased label by referring to "those diagnosed with dyslexia and dysgraphia," rather than to "those with intellectual disabilities." For details, see https://apastyle.apa.org/style-grammar-guidelines/bias-free-language.

The APA style is similar to the MLA style in that it calls for parenthetical documentation within the essay itself, although the information cited in the parentheses differs slightly from that presented according to the MLA format. For example, you will note that in the APA style the date of publication follows the author's last name and precedes the page number in the parentheses. Instead of a Works Cited page, the APA style uses a References page at the end of the essay to list those sources cited in the text. In some instances, your instructor might prefer that you include a Bibliography page, which differs from the References page by listing all works that were consulted. Another important difference concerns capitalization of book and article titles in the reference list: in the MLA style, the first letter of each important word is capitalized, but in the APA style, only proper names, the first word of titles, and the first word appearing after a colon are capitalized.

APA Citations in Your Essay

Here are some guidelines for using the APA parenthetical form within your paper:

1. APA style typically calls for an "author, publication year" method of citation, with the name and date inserted in the text at an appropriate place in the reference.

---

*If you wish a more detailed description of the APA style, consult the *Publication Manual of the American Psychological Association*, 7th ed. (Washington, DC: American Psychological Association, 2020); your school's library probably has a copy. The most up-to-date documentation forms may be found on the APA Web site at https://apastyle.apa.org.

Examples   A later study (Jones, 2012) found no discernible differences in the absentee rate of men and women students on the main campus.

Jones (2012) contrasted the absentee rates of men and women students on the main campus but found no discernible differences.

2. When you are quoting directly, the parenthetical citation includes the page number and follows the quoted material. Note that in APA style, you place commas between the items in the parentheses, and you do include the "p." and "pp." abbreviations for "page" and "pages" (these are omitted in MLA style).

Example   One crucial step in developing an anti-social personality may, in fact, be "the experience of being caught in some act and consequently being publicly labeled as a deviant" (Becker, 2008, p. 31).

3. If you give credit to the author or authors in your sentence, you need give only the date and the page number in parentheses. Note that the publication date follows directly after the name of the author.

Example   According to Green (2006), gang members from upper-class families are rarely convicted for their crimes and are "almost never labeled as delinquent" (p. 101).

4. If you are citing a work with two authors, use "&" (an ampersand) between their names, for example, (Ekman & Friesen). If you are citing a work with more than two authors, use only the first author's last name and "et al." (which means "and others").

Example   Almost half of all the poor households in America today are headed by single women, most of whom are supporting a number of children (Bird et al., 2012, p. 285).

5. If you cite a work that has a corporate or other group author, cite the group responsible for producing the work.

Example   In contrast, the State Highway Research Commission (2012) argues, "The return to the sixty-five-miles-an-hour speed limit on some of our state's highways has resulted in a decrease in traffic fatalities" (p. 3).

6. Private interviews, e-mail messages, and other personal communications should be referred to in your text but *not* in your reference list. Provide the initials and last name of the communicator, the words "personal communication," and the date in your paper.

Example   Sierra Club leader C. L. Byrd confirmed that the fall trip to Cinque Terre would be September 15, 2015 (personal communication, January 18, 2015).

Compiling a Reference List: APA Style

If you are using the APA style, at the end of your essay you should include a page labeled References—a formal listing of the sources you cited in your essay. Arrange the entries alphabetically by the authors' last names; use initials for the authors' first and middle names. All authors' names are inverted (Forst, M. L, & Hall, S. L.). Note that with two to

20 authors, all the authors are included and an ampersand (&) appears before the last author. If a work has more than 20 authors, APA lists the first 19 followed by an ellipsis and the last author's name, omitting the customary ampersand (&). If there are two or more works by one author, list them chronologically, beginning with the earliest publication date. If an author published two or more works in the same year, the first reference alphabetically is designated "a," the second "b," and so on (Feinstein 2012a; Feinstein 2012b). Double-space each entry and between each one. Lines subsequent to the first are indented one-half inch.

Remember in APA style, you italicize book and journal titles, volume numbers, and their associated punctuation, but you do not put the names of articles in quotation marks. Although you do capitalize the major words in the titles of magazines, newspapers, and journals, you do not capitalize any words in the titles of books or articles except the first word in each title, the first word after a colon or dash, and all proper names. Use the full names of publishers, including the words "Books" and "Press," but omit terms such as "Co." or "Inc."

The Parts of a Reference List Entry

Below, you'll find a sample APA entry for an article in an online journal with a DOI (digital object identifier). (For an explanation of DOIs, see page 453 in this chapter.) This sample entry is intended to represent the general format used in APA entries.

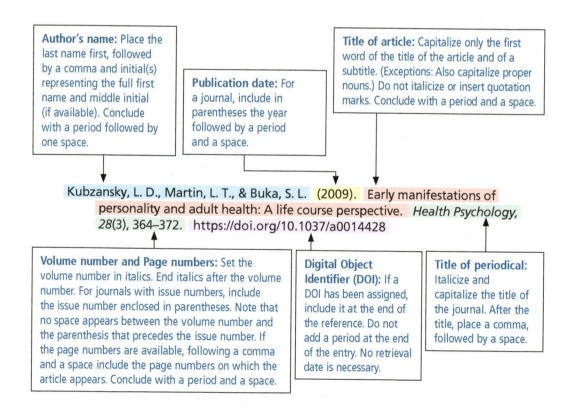

Author's name: Place the last name first, followed by a comma and initial(s) representing the full first name and middle initial (if available). Conclude with a period followed by one space.

Publication date: For a journal, include in parentheses the year followed by a period and a space.

Title of article: Capitalize only the first word of the title of the article and of a subtitle. (Exceptions: Also capitalize proper nouns.) Do not italicize or insert quotation marks. Conclude with a period and a space.

Kubzansky, L. D., Martin, L. T., & Buka, S. L. (2009). Early manifestations of personality and adult health: A life course perspective. *Health Psychology,* *28*(3), 364–372. https://doi.org/10.1037/a0014428

Volume number and Page numbers: Set the volume number in italics. End italics after the volume number. For journals with issue numbers, include the issue number enclosed in parentheses. Note that no space appears between the volume number and the parenthesis that precedes the issue number. If the page numbers are available, following a comma and a space include the page numbers on which the article appears. Conclude with a period and a space.

Digital Object Identifier (DOI): If a DOI has been assigned, include it at the end of the reference. Do not add a period at the end of the entry. No retrieval date is necessary.

Title of periodical: Italicize and capitalize the title of the journal. After the title, place a comma, followed by a space.

Sample Reference List Entries: APA Style

Please note: The *Publication Manual of the American Psychological Association* (seventh edition) provides many examples illustrating APA format for references. APA advises writers to choose the example most like the source in question and to follow that format, offering as much useful information as possible. Checking the APA style Web site (https://apastyle.apa.org) may also prove helpful.

Index of APA Reference List Entries

Books (Print)

- **A book with one author**

    Isaacson, W. (2007). *Einstein: His life and universe.* Simon & Schuster.

- **A book with two authors**

    Forst, M. L., & Blomquist, M. (1991). *Missing children: Rhetoric and reality.* Lexington Books.

- **Books by one author published in the same year**

    Hall, S. L. (2012a). *Attention deficit disorder.* Bald Mountain Press.

    Hall, S. L. (2012b). *Taming your adolescent.* Morrison Books.

- **A book with an editor**

    Banks, A. S. (Ed.). (1988). *Political handbook of the world.* CSA.

- **A chapter from a book with an editor**

    Newcomb, T. M. (1958). Attitude development as a function of reference groups: The Bennington study. In E. Maccoby, T. M. Newcomb, & E. L. Hartley (Eds.), *Readings in social psychology* (pp. 10–12). Holt, Rinehart & Winston.

- **A book with a corporate author**

    Mentoring Group. (1997). *The new mentors and protégés: How to succeed with the new mentoring partnerships.*

    If the corporate author is also the publisher, the name is given only as the author and is not repeated.

- **A reference book**

    Rothman, B. K. (Ed.). (1993). *Encyclopedia of childbearing: Critical perspectives.* Oryx Press.

- **One volume in a multivolume work**

    Venegas, L. (Ed.). (2010). *The principles of animation: A beginner's guide* (Vol. 2). Neman & Hartham.

- **Several volumes in a multivolume work**

    Gregor, T. (Ed.). (2007). *Great thinkers throughout history* (Vols. 1–3). Seville.

- **A translation**

    Zamora, M. (1990). *Frida Kahlo: The brush of anguish* (M. S. Smith, Trans.). Chronicle Books.

- **A reprint**

    Herrera, H. (2002). *Frida: A biography of Frida Kahlo.* Perennial-Harper. (Original work published 1983)

Articles (Print)

APA reference entries for articles in print periodicals (journals, magazines, newspapers, newsletters) follow a pattern similar to that used for books. The author is followed by the date of publication (in parentheses). Note that journals include only the year; magazines and newspapers include the complete date. Do not abbreviate names of months. Next is the article's title, capitalizing the first word and any proper nouns. Then provide the periodical's name and volume number, italicized. If there is also an issue number, place the issue number in parentheses immediately following the volume number. Do not use "p." with page numbers. Unlike MLA style, numbers are not clipped in APA style (e.g., APA prefers 360–378, while MLA favors 360–78).

- **An article in a journal**

> Morrison, G. B., & Byers, B. D. (2007). Criminal justice career fairs: Addressing recruiting challenges through practitioner and academic collaboration. *Law Enforcement Journal, 7*(5), 107–124.

- **A signed article in a magazine**

> Halverson, N. (2009, May). Home gardening: Therapy for the heart and mind. *Today's Gardener, 25*(5), 22–31.

> Khatchadourian, R. (2015, January 19). We know how you feel. *The New Yorker, 90*(44), 50–59.

> Note that the Halverson entry refers to a monthly publication, while the Khatchadourian entry refers to a weekly publication.

- **An unsigned article in a magazine**

> Reduce the risk of breast cancer. (2011, September 1). *Wellness Magazine, 37,* 14–17.

- **A signed article in a newspaper**

> Gascay, G. (2009, June 19). Strong winds, hail damage crops in three counties. *The Athens Eagle,* C1.

> Note the inclusion of the newspaper's entire title as it appears on the masthead.

- **An unsigned article in a newspaper**

> City unveils plans for tourist information center. (2009, May 21). *The Central Courier,* D2, D10–D11.

> If an article is not printed on consecutive pages (for example, if the article begins on page D2, continues on page D10, and concludes on page D11), provide all page numbers with discontinuous numbers separated by a comma and a space.

- **An unsigned editorial**

> Replace bridge is best plan. [Editorial]. (2015, June 2). *Crieff Courier,* C5.

Reference Books, Reports, Dissertations

- **An unsigned article in encyclopedia or reference book**

> Society of Clinical Psychology. (2012). Bullying. In A. Young (Ed.), *Encyclopedia of clinical psychology.* (2nd ed., Vol. 1, pp. 66–69).

- **A corporate or government authored report or document**

  National Oceanic and Atmospheric Administration. (2018). *Ocean acidification research to product development workshop September 2018* (NOAA Technical Memorandum OAR OAP 2). U.S. Department of Commerce.

- **An unpublished dissertation or thesis**

  Wilson, L. M. (2010). *Professional growth and job satisfaction in early career special education teachers* [Unpublished doctoral dissertation]. Arizona State University, Phoenix.

Audio-Visual Media (Films, Television, Radio, Recordings, Artwork)

List the artist or contributor in the author position, using a descriptive word in parentheses to identify the particular role, such as writer or director. Use brackets to enclose the medium, such as film, TV series, or video.

- **A film**

  Lupin, R. J. (Director). (2007). *The red wolf* [Film]. Spotlight Pictures.

- **An episode from a television or radio series**

  Davies, R. (Writer), & Harper, G. (Director). (2006). Doomsday (Season 2, Episode 13) [TV series episode]. In P. Collinson (Producer), *Doctor Who*. British Broadcasting.

  To cite a particular episode, list the writer and director in the author position, and put the producer in the editor position.

- **A music recording**

  Heap, I. (2005). Hide and seek [Song]. On *Speak for yourself*. White Rabbit Recordings.

- **An artwork**

  Carpenter, L. (Artist). (1910). *Country brook* [Watercolor]. Hazel Collection, Texarkana, TX, United States.

  Place the medium (oil, etching, photograph, etc.) in brackets, and identify the location of the artwork (city, state, country, as appropriate, following the name of the museum, private collection, gallery, etc.).

Letters, Lectures, Speeches, and Archived Interviews

- **Letter, private collection**

  Merrill, A. (2012, February 2). [Letter to Jane Wheeler]. Copy in possession of Jane Wheeler.

- **Collection of letters, archived**

  Shulz, E. M. (1983–1994). *Correspondence*. Elizabeth M. Shulz Papers, Green University Archives, Silverton, VT, United States.

- **A speech or presentation**

  Harsin, P. J. (2012, May). *Red Feather Lakes living* [Paper presentation]. Northern Colorado Realtors, Loveland, CO United States.

- **Unpublished papers, lectures**

  Ullman, D. (1999). *Taking action on homelessness and hunger lecture notes.* Daisy Ullman Memoirs (Box L 12), Archives of the Social Work Association, University of Oklahoma, Norman, OK, United States.

- **An interview recorded, archived**

  Scott, J. M. (1972, November 1). *Interview by K. J. Bolin* [Tape recording]. Arts Oral History Project, Peabody Institution, Archives of European Art, Washington, DC, United States.

Electronic Sources: APA Style

As with print versions of periodicals, APA guidelines for citing electronic versions of periodicals differ considerably from MLA methods. Most sources that are available electronically have a DOI (digital object identifier); APA guidelines specify including the DOI if it is available. Publishers who participate in the DOI system assign each publication a unique alphanumeric sequence intended to provide a persistent link to its location on the Internet. To help you recognize a DOI, understand that it begins with a "10" and is often placed on the first page of the article, near the copyright notice.

If the DOI is available, include it in the citation at the location indicated in the following examples. Because the DOI is extremely long, try to copy and paste the DOI for accuracy. Present it as a hyperlink, beginning with "https://doi.org/" as in the example. If you use the DOI, no further retrieval information (such as the URL) is necessary to identify or locate the content.

If the DOI is not available, the APA prefers that you include the URL of the work you are citing. As with DOIs, begin with "https://" or "http://" so readers have a hyperlink.

Do not conclude DOIs or URLs with a period (to avoid confusion that it is part of the DOI or URL).

For more about APA guidelines related to electronic citations, visit the APA Web site at https://apastyle.apa.org.

- **An ebook**

  Walker, M. (2017). *Why we sleep: Unlocking the power of sleep and dreams.* Scribner. https://www.amazon.com/Why-We-Sleep-Unlocking-Dreams/dp/1501144316

  The publishing information, as in the example, will generally be the same as for the print book.

- **A signed entry in an online reference work**

  Brownlee, K. (2007). Civil disobedience. In E. N. Zalta (Ed.), *The Stanford encyclopedia of philosophy* (Winter 2013 ed.). Stanford University. https://plato.stanford.edu/archives/win2013/entries/civil-disobedience/

- **An article in an online journal with DOI**

  > Kubzansky, L. D., Martin, L. T., & Buka, S. L. (2009). Early manifestations of personality and adult health: A life course perspective. *Health Psychology, 28*, 364–372. https://doi.org/10.1037/a0014428

- **A signed article in an online magazine**

  > Lu, Stacy. (2015, February). Erasing bad memories. *Monitor on Psychology, 46*(2). https://www.apa.org/monitor/2015/02/bad-memories

- **An unsigned article in an online magazine**

  > Spend a year working for the federal government. (2014, September). *Monitor on Psychology, 45*(8). https://www.apa.org/monitor/2014/09/upfront-government

- **Non-periodical Web pages/Web documents**

  > Benen, S. (2015, February 9). *Watching an emergency room close.* MSNBC. www .msnbc.com/rachel-maddow-show/watching-emergency-room-close

- **An article in an online newspaper**

  > Kirkpatrick, N. (2015, February 9). See the difference a little rain makes during California's drought. *The Washington Post.* https:// www.washingtonpost.com/news/morning-mix/wp/2015/02/09/ see-the-difference-a-little-rain-makes-during-californias-drought/

  > Psencik, K. (2013, May 29). How much do college students care about online privacy? *USA Today.* https://www.usatoday.com/story/news/nation/2013/05/29/ college-students-online-privacy-debate/2369941/

- **A review of a book, retrieved online**

  > Peterson, B. (2015, February 3). Do no pass go, do not collect $200 [Review of the book *The Monopolists*, by M. Pilon]. *Slate.* https://www.slate.com/ culture/2015/02/mary-pilons-the-monopolists-a-history-of-the-game-monopoly- reviewed.html

- **Social media**

  Podcast episode:

  > Werth, C. (Host). (2015, January 22). Someone else's acid trip (No. 193) [Audio podcast episode]. In *Freakonomics radio.* WYNC. https://freakonomics.com/podcast/ someone-elses-acid-trip-a-new-freakonomics-radio-podcast/

  Facebook post:

  > Soutar, M. (2015, February 9). *Looking forward to GMHG in July. Hope to see you there* [Status update]. Facebook. https://facebook.com/megansoutar/ posts/10294818299020294923

  Twitter tweet:

  > Vaughn, D. (2015, January 17). Kale might be healthy for the body, but it takes more than a spoonful of sugar to make that medicine [Tweet]. Twitter. https://twitter.com/DanVaughn/status/72193483727840503492834

  For the title of a tweet or other social media post, include up to the first 20 words of the post.

YouTube video:

> Scrovegni1305. (2010, November 20). *St. Peter's Basilica: A look at the grandest church in the world* [Video]. YouTube. https://www.youtube.com/watch?v=1D3tUrzr5SM

Footnote and Bibliography Form

Most research papers today use a parenthetical documentation style, as illustrated in the MLA and APA sections of this chapter. However, in the event you face a writing situation that calls for use of traditional footnotes and bibliography page, here is a brief description of one version of that format. This section will also help you understand the citation system of older documents you may be reading, especially those using Latin abbreviations.

If you are writing a paper using this format, each idea you borrow and each quotation you include must be attributed to its author(s) in a footnote that appears at the bottom of the appropriate page.* Number your footnotes consecutively throughout the essay (do not start over with "1" on each new page), and place the number in the text to the right of and slightly above the end of the passage, whether it is a direct quotation, a paraphrase, or a summary. Place the corresponding superscript number, indented one-half inch, before the note at the bottom of the page. Single-space each entry, and double-space after each footnote if more than one appears on the same page. Once you have provided a first full reference, subsequent footnotes for that source may include only the author's last name and page number. (See the examples that follow. Please note that today many word-processing programs include a function for formatting footnotes.)

You may notice the use of Latin abbreviations in the notes of some documents, such as "ibid." ("in the same place") and "op. cit." ("in the work cited"). In such documents, "ibid." indicates the same author's name, title, and publication information as in the preceding footnote; there will be a new page number only if the reference differs from the one in the previous footnote. Writers use "op. cit." with the author's name to substitute for the title in second and subsequent references.

In the Bibliography at the end of the document, sources are listed by author in alphabetical order (or by title if no author is given). The first lines are flush left; subsequent lines are indented a half-inch.

First footnote reference

[5]Garrison Keillor, *Leaving Home* (Viking, 1987), 23.

---

*Some documents use endnotes that appear in a list on a page immediately following the end of the essay, before the bibliography page.

Next footnote

⁶Keillor, 79.   or   ⁶*Ibid.*, 79.

Later reference

¹²Keillor, 135.

Bibliographic entry

Keillor, Garrison. *Leaving Home*. Viking, 1987.

Using Supplementary Notes

Sometimes when writers of research papers wish to give their readers additional information about their topic or about a particular piece of source material, they include *supplementary notes*. If you are using the MLA or APA format, these notes should be indicated by using a superscript number in your text (The study seemed incomplete at the time of its publication.²). The explanations appear on a page called "Notes" that precedes the Works Cited page (MLA) or "Footnotes" that follows the References page (APA); APA style also allows footnotes at the bottom of the page where the relevant superscript occurs. If you are using traditional footnote form, simply include the supplementary notes in your list of footnotes at the bottom of the page or in the list of endnotes following your essay's conclusion.

Supplementary notes can offer a wide variety of additional information.

Sample Notes Page Using MLA Style

Tavares 8

Notes

1. For a different interpretation of this imagery, see Spiller 63-67.

2. Simon and Brown have also contributed to this area of investigation. For a description of their results, see *Report on the Star Wars Project* 98-102.

3. It is important to note here that Brown's study followed Smith's by at least six months.

4. Later in his report Carducci himself contradicts his earlier evaluation by saying, "Our experiment was contaminated from the beginning" (319).

Use supplementary notes only when you think the additional information would be truly valuable to your readers. Obviously, information critical to your essay's points should go in the appropriate body paragraphs. (◆ See pages 455–456 for additional examples.)

Sample Student Essay Using MLA Style

Here is the result of Gabriela Guerrera's research on pervasive computing technology and its role in our lives. As you read this essay, evaluate its effectiveness: does Gabriela successfully support her thesis? Point out major strengths and any weaknesses you see. If you wanted more information on pervasive computing technology, how might Gabriela's sources help you begin your search?

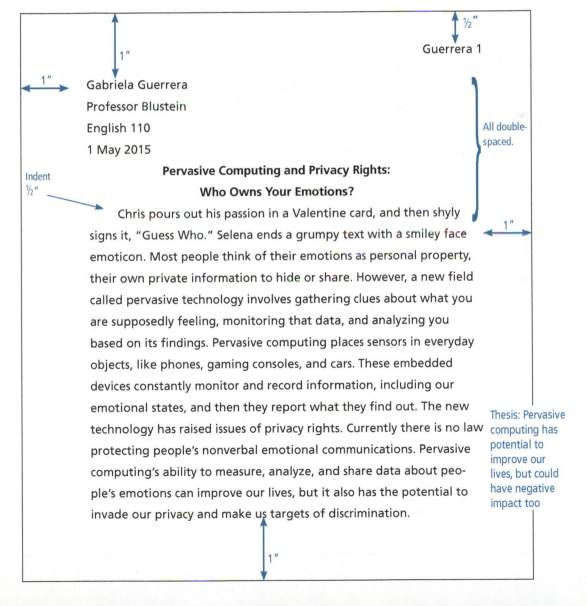

½"

Guerrera 1

1"

1"

Gabriela Guerrera

Professor Blustein

English 110

1 May 2015

All double-spaced.

Indent ½"

Pervasive Computing and Privacy Rights:
Who Owns Your Emotions?

Chris pours out his passion in a Valentine card, and then shyly signs it, "Guess Who." Selena ends a grumpy text with a smiley face emoticon. Most people think of their emotions as personal property, their own private information to hide or share. However, a new field called pervasive technology involves gathering clues about what you are supposedly feeling, monitoring that data, and analyzing you based on its findings. Pervasive computing places sensors in everyday objects, like phones, gaming consoles, and cars. These embedded devices constantly monitor and record information, including our emotional states, and then they report what they find out. The new technology has raised issues of privacy rights. Currently there is no law protecting people's nonverbal emotional communications. Pervasive computing's ability to measure, analyze, and share data about people's emotions can improve our lives, but it also has the potential to invade our privacy and make us targets of discrimination.

1"

Thesis: Pervasive computing has potential to improve our lives, but could have negative impact too

1"

Widespread
use of affective
computing
technology

Although most of us are not aware of its presence, pervasive computing is here to stay, thanks to advances in affective computing technology. The term *affective* means "relating to emotions." An affective computer program detects a user's facial expression, heart rate, and other physical signals. The program then interprets these signals as emotions and responds to them in ways the software developer has decided are appropriate for the situation. For example, it might "see" a user's confused expression through a webcam lens and adjust its behavior to create a more satisfying situation for the user, almost like the seemingly warm and caring computer operating system named Samantha in the 2013 film *Her*. Current affective computing technology has been used to gather data about users' nonverbal communications in a variety of fields, including education, such as monitoring how students respond to e-learning lessons, and psychology, such as helping people track their moods.

Ekman's FACS
database

Internal
reference to
graphic

Pervasive computing is recent, but the theory behind it that gives it credibility draws from the 1960s research of psychologist Paul Ekman, who studied the facial expressions of men and women of different ages and cultures. He asked people to identify emotions in pictures of faces and concluded that people across cultures recognize six emotions: anger, disgust, fear, happiness, sadness, and surprise (see fig. 1). Each emotion has its own facial expression. Fear, for example, equals raised eyebrows, raised upper eyelids, tensed lower eyelids, and a stretched mouth. Ekman added many more expressions to his list, including amusement, confusion, guilt, and relief. His huge database of facial expressions is called the Facial Action Coding System (FACS). The database is so popular that it "is used today by everyone from TSA screeners to animators trying to imbue their characters with more realistic facial expressions" (Miller).

Guerrera 3

Starting in the mid 1990s, Ekman's FACS database became the basis of computer programs that analyzed facial expressions. Researchers like computer scientist Rosalind Picard, a professor at the M.I.T. Media Laboratory, experimented with software that set up an interactive relationship with users by responding to their facial expressions, body movements, heart rates, and muscle tension. For example, one of her experimental programs could sense excitement through how tightly the user squeezed a mouse that measured electrical pulses in the skin, and then alter its response to the user based on what it thought he or she was feeling. Picard's work showed that all kinds of physical signals, not just facial expressions, could be used to interpret user emotions (Khatchadourian 52, 54).

Picard's research

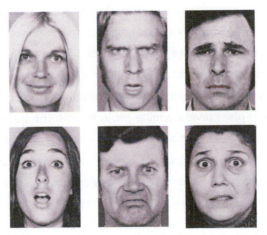

Fig. 1. The facial expressions associated with the six basic emotions identified by psychologist Paul Ekman. Top row, left to right, happiness, anger, sadness; bottom row, left to right, surprise, disgust, fear. Eckman, Paul, and Wallace V. Friesen. *Unmasking the Face: A Guide to Recognizing Emotions from Facial Expressions*. Malor, 2003.

Kaliouby's
research

Picard's colleague at the M.I.T. Media Laboratory, Rana el Kaliouby, saw how affective computing could help people who had trouble recognizing feelings. She developed a so-called emotional aid for people with autism that helped them understand the physical reactions people give off during polite conversation. (People with autism or Asperger's often have trouble noticing social cues and get hung up on talking about favorite subjects others might not relate to.) The emotional aid, which was a mini computer, camera, and earpiece the person wore, would speak to the person with autism and suggest changing the subject when a listener looked bored (Khatchadourian 54).

Emotient's
app used for
marketing

Unfortunately, software developers using affective computing began to turn away from the goal of helping people communicate better. Today's research emphasizes using affective computing for marketing, by analyzing viewers' emotional reactions to advertisements in order to sell more products. A specific instance of this is found in an app designed to help salespeople interpret shoppers' expressions. If this app gains popularity, however, the app's designer (Emotient) plans several similar projects, with the stated aim of becoming the "sentiment analytics engine for 'any connected device with a camera'" (Lunden). Because many people feel uncomfortable when they are observed or recorded, it will be interesting to note if users of this app consider it so annoying that they delete it. Monitoring the success of this app and watching for Emotient's other projects should prove interesting.

Awareness is
important.

Thus, affective computing has been used both to help people with problems and to gather information for profit. Whether the applications are beneficial or manipulative, however, we should be fully aware that we are being monitored. That way, we have the choice to opt out. Unfortunately, with the increasingly common

Guerrera 5

presence of pervasive computing in our lives, it is becoming more difficult for us to protect our privacy rights. That's because pervasive computing devices are easy to take for granted. Consumers might buy the devices willingly, eager to be monitored so that they can have a personalized experience such as being offered product choices or experiences tailored to their tastes. But they might realize that the devices they have brought home are constantly connected and actively recording everything they do. In his investigation, Khatchadourian found that Verizon has drafted plans for a media console featuring a variety of sensors, including a microphone and thermographic camera.

> By scanning a room, the system could determine the occupants' age, gender, weight, height, skin color, hair length, facial features, mannerisms, what language they spoke, and whether they had an accent. It could identify pets, furniture, paintings, even a bag of chips. It could track "ambient actions": eating, exercising, reading, sleeping, cuddling, cleaning, playing a musical instrument. It could probe other devices—to learn what a person might be browsing on the Web, or writing in an e-mail. It could scan for affect, tracking moments of laughter or argument. All of this data would then shape the console's choice of TV ads. A marital fight might prompt an ad for a counselor. Signs of stress might prompt ads for aromatherapy candles. (58)

While some might consider this technology an intrusion into the home, others could view it as an advance in effective marketing. Could all of these tasks be accomplished through an app some day?

Author's name is mentioned in introduction, so citation requires only page number.

Indent left margin additional 1/2" for a quotation of more than four lines.

Maintain 1" right margin indentation.

Double-space

Citation appears after concluding punctuation.

Guerrera 6

One of the most disturbing concerns inherent to pervasive computing is that it uses affective computing technology to read us—accurately or not—without our even noticing. Any new technology we buy could come with sensors that stay on all the time, and we might not be aware of it. This already became issue in 2013 with the Microsoft Xbox One Kinect 2 motion sensor, which used facial recognition to sign in players. Many users didn't understand that their faces, voices, bodies, and actions were being monitored by Microsoft until the company provided, after the fact, a privacy statement to explain what kind of data the Kinect 2 could collect and how it would be used. According to Evan Shamoon in *Rolling Stone*, "Even when your Xbox One is off, the Kinect is still listening, watching and waiting" (Shamoon).

Pervasive computing devices that track our emotions without our permission or understanding pose a genuine problem because we often don't know what will happen to that data after it is gathered. As Picard notes, "Most people will want to retain control over who has access to their expressive information" (123). Even if we agree to participate in a study, we might be horrified if our personal information became public. Think about sitting in a classroom while your instructor gives a boring lecture. You allow your emotional engagement to be measured as you daydream, flirt with the person next to you, and finally fall asleep. Would you like it if your professor then shared that data, labeling you as an unmotivated student? It could happen if you are not part of the decision-making process when it comes to how your personal emotional data is used.

In reporting the findings of their investigation, Jeremy Pitt and Arvind Bhusate point out the privacy issues surrounding pervasive computing: "On the down-side, there is a real risk of privacy invasion if emotions, behaviours, and even intentions are recorded and subject to the same [privacy] rules as telephone calls . . ." (168). Unfortunately,

Affective computing technology in Microsoft Xbox One

Concerns about how data will be used

Author's name is mentioned in the sentence, so only the page number is necessary in citation

Additional privacy concerns

Guerrera 7

this problem doesn't have a clear solution because laws about sharing private information stored on the Internet have not caught up with the reality of affective computing. Although the Electronic Communication Act of 1986 addresses Internet privacy, it is certainly outdated, considering the changes that the Internet has seen in the past three decades—even the past three months. As a recent newspaper editorial points out, "Congress hasn't significantly updated federal privacy law since the Electronic Communications Privacy Act passed 28 years ago, leaving private communications online far less protected than telephone conversations, mail or paper documents stored in an office file drawer" ("Editorial").

If we consider the value of pervasive computing apart from any concerns about privacy rights, we notice clear advantages. Pervasive computing can help society. Embedded devices that sense our motions can help ensure our safety on the road, for example, alerting us if we fall asleep at the wheel. Similarly, using affective computing technology to improve our psychological health by providing feedback about our emotions is also beneficial. Even pervasive computing applications that simply give us satisfying experiences aren't harmful in themselves, as long as we know what is happening. If we agree to the process, the detection of emotion itself isn't an invasion of privacy; the problem lies in recording and sharing it without our permission.

Advantages to pervasive computing

With respect to our privacy rights, pervasive computing can be discriminatory. As Picard notes, too much awareness of someone's emotions holds the potential for alarming consequences:

Potential disadvantages

> As you give computers access to your affective bits, the opportunity arises for someone, somewhere, to know something about your feelings, and possibly to try to control them. . . . One can imagine some malevolent dictator requiring people to wear emotion "meters" of some sort, to monitor their fun, for example. (123)

Guerrera 8

Although it could remind you of a scene in a futuristic novel, it might not be so unlikely, if people don't inform themselves about the pros and cons of pervasive technology.

Potential misuse of this technology in collecting data

Companies involved in pervasive computing are aware of the privacy issues. Affectiva's Rana el Kaliouby says that she objects when clients tell her that they want to collect data about people's emotions without their consent. "When we first started Affectiva, some of our early customers said, 'We don't want to tell people they're being recorded because either they'll opt out or it'll affect their experiences.' We're always adamant that they tell people up front and people have to sign a consent form" (Bosker). While Affectiva's stance is commendable, users cannot rely on the maker of the technology to enforce their rights; instead, we should take an active role in informing ourselves and speaking out about the issue. According to journalist Katey Psencik, by the time computer users hit college age, they expect to have the freedom to use the Internet and social media without exposing their private and personal data. Clearly, college students expect privacy protection when it comes to pervasive computing as well.

Conclusion: Pervasive computing offers distinct advantages, but users must be aware of potential hazards.

In conclusion, pervasive computing has its benefits, but it can also endanger our privacy. It can expose feelings we prefer to keep private, and it can expose us to judgments that are not accurate or taken out of context. The best way to make sure that we deal with pervasive computing in a way that helps us rather than hurts us is to learn more. We should investigate the data-gathering process of any pervasive computing device or program we interact with, investigate how and when it is shared, and consider how it can affect our lives. If companies don't provide this information, we should demand it. Then we can make informed decisions about whether to opt out of the process. Remember, our private lives, including our feelings, belong to us.

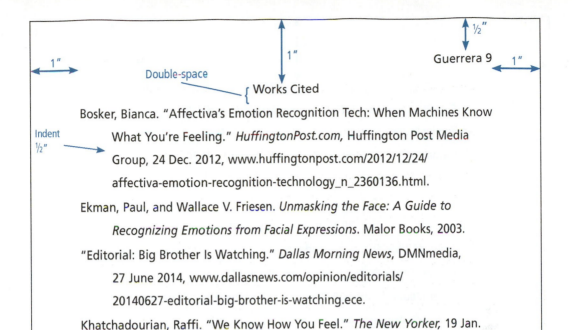

½"

1"

Double-space

1"

1"

{ Works Cited

Bosker, Bianca. "Affectiva's Emotion Recognition Tech: When Machines Know

Indent
½"

What You're Feeling." *HuffingtonPost.com,* Huffington Post Media

Group, 24 Dec. 2012, www.huffingtonpost.com/2012/12/24/

affectiva-emotion-recognition-technology_n_2360136.html.

Ekman, Paul, and Wallace V. Friesen. *Unmasking the Face: A Guide to*

Recognizing Emotions from Facial Expressions. Malor Books, 2003.

"Editorial: Big Brother Is Watching." *Dallas Morning News*, DMNmedia,

27 June 2014, www.dallasnews.com/opinion/editorials/

20140627-editorial-big-brother-is-watching.ece.

Khatchadourian, Raffi. "We Know How You Feel." *The New Yorker,* 19 Jan.

2015, pp. 50–59.

Lunden, Ingrid. "Emotient Raises $6M for Facial Expression Recognition Tech,

Debuts Google Glass Sentiment Analysis App." *TechCrunch.com,* AOL, 6

Mar. 2014, techcrunch.com/2014/03/06/emotient-raises-6m-for-its-facial-

expression-recognition-tech-debuts-sentiment-analysis-app-for-google-

glass/.

Miller, Greg. "This Computer Can Tell When People Are Faking Pain."

Wired.com, Condé Nast, 20 Mar. 2014, www.wired.com/2014/03/

computer-vision-facial-expressions/.

Picard, Rosalind W. *Affective Computing.* MIT P, 1997.

Pitt, Jeremy, and Arvind Bhusate. "Privacy in Pervasive and Affective

Computing Environments." *Information Communication Technology*

Law, Protection and Access Rights: Global Approaches and Issues,

edited by Irene Maria Portela and Maria Manuela Cruz-Cunha, IGI

Global, 2010, pp. 168–87. *Google Book Search,* books.google.com/

books?id= IWa-AQAAQBAJ&lpg=PR14&ots=pcVnkfKjYY&dq=

1"

1"

Some instructors prefer that students do not include location URLs because long URLs can clutter a work's cited list. Follow each instructor's directions for URL citation.

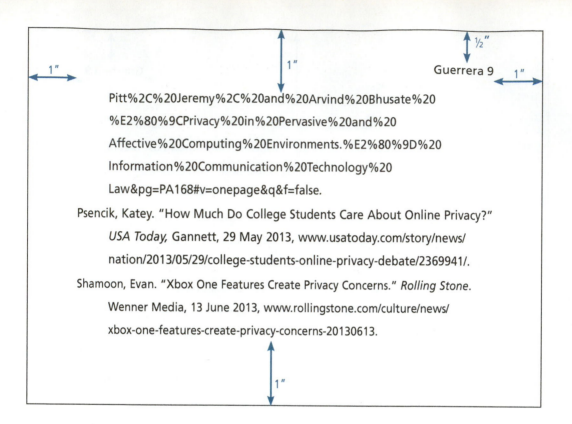

Pitt%2C%20Jeremy%2C%20and%20Arvind%20Bhusate%20
%E2%80%9CPrivacy%20in%20Pervasive%20and%20
Affective%20Computing%20Environments.%E2%80%9D%20
Information%20Communication%20Technology%20
Law&pg=PA168#v=onepage&q&f=false.

Psencik, Katey. "How Much Do College Students Care About Online Privacy?"
USA Today, Gannett, 29 May 2013, www.usatoday.com/story/news/
nation/2013/05/29/college-students-online-privacy-debate/2369941/.

Shamoon, Evan. "Xbox One Features Create Privacy Concerns." *Rolling Stone.*
Wenner Media, 13 June 2013, www.rollingstone.com/culture/news/
xbox-one-features-create-privacy-concerns-20130613.

Sample Student Essay Using APA Style

To illustrate the differences between MLA and APA documentation styles, here is the student essay from the previous pages rewritten to show the most current APA guidelines for in-text citations and a References page. This assignment also includes an abstract, which appears on page 2.

As you read this essay, evaluate its effectiveness: does Gabriela successfully support her thesis? Point out major strengths and any weaknesses you see. If you wanted more information on pervasive computing technology, how might Gabriela's sources help you begin your search?

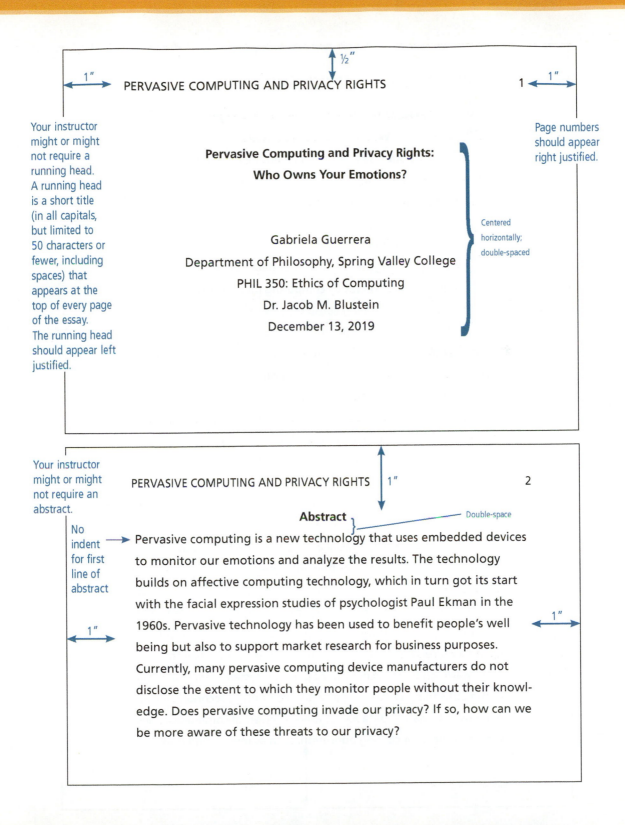

½"

1"   1"

Your instructor might or might not require a running head. A running head is a short title (in all capitals, but limited to 50 characters or fewer, including spaces) that appears at the top of every page of the essay. The running head should appear left justified.

Pervasive Computing and Privacy Rights:
Who Owns Your Emotions?

Gabriela Guerrera
Department of Philosophy, Spring Valley College
PHIL 350: Ethics of Computing
Dr. Jacob M. Blustein
December 13, 2019

Page numbers should appear right justified.

Centered horizontally; double-spaced

Your instructor might or might not require an abstract.

1"

Abstract   Double-space

No indent for first line of abstract

1"

Pervasive computing is a new technology that uses embedded devices to monitor our emotions and analyze the results. The technology builds on affective computing technology, which in turn got its start with the facial expression studies of psychologist Paul Ekman in the 1960s. Pervasive technology has been used to benefit people's well being but also to support market research for business purposes. Currently, many pervasive computing device manufacturers do not disclose the extent to which they monitor people without their knowledge. Does pervasive computing invade our privacy? If so, how can we be more aware of these threats to our privacy?

1"

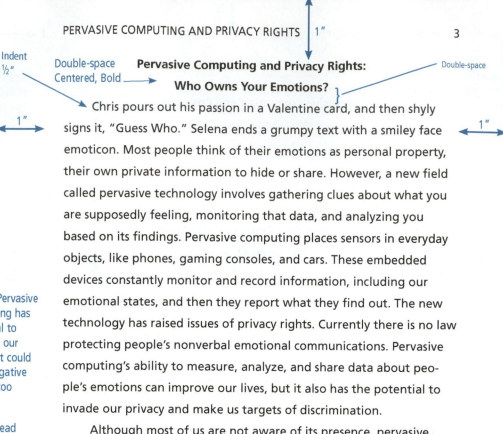

Indent ½"

Double-space Centered, Bold

Double-space

Pervasive Computing and Privacy Rights: Who Owns Your Emotions?

1"

Chris pours out his passion in a Valentine card, and then shyly signs it, "Guess Who." Selena ends a grumpy text with a smiley face emoticon. Most people think of their emotions as personal property, their own private information to hide or share. However, a new field called pervasive technology involves gathering clues about what you are supposedly feeling, monitoring that data, and analyzing you based on its findings. Pervasive computing places sensors in everyday objects, like phones, gaming consoles, and cars. These embedded devices constantly monitor and record information, including our emotional states, and then they report what they find out. The new technology has raised issues of privacy rights. Currently there is no law protecting people's nonverbal emotional communications. Pervasive computing's ability to measure, analyze, and share data about people's emotions can improve our lives, but it also has the potential to invade our privacy and make us targets of discrimination.

1"

Thesis: Pervasive computing has potential to improve our lives, but could have negative impact too

Widespread use of affective computing technology

Although most of us are not aware of its presence, pervasive computing is here to stay, thanks to advances in affective computing technology. An affective computer program (*affective* relates to emotions) detects a user's facial expression, heart rate, and other physical signals. The program then interprets these signals as emotions and responds to them in ways the software developer has decided are appropriate for the situation. For example, it might "see" a user's confused expression through a webcam lens and adjust its behavior to create a more satisfying situation for the user, almost like the seemingly warm and caring computer operating system named Samantha in the 2013 film *Her*. Current affective computing technology has been used to gather data about users' nonverbal communications in a variety of fields, including education, such as monitoring how

1"

PERVASIVE COMPUTING AND PRIVACY RIGHTS   4

students respond to e-learning lessons, and psychology, such as helping people track their moods.

Pervasive computing is recent, but the theory behind it that
gives it credibility draws from the 1960s research of psychologist Paul
Ekman. Ekman studied the facial expressions of men and women of
different ages and cultures. He asked people to identify emotions in
pictures of faces and concluded that people across cultures recognize
six emotions: anger, disgust, fear, happiness, sadness, and surprise
(see Figure 1). Each emotion has its own facial expression. Fear, for
example, equals raised eyebrows, raised upper eyelids, tensed lower
eyelids, and a stretched mouth. Ekman added many more expressions to his list, including amusement, confusion, guilt, and relief. His
huge database of facial expressions is called the Facial Action Coding
System (FACS). The database is so popular that it "is used today by
everyone from TSA screeners to animators trying to imbue their characters with more realistic facial expressions" (Miller, 2014, para. 6).

Figure 1 *Ekman's Universal Facial Expressions*

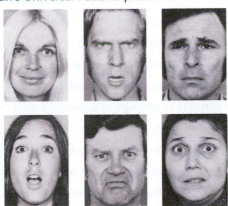

Note. The facial expressions associated with the six basic emotions
identified by psychologist Paul Ekman. Top row, left to right, happiness, anger, sadness; bottom row, left to right, surprise, disgust, fear.

Ekman's FACS
database

Internal
reference to
graphic

PERVASIVE COMPUTING AND PRIVACY RIGHTS   5

Picard's
research

Starting in the mid 1990s, Ekman's FACS database became the basis of computer programs that analyzed facial expressions (Khatchadourian, 2015, p. 52). Researchers like computer scientist Rosalind Picard, a professor at the M.I.T. Media Laboratory, experimented with software that set up an interactive relationship with users by responding to their facial expressions, body movements, heart rates, and muscle tension (Khatchadourian, 2015, p. 54). For example, one of her experimental programs could sense excitement through how tightly the user squeezed a mouse that measured electrical pulses in the skin, and then alter its response to the user based on what it thought they were feeling (Khatchadourian, 2015, p. 54). Picard's work showed that all kinds of physical signals, not just facial expressions, could be used to interpret user emotions.

Kaliouby's
research

Picard's colleague at the M.I.T. Media Laboratory, Rana el Kaliouby, saw how affective computing could help people who had trouble recognizing feelings (Khatchadourian, 2015, p. 54). She developed a so-called emotional aid for people with autism that helped them understand the physical reactions people give off during polite conversation (Khatchadourian, 2015, p. 54). This is because some people with autism may not notice some social cues easily. The emotional aid, which was a mini computer, camera, and earpiece the person wore, would speak to the person with autism and suggest changing the subject when a listener looked bored (Khatchadourian, 2015, p. 54).

Unfortunately, software developers using affective computing began to turn away from the goal of helping people communicate better. Today's research emphasizes using affective computing for marketing, by analyzing viewers' emotional reactions to advertisements in order to sell more products. A specific instance of this is

PERVASIVE COMPUTING AND PRIVACY RIGHTS   6

found in an app designed to help salespeople interpret shoppers'
expressions. If this app gains popularity, however, the app's designer
(Emotient) plans several similar projects, with the stated aim of
becoming the "sentiment analytics engine for 'any connected device
with a camera'" (Lunden, 2014, para. 2). Because many people feel
uncomfortable when they are observed or recorded, it will be interesting
to note if users of this app consider it so annoying that they delete it.
Monitoring the success of this app and watching for Emotient's other
projects should prove interesting.

Thus, affective computing has been used both to help people
with problems and to gather information for profit. Whether the applications are beneficial or manipulative, however, we should be fully
aware that we are being monitored. That way, we have the choice
to opt out. Unfortunately, with the increasingly common presence
of pervasive computing in our lives, it is becoming more difficult for
us to protect our privacy rights. That's because pervasive computing
devices are easy to take for granted. Consumers might buy the devices
willingly, eager to be monitored so that they can have a personalized
experience such as being offered product choices or experiences tailored to their tastes. But they might not realize that the devices they
have brought home are constantly connected and actively recording
everything they do. In his investigation, Khatchadourian (2015) found
that Verizon has drafted plans for a media console featuring a variety
of sensors, including a microphone and thermographic camera.

> By scanning a room, the system could determine the occupants'
> age, gender, weight, height, skin color, hair length, facial features,
> mannerisms, what language they spoke, and whether they had an
> accent. It could identify pets, furniture, paintings, even a bag of
> chips. It could track "ambient actions": eating, exercising, reading,
> sleeping, cuddling, cleaning, playing a musical instrument. It could

Emotient's app used for marketing

Awareness is important.

Indent 1/2" from left margin a quotation of 40 words or more.

Do not insert quotation marks

For long quote, citation appears after concluding punctuation.

probe other devices—to learn what a person might be browsing on the Web, or writing in an e-mail. It could scan for affect, tracking moments of laughter or argument. All of this data would then shape the console's choice of TV ads. A marital fight might prompt an ad for a counselor. Signs of stress might prompt ads for aroma-therapy candles. (p. 58)

Citation requires only page number because author and pub date are in lead-in sentence.

While some might consider this technology an intrusion into the home, others could view it as an advance in effective marketing. Could all of these tasks be accomplished through an app someday?

Affective computing technology in Microsoft Xbox One

One of the most disturbing concerns inherent to pervasive computing is that it uses affective computing technology to read us—accurately or not—without our even noticing. Any new tech-nology we buy could come with sensors that stay on all the time, and we might not be aware of it. This already became issue in 2013 with the Microsoft Xbox One Kinect 2 motion sensor, which used facial recognition to sign in players. Many users didn't understand that their faces, voices, bodies, and actions were being monitored by Microsoft until the company provided, after the fact, a privacy state-ment to explain what kind of data the Kinect 2 could collect and how it would be used. According to Evan Shamoon in *Rolling Stone*, "Even when your Xbox One is off, the Kinect is still listening, watching and waiting" (2013, para. 4).

Author's name is mentioned in the sentence, so only the date is necessary in citation.

Pervasive computing devices that track our emotions without our permission or understanding pose a genuine problem because we often don't know what will happen to that data after it is gathered. As Picard (1997) notes, "Most people will want to retain control over who has access to their expressive information" (p. 123). Even if we agree to participate in a study, we might be horrified if our personal information became public. Think about sitting in a classroom while

Concerns about how data will be used

your instructor gives a boring lecture. You allow your emotional engagement to be measured as you daydream, flirt with the person next to you, and finally fall asleep. Would you like it if your professor then shared that data, labeling you as an unmotivated student? It could happen if you are not part of the decision-making process when it comes to how your personal emotional data is used.

In reporting the findings of their investigation, Jeremy Pitt and Arvind Bhusate (2010) point out the privacy issues surrounding pervasive computing: "On the down-side, there is a real risk of privacy invasion if emotions, behaviours, and even intentions are recorded and subject to the same [privacy] rules as telephone calls" (p. 168). Unfortunately, this problem doesn't have a clear solution because laws about sharing private information stored on the Internet have not caught up with the reality of affective computing. Although the Electronic Communication Act of 1986 addresses Internet privacy, it is certainly outdated, considering the changes that the Internet has seen in the past three decades—even the past three months. As a recent newspaper editorial points out, "Congress hasn't significantly updated federal privacy law since the Electronic Communications Privacy Act passed . . . leaving private communications online far less protected than telephone conversations, mail or paper documents stored in an office file drawer" (Editorial, 2014, para. 2).

Additional privacy concerns

If we consider the value of pervasive computing apart from any concerns about privacy rights, we notice clear advantages. Pervasive computing can help society. Embedded devices that sense our motions can help ensure our safety on the road, for example, alerting us if we fall asleep at the wheel. Similarly, using affective computing technology to improve our psychological health by providing feedback about our emotions is also beneficial. Even pervasive computing applications that simply give us satisfying experiences aren't harmful in themselves,

Advantages to pervasive computing

as long as we know what is happening. If we agree to the process, the detection of emotion itself isn't an invasion of privacy; the problem lies in recording and sharing it without our permission.

Potential disadvantages

With respect to our privacy rights, pervasive computing can be discriminatory. As Picard (1997) notes, too much awareness of someone's emotions holds the potential for alarming consequences:

> As you give computers access to your affective bits, the opportunity arises for someone, somewhere, to know something about your feelings, and possibly to try to control them. . . . One can imagine some malevolent dictator requiring people to wear emotion "meters" of some sort, to monitor their fun, for example. (p. 123)

Although it could remind you of a scene in a futuristic novel, it might not be so unlikely, if people don't inform themselves about the pros and cons of pervasive technology.

Potential misuse of technology in collecting data

Companies involved in pervasive computing are aware of the privacy issues. Rana el Kaliouby says that she objects when clients tell her that they want to get data about people's emotions without their consent. "When we first started Affectiva, some of our early customers said, 'We don't want to tell people they're being recorded because either they'll opt out or it'll affect their experiences.' We're always adamant that they tell people up front and people have to sign a consent form" (Bosker, 2012, para. 22). While Affectiva's stance is commendable, users cannot rely on the maker of the technology to enforce their rights; instead, we should take an active role in informing ourselves and speaking out about the issue. According to journalist Katey Psencik (2013), by the time computer users hit college age, they expect to have the freedom to use the Internet and social media without exposing their private and personal data. Clearly, college students expect privacy protection when it comes to pervasive computing as well.

PERVASIVE COMPUTING AND PRIVACY RIGHTS   10

     In conclusion, pervasive computing has its benefits, but it can also endanger our privacy. It can expose feelings we prefer to keep private, and it can expose us to judgments that are not accurate or are taken out of context. The best way to make sure that we deal with pervasive computing in a way that helps us rather than hurts us is to learn more. We should investigate the data-gathering process of any pervasive computing device or program we interact with, investigate how and when it is shared, and consider how it can affect our lives. If companies don't provide this information, we should demand it. Then we can make informed decisions about whether to opt out of the process. Remember, our private lives, including our feelings, belong to us.

Conclusion: Pervasive computing offers distinct advantages, but users must be aware of potential hazards.

Centered ——————**References** } —————— Double-space

Indent ½″

Bosker, B. (2012, December 24). Affectiva's emotion recognition tech: When machines know what you're feeling. *HuffPost.* https://www.huffpost .com/entry/affectiva-emotion-recognition-technology_n_2360136

1″

Ekman, P., & Friesen W. V. (2003). *Unmasking the face: A guide to recognizing emotions from facial expressions.* Major Books.   1″

Editorial: Big Brother is watching [Editorial]. (2014, June 27). *The Dallas Morning News.* https://www.dallasnews.com/opinion/editorials/ 2014/06/27/editorial-big-brother-is-watching/

Khatchadourian, R. (2015, January 19). We know how you feel. *The New Yorker, 90*(44), 50–59.

Lunden, I. (2014, March 6). Emotient raises $6M for facial expression recognition tech, debuts Google Glass sentiment analysis app. *TechCrunch.* https://techcrunch.com/2014/03/06/emotient-raises-6m-for-its-facial-expression-recognition-tech-debuts-sentiment-analysis-app-for-google-glass/

Miller, G. (2014, March 20). This computer can tell when people are faking pain. *Wired.* https://www.wired.com/2014/03/computer-vision-facial-expressions/

Picard, R. W. (1997). *Affective Computing.* MIT Press.

When available, include the DOI.

Pitt, J., & Bhusate, A. (2010). Privacy in pervasive and affective computing environments. In I. Portela & M. Cruz-Cunha (Eds.), *Information communication technology law, protection and access rights: Global approaches and issues* (pp. 168–187). IGI Global. https://doi .org/10.4018/978-1-61520-975-0.ch011

Psencik, K. (2013, May 29). How much do college students care about online privacy? *USA Today.* https://www.usatoday.com/story/news/ nation/2013/05/29/college-students-online-privacy-debate/2369941/

If no DOI is available, include the URL

Shamoon, E. (2013, June 13). Xbox One features create privacy concerns. *Rolling Stone.* https://www.rollingstone.com/culture/culture-news/ xbox-one-features-create-privacy-concerns-90317/

1″

Chapter 21

Classroom Writing: Exams, Timed Essays, and Presentations

In-class writing assignments call for good writing skills, analytical reading skills, and confidence. When you write essays out of class, you have the luxury of time: you can mull over your ideas, talk about them with friends or classmates, prewrite, plan, revise, or even start over if you wish. Because essay assignments written in class must be planned and composed on the spot under the pressure of a time limit, they may induce anxiety in some students. (One composition-class student characterized his feelings of terror this way: "I felt like a slug caught in a sudden salt storm!") But never fear: this chapter will refresh what you already know about writing the short essay and will offer advice to help you learn to analyze quickly the demands of the task you face, which should substantially reduce your anxiety level. With practice, you may discover that in-class writing assignments are not nearly as threatening as you may have once thought.

This chapter also gives advice for preparing another kind of in-class activity: presentations, in a variety of formats, to your classmates of your written work, research, or drafts in progress. Learning to adapt your out-of-class writing for in-class delivery is an extremely valuable skill—one that you may find useful throughout your academic or professional career whenever you are called upon to speak about your ideas.

Let's first address writing in class with some general suggestions about facing a variety of timed examinations and essays, with specific attention then focused on the "summary-response" essay assignment frequently included in composition courses.

Steps to Writing Well Under Pressure

Consider these steps as you prepare for an in-class writing assignment.

1. First, **clarify for yourself the kind of task you face**. Sometimes your instructor will tell you about the assignment's format or general design in advance. Other times, however, figuring out the demands of the assignment on the spot and following the instructions carefully will be part of the task itself. Understanding the kind of exam or essay question you face will help you plan your response and boost your confidence. Here are some common formats for in-class assignments that call for your writing skills:

- **Short-answer exam questions**

Your instructor might give an exam that asks you to write a well-developed paragraph or two to identify, define, or explain a term or idea. For example, a political science instructor might ask for paragraphs explaining the importance of certain treaties or laws; a literature teacher might ask for paragraphs that explain the significance of certain lines, characters, or symbols in a particular work; a science instructor might ask for extended definitions of important biological terms, and so on. The paragraph skills you learned in Chapter 3—focus, development, unity, and coherence—are all relevant here.

- **Essay exam questions**

Frequently, questions appear on exams that call for more detailed discussion of specific material studied in a course. An essay question on a history exam might ask you to "Explain the major causes of the Civil War." Or in biology you might be asked to "Trace a drop of blood on its circulatory journey from the human heart throughout the body." You would be expected to shape your answer into a multiparagraph essay developed clearly in an easy-to-follow organizational pattern.

- **"Prompted" essays**

Perhaps the most common in-class assignment in composition classes asks students to respond thoughtfully to some *prompt*—that is, students are asked to give their own opinion about a specific topic presented in a written passage or question, such as "Do you think teenage consumers are too influenced by social media?" Other times, students will be asked to read a quotation or proverb ("All that glitters is not gold") and then respond in a personal essay. Other prompts include a statement of a current controversy (students should/should not be assessed a special fee for athletics on this campus) or the description of a hypothetical problem (the developer of a discount superstore has applied for a building permit on the edge of a wildlife preserve). Each student is responsible for explaining and supporting his or her position on the topic presented by the prompt.

- **Summary-and-response essays**

Some in-class essays ask students to do more than voice their opinions in response to a short prompt. One common assignment is known as the *summary-and-response* essay or the *summary-reaction* essay. Students first read an essay by a professional writer (the reading may be done either in or out of class, depending on the instructor's preference). Once in class, students write an essay that begins with a clear summary of the essay they have just read (an activity that demonstrates analytical reading abilities), and then they present a reasoned argument that agrees or disagrees with the professional essay's ideas. Summary-and-response essays are often used as entrance or exit exams for composition classes at many schools throughout the country because they allow students to display critical thinking and both reading and writing skills. Because the summary-and-response essay is so frequently assigned today, additional discussion, illustrated by a student paper, is provided on pages 487–492 of this chapter.

There are numerous kinds and combinations of essay exams and in-class writing assignments. You can best prepare yourself mentally if you know in advance the purpose and format of the writing task you will face. If possible, ask your instructor to clarify the nature of your assignment before you come to class to write. (Also, some teachers allow students to bring dictionaries, outlines, or notes to class, but others don't. Consult your instructor.)

2. **Arrive prepared.** Before class, determine what items you need to take to respond to your writing assignment. For example, do you need loose paper or an exam book, or will paper or a computer be provided? (If you are writing on your own notebook paper, always bring a paper clip or, better, one of those mini-staplers to fasten your pages together.) Were you asked to bring a copy of a reading or essay questions that were handed out in advance? Are dictionaries permitted? Notes? Always try to bring some sort of clock or watch to help you gauge your writing time. If you must provide your own pen, bring several, and carry extra paper as well. Having adequate supplies on hand keeps you from rustling around to borrow from your neighbors, which not only costs you valuable minutes but also disturbs the other writers around you. In addition, speaking to your classmates, especially during an examination, may be erroneously perceived as scholastic dishonesty. To avoid all such problems, bring the right tools to class.

Perhaps this is also a good place to say a little more about classroom atmosphere. Students often complain about their classmates' annoying behaviors during in-class writing assignments or examinations. Repeated pen-clicking, gum snapping, or chair kicking can make life miserable for other writers in the room. Empty soda cans noisily clanking down aisles, musical cell phones, beeping watches, and even crinkling candy wrappers can distract and derail someone else's complex thought. Please be *courteous*: leave the snack bar at home, spit out that gum, and turn off all electronic equipment.

One more piece of advice: many in-class writing situations are "closed door." That is, at the appointed time for the class or exam to begin, the door is closed and no one is permitted to enter late. Consequently, try to arrive at least five minutes early, in case your instructor's clock is faster than yours but also to have the extra minutes to settle yourself mentally as well as physically. ("Closed door" may also mean that no one is permitted to leave and return to the room during the writing session, even for restroom trips, so think carefully about that extra cup of coffee or can of soda just before your class.)

3. Once you are in class ready to write, **read the entire assignment with great care**. First, underline or highlight *key words* that are important to the subject matter of your essay; then circle the *directional words* that give you clues to the primary method of development you might use to organize your response.

Example   Explain the effects of the Triangle Shirtwaist Factory fire on child-labor laws in America from 1912 to 1915.

Example   In *The Grapes of Wrath*, John Steinbeck criticizes the unfair treatment of farm workers by California land owners. Illustrate this criticism with three examples from the novel.

To help you identify some of the frequently used directional words and understand the approaches they suggest, study the following chart.

Directional Word or Phrase	Suggested Method of Development
Illustrate . . . Provide examples of . . . Show a number of . . . Support with references to . . .	Example
Explain the steps . . . Explain the procedure . . . Outline the sequence of . . . Trace the events . . . Review the series of . . . Give the history of . . .	Process or Narration
Discuss the effects of . . . Show the consequences of . . . Give the reasons for . . . Explain why . . . Discuss the causes of . . . Show the influence of . . .	Causal Analysis
Compare the following . . .* Contrast the positions of . . .* Show the differences between . . . Discuss the advantages and disadvantages . . . Show the similarities among . . . Relate X to Y . . .	Comparison/Contrast
Describe the following . . . Re-create the scene . . . Discuss in detail . . . Explain the features of . . .	Description
Agree or disagree . . . Defend or attack . . . Offer proof . . . Present evidence . . . Criticize . . . Evaluate . . . State reasons for . . . Justify your answer . . . What if . . .	Argument

*Remember that the directional word "compare" may indicate a discussion of both similarities and differences; the directional word "contrast" focuses only on the differences.

Discuss the types of . . .
Show the kinds of . . .   } Classification/Division
Analyze the parts of . . .
Classify the following . . .

Define . . .
Explain the meaning of . . .   } Definition
Identify the following . . .
Give the origins of the term . . .

Note that essay questions may demand more than one pattern of development in your response:

> Explain the meaning of the term "hospice" and show the differences between the Hospice Movement in Great Britain and that in the United States. [definition and contrast]

> Discuss Weber's three types of authority, giving examples of societies that illustrate each type. [classification and example]

> Explain President Truman's reasons for dropping H-bombs on Japanese cities during World War II, and then defend or attack Truman's decision. [causal analysis and argument]

Learning to quickly recognize key directional words will help you organize as you begin to focus your essay. Always read the assignment at least twice and ask your instructor for clarification if some part of the assignment seems confusing to you.

4. Once you have read and fully understood the purpose and direction of your assignment, **prepare to write**. The following advice may be helpful:

   - Think positively: remind yourself that the task you face is not unknown to you. You are being asked to write—yes, quickly—the same kind of essay that you have been practicing in your composition class. You *CAN* do this!

   - If you are writing an in-class essay, take the first few minutes to think and plan. Many times it's helpful to formulate a thesis in a direct rephrasing of the exam question or "prompt" you have been assigned. For example:

   Assignment: After reading "How to Make People Smaller Than They Are" by Norman Cousins, write an essay agreeing or disagreeing with Cousins's suggestions for improving higher education today.

   Thesis: In his essay "How to Make People Smaller Than They Are," author Norman Cousins convincingly argues for requiring additional liberal arts courses for all students in college today. His suggestions for improving higher education are uniformly excellent and should be implemented immediately.

Assignment: Discuss Weber's three types of authority, giving examples to clarify your answer.

Thesis: Weber's three types of authority are traditional authority, charismatic authority, and legal authority. The three types may be exemplified, respectively, by the nineteenth-century absolute monarchs of Europe, by a variety of religious groups, and by the constitutional government of the United States.

- After deciding on your thesis, jot down a brief plan or outline that sketches out the main points that will appear in the body of your essay. You might scribble a few key words to remind yourself of the supporting evidence or important details you will use. Don't get too bogged down in detailed outlining—just use enough words to help you stay on track.

- You might also budget your time now—thinking "by 2:30 I should be done with two points in my discussion." Although such figuring is approximate at best, having a general schedule in mind might keep you from drifting or spending too much time on the first parts of your essay. In most cases, you should assume you will not be able to write a rough draft of your essay and then have the time to massively reorganize as you recopy it.

5. As you **begin writing**, remember what you have learned about paragraphing, topic sentences, and supporting evidence. If you have been given multiple tasks, be sure that you are responding to all parts of the assignment. If the assignment asks you to present your own opinion, focus your answer accordingly. In timed-writing situations, you can't take on the world, but you can offer intelligent commentary on selected ideas. If you have only an hour or less to complete your essay, consider aiming for three well-developed points of discussion. You may be writing a rather conventional five-paragraph essay, but such a clear pattern of organization frequently works best when nervous writers are under pressure and time is short.

Stockbyte/SuperStock

Two more suggestions:

- If you are writing by hand, it may be a good idea to compose on one side of your paper only, leaving wide margins on both sides; consider, too, leaving extra lines between paragraphs. If you discover that you have time after finishing your essay, you might wish to add additional information to your exam answer or perhaps another persuasive example to a body paragraph. Leaving plenty of blank spaces will allow you to insert information neatly instead of jamming in handwriting too small for your instructor to decipher.

- If you are writing an essay (rather than a short answer), try to conclude in a satisfactory way. Your conclusion may be brief, but even a few sentences are better than an abrupt midsentence halt when time runs out.

6. In the time remaining after writing the complete draft of your essay, **read what you have written**. Aim for sufficient, appropriate content and clear organization. Insert, delete, or make changes neatly. Once you are reasonably satisfied with the essay's content and flow, take a few minutes to proofread and edit. Although most instructors do not expect an in-class essay to be as polished as one written out of class, you are responsible for the best spelling, grammar, and punctuation you can muster under the circumstances. Take care to apply what you know to sentence problems, especially the run-ons, comma splices, and twisted predicates that tend to surface when writers are composing in a hurry. After all, information too deeply hidden in a contorted sentence is information that may not be counted in your favor.

7. **Concluding tips: If you have handwritten your work,** be sure your name is on every page of your essay or exam so your instructor will know the correct person to praise for a job well done. Include other pertinent information, such as your course name and class section, as appropriate. Always number and clip or staple the loose pages of your essay or exam (do *not* rely on folded corners to hold your pages together!).

Problems to Avoid

Misreading the assignment. Always read the directions and the assignment completely and carefully before you start prewriting. Mark key and directional words. Do you have multiple tasks? Consider numbering the tasks to avoid overlooking any parts. Important choices to make if given options? Perhaps neatly put a line through or bracket the options you don't want. Misreading your assignment may give you as much chance at success as a pig at a barbecue.

Incomplete essay. Don't begin writing an in-class essay without a plan, even if you are excited about the topic and want to dive right in. Having a plan and budgeting your time accordingly will avoid the common problem of not finishing, which, in the end, may cost you dearly. Don't allow yourself to ramble off on a tangent in one part of the assignment. Stay focused on your plan and complete the entire essay or exam. If you are handwriting your assignment and have left blank space as described previously, you can return to a part of the essay to add more information if time permits. Consult your clock or watch regularly; don't depend on a classmate or your instructor to advise you of the time remaining.

Composition amnesia. Writing essays under time pressure causes some students suddenly to forget everything they ever knew about essay organization. This memory loss often wreaks havoc on paragraphing skills, resulting in a half-dozen one- and two-sentence string-bean paragraphs without adequate development; at other times, it results in one long super-paragraph that stretches for pages before the eye like the Mojave Desert; no relief or rest stop in sight. Emphasize your good ideas by presenting them in a recognizable organizational structure, just as you would do in an out-of-class assignment.

Gorilla generalizations. Perhaps the biggest problem instructors find is the lack of adequate, specific evidence to explain or support shaggy, gorilla-sized generalities roaming aimlessly through students' essays. If, for example, you argue, "Team sports are good for kids because they build character," *why* do you believe this? What particular character traits do you mean? Can you offer a personal example or a hypothetical case to clarify and support your claim? ◆ Remember what you learned in Chapter 3 about using evidence—examples, personal experience, testimony—to illustrate or back up any general claims you are making. Your goal is to be as clear and persuasive as you can be—*show* what you know!

Practicing What You've Learned

Underline the key words and circle the directional words or phrases in the following assignments. What pattern(s) of development are suggested in each assignment?

1. Discuss three examples of flower imagery as they clarify the major themes of Toni Morrison's novel *The Bluest Eye*.

2. Trace the events that led to the Bay of Pigs invasion of Cuba.

3. Discuss Louis B. Mayer's major influences on the American film industry during the "Golden Age of Moviemaking."

4. Agree or disagree with the following statement: "The 1957 launching of the Russian satellite *Sputnik* caused important changes in the American educational system."

5. Consider the similarities and differences between the expressionistic techniques of American painters Jaune Quick-to-See Smith and Audrey Flack. Illustrate your answer with references to important works of both artists.

Assignment

Practice planning an in-class essay by selecting one of the quotations in the Assignment on pages 45–47 in Chapter 2 as a brief "prompt" for a personal opinion essay developed by any method(s) you find appropriate. Allow yourself only ten minutes to write a working thesis and a sketch outline for your essay. Would you then be ready to turn your plan into a clearly organized and well-developed in-class essay? Continue to practice responding to the prompts in Chapter 2 until you gain confidence in your ability to think, plan, and write under time pressure.

Writing the Summary-and-Response Essay

The "summary-and-response essay" is such a common assignment today that it merits additional discussion and illustration. As noted earlier in this chapter, this kind of assignment frequently asks students to read a professional article,* summarize its thesis and main points, and write a response expressing agreement or disagreement with the article's ideas.

You may have had experience with some form of this assignment before now. Many college entrance examinations have adopted this kind of essay to evaluate both reading comprehension and writing skills. Many colleges also use this format as their composition placement exam, to direct students into the appropriate writing class. Still other schools employ this kind of essay as a final exam or exit test for their composition requirement. And although this format is often assigned as in-class writing, it certainly is not limited to this use. Many composition classes and other academic courses include this type of essay as an out-of-class paper.

Though the format of this assignment may vary slightly depending on its purpose and occasion, throughout your college and professional life you will almost certainly be asked on more than one occasion to read information, summarize it for others, and then present your reaction to its ideas. To help you prepare for this kind of thinking and writing activity, here are a few suggestions, divided into three sections for clarity.

Reading the Assignment and the Article

1. Read your assignment's directions carefully to discover exactly what you are being asked to do. For example, are you being asked to present a one-paragraph summary of a professional article first and then write a personal response? Or are you being asked to respond to the professional article's major points one at a time? Perhaps you are being asked to critique the author's style as well as ideas. Because formats vary, be sure you understand your complete assignment—all its required parts—before you begin writing.

2. Before you can intelligently respond to any reading you need to thoroughly understand its ideas. ◆ To review suggestions for close reading, take the time now to revisit Chapter 8, "The Reading-Writing Connection," in this text. This chapter will help you identify and evaluate an article's thesis, main points, supporting evidence, and other rhetorical techniques.

3. If you are given an article to read out of class, study it carefully, annotating it as outlined in Chapter 8. If reading the article is part of the in-class activity, you may have only enough time to read it carefully once, underlining and annotating as you move through each paragraph. Minimally, you should mark the thesis and the main ideas of the body paragraphs. Underline or star important claims or supporting evidence. Are the claims logical and well supported, or does the author rely on generalizations or other faulty reasoning? Overall, do you agree or disagree with

---

*To avoid confusion in this discussion between the professional essay used as a prompt and the student's response essay, the word "article" will be used to refer to the professional reading.

the article? Would you call it a weak or strong piece of writing? Why? (◆ For help evaluating claims and supporting evidence, review the discussion of logical falla-cies in Chapter 15, pages 316–319.)

Writing the Summary

If you are to begin with a brief summary of the article, follow the guidelines listed under "Writing a Summary" on pages 192–193 of Chapter 8. Remember that a good summary presents the author's name and full title of the article in the first sentence, which also frequently presents the article's thesis (In his article "Free Speech on Campus," author Clarence Page argues that . . .). The next sentences of your summary should present the article's main ideas, found in the article's body paragraphs. Unless you need to quote a word or phrase for clarity or emphasis, use your own words to present a concise ver-sion of the article. Normally, your summary will be an objective treatment of the article's ideas, so save your opinions for the "response" section.

Writing the Response

1. Before you begin writing the "response" part of your essay, look at the under-lining and any marginal notes you made on the article. What was your general assessment of the article? Do you agree or disagree with the author? Perhaps you only agree with some points and disagree with others? Or perhaps you agree with the main ideas but think that this particular essay is a weak defense of those ideas? After looking over the article and your notes, decide on your overall reaction to this article. This assessment will become your thesis in the "response" portion of your essay.

2. Once you have a working thesis in mind, plan the rest of your essay. For example, if you disagree with the article, you might want to note two or three reasons you reject the author's opinion; these reasons may become the basis for your own body paragraphs. **Important:** Be sure you have evidence of your own to support your positions. Responding with personal examples is perhaps the most common kind of support for essays written in class, but if you know facts, statistics, testi-mony, or other information that would support your position, you may certainly include them.

3. If you have begun your essay with a summary, start the next paragraph with a sentence that clearly indicates the "response" section is now beginning. Present a smooth transition to your thesis and consider using an "essay map" to indicate to your readers the points you will discuss.

   Example   Although in his article "Test!" Paul Perez correctly identifies a growing drug problem in our public schools, his plan to drug-test all students involved in campus activities should be rejected. Such a test could not be implemented fairly and is an unreasonable invasion of students' privacy.

4. In each of your own body paragraphs make clear which of the author's claims or ideas you are refuting or supporting by using "tag lines" to remind the reader.

Example　Although Foxcroft argues that the proposed tuition increase will not discourage prospective students, she fails to understand the economic situation of most IBC applicants, who are sacrificing income to return to school. In a recent survey . . .

5. Once you have signaled the point in question and stated your position, develop each body paragraph with enough specific supporting evidence to make your claim convincing. If you disagree with a point, you must show why and present your position logically (◆ you may wish to review Chapter 15 on argument). If you agree with the article, beware a tendency to simply restate the positions with which you are in agreement ("I think Brower is right when she says housing is too expensive on campus. She is also right about the lack of housing choices . . ."). Find examples, reasons, or information that lend support to the points that you and the author think are valid.

6. Many assignments call for a straightforward personal opinion or "agree-disagree" response. In other assignments, you may be given the option of criticizing or praising an author's logic, style, or even tone. You might, for example, show that a particular argument is ineffective because it is based on a mass of overstated generalities, or you might show why the author's sarcastic tone alienates the reader. On the other hand, an author might deserve credit for a particularly effective supporting example or a brilliantly clever turn of phrase that captures the essence of an idea. Always check your assignment to see if this sort of critique is welcome or even required in your response.

7. Don't forget to write a brief concluding paragraph. If appropriate, you might emphasize the value of the article in question, or call for action for or against its ideas, or project its effects into the future (◆ other suggestions for conclusions appear in Chapter 4). However you end your essay, your conclusion should always be consistent with your overall assessment of the article and its ideas.

Sample Student Essay

The following essay was written by a student in response to the article "College for Grown-Ups" by Mitchell L. Stevens (pages 186–188 in Chapter 8). While the author believed that the premise of Stevens's argument was sound (colleges are perceived as places for the young) ultimately it is his opinion that Stevens exaggerated to make his argument seem more pressing. The student writer reinforces his thesis that colleges aren't discriminating against older students by relying on direct observation and personal experience.

After you read Mitchell Stevens's article and the summary-and-response essay below, what suggestions do you have for the student?

Summary-and-Response Essay on "College for Grown-Ups"

1   In "College for Grown-Ups," Mitchell L. Stevens argues that society should stop thinking of college as being only for students in their teens and early twenties and instead see higher education as an opportunity for people of all ages. Stevens says that college is risky for young people, exposing them to financial, psychological, and physical dangers. According to Stevens, campuses are designed and organized for the youth market, and younger and older people don't get to mix. In his opinion, the idea that college is only for the young is damaging to society and discriminates against both younger and older people. He claims that everyone would be better off if people would stop thinking of college as something that teens jump into right after high school, and he goes on to suggest several different experimental and traditional alternatives to the unfair way higher education is seen now.

2   Although I agree with Stevens that everyone in society is hurt when colleges see themselves as being only for the young, his article presents an exaggerated picture of risks, selective marketing, and discrimination on college campuses. For one thing, I think that Stevens overstates the negative side of Greek life. I go to a public university, and I and several of my friends, male and female, have chosen not to participate in a fraternity or a sorority. When Stevens talks about the "party pathway through college" and its consequences of drug abuse and sexual assault, I think he is very much overstating the negative side of Greek life and college administrators' involvement in it. It seems that Stevens is inflating the negative view of Greek life in order to suggest that teens are too young to make their own decisions when it comes to college activities and safety.

Summary [margin label]

Response begins, focuses on discrimination and Greek Life [margin label]

3   Second, I don't agree with the author's point that residential colleges use selective marketing, targeting everything toward teens. My friend Britt is in her late twenties and is studying engineering at a public university. Britt shares an apartment in a residence hall with a fellow student in her early forties. They don't need to be babied or entertained by their surroundings; they are serious older students who welcome the chance to relax and get work done in an apartment-style setting with their own kitchen and living room. Clearly, their university understood the need for older students to have independent, adult-style living. In fact, Britt's university also offers family housing for students of any age who are couples or have children. So the article's point that residential colleges arrange their environment to appeal to teens is overstated and not well researched, in my opinion.

Response to Stevens's claims about campus life for adult students

4   Third, leaving adult students out of the mix when it comes to admissions is discriminatory, but I disagree with Stevens that this is actually happening. He calls campuses "age-segregated play-grounds," which I think is insulting. On the contrary, I believe that colleges today are making a big effort to attract students of all ages. For example, my oldest sister, Grace, is considering going back to school to get a law degree, and she has discovered a lot of colleges that offer courses in formats that make it easier for adults who work and have small children, like herself, to get degrees. Some colleges offer flexible schedules that offer back-to-back courses that she could take in four-week increments, for example. This interest on the part of colleges to attract and keep adult students is not unique to Grace's experience. Just a quick search on the Web, using "attracting older students," turned up a lot of information on this issue. For example, articles and college Web sites both talk about offering counseling services for older students who may need help with juggling work, family, and academic responsibilities. So with all this interest in reaching older students, I think that Stevens's perception that higher education discriminates against the older student is inaccurate.

Thesis in opposition to Stevens's thesis

Conclusion agrees with one of Stevens's ideas and restates this essay's thesis

5   Even though I disagree with Stevens as to what is actually going on at college campuses today, I think he makes one excellent point that mixing all ages of students together would create "an ever-replenished intergenerational community of personal learners." I think this is a great concept because academic life should not be any different from regular life. In the real world, people of all ages live together and learn from each other, and that's the way it should be at college, as well. The only thing that I think is fundamentally wrong about the argument Stevens puts forth is that I think this is already actually happening; however, he insists that it isn't.

Practicing What You've Learned

A. After reading Mitchell L. Stevens's article "College for Grown-Ups" (pages 186–188), write your own summary-and-response essay. In your opinion, do colleges cater to younger students? Why or why not? Can more be done to attract and retain adult learners? If yes, then please describe any ideas you have for how to do this. Remember to draw on your own knowledge and experience to support or reject Stevens's claims.

B. *Collaborative Activity:* Review Stevens's "College for Grown-Ups" and practice your analytical skills by composing a short list of the essay's major strengths and weaknesses. What are the essay's most effective points? How might Stevens have improved his arguments and supporting evidence? Pair with a classmate and compare lists. Pretend Stevens is a partner in a peer revision workshop who has asked you two for help; give him feedback that includes at least one compliment on something well done and one specific suggestion for an effective change. How does your advice to Stevens compare to the recommendations of the other students in the class?

Assignment

Read and annotate the selection "So What's So Bad about Being So-So?" on pages 212–214 of this textbook and then write your own summary-and-response essay, agreeing or disagreeing (wholly or in part) with the writer's view of competition today. Remember to support your position with logical reasons, persuasive examples, or relevant facts. (If you prefer, you may select some other professional essay from this textbook or from another source, such as a newspaper or magazine, but be sure to obtain your instructor's approval of your selection in advance.)

Writing for Classroom Presentations

In addition to exams and timed essays written in the classroom, you may also be assigned another kind of in-class activity: the oral presentation of your written work to your classmates. Essay summaries, progress reports, panel discussions, and other kinds of in-class speaking based on your written work provide opportunities to practice your critical thinking skills, increase your audience awareness, and refine your prose. Learning to deliver your ideas effectively to your composition peers now may also help you learn to present plans and projects in other classes and throughout your professional life.

iStockphoto.com/Chris Schmidt

Some assignments call for new writing exclusively for presentation; others ask that you adapt in special ways a piece of writing on which you are currently working or one you may have already completed. Whatever the assignment, you may profit from the advice given here regarding the effective shaping of your written work for classroom delivery.

Before you read on, however, let's address a common problem associated with presentations: nervousness. According to many surveys, Americans identify public speaking as their number one fear, even ranking it over fear of death. Comedian Jerry Seinfeld once described the feeling this way: "At a funeral, the average person would rather be in the casket than giving the eulogy"! Speaking to a group is a challenge for most people, but by practicing the advice that follows, you should be up to the task.

Steps to Successful Presentations

1. **Clearly understand your assignment's purpose and format.** What are you being asked to do, and in what way? Purposes and designs of oral presentations may vary widely. Are you being asked to give information, argue a point, offer a solution, or provide instruction? Are you speaking alone, as part of a pair, or as a group or panel member?

Here are some common assignments in composition classes for solo presentations: (a) a summary of a completed essay, (b) an overview of a current draft, (c) a progress report on research, (d) the sharing of the most interesting idea in your examination of a topic, (e) the request of feedback to help you solve a frustrating problem you're having with research or a draft, (f) the teaching of a lesson to your peers (often punctuation or grammar related).

In other assignments, you might be part of a collaborative or team effort exploring a topic by presenting information through (a) a panel discussion, (b) a multi-part group project, (c) a debate with other classmates, (d) a team-generated piece of writing.

2. **Once you understand your purpose and its format, be aware of the presentation's exact logistical requirements.** Will you, for example, speak by yourself standing in front of the class? Will you have a lectern—a speaker's stand—on which to rest your notes? Or will you remain seated at your desk? Perhaps you are part of a panel seated at a table? How much time is allotted for your talk? Should your talk include visual aids or handouts?

3. **Consider your listening audience's needs.** To achieve your assignment's purpose, what does your audience need to know? Do they need any background information or definition of special terms to understand your talk? Remember, too, that listening isn't the same as reading. If your comments are the least bit vague, overly complicated, or disorganized, your audience cannot turn back and reread your point. Clarity, simplicity, and directness are of ultimate importance in most oral presentations.

4. **Practice your critical thinking skills.** Most composition classroom presentations are brief by necessity, so you will likely need to evaluate your own work carefully and select the very best—and most accessible—material for delivery. Whether you are adapting an existing piece of writing or composing anew, start by drafting a one-sentence statement of your primary goal: what do you want your audience to know, feel, or do as a result of your presentation? To achieve this goal, and help your listeners follow your thinking, consider an organizational pattern that allows you to state clearly your main idea early on, make your point(s) directly with easy-to-understand explanations, and then summarize your main point again at the end. Don't forget to use transitional words to signal movement in your discussion (◆ review pages 72–74 and 79–80 if you need suggestions).

5. **Make a written draft of your talk.** Even if it is a summary of an existing essay, your overview is a new, sleeker version, reframed for your listening-audience, not a word-for-word repetition or flat reading of the original work. Once you are satisfied with your draft, then transfer its outline to something you can refer to quickly and easily. In most cases note cards rather than pages are useful; keywords written or underlined in different colored ink can also be helpful. (And always number the note cards in case you drop them moments before your talk begins!)

6. **Practice your delivery.** Give your entire talk, more than once, in front of a mirror, a friend, or a video camera. Time yourself to the minute, knowing that your real talk may be delivered faster or slower than your practice one. Remember that the

best way to sound like you know what you are talking about is to know what you are talking about . . . so if you find yourself stumbling in parts of your talk, look closely at your material to see what needs strengthening or clarifying (more critical thinking). Deliver your material in the best possible manner by following the hints offered in the next section of this discussion.

Guidelines for Effective Delivery

Try to think of your talk as less of a formal production than a conversation with interested peers. You are not an actor hired to perform but rather someone knowledgeable and at ease who sincerely wants to share information and stimulate thought. To communicate your ideas well, here are some suggestions for a pleasing delivery.

1. **Monitor your voice.** You need to speak loud enough to reach the back row in the room, and you need to speak slowly enough to be understood, pronouncing each word clearly. Avoid a monotone; practice pausing to give emphasis to key words or concepts (if it helps, write the word "pause" in red ink in various places in your note cards).

2. **Make eye contact.** Sweep the different parts of the room with your glance so that everyone feels included in your comments. You should know your work well enough that you do not have to read your notes; instead, use your notes or outline as prompts or reminders of what you want to say next.

3. **Avoid distractions.** Practicing your talk so that your words flow smoothly will help rid yourself of annoying verbal tics such as "ummm" and "you know." Gestures can effectively emphasize points but don't overdo them, and if you are standing, try to find a balance between remaining rigid (no hiding behind the lectern) and moving or shifting around too much. You want your listeners to focus on what you are saying, so on the day of your presentation dress neatly and maybe even a bit blandly if your style is normally on the colorful or exotic side. Bring a watch or have a clock somewhere in your line of sight so you can discreetly check that your talk is moving along with time to finish as scheduled.

4. **Consider instructional aids.** Find out in advance if your assignment permits, or even calls for, use of supplementary materials (handouts, outlines, samples, etc.) or audio-visual equipment (flip charts, white boards, posters, PowerPoint, recordings, etc.). Visual aids that present a few key words or lines can be effective in some cases, though tiny print, complex graphs, crowded screens, and overly flashy images can be more distracting than helpful. Remember that you want your audience's close attention on your ideas, not on your props.

5. **Adjust and adapt.** Watch your audience's reactions—their facial expressions and body language. If they seem confused or restless, you might need to slow down, speed up, simplify, or restate a point in a slightly different way.

6. **End well.** Sometimes the concluding restatement of your main point can best be followed with a humorous comment or a serious thought or a call for action, depending on your subject matter and purpose. Some assignments include a brief question-and-answer period after your presentation; if so, as you plan your talk, try to anticipate what some of the questions might be so that you are ready

to succinctly address them. Plan a comment that announces the end of the Q & A session ("If anyone has additional questions, I can answer them after class"), and do thank your audience for listening.

As you prepare to give your presentation, try to relax. Breathe deeply and evenly if you are nervous; as yoga students know, controlling the breath helps focus the mind and body. Visualize success—and unless a somber subject matter dictates otherwise, approach your listeners with a warm, friendly smile.

Practicing What You've Learned

Collaborative Activity: Analyze a draft of an essay or research project on which you are now working. Decide which part of this essay is your Best Idea or Most Surprising Discovery, and adapt this portion of your work into an interesting five-minute presentation to two other classmates in a small group. After each of you has spoken, offer each other suggestions for improving clarity of content and its presentation. Consider using these suggestions to revise your essay so that your prose becomes even more effective for your readers.

Assignment

A. Think about a time when you learned to do something that at first you found difficult or challenging and identify the single most important factor to your success (perhaps a coach helped you learn to throw a curve ball, or hours of repetition and practice helped you master long division, or keeping a positive attitude gave you the confidence to learn the backstroke). Prepare a short presentation in which you describe what you learned, including the challenges or problems you encountered when starting out, and the steps you took that eventually led you to success. Offer ideas for how these steps or strategies can be adapted to help you and your classmates learn new things today (in college, at work, in life); be sure to include specific examples.

B. *Collaborative Activity:* As part of your class as a whole, compile a list of current campus controversies (e.g., Should military representatives be allowed to recruit in the student center? Should students be allowed to opt out of fees for student activities or athletics? Is the upcoming increase in tuition for laboratory courses justified?). With a partner, select and research a topic that interests you both. Together, write a presentation for your class that offers thoughtful examination of at least two conflicting views of the issue. Or, if after your investigation, you find that you and your partner have a strong difference of opinion, offer your classmates a classic debate. (◆ Consulting Chapter 15 on argumentation may be helpful for this assignment.)

Chapter 22

Writing about Literature

People read literature for many, many reasons, including amusement, comfort, escape, new ideas, exploration of values, intellectual challenge, and on and on. Similarly, people write about literature to accomplish a variety of purposes. Literary essays may inform readers about the ideas in a work, analyze its craft, or focus on the work's relationship to the time or culture in which it was written. Other essays might explore biographical, psychological, archetypal, or personal readings of a work.

Although approaches to literature are diverse and may be studied in depth in other English courses, writing essays about literature is worthwhile in the composition classroom as well. Writing about literature offers an opportunity to practice the important skills of close reading, critical thinking, effective use of supporting evidence, and clear expression of ideas.

Using Literature in the Composition Classroom

Teachers of writing most often use literature in their courses in two ways: as "prompts" to inspire personal essay topics and as subjects of interpretative essays.

1. **Prompts:** You may be asked to read a poem or short story and then use some aspect of it—its ideas or characters, for example—as a springboard to discover an essay topic of your own. For instance, after reading John Updike's "A&P," a story about a rather naive young man who receives a real-world lesson, you might write about a coming-of-age experience you had. Or your teacher might assign Shirley Jackson's "The Lottery" and ask you to agree or disagree with the author's views on unexamined conformity to tradition.

2. **Literary Analysis:** Rather than responding to a piece of literature in a personal essay, you might be assigned a literary analysis, asking you to study a piece of literature and then offer your interpretation—that is, your insight into the work (or some important part of it). Your insight becomes your thesis; the body of your essay explains this reading, supported by textual evidence (material from the work) to help your reader understand your view and perhaps gain greater pleasure from, and appreciation of, the work itself.

Literary analysis assignments may be focused in different ways, as well. Some common examples include essays whose main purpose is to show:

- how the various parts or elements of a piece of literature work together to present the main ideas (for example, how the choices of narrator, stanza form, and figurative language in a poem effectively complement each other);

- how one element fits into the complex whole (for example, how setting contributes to a story);

- how two works or two elements may be profitably read together (two poems with similar ideas but different forms; two characters from one story);

- how one interpretation is more insightful than another reading;

- how a work's value has been overlooked or misunderstood.

There are as many possibilities for essay topics as there are readers!

Regardless of the exact assignment, you should feel confident about writing an essay of literary analysis. Working through Part Two of this text, you have already practiced many of the strategies required. For example, to present a particular reading of a poem, you may organize your discussion by *dividing* it into its major literary elements: point of view, setting, structure, language, and so on. Your essay may offer specific lines or images from the work as *examples* illustrating your reading. Working with more than one piece of literature or literary element calls for *comparison and contrast* techniques. And every paper—whether it is a personal response or literary analysis—uses the skills you learned in Part One of this text: a clear thesis, adequate development of ideas, coherent organization, and effective use of language.

Suggestions for Close Reading of Literature

Writing about literature begins with careful reading—and, yes, rereading. The steps suggested here are certainly not exhaustive; one can ask literally hundreds of questions about a complex piece of literature. Rather, these questions are intended to give you a start. Practicing close reading and annotation should help you generate ideas and lead you to additional questions of your own.

Our discussion in this chapter is limited to poems and short stories because composition courses frequently do not have the time to include novels and plays (or long narrative poems, for that matter). However, many of the suggestions for reading short stories and poems may be applied to the reading of longer fiction and drama.

Before you begin reading the suggestions that follow, let's dispel the myth about "hidden meanings." A work of literature is not a trick or puzzle box wherein the author has hidden a message for readers to discover if they can just uncover the right clues. Literary works are open to discussion and interpretation; that's part of their appeal. They contain ideas and images that the author thought important, and some ideas or elements the writer may not have consciously been aware of. You, as the reader, will have insights into a poem or story that your classmates don't. Those insights will emerge as you spend time analyzing both the words and the context of a literary text. It's your job as the writer of your literary analysis to explain not only *WHAT* you see but also *WHY* and *HOW*, supporting your interpretation in ways that seem reasonable, persuasive, and satisfying to your readers.

Steps to Reading a Story

If possible, make your own copy of the story and read with pen in hand. Prepare to make notes, underline important lines, circle revealing words or images, and put stars, question marks, or your own symbols in the margins.

1. Before you begin the piece, read any **biographical information** that may accompany the story. Knowing information about the author and when the story was written or published may offer some insight. Also, note the **title**. Does it offer intriguing hints about the story's content?

2. Read through the story at least once to clearly acquaint yourself with its **plot**, the series of actions and events that make up the narrative. In other words, what happened and to whom? Is there a conflict of some sort? Is it resolved or is the story left open-ended?

3. Many times in a story you'll see words you don't know. Sometimes you can figure them out from their context, but if you find unknown words that might indeed have a critical bearing on your understanding of a character, for example, look them up now.

4. Jot a few notes describing your initial reactions to the story's main idea(s) or major **theme(s)**. (If it's helpful, think of the story in terms of its "about-ness." What do you, as reader, think this story is about? Loss of innocence? The bitterness of revenge? The power of sympathy? Tragic lack of communication? The wonder of first love?) In other words, what comments or observations does this story make about the human condition?

5. As you review the story, begin to think about its parts, always asking yourself "why?": why did the author choose to do it this way? What is gained (or lost) by writing it this way? What does "X" contribute to my understanding of the story? You might begin noting **point of view**—that is, who is narrating this story? Is a character telling this story, or is it told by an all-knowing (omniscient) narrator? A narrator who is partially omniscient, seeing into the thoughts of only some characters? If the story is told by a character, is this narrator informed and trustworthy or "unreliable" to some degree because of ignorance, bias, psychological state, age (a young child, for example), or some other factor? What is gained through the story's choice of narration?

6. Is the story's **structure** in chronological order, or does the writer shift time sequences through flashbacks or multiple points of view? Does the story contain foreshadowing, early indications in the plot that signal later developments? Again, think about the author's choices in terms of communicating the story's ideas.

7. Think about the **characters**, their personalities, beliefs, motivations. How do they interact? Do any of them change—or refuse or fail to change? Look closely at their descriptions, thoughts, and dialogue. Sometimes names are revealing, too.

8. What is the relationship between the **setting** of the story and its action or characters? Remember that setting can include place, time of year, hour of day or night, weather or climate, terrain, culture, and so on. Settings can create mood and even function symbolically to reveal character or foreshadow a coming event.

9. Look closely at the **language** of the story, paying attention to revealing images, metaphors, and similes (◆ for help identifying these, see pages 351–352). Note any use of **symbols**—persons, places, or things that bear a significant meaning beyond their usual meaning. (For example, in a particular story, a dreary rain might be associated with a loss of hope; a soaring bird might emphasize new possibilities.) Overall, would you characterize the story's **style** as realistic or something else? What is the **tone** of the story? Serious? Humorous? Does irony, the discrepancy between appearance and reality, play a part?

10. After you've looked at these and any other important elements of the reading, review your initial reactions. How would you now describe the main ideas or major themes of this story? How do the parts of the story work together to clarify those themes?

Remember to add your own questions to this list, ones that address your specific story in a meaningful way. ◆ To continue improving your reading skills, turn to the "Practicing What You've Learned" exercise on pages 513–515, which offers a story for your analysis. Before you begin drafting any essay of literary analysis, see the guidelines on pages 511–512.

Annotated Story

Using the preceding questions, a composition student annotated the story that follows. Some of the notes she made on imagery became the basis for her short essay, which appears on pages 502–504. Before you read the story, however, cover the marginal notes with a sheet of paper. Then read the story, making your own notes. Next, uncover the student's notes and reread the story. Compare your reactions to those of the student writer. What new or different insights did you have?

The Story of an Hour

Kate Chopin

Kate Chopin was a nineteenth-century American writer whose stories appeared in such magazines as the *Atlantic Monthly, Century,* and the *Saturday Evening Post.* She published two collections of short stories and two novels; one of her novels, *The Awakening* (1899), was considered so shocking in its story of a married woman who desired a life of her own that it was removed from some library shelves. "The Story of an Hour" was first published in 1894.

similar theme

1   Knowing that Mrs. Mallard was afflicted with a heart trouble, great care was taken to break to her as gently as possible the news of her husband's death.

foreshadowing

2   It was her sister Josephine who told her, in broken sentences, veiled hints that revealed in half concealing. Her husband's friend Richards was there, too, near her. It was he who had been in the newspaper office when intelligence of the railroad disaster was received, with Brently Mallard's name leading the list of "killed." He had only taken the time to assure himself of its truth by a second telegram, and had hastened to forestall any less careful, less tender friend in bearing the sad message.

3   She did not hear the story as many women have heard the same, with a paralyzed inability to accept its significance. She wept at once, with sudden, wild abandonment, in her sister's arms. When the storm of grief had spent itself she went away to her room alone. She would have no one follow her.

storm imagery

4   There stood, facing the open window, a comfortable, roomy armchair. Into this she sank, pressed down by a physical exhaustion that haunted her body and seemed to reach into her soul.

5   She could see in the open square before her house the tops of trees that were all aquiver with the new spring life. The delicious breath of rain was in the air. In the street below a peddler was crying his wares. The notes of a distant song which some one was singing reached her faintly, and countless sparrows were twittering in the eaves.

Setting: closed room but open window

—spring
—trees, air
—songs
—blue sky

6   There were patches of blue sky showing here and there through the clouds that had met and piled each above the other in the west facing her window.

7   She sat with her head thrown back upon the cushion of the chair quite motionless, except when a sob came up into her throat and shook her, as a child who has cried itself to sleep continues to sob in its dreams.

8   She was young, with a fair, calm face, whose lines bespoke repression and even a certain strength. But now there was a dull stare in her eyes, whose gaze was fixed away off yonder on one of those patches of blue sky. It was not a glance of reflection, but rather indicated a suspension of intelligent thought.

Mrs. M.: repression and strength

9   There was something coming to her and she was waiting for it, fearfully. What was it? She did not know; it was too subtle and elusive to name. But she felt it, creeping out of the sky, reaching toward her through the sounds, the scents, the color that filled the air.

3rd person narrator—readers know her feelings

new insight from spring sky

10   Now her bosom rose and fell tumultuously. She was beginning to recognize this thing that was approaching to possess her, and she was striving to beat it back with her will—as powerless as her two white slender hands would have been.

conflict within herself

11   When she abandoned herself a little whispered word escaped her slightly parted lips. She said it over and over under her breath: "Free, free, free!" The vacant stare and the look of terror that had followed it went from her eyes. They stayed keen and bright. Her pulses beat fast, and the coursing blood warmed and relaxed every inch of her body.

Revelation: freedom

images of vitality

12   She did not stop to ask if it were not a monstrous joy that held her. A clear and exalted perception enabled her to dismiss the suggestion as trivial.

13   She knew that she would weep again when she saw the kind, tender hands folded in death; the face that had never looked save with love upon her, fixed and gray and dead. But she saw beyond that bitter moment a long procession of years to come that would belong to her absolutely. And she opened and spread her arms out to them in welcome.

more "open" imagery

14   There would be no one to live for during those coming years; she would live for herself. There would be no powerful will bending her in that blind persistence with which men and women believe they have a right to impose a private will upon a fellow creature. A kind intention or a cruel intention made the act seem no less a crime as she looked upon it in that brief moment of illumination.

**self-assertion, wants to control her own life

15   And yet she had loved him—sometimes. Often she had not. What did it matter! What could love, the unsolved mystery, count for in face of this possession of self-assertion which she suddenly recognized as the strongest impulse of her being.

16   "Free! Body and soul free!" she kept whispering.

17   Josephine was kneeling before the closed door with her lips to the keyhole, imploring for admission. "Louise, open the door! I beg; open the door—you will make yourself ill. What are you doing, Louise? For heaven's sake open the door."

18   "Go away. I am not making myself ill." No; she was drinking in a very elixir of life through that open window.

19   Her fancy was running riot along those days ahead of her. Spring days, and summer days, and all sorts of days that would be her own. She breathed a quick prayer that life might be long. It was only yesterday she had thought with a shudder that life might be long.

future: seasons of life, growth

20   She arose at length and opened the door to her sister's importunities. There was a feverish triumph in her eyes, and she carried herself unwittingly like a goddess of Victory. She clasped her sister's waist, and together they descended the stairs. Richards stood waiting for them at the bottom.

victory imagery

21   Some one was opening the front door with a latchkey. It was Brently Mallard who entered, a little travel-stained, composedly carrying his gripsack and umbrella. He had been far from the scene of accident, and did not even know there had been one. He stood

Is he associated with rain?

amazed at Josephine's piercing cry; at Richards' quick motion to screen him from the view of his wife.

22   But Richards was too late.

23   When the doctors came they said she had died of heart disease— of joy that kills.

Irony: She may die from a "broken" heart all right, but readers know it's not from joy.

Initial reactions: Mrs. Mallard is sad about her husband's death, though I'm not sure she really loved him all that much. He wasn't a bad guy—she just wants to be a "free" woman, back when women had few rights, little control over their lives. She dies—of shock? Disappointment?— when he turns up alive.

After rereading: I think Chopin wanted readers to see how confined some nineteenth-century women felt in their traditional roles. I felt sorry for Mrs. Mallard, whose realization that life will not be hers after all is so traumatic that it kills her.

Open window—lets in spring scenes, color, sounds of new life—symbol of future possibilities. Also, lots of sick-versus-well and life-versus-death imagery.

Question: Why is she named "Mallard"—a duck?

Repose, 1911, by John Singer Sargent

Repose by John Singer Sargent (1911). Public Domain.

Sample Student Essay

After studying Chopin's story, this student writer decided to focus her essay on important imagery in the work, to show how contrasting images of illness and health reveal the main character's changes in attitude. Numbers in parentheses following direct quotations refer to the paragraphs in the story.

A Breath of Fresh Air

Introduction: Title and author identified, brief summary of plot and theme

Thesis

1   In Kate Chopin's 1894 story "The Story of an Hour" a young wife grieves over news of her husband's accidental death but soon discovers herself elated at the prospect of a life under her own control. The story ends tragically when the husband's sudden reappearance causes her weak heart to fail—not from joy—but from the devastating realization that her newfound freedom is lost. To help readers understand Mrs. Mallard's all-too-brief transformation to a hopeful "free" woman, Chopin contrasts images of illness and lifelessness with positive images of vitality and victory.

Images of illness and lifelessness, illustrated by lines from the story

2   In the first line of the story, Mrs. Mallard is associated with illness because of her "heart trouble" (1). Following a "storm of grief" (3) on hearing of her husband's death, she isolates herself in her room, lifeless and numb behind a closed door. Chopin describes Mrs. Mallard as feeling "pressed down" (4) and "haunted" (4), exhausted in body and soul; she sits "motionless" (7) with a "dull stare" (8), except for an occasional sob. The lines in her strong, fair face "bespoke repression" (8) and indeed Mrs. Mallard is a young woman who, only the day before, hopelessly shuddered to think "that life might be long" (19).

3   In direct contrast with these images of lifelessness and emotional repression, Chopin introduces images of rebirth and hope. Mrs. Mallard's room has an open window, which becomes the key symbol in the description of Mrs. Mallard's transformation. Chopin uses the open window to provide Mrs. Mallard with both a view

of new life and with fresh air, paralleling the new hopeful feelings that come to her. Through this "open window" (4) Mrs. Mallard sees beyond her house to an "open square" (5) with "trees that were all aquiver with the new spring life" (5). The repetition of the word "open," the budding trees, and the spring season all emphasize the contrast between the world of possibilities and new life and Mrs. Mallard's enclosed room and enclosed spirit. The air after a life-giving spring rain has a "delicious breath" (5), and both people and birds are now singing. "Patches of blue sky" (6) are symbolically breaking through the clouds, but, as yet, Mrs. Mallard can only stare vacantly at the blue sky rather than respond to it.

Contrasting images of rebirth, supported by examples

4   Soon, however, Mrs. Mallard realizes that something—she's not sure what—is "creeping out of the sky, reaching toward her through the sounds, the scents, the color that filled the air" (9). She resists at first but ultimately allows herself the glorious revelation that she is free to live a new life as she, not others, wants it to be. The imagery associated with this revelation shows Mrs. Mallard becoming energized and healthy, in direct contrast to the imagery of lifelessness that characterized her before. The "vacant stare" (11) is replaced by eyes that are "keen and bright" (11). No longer beaten down, "her pulses beat fast, and the coursing blood warmed and relaxed every inch of her body" (11). In contrast to her previous hopeless view of the future, Mrs. Mallard joyfully thinks of the years ahead and "opened and spread her arms out to them in welcome" (13). This open gesture aligns her with the open window and open square, with their images of rebirth and hope.

Contrasting images of vitality, supported by examples and comparison

5   Chopin emphasizes the transformation even further by contrast- ing Mrs. Mallard's description to her sister Josephine's image of her. Symbolically placed on the opposite side of the closed door from the open window and spring sky, her sister tells Mrs. Mallard that "you will make yourself ill" (17). But the images associated with the

Contrast
of illness
imagery to
images of
health, victory

transformed Mrs. Mallard are not of illness but of health and victory. Through the open window, she is drinking in a "very elixir of life" (18), a potion that restores the sick to health, as she thinks of spring and summer, seasons of fertility and growth. She finally emerges from her room with "triumph in her eyes" (20), carrying herself "like a goddess of Victory" (20).

6   Mrs. Mallard's victory is cut short, however, as the return of Mr. Mallard destroys her hopes for her future life. The image of illness once again prevails, as doctors wrongly attribute her death to

Conclusion:
Restatement
of thesis
showing
purpose of
the imagery

"heart disease—of joy that kills" (23). With this ironic last line echoing the story's first line, Chopin's imagery describing her character comes full circle, from illness to life and back to death, to emphasize for readers the tragedy of Mrs. Mallard's momentary gain and then the crushing defeat of her spiritual triumph.

Steps to Reading a Poem

Close reading of a poem is similar to reading a story in many ways. Again, try to read with pen in hand so you can take notes, circle important words, and make comments in the margins.

1. Pay attention to any **biographical information** on the author and the date of publication, which may give you insight into the poem. Also note the **title**, as it may introduce the poem's main idea or tone.

2. Read through the poem at least twice. Poetry does differ from prose in that poets often compress or turn sentence structure in unusual ways, to create new images and fit rhyme and rhythm patterns. You might find it helpful to try to paraphrase (put into your own words) the lines of shorter poems (or summarize distinct parts) so that you have a clear understanding of the basic content. If you're lost in several lines, try to locate the subject, the verb, and objects of the action or description. And, always, before you begin to analyze a poem, be sure you know the meaning of *all* the words. Looking up unfamiliar words is critical here—short poems are compact, so every word counts.

3. Some poems are **narratives** and contain a plot; others, often referred to as **lyrics**, capture a scene, a series of images, an emotion, or a thought that has universal appeal. At this point, what action, situation, or ideas do you see presented in this

poem? Is there a dominant tone or opinion expressed? Make some notes about your initial reactions to the poem's issues, themes, or ideas. As in fiction, poets often offer comments on the human condition or social values.

4. Now begin to analyze the elements of the poem. Identifying the **speaker** (or narrator) of the poem is a good place to start. Is it someone with recognizable characteristics or personality traits? Someone involved in the action of the poem? Young or old? Male or female? Mother, father, lover, friend? Tone of voice (angry, pleading, sad, joyful, etc.)? Remember that a speaker using "I" is not necessarily the poet but rather a persona or role the poet has assumed. Or is the speaker unidentified as she or he unfolds the poem for the reader? And to whom is the poem addressed? A specific person, a group of people, any readers?

5. What is the **setting** or **occasion** of the poem? Is the place, time, season, climate, or historical context important to understanding the poem? Why or why not?

6. What **characters**, if any, appear in the poem? What is the relationship between the speaker and others in the poem? What values, opinions, and motivations do these characters present? What conflicts or changes occur?

7. Look carefully at the poem's **diction** (choice of words). Most poems contain description and figurative language to create imagery, the vivid pictures that create meaning in the reader's mind. ◆ Look for similes and metaphors, as illustrated on pages 176–178 and 351, that make abstract or unfamiliar images clear through comparisons, as well as personification and synecdoche (page 352). Poets often use patterns or groups of **images** to present a dominant impression and concrete objects as **symbols** to represent abstract ideas within the poem (cold rain as death, a spring flower as rebirth). They also use **allusions**, brief references to other well-known persons, places, things, and literary works that shed light on their subject by association (for example, a reference to *Romeo and Juliet* might suggest ill-fated lovers). Underline or circle those words and images that you find most effective in communicating ideas or emotions.

8. How is the poem **structured**? There are too many poetic forms to define each one here (ballads, sonnets, odes, villanelles, etc.), so you might consult a more detailed handbook to help you identify the characteristics of each one. However, to help you begin, here is a brief introduction. Some poems are written in patterns called "fixed" or "closed" form. They often appear in stanzas, recognizable units frequently containing the same number of lines and the same rhyme and rhythm pattern in those lines. They often present one main idea per unit and have a space between each one. Some poems are not divided into stanzas but nevertheless have well-known fixed forms, such as the Shakespearean sonnet, which traditionally challenges the poet to write within fourteen lines, in a predictable line rhythm and rhyme scheme. The modern English version of the Japanese haiku calls for three lines and seventeen syllables but no rhyme. Other poems are written in free verse (or "open" form), with no set line length or regular rhyme pattern; these poems may rely on imagery, line lengths, repetition, and sound devices to maintain unity and show progression of ideas.

Study your poem and try to identify its form. How does its structure help communicate its ideas? Why might the poet have chosen this particular structure?

9. **Sound devices** may help unify a poem, establish tone, emphasize a description, and communicate theme. There are many kinds of rhyme (end, internal, slant, etc.), which often help unify or link ideas and parts of poems. For example, stanzas often have set patterns of end rhyme that pull a unit together; a quatrain (four-line stanza), for example, might rhyme *abab*, as shown here:

     . . . free,   a
     . . . sky,   b
     . . . sea,   a
     . . . fly.   b

The following are four other common sound devices:

- **Alliteration:** repetition of consonant sounds at the beginning of words ("The *S*oul *s*elects her own *S*ociety"), often used to link and emphasize a relationship among words.

- **Assonance:** repetition of vowel sounds ("child bride of time") to link and underscore a relationship among the words.

- **Onomatopoeia:** a word whose sound echoes, and thus emphasizes, its meaning (buzz, rustle, hiss, boom, sigh).

- **Repetition:** the repeating of the same words, phrases, or lines for unity, emphasis, or musical effect ("Sing on, spring! Sing on, lovers!").

Sound devices not only unify poems but also add to their communication of images and meaning. Harsh-sounding, monosyllabic words ("the cold stone tomb") may slow lines and create a tone vastly different from one produced by multisyllabic words with soft, flowing sounds. Poets pick their words carefully for their sounds as well as their connotations and denotations. Ask yourself: what sound devices appear in the poem I'm reading, and why?

10. **Rhythm**, the repetition of stresses and pauses, may also play an important part in the creation of tone and meaning. A poem about a square dance, for example, may reflect the content by having a number of quick stresses to imitate the music and the caller's voice. You can discover patterns of rhythm in lines of poetry by marking the accented (´) and unaccented (ˇ) syllables:

     ˇ   ´   ˇ   ´   ˇ   ´   ˇ   ´   ˇ   ´

     My mistress' eyes are nothing like the sun

Many poems demand a prescribed rhythm as part of their fixed form; lines from a Shakespearean sonnet, as illustrated earlier, contain an often-used pattern called *iambic pentameter*: five units (called *feet*) of an unaccented syllable followed by an accented syllable.

Another device that contributes to the rhythm of a line is the *caesura*, a heavy pause in a line of poetry. Caesuras (indicated by a ‖ mark) may be used to isolate and thus emphasize words or slow the pace. Sometimes they are used to show strong contrasts, as in the following line: "Before, a joy proposed; ‖ behind, a dream." Caesuras may follow punctuation marks such as commas, semicolons, or periods—marks that say "slow down" to the reader.

After you have looked at the various elements of a poem (and there are many others in addition to the ones mentioned here), reassess your initial reaction. Do you understand the poem in a different or better way? Remember that the elements of an effective poem work together, so be sensitive to the poet's choices of point of view, language, structure, and so on. All these choices help communicate the tone and underscore the ideas of the poem. Ask yourself: what is gained through the poet's choice? What might be different—or lost—if the poet had chosen something else?

◆ To continue working on your close-reading skills, you may turn to the "Practicing What You've Learned" exercise on pages 515–516, which includes two poems for your analysis. Before you begin drafting a discussion of a poem, consult the general guidelines for writing about literature on pages 511–512.

Annotated Poem

Using the suggestions of this chapter, a student responded to the Walt Whitman poem "When I Heard the Learn'd Astronomer" that follows. The student essay on pages 508–511 presents an analysis developed from some of the notes shown there.

Starry Night, 1889, by Vincent van Gogh

Digital Image ©The Museum of Modern Art/Licensed by SCALA/Art Resource, NY

educated — someone who studies the stars, sky

When I Heard the Learn'd Astronomer

Walt Whitman

used here, too

Walt Whitman was a nineteenth-century American poet whose free-verse poems often broke with conventional style and subject matter. Some of his most famous poems, including "Song of Myself," "Crossing Brooklyn Ferry," and "Passage to India," extol the virtues of the common people and stress their unity with a universal spirit. This poem was published in 1865.

speaker: "I" in audience

settings: inside lecture hall

> When I heard the learn'd astronomer;
> When the proofs, the figures, were ranged in
>   columns before me;
> When I was shown the charts and diagrams, to
>   add, divide, and measure them;
> When I, sitting, heard the astronomer, where he
>   lectured with much applause in the lecture-room.

scientific images, repetition, long lines, slow pace

outside at night

> ⁵ How soon, unaccountable, I became tired and sick;
> Till rising and gliding out, I wander'd off by myself,
> In the mystical moist night-air, and from time to time,
> Look'd up in perfect silence at the stars.

contrast to 4 lines above: quicker, smoother sounds; nature imagery; appeals to senses, not brain

assonance

multiple uses of alliteration

Initial reaction: The speaker of the poem (a student?) is listening to an astronomer's lecture—lots of facts and figures. He gets tired (bored?) and goes outside and looks at the nice night himself.

After rereading: I see two ways of looking at the sky here, two ways of understanding. You can learn academically and you can use your own senses. I think Whitman prefers the personal experience in this case because the language and images are much more positive in the last lines of the poem when the speaker is looking at nature for himself.

The poem shows the contrast between the two ways by using two stanzas with different styles and tones. Cold vs. warm. Passive vs. active. Facts vs. personal experience.

Sample Student Essay

After studying the Whitman poem, the student writer wrote this essay to show how many poetic elements work together to present the main idea. Do you agree with his analysis? Which of his claims seems the most or least persuasive, and why? What different interpretation(s) might you suggest?

Two Ways of Knowing

1 In the poem "When I Heard the Learn'd Astronomer," nineteenth-century American poet Walt Whitman contrasts two ways people may study the world around them. They can approach the world through lectures and facts, and they can experience nature firsthand through their own senses. Through the use of contrasting structures, imagery, diction, and sound devices in this poem, Whitman expresses a strong preference for personal experience.

2 The poem's structure clearly presents the contrast between the two ways of experiencing the world, or in this specific case, two ways of studying the heavens. The eight-line, free-verse poem breaks into two stanzas, with the first four lines describing an indoor academic setting, followed by a one-line transition to three concluding lines describing an outdoor night scene. The two parts are unified by a first-person narrator who describes and reacts to both scenes.

3 In the first four lines the narrator is described as sitting in "the lecture-room" (l. 4) as part of an audience listening to an astronomer's talk. The dominant imagery of lines 2–3 is scientific and mathematical: "proofs," "figures," "charts," and "diagrams" are presented so that the audience "may add, divide, and measure them" (l. 3). The words, mostly nouns, appear without any colorful modifiers; the facts and figures are carefully arranged "in columns" (l. 2) for objective analysis. This approach to learning is clearly logical and systematic.

4 The structure and word choice of the first four lines of the poem also subtly reveal the narrator's attitude toward the lecture, which he finds dry and boring. To emphasize the narrator's emotional uninvolvement with the material, Whitman presents him passively "sitting" (l. 4), subject of the passive verb "was shown" (l. 3). Lines 2, 3, and 4, which describe the lecture, are much longer than the lines in the second stanza, with many caesuras, commas, and

Introduction: Title, author, brief overview of content

Thesis and essay map

Two-part structure

Stanza 1: Inside lecture hall

Slow pace to emphasize attitude

semicolons that slow the rhythm and pace (for example, l. 3: "When I was shown the charts and diagrams, to add, divide, and measure them;"). The slow, heavy pace of the lines, coupled with the four repetitions of the introductory "when" phrases, emphasizes the narrator's view of the lecture as long, drawn out, and repetitious. Even though the rest of the audience seems to appreciate the astronomer, giving him "much applause" (l. 4), the narrator becomes restless, "tired and sick" (l. 5), and leaves the lecture hall.

Stanza 2: Outside under stars

5   In the last three lines of the poem, the language and sound devices change dramatically, creating positive images of serenity, wonder, and beauty. The narrator leaves the hall by "rising and gliding out" (l. 6), a light, floating, almost spirit-like image that connects him with the "mystical" (l. 7) nature of the heavens. Whitman also uses assonance (repetition of the "i" sound) to strengthen the connection between the "rising and gliding" narrator and the "mystical . . . night-air" (l. 7). In the lecture hall, the narrator was bored, passive, and removed from nature, but now he is spiritually part of the experience himself.

"Mystical" imagery

6   Alone outside in the night, away from the noisy lecture hall, the narrator quietly contemplates the wonder of the sky, using his own senses of sight, touch, and hearing to observe the stars and feel the air. Positive words, such as "mystical" (l. 7) and "perfect" (l. 8), describe the scene, whose beauty is immediately accessible rather than filtered through the astronomer's cold "proofs" and "diagrams." Examples of alliteration tie together flowing images of natural beauty and serenity: "mystical moist night-air" (l. 7), "from time to time" (l. 7), "silence at the stars" (l. 8). Whitman's choice of the soft "m" and "s" sounds here also adds to the pleasing fluid rhythm, which stands in direct, positive contrast to the harsher, choppier sounds ("charts," "add," "divide") and slow, heavy pauses found in the poem's first stanza.

Contrasting diction, flowing lines, smooth sounds

7   Through careful selection and juxtaposition of language, sound, and structure in the two parts of this short poem, Whitman contrasts distinct ways of studying the natural world. One may learn as a student of facts and figures or choose instead to give oneself over to the wonders of the immediate experience itself. Within the context of this poem, it's no contest: first-hand natural experience wins easily over diagrams and lectures. Stars, 1; charts and graphs, 0.

Conclusion: Restatement of thesis and poem's main idea

General Guidelines for Writing about Literature

Here are some suggestions that will improve any essay of literary analysis:

1. **Select a workable topic.** If the choice of subject matter is yours, you must decide if you will approach a work through discussion of several elements or if you will focus on some specific part of it as it relates to the whole work. You must also select a topic that is interesting and meaningful for your readers. If your topic is too obvious or insignificant, your readers will be bored. In other words, your essay should inform your readers and increase their appreciation of the work.

2. **Present a clear thesis.** Remember that your purpose is to provide new insight to your readers. Consequently, they need to know exactly what you see in the work. Don't just announce your topic ("This poem is about love"); rather, put forth your argumentative thesis clearly and specifically ("Through its repeated use of sewing imagery, the story emphasizes the tragedy of a tailor's wasted potential as an artist"). And don't waltz around vaguely talking about something readers may not have seen the first time through ("At first the warehouse scene doesn't look that important, but after reading it a few times you see that it really does contain some of the meaningful ideas in the story"). "Get on with it!" cries your impatient reader. "Tell me what you see!"

3. **Follow literary conventions.** Essays of literary analysis have some customs you should follow, unless instructed otherwise. Always include the full name of the author and the work in your introductory paragraph; the author's last name is fine after that. Titles of short poems and stories are enclosed in quotation marks. Most literary essays are written in present tense ("the poet presents an image of a withered tree"), from third-person point of view rather than the more informal first-person "I." So that your readers may easily follow your discussion, include a copy of the work or at least indicate publication information describing the location of the work (the name of volume, publisher, date, pages, and so forth).

Within your essay, it's also helpful to include a poem's line number following a direct quotation: "the silent schoolyard" (1. 10). Some instructors also request paragraph or page numbers in essays on fiction.

4. **Organize effectively.** Your method of organization may depend heavily on your subject matter. A poem, for example, might be best discussed by devoting a paragraph to each stanza; on the other hand, another work might profit from a paragraph on imagery, another on point of view, another on setting, and so on. You must decide what arrangement makes the best sense for your readers. Experiment by moving your ideas around in your prewriting outlines and drafts.

5. **Use ample evidence.** Remember that you are, in essence, arguing your interpretation—you are saying to your reader, "Understand this work the way I do." Therefore, it is absolutely essential that you offer your reader convincing evidence based on reasonable readings of words in the work itself. The acceptance of your views depends on your making yourself clear and convincing. To do so, include plenty of references to the work through direct quotation and paraphrase. Don't assume that your reader sees what you see—or sees it in the way you do. You must *fight* for your interpretation by offering clearly explained readings substantiated with references to the work.

Unsupported claim	Robert feels sorry for himself throughout the story.
Claim supported with text	Robert's self-pity is evident throughout the story as he repeatedly thinks to himself, "No one on this earth cares about me" (4) and "There isn't a soul I can turn to" (5).

Ask yourself as you work through your drafts: am I offering enough clear, specific, convincing evidence here to persuade my reader to accept my reading?

6. **Find a pleasing conclusion.** At the end of your literary analysis, readers should feel they have gained new knowledge or understanding of a work or some important part of it. You might choose to wrap up your discussion with a creative restatement of your reading, its relation to the writer's craft, or even your assessment of the work's significance within the author's larger body of writing. However you conclude, the readers should feel intellectually and emotionally satisfied with your discussion.

Problems to Avoid

Don't assign meanings. By far the most common problem in essays of literary analysis involves interpretation without clear explanation of supporting evidence. Remember that your readers may not see what you see in a particular line or paragraph; in fact, they may see something quite different. The burden is on you to show cause—how you derived your reading and why it is a valid one. Don't represent claims as truth without support even if they ever-so-conveniently fit your thesis: "It is clear that the moon is used here as a symbol of her family's loss." Clear to whom besides you? If it helps, each time you make an interpretative claim, imagine a classmate who immediately says, "Uh, sorry, but I don't get it. Show me how you see that?" Or imagine a hostile reader with a completely different reading who sneers, "Oh yeah, says who? Convince me."

Use quoted material effectively. Many times your supporting evidence will come from quotations from the text you're analyzing. But don't just drop a quoted line onto your page, as if it had suddenly tumbled off a high cliff somewhere. You run the risk of your readers reading the quoted material and still not seeing in it what you do. Blend the quoted material smoothly into your prose in a way that illustrates or supports your clearly stated point:

Dropped in	Miranda is twenty-four years old. "After working for three years on a morning newspaper she had an illusion of maturity and experience" (280). [What exact point do you want your reader to understand?]
Point clarified	Although Miranda is twenty-four and has worked on a newspaper for three years, she is not as worldly wise as she thinks she is, having acquired only the "illusion of maturity and experience" (280).

◆ Review pages 421–423 for some ways to blend your quotations into your prose. Always double-check to ensure you are quoting accurately; refer to pages 429–430 and 586–587 for help with proper punctuation and block indention of longer quoted material.

Analysis is not plot summary. Sometimes you may want to offer your readers a brief overview of the work before you begin your in-depth analysis. And certainly there will be times in the body of your essay, especially if you are writing about fiction, that you will need to paraphrase actions or descriptions rather than quote long passages directly. Paraphrasing can indeed provide effective support, but do beware a tendency to fall into unproductive plot-telling. Remember that the purpose of your paper is to provide insight into the work's ideas and craft—not merely to present a rehash of the story line. Keep an eye on each of your claims and quote or paraphrase only those particular lines or important passages that illustrate and support your points. Use your editing skill as a sharp stick to beat back plot summary if it begins taking over your paragraphs.

Practicing What You've Learned

Practice your skills of literary analysis on the following story. A few pre-reading questions are offered here to start your thinking.

"Geraldo No Last Name" is an excerpt from Sandra Cisneros's award-winning novel *The House on Mango Street* (1984), which presents a series of scenes often told by Esperanza, a young girl of Mexican heritage growing up in Chicago. In this story, Esperanza's older teenage friend Marin has had a chance meeting with Geraldo. How does this story comment on stereotyping and human misunderstanding? Who "misunderstands"? Overall, what new insights do you think Cisneros wanted her readers to take away from this brief story, and did she succeed? In what way does Geraldo's having no last name universalize this story?

continued on next page

Geraldo No Last Name

Sandra Cisneros

Sandra Cisneros is an award-winning author of poetry, short stories, and novels. Best known for *The House on Mango Street* (1984), she has also published a collection of stories, *Woman Hollering Creek* (1991); two books of poetry, *My Wicked, Wicked Ways* (1992) and *Loose Woman* (1994); a children's book, *Hairs/Pelitos* (1997); and a novel, *Caramelo* (2002). Her most recent work is *Have You Seen Marie?* (2012), an illustrated fable for adults.

1   She met him at a dance. Pretty too, and young. Said he worked in a restaurant, but she can't remember which one. Geraldo. That's all. Green pants and Saturday shirt. Geraldo. That's what he told her.

2   And how was she to know she'd be the last one to see him alive. An accident, don't you know. Hit and run. Marin, she goes to all those dances. Uptown. Logan. Embassy. Palmer. Aragon. Fontana. The Manor. She likes to dance. She knows how to do cumbias and salsas and rancheras even. And he was just someone she danced with. Somebody she met that night. That's right.

3   That's the story. That's what she said again and again. Once to the hospital people and twice to the police. No address. No name. Nothing in his pockets. Ain't it a shame.

4   Only Marin can't explain why it mattered, the hours and hours, for somebody she didn't even know. The hospital emergency room. Nobody but an intern working all alone. And maybe if the surgeon would've come, maybe if he hadn't lost so much blood, if the surgeon had only come, they would know who to notify and where.

5   But what difference does it make? He wasn't anything to her. He wasn't her boyfriend or anything like that. Just another *brazer** who didn't speak English. Just another wetback. You know the kind. The ones who always look ashamed. And what was she doing out at three A.M. anyway? Marin who was sent home with her coat and some aspirin. How does she explain?

6   She met him at a dance. Geraldo in his shiny shirt and green pants. Geraldo going to a dance.

7   What does it matter?

8   They never saw the kitchenettes. They never knew about the two-room flats and sleeping rooms he rented, the weekly money orders sent home, the currency exchange. How could they?

9   His name was Geraldo. And his home is in another country. The ones he left behind are far away, will wonder, shrug, remember. Geraldo—he went north . . . we never heard from him again.

---

*A variant of *bracero*, referring to a Mexican migratory worker in the U.S.

Practicing What You've Learned

Practice your skills of literary analysis on one or both of the following poems. A few pre-reading questions are presented here to help you begin your analysis.

Consider the point of view in both "Those Winter Sundays" by Robert Hayden and "The Road Not Taken" by Robert Frost. Who is speaking in each poem? How old might each speaker be? What actions are described in each poem? What new insight does each person have? What descriptive words and word-sounds help Hayden present vivid images? How might a reader see Frost's "diverging roads" as a metaphor?

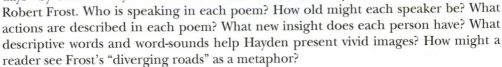

Those Winter Sundays

Robert Hayden

Robert Hayden was a poet and professor at Fisk University and at the University of Michigan; he also served as Poetry Consultant to the Library of Congress. *A Ballad of Remembrance* (1962) first won him international honors at the World Festival of Negro Arts in Senegal; many other volumes of poetry followed, including *Words in Mourning Time* (1970), *American Journal* (1978), and *Complete Poems* (1985). This poem originally appeared in *Angle of Ascent: New and Selected Poems* (1975).

> Sundays too my father got up early
> and put his clothes on in the blueblack cold,
> then with cracked hands that ached
> from labor in the weekday weather made
> 5   banked fires blaze. No one ever thanked him.
>
> I'd wake and hear the cold splintering, breaking.
> When the rooms were warm, he'd call,
> and slowly I would rise and dress,
> fearing the chronic angers of that house,
>
> 10   Speaking indifferently to him,
> who had driven out the cold
> and polished my good shoes as well.
> What did I know, what did I know
> of love's austere and lonely offices?

continued on next page

The Road Not Taken

Robert Frost

Robert Frost was a twentieth-century poet whose poems frequently focus on the characters and scenes of New England. Three of his many volumes of poetry won Pulitzer Prizes: *New Hampshire* (1923), *Collected Poems* (1930), and *A Further Range* (1936). Frost taught at Amherst College, Dartmouth, Yale, and Harvard and was one of the founders of the Bread Loaf School of English in Vermont. This poem was first published in 1916.

> Two roads diverged in a yellow wood,
> And sorry I could not travel both
> And be one traveler, long I stood
> And looked down one as far as I could
> 5 To where it bent in the undergrowth;
>
> Then took the other, as just as fair,
> And having perhaps the better claim,
> Because it was grassy and wanted wear;
> Though as for that the passing there
> 10 Had worn them really about the same,
>
> And both that morning equally lay
> In leaves no step had trodden black.
> Oh, I kept the first for another day!
> Yet knowing how way leads on to way,
> 15 I doubted if I should ever come back.
>
> I shall be telling this with a sigh
> Somewhere ages and ages hence:
> Two roads diverged in a wood, and I—
> I took the one less traveled by,
> 20 And that has made all the difference.

Suggestions for Writing

The two stories and three poems in this chapter may be used as stepping-stones to your own essays. Here are a variety of suggestions:

1. Write an essay of literary analysis presenting your interpretation of "Geraldo No Last Name," "Those Winter Sundays," or "The Road Not Taken." Support your analysis with ample references to the work you've chosen. Consider, if appropriate, discussion of such elements as point of view, characterization, narrative structure, imagery, and diction, among other features.

2. Write an essay comparing/contrasting themes and techniques in two of the literary works from this chapter. For example, how do Hayden and Frost use the past

in their poems? How do Cisneros and Hayden treat the effects of human misunderstanding? How are stereotypical roles examined in Chopin's and Cisneros's stories? Frost and Chopin on life's key choices?

3. Use one of the works in this chapter as a "prompt" for your own personal essay. For example, have you ever taken people for granted or devalued their help, as did the narrator in the Hayden poem? Perhaps the Whitman poem reminded you of a time when you learned something through hands-on experience rather than study? Or perhaps the opposite was true: you didn't fully appreciate an experience until you had studied it? Or, if you prefer, use Cisneros's story "Geraldo No Last Name" to start you thinking about a research essay on some specific aspect of the complex immigration situations facing nations today.

4. *Collaborative Activity:* In both academia and the business world, people are often asked to work together on a joint proposal or committee report. To practice writing with others, meet with another student and discuss the notes you have each taken on "Geraldo No Last Name" or on another story approved by your instructor (many stories are now free and easy to access online). Your assignment calls for a brief essay of analysis (two page maximum) that shows how some significant part of the story (setting, imagery, point of view, a particular character, tone, etc.) contributes to its overall effectiveness. Together, focus a topic and craft a working thesis; then sketch out a plan for presenting your interpretation. Perhaps working on a single computer for ease of revision, draft the mini-essay with your partner, selecting the best supporting evidence from your shared ideas. (Hint: Writing with other people often takes longer than drafting alone, so give this project the time it deserves. ◆ For more discussion of collaborative writing, see pages 119–124 in Chapter 5.)

5. Practice your audience-awareness skills by writing a letter from the point of view of a character whom appears in one of the literary works in this chapter. What, for example, might Marin, the young woman in Cisneros's story, write to Geraldo's family? What might Hayden's narrator say to his father? Frost's narrator, to one of his children on the eve of high school or college graduation?

Chapter 23

Writing in the World of Work

Imagine you are a manager of a business who receives the following memo from one of the sales representatives:

> Our biggest customer in Atlanta asked me to forward the shipment to the company warehouse and I said I could not realizing how serious a decision this was I changed my mind. This OK with you?

Did the salesperson mean to say that at first he thought he could send the shipment, but then changed his mind?

> Our biggest customer in Atlanta asked me to forward the shipment to the company warehouse and I said I could. Not realizing how serious a decision this was, I changed my mind.

Or did he mean he first thought he couldn't but then reconsidered?

> Our biggest customer in Atlanta asked me to forward the shipment to the company warehouse and I said I could not. Realizing how serious a decision this was, I changed my mind.

What would you do as the manager? Very likely, you would stop your current work and contact the salesperson to clarify the situation before you gave final approval. Because of the unclear communication, the extra effort required will cost your business valuable time, energy, and possibly customer satisfaction.

The preceding scenario is not far-fetched; unclear writing hurts businesses and organizations in every country in the world. Consequently, here is a bold claim: *Almost all workplaces today demand employees with good communication skills.*

Although specific writing tasks vary from job to job, profession to profession, successful businesses rely on the effective sharing of information among managers, coworkers, and customers. No employer ever wants to see confusing reports or puzzling messages that result in lost production time, squandered resources, or aggravated clients. To maximize their organization's efficiency, employers look for and reward employees who can demonstrate the very writing skills you have been practicing in this composition course. Without question, your ability to communicate clearly in precise, organized prose will give you a competitive edge in the world of work.

To help you address some of the most common on-the-job writing situations, this chapter offers general guidelines for business letters, office memos, and professional e-mail messages. For job-seekers, a special section at the end of the chapter on the preparation of cover letters, résumés, and post-interview notes will suggest ways to best communicate your experience and skills to any prospective employer.

Insadco Photography/Alamy

Composing Business Letters

Letters in the workplace serve many purposes and audiences, so it isn't possible to illustrate each particular kind. However, it is important to note that all good business letters have some effective qualities in common. And although a business letter is clearly not a personal essay, they share many features: consideration of audience; development of a main idea; organized paragraphs; appropriate tone and diction; and clear, concise expression of thoughts.

Before you begin any letter, prewrite by considering these important questions:

1. What is the main purpose of this letter? What do you want this letter to accomplish? Are you applying for a job, requesting material, offering thanks, lodging a complaint? Perhaps you are answering a request for information about a product, procedure, service, or policy. The occasions for written correspondence are too many to list, but each letter should clearly state its purpose for the reader, just as a thesis in an essay presents your main idea.

2. Who is your "audience," the person to whom you are writing? As discussed in detail on pages 20–23 in Chapter 1, effective writers select the kinds of information, the level of complexity, and even the appropriate "voice" in response to their readers' needs, knowledge, and attitudes. Remember that no matter who the recipient of your letter happens to be, all readers want clarity, not confusion; order, not chaos; and useful information, not irrelevant chitchat. Put yourself in the reader's place: what should she or he know, understand, or decide to do after reading this letter?

3. What overall impression of yourself do you want your letter to present? All business correspondence should be courteous, with a tone that shows your appreciation for the reader's time and attention. Achieving this tone may be more difficult if you are writing a letter of complaint, but remember that to accomplish your purpose (a refund or an exchange of a purchase, for example), you must persuade, not antagonize, your reader. If you're too angry or frustrated to maintain a reasonable tone, give yourself some time to cool off before writing. A respectful tone should not, on the other hand, sound phony or pretentious ("It is indeed

regrettable but I must hereby inform you . . ."). Choose the same level of language you would use in one of your polished academic essays. In short, good business writing is clear, courteous, and direct.

Traditional Business Letter Format

Although much professional correspondence today is conducted through the Internet, you may still compose a variety of letters according to a customary business format. Here is a description of the most common business letter form, for electronic or postal use. Almost all professional letters now use the "block form"—that is, lines of type are flush with the left margin and paragraphs are not indented. If you will be mailing your letter, print on one side of 8½-by-11-inch white bond paper with margins set for a minimum of 1¼ inches at the top and at least one inch on the left and right sides and at the bottom; envelopes should match the letter paper in color and texture.

Business letters (without enclosures or distribution lists) typically have six primary parts:

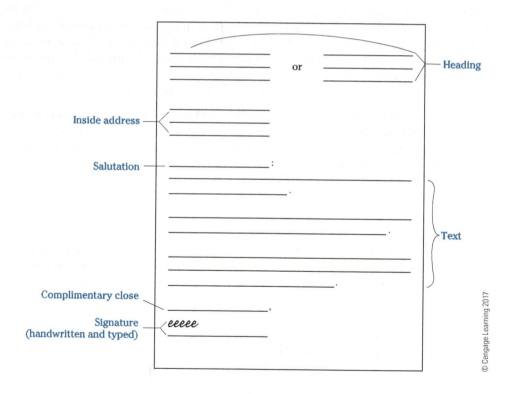

© Cengage Learning 2017

1. The **heading** of a formal letter is your address and the date, placed either above the inside address of the letter or in the upper right corner. If the heading is in the upper right position, the longest line should end at the one-inch margin on the right side of a paper page. All lines in your heading should begin evenly on the left.

If you are using letterhead stationery (paper already imprinted with your business name, address, or logo), you need to add only the date. (In some less-formal letters, it may be permissible to omit the heading and include necessary contact information following your name at the very end of the letter.)

2. The **inside address** contains the name of the person to whom you are writing, the person's title or position, the name of the company or organization, the full address (street or post office box, city, state, ZIP code). The first line of the inside address should appear one or two lines below the last line of the heading. (If you are postally mailing your letter, the inside address information should be repeated exactly on your letter's envelope.)

Correct use of titles and positions can be tricky. Sometimes a person has a title and an additional position; other times, the title is lengthy. In general, if a person's title has more than two words, put it on a separate line:

> Professor Linda Payne
> Dean, College of Liberal Arts
> Wyoming State University

Whenever possible, direct your letter to a specific person. If you do not know the name of the person and cannot discover it before your letter must be sent, you may address the correspondence to the position held by the appropriate person(s): General Manager, Graduate Advisor, Personnel Director, City Council, and so forth.

3. The **salutation** is your letter's greeting to your reader. Begin the salutation one or two lines down from the inside address, and greet the person formally using the word "Dear" plus title and name (Dear Mr. Smith, Dear Ms. Jones,* Dear Dr. Black). The salutation is traditionally followed by a colon rather than the more informal comma:

> Dear Dr. Montoya:
> Dear Personnel Director:

A caution: Be careful to avoid sexist assumptions in your salutations. If you do not know the gender of the person to whom you are writing (initials and many first names—Chris, Pat, Jordan—are used by both men and women), do some research, if possible. When in doubt, use the title or position and last name (Dear Professor Chieu). Use of the full name (Dear Xin Chieu) or organization name (Dear Safety Council) may be preferable to the impersonal "Dear Sir or Madam" or "To Whom It May Concern," phrases that seem stilted today.

---

*If you know that the woman you are writing prefers to be addressed as Mrs. X, address her in this way. However, if you do not know her marital status or preferred title, Ms. may be the best choice. If possible, avoid the matter altogether by using her professional title: Dear Professor Smith, Dear Mayor Alvarez.

4. The "**body**" or **text** of your letter consists of the message that appears in the paragraphs. As in essays, think of your text as having a beginning, a middle, and an ending. Although there is no rule about the number of paragraphs in any business letter, most letters contain the following:

- A first paragraph that clearly states the reason for writing (think about a thesis in an essay).

- One or more paragraphs that present the necessary details or explanation of the reason for writing (think body paragraphs in an essay).

- A last paragraph that sums up the message in a positive way, offers thanks if appropriate, and, on occasion, may provide information to help reader and writer make contact (think conclusion in an essay).

Because professional people receive so much mail, business letters should be brief and to the point. *Above all, readers want clarity!* Scrutinize your prose for any words or phrases that might mislead or confuse your reader. Select precise words and create trim sentences that present your message in the clearest, most straightforward way possible. (◆ For help writing clear, concise prose, review Chapters 6 and 7.)

If possible, without sacrificing clarity or necessary information, keep your letter to one page. Single-spaced paragraphs of eight lines or fewer are easiest to read. Skip a line between paragraphs. If in a paper copy you must go to a second page, type your name, the date, and the page number in an upper corner. If you discover that you have only one or two lines to carry over to the second page, try to condense your text or, if you must, squeeze or expand the margins just a bit. Try not to divide paragraphs or split words between pages. Second and subsequent paper pages should be plain, without any printed letterhead material.

5. The **complimentary closing** of a business letter is a conventional farewell to the reader, typed two lines below the last line of the text. The two most common phrases for closing formal business correspondence are "Sincerely" and "Yours truly." Stick with these unless you have a more informal relationship with the person you are writing. In those cases, you might use such closings as "Cordially" or "Warm regards." The first letter of the first closing word is capitalized, and the closing is followed by a comma.

6. The **signature** part of a business letter presents your name and, if relevant to the situation, your professional title. In a paper copy, you will hand-sign your name in black ink and, beneath that, add your typed name and title, as shown here:

Sincerely,

Jane Doe

Jane Doe
Professor of Philosophy

If you are mailing or delivering a hard-copy, do not forget to sign your letter! Such an oversight not only looks careless but may also suggest to the reader that this is merely a mass-produced form letter.

7. Some letters contain additional information below the signature. Typical notes include the word "enclosure" (or "encl.") to indicate inclusion of additional material (which may be named) or a distribution list to indicate other persons who are receiving a copy of this letter. Distribution is indicated by the word "copy" or by the letters "c" or "cc" (for "courtesy copy"), followed by a colon and the name(s); if more than one person is listed, the names should appear in alphabetical order.

Copy: Mayor Sue Jones
or
cc: Mayor Sue Jones,
  Dr. Inga York

Enclosure: résumé
or
Encl.: résumé

In formal business correspondence, avoid any sort of postscript (P.S.).

Some last advice: Most business letters today may be easily formatted using a document template in Word, and spelling and grammar checker programs can help writers find and fix typos. But, as in any piece of writing, always proofread for errors carefully—and repeatedly! Never trust your spell-checker to catch all possible errors. Don't undercut the message you are sending by failing to revise misspelled words, inaccurate names, ungrammatical sentences, or sloppy punctuation. Also, be sure to select a clear, traditional type font (such as Times New Roman; no fancy script or gothic styles, please), set in a readable size (often 12 point), and use only a printer that can produce dark, high-grade type.

Practicing What You've Learned

Find a recent business letter you or someone you know has received. This letter might be a request for a charitable donation, an announcement of some school policy, a letter of recommendation, or even a parking-violation summons. Assess the effectiveness of the letter: is it clear? Informative? Organized? Write a two-paragraph critique of the letter that identifies both its strengths and any weaknesses you see.

Assignment

Writing business letters becomes easier with practice. Think of an upcoming occasion that will require you to write a professional letter. Perhaps you are asking for a job or accepting one? Applying for a scholarship, grant, or school loan? Requesting an interview or letter of recommendation? Complaining to your landlord? Ordering or returning a product? The choices are many, but try to select a letter that you might indeed send sometime soon. Limit your letter to one page, and revise as many times as necessary to illustrate your thorough understanding of purpose, audience, format, and style. Don't forget to proofread carefully!

Sample Business Letter

Art Tech Studio
802 West Street
Fort Collins, CO 80525
May 10, 2015

Mr. Thomas Valdez
General Manager
Harmony Products, Inc.
645 Monroe Avenue
Little Rock, AR 90056

Dear Mr. Valdez:

Thank you for your May 5 order for twenty of my hand-designed laptop sleeves and for your advance payment check of $250. I am delighted that your company wishes to stock my painted canvas sleeves in both your Little Rock and Fayetteville stores.

The sleeves are being packed in individual boxes this week and should arrive by Air Flight Mail at your main office no later than May 25. If you wish for me to use express mail for quicker arrival, please let me know.

Many thanks again for your interest in my work and for your recent order. I am planning to attend a marketing seminar in Little Rock, June 5–8; I will call you next week to see if we might arrange a brief meeting at your convenience on one of those days. Until then, should you need to contact me, please email me at rzimmerman@gmail.com or call my studio (970/555-6009).

Sincerely,

Rachel Zimmerman

Rachel Zimmerman

Enclosure: receipt

Creating Memos

A memo, short for "memorandum," is a common form of communication *within* a business or an organization. Memos, especially those sent by e-mail, are often more informal in style and tone than business letters, and they may be addressed to more than one person (a committee, a sales staff, an advisory board, etc.). Memos may be sent up or down the chain of command at a particular workplace, or they may be distributed laterally, across a department or between offices. Though the format may vary slightly from organization to organization, paper memos often appear in this way:

TO:	Name of recipient(s) and/or title(s)
FROM:	Name of sender and title
DATE:	Day, month, year
SUBJECT:	Brief identification of the memo's subject matter

The message follows in one or more paragraphs.

Note that in some memos, the term "Re" ("in reference to") may be substituted for the word "Subject." In some paper memos, the name of the sender may be accompanied by the sender's handwritten initials, rather than a full signature as in a business letter.

Many memos are brief, containing important bulletins, announcements, or reminders. Other in-house memos—those explaining policies or procedures, for example—may be long and complex. Lengthy memos may begin with a summary or statement of general purpose and may use headings (such as "Background Information," "Previous Action," or "Recommendations") to identify various parts of the discussion.

All business memos, paper or electronic, regardless of length, share a common goal: the clear, concise communication of useful information from writer to reader.

Sending Professional E-Mail

Although the world of work will never be totally paperless, most businesses today rely on digital communication tools to send or request information, both inside and outside their organizations.

Electronic mail, or e-mail, offers a number of advantages to employees and customers. It's fast, easy, and efficient, as you can compose or forward a message to one person or many people, across the building or across the world, from a variety of sites. Attachment features allow businesses to send documents, forms, graphics, or pictures.

Because e-mail is useful in so many ways to different kinds of businesses and organizations, there is no one-size-fits-all format. Consequently, it's always a good idea to acquaint yourself with customary use of e-mail at your place of work. In addition, here are some suggestions for improving the quality of all professional electronic communications:

1. **Use a helpful subject line.** Successful business leaders today may receive scores of e-mail messages every day; so many that they are tempted to delete any unrecognizable mail that might be "spam" (an unsolicited message or sales offer) or contain a "virus" that might destroy their files. To ensure that your message will be opened and read, always use specific words in the subject line to clearly delineate the central focus or key words of your correspondence ("Project Thunderbolt contracts"). Using a specific subject line will also be helpful if your reader wants to reread your message later and needs to find it quickly in a long list of e-mails.

2. **Begin appropriately.** Unlike a traditional business letter, e-mail normally needs no heading or inside address, but a new communication should begin with an appropriate greeting, depending on the formality of the occasion. For example, if you are writing an officer of another company to ask for information, you might begin with a traditional salutation (Dear Mr. Hall:). An informal memo to a coworker might have a more casual greeting, depending on your relationship to that person (Hello, Bill; Good morning, Ms. Merrill).

3. **Keep your message brief.** Long messages are difficult to read on screens; all that scrolling up and down to check information can be tiresome. If your message is long, consider use of an attachment. Working people are busy, so try to follow the advice given previously in this chapter regarding business letters and memos: clearly state your purpose, explain in a concise manner, and conclude gracefully.

4. **Make it easy to read.** To avoid contributing to your reader's eyestrain, write messages that are visually pleasant. Keep your paragraphs short, and skip a line between each paragraph. If your message is long, break it up with headings, numbered lists, or "bullets." Use a readable, plain font.

5. **Check your tone.** Your e-mail messages should sound professional and cordial. Unlike personal e-mail, which may contain slang, fragments, asides, or funny graphics, business e-mails should be written in standard English and be straight to the point. If you're angry, resist the temptation to fly to the computer and "flame"; cool off and compose a thoughtful, persuasive response instead. Be especially careful about the use of irony or humor: it is easy for readers to misinterpret your words and meaning in an e-mail message and react in a manner opposite the one you intended. In general, strive for a polite, friendly tone, using the clearest, most precise words you can muster.

6. **Sign off.** If your e-mail is performing a task similar to that of a business letter, you may wish to close in a traditional way:

> Yours truly,
> Scott Muranjan

You may also want to create a standard sign-off that not only includes your name but also your title, telephone and fax numbers, and postal and e-mail addresses. Such information is helpful for readers who wish to contact you later.

However, if your e-mail is more akin to an informal memo between coworkers, you may find it appropriate to end with a friendly thought or word of thanks and your first name:

> I'm looking forward to working with you on the Blue file. See you at Tuesday's meeting.
> Scott

Allow your sense of occasion and audience to dictate the kind of closing each e-mail requires.

7. **Revise, proofread, copy, send.** The very ease of e-mail makes it tempting to send messages that may not be truly ready to go. All your professional correspondence should look just that: professional. Take some time to revise for clarity and tone; always proofread. Double-check figures and dates, and run the spell-checker if you have one. If time permits, print out important messages to look over before you hit the Send button. If you need to keep track of your correspondence, make a computer file or a print copy for your office.

Problems to Avoid

Electronic mail is not without its disadvantages. Computers crash, files vaporize, printers freeze, and so on. Work on developing patience and give yourself time to use other methods of communication if necessary. Meanwhile, here are two other tips:

Business e-mail is not private. Perhaps because of individual passwords or because of experience with sealed postal mail, employees often believe that their e-mail is private correspondence. It is not! Employers have the legal right to read any e-mail sent from their organizations. Moreover, you never know when someone may be peering at a screen over the shoulder of the intended recipient. And there's always the danger of hitting the wrong button, sending your thoughts to an entire list of people when you meant to contact only one. To avoid embarrassing yourself—or even endangering your job—never send inappropriate comments, angry responses, petty remarks, or personal information through your business e-mail. Never send confidential or "top secret" business information through e-mail without proper authorization. Learn to use e-mail in a productive way that protects both you and your organization.

Mind your netiquette! Although no one requires that you don your white kid gloves to hit those computer keys, rules of etiquette for e-mail writers are important. Here are a few suggestions for well-behaved writers:

- Don't "shout" your messages in all capital letters. IT'S TOO HARD TO READ A SCREEN FULL OF SAME-SIZED LETTERS. Occasionally, you may type a word in capital letters or bold for emphasis, but use this technique sparingly.
- Be cautious about using Internet and texting shorthand or in-house abbreviations ("the TR6 project"), especially in messages to other organizations. If certain shorthand signs or phrases, such as BTW (by the way), FWIW

(for what it's worth), or G2G (got to go), are routinely used in casual e-mail at your place of work, feel free to adopt them. However, most business correspondence is more formal and not all abbreviations may be universally recognized. When in doubt, spell it out. Business messages depend on clarity and a mutual understanding of all terms. (◆ For more advice regarding texting and Web speak, see pages 170–171.)

- Don't ever, ever use "emoticons" in business or professional writing. Emoticons include typed "smiley" or winky faces read sideways that many people find more annoying than ground glass in a sandwich. Instead of relying on these symbols to communicate emotions of happiness, sadness, surprise, or irony, find the right words instead. Show off your writing skills, not just your ability to arrange type!

- Never forward anyone else's e-mail message without permission, especially if that message contains controversial and/or hurtful statements or confidential material. (Because other people often break this rule, think twice before *you* write.)

Writing Cover Letters and Designing Résumés

Job-seekers often send *cover letters* and *résumés* to potential employers. Although these kinds of documents will vary depending upon the jobs in question, here are some general hints for those in the hunt for employment.

Effective Cover Letters

First, do understand that almost every job application needs a cover letter. Even if a job notice only mentions sending a résumé, your chance of being successfully noticed in a deluge of applications is greatly improved if you "cover" (accompany) your résumé with a professional letter, one that is tailored to fit the employer and job you are seeking.

Next, understand the purposes of your cover letter. You will use it to introduce yourself to your potential employer and explain both why you are applying for a particular job and why you are the best candidate for the position. Unlike a brief résumé, a letter allows you to discuss and emphasize your expertise, special talents, or relevant experience, as well as display your excellent writing and thinking skills.

A cover letter is an exercise in your very best persuasive writing. As such, it calls for some critical thinking about your "audience," the reader(s) of your letter. Do some homework: Find out as much as possible about the job itself so you can make a convincing case for your perfect fit. Research the company to show how you could contribute. (Hint: Going to a potential employer's Web site may reveal a Mission Statement, a record of accomplishments, or a list of goals that will help you shape your letter to speak to their needs.)

To prepare each cover letter, follow the basic steps for writing the traditional business letter, as outlined earlier in this chapter. In the first paragraph, clearly tell your reader why you are writing: the specific job you are applying for and why. Devote one or more paragraphs in the "body" of your letter to explaining why you (a successful product of your education, training, experiences, previous employment, etc.) are a good match for the advertised position and/or how you might benefit the organization. Your concluding paragraph should express thanks for the employer's consideration and briefly reemphasize your interest in the job; in this paragraph you may also mention contact information or explain access to your credentials. In some situations, you may indicate your availability for an interview. If the employer is interested, he or she will read your résumé for more details and possibly distribute copies to others involved in the hiring process.

> REMEMBER: Employers today may receive hundreds of applications for a single job, so it is important to present yourself as positively as possible in your letter and résumé. If your campus has a career center, consider consulting it or its Web site as your first step. Career centers often have extraordinary resources: sample cover letters and résumés, hints for interviews, information on electronic job searching, and much more. Many online professional career services offer similar samples and tips. Because there are multiple ways to arrange a résumé, you will find it useful to familiarize yourself with some representative samples before you begin working on your own.

Effective Résumés

A *résumé* is a document that presents a brief summary of your educational background, work experiences, professional skills, special qualifications, and honors; some résumés also contain a brief list of references and their contact information. You may be asked to submit a résumé on a variety of occasions, most often to supplement your applications for jobs, interviews, promotions, scholarships, grants, fellowships, or other kinds of opportunities. Because prospective employers are the largest target audience for résumés, the following pages offer advice to help job-seekers design the most effective document possible.

Although there is no single blueprint for all résumés, there is one guiding principle: *select and arrange your information in the way that most effectively highlights your strengths to your prospective employer.* Think of your résumé as a concise advertisement for yourself.

To find the best way to "sell" yourself to an employer, you might choose to adopt one of the two most popular arrangement styles:

- **Functional format:** This arrangement places the reader's focus more directly on the job-seeker's education and skills than on limited work experience. It is better suited for job-seekers who are new graduates or those just entering the workforce. Most résumés of this type are one page.

- **Experiential format:** This style emphasizes professional experience by placing work history in the most prominent position, listing the current or most important employment first. This format might be best for students who have a work history before returning to school or for those students who have worked throughout their college careers. If the list of relevant professional experience is lengthy, this kind of résumé may extend to a second page if necessary.

Before you begin drafting your résumé, make a list of the information you want to include. Then think about the best ways to group your material, and select an appropriate title for each section. Some of the common content areas include the following:

1. **Heading.** Located at the top of your résumé, this section identifies you and presents your contact information: your full name, postal address, phone number(s), and e-mail address. You may wish to put your name in slightly bigger type or in bold letters.

2. **Employment objective.** Some job-seekers choose to include a statement describing the kind of employment or specific position they are seeking. Others omit this section, making this information clear in their cover letters. If you do include this section, always substitute a brief, specific objective for trite, overblown language any job-seeker in the world might write:

   Vague Seeking employment with a company offering intellectual challenges and opportunities for professional growth

   Specific A microbiology research position in a laboratory or center working on disease prevention and control

   It's best to customize a résumé for each job announcement you respond to, so you can use this section to show that the position you most want matches the one advertised. However, if you plan to use one résumé for a variety of job applications, beware presenting an employment objective so narrowly focused that it excludes you from a particular application pool.

3. **Education.** If you have no relevant or recent work experience, this section might appear next on your résumé. Begin with the highest degree you have earned or are working on; if you are about to graduate, you may present the anticipated graduation date. Include the name of the school and its location and, if relevant, your major, minor, or special concentration. Some students with a "B" or better grade point average also include that information. This section might also contain any professional certificates or licenses (teaching, real estate, counseling, etc.) you have earned or other educational information you deem relevant to a particular job search (internships, research projects, study-abroad programs, honors classes, or other special training).

4. **Professional experience.** If you wish to emphasize your work history, place this section after your heading or employment objective, rather than your educational background. In this section, list the position title, name of employer, city and state, and employment dates, with the most current job or relevant work experience first. Some résumés include brief statements describing the responsibilities or accomplishments of each position; you may list these statements (with bullets, not numbers) if space is an issue (see page 534 for an example). If you include job descriptions, be specific ("prepared monthly payroll for 35 employees") rather than general ("performed important financial tasks monthly"); use action verbs (supervised, developed, organized, trained, created, etc.) that present your efforts in a strong way. Use past-tense verbs for work completed and present tense for current responsibilities.

   Note that résumés traditionally do not use the word "I"; starting descriptions of your accomplishments with strong verbs ("Supervised"), rather than repeating such phrases as "I was responsible for," saves precious space on your résumé.

5. **Skills.** Because you want to stress your value to a prospective employer, you may wish to note relevant professional skills or special abilities you have to offer. This section may be especially important if you do not have a work history; many recent graduates place this section immediately following the education section to underscore the skills they could bring to the workplace. For example, you might list technical skills you possess or mention expertise in another language.

6. **Honors, awards, activities.** In this section, list awards, scholarships, honors, and prizes to show that others have recognized you as an outstanding worker, student, writer, teacher, and so on. Here (or perhaps in a section for related skills or experiences) you might also add leadership roles in organizations, and even certain kinds of volunteer work, if mentioning these would further your case. Although you don't want to trivialize your résumé by listing irrelevant activities, think hard about your life from a "skills" angle. Coordinating a campus charity project, for example, may indicate just the kinds of managerial skills an employer is looking for. Don't pad your résumé—but don't undersell yourself either.

7. **References.** Some employers ask immediately for references, persons they may contact for more information about you and your work or academic experiences; other employers ask for references later in the hiring process. If references are requested with the initial application letter, the information may be listed at the end of the résumé or on an attached page. Reference information includes the person's full name and title or position, the name and postal address of the person's business or organization, a telephone number, and an e-mail address, if available. In most cases, avoid listing friends or neighbors as references; typically, résumé references should be academics or professionals who are familiar with your work.

Critique Your Page Appeal

Once you have decided on your résumé's content, you also need to consider its visual appeal. Because employers often look over résumés quickly, your page should be not only informative but also professional looking and easy to read. You may highlight your section titles (education, work experiences, skills, etc.) by using boldface or large print, but don't overuse such print. Balance your text and white space in a pleasing arrangement. Unless you have a compelling reason for another choice, always laser print any hard copies you need on high-quality white or off-white paper.

If you have problems arranging your material (too much information jammed on the page or so little that your text looks lonely, for example), go back to campus or online career services to look at ways others handled similar problems. A good page design, like a good haircut, can frame your best features in the most engaging way.

Most important: Always proofread your résumé for errors in grammar, punctuation, spelling, spacing, or typing! Because you want your résumé to look as professional as possible, make a point of having several careful (human) readers proofread your final draft.

Problems to Avoid

Remain ethical. Never lie on a résumé! Never, ever! Although you want to present yourself in the best possible ways, never fib about your experience, forge credentials you don't have, take credit for someone else's work, or overstate your participation in a project. No matter what you have heard about "puffery" in résumés ("Everyone exaggerates, so why shouldn't I?"), avoid embarrassment (or even legal action) by always telling the truth. Instead of misrepresenting yourself, find ways to identify and arrange your knowledge and skills to best highlight your strengths.

Contact your references in advance. You *must* obtain permission from each person before you list him or her as a reference. Even if you know the person well, use your good manners here: in person, by phone, or in a politely written note, ask in advance of your job application if you may name him or her as a reference. Once permission is granted, it's smart to give your references your résumé and any other information that might help them help you if they are contacted by a prospective employer. (Although former bosses or teachers may remember you well, they may be hazy about your exact dates of employment or the semester of your course work. Give them a helpful list of places, dates, skills, and—though you may have to overcome your sense of modesty—tactfully remind them of any outstanding work you did.)

It's also good manners (and smart) to send your references a thank-you note, expressing your appreciation for their part in your job search (such notes are absolutely *required* if people write letters of recommendation for you). In most cases, thank-you notes should be hand-written on stationery and sent through postal mail; e-mail notes are not appropriate except in the most casual circumstances.

Add personal information thoughtfully. Federal law protects you: employers may not discriminate on the basis of ethnicity, race, religion, age, or gender. You should not include on your résumé any personal information (marital status, number of children, birth date, country of origin, etc.) that is not relevant to the job search. Although you may, if you wish, include information on your résumé about relevant personal interests (travel, theatrical experience, volunteer rescue work, etc.), you should be aware that employers may not consider such details useful. Don't squander your résumé space on unessential information! A better plan: if you've spent a great deal of your time in some after-work or extracurricular activity, identify the *skills* you have developed that will transfer to the workplace (customer relations, public speaking, editing, etc.). Instead of just describing yourself, show prospective employers what you can *do* for them.

Special note: A number of Web sites now help employers and job-seekers find each other through the posting of jobs and résumés. If you do post your résumé on such a site, choose your words carefully. Many employers use tracking software to look for keywords in résumés that match their needs, so note the language of a job description and consider repeating, where appropriate, a few important the same key words used in the job description.

Sample Résumés

The resumes that follow were designed by recent college graduates. Because the first graduate did not have an extensive work record, he chose a functional format to emphasize his education, business skills, and scholastic honors. The second résumé briefly notes specific skills from previous academic and work experiences that might interest a prospective employer.

Sample Résumé #1

Brent Monroe

417 Remington Street
Fort Collins, CO 80525

(970) 555-4567
BCMonroe@gmail.com

Education

B.S. in Business Administration, Colorado State University, May 2015. GPA 3.6
A.S., Front Range Community College, May 2012. GPA 3.9

Professional Skills

Accounting

Spreadsheet programs
Amortization schedules
Payroll design and verification
Contracts and invoices

Computer

Microsoft Word, Works, Access, Outlook Express
Spreadsheets: Excel, Select
Presentations: PowerPoint, Macromedia Flash
Web site design

Awards and Activities

Outstanding Student Achievement Award, College of Business, Colorado
    State University, 2012
President's Scholarship, Colorado State University, 2014 and 2015
Treasurer, Business Students Association, Colorado State University, 2014

Employment

Assistant Manager, Poppa's Pizza; Ault, Colorado, 6/13–12/14

References

Professor Gwen Lesser
Department of Accounting
Colorado State University
Fort Collins, CO 80523
(970) 555-7890
Glesser@colostate.edu

Professor Ralph Berber
Department of Finance
Colorado State University
Fort Collins, CO 80523
(970) 555-2344
Rberber@colostate.edu

Mr. Randy Attree
Manager, Poppa's Pizza
630 E. Third Street
Ault, CO 80303
(970) 333-4839

Sample Résumé #2

ROSEMARY SILVA

3000 Colorado Avenue   (720) 555-6428
Boulder, Colorado 80303   Rosesilva@yahoo.com

Objective

A full-time position as a counselor at a mental health or addiction-recovery facility

Education

B.A., University of Colorado, Boulder, May 2015. Major: Psychology. Minor: Spanish.

Internship and Research Experience

Intern Detoxification Counselor, Twin Lakes Recovery Center, Boulder, Colorado; January–May 2015.

- Provided one-on-one counseling for inpatients
- Conducted admission interviews and prepared mental/physical evaluation reports
- Responded to crisis phone line
- Monitored physical vitals of patients; performed basic paramedical techniques
- Referred patients and family members to other community agencies

Psychology Research Lab Assistant, University of Colorado at Boulder, under the direction of Professor Lois Diamond; September–December 2014.

- Helped conduct experiments on CU student-volunteers to measure the relationship of memory and academic success
- Recorded student information and validated research credit slips

Employment

Night Security Dispatcher, University of Colorado, Boulder, Campus Police Department; May 2012–April 2014.

- Accurately received and responded to emergency and non-emergency calls and radio transmissions
- Communicated emergency information to appropriate agencies, such as Boulder Police and the Rape Crisis Center
- Dispatched security units and counselors to disturbances
- Wrote detailed records describing incoming calls and security patrol responses

References Available upon Request

Practicing What You've Learned

A. Prepare a cover letter for a real or dream job you want now, soon, or in the future, perhaps after graduation. Persuade the employer that you are the best person for this job.

B. Prepare a one-page résumé for your professional use at this time or in the near future. While you are in school, you might use this résumé to apply for a scholarship, an internship, a summer job, or a part-time position. Arrange your information to emphasize your strengths, and don't forget to thoroughly proofread several times before you print your final draft. (If you keep a copy of this résumé handy and revise it regularly, you will be ready to respond quickly should a job or other opportunity unexpectedly present itself.)

Assignment

Collaborative Activity: Exchange a cover letter and/or a current résumé (perhaps one—or both—of those you wrote for the preceding "Practicing What You've Learned" assignment) with that of a classmate. Role-play prospective employers, and give each other helpful feedback. Does the cover letter and/or résumé effectively "sell" the job-seeker? Has the information been organized in the most persuasive way? What specific details or action verbs might increase the chances of success? Be sure to proofread carefully, pointing out any typos, mechanical errors, or stylistic inconsistencies.

Preparing Interview Notes and Post-Interview Letters

If a prospective employer wishes to interview you, sketch out a few notes for yourself before the meeting. Try to anticipate questions you may be asked, such as "What are your strengths as a worker?" and "How would you fit into our organization?" You will feel much more confident if you are prepared to discuss specific experiences that show both your skills and your previous work or school successes. Think about important information you wish your interviewer to know; consider making a brief list of the reasons you are the best candidate for the job. Once you have completed your notes, jot down a few key words on a note card to review just before your appointment so you can easily recall the details you want to provide. (◆ For more good suggestions, turn to "Preparing for the Job Interview: Know Thyself" [pages 233–234] by Katy Piotrowski, a career-search consultant.)

After you interview for a job you want, consider writing a follow-up note to the prospective employer. This letter should be a polite thank-you for the interview, and more. Use the opportunity to again emphasize your skills. Begin by thanking the person for his or her time, but then move on to show that you think, now more than ever, that you are the right person for the position and for the organization. Illustrate this claim by showing that during the interview you really listened and observed: "After hearing about your goals for new product X, I know I could contribute because . . . " Or remind your interviewer of reasons to hire you: "You stressed your company's need for someone with XYZ skills. My internship training in that area . . ." In other words, use this follow-up letter not only to offer your thanks but also to advertise yourself (and your good writing skills) one more time.

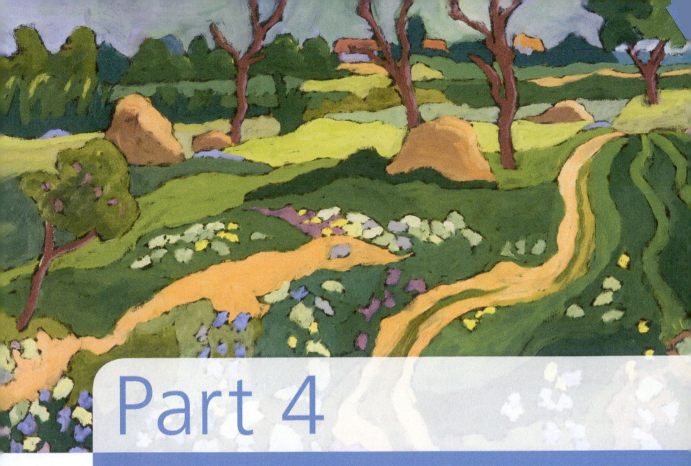

Part 4

A Concise Handbook

Part Four of this text begins with an overview of the parts of speech, followed by a brief discussion of sentence components and types. These pages present explanations, definitions, and illustrations to help you better understand the grammatical conventions and terms used in the handbook chapters that follow. Chapters 24, 25, and 26 will address major errors in grammar, punctuation, and mechanics, showing you how to recognize and correct these problems. Each chapter begins with a diagnostic test to help you identify the rules you may need to review. Then each rule will be explained as simply as possible, with a minimum of technical language. Beside each rule you will find the editing mark or abbreviation that most instructors use to identify that error; each rule is also numbered for easy reference. Exercises placed throughout each chapter offer opportunities to practice the advice; collaborative assignments may also promote improved editing and proofreading skills.

Parts of Speech

The following section offers an overview of the eight groups of words called *parts of speech.* Knowing how a word or phrase is properly used may help you produce sentences that are clear, correct, and pleasing to your readers. In addition, recognizing commonly used grammatical terms may make it easier for you to understand your instructor's advice as well as the explanations of major errors in usage and punctuation that appear in the following handbook chapters.

The eight parts of speech are *nouns, pronouns, verbs, adjectives, adverbs, prepositions, conjunctions,* and *interjections.* The group to which a word belongs is determined by its function in a particular sentence; consequently, a word may be one part of speech in one sentence and a different part of speech in another. (For example, note that "rock" is a noun—a thing—in "Put down that rock!" but also a verb—a word expressing action—in "Don't rock the boat!")

Here is a brief introduction to the parts of speech. You will also see some of these definitions repeated in the various sections on grammatical errors in Chapter 24. Moving back and forth between this overview and the advice in that chapter should help you improve your grammatical skills as you draft and revise your sentences.

1. **Nouns** name persons, places, things, and concepts. *Proper nouns* are the names of particular people, places, and things and should be capitalized; *common nouns,* referring to any person, place, or thing, are not capitalized. *Gerunds* are nouns formed from verbs ending in "-ing."

   Examples of Common Nouns   The *girl* sold her *car* in *town.*
   Examples of Proper Nouns   *Rachel* sold her *Honda* in *Denver.*
   Example of a Gerund   *Dancing* is *fun.*

   (◆ For additional information on the uses of nouns, see pages 552–553.)

2. **Pronouns** take the place of nouns. By using pronouns, you can avoid repeating nouns in the same sentence or group of sentences.

   Example We saw Jennifer across the parking lot and waved to *her.* [Use of "her" avoids the awkward repetition of "We saw Jennifer across the parking lot and waved to Jennifer."]

   There are several classes of pronouns, including these six important kinds:

   - *Personal pronouns* refer to specific people; they include such words as "I," "you," "he," "her," "it," and "them." (*Compound personal pronouns*—sometimes called reflexive pronouns—add "-self" or "-selves" to some of the simple personal ones: "himself," "herself," "themselves.")

     Example   *You* and *I* will meet *him* at the movies.

---

*Some authorities claim nine parts of speech, adding the group of words called *articles:* "a," "an," and "the." In English "a" generally precedes nouns beginning with consonants (*a* cat); "an" generally precedes nouns beginning with vowels (*an* island).

- *Indefinite pronouns* refer to nonspecific people or things and include such words as "everyone," "everything," "someone," "anyone," and "anybody."

  Example   *Everyone* should use caution crossing that busy street.

- *Possessive pronouns* (such as "his," "hers," "its," "ours," "theirs") show ownership.

  Example   *His* passport was about to expire; *its* renewal deadline was March 15.

- *Demonstrative pronouns* refer the reader to previous references.

  Example   *That* is my laptop, *those* are my favorite shoes, and *this* is my bag.

- *Interrogative pronouns* introduce questions.

  Example   *Whose* laptop? *Which* shoes? *Who* is asking all these questions?

- *Relative pronouns* join a dependent clause to the main clause of a sentence and describe a previous noun or pronoun. Commonly used relative pronouns are "who," "which," "that," and "whose."

  Examples   The singer *who* won the competition is holding a free concert.
  I found the wallet *that* I thought I had lost at the restaurant.

  (◆ For more information on the uses of pronouns, see pages 553–557.)

3. **Verbs** express action ("walk," "yell," "swim") and states of being ("am," "is," "are"). A verb phrase may be composed of several words: "should have written," "might have called."

   Three important kinds of verbs include the following:

- *Action verbs* express physical or mental activity.

  Examples   Birds *fly* through the yard.
  I *dream* of beaches in Hawaii.

- *Linking verbs* (such as "is, "are," "was," "were,") show states of being; they may also show connections between ideas or relationships of one thing to another.

  Examples   Shameka *is* twenty-eight years old.
  Austin *was* the youngest child.

- *Auxiliary verbs* are sometimes referred to as "helper verbs" because they assist the main verbs in communicating meaning or time of action. Common auxiliary verbs include forms of "do," "have," "may," "can," and "will."

  Examples (Auxiliary + Main Verbs) Good students *do proofread* their essays.
  Revising *will help* your writing.

  Also note that verbs may be described as being in the *active voice* or the *passive voice.*

- Active voice denotes that the subject of the verb is performing the action:
  The house-sitter *fed* the cat.

- Passive voice denotes that the subject of the verb is acted upon:
  The cat *was fed* by the house-sitter.

Verbs come in many forms, but three to remember as you revise your prose include the *infinitive*, the *participle*, and the *gerund*.

- An infinitive is a verb introduced by the word "to": I like to *read*.

- A participle may share the properties of both a verb and a modifier; present participles end in "-ing": *Watching* the rain fall, we knew we would be late.

- A gerund is a verb plus "-ing" used as a noun: *Swimming* is good exercise.

    (◆ For advice addressing some of the common errors with verbs, see pages 546–548.)

4. **Adjectives** modify or describe nouns and pronouns. *Proper adjectives* derived from proper nouns are usually capitalized. *Predicate adjectives* may follow the word they modify.

    Examples   I bought a *red* sweater, just the *perfect* weight for *Colorado* evenings. Her answer was *wrong*.

5. **Adverbs** most often modify or describe verbs, adjectives, and other adverbs. They frequently answer "how" or "how much" and end in "-ly."

    Examples   My father drove *slowly*. ["Slowly" modifies the verb, describing how he drove.]

    Her answer was *partially* wrong. ["Partially" modifies the adjective "wrong," describing how incorrect the answer was.]

    She appeared *mildly* amused. ["Mildly" modifies the adverb "amused," describing the extent of her delight.]

    (◆ For additional information on the use of adjectives and adverbs, see pages 558–559.)

6. **Prepositions** are words that most often show locations and relationships in time, place, and direction. The following are some common prepositions:

to	under	in	during
on	with	at	upon
about	by	for	since
between	through	from	after
of	before	over	

A preposition and its object make up a *prepositional phrase*, which may be used as an adjective or adverb.

    Example   *During Spring Break,* we took a vacation out of the country. [The first prepositional phrase is used as an adverb to tell when and the other is used as an adjective to describe the place of the vacation.]

Writers should avoid ending sentences with prepositions when possible. Recast the sentence, or simply drop an unnecessary (and ungrammatical) preposition: "Where are you sitting at?" becomes "Where are you sitting?"

7. **Conjunctions** connect words ("dogs *and* cats") or groups of words ("please return package *or* pay for the item").

There are two kinds of conjunctions for you to recognize:

- *Coordinating conjunctions* connect two words, phrases, or clauses of equal kind or rank. The most commonly used coordinating conjunctions are "for," "and," "nor," "but," "or," "yet," and "so."

  Examples He promised an evening of singing *and* dancing. [connecting two words]

  We can either hail a cab *or* catch the subway. [connecting two phrases]

  I have to be home early, *but* you can stay out late. [connecting two clauses]

- *Subordinating conjunctions* connect two clauses of unequal rank; as their name indicates, they connect one clause that is subordinate to—that is, dependent for meaning upon—its main clause. Common subordinating conjunctions include "because," "when," "if," "as," "since," "after," and "although."

  Example *Because* his songs promote violence, I won't buy anything by that singer.

  In most cases when a subordinate clause begins the sentence, it is followed by a comma as shown above.

  (◆ Understanding how to use coordinating and subordinating conjunctions is important as you learn to create sentence variety and also how to avoid fragment, run-on, or spliced sentences. For more information, see pages 561–562 and 563–565.)

8. **Interjections** are exclamatory words that frequently express strong, sudden, or contrary emotions. They may stand alone or they may be part of a sentence.

Examples *Ouch! Help!* Call an ambulance!

Oh, never mind.

OMG! My hair is on fire!

Sentence Components and Classifications

In addition to recognizing the parts of speech, you may find it helpful to understand some of the grammatical terms used to describe sentence components and types. Here are a few common terms, their definitions, and examples.

1. A *sentence* is most often a group of words that expresses a complete thought.

   - The squirrel ate the bird seed.

2. A sentence contains a *subject* and a *predicate*, either expressed or understood. The subject is the performer or receiver of the action or state of being expressed in the predicate, which gives information about the subject.

   - The squirrel [subject] ate the bird seed [predicate].

   A subject may be implied rather than stated.

   - Stop talking! Run for your life! ["You" is implied.]

3. A *direct object* receives the action of the verb. It often answers the question "what?"

   - We caught a *skunk* [direct object] in a trap from the Humane Society.

4. An *indirect object* names the person or thing to whom or for whom the action is done.

   - We gave the *dog* [indirect object] some special treats [direct object].

5. A *modifier* is a word or group of words used to describe, characterize, or change the meaning of other words in the sentence. Adjectives and adverbs are common modifiers.

   - The *starving* child *happily* ate the *cold* pizza.

6. A *phrase* is a group of related words in a sentence that do not contain a subject or predicate. Phrases do not stand alone. Common forms include prepositional, infinitive, and verbal phrases.

   - He accidentally set up the tent *on an ant hill* [prepositional phrase].
   - *Waving frantically,* he ran toward the river. [verbal phrase, using participle "ing" form of the verb "wave"]

7. A *clause* is a group of related words in a sentence that do have a subject and a predicate. Independent clauses stand alone and are complete thoughts; they are, in essence, what we call sentences. Dependent clauses, on the other hand, need to be attached for their meaning to a main clause; they are considered fragments if they stand alone.

   - Abraham Lincoln was the first president to have a beard. [independent clause]
   - Although my history book fails to mention this fact [dependent clause], Abraham Lincoln was the first president to have a beard [independent clause].

8. The word "compound" is often used to indicate parts of sentences that appear in multiple forms, such as compound subjects, predicates, clauses, and objects.

   • *Sarah* and *Kate* received their Master's Degrees on the same day. [compound subject]

   • The girls *found interesting jobs* and *moved to different states*. [compound predicate]

9. Sentences themselves may be classified according to their structures as four types: simple, compound, complex, and compound-complex.

   A *simple sentence* has one independent clause.

   • She practices yoga.

   A *compound sentence* has two or more independent clauses. (Expressed another way, a compound sentence is two simple sentences joined by a conjunction.)

   • Sarah moved to Berkeley, and Kate stayed in Washington.

   A *complex sentence* may consist of one independent clause and one or more dependent clauses.

   • If we are thoughtful enough [dependent clause], we usually can find an important lesson in every disappointment [independent clause].

   A *compound-complex* sentence includes two or more independent clauses and at least one dependent clause.

   • Thomas Jefferson is a much-admired president [independent clause], but he is especially honored in Virginia [independent clause], where he founded the state university [dependent clause].

10. Sentences may also be classified by purpose:

    Declarative: makes a statement (The day is sunny.)

    Imperative: gives a command (Do not pass that car.)

    Interrogative: asks a question (Why are you here?)

    Exclamatory: expresses strong emotion (You look really happy tonight!)

Chapter 24

Major Errors in Grammar

Assessing Your Skills: Grammar

To help you focus your study of this chapter, take the self-graded test that follows. Each of the sentences below contains one or more errors discussed in this chapter. See how much you already know by correcting the sentences (including punctuation) and then checking the answers on pages 569–570. By taking this test, you will be better able to evaluate your knowledge of grammar and direct your attention to those rules governing the errors you missed.*

1. Almost everyone today recognize the Statue of Liberty, but not everybody know its history.

2. Plans for the statue was first began in 1865 by Frenchman Edouard de Laboulaye. In honor of the United States' love of democracy and French-American friendship; according to the National Parks Service.

3. Commissioned to design the work, Bedloe's Island in the New York Harbor was chosen as the location by artist Frederic-Auguste Bartholdi. Because of how it could be seen by boats of immigrants thousands of who was entering the country via Ellis Island and was government owned.

4. The project was a joint effort between the two countries the French agreed to build the statue the U.S. building the pedestal.

5. Money was raised by France by entertainment, selling items with the statue's picture on it, and they charged some public fees. (Though between you and I, this seems difficult and in fact didn't work out so good in the US)

6. The statue has a steel framework designed by Alexandre Gustave Eiffel, who previous had designed the famous Eiffel Tower, covered with a flexible copper skin the width of two pennies that don't crack in high winds.

7. The statue face was modeled on Bartholdi's mother, each of the seven rays of her crown represent one of the seven seas and continents of the world, the torch is

*Historical information included in this assessment test provided by the National Parks Service; for more interesting details about the Statue of Liberty and other famous US landmarks, see the National Parks Service's Web site at <www.nps.gov/>.

a symbol of enlightenment, broken chains at its feet representing freedom from oppression, the tablet in her arm would stand for law.

8. Completed in France in the summer of 1884, the parts had to carefully be disassembled and shipped separate to New York.

9. Reassembled after four months, thousands of spectators watched the massive 305 feet high statue dedication on October 28, 1886.

10. Both you and me can't hardly disagree with the National Parks Service when they call the Statue of Liberty one of the more better recognized icons of democracy in the world, for more information; you may go online to <www.nps.gov/stli/historyculture>.

Errors with Verbs

Verbs express action ("run," "walk," "kick") or state of being ("is," "are," "was").

 24a   Faulty Agreement   S-V Agr

Make your verb agree in number with its subject; a singular subject takes a singular verb, and a plural subject takes a plural verb.

Incorrect	*Ms. Martinez*, principal of the local elementary school, *don't* agree that cell phones should be banned in the classroom.
Correct	*Ms. Martinez*, principal of the local elementary school, *doesn't* agree that cell phones should be banned in the classroom.
Incorrect	The *actions* of the new senator *hasn't* been consistent with her campaign promises.
Correct	The *actions* of the new senator *haven't* been consistent with her campaign promises.

Compound subjects joined by "and" take a plural verb, unless the subject refers to a single person or a single unit.

Examples	*Bean sprouts* and *tofu are* foods Jim Bob won't consider eating. ["Bean sprouts" and "tofu" are a compound subject joined by "and"; therefore, use a plural verb.]
	The *winner* and *new champion refuses* to give up the microphone at the news conference. ["Winner" and "champion" refer to a single person; therefore, use a singular verb.]

Listed here are some of the most confusing subject-verb agreement problems:

1. With a collective noun: a singular noun referring to a collection of elements as a unit generally takes a singular verb.

Incorrect	During boring parts of the Saturday afternoon lecture, the *class* often *look* at the clock.
Correct	During boring parts of the Saturday afternoon lecture, the *class* often *looks* at the clock.
Incorrect	The *army* of the new nation *want* shoes, better food, and weekend passes.
Correct	The *army* of the new nation *wants* shoes, better food, and weekend passes.

2. With a relative pronoun ("that," "which," and "who") used as a subject: the verb agrees with its antecedent, the word being described.

Incorrect	The boss rejected a shipment of *shirts, which* was torn.
Correct	The boss rejected a shipment of *shirts, which* were torn.

3. With "each," "everybody," "everyone," and "neither" as the subject: use a singular verb even when followed by a plural construction.

Incorrect	*Each* of the children *think* Mom and Dad are automatic teller machines.
Correct	*Each* of the children *thinks* Mom and Dad are automatic teller machines.
Incorrect	Although only a few of the students saw the teacher pull out his hair, *everybody know* why he did it.
Correct	Although only a few of the students saw the teacher pull out his hair, *everybody knows* why he did it.
Incorrect	*Neither* have a dime left by the second of the month.
Correct	*Neither has* a dime left by the second of the month.

4. With "either . . . or" and "neither . . . nor": the verb agrees with the nearer item.

Incorrect	Neither rain nor dogs nor *snow keep* the mail carrier from delivering bills.
Correct	Neither rain nor dogs nor *snow keeps* the mail carrier from delivering bills.
Incorrect	Either Jack or *the twins* is playing soccer tonight.
Correct	Either Jack or *the twins* are playing soccer tonight.

5. With "here is (are)" and "there is (are)": the verb agrees with the number indicated by the subject following the verb.

Incorrect	*There is* only two good reasons for missing this law class: death and jury duty.
Correct	*There are* only two good *reasons* for missing this law class: death and jury duty.

Incorrect	To help you do your shopping quickly, Mr. Scrooge, *here are* a list of gifts under a dollar.
Correct	To help you do your shopping quickly, Mr. Scrooge, *here is a list* of gifts under a dollar.

6. With plural nouns intervening between subject and verb: the verb still agrees with the subject.

Incorrect	The *jungle*, with its poisonous plants, wild animals, and biting insects, *make* Bob long for the sidewalks of Topeka.
Correct	The *jungle*, with its poisonous plants, wild animals, and biting insects, *makes* Bob long for the sidewalks of Topeka.

7. With nouns that are plural in form but singular in meaning: a singular verb is usually correct.

Examples	*News travels* slowly if it comes through the post office.
	Physics requires a background in both math and science.
	Politics is a dangerous game.

8. As you revise your writing, use a dictionary if you need help determining whether a word is singular or plural. For example, two common subject–verb agreement errors occur with the words "media" and "data," which, despite colloquial or everyday usage, should be treated as plurals in formal writing.

Correct	The *data were* faulty.
	The *media* often *influence* public opinion polls.

Practicing What You've Learned

Errors with Verbs: Subject–Verb Agreement

The following sentences contain subject–verb agreement errors. Correct the problems by changing the verbs. Some sentences contain more than one error.

1. A recent report on German Shepherds show that they have a sense of smell that is 100,000 times stronger than a human's.

2. The team from Jackson High School are considering switching from wearing shoes to playing barefoot.

3. Neither of the students know that both mystery writer Agatha Christie and inventor Thomas Edison was dyslexic.

4. Each of the twins have read about Benjamin Banneker's contribution to the surveying and design of Washington, D.C., but neither were aware that he also correctly calculated the appearance of a solar eclipse on April 14, 1789.

continued on next page

5. Clarity in speech and writing are absolutely essential in the business world today.

6. Historical data suggests that the world's first money, in the form of coins, were made in Lydia, a country that is now part of Turkey.

7. Bananas, rich in vitamins and low in fat, is rated the most popular fruit in America.

8. There is many people in my dormitory who appreciate a big cheese pizza, but none of my roommates order pineapple as a topping.

9. Either the Labrador Retriever or the German Shepherd hold the honor of being the most popular breed of dogs in the United States, say the American Kennel Club.

10. Many people considers Johnny Appleseed a mythical figure, but now two local historians, authors of a well-known book on the subject, argues that he was a real person named John Chapman.

24b Subjunctive   V Sub

When you make a wish or a statement that is contrary to fact, use the subjunctive verb form "were."

Incorrect	I wish I *was* queen so I could have a diamond crown.
Correct	I wish I *were* queen so I could have a diamond crown. [This expresses a wish.]
Incorrect	If "Fightin' Henry" *was* a foot taller and thirty pounds heavier, we would all be in trouble.
Correct	If "Fightin' Henry" *were* a foot taller and thirty pounds heavier, we would all be in trouble. [This proposes a statement contrary to fact.]

24c Tense Shift   T

In most cases, the first verb in a sentence establishes the tense of any later verb. Keep your verbs within the same time frame to avoid confusing your readers.

Incorrect	Big Joe *saw* the police car coming up behind, so he *turns* into the next alley.
Correct	Big Joe *saw* the police car coming up behind, so he *turned* into the next alley.
Incorrect	Horace *uses* an artificial sweetener in his coffee all day, so he *felt* a pizza and ice cream *were* fine for dinner.
Correct	Horace *uses* an artificial sweetener in his coffee all day, so he *feels* a pizza and ice cream *are* fine for dinner.

| Incorrect | The new manager *was* obviously very smart because he *finds* all of the mistakes in the report. |
| Correct | The new manager *was* obviously very smart because he *found* all of the mistakes in the report. |

24d Split Infinitive   Sp I

Many grammar experts insist that "to" never be separated from its verb; today, however, some grammarians allow the split infinitive except in the most formal kinds of writing.

Nevertheless, because the split offends some readers, it is probably best to avoid the construction unless clarity or emphasis is clearly served by its use.

| Traditional | A swift kick is needed *to start* the machine properly. |
| Untraditional | A swift kick is needed *to* properly *start* the machine. |

| Traditional | The teacher wanted Lori *to communicate* her ideas clearly. |
| Untraditional | The teacher wanted Lori *to* clearly *communicate* her ideas. |

24e Double Negatives   D Neg

1. Rewrite sentences that use two negatives to communicate a single negative idea.

| Incorrect | He *didn't* need *no* fancy car to impress her. |
| Correct | He *didn't* need a fancy car to impress her. |

Incorrect	They *couldn't* find *no* record of my birth.
Correct	They *could* find *no* record of my birth.
Also Correct	They *couldn't* find *any* record of my birth.

2. Don't use a negative verb and a negative qualifier ("hardly," "barely," "scarcely") together.

| Incorrect | I *can't hardly* wait until Linda learns to swim, so I can challenge her to a race. |
| Correct | I *can hardly* wait until Linda learns to swim, so I can challenge her to a race. |

| Incorrect | Even when he flew his helicopter upside-down over her house, she *wouldn't barely* look at him. |
| Correct | Even when he flew his helicopter upside-down over her house, she *would barely* look at him. |

24f Passive Voice   Pass

"Active voice" refers to sentences in which the subject performs the action. "Passive voice" refers to sentences in which the subject is acted upon.

Active	The police *pulled over* the speeding van full of students.
Passive	The speeding van full of students *was pulled over* by the police.

The passive voice is a logical construction when the person or thing performing the action is unknown or of lesser importance than the event or action.

Examples	My car was stolen last night.
	The soldier was buried with full military honors.

Some verbs such as "happen" or "occur" may only be used in the active voice.

Incorrect	An earthquake *was occurred* last night.
Correct	An earthquake *occurred* last night.

Some disciplines, particularly those in science and engineering, may prefer the passive voice: "All results were triple verified." Nevertheless, your writing style will improve if you choose strong, active-voice verbs over wordy, awkward, or unclear passive constructions.

Awkward Passive Construction	The call for volunteers was responded to by many students.
Active Verb	Many students responded to the call for volunteers.
Unclear Passive Construction	Much protest is being voiced over the new electric fireworks. [Who is protesting?]
Active Verb	Members of the Houston Fire Department are protesting the new electric fireworks.

(◆ For more examples of active- and passive-voice verbs, see pages 143–144.)

24g Irregular Verbs   Irreg V

Most verbs form their past tense by adding "-ed" ("ask/asked," "walk/walked"). However, some verbs form their past tenses by changing a vowel ("begin/began," "write/wrote"); others indicate past tense with an entirely new spelling or word ("go/went," "strike/struck").

Consult your dictionary when you are uncertain of the correct verb form you need. Remember that some verbs simply do not behave themselves!

Incorrect	Irregular verbs have *creeped* into our language.
Correct	Irregular verbs have *crept* into our language.
Incorrect	She *shaked* the piggy bank as hard as she could.
Correct	She *shook* the piggy bank as hard as she could.
Incorrect	I don't know the current price of baseball bats because I haven't *boughten* one since high school.
Correct	I don't know the current price of baseball bats because I haven't *bought* one since high school.

Practicing What You've Learned

Errors with Verbs: Form, Tense Shift, and Double Negatives

A. The following sentences contain incorrect verb forms, tense shifts, and double negatives. Correct any problems you see, and rewrite any sentences whose clarity or conciseness would be improved by using active rather than passive verbs.

1. By the time Janice got home, her ice cream has already melted in the car. She couldn't hardly wait to have a dish of ice cream, but she was very disappointed.

2. "If you was in Wyoming and couldn't hear no wind blowing, what would people call you?" asked Jethro. "Dead," replies his buddy Herman.

3. It was believed by Aztec ruler Montezuma that chocolate had magical powers and can act as an aphrodisiac.

4. The hurricane that was happened off the coast of Florida destroyed over 5,000 homes. Bob couldn't barely find any pieces of his house a week later.

5. Suspicions of arson are being raised by the fire department following the burning of the new Chip and Dale Furniture Factory.

B. Revise any incorrect verbs in the following sentences.

1. I seen what she was hiding behind her back.

2. He come around here yesterday asking questions, but we're use to that.

3. Having forget the key to his house, the man quietly sneeked back to his car to look for a spare.

4. Austin don't like to be awokened until noon.

5. The kids done good work all day.

Errors with Nouns   N

Nouns name people, places, and things ("boy," "kitchen," "car"). Proper nouns name specific people, places, and things ("Zora Neale Hurston," "Texas," "Chevrolet") and are capitalized.

24h Possessive with "-ing" Nouns

When the emphasis is on the action, use the possessive pronoun plus the "-ing" noun.

Example   He hated *my* singing around the house, so I made him live in the garage. [The emphasis is on *singing*.]

When the emphasis is not on the action, you may use a noun or pronoun plus the "-ing" noun.

Example   He hated *me* singing around the house, so I made him live in the garage. [The emphasis is on the person singing—*me*—not the action; he might have liked someone else singing.]

24i   Misuse of Nouns as Adjectives

Some nouns may be used as adjectives modifying other nouns ("horse show," "movie star," "theater seats"). But some nouns used as adjectives sound awkward or like jargon. To avoid such awkwardness, you may need to change the noun to an appropriate adjective or reword the sentence.

Awkward   The group decided to work on local *environment* problems.
Better   The group decided to work on local *environmental* problems.

Jargon   The executive began a *cost estimation comparison study* of the two products.
Better   The executive began a *comparison study* of the two products' costs.

(◆ For more information on ridding your prose of multiple nouns, see pages 148–149.)

24j   Plurals of Proper Nouns

Add an "s" to indicate plural proper nouns.

Examples   Both *Keishas* volunteered for the charity drive.

The *Halls* were home for the holidays, enjoying their new *Frisbees* every afternoon.

(◆ For practice correcting errors with nouns, turn to pages 557–558.)

Errors with Pronouns

A pronoun ("he," "she," "it") takes the place of a noun. Possessive pronouns ("his," "hers," "its," "theirs") show ownership.

24k   Faulty Agreement   **Pro Agr**

A pronoun should agree in number and gender with its antecedent (that is, the word the pronoun stands for).

Incorrect	To get a temperamental *actress* to sign a contract, the director would lock *them* in the dressing room.
Correct	To get a temperamental *actress* to sign a contract, the director would lock *her* in the dressing room.

Use the singular pronoun with "everyone," "anyone," and "each."

Incorrect	When the belly dancer asked for a volunteer partner, *everyone* in the men's gym class raised *their* hand.
Correct	When the belly dancer asked for a volunteer partner, *everyone* in the men's gym class raised *his* hand.

Incorrect	*Each* of the new wives decided to keep *their* own name.
Correct	*Each* of the new wives decided to keep *her* own name.

In the past, writers have traditionally used the masculine pronoun "he" when the gender of the antecedent is unknown, as in the following: "If a *spy* refuses to answer questions, *he* should be forced to watch James Bond movies until *he* cracks." Today, however, some authorities prefer the nonsexist "she or he," even though the construction can be awkward when maintained over a stretch of prose. Perhaps the best solution is to use the impersonal "one" when possible or simply rewrite the sentence in the plural: "If *spies* refuse to answer questions, *they* should be forced to watch James Bond movies until *they* crack." (◆ For more advice and examples, see pages 174–176.)

 ## 24l   Vague Reference   Ref

Your pronoun references should be clear.

Vague	If the trained seal won't eat its dinner, throw *it* into the lion's cage. [What goes into the lion's cage? Do you throw the seal or the food?]
Clear	If the trained seal won't eat its dinner, throw *the food* into the lion's cage.

Vague	After the dog bit Harry, *he* raised such a fuss at the police station that the sergeant finally had *him* impounded. [Who raised the fuss? Who was impounded?]
Clear	After being bitten, *Harry* raised such a fuss at the police station that the sergeant finally had the *dog* impounded.

Sometimes you must add a word or rewrite the sentence to make the pronoun reference clear:

Vague	I'm a lab instructor in the biology department and am also taking a statistics course. *This* has always been difficult for me. [What is difficult?]
Clear	I'm a lab instructor in the biology department and am also taking statistics, a *course* that has always been difficult for me.
Clear	I'm a lab instructor in the biology department and am also taking a statistics course. Being a teacher and a student at the same time has always been difficult for me.

In many cases, simply inserting a noun after a vague use of "this" or "that" will clarify meaning.

Vague   I visited with my grandmother while we watched the lunar eclipse. That was so special. [What was special? The visit? The eclipse?]

Clear   I visited with my grandmother while we watched the lunar eclipse. That *evening* was so special.

As you revise your prose, train yourself to catch any sentences that begin with "this" or "that" and see whether adding a noun or phrase will help communicate your meaning more effectively.

 24m   Shift in Pronouns   P Sh

Be consistent in your use of pronouns; don't shift from one person to another.

Incorrect   *One* shouldn't eat pudding with *your* fingers.
Correct   *One* shouldn't eat pudding with *one's* fingers.
Correct   *You* shouldn't eat pudding with *your* fingers.

Incorrect   *We* left-handed people are at a disadvantage because most of the time *you* can't rent left-handed golf clubs or bowling balls.

Correct   *We* left-handed people are at a disadvantage because most of the time *we* can't rent left-handed golf clubs or bowling balls.

(◆ For additional examples, see pages 148–149.)

 24n   Incorrect Case   Ca

1. The case of a pronoun is determined by its function in the particular sentence. If the pronoun is a subject, use the nominative case: "I," "he," "she," "we," and "they"; if the pronoun is an object, use the objective case: "me," "him," "her," "us," and "them." To check your usage, all you need to do in many instances is isolate the pronoun in the manner shown here and determine whether it sounds correct alone.

Incorrect   Give the treasure map to Frankie and *I*.
Isolated   Give the treasure map to *I*. [awkward]
Correct   Give the treasure map to Frankie and *me*.

Incorrect   Paul and *her* suspect that the moon is hollow.
Isolated   *Her* suspects that the moon is hollow. [awkward]
Correct   Paul and *she* suspect that the moon is hollow.

Incorrect   The gift is from Annette and *I*.
Isolated   The gift is from *I*. [awkward]
Correct   The gift is from Annette and *me*.

Sometimes the "isolation test" doesn't work, so you just have to remember the rules. A common pronoun problem involves use of the preposition "between" and the choice of "me" or "I." Perhaps you can remember this rule by recalling there is no "I" in "between," only "e's" as in "me."

Incorrect   Just *between you and I*, the new housekeeper is a good cook, but she won't iron anything.

Correct   Just *between you and me*, the new housekeeper is a good cook, but she won't iron anything.

In other cases, to determine the correct pronoun, you will need to add implied but unstated sentence elements:

Examples   Mother always liked Richard more than *me*. [Mother liked Richard more than *she liked* me.]

She is younger than *I* by three days. [She is younger than I *am* by three days.]

Telephone exchange: May I speak to Kate? This is *she*. [This is she *speaking*.]

2. To solve the confusing *who/whom* pronoun problem, first determine the case of the pronoun in its own clause in each sentence.

A. If the pronoun is the subject of a clause, use "who" or "whoever."

Examples   I don't know *who* spread the peanut butter on my English paper. ["Who" is the subject of the verb "spread" in the clause "who spread the peanut butter on my English paper."]

Rachel is a librarian *who* only likes books with pictures. ["Who" is the subject of the verb "likes" in the clause "who only likes books with pictures."]

He will sell secrets to *whoever* offers the most money. ["Whoever" is the subject of the verb "offers" in the clause "whoever offers the most money."]

B. If the pronoun occurs as the object of a preposition, use "whom," especially when the preposition immediately precedes the pronoun.

Examples   *With whom* am I speaking?

To whom is the letter addressed?

Do not ask *for whom* the bell tolls.

C. If the pronoun is the object of a verb, use "whom" or "whomever."

Examples   Sid is a man *whom* I distrust. ["Whom" is the direct object of the verb "distrust."]

Who's calling *whom* a sore loser now? ["Whom" is the direct object of the verb "calling."]

24o Incorrect Compound Forms

Compound personal pronouns are formed by adding "-self" or "-selves" to some of the simple personal pronouns ("my," "you," "her," "him"). Use a dictionary if you are unsure of a correct form.

Correct   myself, yourself, himself, themselves
Incorrect hisself, theirselves

Practicing What You've Learned

Errors with Nouns and Pronouns

A. In the following sentences, select the proper nouns and pronouns.

1. Please buy a copy of the book *The Never Ending Story* for my sister and (I, me).

2. Between you and (I, me), some people tell you they are honest, but they talk behind your back.

3. (Who, Whom) is the singer of the country song "A Real Good Man"?

4. My grandmother makes better cookies than (I, me).

5. (Her and me, She and I) are going to the movies to see *Attack of the Killer Crabgrass.*

6. I'm giving my tuba to (whoever, whomever) is carrying a grudge against our new neighbors, the (Smith's, Smiths).

7. The Botox surprise party was given by Paige Turner, Justin Case, and (I, me).

8. She is the kind of person for (who, whom) preparing dinner meant making reservations.

9. (Her and him, She and he) are twins (who, whom) are always finding (theirselves, themselves) in trouble with the law.

10. The judge of the ugly feet contest announced (his self, him self, himself) the winner.

B. The following sentences contain a variety of errors with nouns and pronouns. Some sentences contain more than one error; skip any correct sentences you may find.

1. My sister and me have nothing in common but our last name.

2. Of whom did Oscar Wilde once say, "He hasn't a single redeeming vice"?

continued on next page

3. It was a surprise to both Mary and I to learn that Switzerland didn't give women the right to vote until 1971.

4. Each of the young women in the Family Life class decided not to marry after they read that couples today have 2.3 children.

5. I went to the store to look for a new computer, but I discovered that each of the new models has their problems.

6. Either of the men could have switched their seat with the disabled person.

7. The stranger gave the free movie tickets to Louise and I after he saw people standing in line to leave the theater.

8. The personnel director told each of the employees, most of who opposed him, to signify their "no" vote by saying, "I resign."

9. Neither Luisa nor Nancy felt they had been treated fairly by the dean's assistant.

10. One of the first movies to gross over one million dollars was *Tarzan of the Apes* (1932), starring Johnny Weissmuller, a former Olympic star who became an actor. This didn't happen often in the movie industry at that time.

Errors with Adverbs and Adjectives

 24p   Incorrect Usage   Adv Adj

Incorrect use of adverbs and adjectives often occurs when you confuse the two modifiers. Adverbs qualify the meanings of verbs, adjectives, and other adverbs; they often answer the questions "how?" "when?" or "where?" and they frequently end in "-ly."

Incorrect   After Kay argued with the mechanic, she drove *slow* all the way home.
Correct   After Kay argued with the mechanic, she drove *slowly* all the way home.

Adjectives, on the other hand, commonly describe or qualify the meanings of nouns only.

Example   The *angry* mechanic neglected to put oil into Kay's *old* car.

One of the most confusing pairs of modifiers is "well" and "good." We often use "good" as an adjective modifying a noun and "well" as an adverb modifying a verb.

Examples   *Wind in the Willows* is a *good* book for children, although it is not *well* illustrated.

Mike was such a *good* teacher his classes always had a waiting list.

After studying in Spain for two years, Susie speaks Spanish exceptionally *well*.

Did you do *well* on your math test?

If you cannot determine whether a word is an adverb or an adjective, consult your dictionary.

24q Faulty Comparison   Comp

When you compare two elements to a higher or lower degree, you often add "-er" or "-r" to the adjective.

Incorrect   Of the two sisters, Selene is the *oldest*.
Correct   Of the two sisters, Selene is the *older*.

When you compare more than two elements, you often add "-est" to the adjective.

Example   Selene is the *oldest* of the four children in the family.

Other adjectives use the words "more," "most," "less," and "least" to indicate comparison.

Examples   Béla Lugosi is *more* handsome than Lon Chaney but *less* handsome than Vincent Price.

Of all the horror film stars, Boris Karloff is the *most* handsome, and Christopher Lee is the *least* handsome.

Beware using a double comparison when it is unnecessary:

Incorrect   It was the *most saddest* song I've ever heard.
Correct   It was the *saddest* song I've ever heard.

Note, too, that the word "unique" is a special adjective, one without a degree of comparison. Despite common usage to the contrary, an experience or thing may be unique—that is, one of a kind—but it may not be "very unique."

Practicing What You've Learned

Errors with Adverbs and Adjectives
Choose the correct adverbs and adjectives in the following sentences.

1. After losing her contact lens, Julie couldn't see very (good, well) in the movie theater.

2. Which is the (worser, worse, worst) food, liver or buttermilk?

3. I didn't do (good, well) on my nature project because my bonsai sequoia tree grew (bad, badly) in its tiny container.

4. Don't forget to dress (warm, warmly) for the Arctic freestyle race.

5. Leading economic indicators show that the rate of inflation was (slightly, awful) higher than usual last month.

6. Watching Joe drive made Kate feel (real, really) ill, and his way of parking the car did not make her feel (more better, better).

7. The Roman toothpick holder was (very unique, the uniquest, unique).

continued on next page

8. That was the (funniest, most funniest) movie trailer I have ever seen.

9. Does the instructional guide *Bobbing for Doughnuts* still sell (good, well)?

10. The team members had (well, good) coaches, but they just didn't take practices (serious, seriously).

Errors in Modifying Phrases

 24r **Dangling Modifiers**   **DM**

A modifying—or descriptive—phrase must have a logical relationship to some specific words in the sentence. When those words are omitted, the phrase "dangles" without anything to modify. Dangling modifiers frequently occur at the beginnings of sentences and often can be corrected by adding the proper subjects to the main clauses.

Dangling	Not knowing how to swim, buying scuba gear was foolish.
Correct	Not knowing how to swim, *we* decided that buying scuba gear was foolish.
Dangling	Feeling too sick to ski, her vacation to the mountains was postponed.
Correct	Feeling too sick to ski, *she* postponed her vacation to the mountains.

(◆ For additional examples, see page 136.)

24s **Misplaced Modifiers**   **MM**

When modifying words, phrases, or clauses are not placed near the word they describe, confusion or unintentional humor often results.

Misplaced	Teddy swatted the fly still dressed in his pajamas.
Correct	Still dressed in his pajamas, Teddy swatted the fly.
Misplaced	There are many things people won't eat, especially children.
Correct	There are many things people, especially children, won't eat.

(◆ For additional examples, see page 137.)

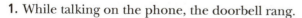

Practicing What You've Learned

Errors in Modifying Phrases
Correct the errors in dangling and misplaced modifiers by rearranging or rewriting the following sentences.

1. While talking on the phone, the doorbell rang.

2. Here is the new phone number for notifying the fire department of any fires that may be attached to your office telephone.

continued on next page

3. The prize-winning ice sculptor celebrated her new open-air studio in Aspen, where she lives with her infant daughter, purchased for $10,000.

4. The movie star showed off letters from admirers that were lying all over his desk.

5. While taking out the garbage, the bag broke.

6. Mary served cupcakes to the children on paper plates.

7. Baggy, wrinkled, and hopelessly out of style, Jean tossed the skirt from her closet.

8. He likes to listen to music doing his homework.

9. Blanche plans to teach a course next spring incorporating her research into the mating habits of Big Foot on the campus of Slippery Rock College.

10. After spending all night in the library, Kate's friends knew she'd need a trip to Special Coffee.

11. Standing near the window, the ocean view was wonderful.

12. From birth to twelve months, parents don't have to worry about solid food.

13. Piled up next to the washing machine, I began to do the laundry.

14. I've read that a number of modern sailors, like Thor Heyerdahl, have sailed primitive vessels across the ocean in books from the public library.

15. Proofreading carefully, dangling modifiers may be spotted and corrected easily.

Errors in Sentences

24t   Fragments   Frag

A complete sentence must contain a subject and a verb. A fragment is an incomplete sentence; it is often a participial ("-ing") phrase or dependent clause that belongs to the preceding sentence. To check for fragments, try reading your prose one sentence at a time, starting at the *end* of your essay. If you find a "sentence" that makes no sense alone, it's probably a fragment that should be either rewritten or connected to another sentence.

Incorrect	Robert's parents refuse to send him to a psychiatrist. Although they both know he eats dirt and chalk.
Correct	Robert's parents refuse to send him to a psychiatrist, although they both know he eats dirt and chalk.
Incorrect	This recording of the symphony's latest concert is so clear you can hear every sound. Including the coughs and whispers of the audience.
Correct	This recording of the symphony's latest concert is so clear you can hear every sound, including the coughs and whispers of the audience.

Incorrect   Barbara named her new mutt Super Dog. Because he could leap fences in a single bound.

Correct   Barbara named her new mutt Super Dog because he could leap fences in a single bound.

You can also try this test to see whether a group of words is a fragment: say the phrase "It is true that" in front of the words in question. In most cases, a complete sentence will still make sense, but a fragment won't.

Example   Barbara named her new mutt Super Dog. Because he could leap fences in a single bound. [Which is a fragment?]

It is true that *Barbara named her new mutt Super Dog.* [This sentence makes sense, so it is not a fragment.]

It is true that *because he could leap fences in a single bound.* [This sentence does not make sense. So, yes, it is a fragment.]

Sentence fragments are often used in conversations ("yes," "maybe," "just a minute") and in informal or personal writing (notes, letters, e-mail, etc.). In some professional and academic writing, *intentional fragments* or abbreviated sentences may be used occasionally for emphasis or to convey a particular tone, such as playfulness, anger, or scorn. However, intentional fragments should be just that: created on purpose to achieve a specific rhetorical goal.

Intentional Fragments   After cleaning out the attic, Eloise felt terrible. *Hot. Tired. Angry with the world.*

She agreed to hand over the jewels. *Just exactly what he had had in mind all along.*

As a general rule, fragments should be avoided in formal writing. Ask your instructor whether intentional fragments are permitted in your essays.

(◆ For more discussion of fragments, see pages 134–135.)

Practicing What You've Learned

Sentence Fragment Errors

A. Using the "It is true that" test, identify the fragments and the complete sentences in the following samples.

1. The Polynesians settled the islands that we know today as Hawaii. Arriving as early as the fifth century.

2. These early Hawaiians traveled the ocean in long canoes. Which were as long as 100 feet.

3. Special parts on the side. Many canoes were double or had outriggers for stability in the ocean waves.

continued on next page

4. These travelers carried supplies with them. For instance, seeds, plants, and small animals. Including bananas and coconuts.

5. They brought their culture. Which can be seen in the customs of the Hawaiian people.

B. Rewrite the following sentences so that there are no fragments.

1. An underground mail tube system was introduced in London in the 1860s. Designed to move mail and packages under the city.

2. Because New York's streets were crowded with people, horses, carriages, and trolleys. Alfred Beach, an American inventor, wanted to build an underground subway system in New York City.

3. Beach designed a model of this tube big enough to hold people. Thinking that this would solve New York's transportation problem.

4. Even though people enjoyed riding the model. The mayor of New York was against the idea of building a whole subway system.

5. Beach opened his subway for everyone to see on February 28, 1870. But the governor closed the project. The official New York City subway opened years later in 1904.

24u   Run-on (or Fused) Sentence   R-O

Don't run two sentences together without any punctuation. Use a period, a semicolon, or a comma plus a coordinating conjunction (if appropriate), or subordinate one clause.

Incorrect	The indicted police chief submitted his resignation the mayor accepted it gratefully.
Correct	The indicted police chief submitted his resignation. The mayor accepted it gratefully.
Correct	The indicted police chief submitted his resignation; the mayor accepted it gratefully.
Correct	The indicted police chief submitted his resignation, and the mayor accepted it gratefully.
Correct	When the indicted police chief submitted his resignation, the mayor accepted it gratefully.

Do not try to correct a run-on by inserting a comma between the two sentences; doing so without a coordinating conjunction will produce an error called a *comma splice*, discussed below and on page 135. Punctuate correctly or rewrite the run-on to best communicate your meaning.

Incorrect (run-on)	Victoria Woodhull was the first American woman to run for the presidency she was defeated in 1872 by Ulysses S. Grant.
Incorrect (comma splice)	Victoria Woodhull was the first American woman to run for the presidency, she was defeated in 1872 by Ulysses S. Grant.
Correct	Victoria Woodhull was the first American woman to run for the presidency. She was defeated in 1872 by Ulysses S. Grant.
Correct	Victoria Woodhull was the first American woman to run for the presidency; she was defeated in 1872 by Ulysses S. Grant.
Correct	Victoria Woodhull was the first American woman to run for the presidency, but she was defeated in 1872 by Ulysses S. Grant.
Correct	Victoria Woodhull, the first American woman to run for the presidency, was defeated in 1872 by Ulysses S. Grant.

Practicing What You've Learned

Run-On Errors

Correct the following run-on sentences. Try to use several different methods of correcting the errors. (◆ For additional practice, turn to exercise "B" on page 565.)

1. Many scientists are convinced that global warming exists some people doubt they are right.

2. In 1901 a schoolteacher named Annie Edson Taylor became the first person to go over Niagara Falls in a wooden barrel she is the only woman known to have survived this risky adventure.

3. My professor read my paper he said it was excellent.

4. The first microwave oven marketed in 1959 was a built-in unit it cost an incredible $2,595.

5. Many students think that a long sentence will look better in a research paper they are often wrong about that.

24v Comma Splice CS

A comma splice occurs when two sentences are linked with a comma. To correct this error, you can (1) separate the two sentences with a period, (2) separate the two sentences with a semicolon, (3) insert a coordinating conjunction ("for," "but," "and," "or," "nor," "so," "yet") after the comma, or (4) subordinate one clause.

Incorrect	George won a stuffed snake at the carnival, his mother threw it away the next day while he was in school.
Correct	George won a stuffed snake at the carnival. His mother threw it away the next day while he was in school.
Correct	George won a stuffed snake at the church carnival; his mother threw it away the next day while he was in school.

| Correct | George won a stuffed snake at the carnival, but his mother threw it away the next day while he was in school. |
| Correct | Although George won a stuffed snake at the carnival, his mother threw it away the next day while he was in school. |

(◆ For more help on correcting comma splices, see page 574 in the following chapter on punctuation; coordination and subordination are discussed in detail on pages 151–154.)

Practicing What You've Learned

Comma Splice Errors

A. Correct the comma splices that appear in the following sentences. Use more than one method of correcting the errors.

1. Most people know that the likeness of Susan B. Anthony appeared on an American dollar coin in the 1990s, fewer people know exactly who she was or why she is so important.

2. For most of her life Anthony fought for women to obtain the right to vote, she was an organizer of the world's first women's rights convention in 1848.

3. Anthony often risked her safety and her freedom for her beliefs, she was arrested in 1872 for the crime of voting in an election.

4. She also worked to secure laws to protect working women, at that time all of a woman's wages automatically belonged to her husband.

5. Unfortunately, Anthony did not live to see the 1920 passage of the Nineteenth Amendment giving women the right to vote, she died in 1906.

B. Correct any run-on sentences or comma splice errors you see. Skip any correct sentences you find.

1. I got up late this morning, I had to rush to class without eating breakfast.

2. Mary Lou decided not to eat the alphabet soup the letters spelled out "botulism."

3. A dried gourd containing seeds probably functioned as the first baby rattle, ancient Egyptian wall paintings show babies with such gourds clutched in their fingers.

4. Opportunists who came to the South after the Civil War were often called "carpetbaggers," they carried their belongings in cheaply produced travel bags made of Belgian carpet.

5. The goal of the new president of the company was to expand cell phone sales, it was a good plan.

6. When English scientist James Smithson died in 1829, he willed his entire fortune to the United States to establish a foundation for knowledge, that's how the Smithsonian Institution was started.

continued on next page

7. After talking with his father, Pete felt more comfortable about moving overseas for medical school.

8. Many people know that Bill Gates dropped out of college to start Microsoft, fewer people know just how angry this decision made his mother.

9. According to a study by the Fish and Wildlife Service, Americans' favorite animals are dogs, horses, swans, robins, and butterflies; their least favorite are cockroaches, mosquitos, rats, wasps, and rattlesnakes.

10. Jack London, the famous American author, worked at many different jobs, he went to Japan as a sailor, rode trains as a hobo, and tried to find gold in Canada's Yukon territory.

Assignment

Collaborative Activity: To continue practicing revision of major sentence errors, join two classmates, each with a current essay draft in hand. Each person should select and then study independently one of the following sections in this chapter: sentence fragments (pages 561–562), run-on sentences (pages 563–564), or comma splices (pages 564–565). After a study period of ten minutes, regroup and take turns explaining each error—and a way to eliminate it. Next, pass around and read all three essay drafts, marking the particular sentence error you studied if you find it in a classmate's paper. How might you help your classmate correct this error?

24w   Faulty Parallelism   //

Parallel thoughts may be expressed in similar grammatical constructions. Repeated sentence elements, such as verbs, nouns, pronouns, and phrases, often appear in parallel form to emphasize meaning and to promote sentence flow.

Parallel verbs	In his vaudeville act he *sang, danced,* and *juggled.*
Parallel prepositional phrases	She ran *through the door, across the yard,* and *into the limo.*

You might find it helpful to isolate the repeated elements in a sentence to see whether they are parallel.

She ran

Isolated   (1) through the door
                  (2) across the yard   } [parallel]
                  (3) into the limo

Faulty Parallelism   Boa constrictors like *to lie* in the sun, *to hang* from limbs, and *swallowing* small animals.

Isolated   (1) to lie
(2) to hang
(3) swallowing [not parallel to #1 and #2]

Revised   Boa constrictors like *to lie* in the sun, *to hang* from limbs, and *to swallow* small animals.

Faulty Parallelism   Whether *working* on his greasy car, *fistfighting* at the hamburger stand, or *in bed*, my brother always kept his hair combed.

Revised   Whether *working* on his greasy car, *fistfighting* at the hamburger stand, or *lounging* in bed, my brother always kept his hair combed.

Practicing What You've Learned

Errors in Parallelism

Revise the following sentences so that the parallel ideas are expressed in similar grammatical constructions.

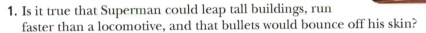

1. Is it true that Superman could leap tall buildings, run faster than a locomotive, and that bullets would bounce off his skin?

2. The disadvantages of using credit cards are overspending and you pay high interest rates.

3. My Aunt Clara swears she has seen Elvis snacking at the deli, browsing at the supermarket, munching at the pizza parlor, and in the cookbook section of a local bookstore.

4. Every Saturday, I run three miles, walk two miles, and a mile on the bike.

5. People often try to avoid eye contact with others, whether riding on a subway, walking through a park, or when they are in an elevator.

6. Yoga encourages its participants to work on their flexibility, strength, and how they can reduce their stress levels.

7. Drivers should hang up their cell phones, refrain from eating, and drinking too, leaving the radio buttons alone.

8. Smart people learn from their own mistakes; learning from the mistakes of others is what even smarter people do.

9. His dorm room was filled with old pizza boxes and computers that don't work.

10. The writer Oscar Wilde, the dancer Isadora Duncan, the painter Max Ernst, and Jim Morrison, who was a rock star, are all buried in the same Paris cemetery.

24x False Predication   Pred

This error occurs when the predicate (that part of the sentence that says something about the subject) doesn't fit properly with the subject. Illogical constructions result.

If it's helpful in some cases, remember that the verbs "is" and "was" often mean "equates to."

Incorrect	Energy is one of the world's biggest problems. ["Energy" itself is not a problem.]
Correct	The lack of fuel for energy is one of the world's biggest problems.
Incorrect	My roommate is why I'm moving to a new apartment. [A roommate is not a reason.]
Correct	My roommate's habit of talking nonstop is driving me to find a new apartment.
Also Correct	Because of my annoying roommate, I'm moving to a new apartment.
Incorrect	Her first comment after winning the lottery was exciting. [Her comment wasn't exciting; she was excited.]
Correct	Her first comment after winning the lottery expressed her excitement.
Incorrect	True failure is when you make an error and don't learn anything from it. [Avoid all "is when" and "is where" constructions. The subject does not denote a time, so the predicate is faulty.]
Correct	You have truly failed only when you make an error and don't learn anything from it.

(◆ For other examples of faulty predication, see pages 137–139.)

24y Mixed Structure   Mix S

"Mixed structure" is a catchall term that applies to a variety of sentence construction errors. Usually, the term refers to a sentence in which the writer begins with one kind of structure and then shifts to another in midsentence. Such a shift often occurs when writers are in a hurry and their minds have already jumped ahead to the next thought.

Confused	By the time one litter of cats is given away seems to bring a new one.
Clear	Giving away one litter of cats seems to tell the mother cat that it's time to produce a new batch.
Confused	The bank robber realized that in his crime spree how very little fun he was having.
Clear	The bank robber realized that he was having very little fun in his crime spree.
Confused	The novel is too difficult for what the author meant.
Clear	The novel is too difficult for me to understand what the author meant.

Confused	Children with messages from their parents will be stapled to the bulletin board.
Clear	To find messages from their parents, children should look at the bulletin board.

(◆ For other examples of mixed structure, see pages 137–139.)

Practicing What You've Learned

Errors of False Predication and Mixed Structure

Rewrite the following sentences so that each one is clear and coherent.

1. The team's quarterback A. M. Hall's broken finger, which sidelined him last week for the Raiders' game, is expected to play in tonight's game.

2. The groom is a graduate of Centerville High School where he lived all his life.

3. On my way to the doctor's office, my universal joint went out, causing even more body damage after hitting the tree.

4. He failed calculus for the reason that he didn't study every night.

5. For those new residents who have children and don't know about it, the town offers low-cost daycare services.

6. The organization believes that more anti-malaria vaccine must be produced right away.

7. Another situation when I get so mad is the plumber showing up three hours late.

8. The purpose of GPS devices was invented to help people find the right location.

9. A vacation is where people get away from work to relax.

10. Hearing his cries for help is how he came to be found in a ditch by some stray cows.

Answers to the Grammar Assessment, Pages 545–546

Please note that some of the problems in grammar and sentence construction in this test could be corrected in more than one way. Here are some sample corrections.

1. Almost everyone today recognizes the Statue of Liberty, but not everybody knows its history.

2. According to the National Parks Service, plans for the statue were first begun in 1865 by Frenchman Edouard de Laboulaye in honor of the United States' love of democracy and French-American friendship.

3. Commissioned to design the work, artist Frederic-Auguste Bartholdi chose Bedloe's Island in the New York Harbor as the location because the island was

government owned and the statue would be seen by thousands of immigrants entering the country through Ellis Island.

4. The project was a joint effort between the two countries: the French agreed to build the statue, and the US agreed to build the pedestal.

5. The French raised money by sponsoring entertainment events, by selling souvenir items, and by charging some public fees. (Between you and me, these fund-raising methods seem difficult, and in fact didn't work very well in the US.)

6. Alexandre Gustave Eiffel, who had previously designed the famous Eiffel Tower, designed the statue's steel framework, which was covered with a flexible copper skin the width of two pennies so that the statue would not crack in high winds.

7. The statue's face is modeled on Bartholdi's mother. Each of the seven rays of her crown represents one of the seven seas and continents of the world; the torch symbolizes enlightenment; the broken chains at her feet signify freedom from oppression; the tablet in her arm stands for law.

8. Completed in France in the summer of 1884, the statue had to be carefully disassembled and the parts shipped separately to New York.

9. Following a reassembly process that took four months, thousands of spectators watched the massive 305-feet-high statue's dedication ceremony on October 28, 1886.

10. Both you and I can hardly disagree with the National Parks Service when it calls the Statue of Liberty one of the most recognized icons of democracy in the world. For more information, you may go online to <www.nps.gov/stli/historyculture>.

Chapter 25

A Concise Guide to Punctuation

Assessing Your Skills: Punctuation

To help you focus your study of this chapter, take the self-graded test that follows. Each of the sentences below contains one or more errors discussed in this chapter. See how much you already know by correcting the sentences and then checking the answers on page 597. By taking this test, you will be better able to evaluate your knowledge of punctuation and direct your attention to those rules governing the errors you missed.*

1. An interesting article appeared recently in the online version of The Writer's Almanac, it gave a brief history of sliced bread

2. Before 1928 bread was sold in solid loaves; or, baked at home.

3. Otto F. Rohwedder [a jeweler from Iowa] had invented a bread slicing machine, however, bakers' rejected it because they thought the bread would go dry stale or moldy too quickly.

4. Rohwedder tried many solutions to the dry—bread problem. Including sticking the slices together with hatpins.

5. He ultimately solved the problem by wrapping the sliced bread in wax paper but he still couldn't sell his machine.

6. Finally a baker in Chillicothe Missouri agreed to try Rohwedders plan.

7. The baker (Frank Bench installed the machine in his bakery. Despite it's bulky size. (three by five feet)

8. Newspaper ad's announced the machines arrival; The Greatest Step Forward in the Baking Industry Since Bread Was Wrapped-Sliced Kleen Maid Bread."

9. Sales' were huge, a modern convenience was born.

10. Moreover the English-language gained an emphatic new phrase to express brilliance . . . Its the best thing since sliced bread

---

*Historical information included in this assessment test provided by *The Writer's Almanac with Garrison Keillor* on July 7, 2011, and may be accessed at <http://writersalmanac.publicradio.org/index.php?date=2011/07/07>.

Punctuation Guidelines

Punctuation marks do not exist to make your life complicated. They are used to clarify your written thoughts so that the reader understands your meaning. Just as traffic signs and signals tell a driver to slow down, stop, or go, so punctuation is intended to guide the reader through your writing. Look, for example, at the confusion in the following sentences when the necessary punctuation marks are omitted:

Confusing	Has the tiger been fed Bill? [Bill was the tiger's dinner?]
Clear	Has the tiger been fed, Bill?
Confusing	After we had finished raking the dog jumped into the pile of leaves. [Raking the dog?]
Clear	After we had finished raking, the dog jumped into the pile of leaves.
Confusing	The coach called the swimmers names. [Was the coach fired for verbally abusing the swimmers?]
Clear	The coach called the swimmers' names.

Because punctuation helps you communicate clearly with your reader, you should familiarize yourself with the following rules.

25a The Period (.) P

1. Use a period to end a sentence that makes a statement.

Examples   Employees at that company are not allowed to go on coffee breaks.

It takes too long to retrain them.

2. Use a period at the end of a sentence that makes a direct command or request.

Examples   Don't walk on the grass.

Please give me your new address.

3. Use a period after initials and many abbreviations.

Example   W. B. Yeats, 12 a.m., Dr., etc., Ms.

4. Only one period is necessary if the sentence ends with an abbreviation.

Examples   The elephant was delivered C.O.D.

To find a good job, you should obtain a B.S. or B.A.

25b The Question Mark (?) P

1. Use a question mark after every direct question.

Examples   May I borrow your boots?

Is the sandstorm over now?

2. No question mark is necessary after an indirect question.

Examples   Jean asked why no one makes a paper milk carton that opens without tearing.

Dave wondered how the television detective always found a parking place next to the scene of the crime.

25c   The Exclamation Point (!)   P

The exclamation point follows words, phrases, or sentences to show strong feelings.

Examples   Fire! Call the rescue squad!

The Broncos finally won the Super Bowl!

Practicing What You've Learned

Errors Using Periods, Question Marks, and Exclamation Points

Correct the following sentences by adding, deleting, or changing periods, question marks, or exclamation points, where appropriate.

1. Take care of your body it's the only place you have to live in.

2. Ms Anita Bath wants to know why erasers never outlast their pencils?

3. Her French class at St Claire's School on First Ave was taught by Madame Beau V Rhee, Ph.D. .

4. Where do all the birds go when it's raining

5. I have wonderful news I won the lottery

25d   The Comma (,)   P

1. Use a comma to separate two independent clauses* joined by a coordinating conjunction. To remember the coordinating conjunctions, think of the acronym FANBOYS: "for," "and," "nor," "but," "or," "yet," and "so." Always use one of the FANBOYS and a comma when you join two independent clauses.

---

*An independent clause looks like a complete sentence; it contains a subject and a verb, and it makes sense by itself.

Examples   You can bury your savings in the backyard, *but* don't expect Mother Nature to pay interest.

I'm going home tomorrow, *and* I'm never coming back.

After six weeks Louie's diet was making him feel lonely and depressed, *so* he had a bumper sticker printed that said, "Honk if you love groceries."

Do *not* join two sentences with a comma only; such an error is called a *comma splice*. Use a comma plus one of the coordinating conjunctions listed previously, a period, a semicolon, or subordination.

Comma Splice   Beatrice washes and grooms the chickens, Samantha feeds the spiders.
Correct   Beatrice washes and grooms the chickens, and Samantha feeds the spiders.
Correct   Beatrice washes and grooms the chickens. Samantha feeds the spiders.
Correct   Beatrice washes and grooms the chickens; Samantha feeds the spiders.
Correct   When Beatrice washes and grooms the chickens, Samantha feeds the spiders.

Comma Splice   Juan doesn't like singing groups, he won't go with us to hear the Tahitian Choir.
Correct   Juan doesn't like singing groups, so he won't go with us to hear the Tahitian Choir.
Correct   Juan doesn't like singing groups. He won't go with us to hear the Tahitian Choir.
Correct   Juan doesn't like singing groups; he won't go with us to hear the Tahitian Choir.
Correct   Because Juan doesn't like singing groups, he won't go with us to hear the Tahitian Choir.

(◆ For additional help, see pages 564–565; for practice exercises, see pages 565–566 and 578–579.)

Beware the tricky word "however." "However" is *not* one of the FANBOYS (coordinating conjunctions) and consequently can never be used to join two independent clauses. Incorrect use of "however" most often results in a comma splice.

Comma Splice   The police arrested the thief, *however*, they had to release him because the witness wouldn't talk.
Correct   The police arrested the thief; *however*, they had to release him because the witness wouldn't talk.
Also Correct   The police arrested the thief. *However*, they had to release him because the witness wouldn't talk.

2. Set off with a comma an introductory phrase or clause.

Examples   After we had finished our laundry, we discovered that one sock was missing.

> According to the owner of the Hall Laundry House, customers have conflicting theories about missing laundry.
>
> For example, one man claims his socks make a break for freedom when no one is watching the dryers.

3. Set off nonessential phrases and clauses. If the information can be omitted without changing the meaning of the main clause, then the phrase or clause is nonessential. Do not set off clauses or phrases that are essential to the meaning of the main clause.

Essential
He looked worse than my friend *who gets his clothes from the "lost and found" at the bus station*. [The "who" clause is essential to explain which friend.]

The storm *that destroyed Mr. Peartree's garage* left him speechless with anger. [The "that" clause is essential to explain which storm angered Mr. Peartree.]

The movie *now showing at the Ritz* is very obscene and very popular. [The participial phrase is essential to identify the particular movie.]

Nonessential
Joe Medusa, *who won the jalapeno-eating contest last year*, is this year's champion bull rider. [The "who" clause is nonessential because it only supplies additional information to the main clause.]

Black widow spiders, *which eat their spouses after mating*, are easily identifiable by the orange hourglass design on their abdomens. [The "which" clause is nonessential because it only supplies additional information.]

The jukebox, *now reappearing in local honky-tonks*, first gained popularity during the 1920s. [The participial phrase is nonessential because it only supplies additional information.]

4. Conjunctive adverbs, such as "however," "moreover," "thus," "consequently," and "therefore," are used to show continuity and are frequently set off by commas when they appear in midsentence.

Examples
She soon discovered, *however*, that he had stolen her laptop in addition to her cell phone.

She felt, *consequently*, that he was not trustworthy.

When a conjunctive adverb occurs at the beginning of a sentence, it may be followed by a comma, especially if a pause is intended. If no pause is intended, you may omit the comma, but inserting the comma is never wrong.

Examples
Thus, she resolved never to speak to him again.
Thus she resolved never to speak to him again.

Therefore, he resolved never to speak to her again.
Therefore he resolved never to speak to her again.

(◆ For practice of comma rules 1–4, turn to pages 578–579.)

5. Use commas to separate items in a series of words, phrases, or clauses.

Examples   Julio collects coins, stamps, foreign money, and old license plates.

Mrs. Jones chased the burglar out the window, around the ledge, down the fire escape, and into the busy street.

Do note that there is no comma separating "such as" and the first word in the list of items that follow.

Incorrect   Sarah eats a variety of vegetarian foods, such as, tofu, nuts, and fruit.
Correct   Sarah eats a variety of vegetarian foods such as tofu, nuts, and fruit.

Although journalists and some grammarians permit the omission of the last comma before the "and," many authorities believe the comma is necessary for clarity. For example, how many pints of ice cream are listed in the sentence below?

Please buy the following pints of ice cream: strawberry, peach, coffee, vanilla and chocolate swirl.

Four or five pints? Without a comma before the "and," the reader doesn't know whether vanilla and chocolate swirl are (is?) one item or two. By inserting the last comma, you clarify the sentence:

Please buy the following pints of ice cream: strawberry, peach, coffee, vanilla, and chocolate swirl.

6. Use commas to separate adjectives of equal emphasis that modify the same noun. To determine whether a comma should be used, see if you can insert the word "and" between the adjectives; if the phrase still makes proper sense with the substituted "and," use a comma.

Examples   She finally moved out of her cold, dark apartment.
She finally moved out of her cold and dark apartment.

I have a sweet, handsome husband.
I have a sweet and handsome husband.

He called from a convenient telephone booth.
But not: He called from a convenient and telephone booth. ["Convenient" modifies the unit "telephone booth," so there is no comma.]

Hand me some of that homemade pecan pie.
But not: Hand me some of that homemade and pecan pie. ["Homemade" modifies the unit "pecan pie," so there is no comma.]

7. Set off a direct address with commas.

Examples   Gentlemen, keep your seats.

Houston, we have a problem.

Not now, Eleanor, I'm busy.

8. Use commas to set off items in addresses and dates.

Examples   The sheriff followed me from Austin, Texas, to question me about my uncle.

He found me on February 2, 2014, when I stopped in Fairbanks, Alaska, to buy sunscreen.

9. Use commas to set off a degree or title following a name.

Examples   John Dough, M.D., was audited when he reported only $9,000 in taxable income last year.

The Neanderthal Award went to Samuel Lyle, Ph.D.

10. Use commas to set off dialogue from the speaker.

Examples   Alexander announced, "I don't think I want a second helping of turkey."

"Eat hearty," said Marie, "because this is the last of the food."

Note that you do not use a comma before an indirect quotation or before titles in quotation marks following the verbs "read," "sang," or "wrote."

Incorrect   Bruce said, that cockroaches have portions of their brains scattered throughout their bodies.

Correct   Bruce said that cockroaches have portions of their brains scattered throughout their bodies.

Incorrect   One panel member read, "Aunt Jennifer's Tigers," and the other sang, "Song for My Father."

Correct   One panel member read "Aunt Jennifer's Tigers," and the other sang "Song for My Father."

11. Use commas to set off "yes," "no," "well," and other weak exclamations.

Examples   Yes, I am in the cat condo business.

No, all the units with decks are sold.

Well, perhaps one with a pool will do.

12. Set off interrupters or parenthetical elements appearing in the middle of a sentence. A parenthetical element is additional information placed as explanation or comment within an already complete sentence. This element may be a word (such as "certainly" or "fortunately"), a phrase ("for example" or "in fact"), or a clause ("I believe" or "you know"). The word, phrase, or clause is parenthetical if the sentence parts before and after it fit together and make sense.

Examples   Jack is, *I think*, still a compulsive gambler.

Harvey, *my brother*, sometimes has breakfast with him.

Jack cannot, *for example*, resist shuffling the toast or dealing the pancakes.

13. Resist the temptation to pepper your prose with commas when you have no good reason to use them. Not all sentences containing "and" take a comma. In the following sentence, for example, "and" separates a compound predicate; it is not used as one of the FANBOYS (a coordinating conjunction, see page 573) separating two independent clauses.

Incorrect	She ate a biscuit, and drank a cup of tea. [The comma here incorrectly separates the verb "drank" from its subject "she."]
Correct	She ate a biscuit and drank a cup of tea.

On the other hand, writers may use commas when necessary to improve sentence clarity.

Confusing	Unlike Mary Jo never learned to cook.
Clear	Unlike Mary, Jo never learned to cook.

Confusing	Whatever will be will be.
Clear	Whatever will be, will be.

Practicing What You've Learned

Comma Errors

A. Study the comma rules numbered 1–4 on pages 573–575. Correct any comma errors you see in the following sentences.

1. In 1886 temperance leader Harvey Wilcox left Kansas, he purchased 120 acres near Los Angeles to develop a new town.

2. Although there were no holly trees growing in that part of California Mrs. Wilcox named the area Hollywood.

3. Mrs. Wilcox may have named the place after a home, owned by a friend living in Illinois.

4. During the early years settlers who shared the Wilcoxes' values moved to the area and banned the recreational drinking of alcoholic beverages, however, some alcohol consumption was allowed for medicinal purposes.

5. Nevertheless by 1910 the first film studio opened its doors inside a tavern on Sunset Boulevard, within seven short years the quiet community started by the Wilcoxes had vanished.

B. Study the comma rules 5–13 on pages 576–578. Correct any comma errors you see in the following sentences.

1. Yes students in the 1960s many juniors took a year off from college travelled around the world and learned about other cultures.

2. In 1961 John F. Kennedy inspired many people when he declared "Ask not what your country can do for you ask what you can do for your country."

continued on next page

3. Jane Marian Donna Ann and Cissy graduated from high school on June 5 1989 in Texarkana Texas in the old Walnut Street Auditorium.

4. "I may be a man of few opinions" said Henry "but I insist that I am neither for nor against apathy."

5. Did you know that the potato originated in South America not North America?

C. The following sentences contain many kinds of comma errors, including the comma splice. Correct any errors you see by adding, deleting, or changing the commas as needed.

1. Statistics prove that women are in fact safer drivers than men.

2. Although ice cream didn't appear in America until the 1700s our country now leads the world in ice cream consumption, Australia is second I think.

3. Last week the couple that lives in the apartment downstairs went to Las Vegas, however, their two large dogs stayed with me.

4. Researchers in Balboa, Panama have discovered that the poisonous, yellow-belly, sea snake which descended from the cobra, is the most deadly serpent in the world.

5. Mary Jeffers, my co-worker, spent the week of April 8–15, 2014 in the storage unit near her apartment looking for old tax paperwork, however, she wasn't successful in finding the small pink receipt she needed.

(◆ For additional practice correcting comma splice errors, see pages 565–566 in Chapter 24.)

25e The Semicolon (;) P

1. Use a semicolon to link two closely related independent clauses.

Examples   Anthropologists believe popcorn originated in Mexico; they have found popcorn poppers that are over 1,500 years old.

Kate's mother does not have to begin a jogging program; she gets all the exercise she needs by walking to and from her job.

Avoid a "semicolon fragment" error by making sure there is an independent clause—a complete sentence, not a fragment—on either side of the semicolon.*

---

*Some folks have noted that the semicolon might be better named the "semi-period" in that it functions like a weak period, joining two complete sentences together but with a weaker stop between thoughts than a period demands.

Semicolon fragment	Cutting your lawn with a push mower burns 420 calories; according to *Vitality* magazine. ["According to *Vitality* magazine" is a fragment. In this case, a comma, not a semicolon, is needed.]
Correct	Cutting your lawn with a push mower burns 420 calories, according to *Vitality* magazine.

◆ If you are unsure about recognizing a fragment, try using the "It is true that" test as described on page 562.

2. Use a semicolon to avoid a comma splice when connecting two independent clauses with words like "however," "moreover," "thus," "therefore," and "consequently."

Examples	Vincent van Gogh sold only one painting in his entire life; however, in 1987 his *Sunflowers* sold for almost $40 million.
	All Esmeralda's plants die shortly after she gets them home from the store; consequently, she has the best compost heap in town.
	This town is not big enough for both of us; therefore, I suggest we expand the city limits.

3. Use a semicolon in a series between items that already contain internal punctuation.

Examples	Last year the Wildcats suffered enough injuries to keep them from winning the pennant, as Jake Pritchett, third baseman, broke his arm in a fight; Hugh Rosenbloom, starting pitcher, sprained his back on a trampoline; and Boris Baker, star outfielder, ate rotten clams and nearly died.
	Her children were born a year apart: Moe, 1936; Curley, 1937; and Larry, 1938.

Practicing What You've Learned

Semicolon Errors

Correct the sentences that follow by adding, deleting, or changing the semicolons.

1. The soloist sang the well-known hymn "I Will Not Pass This Way Again" at her concert last night the audience was delighted.

2. Apples have long been associated with romance for example, one legend says if you throw an apple peel over your shoulder, it will fall into the shape of your true love's initial.

3. According to a report by the ASPCA, pet ownership in the US has more than tripled from the 1970s when 67 million households owned pets, however, the report did not specify which animals were considered to be pets.

continued on next page

4. In 2010, there were 53, 364 Americans older than 100, in 1980 there were only 32,194; according to data from the Census Bureau.

5. The sixth-grade drama club will present their interpretation of *Hamlet* tonight in the school cafeteria all parents are invited to see this tragedy.

6. Some inventors who named weapons after themselves include Samuel Colt, the Colt revolver, Henry Derringer, Jr., the derringer pistol, Dr. Richard J. Gatling, the crank machine gun, Col. John T. Thompson, the submachine or "tommy" gun, and Oliver F. Winchester, the repeating rifle.

7. My brother changed his major from pre-med to chemistry, he discovered he could not stand the sight of blood.

8. The highest point in the United States is Mt. McKinley at 20,320 feet, in contrast, the lowest point is Death Valley at 282 feet below sea level.

9. As we drove down the highway, we saw a sign that said "Last Gas for 100 Miles," however we didn't stop.

10. The next billboard read "Last Chance for Fresh Coffee"; making us want to stop.

25f The Colon (:) P

1. Use a colon to introduce a long or formal list, but do not use one after "to be" verbs.

Example	Please pick up these items at the store: garlic, wolfbane, mirrors, a prayer book, a hammer, and a wooden stake.
Incorrect	Jean is such a bad cook that she thinks the four basic food groups are: canned, frozen, ready-to-mix, and take-out.
Correct	Jean is such a bad cook that she thinks the four basic food groups are canned, frozen, ready-to-mix, and take-out.

Avoid needless colons.

| Incorrect | At the store I couldn't find: wolfbane or a wooden stake. |
| Correct | At the store I couldn't find wolfbane or a wooden stake. |

2. A colon may be used to introduce a quotation or definition.

Examples	Nineteenth-century writer Ambrose Bierce offers this definition of a bore: "A person who talks when you wish him to listen."
	Critic Dorothy Parker was unambiguous in her review of the book: "This is not a novel to be tossed aside lightly; it should be thrown with great force."
	In singer Jimmy Buffett's Margaritaville store in Key West, a sign warns: "Shoplifters will be forced to listen to Barry Manilow."

3. Use a colon to introduce a word, phrase, or sentence that emphatically or humorously explains, summarizes, or amplifies the preceding sentence.

Examples   To her delight, we fed our pet cat her favorite dish: tuna surprise.

According to Kira, Colorado has four seasons: last winter, this winter, next winter, and July.

After marrying nine times, glamour queen Zsa Zsa Gabor had simple advice for becoming a marvelous housekeeper: every time you leave a relationship, keep the house.

4. Use a colon in the salutations of business or professional correspondence. Colons may also follow headings in memos.

Examples   Dear Professor Stallone:

To:

Subject:

Date:

Practicing What You've Learned

Errors with Colons

Correct the following errors by adding, deleting, or substituting colons for faulty punctuation. Skip any correct sentences.

1. Experts have discovered over thirty different kinds of clouds but have separated them into three main types cirrus, cumulus, and stratus.

2. To those folks who may talk too much, Abraham Lincoln gives the following advice: "It is better to remain silent and be thought a fool than to speak out and remove all doubt."

3. A recent *USA Today* study found that Americans consider only one activity more stressful than visiting the dentist making a speech in front of a group.

4. My brother always received the same birthday gift from our aunt seven pairs of black socks.

5. Dr. Field is on vacation, however, Dr. Sanders, who works in the same office, will be happy to see you.

6. A Director of Academic Services at Pennsylvania State University once nominated this sentence for Punctuation Error of the Year; "I had to leave my good friend's behind and find new ones."

continued on next page

7. Some of the cars manufactured between 1907 and 1912 that didn't achieve the popularity of the Model T were: the Black Crow, the Swallow, the Bugmobile, and the Carnation.

8. There's only one thing that can make our lawn look as good as our neighbor's; snow.

9. In a Thurmont, Maryland, cemetery can be found this epitaph "Here lies an Atheist, all dressed up, and no place to go."

10. George Bernard Shaw, the famous playwright, claimed he wanted the following epitaph on his tombstone: "I knew if I stayed around long enough, something like this would happen."

25g   The Apostrophe (')   AP

1. Use an apostrophe to indicate omitted letters in a contraction ("cannot" = "can't").

Examples   *It's* too bad your car burned.

Wouldn't the insurance company believe your story?

Many people today confuse "it's" (the contraction for "it is") and "its" (the possessive pronoun, which never takes an apostrophe).

- Its = shows possession, functioning like "his" or "her"

- It's = contraction for "it is"

Examples   The car is old, but *its* paint is new. ["Its" shows the car's possession of paint.]

The car is old, but *it's* reliable. ["It's" is a contraction for "it is."]

If you are ever in doubt about your choice, read the sentence aloud, saying the words "it is" in place of the *its/it's* in question. If the sentence becomes nonsensical (The car is old but it is coat of paint is new), then the possessive form "its" is probably what you need.

Special note: There is no "its'." No such word exists in the English language! Forget you even thought about it!

2. Add an apostrophe plus "s" to a noun to show possession.

Examples   *Jack's* dog ate the *cat's* dinner.

The *veterinarian's* assistant later doctored the *puppy's* wounds.

3. Add only an apostrophe to a plural noun ending in "s" to show possession.

Examples   Goldilocks invaded the *bears'* house.

She ignored her *parents'* warning about breaking and entering.

4. To show joint possession between two people or things, you need to add an apostrophe and "s" only to the second noun. To show separate ownership, add an apostrophe plus "s" to both nouns.

Examples   Isabel and *Sharona's* design project will be presented today. [one project]

Isabel's and *Sharona's* design projects will be presented today. [separate projects]

5. Be careful to avoid adding an apostrophe when the occasion simply calls for the plural use of a word.

Incorrect   *Apple's* are on sale now.
Correct   *Apples* are on sale now.

Incorrect   We ordered *chip's* and dip.
Correct   We ordered *chips* and dip.

6. In some cases you may add an apostrophe plus "s" to a singular word ending in "s," especially when the word is a proper name or for ease of pronunciation.

Examples   *Doris's* name was popular in the 1950s.

The silent screen *actress's* favorite flowers were mums.

7. To avoid confusion, you may use an apostrophe plus "s" to form the plurals of letters and words discussed as words. An apostrophe is not used on plural numbers (1960s, 80s, nines) or abbreviations (MAs, DVDs, CDs).

Examples   He made four *"C's" last fall.* [or "Cs"]

You use too many *"and's"* in your sentence. [or "ands"]

Practicing What You've Learned

Errors with Apostrophes

A. Correct the apostrophe errors you see in the following phrases.

1. A babies' pajamas

2. The queens throne

3. A families' vacation

4. Ten students grades

5. The Depression of the 1930s' was over.

6. That dress of hers'

continued on next page

7. The childrens' shoes

8. Worm's for sale

9. Bill Jones car

10. All essay's are due today.

11. Sign both the painters and the roofer's contracts.

12. Womens hats with feather's for decoration

B. Show that you understand the difference between "it's" and "its" by correcting any errors in the sentences that follow. Skip any correct use you see.

1. Its unfortunate that the game ended in a tie.

2. The tree lost its leaves.

3. Its beginning to feel like fall now.

4. The coffee shop was closing its' doors.

5. I realize its none of my business.

(◆ For more practice, turn to pages 587–588.)

Assignment

Collaborative Activity: Continue working on your punctuation skills by editing the following paragraph for errors in commas, semicolons, colons, and apostrophes. Form a group with two other students and compare your corrections. Did you find and fix the same errors? If your group disagrees about a particular punctuation mark, consult the appropriate pages in this chapter. Once your group has agreed on a corrected paragraph, compare your work with that of other groups in the class. Later, when you are revising your own writing, proofread carefully for any of the errors you found in this exercise.

During winter parties theres often one ignored dessert on the buffet table; the fruitcake. If you're a fruitcake-hater on someones' annual holiday gift list don't just throw it out—dump it in style! Attend the Great Fruitcake Toss in Manitou Springs Colorado; a whacky series of contests held every first Saturday in January since 1996. Contestants' vie for the longest throw for the most accurate toss and for the most creative launching device. In years past hurlers have used catapults, cannons slingshots, bows and arrows, and giant rubber-band contraptions to fling their fruitcakes, only eating is strictly forbidden. Its all done for charity, the entrance fee of one nonperishable item for the towns local food bank fills the shelves for weeks.

25h   Quotation Marks (" " and ' ')   P

1. Use quotation marks to enclose someone's spoken or written words.

Examples   "Watch out for that left hook," said Tinkerbell to Peter Pan, just before his fight with the pirate captain.

Upon the opening of the world's first underground passenger train in 1863, the editor of the *London Times* wrote that it was "an insult to common sense to think that people would choose to travel in darkness across London."

Note that when a quotation is interrupted, an extra set of marks should be used.

Example   "Today, American coins of ten cents or more have grooved edges," explained the numismatist, "because decades ago our government wanted to stop thieves from shaving the edges of silver and gold coins."

Use quotation marks around the titles of essays,* articles, chapter headings, short stories, short poems, and songs.

Examples   "How to Paint Used Furniture"

"The Fall of the House of Usher"

"Stopping by Woods on a Snowy Evening"

"Come Away with Me"

2. Place quotation marks around a word, phrase, or letter used as the subject of discussion when italics are not available or preferred.

Examples   Never use "however" as a coordinating conjunction.

The word "bigwig," meaning an important person, is derived from the large wigs worn by seventeenth-century British judges.

Is your middle initial "X" or "Y"?

Her use of such adjectives as "silly," "girly-girl," and "fabulous" makes the character sound less serious.

3. Place quotation marks around uncommon nicknames and words used ironically. Do not, however, try to apologize for slang or clichés by enclosing them in quotation marks; instead, substitute specific words.

Examples   "Scat-cat" Malone takes candy from babies.

Her "friend" was an old scarecrow in an abandoned barn.

Slang   After work Chuck liked to "chill out" in front of the television.
Specific   After work Chuck liked to relax by watching old movies on television.

---

*Do *not*, however, put quotation marks around your own essay's title on either the title page or the first page of your paper.

4. The period and the comma go inside quotation marks; the semicolon and the colon go outside. If the quoted material is a question, the question mark goes inside; if the quoted material is a part of a whole sentence that is a question, the mark goes outside. The rules for exclamation points are the same as those for question marks.

Examples   According to cartoonist Matt Groening, "Love is a snowmobile racing across the tundra; suddenly it flips over, pins you underneath, and at night the ice weasels come."

"Love is a snowmobile racing across the tundra; suddenly it flips over, pins you underneath, and at night the ice weasels come," says cartoonist Matt Groening.

According to cartoonist Matt Groening, "Love is a snowmobile . . . suddenly it flips over, pins you underneath, and at night the ice weasels come"; Groening also advises that bored friends are one of the first signs that you're in love.

Did he really say, "At night the ice weasels come"?

Lisa asked, "Do you think you're in love or just in a snowmobile?"

As usual, Homer replied, "D'oh!"

5. Use single quotation marks to enclose a quotation (or words requiring quotation marks) within a quotation.

Examples   Professor Hall asked his class, "Do you agree with Samuel Johnson, who once said that a second marriage represents 'the triumph of hope over experience'?"

"One of my favorite songs is 'In My Life' by the Beatles," said Jane.

"I'm so proud of the 'A' on my grammar test," Sue told her parents.

6. If you are quoting fewer than four lines of poetry, enclose them within quotation marks, using a slash to indicate each line division.

Example   In possibly the first love poem ever published in America, Anne Bradstreet wrote these opening lines in 1678: "If ever two were one, then surely we. / If ever man were loved by wife, then thee."

Practicing What You've Learned

Errors with Apostrophes and Quotation Marks

Correct the following errors by adding, changing, or deleting apostrophes and quotation marks.

1. Its true that when famous wit Dorothy Parker was told that President Coolidge, also known as Silent Cal, was dead, she exclaimed, How can they tell?

continued on next page

2. When a woman seated next to Coolidge at a dinner party once told him she had made a bet with a friend that she could get more than two words out of him, he replied You lose.

3. Twenty-one of Elvis Presleys albums have sold over a million copies; twenty of the Beatles albums have also done so.

4. The Campus Medical Director argued strongly in favor of a smoke-free campus, "We must protect students from the dangers of second-hand smoke—she said.

5. Wasn't it Mae West who said, When choosing between two evils, I always like to try the one I've never tried before? asked Olivia.

6. The sheriff explained Its better to do as I say and call me Sir than to spend the night in the county jail.

7. A scholars research has revealed that the five most commonly used words in written English are the, of, and, a, and to.

8. The triplets mother said that while its' hard for her to choose, O. Henrys famous short story The Ransom of Red Chief is probably her favorite.

9. Despite both her lawyers advice, she used the words terrifying, hideous, and unforgettable to describe her latest flight on Golden Fleece Airways, piloted by Jack Eagle-Eye Marcus.

10. Its clear that Paul didnt know whether the Christmas' tree thrown in the neighbors yard was ours, theirs,' or your's.

25i Parentheses ( ) P

1. Use parentheses to set off words, dates, or statements that give additional information, explain, or qualify the main thought.

Examples   To encourage sales, some automobile manufacturers named their cars after fast or sleek animals (Impala, Mustang, and Thunderbird, for example).

Popular American author Mark Twain (Samuel Clemens) described many of his childhood experiences in *Tom Sawyer* (1876).

The Founding Fathers rejected the turkey as the national bird, choosing instead to select the bald eagle (a very wise decision).

2. The period comes inside the close parenthesis if a complete sentence is enclosed; it occurs after the close parenthesis when the enclosed matter comes at the end of the main sentence and is only a part of the main sentence.

Examples   The Colorado winters of 1978 and 1979 broke records for low temperatures. (See pages 72–73 for temperature charts.)

Jean hates Colorado winters and would prefer a warmer environment (such as Alaska, the North Pole, or a meat locker in Philadelphia).

3. If you are confused trying to decide whether information should be set off by commas, parentheses, or dashes, here are three guidelines:

   a. Use commas to set off information closely related to the rest of the sentence.

   Example   When Bill married Patty, his brother's young widow, the family was shocked. [The information identifies Patty and tells why the family was shocked.]

   b. Use parentheses to set off information loosely related to the rest of the sentence or material that would disturb the grammatical structure of the main sentence.

   Examples   Bill married Patty (his fourth marriage, her second) in Las Vegas on Friday. [The information is merely additional comment not closely related to the meaning of the sentence.]

   Bill married Patty (she was previously married to his brother) in Las Vegas on Friday. [The information is an additional comment that would also disturb the grammatical structure of the main sentence were it not enclosed in parentheses.]

   c. Use dashes to set off information dramatically or emphatically.

   Example   Bill eloped with Patty—only three days after her husband's funeral—without saying a word to anyone in the family.

4. For clarity, parentheses may be used to set off numbers in a list that appears within prose.

   Example   Urban legends are popular stories that almost always share these characteristics: (1) they are spread through person-to-person communication; (2) they are virtually untraceable to a single source, such as a book or newspaper; (3) they involve outlandish, humorous, or terrifying events; and (4) they carry an unstated warning or moral.

5. Parentheses may enclose the first-time use of acronyms (words formed from the initials of several words) or abbreviations.

   Examples   National Aeronautics and Space Administration (NASA)

   University of California at Los Angeles (UCLA)

   Museum of Modern Art (MoMA)

25j Brackets [ ] P

1. Use brackets to set off editorial explanations in the work of another writer.

   Examples   According to the old letter, the treasure map could be found "in the library taped to the back of the portrait [of Gertrude the Great] that faces north."

   The country singer ended the interview by saying, "My biggest hit so far is 'You're the Reason Our Kids Are Free' [original version by Sarah Bellham]."

2. Use brackets to set off editorial corrections in quoted material. By placing the bracketed word "sic" (meaning "thus") next to an error, you indicate that the mistake appeared in the original text and that *you* are not misquoting or misspelling.

Examples   The student wrote, "I think it's unfair for teachers to count off for speling [sic]." ["Sic" in brackets indicates that the student who is quoted misspelled the word "spelling."]

The highway advertisement read as follows: "For great stakes [sic], eat at Joe's, located right behind Daisy's Beef Buffet." [Here, "sic" in brackets indicates an error in word choice; the restaurant owner incorrectly advertised "stakes" instead of "steaks."]

3. If additional information needs to appear in material already enclosed in parentheses, use brackets to avoid the confusion of double parenthesis marks.

Example   Nineteenth-century author Kate Chopin often found herself in the midst of controversy. (For example, *The Awakening* [1899] was considered so scandalous that it was banned by the St. Louis Library.)

25k The Dash (—)* P

1. Use a dash to indicate a strong or sudden shift in thought.

Examples   Now, let's be reasonable—wait, put down that ice pick!

"It's not athlete's foot—it's deadly coreopsis!" cried Dr. Mitty.

2. Use dashes to set off parenthetical matter that deserves more emphasis than parentheses denote.

Examples   Wanda's newest guru—the one who practiced catatonic hedonism—taught her to rest and play at the same time.

He was amazed to learn his test score—a pitiful 43.

(◆ To clear up any confusion over the uses of dashes, commas, and parentheses, see the guidelines on page 589.)

3. Use a dash before a statement that summarizes or amplifies the preceding thought. (Dashes can also be used to introduce a humorous or ironic twist on the first idea in the sentence.)

Examples   Aged wine, delicious food, someone else picking up the check—the dinner was perfect.

---

*Do not confuse the dash with the hyphen. In typed work, a dash is indicated by *two* bar marks ("--"); one bar mark ("-") indicates a hyphen. Some word processing programs will automatically convert two bar marks to a dash.

Not everyone agrees with football coach Vince Lombardi, who said, "Winning isn't everything—it's the only thing."

According to Hollywood star Cher, "The trouble with some women is that they get all excited about nothing—and then marry him."

Practicing What You've Learned

Errors with Parentheses, Brackets, and Dashes

Show that you understand the different uses of parentheses, brackets, and dashes by selecting the best choice in the sentences that follow. Skip any correct sentences you see. (◆ For additional practice, see also the exercise that appears on pages 596–597.)

1. George Eliot (the pen name of Mary Ann Evans) wrote the novel *Middlemarch.*

2. The Apostrophe Protection Society, founded in London in 2001, fights against the gross misuse of this mark of punctuation. Editor's note: For help with apostrophes, see pages 583–584 in this text.

3. A Russian woman holds the record for the highest number of children born to one mother: sixty-nine babies in a total of twenty-seven pregnancies sixteen pairs of twins, seven sets of triplets, and four sets of quadruplets. (That woman must have been very tired.)

4. More men holding first-class tickets on the *Titanic* were saved than childrens (sic) in the third-class section of the ship.

5. Bill could stay married to Marie as long as he played his cards right [his Visa card, his Mastercard, his American Express card.]

25l   The Hyphen (-)*   P

1. Use a hyphen to join words into a single adjective before a noun.

Examples	a wind-blown wig	a well-written essay
	a two-hour test	a five-year-old boy
	a made-for-television movie	

Do not use a hyphen when the modifier ends in "-ly."

Examples	a highly regarded worker
	a beautifully landscaped yard

---

*Do not confuse the hyphen with the dash. In typed work, a hyphen is indicated by *one* bar mark ("-"); a dash is indicated by *two* bar marks or one long mark ("--" or "—").

2. Writers who create original compound adjectives often join the words with hyphens.

Examples   Compulsive shoppers suffer from stuff-lust syndrome.

She prefers novels with they-lived-wretchedly-ever-after endings.

3. Some compound words are always spelled with a hyphen; check your dictionary when you're in doubt. Note that compound numbers from twenty-one to ninety-nine use a hyphen.

Examples   mother-in-law   runner-up   twenty-nine

president-elect   good-for-nothing

Compound words made from combining verb forms are frequently hyphenated:

The psychiatrist insisted his birthday presents be *shrink-wrapped*.

4. Some words with prefixes use a hyphen; again, check your dictionary if necessary. (Hint: If the second word begins with a capital letter, a hyphen is almost always used.)

Examples   ex-wife   all-American

self-esteem   non-English

5. In a series of compound adjectives, place a space (or a comma and a space, when appropriate) following the hyphen in every item except the last one.

Examples   They surveyed students at both two- and four-year colleges.

She found herself on both the best- and the worst-dressed lists.

He suffered first-, second-, and third-degree burns on his arms.

6. Use a hyphen to mark the separation of syllables when you divide a word at the end of a line. Do not divide one-syllable words; do not leave one or two letters at the end of a line. (In most dictionaries, dots are used to indicate the division of syllables: va • ca • tion.)

Examples   In your essays you should avoid using fragment sentences.

Did your father try to help you with your homework?

Practicing What You've Learned

Errors with Hyphens

Correct the errors in the phrases that follow by adding, deleting, or changing hyphens. Skip any correct uses you see.

1. A first class event

2. The well done steak

continued on next page

3. A self employed person

4. His completely fabricated story

5. Her one word answer

6. Pre-Columbian art

7. A once in a lifetime experience

8. A fifteen year-old girl

9. The overly-excited dog

10. His fifty sixth birthday

11. fourth- and fifth-place trophies

12. The student o- mitted an important detail in his re-search paper.

(◆ For additional practice, turn to the exercise on pages 596–597.)

25m Italics (Ital) and Underlining (Und)   P

Today, many style manuals recommend the use of italics in printed matter in place of underlining. Ask your instructor whether the use of italics or underlining is preferred. In handwritten material, you may use underlining in the cases described below.

1. Underline, italicize, or place quotation marks around a word, phrase, or letter used as the subject of discussion. Whether you underline, italicize, or use quotation marks, always be consistent. (◆ See also pages 586–587.)

   Examples   No matter how I spell <u>offered</u>, it always looks wrong.

   Is your middle initial "X" or "Y"?

   Her use of such words as *drab, bleak,* and *musty* give the poem a somber tone.

2. Underline or italicize the title of books, plays, magazines, newspapers, movies, works of art, television programs (but use quotation marks for individual episodes), airplanes, trains, and ships.

   Examples   <u>Moby-Dick</u>   or   *Moby-Dick*
   <u>Reader's Digest</u>   *Reader's Digest*
   <u>Texarkana Gazette</u>   *Texarkana Gazette*
   <u>Gone with the Wind</u>   *Gone with the Wind*
   <u>Mona Lisa</u>   *Mona Lisa*
   <u>60 Minutes</u>   *60 Minutes*
   <u>Spirit of St. Louis</u>   *Spirit of St. Louis*
   <u>Titanic</u>   *Titanic*

Exceptions: Do not italicize or underline the names of sacred texts (Bible, Torah, Koran), the titles of legal documents (United States Constitution, Magna Carta), or the name of your own essay when it appears on your title page. Do not italicize or underline the city in a newspaper title unless the city's name is actually part of the newspaper's title.

3. Underline or italicize foreign words that are not commonly regarded as part of the English language.

Examples   He shrugged and said, *"C'est la vie."*

Under the "For Sale" sign on the old rusty truck, the farmer had written *caveat emptor*, meaning "let the buyer beware."

4. Use underlining or italics sparingly to show emphasis.

Examples   Everyone was surprised to discover that the butler <u>didn't</u> do it.

"Do you realize that *your* son just ate a piece of my priceless sculpture?" the artist screamed at the museum director.

Practicing What You've Learned

Errors with Italics and Underlining

Which of the following words should be italicized or underlined in your essay?

1. page six of the New York Times

2. the popular novel The Great Gatsby

3. an article in Time magazine

4. watching the episode The Puffy Shirt on Seinfeld

5. movie stars in The Dark Knight

6. confusing the words to, too, and two

7. the first act of Romeo and Juliet

8. remembering the words to The Star-Spangled Banner

9. the sinking of the Edmund Fitzgerald

10. missing my abuela in Texas

(◆ For additional practice, turn to pages 596–597.)

25n   Ellipsis Points (. . . or . . . .)   P

1. To show an omission in quoted material within a sentence, use three periods, with spaces before and after each one.

Original Source	Every time my father told the children about his having to trudge barefooted to school in the snow, the walk got longer and the snow got deeper.
Quoted with Omission	In her autobiography, she noted, "Every time my father told the children about his having to trudge barefooted to school . . . the snow got deeper."

Note: Never begin a sentence with ellipsis points.

2. Three points with spaces may be used to show an incomplete or interrupted thought.

Example   My wife is an intelligent, beautiful woman who wants me to live a long time. On the other hand, Harry's wife . . . oh, never mind.

3. If you omit any words at the end of a quotation and you are also ending your sentence, use three points plus a fourth to indicate the period.

Example   Lincoln wrote, "Four score and seven years ago our fathers brought forth, upon this continent, a new nation . . . ."

Note: If a parenthetical reference follows ellipses at the end of your sentence, use three points with a space before each and put a period after the parenthesis:

Example   Lincoln wrote, "Four score and seven years ago our fathers brought forth, upon this continent, a new nation . . ." (139-140).

4. If the omission of one or more sentences occurs at the end of a quoted sentence, use four points with no space before the first point.

Example   "The Lord is my shepherd; I shall not want. . . . I will fear no evil."

5. Use a row of ellipsis points to indicate one or more missing lines of poetry.

Example   Failing to fetch me at first keep encouraged.
. . . .
I stop somewhere waiting for you.
            —*Walt Whitman, "Song of Myself"*

6. Ellipsis points can occasionally be used to show hesitation or a pause in thought.

Example   "Yes, I'm leaving . . . I need to find myself," said Waldo.

25o   The Slash (/)   P

1. Use a slash between terms to indicate that either is acceptable. Do not put a space on either side of the slash.

Examples   Bring a salad *and/or* a dessert to share at the picnic.

Be careful to avoid the *either/or* fallacy in your argument paper.

2. Use a slash to mark line divisions in quoted poetry. Do use a space both before and after the slash.

Example   In this poem Shakespeare describes love as "an ever-fixed mark / That looks on tempests and is never shaken."

Practicing What You've Learned

Errors with Parentheses, Brackets, Dashes, Hyphens, Italics, Ellipses, and Slashes

Correct the following errors by adding, changing, or deleting parentheses, brackets, dashes, hyphens, italics, ellipsis points, and slashes.

1. Many moviegoers know that the ape in King Kong the original 1933 version, not the re-make was only an eighteen inch tall animated figure, but not everyone realizes that the Red Sea Moses parted in the 1923 movie of The Ten Commandments was a quivering slab of Jell O sliced down-the-middle.

2. We recall the last words of General John B. Sedgwick at the Battle of Spotsylvania in 1864: "They couldn't hit an elephant at this dist."

3. In a face to face conversation, the Oscar nominated actor promised the reporter that he would "tell the truth . . . and nothing but the truth" about the mistaken use of live bullets on the set of Soldier in the Jungle.

4. While sailing across the Atlantic on board the celebrity filled yacht Titanic II, Dottie Mae Haskell she's the author of the popular new self help book Finding Wolves to Raise Your Children confided that until recently she thought chutzpah was an Italian side dish.

5. During their twenty four hour sit in at the melt down site, the anti-nuclear protestors began to sing, "Oh, say can you see . . ."

6. Few people remember that George Clooney was a character in the T.V. show Roseanne. Most people think he first started acting in the long-running television series E. R. playing the emergency room doctor, Doug Ross.

continued on next page

7. If you do not pay your rent on time, your landlord has the right to charge a late fee and-or begin an eviction procedure.

8. A French chemist named Georges Claude invented the first neon sign in 1910. For additional information on his unsuccessful attempts to use seawater to generate electricity, see pages 200–205.

9. When Lucille Ball, star of I Love Lucy, became pregnant with her first child, the network executives decided that the word expecting could be used on the air to refer to her condition, but not the word pregnant.

10. In police shows on television, the detectives often talk about the motives of the unsub. Editor's note: Unsub means "unknown subject."

Answers to the Punctuation Assessment, Page 571

Please note that some of the punctuation errors in this test could be corrected in more than one way. Here are some sample corrections.

1. An interesting article appeared recently in the online version of *The Writer's Almanac*; it gave a brief history of sliced bread.

2. Before 1928, bread was sold in solid loaves or baked at home.

3. Otto F. Rohwedder, a jeweler from Iowa, had invented a bread-slicing machine; however, bakers rejected it because they thought the bread would go dry, stale, or moldy too quickly.

4. Rohwedder tried many solutions to the dry-bread problem, including sticking the slices together with hatpins.

5. He ultimately solved the problem by wrapping the sliced bread in wax paper, but he still couldn't sell his machine.

6. Finally, a baker in Chillicothe, Missouri, agreed to try Rohwedder's plan.

7. The baker, Frank Bench, installed the machine in his bakery, despite its bulky size (three by five feet).

8. Newspaper ads announced the machine's arrival: "The Greatest Step Forward in the Baking Industry Since Bread Was Wrapped—Sliced Kleen Maid Bread."

9. Sales were huge; a modern convenience was born.

10. Moreover, the English language gained an emphatic new phrase to express brilliance: "It's the best thing since sliced bread!"

Chapter 26

A Concise Guide to Mechanics

Assessing Your Skills: Mechanics

To help you focus your study of this chapter, take the self-graded test that follows. Each of the sentences below contains one or more errors discussed in this chapter. See how much you already know by correcting the sentences and then checking the answers on page 607. By taking this test, you will be better able to evaluate your knowledge of mechanics and direct your attention to those rules governing the errors you missed.*

1. According to "a monopoly anniversary," a december 1, 2010 article in the *denver post* newspaper, the board game called monopoly is 75 years old.

2. charles darrow of Pa. was struggling through the great depression and looking for extra income to support his Family.

3. he sketched a game on a tablecloth, including street names, such as baltic avenue, found in atlantic city, a favorite vacation spot.

4. Darrow and his wife invited neighbors to play, & alot of them wanted there own set to keep at home.

5. The inventor made 2 sets a day and sold them to a store in philadelphia.

6. 5,000 people bought the game from Darrow before the parker bros. company agreed to manufacture and sell the game for him in 1935.

7. Some people believe that Darrow based his game on one called the landlord's game designed by a quaker woman named lizzie j. magie in 1903.

8. Today monopoly is not only produced in english and spanish but in more than 40 other languages, as well as in a braille version for people who are visually impaired.

---

*Historical information in this assessment test originally found in "A Monopoly Anniversary," a December 1, 2010, article in "The Mini Page," a weekly section for young readers and adults in the *Denver Post* newspaper.

9. Mister Green likes to play the game with his friends in the conservatory on new year's day.

10. Ms. Scarlett, who grew up in the south, asks, "would you rather play a board game or watch the nfl game?"

26a Capitalization   Cap

1. Capitalize the first word of every sentence.

   Example   The lazy horse leans against a tree all day.

2. Capitalize proper nouns—the specific names of people, places, and products— and also the adjectives formed from proper nouns.

   Examples   John Doe   Toyotas

   Austin, Texas   Japanese cameras

   First National Bank   Spanish class

   the Eiffel Tower   an English major

3. Always capitalize the days of the week, the names of the months, and holidays.

   Examples   Saturday, December 14

   Tuesday's meeting

   Halloween parties

   Special events are often capitalized: Super Bowl, World Series, Festival of Lights.

4. Capitalize titles when they are accompanied by proper names.

   Examples   President Jones, Major Smith, Governor Brown, Judge Wheeler, Professor Plum, Queen Elizabeth

5. Capitalize all the principal words in titles of books, articles, stories, plays, movies, and poems. Prepositions, articles, and conjunctions are not capitalized unless they begin or end the title.

   Examples   "The Face on the Barroom Floor"

   A Short History of the Civil War

   For Whom the Bell Tolls

6. Capitalize the first word of a direct quotation.

   Examples   Shocked at actor John Barrymore's use of profanity, the woman said, "Sir, I'll have you know I'm a lady!"

   Barrymore replied, "Your secret is safe with me."

7. Capitalize "east," "west," "north," and "south" when they refer to particular sections of the country but not when they merely indicate direction.

Examples   The South has produced many excellent writers, including William Faulkner and Flannery O'Connor. ["South" here refers to a section of the country.]

If you travel south for ten miles, you'll see the papier-mâché replica of the world's largest hamburger. [In this case, "south" is a direction.]

Capitalize a title when referring to a particular person;* do not capitalize a title if a pronoun precedes it.

Examples   The President announced a new national holiday honoring Frank H. Fleer, inventor of bubble gum.

The new car Dad bought is guaranteed for 10,000 miles or until something goes wrong.

My English teacher told us about a Hollywood party during which Zelda and F. Scott Fitzgerald collected and boiled all the women's purses.

8. Capitalize important historic movements, documents, and events.

Examples   the Civil Rights Movement

World War I

Impressionism

Declaration of Independence

D-Day

9. Capitalize the names of religions, their followers, revered books, and holidays.

Examples   Islam

Methodists

Torah

Bible

Easter

10. Capitalize the letters that make up abbreviations for organizations, companies, agencies, and well-known people, places, and events.

Examples   NFL   JFK

CBS   USA

FEMA   WW II

*Some authorities disagree; others consider such capitalization optional.

Practicing What You've Learned

Errors with Capitalization

A. Correct the errors in capitalization in the following phrases.

1. delicious korean food
2. memorial day memories
3. fiery southwestern salsa
4. his latest novel, entitled *a prince at work*
5. bible study at the baptist church
6. count Dracula's castle in transylvania
7. african american heritage
8. a dodge van driven across the golden gate bridge
9. sunday morning programs on abc
10. the british daughter-in-law of senator Sanders

B. Write a sentence in which the following pairs of words are capitalized correctly. Example: He joined the US Navy wearing his best white shirt and navy pants.

1. street, Street
2. lake, Lake
3. mustang, Mustang
4. south, South
5. president, President

26b Abbreviations   Ab

1. Abbreviate the titles "Mr.," "Mrs.," "Ms.," "St.," and "Dr." when they precede names.

   Examples   Dr. Scott, Ms. Steinham, Mrs. White, St. Jude

2. Abbreviate titles and degrees when they follow names.

   Examples   Charles Byrd, Jr.; David Hall, Ph.D.; Dudley Carpenter, D.D.S.

3. You may abbreviate the following in even the most formal writing: "A.M." (*ante meridiem*, before noon), "P.M." (*post meridiem*, after noon), "A.D." (*anno Domini*, in the year of our Lord), "B.C." (before Christ), "C.E." (common era), "B.C.E." (before the common era), "etc." (*et cetera*, and others), "i.e." (*id est*, that is), and "e.g." (*exempli gratia*, for example).

4. In formal writing, do *not* abbreviate the names of days, months, centuries, states, countries, or units of measure. Do *not* use an ampersand (&) unless it is an official part of a title.

Incorrect in formal writing	Tues., Sept., 18th century, Ark., Mex., lbs.
Correct	Tuesday, September, eighteenth century, Arkansas, Mexico, pounds

Incorrect	Kate & Debbie went to the mall to buy shoes.
Correct	Kate and Debbie went to H&M to buy shoes. [The "&" in "H&M" is correct because it is part of the store's official name.]

5. In formal writing, do *not* abbreviate the words "page," "chapter," "volume," and so forth, except in footnotes and bibliographies, which have prescribed rules of abbreviation.

6. Except in formal writing, it is often permissible to use abbreviations or acronyms for well-known organizations or people. However, you should spell out the abbreviation the first time, to avoid any confusion.

Examples	Franklin Delano Roosevelt (FDR)
	National Public Radio (NPR)
	North Atlantic Treaty Organization (NATO)

(For additional information on proper abbreviation, consult your dictionary.)

26c Numbers   Num

1. Use figures for dates; street, room, and apartment numbers; page numbers; phone numbers; numbers by percentage signs; and decimals.

Examples	April 22, 1946	626-476–1423
	710 West 14th Street	40%
	page 242	3.78 GPA
	room 17	

2. Use figures for hours with "A.M." and "P.M." but write out the time when you use "o'clock."

Examples	8:00 A.M. or 8 A.M.
	eight o'clock in the morning

3. Some authorities say to spell out numbers that can be expressed in one or two words; others say to spell out numbers under one hundred.

Examples	ten thousand dollars or $10,000
	twenty-four hours
	thirty-nine years
	five partridges
	1,294 essays

4. When several numbers are used in a short passage, use figures.

Examples   In the anchovy-eating contest, Jennifer ate 22, Juan ate 21, Pete ate 16, and I ate 6.

According to the US Census Bureau, on an average day 11,000 babies are born, 6,000 people die, 7,000 couples marry, and 3,000 couples divorce.

5. Never begin a sentence with a figure.

Incorrect   50 spectators watched the surfing exhibition in Hawaii.
Correct   Fifty spectators watched the surfing exhibition in Hawaii.

6. When a date containing a month, a day, and a year appears in that order within a sentence, always set off the year by placing commas on each side. No comma is necessary between a month or season and a year.

Examples   She married her first husband on February 2, 1978, in Texas.

The first birth on a commercial airliner occurred on October 28, 1929, as the plane cruised over Miami.

I graduated spring 2011; the job began May 2012.

Practicing What You've Learned

Errors in Capitalization, Abbreviations, and Numbers

Correct the following errors by adding, deleting, or changing capitals, abbreviations, and numbers. Skip any correct words, letters, or numbers you may find.

1. Speaking to students at Gallaudet university, Marian Wright Edelman, Founder and president of the Children's Defense Fund, noted that an american child is born into poverty every thirty seconds, is born to a teen mother every 60 seconds, is abused or neglected every 26 seconds, is arrested for a violent crime every five minutes, and is killed by a gun every two hours.

continued on next page

2. My sister, who lives in the east, was amazed to read studies by Thomas Radecki, MD, showing that 12-year-olds commit 300 percent more murders than did the same age group 30 years ago.

3. In C.E. sixty-seven the roman emperor Nero entered the chariot race at the olympic games, and although he failed to finish the race, the judges unanimously declared him the Winner.

4. According to John Alcock, a Behavioral Ecologist at Arizona State University, in the U.S.A. the chance of being poisoned by a snake is 20 times less than that of being hit by lightning and 300 times less than the risk of being murdered by a fellow American.

5. There is an urban legend that states, "a woman over age forty has a better chance of getting shot by a terrorist than of getting married." Originally published in a newsweek article, this statement was based partially on a study conducted by professors from harvard and yale in nineteen eighty five. 1 problem with this study is that it was based on University-educated women, not all U.S. women. A Second problem is that Terrorism was not part of the study; newsweek introduced the comparison to sell Magazines.

6. 231 electoral votes were cast for James Monroe but only 1 for John Quincy Adams in the 1820 Presidential race.

7. The british soldier T. E. Lawrence, better known as "lawrence of arabia," stood less than 5 ft. 6 in. tall.

8. Before my 9 a.m. French class, held in st. thomas hall every Monday and wed., I eat 2 english muffins.

9. When a political opponent once called him "two-faced," president Lincoln retorted, "if I had another face, do you think I would wear this one?"

10. Alexander Graham Bell, inventor of the telephone, died on aug. 2, 1922 in nova scotia; 2 days later, on the day of his burial, for 1 minute no telephone in north america was allowed to ring.

Assignment

Collaborative Activity: After studying the rules in this chapter, write a paragraph of at least five sentences containing the following data. Create the information for a mythical person (Captain Glass Half-Full born in Optimism, Indiana? Your Evil Twin raised in Elbonia?). Exchange paragraphs with a classmate, and circle any errors you see in capitalization, abbreviations, or numbers. Work together to correct any errors you find.

continued on next page

Include this data:

- City, state/province, and country of birth
- Day, month, year, and century of birth
- Exact time of birth
- Current professional title and salary
- Favorite holiday, book, and movie
- Membership in a sports league or organization, name abbreviated
- Number and kinds of pets

 26d Spelling **Sp**

For some folks, learning to spell correctly is harder than trying to herd cats. Entire books have been written to teach people to become better spellers, and some of these are available at your local bookstore. Here, however, are a few suggestions that seem to work for many students:

1. Keep a list of the little beasties you misspell. After a few weeks, you may notice that you tend to misspell the same words again and again or that the words you misspell tend to fit a pattern—that is, you can't remember when the *i* goes before the *e* or when to change the *y* to *i* before *-ed*. Try to memorize the words you repeatedly misspell, or at least keep the list somewhere handy (your journal?) so you can refer to it when you're editing your last draft (listing the words in a computer file or on the inside cover of your desk dictionary also makes sense).

2. Become aware of a few rules that govern some of our spelling in English. For example, many people know the rule in the jingle "*I* before *E* except after *C* or when sounded like *A* as in *neighbor* and *weigh*." Not everyone, however, knows the follow-up line, which contains many of the exceptions to that jingle: "Neither the weird financier nor the foreigner seizes leisure at its height."

3. Here are some other rules, without jingles, for adding suffixes (new endings to words), a common plague for poor spellers:
   - Change final *y* to *i* if the *y* follows a consonant.*

     bury → buried

     marry → marries
   - But if the suffix is *-ing*, keep the *y*.

     marry + ing = marrying

     worry + ing = worrying

---

*Reminder: Consonants are all the letters that are not vowels (*a, e, i, o, u*, and sometimes *y*).

- If the word ends in a single consonant after a single vowel and the accent is on the last syllable, double the consonant before adding the suffix.

  occur → occurred

  cut → cutting

  swim → swimmer

- If a word ends in a silent *e*, drop the *e* before adding -*able* or -*ing*.

  love + able = lovable

  believe + able = believable

4. And here's an easy rule governing the doubling of letters with the addition of prefixes (new beginning syllables): Most of the time, you simply add all the letters you've got when you mix the word and the prefix.

   mis + spell = misspell

   un + natural = unnatural

   re + entry = reentry

5. Teach yourself to spell the words that you miss often by making up your own silly rules or jingles. For instance:

   - dessert (one *s* or two?): I always want two helpings so I double the *s*.
   - apparently (apparantly?): Ap*parent*ly, my *parent* knows the whole story.
   - separate (seperate?): I'd be *a rat* to sep*arat*e from you.
   - a lot (or alot?): A cot (not *acot*) provides *a lot* of comfort in a tent.
   - all right (or alright?): Think of the rhyme "all right, good night" and remember that both these phrases have two words. (No matter what Roger Daltrey and The Who said, the line should be "The kids are all right"!)
   - questionnaire (one *n* or two?): Questio*nn*aires have *n*umerous *n*umbered questions (two *n*'s).

   And so on.

6. Proofread your papers carefully. Anything that looks misspelled probably is and deserves to be looked up in your dictionary. Reading your paper one sentence at a time from the end helps, too, because you tend to start thinking about your ideas when you read from the beginning of your paper. If you are writing on a word processor that has a spell-checking program, don't forget to run it; however, do remember that such programs will skip over confused words (*to* for *too*, *there* for *their*) that are spelled correctly.

Although these few suggestions won't completely cure your spelling problems, they can make a dramatic improvement in the quality of your papers and give you the confidence to continue learning and practicing other rules that govern the spelling of our language. Good luck!

Answers to the Mechanics Assessment, Pages 598–599

1. According to "A Monopoly Anniversary," a December 1, 2010, article in the *Denver Post* newspaper, the board game called Monopoly is seventy-five years old.

2. Charles Darrow of Pennsylvania was struggling through the Great Depression and looking for extra income to support his family.

3. He sketched a game on a tablecloth, including street names such as Baltic Avenue, found in Atlantic City, a favorite vacation spot.

4. Darrow and his wife invited neighbors to play, and a lot of them wanted their own set to keep at home.

5. The inventor made two sets a day and sold them to a store in Philadelphia.

6. Five thousand people bought the game from Darrow before the Parker Brothers Company agreed to manufacture and sell the game for him in 1935.

7. Some people believe that Darrow based his game on one called The Landlord's Game designed by a Quaker woman named Lizzie J. Magie in 1903.

8. Today Monopoly is not only produced in English and Spanish but in more than forty other languages, as well as in a Braille version for people who are visually impaired.

9. Mr. Green likes to play the game with his friends in the conservatory on New Year's Day.

10. Ms. Scarlett, who grew up in the South, asks, "Would you rather play a board game or watch the NFL game?"

Part 5

Additional Readings

Part Five offers thirty-one additional readings to help you improve your writing skills. In Chapters 27–35, selections illustrate each of the modes and strategies previously explained in Part Two. Chapter 36 includes essays illustrating multiple strategies and styles for further analysis, and Chapter 37 offers two poems and a story to supplement literary assignments. Overall, the readings in Part Five were selected not only to model methods of development but also to illustrate a variety of purposes, styles, and tones, including humor and irony.

A close reading of these selections can help you become a better writer in several ways. Identifying the various methods by which these writers focused, organized, and developed their material may spark new ideas as you plan and shape your own essay. Familiarizing yourself with different styles and voices may encourage new uses of language. Analyzing the rhetorical choices of other writers will also help you revise your prose because it promotes the habit of asking questions from the reader's point of view. Moreover, reading the opinions or sharing the experiences of these authors may suggest interesting topics for your own essays. In other words, to help yourself become a more effective writer, read as much and as often as you can.

Chapter 27

Development by Example

Black Men and Public Space

Brent Staples

Brent Staples is an editorial writer for the *New York Times* and has published essays and reviews in a number of other newspapers and magazines, including the *Chicago Sun-Times*, the *New York Review of Books*, and *Slate* magazine. He holds a Ph.D. in psychology from the University of Chicago, and his memoir *Parallel Time: Growing Up in Black and White* (1994) won the Anisfield-Wolf Book Award. This essay first appeared in *Ms.* magazine in 1986.

1   My first victim was a woman—white, well dressed, probably in her late twenties. I came upon her late one evening on a deserted street in Hyde Park, a relatively affluent neighborhood in an otherwise mean, impoverished section of Chicago. As I swung onto the avenue behind her, there seemed to be a discreet, uninflammatory distance between us. Not so. She cast back a worried glance. To her, the youngish black man—a broad six feet two inches with a beard and billowing hair, both hands shoved into the pockets of a bulky military jacket—seemed menacingly close. After a few more quick glimpses, she picked up her pace and was soon running in earnest. Within seconds she disappeared into a cross street.

2   That was more than a decade ago. I was twenty-two years old, a graduate student newly arrived at the University of Chicago. It was in the echo of that terrified woman's footfalls that I first began to know the unwieldy inheritance I'd come into—the ability to alter public space in ugly ways. It was clear that she thought herself the quarry of a mugger, a rapist, or worse. Suffering a bout of insomnia, however, I was stalking sleep, not defenseless wayfarers. As a softy who is scarcely able to take a knife to a raw chicken—let alone hold one to a person's throat—I was surprised, embarrassed, and dismayed all at once. Her flight made me feel like an accomplice in tyranny. It also made it clear that I was indistinguishable from the muggers who occasionally seeped into the area from the surrounding ghetto. That first encounter, and those that followed, signified that a vast, unnerving gulf lay between nighttime pedestrians—particularly women—and me. And I soon gathered that being perceived as dangerous is a hazard in itself. I only needed to turn a corner into a dicey situation, or crowd some frightened, armed person in a foyer somewhere, or make an errant move after being pulled over by a policeman. Where fear and weapons meet—and they often do in urban America—there is always the possibility of death.

3   In that first year, my first away from my hometown, I was to become thoroughly familiar with the language of fear. At dark, shadowy intersections, I could cross in front of a car stopped at a traffic light and elicit the *thunk, thunk, thunk, thunk* of the driver—black, white, male, or female—hammering down the door locks. On less traveled streets after dark, I grew accustomed to but never comfortable with people crossing to the other side of the street rather than pass me. Then there were the standard unpleasantries with policemen, doormen, bouncers, cabdrivers, and others whose business it is to screen out troublesome individuals *before* there is any nastiness.

4   I moved to New York nearly two years ago and I have remained an avid night walker. In central Manhattan, the near-constant crowd cover minimizes tense one-on-one street encounters. Elsewhere—in SoHo, for example, where sidewalks are narrow and tightly spaced buildings shut out the sky—things can get very taut indeed.

5   After dark, on the warrenlike streets of Brooklyn where I live, I often see women who fear the worst from me. They seem to have set their faces on neutral, and with their purse straps strung across their chests bandolier-style, they forge ahead as though bracing themselves against being tackled. I understand, of course, that the danger they perceive is not a hallucination. Women are particularly vulnerable to street violence, and young black males are drastically overrepresented among the perpetrators of that violence. Yet these truths are no solace against the kind of alienation that comes of being ever the suspect, a fearsome entity with whom pedestrians avoid making eye contact.

6   It is not altogether clear to me how I reached the ripe old age of twenty-two without being conscious of the lethality nighttime pedestrians attributed to me. Perhaps it was because in Chester, Pennsylvania, the small, angry industrial town where I came of age in the 1960s, I was scarcely noticeable against a backdrop of gang warfare, street knifings, and murders. I grew up one of the good boys, had perhaps a half-dozen fistfights. In retrospect, my shyness of combat has clear sources.

7   As a boy, I saw countless tough guys locked away; I have since buried several, too. They were babies, really—a teenage cousin, a brother of twenty-two, a childhood friend in his mid-twenties—all gone down in episodes of bravado played out in the streets. I came to doubt the virtues of intimidation early on. I chose, perhaps unconsciously, to remain a shadow—timid, but a survivor.

8   The fearsomeness mistakenly attributed to me in public places often has a perilous flavor. The most frightening of these confusions occurred in the late 1970s and early 1980s, when I worked as a journalist in Chicago. One day, rushing into the office of a magazine I was writing for with a deadline story in hand, I was mistaken for a burglar. The office manager called security and, with an ad hoc posse, pursued me through the labyrinthine halls, nearly to my editor's door. I had no way of proving who I was. I could only move briskly toward the company of someone who knew me.

9   Another time I was on assignment for a local paper and killing time before an interview. I entered a jewelry store on the city's affluent Near North Side. The proprietor excused herself and returned with an enormous red Doberman pinscher straining at the end of a leash. She stood, the dog extended toward me, silent to my questions, her eyes bulging nearly out of her head. I took a cursory look around, nodded, and bade her good night.

10   Relatively speaking, however, I never fared as badly as another black male journalist. He went to nearby Waukegan, Illinois, a couple of summers ago to work on a story about

a murderer who was born there. Mistaking the reporter for the killer, police officers hauled him from his car at gunpoint and but for his press credentials would probably have tried to book him. Such episodes are not uncommon. Black men trade tales like this all the time.

11   Over the years, I learned to smother the rage I felt at so often being taken for a criminal. Not to do so would surely have led to madness. I now take precautions to make myself less threatening. I move about with care, particularly late in the evening. I give a wide berth to nervous people on subway platforms during the wee hours, particularly when I have exchanged business clothes for jeans. If I happen to be entering a building behind some people who appear skittish, I may walk by, letting them clear the lobby before I return, so as not to seem to be following them. I have been calm and extremely congenial on those rare occasions when I've been pulled over by the police.

12   And on late-evening constitutionals I employ what has proved to be an excellent tension-reducing measure: I whistle melodies from Beethoven and Vivaldi and the more popular classical composers. Even steely New Yorkers hunching toward nighttime destinations seem to relax, and occasionally they even join in the tune. Virtually everybody seems to sense that a mugger wouldn't be warbling bright, sunny selections from Vivaldi's *Four Seasons*. It is my equivalent of the cowbell that hikers wear when they know they are in bear country.

Rhetorical Reasons that Slogans Stick

Mark Forsyth

Best-selling British author Mark Forsyth is a word nerd who claims he once drew a diagram "to explain what the name Philip has to do with a hippopotamus." Also known as The Inky Fool, after his blog of the same name, he reveals the hidden meanings, connections, and stories behind English words. Forsyth is the author of *The Etymologicon: A Circular Stroll Through the Hidden Connections of the English Language,* 2011; *The Horologicon: A Day's Jaunt Through the Lost Words of the English Language,* 2012; and *The Elements of Eloquence: Secrets of the Perfect Turn of Phrase,* 2014. The following selection, exploring the rhetoric of advertising slogans and what makes the good ones memorable, was published in 2014 in the *New York Times*.

1   Slogan is an ancient Gaelic word. It means, or at least it meant, battle cry. When medieval Scotsmen were charging their enemies in remote and warlike glens, they would shout the name of their clan or their chieftain again and again and again. "Campbell! Campbell! Campbell!" or "McDonald! McDonald! McDonald!" These days, in the battles of global corporations, there's slightly less killing, and certainly fewer kilts. But otherwise it's pretty much the same clamoring to be heard above the competitive fray. Imagine an army of Apple employees, brandishing iPhone 6s and bellowing "Bigger than bigger!" as they storm a counterattacking legion of Samsung smartphone reps wielding Galaxy S5s and urging one another onward with "The next big thing is here!"

2   A slogan, a good one at least, is at the heart of a company. It doesn't just face outward to the consumer, but inward to the employees. One sentence becomes the company identity, the corporate motto and the battle cry. So it had better be a cracking good sentence.

And many are. In fact you can often use the techniques of classical rhetoric to slice them apart and explain exactly how and why they work. Sometimes, they can be pretty simple.

3   You don't need to be Cicero,* for instance, to see the common thread running through "Intel Inside," United Airlines' "Fly the friendly skies" or the nut purveyor Planters's "Famously Fresh." All three phrases rely on alliteration, which can be especially effective when, like those last two, they repeat an F sound. They are slogans that Shakespeare might have penned.

4   Think I'm getting carried away? Consider "Full fathom five thy father lies." There's no real content there. All Shakespeare is saying is "Your father's body is 9.144 meters under water." But putting it that way wouldn't have made it one of the most enduring lines in English literature. Shakespeare knew what any good slogan writer knew: Alliteration works. And if you sat him down to write a slogan, or to name a product or a company, that's probably where he would start. Coca-Cola, Kit Kat, Paypal: the alliterative allure is alive.

5   The Bard would also have heartily endorsed the international ad slogan that Reebok rolled out nearly a decade ago: "I am what I am." It is, after all, almost exactly the same as "To be or not to be." That's a trick called diacope, a verbal sandwich of two words or phrases with something else tucked in the middle. And it's almost guaranteed to give you a memorable line—whether you're saying "Bond, James Bond" or "Be all you can be," or "Home, sweet home," or "Bigger than bigger." Even a line like "I am what I am"—which let's be frank, doesn't actually mean that much—can enter the public consciousness because of its shape. Shakespeare knew that. If he were around to write a slogan for Walmart, he might come up with something along the lines of the very one the company used for years: "Always low prices. Always."

6   Diacope is just one of the figures of rhetoric—little tricks that don't change the meaning of a sentence, but make it more memorable. The ancient Greeks and the Romans loved identifying and collecting these patterns. They didn't invent them exactly, they simply observed that some lines are memorable, others are not, and that the memorable lines tend to follow certain formulas. In Shakespeare's day rhetoric was still part of the standard school curriculum, so when he used diacope, he knew he was using diacope. These days we tend to thrash about until we get there by accident.

7   For a figure called chiasmus, a perfect example is "I am stuck on Band-Aids 'cause Band-Aid's stuck on me." If you put it next to J.F.K.'s inaugural speech, you'll see exactly what I mean. "Mankind must put an end to war, or war will put an end to mankind." "We must never negotiate out of fear, but we must never fear to negotiate." "Ask not what your country can do for you. . . . " You get the picture. But when I contacted Mike Becker, the man who actually came up with the Band-Aid phrase in the mid-1970s, he told me that he'd never thought of the J.F.K. parallels. "It just had a kind of magic to it," he told me. And he denied ever having heard of chiasmus.

---

*Marcus Tullius Cicero lived from 106 BCE to 43 BCE and was a famous Roman orator, statesman, and scholar.

8   Instead, like a true adman, Becker was concentrating on the unique selling point: that Band-Aids stuck better than their competitors. So he wanted to get the word in twice with the different senses of "stuck on" meaning both "in love with" and "glued to." Once you work out the pattern, you can see that the pattern works. But unlike Mr. Becker, Shakespeare would have known that the pattern was called chiasmus, because he would have had it firmly beaten into him at school.

9   These days, slogans and corporate mottos tend to evolve through a form of natural selection. If one slogan isn't memorable, it's replaced with another and another and another until something comes along that hits the rhetorical sweet spot.

10   "Byte into an Apple" isn't the best pun ever, which might be one reason Apple Computer in the late 1970s wasn't a household name. "Think different," which the company used more recently, worked—and it worked for a very precise reason. The other day I told a friend I was writing an article on corporate slogans. He immediately told me that the one he hated, absolutely hated, was "Think different" because it should be "think differently." He's right, grammatically. But the fact that he's nursing a grudge over an ad slogan Apple hasn't run for a dozen years proves just how memorable it was.

11   Same for a long-popular British slogan, "Beanz Meanz Heinz," which grammar would have insisted on as "Beanz Mean Heinz." For that matter "Got milk?" is substandard speech. So is Subway's "Eat fresh." Probably the most memorable ad in Britain in the last few years uses the one-word tagline "Simples"—uttered by an anthropomorphic Russian meerkat on behalf of an insurance website, comparethemarket.com.

12   It's a trick called enallage: a slight deliberate grammatical mistake that makes a sentence stand out. "We was robbed." "Mistah Kurtz—he dead." "Thunderbirds are go." All of these stick in our minds because they're just wrong—wrong enough to be right. T.S. Eliot's "Let us go then, you and I" is perhaps his best line. Why? Maybe because it's wrong. It should be "Let us go then, you and me." Thank the Muses, he didn't have a literal-minded proof reader.

13   Isn't it beautiful how these ancient figures of rhetoric still do their work, if now only to give euphony to the corporate canon?

14   Shakespeare's tricolon—the rule of three that gave him "Friends, Romans, countrymen" and that inspired the French revolution's "Liberté, Egalité, Fraternité"—lives on in eBay's "Buy it. Sell it. Love it." and in Fisher Price's "Play. Laugh. Grow."

15   Shakespeare also had paradoxes, like "Heavy lightness! Serious vanity!" We have HSBC's "The world's local bank" and "If you want to capture someone's attention, whisper." Rhetoric survives.

16   But rhetoric doesn't explain absolutely everything. There's no classical explanation for the long success of Nike's "Just do it" and no figure of rhetoric to account for the wondrously smug understatement of British Airways' "The world's favourite airline." Sometimes the rhetorical explanation system simply breaks down.

17   Or maybe it just goes back to the other great, old rule of advertising:

18   It's not what you say, it's how many times you say it.

19   It's not what you say, it's how many times you say it.

20   It's not what you say, it's . . .

A Look into the "Double Lives" of America's Homeless College Students

Shadee Ashtari

Shadee Ashtari is an associate politics editor at the *Huffington Post*. This article is based on research that she conducted for her senior thesis as a Communications major at the University of California at Los Angeles (UCLA). Ashtari was the editor-in-chief of UCLA's foreign affairs publication, *The Generation*, and was herself a scholarship recipient. She is currently pursuing an advanced degree at the Johns Hopkins Bloomberg School of Public Health. This article was published in the *Huffington Post* in December 2014.

1   Sean McLean's first day of college at the University of Massachusetts Boston came on the heels of sobering news: The night before, he and his family were evicted from their home in Woburn, 9 miles north of Boston.

2   "I went to school knowing that later that day I would be packing up everything I owned and going to a shelter," said McLean, now 19.*

3   McLean is one of more than 58,000 homeless college students in America today, according to Free Application for Federal Student Aid data from the 2012–2013 academic year. The figure—which does not account for students who either do not realize they qualify as homeless (i.e., couch-surfers) or those who choose not to report their cases out of fear or shame—marks a more than 75 percent increase over the previous three years. Administrators and poverty advocates nationwide attribute the recent spike in homelessness among college students to several leading factors: a parent losing a job, a lack of affordable housing and rising tuition costs.

4   Unlike the homeless population at large, homeless college students are largely indistinguishable from their peers. Many live out of their cars. Some spend nights in the school library pretending they fell asleep studying; others couch-surf at friends' houses. The rest shack up on the streets or in shelters or motels.

5   McLean found himself in the latter group last fall. His mother was no longer able to work after taking custody of her infant granddaughter in 2012, and McLean's part-time job as a maintenance assistant at a school for students with special needs became their primary source of income. They were evicted from their home in September 2013 after falling behind on rent. The state Department of Housing and Community Development placed McLean, his mother and his 2-year-old niece at the Bedford Plaza Hotel in Bedford, Mass., which operates as a family shelter.

6   McLean's counselor at UMass Boston, Shirley Fan-Chan, is the director of U-ACCESS, a college support center for disadvantaged students, which provides free meals and guidance on financial aid, among other resources. Fan-Chan has worked with roughly 60 homeless or nearly homeless students at UMass in the past year.

7   Due to misperceptions, Fan-Chan says, homeless students in higher education lead "double lives." Indeed, the stigmas associated with homelessness lead the majority to hide their living situations from their peers. Many resist financial aid out of pride, while others do not qualify because they are undocumented, lack a co-signer or have bad credit.

---

*Interviews for this article were conducted in May 2014.

8   "They're embarrassed, they're afraid and they don't want people to look at them like they're waiting for the free handout," Fan-Chan said.

9   They're also uniquely motivated to succeed.

10   "These are people who get it," said Kathleen O'Neill, who directs Single Stop USA for Massachusetts' Bunker Hill Community College. The national nonprofit organization assists low-income families. "The way out of poverty is education and they are committed to doing whatever it is they need to do to get there."

11   Twenty-four-year-old Stephanie, who requested her last name not be used, is a dean's list student entering her senior year at UMass and a mother of two. Stephanie and her family lost their home in 2011 after falling behind on payments, and the state placed them in a motel in Brighton.

12   "Only 2 percent of teen mothers graduate college—I refuse to be that 98 percent," she said. "There is just no way I'm going to be able to afford rent without a college degree. It's the only way I'm going to be able to compete for a job with a family sustaining wage."

13   McLean also views college as his ticket to a stable life. "I don't want to be a millionaire," he insisted. "I want to be known as the person who never made his family stress about having money."

14   In the meantime, he keeps his living situation hidden from his school friends and professors. He has to catch a bus home by 6:30 p.m. every day, limiting his ability to make plans with friends, attend on-campus events, or even meet his classmates to work on group projects. The shelter's 10 p.m. curfew adds another barrier to socializing. But McLean says he's most responsible for alienating himself.

15   "I don't want to be around people," he said, "if for any reason because eventually I'm going to have to tell them what's going on. I don't know where I get it from, but I do have a lot of pride."

16   Stephanie's friends, and most of her family, are not aware she is homeless either. "Who wants to walk around telling people they're homeless?" she asked. "I will probably take it to the grave with me."

17   For most people in her situation, Stephanie's question is a no-brainer: Why broadcast a label that you're looking to shirk as soon as possible?

18   A majority of homeless college students come from lower-middle-class families and do not have a history of homelessness or extreme poverty. Many were severely affected by the 2008 recession—a parent lost a job and was then unable to assist the student in paying for tuition or housing. Almost all were not homeless before they started school, and would not be now if they had opted for full-time jobs over college.

19   "People think this is the population that is stuck in a situation because they have drugs problems or they're lazy," Fan-Chan said. "But the only issue they have is that they're poor."

Chapter 28

Process Analysis

College Students: Protect Yourself from Identity Theft

Luanne Kadlub

Luanne Kadlub is the Media Relations Manager at the Better Business Bureau (BBB) serving Northern Colorado and Wyoming, representing a national organization whose mission is "advancing marketplace trust." Kadlub wrote this *Coloradoan* newspaper article in 2011, in early August, just prior to the start of most college students' academic year, as part of the BBB's commitment to consumer education and protection.

1   In a few short weeks, college students will say goodbye to their families and head off to colleges near and far. But their academic adventures are not without risks, which makes now a good time for a refresher course on the importance of protecting their identities from potential identity thieves.

2   In 2010, 8.1 million Americans—or 3.5 percent of the population—became victims of identity theft, according to the 2011 Identity Fraud Survey conducted by Javelin Strategy & Research and sponsored by the Better Business Bureau.* The average mean cost of identity theft is $631, and the average time to resolve identity fraud is 33 hours—valuable study time.

3   "Friendly fraud" accounts for 14 percent of all ID theft crimes. This means that new roommates and friends have just as much potential of being as dastardly as a foreign-based scam artist phishing on the Internet. And identity thieves—friend or foe—think nothing of Dumpster diving (or rifling through unattended trash cans) for unshredded paperwork or even taking mail from unlocked mailboxes (or off a desk). They even cruise social networking sites looking for some personal tidbit that can unlock a wealth of information elsewhere.

4   What to do?

5   • Keep sensitive information from prying eyes. Store personal and financial records in a locked storage device or in a password-protected file. Shred sensitive documents you don't intend to keep. (Note to parents: A paper shredder makes a great last-minute going-away gift for college students.)

---

* Editor's Note: According to a 2015 identity fraud study conducted by Javelin Strategy & Research, 12.7 million Americans were victims of identity fraud in 2014, and over $16 billion was stolen from fraud victims in 2014.

6   • Be mindful of people in close proximity who could overhear or watch as sensitive financial or personal information is provided on the phone, websites or while shopping.

7   • Avoid providing your full nine-digit Social Security number whenever possible. Ask if you can provide alternate information instead.

8   • Don't carry Social Security cards or unnecessary credit cards or checks.

9   • Request electronic financial statements and use online bill pay whenever possible. Enroll in direct deposit, shred sensitive paper documents, and don't put checks in an unlocked mailbox.

10   • Install and update anti-virus and anti-malware software on your computer. Keep firewalls, browsers, applications and software updated as well.

11   • Don't publish birth date, email address, mother's maiden name, pet's name or other identifying personal information on social networking sites. Use privacy settings to control who has access to your profile.

12   • Use strong passwords that combine letters, numbers and symbols, and change them regularly. Don't access unsecure websites or type in personally identifiable information while using public Wi-Fi on mobile devices, laptops or computers. Turn off Bluetooth and Wi-Fi when they're not being used.

13   • If conducting business online, provide personal or financial information only on secure sites. To recognize these sites, look for a padlock symbol and an "s" after the "http" in the address bar.

14   • Be vigilant in monitoring bank and credit card statements to spot unauthorized activity. The most common method for fraudsters to take over a victim's account is by changing the physical address, so sign up for security alerts that are sent to your mobile phone or email account whenever changes are made to your account or personal information.

15   College students—and others—who believe they are victims of identity theft should immediately contact their bank and credit card companies, contact the Federal Trade Commission to fill out a complaint form, place a fraud alert on their credit report, and file a police report.

Bite-Sized History

Carlton Stowers

Carlton Stowers is the author of more than two dozen works of nonfiction, including two Edgar Award-winning books, *Careless Whispers* (1986) and *To the Last Breath* (1998), and the Pulitzer Prize-nominated *Innocence Lost* (1990). As a journalist and feature writer, he has published stories in the *Dallas Morning News,* the *Dallas Observer, Time, Sports Illustrated,* and many other magazines. This article first appeared in *American Way* magazine in 2010.

1   For the most part, our historians have done a commendable job of reminding us of the milestone achievements that have greatly affected American lives. We know that Thomas Edison brought us out of the darkness with the invention of the lightbulb. Were

it not for Alexander Graham Bell, our kids couldn't talk endlessly on the phone. We've duly credited Henry Ford for freeway traffic jams and the Wright brothers for [air travel].

2   But in no history book can I find mention of Charles Elmer Doolin and his Great Depression brainstorm that forever changed our nation's eating habits. If you ask me, the guy deserves a statue and a parade.

3   True, he may not have done my waistline much good, but over the years, he's added greatly to my enjoyment of county fairs, ballgames, late-night TV watching, backyard cookouts and long cross-country drives. His food-on-the-run invention has been my constant companion since boyhood days.

4   Think about it for a minute: Where would we be today without his crispy, salted corn chips, Fritos? If there were a Snack Food Hall of Fame, Doolin would get my vote for immediate induction.

5   His proud daughter, Kaleta, an accomplished Dallas artist and careful keeper of the family history, agrees. Her dad and his story are, she rightfully boasts, a need-to-know part of Americana. And she's the go-to source for how it all came about; she's even written a book, *Fritos Pie: Stories, Recipes and More*, that Texas A&M University Press will publish next fall.

6   You want an honest-to-goodness success tale, she's got a dandy.

7   In the early 1930s, C.E. Doolin was the proprietor of San Antonio's Highland Park Confectionary, constantly in search of new ways to lure customers into his establishment. In addition to the pastries, ice creams, soft drinks and candies he had to offer, he wanted some kind of bite-size treat he could place on his counter for arriving patrons.

8   Down the street, at a neighborhood service station, Gustavo Olguin had just the thing. Originally from Mexico, Olguin had brought the ideas of a popular Mexican beach food that he cooked, packaged and sold. It wasn't exactly the culinary version of rocket science. He shaped masa (a corn and water mixture) into small strips using a converted potato ricer, deep-fried and salted them, and then put the crispy chips into small bags. Records show that he started with a grand total of only nineteen customers. Aware that Olguin wanted badly to return to his homeland and to his love of coaching soccer, Doolin offered to buy him out. After considerable negotiation, the owner agreed to sell his recipe, customer list and cooking utensils for $100 cash.

9   Doolin's only problem was in getting his hands on that kind of money. Which is where his mother, Daisy Dean Doolin, enters our story. Demonstrating remarkable faith in her son's plan, she offered to pawn her wedding ring, an above-and-beyond gesture that raised $80. Gustavo Olguin loaned C.E. the additional $20, and thus was born The Frito Co. Its first headquarters was Daisy Doolin's kitchen when ten pounds of *fritos* (Spanish translation: "fried things") could be produced daily. Priced to sell for a nickel per package, on a good day the chips brought in a profit of two bucks.

10   That, as historians like to say, was how it all began.

11   In the years to come, Doolin became consumed with the notion that he had struck a food product gold mine. Eventually, production moved into a rented building that would house Doolin-designed cooking facilities, assembly-line conveyor belts, a packaging process and its own test kitchen for continued experimenting with the recipe. He even began growing and testing various types of corn in his search for the perfect masa. "We kids were his taste testers," recalls Kaleta. "He'd bring samples home, straight off the conveyor belt."

12   Fritos were a hit in the Doolin home as well as in food outlets nationwide. And not just as a snack but as an ingredient in recipes Daisy Doolin was coming up with to be printed on the back of each package. There were her Fritos Meatloaf, Fritos Squash and, most important, her famed Fritos Pie, that simple and tasty treat that remains the favorite of every high school football-stadium concession stand in the nation. You don't even need to write it down to remember it: Open a pack of Fritos, pour in a little chili, stir and enjoy. I can do it with my eyes closed.

13   But, back to our history lesson.

14   In 1934, the farsighted Doolin moved his operation to Dallas and ultimately had a fleet of delivery trucks on the road. By 1950, Fritos were being sold in every state in the U.S. A decade later, distribution had expanded to forty-eight countries.

15   Such was the ever-growing demand that he eventually sold a dozen manufacturing franchises. Among those who bought in was Herman Lay, a Nashville businessman who was also pioneering in the snack-food business. If you bought a bag of potato chips in the southeastern U.S. back in those days, it was most likely distributed by Lay's company. Ultimately, it was at Lay's suggestion that the companies merged into what would become the famous and mega-successful Frito-Lay Co.

16   Not a bad return on a $100 investment.

Chapter 29

Comparison and Contrast

Us and Them

David Sedaris

David Sedaris is an American author, humorist, and radio personality. Born in 1956 and raised in suburban North Carolina, Sedaris's stories and essays are collected in works such as *Naked, Me Talk Pretty One Day, Dress Your Family in Corduroy and Denim,* and *When You are Engulfed in Flames,* all of which have become *New York Times* bestsellers. Based on his personal experiences as a middle-class suburbanite, Sedaris's essays are wildly humorous and often subtly poignant. After his National Public Radio debut in 1992, Sedaris became a regular contributor to NPR's *This American Life.* The essay below is from *Dress Your Family in Corduroy and Denim.*

1   When my family first moved to North Carolina, we lived in a rented house three blocks from the school where I would begin the third grade. My mother made friends with one of the neighbors, but one seemed enough for her. Within a year we would move again and, as she explained, there wasn't much point in getting too close to people we would have to say good-bye to. Our next house was less than a mile away, and the short journey would hardly merit tears or even good-byes, for that matter. It was more of a "see you later" situation, but still I adopted my mother's attitude, as it allowed me to pretend that not making friends was a conscious choice. I could if I wanted to. It just wasn't the right time.

2   Back in New York State, we had lived in the country, with no sidewalks or street-lights; you could leave the house and still be alone. But here, when you looked out the window, you saw other houses, and people inside those houses. I hoped that in walking around after dark I might witness a murder, but for the most part our neighbors just sat in their living rooms, watching TV. The only place that seemed truly different was owned by a man named Mr. Tomkey, who did not believe in television. This was told to us by our mother's friend, who dropped by one afternoon with a basketful of okra. The woman did not editorialize—rather, she just presented her information, leaving her listener to make of it what she might. Had my mother said, "That's the craziest thing I've ever heard in my life," I assume that the friend would have agreed, and had she said, "Three cheers for Mr. Tomkey," the friend likely would have agreed as well. It was a kind of test, as was the okra.

3   To say that you did not believe in television was different from saying that you did not care for it. Belief implied that television had a master plan and that you were against it. It also suggested that you thought too much. When my mother reported that Mr. Tomkey did not believe in television, my father said, "Well, good for him. I don't know that I believe in it, either."

4   "That's exactly how I feel," my mother said, and then my parents watched the news, and whatever came on after the news.

5   Word spread that Mr. Tomkey did not own a television, and you began hearing that while this was all very well and good, it was unfair of him to inflict his beliefs upon others, specifically his innocent wife and children. It was speculated that just as the blind man develops a keener sense of hearing, the family must somehow compensate for their loss. "Maybe they read," my mother's friend said. "Maybe they listen to the radio, but you can bet your boots they're doing something."

6   I wanted to know what this something was, and so I began peering through the Tomkeys' windows. During the day I'd stand across the street from their house, acting as though I were waiting for someone, and at night, when the view was better and I had less chance of being discovered, I would creep into their yard and hide in the bushes beside their fence.

7   Because they had no TV, the Tomkeys were forced to talk during dinner. They had no idea how puny their lives were, and so they were not ashamed that a camera would have found them uninteresting. They did not know what attractive was or what dinner was supposed to look like or even what time people were supposed to eat. Sometimes they wouldn't sit down until eight o'clock, long after everyone else had finished doing the dishes. During the meal, Mr. Tomkey would occasionally pound the table and point at his children with a fork, but the moment he finished, everyone would start laughing. I got the idea that he was imitating someone else, and wondered if he spied on us while we were eating.

8   When fall arrived and school began, I saw the Tomkey children marching up the hill with paper sacks in their hands. The son was one grade lower than me, and the daughter was one grade higher. We never spoke, but I'd pass them in the halls from time to time and attempt to view the world through their eyes. What must it be like to be so ignorant and alone? Could a normal person even imagine it? Staring at an Elmer Fudd* lunch box, I tried to divorce myself from everything I already knew: Elmer's inability to pronounce the letter *r*, his constant pursuit of an intelligent and considerably more famous rabbit. I tried to think of him as just a drawing, but it was impossible to separate him from his celebrity.

9   One day in class a boy named William began to write the wrong answer on the blackboard, and our teacher flailed her arms, saying, "Warning, Will. Danger, danger."** Her voice was synthetic and void of emotion, and we laughed, knowing that she was imitating the robot in a weekly show about a family who lived in outer space. The Tomkeys,

---

* Elmer Fudd is a cartoon character in the *Looney Tunes* series. Elmer is a hunter in constant, but always unsuccessful, pursuit of Bugs Bunny (the "more famous rabbit" mentioned above).
** The television series *Lost In Space* (1965–1968) featured a family lost in space and trying to get back to Earth, and included a robot which would wave its arms and say the line,"Warning. Danger. Danger."

though, would have thought she was having a heart attack. It occurred to me that they needed a guide, someone who could accompany them through the course of an average day and point out all the things they were unable to understand. I could have done it on weekends, but friendship would have taken away their mystery and interfered with the good feeling I got from pitying them. So I kept my distance.

10   In early October the Tomkeys bought a boat, and everyone seemed greatly relieved, especially my mother's friend, who noted that the motor was definitely secondhand. It was reported that Mr. Tomkey's father-in-law owned a house on the lake and had invited the family to use it whenever they liked. This explained why they were gone all weekend, but it did not make their absences any easier to bear. I felt as if my favorite show had been canceled.

11   Halloween fell on a Saturday that year, and by the time my mother took us to the store, all the good costumes were gone. My sisters dressed as witches and I went as a hobo. I'd looked forward to going in disguise to the Tomkeys' door, but they were off at the lake, and their house was dark. Before leaving, they had left a coffee can full of gumdrops on the front porch, alongside a sign reading DON'T BE GREEDY. In terms of Halloween candy, individual gumdrops were just about as low as you could get. This was evidenced by the large number of them floating in an adjacent dog bowl. It was disgusting to think that this was what a gumdrop might look like in your stomach, and it was insulting to be told not to take too much of something you didn't really want in the first place. "Who do these Tomkeys think they are?" my sister Lisa said.

12   The night after Halloween, we were sitting around watching TV when the door-bell rang. Visitors were infrequent at our house, so while my father stayed behind, my mother, sisters, and I ran downstairs in a group, opening the door to discover the entire Tomkey family on our front stoop. The parents looked as they always had, but the son and daughter were dressed in costumes—she as a ballerina and he as some kind of a rodent with terry-cloth ears and a tail made from what looked to be an extension cord. It seemed they had spent the previous evening isolated at the lake and had missed the opportunity to observe Halloween. "So, well, I guess we're trick-or-treating now, if that's okay," Mr. Tomkey said.

13   I attributed their behavior to the fact that they didn't have a TV, but television didn't teach you everything. Asking for candy on Halloween was called trick-or-treating, but asking for candy on November first was called begging, and it made people uncomfortable. This was one of the things you were supposed to learn simply by being alive, and it angered me that the Tomkeys did not understand it.

14   "Why of course it's not too late," my mother said. "Kids, why don't you . . . run and get . . . the candy."

15   "But the candy is gone," my sister Gretchen said. "You gave it away last night."

16   "Not that candy," my mother said. "The other candy. Why don't you run and go get it?"

17   "You mean our candy?" Lisa said. "The candy that we earned?"

18   This was exactly what our mother was talking about, but she didn't want to say this in front of the Tomkeys. In order to spare their feelings, she wanted them to believe that we always kept a bucket of candy lying around the house, just waiting for some-one to knock on the door and ask for it. "Go on, now," she said. "Hurry up."

19   My room was situated right off the foyer, and if the Tomkeys had looked in that direction, they could have seen my bed and the brown paper bag marked MY CANDY. KEEP OUT. I didn't want them to know how much I had, and so I went into my room and shut the door behind me. Then I closed the curtains and emptied my bag onto the bed, searching for whatever was the crummiest. All my life chocolate has made me ill. I don't know if I'm allergic or what, but even the smallest amount leaves me with a blinding headache. Eventually, I learned to stay away from it, but as a child I refused to be left out. The brownies were eaten, and when the pounding began I would blame the grape juice or my mother's cigarette smoke or the tightness of my glasses—anything but the chocolate. My candy bars were poison but they were brand-name, and so I put them in pile no. 1, which definitely would not go to the Tomkeys.

20   Out in the hallway I could hear my mother straining for something to talk about. "A boat!" she said. "That sounds marvelous. Can you just drive it right into the water?"

21   "Actually, we have a trailer," Mr. Tomkey said. "So what we do is back it into the lake."

22   "Oh, a trailer. What kind is it?"

23   "Well, it's a boat trailer," Mr. Tomkey said.

24   "Right, but is it wooden or, you know . . . I guess what I'm asking is what style trailer do you have?"

25   Behind my mother's words were two messages. The first and most obvious was "Yes, I am talking about boat trailers, but also I am dying." The second, meant only for my sisters and me, was "If you do not immediately step forward with that candy, you will never again experience freedom, happiness, or the possibility of my warm embrace."

26   I knew that it was just a matter of time before she came into my room and started collecting the candy herself, grabbing indiscriminately, with no regard to my rating system. Had I been thinking straight, I would have hidden the most valuable items in my dresser drawer, but instead, panicked by the thought of her hand on my doorknob, I tore off the wrappers and began cramming the candy bars into my mouth, desperately, like someone in a contest. Most were miniature, which made them easier to accommodate, but still there was only so much room, and it was hard to chew and fit more in at the same time. The headache began immediately, and I chalked it up to tension.

27   My mother told the Tomkeys she needed to check on something, and then she opened the door and stuck her head inside my room. "What the hell are you doing?" she whispered, but my mouth was too full to answer. "I'll just be a moment," she called, and as she closed the door behind her and moved toward my bed, I began breaking the wax lips and candy necklaces pulled from pile no. 2. These were the second-best things I had received, and while it hurt to destroy them, it would have hurt even more to give them away. I had just started to mutilate a miniature box of Red Hots when my mother pried them from my hands, accidentally finishing the job for me. BB-size pellets clattered onto the floor, and as I followed them with my eyes, she snatched up a roll of Necco wafers.

28   "Not those," I pleaded, but rather than words, my mouth expelled chocolate, chewed chocolate, which fell onto the sleeve of her sweater. "Not those. Not those."

29   She shook her arm, and the mound of chocolate dropped like a horrible turd upon my bedspread. "You should look at yourself," she said. "I mean, really look at yourself."

30   Along with the Necco wafers she took several Tootsie Pops and half a dozen caramels wrapped in cellophane. I heard her apologize to the Tomkeys for her absence, and then I heard my candy hitting the bottom of their bags.

31   "What do you say?" Mrs. Tomkey asked.

32   And the children answered, "Thank you."

33   While I was in trouble for not bringing my candy sooner, my sisters were in more trouble for not bringing theirs at all. We spent the early part of the evening in our rooms, then one by one we eased our way back upstairs, and joined our parents in front of the TV. I was the last to arrive, and took a seat on the floor beside the sofa. The show was a Western, and even if my head had not been throbbing, I doubt I would have had the wherewithal to follow it. A posse of outlaws crested a rocky hilltop, squinting at a flurry of dust advancing from the horizon, and I thought again of the Tomkeys and of how alone and out of place they had looked in their dopey costumes. "What was up with that kid's tail?" I asked.

34   "Shhhh," my family said.

35   For months I had protected and watched over these people, but now, with one stupid act, they had turned my pity into something hard and ugly. The shift wasn't gradual, but immediate, and it provoked an uncomfortable feeling of loss. We hadn't been friends, the Tomkeys and I, but still I had given them the gift of my curiosity. Wondering about the Tomkey family had made me feel generous, but now I would have to shift gears and find pleasure in hating them. The only alternative was to do as my mother had instructed and take a good look at myself. This was an old trick, designed to turn one's hatred inward, and while I was determined not to fall for it, it was hard to shake the mental picture snapped by her suggestion: here is a boy sitting on a bed, his mouth smeared with chocolate. He's a human being, but also he's a pig, surrounded by trash and gorging himself so that others may be denied. Were this the only image in the world, you'd be forced to give it your full attention, but fortunately there were others. This stagecoach, for instance, coming round the bend with a cargo of gold. This shiny new Mustang convertible. This teenage girl, her hair a beautiful mane, sipping Pepsi through a straw, one picture after another, on and on until the news, and whatever came on after the news.

The Myth of the Latin Woman: I Just Met a Girl Named Maria

Judith Ortiz Cofer

Judith Ortiz Cofer is an award-winning poet, essayist, fiction writer, and professor emerita of English and creative writing at the University of Georgia. Cofer often draws upon her Puerto Rican heritage as she explores cultural diversity issues in America. Her works include *If I Could Fly* (2011), *A Love Story Beginning in Spanish* (2005), *The Meaning of Consuelo* (2003), and *The Latin Deli* (1993), from which this essay is taken.

1   On a bus trip to London from Oxford University, where I was earning some graduate credits one summer, a young man, obviously fresh from a pub, spotted me and as if struck by inspiration went down on his knees in the aisle. With both hands over

his heart he broke into an Irish tenor's rendition of "Maria" from *West Side Story*.* My politely amused fellow passengers gave his lovely voice the round of gentle applause it deserved. Though I was not quite as amused, I managed my version of an English smile: no show of teeth, no extreme contortions of the facial muscles—I was at this time of my life practicing reserve and cool. Oh, that British control, how I coveted it. But Maria had followed me to London, reminding me of a prime fact of my life: you can leave the Island [Puerto Rico], master the English language, and travel as far as you can, but if you are Latina, especially one like me who so obviously belongs to Rita Moreno's gene pool, the Island travels with you.

2   This is sometimes a very good thing—it may win you that extra minute of someone's attention. But with some people, the same things can *make you* an island—not so much a tropical paradise as an Alcatraz, a place nobody wants to visit. As a Puerto Rican girl growing up in the United States and wanting like most children to "belong," I resented the stereotype that my Hispanic appearance called forth from many people I met.

3   Our family lived in a large urban center in New Jersey during the sixties, where life was designed as a microcosm of my parents' *casas* [households] on the island. We spoke in Spanish, we ate Puerto Rican food bought at the *bodega* [grocery], and we practiced strict Catholicism complete with Saturday confession and Sunday mass at a church where our parents were accommodated into a one-hour Spanish mass slot, performed by a Chinese priest trained as a missionary for Latin America.

4   As a girl I was kept under strict surveillance, since virtue and modesty were, by cultural equation, the same as family honor. As a teenager I was instructed on how to behave as a proper señorita. But it was a conflicting message girls got, since the Puerto Rican mothers also encouraged their daughters to look and act like women and to dress in clothes our Anglo friends and their mothers found too "mature" for our age. It was, and is, cultural, yet I often felt humiliated when I appeared at an American friend's party wearing a dress more suitable to a semiformal than a playroom birthday celebration. At Puerto Rican festivities, neither the music nor the colors we wore could be too loud. I still experience a vague sense of letdown when I'm invited to a "party" and it turns out to be a marathon conversation in hushed tones rather than a fiesta with salsa, laughter, and dancing—the kind of celebration I remember from my childhood.

5   I remember Career Day in our high school, when teachers told us to come dressed as if for a job interview. It quickly became obvious that to the barrio girls, "dressing up" sometimes meant wearing ornate jewelry and clothing that would be more appropriate (by mainstream standards) for the company Christmas party than as daily office attire. That morning I had agonized in front of my closet, trying to figure out what a "career girl" would wear because, essentially, except for Marlo Thomas** on TV, I had no models on which to base my decision. I knew how to dress for school: at the Catholic school I attended we all wore uniforms; I knew how to dress for Sunday mass, and I knew what dresses to wear for parties at my relatives' homes. Though I do not recall

---

* *West Side Story* is a well-known musical (and movie) that sets the Romeo and Juliet story on the streets of New York amid gang rivalry. Puerto Rico-born actress Rita Moreno won an Oscar for her supporting role in the film version.

** Marlo Thomas starred in the 1965–1971 series *That Girl* as a young single woman seeking an acting career in New York City.

the precise details of my Career Day outfit, it must have been a composite of the above choices. But I remember a comment my friend (an Italian American) made in later years that coalesced my impressions of that day. She said that at the business school she was attending the Puerto Rican girls always stood out for wearing "everything at once." She meant, of course, too much jewelry, too many accessories. On that day at school, we were simply made the negative models by the nuns who were themselves not credible fashion experts to any of us. But it was painfully obvious to me that to the others, in their tailored skirts and silk blouses, we must have seemed "hopeless" and "vulgar." Though I now know that most adolescents feel out of step much of the time, I also know that for the Puerto Rican girls of my generation that sense was intensified. The way our teachers and classmates looked at us that day in school was just a taste of the culture clash that awaited us in the real world, where prospective employers and men on the street would often misinterpret our tight skirts and jingling bracelets as a come-on.

6   Mixed cultural signals have perpetuated certain stereotypes—for example, that of the Hispanic woman as the "Hot Tamale" or sexual firebrand. It is a one-dimensional view that the media have found easy to promote. In their special vocabulary, advertisers have designated "sizzling" and "smoldering" as the adjectives of choice for describing not only the foods but also the women of Latin America. From conversations in my house I recall hearing about the harassment that Puerto Rican women endured in factories where the "boss men" talked to them as if sexual innuendo was all they understood and, worse, often gave them the choice of submitting to advances or being fired.

7   It is custom, however, not chromosomes, that leads us to choose scarlet over pale pink. As young girls, we were influenced in our decisions about clothes and colors by the women— older sisters and mothers who had grown up on a tropical island where the natural environment was a riot of primary colors, where showing your skin was one way to keep cool as well as to look sexy. Most important of all, on the island, women perhaps felt freer to dress and move more provocatively, since, in most cases, they were protected by the traditions, mores, and laws of a Spanish/Catholic system of morality and machismo whose main rule was: *You may look at my sister, but if you touch her I will kill you.* The extended family and church structure could provide a young woman with a circle of safety in her small pueblo on the island; if a man "wronged" a girl, everyone would close in to save her family honor.

8   This is what I have gleaned from my discussions as an adult with older Puerto Rican women. They have told me about dressing in their best party clothes on Saturday nights and going to the town's plaza to promenade with their girlfriends in front of the boys they liked. The males were thus given an opportunity to admire the women and to express their admiration in the form of *piropos*: erotically charged street poems they composed on the spot. I have been subjected to a few *piropos* while visiting the Island and they can be outrageous, although custom dictates that they must never cross into obscenity. This ritual, as I understand it, also entails a show of studied indifference on the woman's part; if she is "decent," she must not acknowledge the man's impassioned words. So I do understand how things can be lost in translation. When a Puerto Rican girl dressed in her idea of what is attractive meets a man from the mainstream culture who has been trained to react to certain types of clothing as a sexual signal, a clash is likely to take place. The line I first heard based on this aspect of the myth happened when the boy who took me to my first formal dance leaned over to plant a sloppy overeager kiss painfully on my mouth, and when I didn't respond with sufficient passion said

in a resentful tone: "I thought you Latin girls were supposed to mature early"—my first instance of being thought of as a fruit or vegetable—I was supposed to *ripen*, not just grow into womanhood like other girls.

9   It is surprising to some of my professional friends that some people, including those who should know better, still put others "in their place." Though rarer, these incidents are still commonplace in my life. It happened to me most recently during a stay at a very classy metropolitan hotel favored by young professional couples for their weddings. Late one evening after the theater, as I walked toward my room with my new colleague (a woman with whom I was coordinating an arts program), a middle-aged man in a tuxedo, a young girl in satin and lace on his arm, stepped directly into our path. With his champagne glass extended toward me, he exclaimed, "Evita!"*

10   Our way blocked, my companion and I listened as the man half-recited, half-bellowed "Don't Cry for Me, Argentina." When he finished, the young girl said: "How about a round of applause for my daddy?" We complied, hoping this would bring the silly spectacle to a close. I was becoming aware that our little group was attracting the attention of the other guests. "Daddy" must have perceived this too, and he once more barred the way as we tried to walk past him. He began to shout-sing a ditty to the tune of "La Bamba"—except the lyrics were about a girl named Maria whose exploits all rhymed with her name and gonorrhea. The girl kept saying "Oh, Daddy" and looking at me with pleading eyes. She wanted me to laugh along with the others. My companion and I stood silently waiting for the man to end his offensive song. When he finished, I looked not at him but at his daughter. I advised her calmly never to ask her father what he had done in the army. Then I walked between them and to my room. My friend complimented me on my cool handling of the situation. I confessed to her that I really had wanted to push the jerk into the swimming pool. I knew that this same man—probably a corporate executive, well educated, even worldly by most standards—would not have been likely to regale a white woman with a dirty song in public. He would perhaps have checked his impulse by assuming that she could be somebody's wife or mother, or at least *somebody* who might take offense. But to him, I was just an Evita or a Maria; merely a character in his cartoon-populated universe.

11   Because of my education and my proficiency with the English language, I have acquired many mechanisms for dealing with the anger I experience. This was not true for my parents, nor is it true for the many Latin women working at menial jobs who must put up with stereotypes about our ethnic group, such as "They make good domestics." This is another facet of the myth of the Latin woman in the United States. Its origin is simple to deduce. Work as domestics, waitressing, and factory jobs are all that's available to women with little English and few skills. The myth of the Hispanic menial has been sustained by the same media phenomenon that made Mammy from *Gone with the Wind* America's idea of the black woman for generations: Maria, the housemaid or counter girl, is now indelibly etched into the national psyche. The big and the little screens have presented us with the picture of the funny Hispanic maid, mispronouncing words and cooking up a spicy storm in a shiny California kitchen.

---

* "Evita" refers to Eva Perón, popular wife of former Argentinean president Juan Perón, whose rags-to-riches life story was made into a hit musical and movie.

12   This media-engendered image of the Latina in the United States has been documented by feminist Hispanic scholars, who claim that such portrayals are partially responsible for the denial of opportunities for upward mobility among Latinas in the professions. I have a Chicana friend working on a Ph.D. in philosophy at a major university. She says her doctor still shakes his head in puzzled amazement at all the "big words" she uses. Since I do not wear my diplomas around my neck for all to see, I too have on occasion been sent to that "kitchen," where some think I obviously belong.

13   One such incident that has stayed with me, though I recognize it as a minor offense, happened on the day of my first public poetry reading. It took place in Miami in a boat-restaurant where we were having lunch before an event. I was nervous and excited as I walked in with my notebook in my hand. An older woman motioned me to her table. Thinking (foolish me) that she wanted me to autograph a copy of my brand-new slender volume of verse, I went over. She ordered a cup of coffee from me, assuming that I was the waitress. Easy enough to mistake my poems for menus, I suppose. I know that it wasn't an intentional act of cruelty, yet of all the good things that happened that day, I remember that scene most clearly, because it reminded me of what I had to overcome before anyone would take me seriously. In retrospect I understand that my anger gave my reading fire, that I have almost always taken doubts in my abilities as a challenge—and that the result is, most times, a feeling of satisfaction at having won a convert when I see the cold, appraising eyes warm to my words, the body language change, the smile that indicates that I have opened some avenue for communication. That day I read to that woman and her lowered eyes told me that she was embarrassed at her little faux pas, and when I willed her to look up at me, it was my victory, and she graciously allowed me to punish her with my full attention. We shook hands at the end of the reading, and I never saw her again. She has probably forgotten the whole thing, but maybe not.

14   Yet I am one of the lucky ones. My parents made it possible for me to acquire a stronger footing in the mainstream culture by giving me the chance at an education. And books and art have saved me from the harsher forms of ethnic and racial prejudice that many of my Hispanic *compañeras* [friends] have had to endure. I travel a lot around the United States, reading from my books of poetry and my novel, and the reception I most often receive is one of positive interest by people who want to know more about my culture. There are, however, thousands of Latinas without the privilege of an education or the entrée into society that I have. For them life is a struggle against the misconceptions perpetuated by the myth of the Latina as whore, domestic, or criminal. We cannot change this by legislating the way people look at us. The transformation, as I see it, has to occur at a much more individual level. My personal goal in my public life is to try to replace the old pervasive stereotypes and myths about Latinas with a much more interesting set of realities. Every time I give a reading, I hope the stories I tell, the dreams and fears I examine in my work, can achieve some universal truth which will get my audience past the particulars of my skin color, my accent, or my clothes.

15   I once wrote a poem in which I called us Latinas "God's brown daughters." This poem is really a prayer of sorts, offered upward but also, through the human-to-human channel of art, outward. It is a prayer for communication, and for respect. In it, Latin women pray "in Spanish to an Anglo God / with a Jewish heritage," and they are "fervently hoping / that if not omnipotent, / at least He be bilingual."

Once More to the Lake

E. B. White

Elwyn Brooks White was an editor and writer for *The New Yorker* and a columnist for *Harper's* magazine. He is well known for his essays, collected in volumes including *One Man's Meat* (1943), *The Second Tree from the Corner* (1954), and *The Points of My Compass* (1962), and for his children's books, *Stuart Little* (1945) and *Charlotte's Web* (1952). This essay, written in 1941, originally appeared in *Harper's*.

1   One summer, along about 1904, my father rented a camp on a lake in Maine and took us all there for the month of August. We all got ringworm from some kittens and had to rub Pond's Extract on our arms and legs night and morning, and my father rolled over in a canoe with all his clothes on; but outside of that the vacation was a success and from then on none of us ever thought there was any place in the world like that lake in Maine. We returned summer after summer—always on August 1st for one month. I have since become a salt-water man, but sometimes in summer there are days when the restlessness of the tides and the fearful cold of the sea water and the incessant wind which blows across the afternoon and into the evening make me wish for the placidity of a lake in the woods. A few weeks ago this feeling got so strong I bought myself a couple of bass hooks and a spinner and returned to the lake where we used to go, for a week's fishing and to revisit old haunts.

2   I took along my son, who had never had any fresh water up his nose and who had seen lily pads only from train windows. On the journey over to the lake I began to wonder what it would be like. I wondered how time would have marred this unique, this holy spot—the coves and streams, the hills that the sun set behind, the camps and the paths behind the camps. I was sure the tarred road would have found it out and I wondered in what other ways it would be desolated. It is strange how much you can remember about places like that once you allow your mind to return into the grooves which lead back. You remember one thing, and that suddenly reminds you of another thing. I guess I remembered clearest of all the early mornings, when the lake was cool and motionless, remembered how the bedroom smelled of the lumber it was made of and of the wet woods whose scent entered through the screen. The partitions in the camp were thin and did not extend clear to the top of the rooms, and as I was always the first up I would dress softly so as not to wake the others, and sneak out into the sweet outdoors and start out in the canoe, keeping close along the shore in the long shadows of the pines. I remembered being very careful never to rub my paddle against the gunwale for fear of disturbing the stillness of the cathedral.

3   The lake had never been what you would call a wild lake. There were cottages sprinkled around the shores, and it was in farming country although the shores of the lake were quite heavily wooded. Some of the cottages were owned by nearby farmers, and you would live at the shore and eat your meals at the farmhouse. That's what our family did. But although it wasn't wild, it was a fairly large and undisturbed lake and there were places in it which, to a child at least, seemed infinitely remote and primeval.

4   I was right about the tar; it led to within half a mile of the shore. But when I got back there, with my boy, and we settled into a camp near a farmhouse and into the kind of summertime I had known, I could tell that it was going to be pretty much the same as

it had been before—I knew it, lying in bed the first morning, smelling the bedroom, and hearing the boy sneak quietly out and go off along the shore in a boat. I began to sustain the illusion that he was I, and therefore by simple transposition, that I was my father. This sensation persisted, kept cropping up all the time we were there. It was not an entirely new feeling, but in this setting it grew much stronger. I seemed to be living a dual existence. I would be in the middle of some simple act, I would be picking up a bait box or laying down a table fork, or I would be saying something, and suddenly it would be not I but my father who was saying the words or making the gesture. It gave me a creepy sensation.

5   We went fishing the first morning. I felt the same damp moss covering the worms in the bait can, and saw the dragonfly alight on the tip of my rod as it hovered a few inches from the surface of the water. It was the arrival of this fly that convinced me beyond any doubt that everything was as it always had been, that the years were a mirage and there had been no years. The small waves were the same, chucking the rowboat under the chin as we fished at anchor, and the boat was the same boat, the same color green and the ribs broken in the same places, and under the floor-boards the same fresh-water leavings and debris—the dead helgramite,* the wisps of moss, the rusty discarded fish-hook, the dried blood from yesterday's catch. We stared silently at the tips of our rods, at the dragonflies that came and went. I lowered the tip of mine into the water, tentatively, pensively dislodging the fly, which darted two feet away, poised, darted two feet back, and came to rest again a little farther up the rod. There had been no years between the ducking of this dragonfly and the other one—the one that was part of memory. I looked at the boy, who was silently watching his fly, and it was my hands that held his rod, my eyes watching. I felt dizzy and didn't know which rod I was at the end of.

6   We caught two bass, hauling them in briskly as though they were mackerel, pulling them over the side of the boat in a businesslike manner without any landing net, and stunning them with a blow on the back of the head. When we got back for a swim before lunch, the lake was exactly where we had left it, the same number of inches from the dock, and there was only the merest suggestion of a breeze. This seemed an utterly enchanted sea, this lake you could leave to its own devices for a few hours and come back to, and find that it had not stirred, this constant and trustworthy body of water. In the shallows, the dark, water-soaked sticks and twigs, smooth and old, were undulating in clusters on the bottom against the clean ribbed sand, and the track of the mussel was plain. A school of minnows swam by, each minnow with its small individual shadow, doubling the attendance, so clear and sharp in the sunlight. Some of the other campers were in swimming, along the shore, one of them with a cake of soap, and the water felt thin and clear and unsubstantial. Over the years there had been this person with the cake of soap, this cultist, and here he was. There had been no years.

7   Up to the farmhouse to dinner through the teeming, dusty field, the road under our sneakers was only a two-track road. The middle track was missing, the one with the marks of the hooves and the splotches of dried, flaky manure. There had always been three tracks to choose from in choosing which track to walk in; now the choice was narrowed down to two. For a moment I missed terribly the middle alternative. But the way led past the tennis court, and something about the way it lay there in the sun reassured

---

* A helgramite is an insect sometimes used for bait.

me; the tape had loosened along the backline, the alleys were green with plantains and other weeds, and the net (installed in June and removed in September) sagged in the dry noon, and the whole place steamed with mid-day heat and hunger and emptiness. There was a choice of pie for dessert, and one was blueberry and one was apple, and the waitresses were the same country girls, there having been no passage of time, only the illusion of it as in a dropped curtain—the waitresses were still fifteen; their hair had been washed, that was the only difference—they had been to the movies and seen the pretty girls with the clean hair.

8   Summertime, oh summertime, pattern of life indelible, the fade-proof lake, the woods unshatterable, the pasture with the sweet-fern and the juniper forever and ever, summer without end; this was the background, and the life along the shore was the design, the cottages with their innocent and tranquil design, their tiny docks with the flagpole and the American flag floating against the white clouds in the blue sky, the little paths over the roots of the trees leading from camp to camp and the paths leading back to the outhouses and the can of lime for sprinkling, and at the souvenir counters at the store the miniature birch-bark canoes and the post cards that showed things looking a little better than they looked. This was the American family at play, escaping the city heat, wondering whether the newcomers in the camp at the head of the cove were "common" or "nice," wondering whether it was true that the people who drove up for Sunday dinner at the farmhouse were turned away because there wasn't enough chicken.

9   It seemed to me, as I kept remembering all this, that those times and those summers had been infinitely precious and worth saving. There had been jollity and peace and goodness. The arriving (at the beginning of August) had been so big a business in itself, at the railway station the farm wagon drawn up, the first smell of the pine-laden air, the first glimpse of the smiling farmer, and the great importance of the trunks and your father's enormous authority in such matters, and the feel of the wagon under you for a long ten-mile haul, and at the top of the last long hill catching the first view of the lake after eleven months of not seeing this cherished body of water. The shouts and cries of the other campers when they saw you, and the trunks to be unpacked, to give up their rich burden. (Arriving was less exciting nowadays, when you sneaked up in your car and parked it under a tree near the camp and took out the bags and in five minutes it was all over, no fuss, no loud wonderful fuss about trunks.)

10   Peace and goodness and jollity. The only thing that was wrong now, really, was the sound of the place, an unfamiliar nervous sound of the outboard motors. This was the note that jarred, the one thing that would sometimes break the illusion and set the years moving. In those other summertimes all motors were inboard; and when they were at a little distance, the noise they made was a sedative, an ingredient of summer sleep. They were one-cylinder and two-cylinder engines, and some were make-and-break and some were jump-spark, but they all made a sleepy sound across the lake. The one-lungers throbbed and fluttered, and the twin-cylinder ones purred and purred, and that was a quiet sound too. But now the campers all had outboards. In the daytime, in the hot mornings, these motors made a petulant, irritable sound; at night, in the still evening when the afterglow lit the water, they whined about one's ears like mosquitoes. My boy loved our rented outboard, and his great desire was to achieve singlehanded mastery over it, and authority, and he soon learned the trick of choking it a little (but not too much), and the adjustment of the needle valve. Watching him I would remember the

things you could do with the old one-cylinder engine with the heavy flywheel, how you could have it eating out of your hand if you got really close to it spiritually. Motor boats in those days didn't have clutches, and you would make a landing by shutting off the motor at the proper time and coasting in with a dead rudder. But there was a way of reversing them, if you learned the trick, by cutting the switch and putting it on again exactly on the final dying revolution of the flywheel, so that it would kick back against compression and begin reversing. Approaching a dock in a strong following breeze, it was difficult to slow up sufficiently by the ordinary coasting method, and if a boy felt he had complete mastery over his motor, he was tempted to keep it running beyond its time and then reverse it a few feet from the dock. It took a cool nerve, because if you threw the switch a twentieth of a second too soon you would catch the flywheel when it still had speed enough to go up past center, and the boat would leap ahead, charging bull-fashion at the dock.

11   We had a good week at the camp. The bass were biting well and the sun shone endlessly, day after day. We would be tired at night and lie down in the accumulated heat of the little bedrooms after the long hot day and the breeze would stir almost imperceptibly outside and the smell of the swamp drift in through the rusty screens. Sleep would come easily and in the morning the red squirrel would be on the roof, tapping out his gay routine. I kept remembering everything, lying in bed in the mornings—the small steamboat that had a long rounded stern like the lip of a Ubangi, and how quietly she ran on the moonlight sails, when the older boys played their mandolins and the girls sang and we ate doughnuts dipped in sugar, and how sweet the music was on the water in the shining night, and what it had felt like to think about girls then. After breakfast we would go up to the store and the things were in the same place—the minnows in a bottle, the plugs and spinners disarranged and pawed over by the youngsters from the boys' camp, the fig newtons and the Beeman's gum. Outside, the road was tarred and cars stood in front of the store. Inside, all was just as it had always been, except there was more Coca-Cola and not so much Moxie and root beer and birch beer and sarsaparilla. We would walk out with a bottle of pop apiece and sometimes the pop would backfire up our noses and hurt. We explored the streams, quietly, where the turtles slid off the sunny logs and dug their way into the soft bottom; and we lay on the town wharf and fed worms to the tame bass. Everywhere we went I had trouble making out which was I, the one walking at my side, the one walking in my pants.

12   One afternoon while we were there at that lake a thunderstorm came up. It was like the revival of an old melodrama that I had seen long ago with childish awe. The second-act climax of the drama of the electrical disturbance over a lake in America had not changed in any important respect. This was the big scene, still the big scene. The whole thing was so familiar, the first feeling of oppression and heat and a general air around camp of not wanting to go very far away. In midafternoon (it was all the same) a curious darkening of the sky, and a lull in everything that had made life tick; and then the way the boats suddenly swung the other way at their moorings with the coming of a breeze out of the new quarter, and the premonitory rumble. Then the kettle drum, then the snare, then the bass drum and cymbals, then crackling light against the dark, and the gods grinning and licking their chops in the hills. Afterward the calm, the rain steadily rustling in the calm lake, the return of light and hope and spirits, and the campers running out in the joy and relief to go swimming in the rain, their bright cries

perpetuating the deathless joke about how they were getting simply drenched, and the children screaming with delight at the new sensation of bathing in the rain, and the joke about getting drenched linking the generations in a strong indestructible chain. And the comedian who waded in carrying an umbrella.

13   When the others went swimming my son said he was going in too. He pulled his dripping trunks from the line where they had hung all through the shower, and wrung them out. Languidly, and with no thought of going in, I watched him, his hard little body, skinny and bare, saw him wince slightly as he pulled up around his vitals the small, soggy, icy garment. As he buckled the swollen belt suddenly my groin felt the chill of death.

Chapter 30

Definition

Celebrating Nerdiness

Tom Rogers

A former chemical engineer, Tom Rogers now teaches advanced courses in physics, computer science, and statistics at a South Carolina high school and maintains a popular Web site, *Insultingly Stupid Movie Physics*, that has been featured on National Public Radio and in the *New York Times*. A companion book to the site was published in 2007. This essay appeared in *Newsweek* in 2000.

1   I'm a nerd. While the Internet boom has lent some respectability to the term, narrow-minded and thoughtless stereotypes still linger. Nerds are supposedly friendless, book-smart sissies who suck up to authority figures. Some of our image problems stem from our obsession with mastering every inane detail of our interests. But to call us suck-ups is nonsense. We often horrify those in authority with our inability to understand, let alone follow, societal norms.

2   Like most nerds, I didn't know I was one until I started school. There I quickly found out that my enthusiasm for answering the teacher's questions made others feel I was deliberately trying to make them look bad. My classmates were not shy about expressing their feelings on the playground. Fortunately, I was tall and stood my ground, a bluff that helped repel bullies. But mostly I survived by learning to keep quiet in the classroom.

3   I became a high-school teacher because I realized there were lots of young nerds growing up who needed to know that being a nerd was not just OK but something wonderful. Unfortunately, they weren't likely to hear this even from teachers, although virtually every modern blessing from democracy to electric motors originated with a nerd. Some, like Thomas Paine, were idealistic; others, like Tesla, eccentric. Newton was arrogant and Einstein absent-minded. All of them are now considered geniuses. But make no mistake: 17-year-old versions of these men, placed in modern American high schools, would instantly be labeled as nerds.

4   I raised two nerd sons and a daughter, who describes herself as a nerd sympathizer, partly because I didn't have the cleverness to raise "cool" kids, but also because, selfishly, I wanted nerds to talk to. Every year I invite my Advanced Placement physics students to my house for study sessions before the AP test. Last year one student nerd's mother told me that her son had returned home and talked for hours about how awesome it was

to have found a nerd family. Unfortunately, the world's response to our family has not always been so enthusiastic.

5   When my sons were still in school, they were often picked on by classmates. My older boy, a pale and unathletic kid, was an easy target. When his middle-school science teacher asked if anyone could name some elements, my son recited the periodic table from memory. Thanks to events like that, he endured nerd hell at the hands of bullies when waiting for the school bus every afternoon. We tried karate classes and pep talks to bolster his defenses, but he was never able to win his tormentors' respect. He was just too small.

6   My boys were often misunderstood by their teachers, too. My younger son's middle-school social-studies teacher rigidly insisted that he take notes. When he refused, she publicly told him he would never graduate from high school. My son was perfectly capable of taking notes, but in typical nerd fashion, he couldn't bring himself to comply because it was illogical. He could easily remember what the teacher had said. Writing it down cut into his thinking time.

7   Clearly, my son would have to give his teacher what she wanted, but it had to be done with style. We discussed options. These included taking notes in one of the foreign languages he studied as a hobby. I discouraged it because he had learned some colorful foreign terms and was capable of describing his teacher in ways that could make a sailor blush. Finally, we agreed he would write his notes backward.

8   For six months he transcribed his teacher's lectures backward. When I held my son's notes up to a mirror, they were perfectly readable. I shouldn't have been surprised. As a small child he'd entertained us by turning books upside down and reading them backward. I waited for a complaint from his teacher, but she never noticed.

9   Despite childhood trials, both of my sons remain devoted nerds. My older son became conversational in four foreign languages and has hitchhiked around Europe three times. And these days no one would mistake him for a sissy. On one occasion a group of Russian policemen threw him a party after he accepted their invitation to take a mid-December dip in a spring filled with near-freezing water.

10   My younger son proved his teacher wrong and graduated from high school. He scored 1600 on the SAT and was asked to give a speech before 500 educators and politicians who had gathered to honor education. It was his one moment of visibility. As I waited for him to talk, my stomach flip-flopped. I had no idea what he was going to say. He rose from his seat and delivered 10 minutes of stand-up comedy on being a nerd. The audience laughed until they cried. I cried. Afterward a young nerd paid him his highest compliment: "Thank you for what you've done for our people." No, our kind doesn't fit the stereotypes, but yes, there is something wonderful about being a nerd.

The Exam Dream

Eric Hoover

Eric Hoover is a senior writer for *The Chronicle of Higher Education*, a weekly news source for college faculty, administrators, staff, and students. Hoover often writes about college admissions, enrollment management, standardized testing, and issues facing non-traditional age students. Previously, he worked for the *C-VILLE Weekly* (Charlottesville, Va.) and for the *Washington* [D.C.] *City Paper*. This article appeared in the *Chronicle* in March 2011.

1   *Once more I find myself on this strange but familiar campus. As always, I'm running, a madman with a bookbag, late for an appointment. . . . Down a hallway lies a classroom, and inside waits a desk—the desk of my doom. I sit down; then someone passes me the final exam. All semester I have not cracked a single book. Before me lie pages of questions for which I have no answers. I grip my pen. The pale eye of the clock glares. My palms turn to sponges, and—and then . . . sweet relief . . . I wake up.*

2   So goes my "exam dream," which I've had about once a month since the late 1990s. Odds are you've had some version of it, too. In this nation of tests, few dreams are so familiar, recurring long after we put away our No. 2 pencils and textbooks. For many of us, the exam dream is an albatross gliding evermore over the dark seas of sleep, calling us back to the long ago.

3   In sleep we return to the classrooms where we once fretted over questions and fumbled for the answers. And these settings are no coincidence. "Children start with test-taking very early—it's often their first school experience," says Eleanor Rosch, a professor of psychology at the University of California at Berkeley. Ms. Rosch recalls taking a spelling test in second or third grade. She wrote down the first few words, but then she froze. "There was this mounting terror of figuring out the next word," she says. Such moments, she explains, can imprint themselves in our memories, becoming symbols of emotions and fears we experience years, or even decades, later.

4   The dream can be especially powerful among those who never leave the land of learning. After all, even the highest positions come with scrutiny; the tenured merely trade tests for other trials. "You're being evaluated on your evaluation of someone else's journal article," Ms. Rosch says.

5   Like real exams, the exam dream may take many forms. William G. Durden, president of Dickinson College, sometimes dreams that he's an anxious student who's forgotten to write a paper. He must finish the assignment to graduate, but he cannot. That dream merges with another in which he's a college president with no degrees—a phony in plain sight. These nightmares, Mr. Durden believes, speak to his past: He was the first in his family to attend college, so he had grown up with no narrative for his eventual success. "At a very primordially emotional level," he says, "I appear to find it very hard to believe that I actually have a degree."

6   Over time, some dreamers of exam dreams experience a shift in perspective. As a history professor at Grinnell College, Marci Sortor long dreamed that she had exams in geometry and Spanish but had not been attending either class. In the dream, she couldn't remember where the classrooms were, or how to find her locker, which contained her textbooks. Eventually, Ms. Sortor's dream-self resolved to drop one course and study hard for the other. "Somehow my subconscious was satisfied," she says. The dream vanished, only to return as the professor's version, in which she was late for class, frantically wondering how she would explain herself to her students and her department chair. "Meanwhile, I'm climbing mountains, jumping over crevasses, and swimming across moats," she says. That dream faded after Ms. Sortor became vice president for institutional planning. Now she dreams that she's late for an administrative meeting, a horror within a horror, if you will.

7   The venues of dreams may vary according to one's interests. Benjamin B. Dunlap, president of Wofford College, suspects that he's never had the exam dream because

he's rarely doubted his intellectual abilities or verbal skills (Rhodes Scholars are like that, you know). Yet Mr. Dunlap—who's published poems, written television scripts, and danced for a ballet company—has long valued artistic excellence above other kinds. So perhaps it's not surprising that in his own recurring dream he's a pianist faking his way through a concerto before a large audience. "I'm improvising along with the orchestra, then I realize I've run out of gas, I'm not able to keep up, and I'm just seconds away from people discovering that I'm a total fraud," he says. "It's dreadful."

8   In other words, Mr. Dunlap, who likes to noodle about on the Steinway in the president's house, believes anxiety follows one's most profound aspirations into slumber. But that doesn't mean his dream lacks metaphysical ties to the present. After all, his job demands constant improvisation and buckets of confidence; he describes being a college president as "performance art." "These dreams represent a kind of psychic modesty or intellectual integrity," he says, "the uneasy feeling that you're getting away with something and might get called out."

9   That uneasy feeling can creep over anyone, be it a president or a plumber. By no means are dreams set in school or college the exclusive bane of those who work in education. Merely attending college is enough to get you into the club. My brother-in-law Greg Stuckey, a computer-systems analyst in Illinois, still dreams that he failed a college course, usually English, that kept him from graduation. Every couple of months, Elizabeth Brotherton, a writer I know in Washington, dreams that she must take an exam for a class she's skipped all semester; often the dream comes when she's feeling overwhelmed.

10   Ann McClure, a real-estate agent I know in Virginia, sometimes dreams that she's standing in her cap and gown when she realizes that she hasn't passed a class she needed to graduate. Martha Floyd, who works in the same office, still dreams about taking a big test for which she's not prepared, 32 years after graduating from college. And my dear friend Bryn Chalkley has a jarring version of the exam dream about twice a month, "Going into a situation blind definitely makes me nervous," she says, "and I guess this scenario is an easy or tangible experience for me to apply that kind of anxiety."

11   In some form, the exam dream may be more common among Americans than all but one other type—the nightmare in which we are running from someone or something. This is according to Dierdre Barrett, an assistant clinical professor of psychology at Harvard Medical School, who has reviewed more dream-frequency studies and surveys of dreamers than you ever knew existed. She suspects that people go on dreaming of academic tasks because much of our "symbolic imagery" is set during adolescence, when tests are literally an everyday burden. "This is when our emotional wiring is getting laid down, and a lot of our emotions are associated with certain visual imagery," Ms. Barrett says. "People have basic anxieties about other people evaluating them. And our society puts a pretty strong value on test-taking."

12   A defining feature of many exam dreams is the dreamer's role in his or her own demise. The psychic gist isn't so much that the big test is a monster, but that one has somehow ushered the monster in, by skipping class or failing to prepare for a task. In the end, we seem to judge ourselves more harshly than the grader of any exam might.

13   So those who've never had such a dream should be very glad. To everyone else, there's just one more thing to say: See you in class.

What Is Poverty?

Jo Goodwin Parker

When George Henderson, a professor at the University of Oklahoma, was writing his 1971 book, *America's Other Children: Public Schools outside Suburbia*, he received the following essay in the mail. It was signed "Jo Goodwin Parker" and had been mailed from West Virginia. No further information was ever discovered about the essay or its source. Whether the author of this essay was in reality a woman describing her own painful experiences or a sympathetic writer who had adopted her persona, Jo Goodwin Parker remains a mystery.

1   You ask me what is poverty? Listen to me. Here I am, dirty, smelly, and with no "proper" underwear on and with the stench of my rotting teeth near you. I will tell you. Listen to me. Listen without pity. I cannot use your pity. Listen with understanding. Put yourself in my dirty, worn out, ill-fitting shoes, and hear me.

2   Poverty is getting up every morning from a dirt- and illness-stained mattress. The sheets have long since been used for diapers. Poverty is living with a smell that never leaves. This is the smell of urine, sour milk, and spoiling food sometimes joined with the strong smell of long-cooked onions. Onions are cheap. If you have smelled this smell, you did not know how it came. It is the smell of the outdoor privy. It is the smell of young children who cannot walk the long dark way in the night. It is the smell of the mattresses where years of "accidents" have happened. It is the smell of the milk which has gone sour because the refrigerator long has not worked, and it costs money to get it fixed. It is the smell of rotting garbage. I could bury it, but where is the shovel? Shovels cost money.

3   Poverty is being tired. I have always been tired. They told me at the hospital when the last baby came that I had chronic anemia caused from poor diet, a bad case of worms, and that I needed a corrective operation. I listened politely—the poor are always polite. The poor always listen. They don't say that there is no money for iron pills, or better food, or worm medicine. The idea of an operation is frightening and costs so much that, if I had dared, I would have laughed. Who takes care of my children? Recovery from an operation takes a long time. I have three children. When I left them with "Granny" the last time I had a job, I came home to find the baby covered with fly specks, and a diaper that had not been changed since I left. When the dried diaper came off, bits of my baby's flesh came with it. My other child was playing with a sharp bit of broken glass, and my oldest was playing alone at the edge of a lake. I made twenty-two dollars a week, and a good nursery school costs twenty dollars a week for three children. I quit my job.

4   Poverty is dirt. You say in your clean clothes coming from your clean house, "Anybody can be clean." Let me explain about housekeeping with no money. For breakfast I give my children grits with no oleo or cornbread without eggs and oleo. This does not use up many dishes. What dishes there are, I wash in cold water and with no soap. Even the cheapest soap has to be saved for the baby's diapers. Look at my hands, so cracked and red. Once I saved for two months to buy a jar of Vaseline for my hands and the baby's diaper rash. When I had saved enough, I went to buy it and the price had gone up two cents. The baby and I suffered on. I have to decide every day if I can bear to put my cracked, sore hands into the cold water and strong soap. But you ask, why not hot water? Fuel costs money. Hot water is a luxury. I do not have luxuries. I know you will be surprised when I tell you how young I am. I look so much older. My back has been bent over the wash tubs for so long, I cannot remember when I ever

did anything else. Every night I wash every stitch my school age child has on and just hope her clothes will be dry by morning.

5   Poverty is staying up all night on cold nights to watch the fire, knowing one spark on the newspaper covering the walls means your sleeping children die in flames. In summer poverty is watching gnats and flies devour your baby's tears when he cries. The screens are torn and you pay so little rent you know they will never be fixed. Poverty means insects in your food, in your nose, in your eyes, and crawling over you when you sleep. Poverty is hoping it never rains because diapers won't dry when it rains and soon you are using newspapers. Poverty is seeing your children forever with runny noses. Paper handkerchiefs cost money and all your rags you need for other things. Even more costly are antihistamines. Poverty is cooking without food and cleaning without soap.

6   Poverty is asking for help. Have you ever had to ask for help, knowing your children will suffer unless you get it? Think about asking for a loan from a relative, if this is the only way you can imagine asking for help. I will tell you how it feels. You find out where the office is that you are supposed to visit. You circle that block four or five times. Thinking of your children, you go in. Everyone is very busy. Finally, someone comes out and you tell her that you need help. That never is the person you need to see. You go see another person, and after spilling the whole shame of your poverty all over the desk between you, you find that this isn't the right office after all—you must repeat the whole process, and it never is any easier at the next place.

7   You have asked for help, and after all it has a cost. You are again told to wait. You are told why, but you don't really hear because of the red cloud of shame and the rising black cloud of despair.

8   Poverty is remembering. It is remembering quitting school in junior high because "nice" children had been so cruel about my clothes and my smell. The attendance officer came. My mother told him I was pregnant. I wasn't but she thought that I could get a job and help out. I had jobs off and on, but never long enough to learn anything. Mostly I remember being married. I was so young then. I am still young. For a time, we had all the things you have. There was a little house in another town, with hot water and everything. Then my husband lost his job. There was unemployment insurance for a while and what few jobs I could get. Soon, all our nice things were repossessed and we moved back here. I was pregnant then. This house didn't look so bad when we first moved in. Every week it gets worse. Nothing is ever fixed. We now had no money. There were a few odd jobs for my husband, but everything went for food then, as it does now. I don't know how we lived through three years and three babies, but we did. I'll tell you something, after the last baby I destroyed my marriage. It had been a good one, but could you keep on bringing children in this dirt? Did you ever think how much it costs for any kind of birth control? I knew my husband was leaving the day he left, but there were no good-byes between us. I hope he has been able to climb out of this mess somewhere. He never could hope with us to drag him down.

9   That's when I asked for help. When I got it, you know how much it was? It was, and is, seventy-eight dollars a month for the four of us; that is all I ever can get. Now you know why there is no soap, no needles and thread, no hot water, no aspirin, no worm medicine, no hand cream, no shampoo. None of these things forever and ever and ever. So that you can see clearly, I pay twenty dollars a month rent, and most of the rest goes for food. For grits and cornmeal, and rice and milk and beans. I try my best to use only the minimum electricity. If I use more, there is that much less for food.

10   Poverty is looking into a black future. Your children won't play with my boys. They will turn to other boys who steal to get what they want. I can already see them behind the bars of their prison instead of behind the bars of my poverty. Or they will turn to the freedom of alcohol or drugs, and find themselves enslaved. And my daughter? At best, there is for her a life like mine.

11   But you say to me, there are schools. Yes, there are schools. My children have no extra books, no magazines, no extra pencils, or crayons, or paper and the most important of all, they do not have health. They have worms, they have infections, they have pinkeye all summer. They do not sleep well on the floor, or with me in my one bed. They do not suffer from hunger, my seventy-eight dollars keeps us alive, but they do suffer from malnutrition. Oh yes, I do remember what I was taught about health in school. It doesn't do much good. In some places there is a surplus commodities program. Not here. The county said it cost too much. There is a school lunch program. But I have two children who will already be damaged by the time they get to school.

12   But, you say to me, there are health clinics. Yes, there are health clinics and they are in the towns. I live out here eight miles from town. I can walk that far (even if it is sixteen miles both ways), but can my little children? My neighbor will take me when he goes; but he expects to get paid, *one way or another*. I bet you know my neighbor. He is that large man who spends his time at the gas station, the barbershop, and the corner store complaining about the government spending money on the immoral mothers of illegitimate children.

13   Poverty is an acid that drips on pride until all pride is worn away. Poverty is a chisel that chips on honor until honor is worn away. Some of you say that you would do *something* in my situation, and maybe you would, for the first week or the first month, but for year after year after year?

14   Even the poor can dream. A dream of a time when there is money. Money for the right kinds of food, for worm medicine, for iron pills, for toothbrushes, for hand cream, for a hammer and nails and a bit of screening, for a shovel, for a bit of paint, for some sheeting, for needles and thread. Money to pay *in money* for a trip to town. And, oh, money for hot water and money for soap. A dream of when asking for help does not eat away the last bit of pride. When the office you visit is as nice as the offices of other governmental agencies, when there are enough workers to help you quickly, when workers do not quit in defeat and despair. When you have to tell your story to only one person, and that person can send you for other help and you don't have to prove your poverty over and over and over again.

15   I have come out of my despair to tell you this. Remember I did not come from another place or another time. Others like me are all around you. Look at us with an angry heart, anger that will help you help me. Anger that will let you tell of me. The poor are always silent. Can you be silent too?

Chapter 31

Division and Classification

Virtual Unreality: The Online Sockpuppets That Trick Us All

Charles Seife

Charles Seife is a mathematician, science writer, and New York University journalism professor. He is the author of several books, including *Zero: The Biography of a Dangerous Idea* (2000) and *Proofiness: How You're Being Fooled by the Numbers* (2010). Seife focuses on digital gullibility in *Virtual Unreality: Just Because the Internet Told You, How Do You Know It's True?* (2014). In the following excerpt from that book, published on *Wired.com* in 2014, Seife discusses different types of online false identities and warns against the consequences of hiding behind such false personas.

1   Sockpuppetry—using false identities for deception—is centuries old, but the advent of the web has made creating sockpuppets, and falling for their tricks, easier than ever before. We can't physically meet most of the people we interact with on the internet. So we create avatars who represent us in the online world, personae that are designed—on some level, conscious or subconscious—to shape others' ideas about who we really are. Indeed, it's natural for us to create avatars that represent what we want to be rather than what we are. And it's only a short step from there to manipulating others' perceptions of us to give ourselves an advantage of some sort, to deceive. To become puppet masters.

The daring political rebel who was not what she seemed

2   Take Amina Arraf. She was a 35-year-old Syrian American who had become a prominent blogger. Her blog, *Gay Girl in Damascus*, described life in Syria during the beginning of the uprising against Bashar al-Assad. Liberal and lesbian, she was in a precarious position as a protester in a conservative and unstable society. She kept writing, and in May, The Guardian dubbed her "an unlikely hero of revolt in a conservative country."

3   But in the early evening of Monday, June 6, 2011, she was walking to meet a friend in downtown Damascus when three young men wrestled her into a red minivan, which screeched off into the dusk. Arraf's cousin posted details to Amina's blog. The outcry was immediate. The *Guardian* reported the kidnapping, and so did the *New York Times*, Fox News, *Gawker*, CNN, and several other news organizations. The *International Business Times* asked how the United States should respond to the abduction, and "Free Amina" websites and posters began to spring up.

4   Within a few hours, though, Andy Carvin, an NPR journalist, noted on Twitter that none of the people who had ever interviewed Arraf had met her or even spoken to her over the phone. Once someone began to question Arraf's identity, the illusion shattered. By the morning of June 8, the *Wall Street Journal* had discovered that photos purportedly of Arraf were, in fact, snapshots of a woman living in London. Shortly thereafter, a website in communication with Arraf was able to show that her computer was in Scotland. Soon it became clear that Arraf wasn't a "she" at all. She was the creation of Tom MacMaster, a Ph.D. student at the University of Edinburgh.

5   Everything about Arraf was completely made up—MacMaster had created Arraf's *Facebook* page, her *Twitter* account, her email address—and had conducted interviews with numerous journalists in her name. Why? It was a matter of authority. MacMaster had some very strong views on Middle Eastern affairs, so he created Amina Arraf to give his ideas credibility.

6   Tom MacMaster's Amina Arraf is fairly typical of one kind of false persona: what I call "Type 1" sockpuppetry. In Type 1 sockpuppetry, the puppet master fabricates a phony persona who has a specific attribute or experience that the puppet master himself lacks—an attribute or experience that gives the puppet master extra authority in a conversation or extra ability to generate a reaction from others. In all cases, the point seems to be to seek either authority, attention, or profit.

A wonderland for pathological liars and attention seekers

7   Debbie Swenson was after attention when she created a Type 1 sockpuppet, a fictitious teenage girl named Kaycee Nicole, in 1999. In a blog she called Living Colours, Kaycee described in detail the ups and downs of her battle with leukemia, which attracted a great deal of attention and sympathy. When Kaycee finally died on May 14, 2001, the outpouring of grief from her online fans was real and palpable. Denizen after denizen of the popular website *MetaFilter* expressed heartbreak.

8   Then, on May 19, the user "acridrabbit" posted a simple question: "Is it possible that Kaycee did not exist?" Not only were there some inconsistencies in Kaycee's story—some odd-sounding descriptions of how the doctors talked about leukemia, the difficulty people were having in finding an address for flowers and cards—but it also appeared that nobody had ever met Kaycee in person. Immediately, some *MetaFilter* sleuths started picking apart the story, even as Kaycee believers, like "bwg," appeared to suffer genuine anguish because of the cynicism: "STOP! STOP!! STOP!!! this is deplorable. it's making me sick to my stomach! i have spoken to kaycee on the phone, as well as her mother, numerous times. i can assure you kaycee was quite real." But the truth was that Kaycee simply didn't exist. Debbie Swenson admitted the next day that Kaycee had been a fabrication.

9   Stories like Kaycee's are surprisingly common, to the point that psychiatrists and psychologists have started noticing a pattern—a syndrome that's now called "virtual factitious disorder" or, more snappily, "Munchausen by internet." In the syndrome someone creates an online persona who suffers some kind of tragedy and milks the resulting outpouring of sympathy and concern. It's almost guaranteed to cause a big stir, so it becomes irresistible to the extreme attention seeker. Any sufficiently large online community will encounter one of these sooner or later.

How to destroy your enemies and look good doing it

10   More common than Type 1 sockpuppetry is Type 2 sockpuppetry, in which the only one thing that matters is that the the fictional personality must be someone other than the puppet master. Type 2 sockpuppets are often deployed as reinforcements in an online feud. Because these sockpuppets are meant to seem independent of the puppet master, these false personae give the impression of a group of online people who agree with and bolster the puppet master's position—or attack his enemies.

11   John Lott, a gun researcher, created a fake student who defended his writing online and gave him positive reviews on *Amazon.com*. (Bing Liu, a computer scientist who studied *Amazon* reviews, told the *New York Times* that approximately a third of reviews on the internet were likely fake. These are either created by sockpuppets or purchased wholesale.)

12   Mystery writer R. J. Ellory used a brigade of sockpuppets not only to give his own books glowing reviews, but also to depress his rivals' ratings. Professor Orlando Figes, an esteemed British historian, lost much of that esteem by doing precisely the same thing, and in a legal settlement Figes apologized and agreed to pay his rivals' legal bills.

13   The Type 2 sockpuppet is an easy weapon for an online skirmisher with a fragile ego. It's also a great sales booster for a company that wants to tinker with its online reviews. But don't make the mistake of thinking that these are the only people who deploy sockpuppets. In fact, sockpuppets are now being used for intelligence and for defense.

We're all caught up in a sockpuppet cyberwar

14   Social media sites often reveal more information about you to your friends or followers than they do to the general public. This means that people who have an interest in knowing something about you have a vested interest in trying to get you to invite them into your inner circle.

15   In 2012, Raymond Kelly, commissioner of the New York City Police Department, declared that officers could create false identities to hang out on social media sites in hopes of spotting crime. Police have been using similar tricks for years—impersonating underage children on the internet, for example, in hopes of catching pedophiles—but the ease of creating a large number of sockpuppets for the express purpose of infiltrating social media sites is making civil libertarians nervous.

16   Some sockpuppets have even bigger targets. In March 2012, unknown parties repeatedly tried to get sensitive information about NATO's supreme allied commander in Europe, Admiral James Stavridis, by impersonating him on *Facebook* and insinuating themselves into his circle of friends and colleagues. NATO sources said they didn't know who was responsible, but other experts suggested that the culprit may have been China. China has acquired a reputation—probably justly—for gathering information on its enemies and rivals through sockpuppeteering and other underhanded internet tricks. But it's not the only state in the sockpuppet game. The U.S. is in it, too.

17   In late 2010 or early 2011, the United States Central Command (Centcom)—the branch of the military responsible for operations in Iran, Iraq, Afghanistan, Pakistan, and the Middle East—signed a $2.76 million contract with Ntrepid, a California company, to provide the ultimate sockpuppeteering software. According to the original proposal, Centcom was looking for a software suite that would allow 50 users to create 10 sockpuppets

each, "replete with background, history, supporting details, and cyber presences that are technically, culturally and geographacilly [sic] consistent. Individual applications will enable an operator to exercise a number of different online persons from the same workstation and without fear of being discovered by sophisticated adversaries."

18   The internet has become a battlefield for virtual personalities—sockpuppets all attempting to gather information and using that information to help their causes and hurt their enemies. It's a war without bystanders, for we're all caught up in the fighting, whether we're aware of it or not.

Party Manners

Richard L. Grossman

Richard L. Grossman was a psychotherapist, medical educator, author and publisher. He wrote a number of books, many on health-related issues, including *Choosing & Changing: A Guide to Self-Reliance* (1978) and *The Other Medicines* (1986). He edited *A Year with Emerson* (2003), an introduction to the writings of philosopher–poet Ralph Waldo Emerson, and *The Tao of Emerson* (2007). This 1983 article first appeared in *Health* magazine as part of Grossman's column called "Richard's Almanac."

1   The Romans had their Colosseum, the Elizabethans their village promenades and their Globe Theater. For centuries the French and Germans had their spectacular court balls. Queens and Presidents have their state dinners, complete with chamber music. And we ordinary moderns? We have *parties*.

2   From college "mixers" to suburban cocktail "standarounds," from children's ice-cream splattered birthday celebrations to retirement dinners, from political fund-raisers to bridal showers, the party has become as ubiquitous an institution as the Internal Revenue Service. And familiar though it is, the party has a psychologically transforming effect on many of us. Somehow our attendance at a gathering called a "party" causes us to behave in ways we never do elsewhere, as though we were players in a drama meant to reveal some of the hidden parts of our personalities. The party setting seems to provide a license to unveil attitudes that we would never display at the office or the family dinner table. And though party behavior may not be a reliable guide to all our psychological tics, it is nevertheless a place to see how we "go public" with some of our unresolved problems. Consider this cast of characters, for example:

The cartoonist

3   Here's the person who has no other arena in his life in which to be a vocal social critic, who sees every party as an opportunity to be the local Andy Rooney.* No dancing or merrymaking for this one, but rather a steady stream of mini-lectures on the foibles and deficiencies of all the other guests. The Cartoonist is someone who does not want to be part of

---

* Andy Rooney, a television commentator on *60 Minutes* for over thirty years, was known for his cranky observations on the annoyances of everyday life.

the crowd, but needs to keep his distance and act the reporting observer, drawing verbal caricatures of "them" as though he were sending communiqués back to Mars on the tribal rituals of the "Earthlings." What's really going on, of course, is that the fear of spontaneity and the relaxation of conventions are just too threatening, so the only safe stance is to play the part of the uninvolved expert.

The spotter

4   This character is the familiar shopper for greener pastures. She is talking to you, but is looking over your shoulder the whole time, ever alert to someone just a little more interesting or a little more important who may be on the other side of the room. This person is usually the inside-dopester, the one who craves the latest information, who drops the trendiest names, who goes to the hottest events. The Spotter has the attention span of an alcoholic mayfly and cannot wait to move on, fearful that she is missing out on something better. The usual result, of course, is that she has a terrible time at parties and can't understand why all those other folks are laughing.

The performer

5   He's often known as "the life of the party" and is the one for whom every party is the high school play in which he didn't get a part. Parties for this type are only an opportunity to grab the spotlight that he wants desperately but is being denied elsewhere. There are variations, of course: The Practical Joker, The Bathroom Comedian, The Barroom Baritone, The Poor Man's Rich Little*—but all are revealing only one sad fact: They are yearning for notoriety and attention.

The wallflower

6   Here you have the reverse image of The Performer: The person who gains attention by a silent, martyred withdrawal from the center of the party. Sooner or later, someone will spot her standing in a corner with a rueful smile on her face, just waiting to be asked if something is wrong. If you should inquire, you'll hear that she "just isn't good in crowds," or "hates all that noise," or "never could learn to disco." Do not be deceived into thinking that you've discovered an authentically shy or lonely person. This routine is simply a device to get attention with a passive strategy. (The *really* shy one didn't come to the party.)

The swashbuckler

7   Also known as "The Last of the Big Benders," this is a person who may be in real trouble. Something has gone drastically wrong somewhere in his life, and he is frightened or even desperate about the outcome. If he is not working on the problem in another corner of life or getting the help he really needs, then the only place for that terrified energy to go is into uncharacteristically heavy drinking and raucous, high-pitched haranguing. There are

---

* Rich Little is a comedian known for his impersonations of famous celebrities.

usually very real and troubling issues underlying this kind of behavior, and the party can, unfortunately, provide a convenient setting for acting out.

The scarlet pimpernel*

8   She's the person who sees every party invitation as an opportunity to project her romantic fantasy. Feeling frustrated by a humdrum, uneventful existence, such a person mentally writes out a script for Meryl Streep or Julie Christie** and goes off to the party prepared to try out the new role, altering the voice to sound sultry or provocative, speaking in cryptic or poetic language, gliding around the room like a visitor from the Court of St. James. Sometimes this is just playfulness or harmless flirtatiousness, but usually the pseudo-romantic is simply saying through her behavior that the rest of her life is dull and gray, and needs spicing up.

9   Now, a certain amount of nervousness and unease about going to a party is clearly normal, and it would be simple-minded to claim that even the types described above are necessarily displaying secret pathology. But if parties regularly call up odd or extraordinary behavior in you, or become a theater for exposing subterranean needs, it might be a good idea to look at the usual, non-partying areas of your life and see what's troubling you. Some parties are boring, to be sure, and a dose of silly, unplanned frolicking may liven them up. But we should remember that parties are usually designed as a means to gather in a friendly, open, genuine way; as a chance to enjoy the warmth and closeness of other human beings. If those are not reasons enough for going, if we need parties to ventilate other feelings, perhaps we should consider group therapy instead.

The Colorful Plate

Dianne Moeller

Dianne Moeller spent many years as a registered dietitian at the Health District of Northern Larimer County, serving communities in northern Colorado. In addition to offering nutritional counseling to Health District clients, Moeller wrote a newspaper column called "Health and Fitness," in which she presented a variety of suggestions for improving and maintaining her readers' physical wellbeing. This column appeared in the Fort Collins, Colorado, *Coloradoan* in March 2011.

1   Spring is here, and with it comes the promise of more color in our yards and gardens. There's one place we should try to keep colorful throughout the year: the meal plate.

---

* This name is drawn from a 1905 novel by Baroness Emmuska Orczy, in which a British nobleman leads a double life as "the Scarlet Pimpernel," a sword-fighting rescuer of innocent people condemned to the guillotine during the French Revolution's Reign of Terror. Often credited as the first popular novel to establish the "dual identity" hero, the story paved the way for Superman, Batman, Zorro, and other modern superheroes in disguise.

** Meryl Streep is one of America's most highly regarded actresses, having won three Academy Awards; Julie Christie is a British actress, also an Academy Award winner, but possibly best known in this country for her role as Lara in the classic 1965 film *Dr. Zhivago*.

2   The vibrant hues of fruits and vegetables aren't just a feast for the eyes—they're a source of powerful compounds packed with health benefits. These compounds, called phytonutrients (or phytochemicals), help protect plants while they are growing. As part of our diet, they can help protect us from disease, and they are most heavily concentrated in colorful fruits and vegetables.

3   Phytonutrients can be grouped into families represented by different colors and health benefits. Generally the brighter the color, the bigger the benefit (as long as the color doesn't come from a dye). As with all foods we eat, variety is key. You get the most benefit by eating fruits and vegetables from several families. That's why experts now recommend that we "eat a rainbow" everyday.

4   Let's take a look at the color families.

5   **Red**—Tomatoes, watermelon and red grapefruit are rich in the antioxidant lycopene. Diets high in lycopene have been associated with reduced incidence of prostate and other cancers, cardiovascular disease and macular degeneration. Using salsa or other tomato products generously helps you get more lycopene. Also, cooking concentrates lycopene, so foods such as pasta sauce offer a bigger dose of this phytonutrient.

6   **Blue/Purple**—This family includes all berries (not just blue ones) because they contain similar compounds, which might help slow the aging process, protect against heart disease and cancer, prevent blood clots and fight inflammation and allergies. Use berries as toppings, snacks, or ingredients in smoothies. Juices, including grape and cranberry, are another way to get benefits from the blue/purple family. This family also extends to vegetables, including eggplant and purple cabbage.

7   **Orange**—Carrots, cantaloupe, apricots, sweet potatoes and squashes contain carotenoids and other compounds that are important for eye health and might protect against sun damage to the eyes and skin. Your best and safest source for carotenoids is food, as evidence suggests that beta-carotene supplements might have harmful effects, at least in smokers. Carrots, cooked or raw, shredded on salads or eaten as snacks, deliver plenty of carotenoids.

8   **Yellow**—Yellow fruits and vegetables, including citrus, pineapple, and white grapefruit, contain substances that inhibit cancer, macular degeneration and cataracts.

9   **Green**—Here darker is better. Green vegetables, whether cruciferous—such as broccoli—or leafy (spinach, kale, chard), offer up a host of powerful health-promoting compounds. The green family contains nutrients that protect against many cancers, help strengthen bones and teeth, sharpen eyesight and fight birth defects.

10   **White**—Yes, white is a color. Foods such as onions, garlic and mushrooms contain allicin, flavonoids and quercitin, which provide protection against heart disease and cancer. Other white foods, including bananas, cauliflower, and white peaches, have important phytonutrients.

11   So go ahead and turn your plate into a palette. The colorful scenes you create will help keep you healthy in addition to making your meals more attractive.

Chapter 32

Causal Analysis

Some Lessons from the Assembly Line

Andrew Braaksma

Andrew Braaksma, from Portage, Michigan, was a junior at the University of Michigan studying history and French in the College of Literature, Science, and Arts when he won first place in a "Back to School" essay contest sponsored by *Newsweek* magazine. The award-winning essay was then published in *Newsweek's* "My Turn" column in September 2005.

1   Last June, as I stood behind the bright orange guard door of the machine, listening to the crackling hiss of the automatic welders, I thought about how different my life had been just a few weeks earlier. Then, I was writing an essay about French literature to complete my last exam of the spring semester at college. Now I stood in an automotive plant in southwest Michigan, making subassemblies for a car manufacturer.

2   I have worked as a temp in the factories surrounding my hometown every summer since I graduated from high school, but making the transition between school and full-time blue-collar work during the break never gets any easier. For a student like me who considers any class before noon to be uncivilized, getting to a factory by 6 o'clock each morning, where rows of hulking, spark-showering machines have replaced the lush campus and cavernous lecture halls of college life, is torture. There my time is spent stamping, cutting, welding, moving or assembling parts, the rigid work schedules and quotas of the plant making days spent studying and watching *SportsCenter* seem like a million years ago.

3   I chose to do this work, rather than bus tables or fold sweatshirts at the Gap, for the overtime pay and because living at home is infinitely cheaper than living on campus for the summer. My friends who take easier, part-time jobs never seem to understand why I'm so relieved to be back at school in the fall or that my summer vacation has been anything but a vacation.

4   There are few things as cocksure as a college student who has never been out in the real world, and people my age always seem to overestimate the value of their time and knowledge. After a particularly exhausting string of 12-hour days at a plastics factory, I remember being shocked at how small my check seemed. I couldn't believe how little I was taking home after all the hours I spent on the sweltering production floor. And all the classes in the world could not have prepared me for my battles with the machine

I ran in the plant, which would jam whenever I absent-mindedly put in a part back-ward or upside down. As frustrating as the work can be, the most stressful thing about blue-collar life is knowing your job could disappear overnight. Issues like downsizing and overseas relocation had always seemed distant to me until my co-workers at one factory told me that the unit I was working in would be shut down within six months and moved to Mexico, where people would work for 60 cents an hour.

5   Factory life has shown me what my future might have been like had I never gone to college in the first place. For me, and probably many of my fellow students, higher edu-cation always seemed like a foregone conclusion: I never questioned if I was going to college, just where. No other options ever occurred to me. After working 12-hour shifts in a factory, the other options have become brutally clear. When I'm back at the univer-sity, skipping classes and turning in lazy rewrites seems like a cop-out after seeing what I would be doing without school. All the advice and public-service announcements about the value of an education that used to sound trite now ring true.

6   These lessons I am learning, however valuable, are always tinged with a sense of guilt. Many people pass their lives in the places I briefly work, spending 30 years where I spend only two months at a time. When fall comes around, I get to go back to a sunny and beautiful campus, while work in the factories continues. At times I feel almost voy-euristic, like a tourist dropping in where other people make their livelihoods. My les-sons about education are learned at the expense of those who weren't fortunate enough to receive one. "This job pays well, but it's hell on the body," said one co-worker. "Study hard and keep reading," she added, nodding at the copy of Jack Kerouac's *On the Road** I had wedged into the space next to my machine so I could read discreetly when the line went down.

7   My experience will stay with me long after I head back to school and spend my wages on books and beer. The things that factory work has taught me—how lucky I am to get an education, how to work hard, how easy it is to lose that work once you have it—are by no means earth-shattering. Everyone has to come to grips with them at some point. How and when I learned these lessons, however, has inspired me to make the most of my college years before I enter the real world for good. Until then, the summer months I spend in the factories will be long, tiring and every bit as educational as a French-lit class.

Mystery!

Nicholas Meyer

Nicholas Meyer is a novelist, screenwriter, and film director-producer. Two of his three mystery novels, *The Seven-PerCent Solution* (1974) and *The West End Horror* (1976), have been made into successful movies. Meyer, also known for his contributions as a director and co-writer of the sci-fi movies *Star Trek II, IV*, and *VI*, has published *The View from the Bridge: Memories of Star Trek and a Life in Hollywood* (2009). This essay, originally

---

* American novelist and poet Jack Kerouac was one of the 1950s "Beat Generation" writers.

published in *TV Guide* magazine in 1980, appeared in an earlier edition of this textbook and has returned in response to readers' requests.

1   Reading mysteries is a bedtime recreation for all segments of society—high, low and middle brow. It is the *divertissement** of prime ministers and plumbers. Mysteries, whether they are on television, paper or movie screens, delight almost all of us. Everyone likes to "curl up" with a good mystery, and that makes this particular kind of literature unique in its ubiquitous appeal. No other genre so transcends what might otherwise appear to be significant differences in the social, educational and economic backgrounds of its audience.

2   Why, for heaven's sake? What is there about mystery and detective stories that fascinate so many of us, regardless of age, sex, color and national origin?

3   On the surface, it seems highly improbable that detective novels should provide such broad-based satisfaction. Their jacket blurbs and ad copy contain plenty of violent, even gory, references: "The body lay inert, the limbs dangling at unnatural angles, the head bashed in, clearly the result of a blunt instrument . . ." Who wants to read this stuff? Even assuming that there is a certain segment of society that delights in sadistic imagery and rejoices in thrills and chills and things that go bump in the night, it is hard to imagine that these sensibilities are in the majority.

4   As the Great Detective** himself might have observed, "It is a singular business, Watson, and on the surface, most unlikely." Yet as Holmes was wont to remark, evidence that appears to point in one unerring direction may, if viewed from a slightly altered perspective, admit of precisely the opposite interpretation. People do, in fact, like to "curl up" with a good mystery. They take the corpses and the murderers to bed with them as favorite nighttime reading. One could hardly imagine a more intimate conjunction!

5   But the phrase "curling up" does not connote danger; say rather the reverse. It conjures up snug, warm, secure feelings. Curling up with a good mystery is not exciting or thrilling; it is in fact oddly restful. It is reassuring.

6   Now why should this be? How is it possible that detective stories, with all the murder and blackmail and mayhem and mystery that pervades them, should provide us with feelings of security, coziness and comfort?

7   Well, detective stories have other things in them besides violence and blood. They have solutions, for one thing. Almost invariably, the murderer is caught, or at the very least identified. *As sure as God made little green apples, it all adds up to something.* If it doesn't, we aren't happy with the piece. A good detective story ties up all the loose ends; we resent motives and clues left unconnected.

8   Yes, detective stories have solutions. But life does not. On the contrary, life is an anarchic proposition in which meaningless events conspire daily to alter our destiny without rhyme or reason. Your plane crashes, or the one you were booked on crashes but you missed it; a flat tire, a missed phone call, an open manhole, a misunderstanding—these are the chaotic commonplaces of everyday existence. But they have no place in the mystery novel. In detective novels, nothing happens without a reason. Detective literature, though

---

* A French word for diversion or entertainment.
** Sherlock Holmes

it may superficially resemble life, in fact has effected at least one profound alteration: mystery stories *organize* life and provide it with meaning and answers. The kind of confusion in which real people are forced to exist doesn't occur in detective stories. Whatever the various people's problems, the only serious difficulty confronting them in detective stories is the fact that they are suspected of committing the crime involved. Once cleared of that lowering cloud, they are free to pursue their lives with, presumably, successful results.

9   So we see that the coziness of detective and mystery stories is not entirely incomprehensible or inappropriate, after all. If we like to take such literature to bed with us and cuddle up with it, what we are really cuddling up to is a highly stylized literary formula, which is remarkably consistent in delivering to us that reassuring picture we all crave of an ordered world.

10   Sherlock Holmes, Philip Marlow, Miss Marple or Columbo*—the stories in which these characters appear all manage to delight us by reassuring us. The victim is usually only slightly known or not very well liked. The world seems better off without him, or else he is so sorely missed that tracking his (or her) murderer will be, in Oscar Wilde's** words, more than a duty, it will be a pleasure.

11   And pleasurable indeed is the process of watching the tracking. There are some highfalutin apologists of the detective genre who would have us believe it is the intellectual exercise of following the clues along with the detective—the reader's or viewer's participation in a kind of mental puzzle—that provides the satisfaction associated with detective stories. I believe such participation is largely illusory. We don't really ever have all the pieces at our disposal and most of us are not inclined to work with them very thoroughly, even in those rare cases when the author has been scrupulously "fair" in giving them to us. We enjoy the *illusion* of participation without really doing any of the mental legwork beyond the normal wondering "Whodunit?"

12   In any event, such a theory to justify the fascination exerted by detective and mystery stories is elitist and falsely elitist into the bargain. It distracts our attention with a pretentious and tenuous explanation in place of a much more interesting and persuasive one; namely, that detective stories are appealing because they depict life not as it is but in some sense as it ought to be.

The Mind Game

Joshua Bell

Award-winning contemporary musician Joshua Bell has been called "the poet of the violin." Since the age of fourteen, he has appeared as a star performer with the premier orchestras of the world and is a frequent guest on popular television shows. He has recorded more than forty albums, winning both a Grammy and an Oscar for his music. This

---

* These four characters are famous fictional detectives: Sherlock Holmes created by Arthur Conan Doyle; Philip Marlowe, by Raymond Chandler; Miss Marple, by Agatha Christie. Columbo solved crimes in a popular television series of the same name.
**Oscar Wilde was a nineteenth-century English author and wit.

essay, on the mind game of performing, was published in *Newsweek* magazine's column called "My Favorite Mistake," in January 2012.

1   When I was twelve years old I entered my first violin competition, the Stulberg International String Competition. Almost everyone else was college-age, so I wasn't expecting to do very well. I was playing a violin concerto called *Symphonie Espagnole* by Lalo. It starts with a very difficult opening right off the bat, sort of like if a skating routine started with a triple axel. I began playing, and I messed it up worse than I ever could have imagined. I had never made such a terrible mistake at the beginning of a piece. My parents came all the way to Michigan for me to be in my first big competition, and it was a completely embarrassing way to start.

2   No one tells you what to do if you completely flop at the beginning of a performance. My teachers had never taught me, and I didn't know the etiquette, but I think I did the right thing in the moment. Instead of just playing on, finishing the piece, and feeling lousy, I completely stopped. I turned to the audience and said, "I'd really like to start over." I already felt like I'd lost the competition and the chance to do well, but I really wanted to try again.

3   It was a quick decision and could have been the worst performance after that because my confidence was down. I screwed up, and when you do something like that it can psychologically totally ruin your performance. But somehow it turned in the other direction. I got into this zone of feeling completely liberated and relaxed because I knew I had lost. I played the best I had ever played in my life. I felt like I couldn't make a mistake. I was elated, and it could have been the worst day of my twelve-year-old life.

4   I actually ended up getting third prize in the competition and went back the next year and won first prize, but that's not really the point. For me it was a major revelation, and it taught me that when you take your mind off worrying about being perfect all the time, sometimes amazing things can happen. So much of performing is a mind game. You're memorizing thousands of notes, and if you start thinking about it in the wrong way, everything can blow up in your face.

5   When I'm onstage and make a mistake, I remember back to that moment. I learned from that experience how to get into that zone. The competition ended up launching my career and my confidence in a lot of ways. It was a turning point and a lesson I use to this day.

Chapter 33

Argumentation

The Lost Language of Privacy

David Brooks

David Brooks is a journalist and Opinion-Editorial columnist for the *New York Times*, a political commentator on television's *PBS NewsHour*, and a frequent contributor to National Public Radio's *All Things Considered*. He has been an editor at the *Wall Street Journal*, the *Weekly Standard*, the *Atlantic Monthly* magazine, and *Newsweek*. His most recent book is *The Road to Character* (2015). This essay was published on April 14, 2015, in the *New York Times*.

1   Like a lot of people, I've come to believe that it would be a good idea to put body-mounted cameras on police officers. I now believe this for several reasons. First, there have been too many cases in which police officers have abused their authority and then covered it up. Second, it seems probable that cops would be less likely to abuse their authority if they were being tracked. Third, human memory is an unreliable faculty. We might be able to reduce the number of wrongful convictions and acquittals if we have cameras recording more events.

2   I've come to this conclusion, but I haven't come to it happily. And, as the debate over cop-cams has unfolded, I've been surprised by how many people don't see the downside to this policy. Most people don't even seem to recognize the damage these cameras will do both to police-civilian relations and to privacy. As the debate has unfolded, it's become clear that more and more people have lost even the language of privacy, and an understanding of why privacy is important.

3   Let's start with the basics. Privacy is important to the development of full individuals because there has to be an interior zone within each person that other people don't see. There has to be a zone where half-formed thoughts and delicate emotions can grow and evolve, without being exposed to the harsh glare of public judgment. There has to be a place where you can be free to develop ideas and convictions away from the pressure to conform. There has to be a spot where you are only yourself and can define yourself.

4   Privacy is important to families and friendships because there has to be a zone where you can be fully known. There has to be a private space where you can share your doubts and secrets and expose your weaknesses with the expectation that you will still be loved and forgiven and supported.

5   Privacy is important for communities because there has to be a space where people with common affiliations can develop bonds of affection and trust. There has to be a

boundary between us and them. Within that boundary, you look out for each other; you rally to support each other; you cut each other some slack; you share fierce common loyalties.

6   All these concentric circles of privacy depend on some level of shrouding. They depend on some level of secrecy and awareness of the distinction between the inner privileged space and the outer exposed space. They depend on the understanding that what happens between us stays between us.

7   Cop-cams chip away at that. The cameras will undermine communal bonds. Putting a camera on someone is a sign that you don't trust him, or he doesn't trust you. When a police officer is wearing a camera, the contact between an officer and a civilian is less likely to be like intimate friendship and more likely to be oppositional and transactional. Putting a camera on an officer means she is less likely to cut you some slack, less likely to not write that ticket, or to bend the regulations a little as a sign of mutual care.

8   Putting a camera on the police officer means that authority resides less in the wisdom and integrity of the officer and more in the videotape. During a trial, if a crime isn't captured on the tape, it will be presumed to never have happened.

9   Cop-cams will insult families. It's worth pointing out that less than 20 percent of police calls involve felonies, and less than 1 percent of police-citizen contacts involve police use of force. Most of the time cops are mediating disputes, helping those in distress, dealing with the mentally ill or going into some home where someone is having a meltdown. When a police officer comes into your home wearing a camera, he's trampling on the privacy that makes a home a home. He's recording people on what could be the worst day of their lives, and inhibiting their ability to lean on the officer for care and support.

10   Cop-cams insult individual dignity because the embarrassing things recorded by them will inevitably get swapped around. The videos of the naked crime victim, the berserk drunk, the screaming maniac will inevitably get posted online — as they are already. With each leak, culture gets a little coarser. The rules designed to keep the videos out of public view will inevitably be eroded and bent.

11   So, yes, on balance, cop-cams are a good idea. But, as a journalist, I can tell you that when I put a notebook or a camera between me and my subjects, I am creating distance between me and them. Cop-cams strike a blow for truth, but they strike a blow against relationships. Society will be more open and transparent, but less humane and trusting.

Putting Up with Hate

The Denver Post *Editorial Board*

The *Denver Post* Editorial Board currently consists of William Dean Singleton, chairman and publisher; Mac Tully, publisher and CEO; and eight of the newspaper's editors and columnists. This editorial, which appeared in March 2011, was the Board's response to the Supreme Court ruling that even the most vile protests near a soldier's funeral should be protected by the First Amendment to the Constitution, which guarantees the right of free speech.

1   The despicable Rev. Fred W. Phelps Sr. and his followers are a difficult price to pay for the First Amendment.

2   Their ugly protests at the funerals of dead soldiers are designed to shock and get attention for their anti-gay agenda. And even though their hateful words and actions have hurt and angered grieving families, they ought to be constitutionally protected.

3   The U.S. Supreme Court last week agreed, ruling that the First Amendment protects the church members who protest outside funerals. The 8-1 decision, with Justice Samuel Alito dissenting, upheld an appeals court ruling that tossed out a $5 million judgment to the father of a dead Marine who sued church members after they picketed his son's funeral.

4   In the court of public opinion, Phelps and his followers, most of whom are his extended family, lose. These characters flew 1,000 miles from the Westboro Baptist Church in Kansas to picket the 2006 funeral of Lance Cpl. Matthew Snyder, carrying signs with messages such as "Thank God for Dead Soldiers" and "You're going to hell." Somehow, according to the twisted beliefs of Phelps, Snyder's death was punishment from God for this country's tolerance of gays and lesbians, especially in the military. It doesn't matter that Snyder was not gay.

5   But in writing the court's opinion Chief Justice John Roberts said that free-speech rights shield the funeral protests, noting that they obeyed police directions and were 1,000 feet from the church. "Speech is powerful. It can stir people to action, move them to tears of both joy and sorrow, and—as it did here—inflict great pain. On the facts before us, we cannot react to that pain by punishing the speaker," Roberts said. "As a nation we have chosen a different course—to protect even hurtful speech on public issues to ensure that we do not stifle public debate."

6   The central question before the high court was whether Phelps' speech should lose its constitutional protections if it was deemed to be outrageous or cause severe emotional distress. Had a majority of the court sided with Alito, it would have set a dangerous precedent. If speech can be squelched because it is deemed to be "outrageous," how long would it be before other "outrageous" speech was curbed?

7   Rather than curbing speech, we prefer the way communities have neutralized the Phelps gang—with citizens lining the streets surrounding the funeral. They form a barrier between the ugly shouts of protesters and the grieving family members.

Judging by the Cover

Bonny Gainley

Bonny Gainley is a marketing and management consultant, speaker, and author who writes on topics relating to the family and the workplace. In addition to articles based on her experiences in the high-tech industry, she has published *Look Before You Step: Advice for Potential Stepparents and Their Partners* (2002) and *Firefly Whispers* (2011). This essay originally appeared in 2003 as an opinion column in the Fort Collins, Colorado, newspaper, the *Coloradoan*.

1   Spring is in the air, and those about to graduate are looking for jobs just like many of the rest of us. Competition is tough, so jobs seekers must carefully consider their personal choices.

2   Every person has a need to be accepted, ideally just as he or she is. Our family and friends may do that, but the workplace does not. An editorial a while back in one of our high school newspapers claimed it is unfair for professions such as business, public relations, teaching and others to discourage visible tattoos. While not specifically mentioned, piercings and perhaps even certain hairstyles or garments would fall into the same category.

3   They say you can't judge a book by its cover, yet some people "cover" themselves in ways intended to convey certain messages. The message may be "my uniform says I am a police officer" or "I like the latest fashions" or "I am a gang member."

4   We make assumptions about people based on their appearance every day, and often we assume exactly what they want us to assume. Just as people project messages about themselves with their appearance, so do businesses. Dress codes and standards exist in the professional world for a number of reasons. Sometimes the issue is safety; sometimes it is a matter of what clients will accept. As long as parents don't want pre-school teachers waving visible skull or profanity tattoos in front of their small children, those tattoos will be deemed inappropriate for that profession.

5   Some say this is an issue of human rights and freedom, but it is really about free enterprise. The bottom line is that businesses exist to make money. Whether it seems fair or not, most employers do care about the personal appearances of the people they hire because those people represent the business to its customers.

6   Discrimination on the basis of factors an applicant can't control is wrong and illegal. Choosing the candidate who displays the attributes and skills that best match a job description is not. Just as runners would put themselves at a disadvantage by choosing to run the 100 meters in combat boots, people who choose to wear rings through their noses are putting themselves at a disadvantage in the professional job market. Each of us can choose whether to conform to the rules of any organization, but that organization is also free to choose whether they want us associated with it.

7   I don't personally have issues with visible tattoos or piercings, but as a hiring manager I was paid to choose the people who would make the best impression on our customers. It comes down to this—there are plenty of well-qualified applicants and most present themselves in a way my industry considers professional, so there was no compelling reason to choose someone who might offend my customers or poorly represent my company. Even though I may be open minded, I can't count on my customers to be.

8   If people continue to tattoo and pierce, attitudes about the appropriateness of those adornments in the professional workplace will change over time, in the same way that pants have become appropriate for women, for example. When tattoos and piercings are generally accepted in the business world, there will be new things that aren't—maybe nudity or some other trend we can't even imagine. Whether our personal choices will be accepted or not, we each have the right to make them, but must also be willing to accept the related consequences.

9   How we dress, tattoo or pierce is an expression of who we are and a message to the people we encounter. Freedom of choice is a dual-edged sword—individuals are free to present their desired image, and others are free to react to it.

10   There is nobody to blame but yourself if your set of choices does not match those desired by your preferred employers. No organization should have to change to accommodate a candidate simply because that person is unwilling to respect its standards, as long as its standards are legal.

Chapter 34

Description

Still Learning from My Mother

Cliff Schneider

Cliff Schneider is a graduate of Cornell and a retired freshwater fisheries biologist who worked for the Department of Environmental Conservation in New York. Much of his research and writing has focused on his work studying Lake Ontario. This essay, a personal tribute to his then 79-year-old mother, was first published in the "My Turn" column of *Newsweek* magazine in March 2000.

1   When I was a young boy growing up on New York's Long Island in the 1950s, it was common to see boys and their fathers gathering in the roads in front of their homes on warm summer evenings to "have a catch." That was the term we had for tossing a baseball while we talked about school, jobs and life in general. Although my dad and I had many catches together, my most memorable ones were with my mother. She would happily grab a glove, run out to the road and then fire fastballs at me that cracked my glove and left my hand stinging. She never showed any motherly concern, though, just a broad grin with the tip of her tongue exposed in the corner of her mouth. This was her game face. I can still recall how delighted I was tossing the ball with Mom and hearing the comments from my friends and neighbors: "Where did your mother learn to throw a ball like that?"

2   My mother, you see, was a jock long before Title IX unleashed the explosion of modern women's athletics. She lettered in field hockey and basketball while attending Hofstra University in the late 1930s. This was a time when it wasn't very fashionable for women to go running after a ball and work up a sweat. Luckily for me, Mom never worried about what was fashionable. She loved sports, loved being active and, most of all, loved the competition. Mom was kind to her kids until we played ball. Then we'd notice this gleam in her eye, the broad grin and the familiar tongue that told us she was ready for action and ready to have some fun. No matter what game she played, Mom had class. She played hard, she laughed a lot and, win or lose, she was always gracious.

3   The years have diminished Mom's physical abilities, as they would have for anyone who is about to become an octogenarian. Her back is a little bent, and she complains occasionally about her hip. Her biggest concession to the aging process, however, is that she has had to lighten up on her bowling ball. As a young mother in suburban

bowling leagues she toted a 15-pound ball, carried a 160 average and had a high game of 212. As she's grown older, her scores have declined. In recent years she's had to start using an eight-pound ball, which she protests is too light and "doesn't give enough pin action."

4   For years I have had to listen to my mother's perennial battle cry as she begins each new bowling season—"This is the year I'm going to bowl a 200 game!" I've always smiled and nodded in agreement, which was my way of acknowledging her determination. During our regular Thursday-evening phone conversations (she bowls on Thursdays), she gives me a frame-by-frame description of her games, and gripes that she can't bowl the way she used to. She almost always slips in the comment "I'm going to make 200 if it kills me." I try to explain that she should be satisfied that she is at least able to play the game. "Try to make some concession to your age, Mom," I say. Of course, she will have none of this talk and this year bought a 10-pound ball in pursuit of her dream. Vince Lombardi would be proud.

5   A week after she started bowling with her new ball, I called to check on her progress. She no sooner said "Hi" than I could tell something big had happened in her life. I could feel the smile all the way from Hendersonville, N.C., to upstate New York. I shouted, "You bowled a 200 game!" knowing it could be the only reason for such a happy voice. She corrected me: "Not a 200 game; I got a 220." It was her highest score ever! She gave me a strike-by-strike description of her game, and we both celebrated over the phone. As she signed off and said her goodbyes, I could still sense the smile on her face. Her grin will probably fade in another month or two.

6   After some reflection, I am amazed by my mother's accomplishment. Whether it is baseball, tennis, golf or even bowling, I have never heard of anyone's peaking at 79. Yes, there is some degree of luck in every game, but in Mom's case she had the best game of her life because she persevered. Mom's achievement has lifted her spirits and made her feel young again. For someone who is too frequently reminded that she can't do what she used to, this experience could not have come at a better time in her life. I guess I'm not surprised that I can still learn from Mom—that you are never too old to dream and never too old to realize those dreams. I am not surprised, either, that in our most recent calls she talks about bowling a 250 game.

A Day at the Theme Park

W. Bruce Cameron

W. Bruce Cameron began writing humorous features for the Denver newspaper the *Rocky Mountain News* in 1999; his column is now in national syndication. His book *8 Simple Rules for Dating My Teenage Daughter* (2001) was adapted into a television show of the same name; other books include *How to Remodel a Man* (2004), *A Dog's Purpose* (2010), *Emory's Gift* (2011) and *The Dog Master* (2015). As a father of three, Cameron often writes about the challenges facing parents, as illustrated in this 1999 column.

1   One of the most endearing traits of children is their utter trust that their parents will provide them with all of life's necessities, meaning food, shelter, and a weekend at a theme park.

2   A theme park is a sort of artificial vacation, a place where you can enjoy all your favorite pastimes at once, such as motion sickness and heat exhaustion. Adult tolerance for theme parks peaks at about an hour, which is how long it takes to walk from the parking lot to the front gate. You fork over an obscene amount of money to gain entrance to a theme park, though it costs nothing to leave (which is odd, because you'd pay anything to escape). The two main activities in a theme park are (a) standing in line, and (b) sweating. The sun reflects off the concrete with a fiendish lack of mercy. You're about to learn the boiling point of tennis shoes. Your hair is sunburned, and when a small child in front of you gestures with her hand she smacks you in the face with her cotton candy; now it feels like your cheeks are covered with carnivorous sand.

3   The ride your children have selected for you is a corkscrewing, stomach-compressing roller coaster built by the same folks who manufactured the baggage delivery system at DIA.* Apparently the theme of this particular park is "Nausea." You sit down and are strapped in so tightly you can feel your shoulders grinding against your pelvis. Once the ride begins you are thrown about with such violence it reminds you of your teenager's driving. When the ride is over your children want to get something to eat, but first the ride attendants have to pry your fingers off the safety bar. "Open your eyes, please, sir," they keep shouting. They finally persuade you to let go, though it seems a bit discourteous of them to have used pepper spray. Staggering, you follow your children to the Hot Dog Palace for some breakfast.

4   Food at a theme park is so expensive it would be cheaper to just eat your own money. Your son's meal costs a day's pay and consists of items manufactured of corn syrup, which is sugar; sucrose, which is sugar; fructose, which is sugar; and sugar, which is sugar. He also consumes large quantities of what in dog food would be called "meat byproducts." When, after a couple of rides, he announces that he feels like he is going to throw up, you're very alarmed. Having seen his meal once, you're in no mood to see it again.

5   With the exception of that first pummeling, you manage to stay off the rides all day, explaining to your children that it isn't good for you when your internal organs are forcibly rearranged. Now, though, they coax you back in line, promising a ride that doesn't twist, doesn't hang you upside down like a bat, doesn't cause your brain to flop around inside your skull; it just goes up and then comes back down. That's it, Dad, no big deal. What they don't tell you is HOW it comes back down. You're strapped into a seat and pulled gently up into acrophobia, the city falling away from you. Okay, not so bad, and in the conversation you're having with God you explain that you're thankful for the wonderful view but you really would like to get down now.

6   And that's just how you descend: NOW. Without warning, you plummet to the ground in an uncontrolled free fall. You must be moving faster than the speed of sound because when you open your mouth, nothing comes out. Your life passes before your eyes, and your one regret is that you will not have an opportunity to punish your children for bringing you to this hellish place. Brakes cut in and you slam to a stop. You gingerly touch your face to confirm it has fallen off. "Wasn't that fun, Dad?" your kids ask. "Why are you kissing the ground?"

7   At the end of the day, you let your teenager drive home. (After the theme park, you are impervious to fear.)

---

* Denver International Airport

The Battle of the Ants

Henry David Thoreau

Henry David Thoreau was a nineteenth-century American author, naturalist, and proponent of Transcendentalism, a philosophical movement of the 1830s–1840s that emphasized the inherent goodness of humankind. Thoreau is perhaps best known today for his essay "Civil Disobedience" (1849) and for *Walden, or Life in the Woods* (1854), a memoir of living simply in nature, based on his two years in a cabin at Walden Pond, near Concord, Massachusetts. This excerpt is from Chapter 12 of that work.

1   You only need sit still long enough in some attractive spot in the woods that all its inhabitants may exhibit themselves to you by turns.

2   I was witness to events of a less peaceful character. One day when I went out to my wood-pile, or rather my pile of stumps, I observed two large ants, the one red, the other much larger, nearly half an inch long, and black, fiercely contending with one another. Having once got hold they never let go, but struggled and wrestled and rolled on the chips incessantly. Looking farther, I was surprised to find that the chips were covered with such combatants, that it was not a *duellum,** but a *bellum,* a war between two races of ants, the red always pitted against the black, and frequently two red ones to one black. The legions of these Myrmidons** covered all the hills and vales in my wood-yard, and the ground was already strewn with the dead and dying, both red and black. It was the only battle which I have ever witnessed, the only battle-field I ever trod while the battle was raging; internecine war; the red republicans on the one hand, and the black imperialists on the other. On every side they were engaged in deadly combat, yet without any noise that I could hear, and human soldiers never fought so resolutely. I watched a couple that were fast locked in each other's embraces, in a little sunny valley amid the chips, now at noonday prepared to fight till the sun went down, or life went out. The smaller red champion had fastened himself like a vice to his adversary's front, and through all the tumblings on that field never for an instant ceased to gnaw at one of his feelers near the root, having already caused the other to go by the board; while the stronger black one dashed him from side to side, and, as I saw on looking nearer, had already divested him of several of his members. They fought with more pertinacity than bulldogs. Neither manifested the least disposition to retreat. It was evident that their battle-cry was "Conquer or die."

3   In the meanwhile there came along a single red ant on the hillside of this valley, evidently full of excitement, who either had dispatched his foe, or had not yet taken part in the battle; probably the latter, for he had lost none of his limbs; whose mother had charged him to return with his shield or upon it.† Or perchance he was some Achilles, who had nourished his wrath apart, and had now come to avenge or rescue his Patroclus.†† He saw this unequal combat from afar—for the blacks were nearly

---

* Latin word for "duel."

** The Myrmidons were the troops led by the Greek hero, Achilles, during the Trojan War. Achilles is the central character in Homer's *Iliad*.

† Mothers of Spartan warriors supposedly told their sons to return from battle as either victors or dead soldiers (i.e., carried home upon their shields).

†† In Homer's epic, Achilles had remained in camp until the death of his friend Patroclus, who had worn Achilles' armor into battle. Enraged over his friend's death, Achilles sought revenge.

twice the size of the red—he drew near with rapid pace till be stood on his guard within half an inch of the combatants; then, watching his opportunity, he sprang upon the black warrior, and commenced his operations near the root of his right foreleg, leaving the foe to select among his own members; and so there were three united for life, as if a new kind of attraction had been invented which put all other locks and cements to shame.

4   I should not have wondered by this time to find that they had their respective musical bands stationed on some eminent chip, and playing their national airs the while, to excite the slow and cheer the dying combatants. I was myself excited somewhat even as if they had been men. The more you think of it, the less the difference. And certainly there is not the fight recorded in Concord* history, at least, if in the history of America, that will bear a moment's comparison with this, whether for the numbers engaged in it, or for the patriotism and heroism displayed. For numbers and for carnage it was an Austerlitz or Dresden.** Concord Fight! Two killed on the patriots' side, and Luther Blanchard wounded! Why here every ant was a Buttrick—"Fire! for God's sake fire!"—and thousands shared the fate of Davis and Hosmer.† There was not one hireling there. I have no doubt that it was a principle they fought for, as much as our ancestors, and not to avoid a three-penny tax on their tea; and the results of this battle will be as important and memorable to those whom it concerns as those of the battle of Bunker Hill, at least.

5   I took up the chip on which the three I have particularly described were struggling, carried it into my house, and placed it under a tumbler [a drinking glass] on my window-sill, in order to see the issue. Holding a microscope [a magnifying glass] to the first-mentioned red ant, I saw that, though he was assiduously gnawing at the near foreleg of his enemy, having severed his remaining feeler, his own breast was all torn away, exposing what vitals he had there to the jaws of the black warrior, whose breastplate was apparently too thick for him to pierce; and the dark carbuncles of the sufferer's eyes shone with ferocity such as war only could excite. They struggled half an hour longer under the tumbler, and when I looked again the black soldier had severed the heads of his foes from their bodies, and the still living heads were hanging on either side of him like ghastly trophies at his saddle-bow, still apparently as firmly fastened as ever, and he was endeavoring with feeble struggles, being without feelers and with only the remnant of a leg, and I know not how many other wounds, to divest himself of them, which at length, after half an hour more, he accomplished. I raised the glass, and he went off over the window-sill in that crippled state. Whether he finally survived that combat, and spent the remainder of

---

* Concord, Massachusetts, was the site of the first shots fired in the American Revolution, in 1775.

** Austerlitz and Dresden were the sites of famous battles during the Napoleonic wars.

† Thoreau includes various references to the American Revolution, including names of people, places, and issues his readers might recognize. During the Battle of Concord, British troops first wounded Luther Blanchard, though perhaps aiming for Major John Buttrick, militia commander, who then gave the order to return fire. Davis and Hosmer were the only colonists killed that day. Bunker Hill was another battle site in the American Revolution.

his days in some Hôtel des Invalides,* I do not know; but I thought that his industry would not be worth much thereafter.

6   I never learned which party was victorious, nor the cause of the war; but I felt for the rest of that day as if I had had my feelings excited and harrowed by witnessing the struggle, the ferocity and carnage, of a human battle before my door.

---

* Originally, the Paris hospital for veterans; now most famous as the site of Napoleon's elaborate 1840 tomb.

Chapter 35

Narration

---

37 Who Saw Murder Didn't Call the Police*

Martin Gansberg

Martin Gansberg was a reporter and editor for the *New York Times* for over 40 years, until his retirement in 1985. He also wrote for such magazines as *Diplomat*, *Catholic Digest*, and *Facts*. This often-reprinted article was first published in the *New York Times* in 1964, shortly after the murder of Kitty Genovese. Since then, some of the facts reported in this article have been disputed, including the number of people who could have and did actually witness the crime, the number of times the victim was attacked (two, not three), and the number of people who called the police. Nevertheless, this crime has become a famous example of the tendency of onlookers to turn away from bad events and of the way that people in groups can feel "a diffusion of responsibility" and thus be slow to speak up or take action.

1   For more than half an hour 38 respectable, law-abiding citizens in Queens watched a killer stalk and stab a woman in three separate attacks in Kew Gardens.

2   Twice the sound of their voices and the sudden glow of their bedroom lights interrupted him and frightened him off. Each time he returned, sought her out and stabbed her again. Not one person telephoned the police during the assault; one witness called after the woman was dead.

3   That was two weeks ago today. But Assistant Chief Inspector Frederick M. Lussen, in charge of the borough's detectives and a veteran of 25 years of homicide investigations, is still shocked.

4   He can give a matter-of-fact recitation of many murders. But the Kew Gardens slaying baffles him—not because it is a murder, but because the "good people" failed to call the police.

5   "As we have reconstructed the crime," he said, "the assailant had three chances to kill this woman during a 35-minute period. He returned twice to complete the job. If we had been called when he first attacked, the woman might not be dead now."

6   This is what the police say happened beginning at 3:20 a.m. in the staid, middle-class, tree-lined Austin Street area:

---

* Although this article has sometimes been reprinted with the title "38 Who Saw Murder Didn't Call the Police," the original 1964 article in the *New York Times* does, in fact, use the title shown here.

7   Twenty-eight-year-old Catherine Genovese, who was called Kitty by almost everyone in the neighborhood, was returning home from her job as manager of a bar in Hollis. She parked her red Fiat in a lot adjacent to the Kew Gardens Long Island Rail Road Station, facing Mowbray Place. Like many residents of the neighborhood, she had parked there day after day since her arrival from Connecticut a year ago, although the railroad frowns on the practice.

8   She turned off the lights of her car, locked the door and started to walk the 100 feet to the entrance of her apartment at 82–70 Austin Street, which is in a Tudor building, with stores on the first floor and apartments on the second.

9   The entrance to the apartment is in the rear of the building because the front is rented to retail stores. At night the quiet neighborhood is shrouded in the slumbering darkness that marks most residential areas.

10   Miss Genovese noticed a man at the far end of the lot, near a seven-story apartment house at 82–40 Austin Street. She halted. Then, nervously, she headed up Austin Street toward Lefferts Boulevard, where there is a call box to the 102nd Police Precinct in nearby Richmond Hill.

"He stabbed me"

11   She got as far as a street light in front of a bookstore before the man grabbed her. She screamed. Lights went on in the 10-story apartment house at 82–67 Austin Street, which faces the bookstore. Windows slid open and voices punctuated the early-morning stillness.

12   Miss Genovese screamed: "Oh, my God, he stabbed me! Please help me! Please help me!"

13   From one of the upper windows in the apartment house, a man called down: "Let that girl alone!"

14   The assailant looked up at him, shrugged and walked down Austin Street toward a white sedan parked a short distance away. Miss Genovese struggled to her feet.

15   Lights went out. The killer returned to Miss Genovese, now trying to make her way around the side of the building by the parking lot to get to her apartment. The assailant stabbed her again.

16   "I'm dying!" she shrieked. "I'm dying!"

A city bus passed

17   Windows were opened again, and lights went on in many apartments. The assailant got into his car and drove away. Miss Genovese staggered to her feet. A city bus, Q-10, the Lefferts Boulevard line to Kennedy International Airport, passed. It was 3:35 A.M.

18   The assailant returned. By then, Miss Genovese had crawled to the back of the building, where the freshly painted brown doors to the apartment house held out hope of safety. The killer tried the first door; she wasn't there. At the second door, 82–62 Austin Street, he saw her slumped on the floor at the foot of the stairs. He stabbed her a third time—fatally.

19   It was 3:50 by the time the police received their first call, from a man who was a neighbor of Miss Genovese. In two minutes they were at the scene. The neighbor, a 70-year-old woman and another woman were the only persons on the street. Nobody else came forward.

20   The man explained that he had called the police after much deliberation. He had phoned a friend in Nassau County for advice and then he had crossed the roof of the building to the apartment of the elderly woman to get her to make the call.

21   "I didn't want to get involved," he sheepishly told the police.

Suspect is arrested

22   Six days later, the police arrested Winston Moseley, a 29-year-old business-machine operator, and charged him with homicide. Moseley had no previous record. He is married, has two children and owns a home at 133–19 Sutter Avenue, South Ozone Park, Queens. On Wednesday, a court committed him to Kings County Hospital for psychiatric observation.

23   When questioned by the police, Moseley also said that he had slain Mrs. Annie May Johnson, 24, of 146–12 133d Avenue, Jamaica, on Feb. 29 and Barbara Kralik, 15, of 174–17 140th Avenue, Springfield Gardens, last July. In the Kralik case, the police are holding Alvin L. Mitchell, who is said to have confessed [to] that slaying.

24   The police stressed how simple it would have been to have gotten in touch with them. "A phone call," said one of the detectives, "would have done it." The police may be reached by dialing "O" for operator or SPring 7-3100.

25   The question of whether the witnesses can be held legally responsible in any way for failure to report the crime was put to the Police Department's legal bureau. There, a spokesman said: "There is no legal responsibility with few exceptions, for any citizen to report a crime."

Statutes explained

26   Under the statutes of the city, he said, a witness to a suspicious or violent death must report it to the medical examiner. Under state law, a witness cannot withhold information in a kidnapping.

27   Today witnesses from the neighborhood, which is made up of one-family homes in the $35,000 to $60,000 range with the exception of the two apartment houses near the railroad station, find it difficult to explain why they didn't call the police.

28   Lieut Bernard Jacobs, who handled the investigation by the, detectives, said: "It is one of the better neighborhoods. There are few reports of crimes. You only get the usual complaints about boys playing or garbage cans being turned over."

29   The police said most persons had told them they had been afraid to call, but had given meaningless answers when asked what they had feared.

30   "We can understand the reticence of people to become involved in an area of violence," Lieutenant Jacobs said, "but where they are in their homes, near phones, why should they be afraid to call the police?"

31   He said his men were able to piece together what happened – and capture the suspect – because the residents furnished all the information when detectives rang doorbells during the days following the slaying.

32   "But why didn't someone call us that night ?" he asked unbelievingly.

33   Witnesses—some of them unable to believe what they had allowed to happen—told a reporter why.

34   A housewife, knowingly if quite casual[ly], said, "We thought it was a lover's quarrel." A husband and wife both said, "Frankly, we were afraid." They seemed aware of the fact

that events might have been different. A distraught woman, wiping her hands in her apron, said, "I didn't want my husband to get involved."

35   One couple, now willing to talk about that night, said they heard the first screams. The husband looked thoughtfully at the bookstore where the killer first grabbed Miss Genovese.

36   "We went to the window to see what was happening," he said, "but the light from our bedroom made it difficult to see the street." The wife, still apprehensive, added: "I put out the light and we were able to see better."

37   Asked why they hadn't called the police, she shrugged and replied: "I don't know."

38   A man peeked out from a slight opening in the doorway to his apartment and rattled off an account of the killer's second attack. Why hadn't he called the police at the time? "I was tired," he said without emotion. "I went back to bed."

39   It was 4:25 A.M. when the ambulance arrived to take the body of Miss Genovese. It drove off. "Then," a solemn police detective said, "the people came out."

Salvation

Langston Hughes

Langston Hughes was a poet and fiction writer who was an important part of the Harlem Renaissance of the 1920s. Creating innovative poetry that often incorporated the rhythms of jazz and vibrant dialect into his work, Hughes is admired for his insightful presentations of black life in America; his most famous poem is known as "Dream Deferred." This essay was first published as part of his autobiography, *The Big Sea* (1940).

1   I was saved from sin when I was going on thirteen. But not really saved. It happened like this. There was a big revival at my Auntie Reed's church. Every night for weeks there had been much preaching, singing, praying, and shouting, and some very hardened sinners had been brought to Christ, and the membership of the church had grown by leaps and bounds. Then just before the revival ended, they held a special meeting for children, "to bring the young lambs to the fold." My aunt spoke of it for days ahead. That night I was escorted to the front row and placed on the mourners' bench* with all the other young sinners, who had not yet been brought to Jesus.

2   My aunt told me that when you were saved you saw a light, and something happened to you inside! And Jesus came into your life! And God was with you from then on! She said you could see and hear and feel Jesus in your soul. I believed her. I had heard a great many old people say the same thing and it seemed to me they ought to know. So I sat there calmly in the hot, crowded church, waiting for Jesus to come to me.

3   The preacher preached a wonderful rhythmical sermon, all moans and shouts and lonely cries and dire pictures of hell, and then he sang a song about the ninety and nine safe in the fold, but one little lamb was left out in the cold. Then he said: "Won't you come? Won't you come to Jesus? Young lambs, won't you come?" And he held out his

---

* At some revivals, a bench near the front of the church provided reserved seating for repentant sinners and others in sorrow.

arms to all us young sinners there on the mourners' bench. And the little girls cried. And some of them jumped up and went to Jesus right away. But most of us just sat there.

4   A great many old people came and knelt around us and prayed, old women with jet-black faces and braided hair, old men with work-gnarled hands. And the church sang a song about the lower lights are burning, some poor sinners to be saved. And the whole building rocked with prayer and song.

5   Still I kept waiting to *see* Jesus.

6   Finally all the young people had gone to the altar and were saved, but one boy and me. He was a rounder's [drunkard's] son named Westley. Westley and I were surrounded by sisters and deacons praying. It was very hot in the church, and getting late now. Finally Westley said to me in a whisper: ". . . I'm tired o' sitting here. Let's get up and be saved." So he got up and was saved.

7   Then I was left all alone on the mourners' bench. My aunt came and knelt at my knees and cried, while prayers and song swirled all around me in the little church. The whole congregation prayed for me alone, in a mighty wail of moans and voices. And I kept waiting serenely for Jesus, waiting, waiting—but he didn't come. I wanted to see him, but nothing happened to me. Nothing! I wanted something to happen to me, but nothing happened.

8   I heard the songs and the minister saying: "Why don't you come? My dear child, why don't you come to Jesus? Jesus is waiting for you. He wants you. Why don't you come? Sister Reed, what is this child's name?"

9   "Langston" my aunt sobbed.

10   "Langston, why don't you come? Why don't you come and be saved? Oh, Lamb of God! Why don't you come?"

11   Now it was really getting late. I began to be ashamed of myself, holding everything up so long. I began to wonder what God thought about Westley, who certainly hadn't seen Jesus either, but who was now sitting proudly on the platform, swinging his knickerbock-ered legs and grinning down at me, surrounded by deacons and old women on their knees praying. God had not struck Westley dead for taking his name in vain or for lying in the temple. So I decided that maybe to save further trouble, I'd better lie, too, and say that Jesus had come, and get up and be saved.

12   So I got up.

13   Suddenly the whole room broke into a sea of shouting, as they saw me rise. Waves of rejoicing swept the place. Women leaped in the air. My aunt threw her arms around me. The minister took me by the hand and led me to the platform.

14   When things quieted down, in a hushed silence, punctuated by a few ecstatic "Amens," all the new young lambs were blessed in the name of God. Then joyous singing filled the room.

15   That night, for the last time in my life but one—for I was a big boy twelve years old—I cried. I cried, in bed alone, and couldn't stop. I buried my head under the quilts, but my aunt heard me. She woke up and told my uncle I was crying because the Holy Ghost had come into my life, and because I had seen Jesus. But I was really crying because I couldn't bear to tell her that I had lied, that I had deceived everybody in the church, that I hadn't seen Jesus, and that now I didn't believe there was a Jesus any more, since he didn't come to help me.

———————————

* An older brother.

Arrival at Manzanar

Jeanne Wakatsuki Houston and James D. Houston

Born in California, Jeanne Wakatsuki Houston was seven years old when, during World War II, her family was moved to a Japanese-American internment camp, where they were held for four years. In collaboration with her husband, novelist James D. Houston, she recounts these experiences in *Farewell to Manzanar* (1973), from which this excerpt is taken. Individually and together, the couple has written a variety of books, films, and magazine articles. Wakatsuki Houston's most recent work is *The Legend of Fire Horse Woman* (2004); Houston's is *A Queen's Journey* (2011).

1   In December of 1941 Papa's disappearance didn't bother me nearly so much as the world I soon found myself in.

2   He had been a jack-of-all-trades. When I was born he was farming near Ingelwood. Later, when he started fishing, we moved to Ocean Park, near Santa Monica, and until they [the FBI] picked him up, that's where we lived, in a big frame house with a brick fireplace, a block back from the beach. We were the only Japanese family in the neighborhood. Papa liked it that way. He didn't want to be labeled or grouped by anyone. But with him gone and no way of knowing what to expect, my mother moved all of us down to Terminal Island. Woody* already lived there, and one of my older sisters had married a Terminal Island boy. Mama's first concern now was to keep the family together; and once the war began, she felt safer there than isolated racially in Ocean Park.

3   But for me, at age seven, the island was a country as foreign as India or Arabia would have been. It was the first time I had lived among other Japanese, or gone to school with them, and I was terrified all the time. . . .

4   At the time it seemed we had been living under this reign of fear for years. In fact, we lived there about two months. Late in February the navy decided to clear Terminal Island completely. Even though most of us were American-born, it was dangerous having that many Orientals so close to the Long Beach Naval Station, on the opposite end of the island. We had known something like this was coming. But, like Papa's arrest, not much could be done ahead of time. There were four of us kids still young enough to be living with Mama, plus Granny, her mother, sixty-five then, speaking no English, and nearly blind. Mama didn't know where else she could get work, and we had nowhere else to move *to*. On February 25 the choice was made for us. We were given forty-eight hours to clear out.

5   The secondhand dealers had been prowling around for weeks, like wolves, offering humiliating prices for goods and furniture they knew many of us would have to sell sooner or later. Mama had left all but her most valuable possessions in Ocean Park, simply because she had nowhere to put them. She had brought along her pottery, her silver, heirlooms like the kimonos Granny had brought from Japan, tea sets, lacquered tables, and one fine old set of china, blue and white porcelain, almost translucent. On the day we were leaving, Woody's car was so crammed with boxes and luggage and kids we had just run out of room. Mama had to sell this china.

6   One of the dealers offered her fifteen dollars for it. She said it was a full setting for twelve and worth at least two hundred. He said fifteen was his top price. Mama started to quiver. Her eyes blazed up at him. She had been packing all night and trying to calm down Granny, who didn't understand why we were moving again and what all the rush

was about. Mama's nerves were shot, and now Navy jeeps were patrolling the streets. She didn't say another word. She just glared at this man, all the rage and frustration channeled at him through her eyes.

7   He watched her for a moment and said he was sure he couldn't pay more than seventeen fifty for that china. She reached into the red velvet case, took out a dinner plate and hurled it at the floor right in front of his feet.

8   The man leaped back shouting, "Hey! Hey, don't do that! Those are valuable dishes!"

9   Mama took out another dinner plate and hurled it at the floor; then another and another, never moving, never opening her mouth, just quivering and glaring at the retreating dealer, with tears streaming down her cheeks. He finally turned and scuttled out the door, heading for the next house. When he was gone she stood there smashing cups and bowls and platters until the whole set lay in scattered blue and white fragments across the wooden floor.

10   The American Friends Service helped us find a small house in Boyle Heights, another minority ghetto, in downtown Los Angeles, now inhabited briefly by a few hundred Terminal Island refugees. Executive Order 9066 had been signed by President Roosevelt, giving the War Department authority to define military areas in the western states and to exclude from them anyone who might threaten the war effort. There was a lot of talk about internment, or moving inland, or something like that in store for all Japanese Americans. I remember my brothers sitting around the table talking very intently about what we were going to do, how we would keep the family together. They had seen how quickly Papa was removed, and they knew now that he would not be back for quite a while. Just before leaving Terminal Island Mama had received her first letter, from Bismarck, North Dakota. He had been imprisoned at Fort Lincoln, in an all-male camp for enemy aliens.

11   Papa had been the patriarch. He had always decided everything in the family. With him gone, my brothers, like councilors in the absence of a chief, worried about what should be done. The ironic thing is, there wasn't much left to decide. These were mainly days of quiet, desperate waiting for what seemed at the time to be inevitable. There is a phrase the Japanese use in such situations, when something difficult must be endured. You would hear the older heads, the Issei, telling others very quietly, "*Shikato ga nai*" (It cannot be helped). "*Shikata ga nai*" (It must be done).

12   Mama and Woody went to work packing celery for a Japanese produce dealer. Kiyo and my sister May and I enrolled in the local school, and what sticks in my memory from those few weeks is the teacher—not her looks, her remoteness. In Ocean Park my teacher had been a kind, grandmotherly woman who used to sail with us in Papa's boat from time to time and who wept the day we had to leave. In Boyle Heights the teacher felt cold and distant. I was confused by all the moving and was having trouble with the classwork, but she would never help me out. She would have nothing to do with me.

13   This was the first time I had felt outright hostility from a Caucasian. Looking back, it is easy enough to explain. Public attitudes toward the Japanese in California were shifting rapidly. In the first few months of the Pacific war, America was on the run. Tolerance had turned to distrust and irrational fear. The hundred-year-old tradition of anti-Orientalism on the west coast soon resurfaced, more vicious than ever. Its result became clear about a month later, when we were told to make our third and final move.

14   The name Manzanar meant nothing to us when we left Boyle Heights. We didn't know where it was or what it was. We went because the government ordered us to. And, in the

case of my older brothers and sisters, we went with a certain amount of relief. They had all heard stories of Japanese homes being attacked, of beatings in the streets of California towns. They were as frightened of the Caucasians as Caucasians were of us. Moving, under what appeared to be government protection, to an area less directly threatened by the war seemed not such a bad idea at all. For some it actually sounded like a fine adventure.

15   Our pickup point was a Buddhist church in Los Angeles. It was very early, and misty, when we got there with our luggage. Mama had bought heavy coats for all of us. She grew up in eastern Washington and knew that anywhere inland in early April would be cold. I was proud of my new coat, and I remember sitting on a duffel bag trying to be friendly with the Greyhound driver. I smiled at him. He didn't smile back. He was befriending no one. Someone tied a numbered tag to my collar and to the duffel bag (each family was given a number, and that became our official designation until the camps were closed), someone else passed out box lunches for the trip, and we climbed aboard.

16   I had never been outside Los Angeles County, never traveled more than ten miles from the coast, had never even ridden on a bus. I was full of excitement, the way any kid would be, and wanted to look out the window. But for the first few hours the shades were drawn. Around me other people played cards, read magazines, dozed, waiting. I settled back, waiting too, and finally fell asleep. The bus felt very secure to me. Almost half its passengers were immediate relatives. Mama and my older brothers had succeeded in keeping most of us together, on the same bus, headed for the same camp. I didn't realize until much later what a job that was. The strategy had been, first, to have everyone living in the same district when the evacuation began, and then to get all of us included under the same family number, even though names had been changed by marriage. Many families weren't as lucky as ours and suffered months of anguish while trying to arrange transfers from one camp to another.

17   We rode all day. By the time we reached our destination, the shades were up. It was late afternoon. The first thing I saw was a yellow swirl across a blurred, reddish setting sun. The bus was being pelted by what sounded like splattering rain. It wasn't rain. This was my first look at something I would soon know very well, a billowing flurry of dust and sand churned up by the wind through Owens Valley.

18   We drove past a barbed-wire fence, through a gate, and into an open space where trunks and sacks and packages had been dumped from the baggage trucks that drove out ahead of us. I could see a few tents set up, the first rows of black barracks, and beyond them, blurred by sand, rows of barracks that seemed to spread for miles across this plain. People were sitting on cartons or milling around, with their backs to the wind waiting to see which friends or relatives might be on this bus. As we approached, they turned or stood up, and some moved toward us expectantly. But inside the bus no one stirred. No one waved or spoke. They just stared out the windows, ominously silent. I didn't understand this. Hadn't we finally arrived, our whole family intact? I opened a window, leaned out, and yelled happily. "Hey! This whole bus is full of Wakatsukis!"

19   Outside, the greeters smiled. Inside there was an explosion of laughter, hysterical, tension-breaking laughter that left my brothers choking and whacking each other across the shoulders.

20   We had pulled up just in time for dinner. The mess halls weren't completed yet. An outdoor chow line snaked around a half-finished building that broke a good part of the wind. They issued us army mess kits, the round metal kind that fold over, and plopped in scoops

of canned Vienna sausage, canned string beans, steamed rice that had been cooked too long, and on top of the rice a serving of canned apricots. The Caucasian servers were thinking that the fruit poured over rice would make a good dessert. Among the Japanese, of course, rice is never eaten with sweet foods, only with salty or savory foods. Few of us could eat such a mixture. But at this point no one dared protest. It would have been impolite. I was horrified when I saw the apricot syrup seeping through my little mound of rice. I opened my mouth to complain. My mother jabbed me in the back to keep quiet. We moved on through the line and joined the others squatting in the lee of half-raised walls, dabbing courteously at what was, for almost everyone there, an inedible concoction.

21   After dinner we were taken to Block 16, a cluster of fifteen barracks that had just been finished a day or so earlier—although finished was hardly the word for it. The shacks were built of one thickness of pine planking covered with tarpaper. They sat on concrete footings, with about two feet of open space between the floorboards and the ground. Gaps showed between the planks, and as the weeks passed and the green wood dried out, the gaps widened. Knotholes gaped in the uncovered floor.

22   Each barracks was divided into six units, sixteen by twenty feet, about the size of a living room, with one bare bulb hanging from the ceiling and an oil stove for heat. We were assigned two of these for the twelve people in our family group; and our official family "number" was enlarged by three digits—6 plus the number of this barracks. We were issued steel army cots, two brown army blankets each, and some mattress covers, which my brothers stuffed with straw.

23   The first task was to divide up what space we had for sleeping. Bill and Woody contributed a blanket each and partitioned off the first room: one side for Bill and Tomi, one side for Woody and Chizu and their baby girl. Woody also got the stove, for heating formulas.

24   The people who had it hardest during the first few months were young couples like these, many of whom had married just before the evacuation began, in order not to be separated and sent to different camps. Our two rooms were crowded, but at least it was all in the family. My oldest sister and her husband were shoved into one of those sixteen-by-twenty-foot compartments with six people they had never seen before—two other couples, one recently married like themselves, the other with two teenage boys. Partitioning off a room like that wasn't easy. It was bitter cold when we arrived, and the wind did not abate. All they had to use for room dividers were those army blankets, two of which were barely enough to keep one person warm. They argued over whose blanket should be sacrificed and later argued about noise at night—the parents wanted their boys asleep by 9:00 P.M.—and they continued arguing over matters like that for six months, until my sister and her husband left to harvest sugar beets in Idaho. It was grueling work up there, and wages were pitiful, but when the call came through camp for workers to alleviate the wartime labor shortage, it sounded better than their life at Manzanar. They knew they'd have, if nothing else, a room, perhaps a cabin of their own.

25   That first night in Block 16, the rest of us squeezed into the second room—Granny, Lillian, age fourteen, Ray, thirteen, May, eleven, Kiyo, ten, Mama, and me. I didn't mind this at all at the time. Being youngest meant I got to sleep with Mama. And before we went to bed I had a great time jumping up and down on the mattress. The boys had stuffed so much straw into hers, we had to flatten it some so we wouldn't slide off. I slept with her every night after that until Papa came back.

Chapter 36

Essays Using Multiple Strategies and Styles

Courage in Greensboro

Owen Edwards

Owen Edwards is a freelance writer and author of *Elegant Solutions* (1989). For over a decade he has written the "Object at Hand" column for the *Smithsonian*, a magazine that supports the Smithsonian Institute.* This column highlights the stories behind historical and cultural objects in the Smithsonian's museum collections, ranging from George Washington's bed to Mr. Rogers' cardigan sweater. This February 2010 column focuses on the lunch counter from a Woolworth's discount store, the scene of a 1960 protest considered a landmark event in the Civil Rights Movement.

1   On February 1, 1960, four young African-American men, freshmen at the Agricultural and Technical College of North Carolina, entered the Greensboro Woolworth's and sat down on stools that had, until that moment, been occupied exclusively by white customers. The four—Franklin McCain, Ezell Blair Jr., Joseph McNeil and David Richmond—asked to be served, and were refused. But they did not get up and leave. Indeed, they launched a protest that lasted six months and helped change America. A section of that historic counter is now held by the National Museum of American History, where the chairman of the division of politics and reform, Harry Rubenstein, calls it "a significant part of a larger collection about participation in our political system." The story behind it is central to the epic struggle of the civil rights movement.

2   William Yeingst, chairman of the museum's division of home and community life, says the Greensboro protest "inspired similar actions in the state and elsewhere in the South. What the students were confronting was not the law, but rather a cultural system that defined racial relations."

---

* Located on the National Mall in Washington, D.C., the Smithsonian Institute is the world's largest museum complex, containing nineteen museums and galleries, including the American History Museum, the National History Museum, and the National Air and Space Museum. These museums are free and open every day except Dec. 25. The Smithsonian was originally funded by British scientist James Smithson (1765–1829), who left his estate to create an "institution for the increase and diffusion of knowledge." Mysteriously, Smithson had never visited America nor even corresponded with anyone in this country.

3   Joseph McNeil, 67, now a retired Air Force major general living on Long Island, New York, says the idea of staging a sit-in to protest the ingrained injustice had been around awhile. "I grew up in Wilmington, North Carolina, and even in high school, we thought about doing something like that," he recalls. After graduating, McNeil moved with his family to New York, then returned to the South to study engineering physics at the technical college in Greensboro.

4   On the way back to school after Christmas vacation during his freshman year, he observed the shift in his status as he traveled south by bus. "In Philadelphia," he remembers, "I could eat anywhere in the bus station. By Maryland, that had changed." And in the Greyhound depot in Richmond, Virginia, McNeil couldn't buy a hot dog at a food counter reserved for whites. "I was still the same person, but I was treated differently." Once at school, he and three of his friends decided to confront segregation. "To face this kind of experience and not challenge it meant we were part of the problem," McNeil recalls.

5   The Woolworth's itself, with marble stairs and 25,000 square feet of retail space, was one of the company's flagship stores. The lunch counter, where diners faced rose-tinted mirrors, generated significant profits. "It really required incredible courage and sacrifice for those four students to sit down there," Yeingst says.

6   News of the sit-in spread quickly, thanks in part to a photograph taken the first day by Jack Moebes of the *Greensboro Record* [shown here] and stories in the paper by Marvin Sykes and Jo Spivey. Nonviolent demonstrations cropped up outside the store, while other protesters had a turn at the counter. Sit-ins erupted in other North Carolina cities and segregationist states.

7   By February 4, African-Americans, mainly students, occupied 63 of the 66 seats at the counter (waitresses sat in the remaining three). Protesters ready to assume their place crowded the aisles. After six months of diminished sales and unflattering publicity, Woolworth's desegregated the lunch counter—an astonishing victory for nonviolent protest. "The sit-in at the Greensboro Woolworth's was one of the early and pivotal events that inaugurated the student-led phase of the civil rights movement," Yeingst says.

Jack Moebes/Historical/Corbis

Four African-American students launched a six-month protest that helped change America.

8   More than three decades later, in October 1993, Yeingst learned Woolworth's was closing the Greensboro store as part of a company-wide downsizing. "I called the manager right away," he recalls, "and my colleague Lonnie Bunch and I went down and met with African-American city council members and a group called Sit-In Movement Inc." (Bunch is now the director of the National Museum of African American History and Culture.) Woolworth's officials agreed that a piece of the counter belonged at the Smithsonian, and volunteers from the local carpenters' union removed an eight-foot

section with four stools. "We placed the counter within sight of the flag that inspired the national anthem," Yeingst says of the museum exhibit.

9   When I asked McNeil if he had returned to Woolworth's to eat after the sit-in ended, he laughed, saying: "Well, I went back when I got to school the next September. But the food was bland, and the apple pie wasn't that good. So it's fair to say I didn't go back often."

A Modest Proposal

Jonathan Swift

Born in 1667 in Ireland, Jonathan Swift was an Anglican priest who eventually became dean of St. Patrick's Cathedral in Dublin. He is best known for his satires, often addressing the English exploitation of the Irish, including his masterpiece *Gulliver's Travels* (1726). This essay, originally a pamphlet written in 1729 during a terrible famine and at a time when the English were proposing a severe tax on the Irish, uses irony and satiric exaggeration to emphasize Ireland's desperation and England's greed.

For Preventing the Children of
Poor People in Ireland
from Being a Burden to Their Parents
or Country,
and for Making Them Beneficial to the Public

1   It is a melancholy object to those who walk through this great town or travel in the country, when they see the streets, the roads, and cabin doors, crowded with beggars of the female sex, followed by three, four, or six children, all in rags and importuning every passenger for an alms. These mothers, instead of being able to work for their honest livelihood, are forced to employ all their time in strolling to beg sustenance for their helpless infants, who, as they grow up, either turn thieves for want of work, or leave their dear native country to fight for the Pretender in Spain, or sell themselves to the Barbadoes.

2   I think it is agreed by all parties that this prodigious number of children in the arms, or on the backs, or at the heels of their mothers, and frequently of their fathers, is in the present deplorable state of the kingdom a very great additional grievance; and therefore whoever could find out a fair, cheap, and easy method of making these children sound, useful members of the commonwealth would deserve so well of the public as to have his statue set up for a preserver of the nation.

3   But my intention is very far from being confined to provide only for the children of professed beggars; it is of a much greater extent, and shall take in the whole number of infants at a certain age who are born of parents in effect as little able to support them as those who demand our charity in the streets.

4   As to my own part, having turned my thoughts for many years upon this important subject, and maturely weighed the several schemes of other projectors, I have always found them grossly mistaken in the computation. It is true, a child just dropped from its dam may be supported by her milk for a solar year, with little other nourishment; at most not above the value of two shillings, which the mother may certainly get, or the

value in scraps, by her lawful occupation of begging; and it is exactly at one year old that I propose to provide for them in such a manner as instead of being a charge upon their parents or the parish, or wanting food and raiment for the rest of their lives, they shall on the contrary contribute to the feeding, and partly to the clothing, of many thousands.

5   There is likewise another great advantage in my scheme, that it will prevent those voluntary abortions, and that horrid practice of women murdering their bastard children, alas, too frequent among us, sacrificing the poor innocent babes I doubt, more to avoid the expense than the shame, which would move tears and pity in the most savage and inhuman breast.

6   The number of souls in this kingdom being usually reckoned one million and a half, of these I calculate there may be about two hundred thousand couples whose wives are breeders; from which number I subtract thirty thousand couples who are able to maintain their own children, although I apprehend there cannot be so many under the present distress of the kingdom; but this being granted, there will remain an hundred and seventy thousand breeders. I again subtract fifty thousand for those women who miscarry, or whose children die by accident or disease within the year. There only remain an hundred and twenty thousand children of poor parents annually born. The question therefore is, how this number shall be reared and provided for, which, as I have already said, under the present situation of affairs, is utterly impossible by all the methods hitherto proposed. For we can neither employ them in handicraft nor agriculture; we neither build houses (I mean in the country) nor cultivate land. They can very seldom pick up a livelihood by stealing till they arrive at six years old, except where they are of towardly parts; although I confess they learn the rudiments much earlier, during which time they can however be looked upon only as probationers, as I have been informed by a principal gentleman in the county of Cavan, who protested to me that he never knew above one or two instances under the age of six, even in a part of the kingdom so renowned for the quickest proficiency in that art.

7   I am assured by our merchants that a boy or a girl before twelve years old is no salable commodity; and even when they come to this age, they will not yield above three pounds, or three pounds and half a crown at most on the Exchange; which cannot turn to account either to the parents or kingdom, the charge of nutriment and rags having been at least four times that value.

8   I shall now therefore humbly propose my own thoughts, which I hope will not be liable to the least objection.

9   I have been assured by a very knowing American of my acquaintance in London, that a young healthy child well nursed is at a year old a most delicious, nourishing, and wholesome food, whether stewed, roasted, baked, or boiled; and I make no doubt that it will equally serve in a fricassee or a ragout.

10   I do therefore humbly offer it to public consideration that of the hundred and twenty thousand children, already computed, twenty thousand may be reserved for breed, whereof only one fourth part to be males, which is more than we allow to sheep, black cattle, or swine; and my reason is that these children are seldom the fruits of marriage, a circumstance not much regarded by our savages, therefore one male will be sufficient to serve four females. That the remaining hundred thousand may at a year old be offered in sale to the persons of quality and fortune through the kingdom,

always advising the mother to let them suck plentifully in the last month, so as to render them plump and fat for a good table. A child will make two dishes at an entertainment for friends; and when the family dines alone, the fore or hind quarter will make a reasonable dish, and seasoned with a little pepper or salt will be very good boiled on the fourth day, especially in winter.

11   I have reckoned upon a medium that a child just born will weigh twelve pounds, and in a solar year if tolerably nursed increaseth to twenty-eight pounds.

12   I grant this food will be somewhat dear, and therefore very proper for landlords, who, as they have already devoured most of the parents, seem to have the best title to the children.

13   Infant's flesh will be in season throughout the year, but more plentiful in March, and a little before and after. For we are told by a grave author, an eminent French physician, that fish being a prolific diet, there are more children born in Roman Catholic countries about nine months after Lent, than at any other season; therefore, reckoning a year after Lent, the markets will be more glutted than usual, because the number of popish infants is at least three to one in this kingdom; and therefore it will have one other collateral advantage, by lessening the number of Papists among us.

14   I have already computed the charge of nursing a beggar's child (in which list I reckon all cottagers, laborers, and four-fifths of the farmers) to be about two shillings per annum, rags included; and I believe no gentleman would repine to give ten shillings for the carcass of a good fat child, which, as I have said, will make four dishes of excellent nutritive meat, when he hath only some particular friend or his own family to dine with him. Thus the squire will learn to be a good landlord, and grow popular among his tenants; the mother will have eight shillings net profit, and be fit for work till she produces another child.

15   Those who are more thrifty (as I must confess the times require) may flay the carcass; the skin of which artificially dressed will make admirable gloves for ladies, and summer boots for fine gentlemen.

16   As to our city of Dublin, shambles may be appointed for this purpose in the most convenient parts of it, and butchers we may be assured will not be wanting; although I rather recommend buying the children alive, and dressing them hot from the knife as we do roasting pigs.

17   A very worthy person, a true lover of his country, and whose virtues I highly esteem, was lately pleased in discoursing on this matter to offer a refinement upon my scheme. He said that many gentlemen of this kingdom, having of late destroyed their deer, he conceived that the want of venison might be well supplied by the bodies of young lads and maidens, not exceeding fourteen years of age nor under twelve, so great a number of both sexes in every country being now ready to starve for want of work and service; and these to be disposed of by their parents, if alive, or otherwise by their nearest relations. But with due deference to so excellent a friend and so deserving a patriot, I cannot be altogether in his sentiments; for as to the males, my American acquaintance assured me from frequent experience that their flesh was generally tough and lean, like that of our schoolboys, by continual exercise, and their taste disagreeable; and to fatten them would not answer the charge. Then as to the females, it would, I think with humble submission, be a loss to the public, because they soon would become breeders themselves; and besides, it is not improbable that some scrupulous people might be apt to censure such a practice

(although indeed very unjustly) as a little bordering upon cruelty; which, I confess, hath always been with me the strongest objection against any project, how well soever intended.

18   But in order to justify my friend, he confessed that this expedient was put into his head by the famous Psalmanazar, a native of the island Formosa, who came from thence to London above twenty years ago, and in conversation told my friend that in his country when any young person happened to be put to death, the executioner sold the carcass to persons of quality as a prime dainty; and that in his time the body of a plump girl of fifteen, who was crucified for an attempt to poison the emperor, was sold to his Imperial Majesty's prime minister of state, and other great mandarins of the court, in joints from the gibbet, at four hundred crowns. Neither indeed can I deny that if the same use were made of several plump young girls in this town, who without one single groat to their fortunes cannot stir abroad without a chair, and appear at the playhouse and assemblies in foreign fineries which they never will pay for, the kingdom would not be the worse.

19   Some persons of a desponding spirit are in great concern about that vast number of poor people who are aged, diseased, or maimed, and I have been desired to employ my thoughts what course may be taken to ease the nation of so grievous an encumbrance. But I am not in the least pain upon that matter, because it is very well known that they are every day dying and rotting by cold and famine, and filth and vermin, as fast as can be reasonably expected. And as to the young laborers, they are now in almost as hopeful a condition. They cannot get work, and consequently pine away for want of nourishment to a degree that if at any time they are accidentally hired to common labor, they have not strength to perform it; and thus the country and themselves are happily delivered from the evils to come.

20   I have too long digressed, and therefore shall return to my subject. I think the advantages by the proposal which I have made are obvious and many, as well as of the highest importance.

21   For first, as I have already observed, it would greatly lessen the number of Papists, with whom we are yearly overrun, being the principal breeders of the nation as well as our most dangerous enemies; and who stay at home on purpose to deliver the kingdom to the Pretender, hoping to take their advantage by the absence of so many good Protestants, who have chosen rather to leave their country than to stay at home and pay tithes against their conscience to an Episcopal curate.

22   Secondly, the poorer tenants will have something valuable of their own, which by law may be made liable to distress, and help to pay their landlord's rent, their corn and cattle being already seized and money a thing unknown.

23   Thirdly, whereas the maintenance of an hundred thousand children, from two years old and upwards, cannot be computed at less than ten shillings a piece per annum, the nation's stock will be thereby increased fifty thousand pounds per annum, besides the profit of a new dish introduced to the tables of all gentlemen of fortune in the kingdom who have any refinement in taste. And the money will circulate among ourselves, the goods being entirely of our own growth and manufacture.

24   Fourthly, the constant breeders, besides the gain of eight shillings sterling per annum by the sale of their children, will be rid of the charge for maintaining them after the first year.

25   Fifthly, this food would likewise bring great custom to taverns; where the vintners will certainly be so prudent as to procure the best receipts for dressing it to perfection, and

consequently have their houses frequented by all the fine gentlemen, who justly value themselves upon their knowledge in good eating; and a skillful cook, who understands how to oblige his guests, will contrive to make it as expensive as they please.

26 Sixthly, this would be a great inducement to marriage, which all wise nations have either encouraged by rewards or enforced by laws and penalties. It would increase the care and tenderness of mothers toward their children, when they were sure of a settlement for life to the poor babes, provided in some sort by the public, to their annual profit instead of expense. We should see an honest emulation among the married women, which of them could bring the fattest child to the market. Men would become as fond of their wives during the time of their pregnancy as they are now of their mares in foal, their cows in calf, or sows when they are ready to farrow; nor offer to beat or kick them (as is too frequent a practice) for fear of a miscarriage.

27 Many other advantages might be enumerated. For instance, the addition of some thousand carcasses in our exportation of barreled beef, the propagation of swine's flesh, and improvements in the art of making good bacon, so much wanted among us by the great destruction of pigs, too frequent at our tables, which are no way comparable in taste or magnificence to a well-grown, fat, yearling child, which roasted whole will make a considerable figure at a lord mayor's feast or any other public entertainment. But this and many others I omit, being studious of brevity.

28 Supposing that one thousand families in this city would be constant customers for infants' flesh, besides others who might have it at merry meetings, particularly weddings and christenings, I compute that Dublin would take off annually about twenty thousand carcasses, and the rest of the kingdom (where probably they will be sold somewhat cheaper) the remaining eighty thousand.

29 I can think of no one objection that will possibly be raised against this proposal, unless it should be urged that the number of people will be thereby much lessened in the kingdom. This I freely own, and it was indeed one principal design in offering it to the world. I desire the reader will observe, that I calculate my remedy for this one individual kingdom of Ireland and for no other that ever was, is, or I think ever can be upon earth. Therefore, let no man talk to me of other expedients: of taxing our absentees at five shillings a pound: of using neither clothes nor household furniture except what is of our own growth and manufacture: of utterly rejecting the materials and instruments that promote foreign luxury: of curing the expensiveness of pride, vanity, idleness, and gaming in our women: of introducing a vein of parsimony, prudence, and temperance: of learning to love our country, in the want of which we differ even from Laplanders and the inhabitants of Topinamboo: of quitting our animosities and factions, nor acting any longer like the Jews, who were murdering one another at the very moment their city was taken: of being a little cautious not to sell our country and conscience for nothing: of teaching our landlords to have at least one degree of mercy towards their tenants: lastly, of putting a spirit of honesty, industry, and skill into our shopkeepers; who, if a resolution could now be taken to buy only our native goods, would immediately unite to cheat and exact upon us in the price, the measure, and the goodness, nor could ever yet be brought to make one fair proposal of just dealing, though often and earnestly invited to it.

30   Therefore, I repeat, let no man talk to me of these and the like expedients, till he hath at least some glimpse of hope that there will ever be some hearty and sincere attempt to put them into practice.

31   But as to myself, having been wearied out for many years with offering vain, idle, visionary thoughts, and at length utterly despairing of success, I fortunately fell upon this proposal, which, as it is wholly new, so it hath something solid and real, of no expense and little trouble, full in our own power, and whereby we can incur no danger in disobliging England. For this kind of commodity will not bear exportation, the flesh being of too tender a consistence to admit a long continuance in salt, although perhaps I could name a country which would be glad to eat up our whole nation without it.

32   After all, I am not so violently bent upon my own opinion as to reject any offer proposed by wise men, which shall be found equally innocent, cheap, easy, and effectual. But before something of that kind shall be advanced in contradiction to my scheme, and offering a better, I desire the author or authors will be pleased maturely to consider two points. First, as things now stand, how they will be able to find food and raiment for an hundred thousand useless mouths and backs. And secondly, there being a round million of creatures in human figure throughout this kingdom, whose sole subsistence put into a common stock would leave them in debt two millions of pounds sterling, adding those who are beggars by profession to the bulk of farmers, cottagers, and laborers, with their wives and children who are beggars in effect; I desire those politicians who dislike my overture, and may perhaps be so bold as to attempt an answer, that they will first ask the parents of these mortals whether they would not at this day think it a great happiness to have been sold for food at a year old in this manner I prescribe, and thereby have avoided such a perpetual scene of misfortunes as they have since gone through by the oppression of landlords, the impossibility of paying rent without money or trade; the want of common sustenance, with neither house nor clothes to cover them from the inclemencies of the weather, and the most inevitable prospect of entailing the like or greater miseries upon their breed forever.

33   I profess, in the sincerity of my heart, that I have not the least personal interest in endeavoring to promote this necessary work, having no other motive than the public good of my country, by advancing our trade, providing for infants, relieving the poor, and giving some pleasure to the rich. I have no children by which I can propose to get a single penny; the youngest being nine years old, and my wife past childbearing.

Chapter 37

Literature

Bilingual/Bilingüe

Rhina P. Espaillat

Bilingual poet Rhina P. Espaillat was born in the Dominican Republic, and immigrated to New York City after dictator Rafael Trujillo exiled her family for opposing his regime. Espaillat is the author of eleven poetry collections, including *Mundo y Palabra/The World and the Word* (2001) and the recipient of several awards, including three Poetry Society of America prizes. She has also published critically acclaimed Spanish translations of Robert Frost's poetry. This poem, from *Where Horizons Go* (1998), explores language as both a bridge and a wall between father and daughter.

> My father liked them separate, one there,
> one here (allá y aquí), as if aware
>
> that words might cut in two his daughter's heart
> (el corazón) and lock the alien part
>
> to what he was—his memory, his name
> (su nombre)—with a key he could not claim.
>
> "English outside this door, Spanish inside,"
> he said, "y basta."* But who can divide
>
> the world, the word (mundo y palabra) from
> any child? I knew how to be dumb
>
> and stubborn (testaruda); late, in bed,
> I hoarded secret syllables I read
>
> until my tongue (mi lengua) learned to run
> where his stumbled. And still the heart was one.
>
> I like to think he knew that, even when,
> proud (orgulloso) of his daughter's pen,
>
> he stood outside mis versos,** half in fear
> of words he loved but wanted not to hear

---

* "y basta" – translation: "and enough."
** mis versos – translation: my poems.

Poem for an Inked Daughter

Jane Wheeler

Jane Wheeler is a northern Colorado teacher and writer, whose prose and poetry have been published nationally in a variety of venues, from books to buses. This poem, written to her teenage daughter, was first published in *UU World* in 2006; since then it has been reprinted frequently and has been taught in both college and community writing courses.

1   I did it too you know, just differently.
Way back then
when I was angry young
I pierced my ears with a rusty ice pick,
5   and willfully wore dangly earrings
(and a smirk) to Christmas dinner.
My scandalized Mother
referred to me for days as
"my daughter, the dirty gypsy."
10   I let my ears jingle silver music, ultimately
dancing right over her Victorian disapproval
out of that house forever.

And now here you are,
fresh from a different kind of parlor,
15   with that defiant dragon
curling dark over your shoulder.
No, of course you know I don't like it.
Another gauntlet thrown down
in the ongoing Mother-Daughter Wars.

20   But hear this, my own gypsy girl:
I know something you don't.
That under that fierce fire-breathing dragon,
claws bared, ready for the next battle,
under the skin where the purple ink turns to blood,
25   your blood is my blood,
rushing red to red, flowing in a long bond
linking my heart to you no matter what,
like the swirling, twisting lines
of an intricate intimate tattoo,
30   invisible, indelible, forever permanent.

A Jury of Her Peers*

Susan Glaspell

Susan Glaspell was a novelist, playwright, and co-founder of the innovative Provincetown Playhouse. She published nine novels, over a dozen plays, and more than forty short stories; her play *Alison's House* won the Pulitzer Prize in 1931. As a young woman, Glaspell was a reporter in Iowa, where she covered the trial of Margaret Hossack, accused of murdering her husband. From that experience Glaspell wrote her play *Trifles* (1916), followed the next year by the short-story version reprinted here.

1   When Martha Hale opened the storm door and got a cut of the north wind, she ran back for her big woolen scarf. As she hurriedly wound that round her head her eye made a scandalized sweep of her kitchen. It was no ordinary thing that called her away—it was probably farther from ordinary than anything that had ever happened in Dickson County. But what her eye took in was that her kitchen was in no shape for leaving: her bread all ready for mixing, half the flour sifted and half unsifted.

2   She hated to see things half done; but she had been at that when the team from town stopped to get Mr. Hale, and then the sheriff came running in to say his wife wished Mrs. Hale would come too—adding, with a grin, that he guessed she was getting scary and wanted another woman along. So she had dropped everything right where it was.

3   "Martha!" now came her husband's impatient voice. "Don't keep folks waiting out here in the cold."

4   She again opened the storm door, and this time joined the three men and the one woman waiting for her in the big two-seated buggy.

5   After she had the robes tucked around her she took another look at the woman who sat beside her on the back seat. She had met Mrs. Peters the year before at the county fair, and the thing she remembered about her was that she didn't seem like a sheriff's wife. She was small and thin and didn't have a strong voice. Mrs. Gorman, sheriff's wife before Gorman went out and Peters came in, had a voice that somehow seemed to be backing up the law with every word. But if Mrs. Peters didn't look like a sheriff's wife, Peters made it up in looking like a sheriff. He was to a dot the kind of man who could get himself elected sheriff—a heavy man with a big voice, who was particularly genial with the law-abiding, as if to make it plain that he knew the difference between criminals and non-criminals. And right there it came into Mrs. Hale's mind, with a stab, that this man who was so pleasant and lively with all of them was going to the Wrights' now as a sheriff.

6   "The country's not very pleasant this time of year," Mrs. Peters at last ventured, as if she felt they ought to be talking as well as the men.

7   Mrs. Hale scarcely finished her reply, for they had gone up a little hill and could see the Wright place now, and seeing it did not make her feel like talking. It looked very lonesome this cold March morning. It had always been a lonesome-looking place. It was down in a hollow, and the poplar trees around it were lonesome-looking trees. The men were looking at it and talking about what had happened. The county attorney was bending to one side of the buggy, and kept looking steadily at the place as they drew up to it.

_____

* Readers might see several ironies at work in Glaspell's choice of titles. Recall that at this time women in Iowa could neither serve on juries nor vote.

8   "I'm glad you came with me," Mrs. Peters said nervously, as the two women were about to follow the men in through the kitchen door.

9   Even after she had her foot on the doorstep, her hand on the knob, Martha Hale had a moment of feeling she could not cross the threshold. And the reason it seemed she couldn't cross it now was simply because she hadn't crossed it before. Time and time again it had been in her mind, "I ought to go over and see Minnie Foster"—she still thought of her as Minnie Foster, though for twenty years she had been Mrs. Wright. And then there was always something to do and Minnie Foster would go from her mind. But *now* she could come.

10   The men went over to the stove. The women stood close together by the door. Young Henderson, the county attorney, turned around and said, "Come up to the fire, ladies."

11   Mrs. Peters took a step forward, then stopped. "I'm not—cold," she said.

12   And so the two women stood by the door, at first not even so much as looking around the kitchen.

13   The men talked for a minute about what a good thing it was the sheriff sent his deputy out that morning to make a fire for them, and then Sheriff Peters stepped back from the stove, unbuttoned his outer coat, and leaned his hands on the kitchen table in a way that seemed to mark the beginning of official business. "Now, Mr. Hale," he said in a sort of semiofficial voice, "before we move things about, you tell Mr. Henderson just what it was you saw when you came here yesterday morning."

14   The county attorney was looking around the kitchen.

15   "By the way," he said, "has anything been moved?" He turned to the sheriff. "Are things just as you left them yesterday?"

16   Peters looked from cupboard to sink; from that to a small worn rocker a little to one side of the kitchen table.

17   "It's just the same."

18   "Somebody should have been left here yesterday," said the county attorney.

19   "Oh—yesterday," returned the sheriff, with a little gesture as of yesterday having been more than he could bear to think of. "When I had to send Frank to Morris Center for that man who went crazy—let me tell you, I had my hands full *yesterday*. I knew you could get back from Omaha by today, George, and as long as I went over everything here myself—"

20   "Well, Mr. Hale," said the county attorney, in a way of letting what was past and gone go, "tell just what happened when you came here yesterday morning."

21   Mrs. Hale, still leaning against the door, had that sinking feeling of the mother whose child is about to speak a piece. Lewis often wandered along and got things mixed up in a story. She hoped that he would tell this straight and plain, and not say unnecessary things that would just make things harder for Minnie Foster. He didn't begin at once, and she noticed that he looked queer—as if standing in that kitchen and having to tell what he had seen there yesterday morning made him almost sick.

22   "Yes, Mr. Hale?" the county attorney reminded.

23   "Harry and I had started to town with a load of potatoes," Mrs. Hale's husband began.

24   Harry was Mrs. Hale's oldest boy. He wasn't with them now, for the very good reason that those potatoes never got to town yesterday and he was taking them this morning, so he hadn't been home when the sheriff stopped to say he wanted Mr. Hale to come over to the Wright place and tell the county attorney his story there, where he could point it all out. With all Mrs. Hale's other emotions came the fear now that maybe Harry wasn't dressed warm enough—they hadn't any of them realized how that north wind did bite.

25   "We come along this road," Hale was going on, with a motion of his hand to the road over which they had just come, "and as we got in sight of the house I says to Harry, 'I'm goin' to see if I can't get John Wright to take a telephone.' You see," he explained to Henderson, "unless I can get somebody to go in with me they won't come out this branch road except for a price *I* can't pay. I'd spoke to Wright about it once before; but he put me off, saying folks talked too much anyway, and all he asked was peace and quiet—guess you know about how much he talked himself. But I thought maybe if I went to the house and talked about it before his wife, and said all the women-folks liked the telephones, and that in this lonesome stretch of road it would be a good thing—well, I said to Harry that that was what I was going to say—though I said at the same time that I didn't know as what his wife wanted made much difference to John—"

26   Now, there he was!—saying things he didn't need to say. Mrs. Hale tried to catch her husband's eye, but fortunately the county attorney interrupted with:

27   "Let's talk about that a little later, Mr. Hale. I do want to talk about that, but I'm anxious now to get along to just what happened when you got here."

28   When he began this time, it was very deliberately and carefully:

29   "I didn't see or hear anything. I knocked at the door. And still it was all quiet inside. I knew they must be up—it was past eight o'clock. So I knocked again, louder, and I thought I heard somebody say 'Come in.' I wasn't sure—I'm not sure yet. But I opened the door—this door," jerking a hand toward the door by which the two women stood, "and there, in that rocker"—pointing to it—"sat Mrs. Wright."

30   Every one in the kitchen looked at the rocker. It came into Mrs. Hale's mind that that rocker didn't look in the least like Minnie Foster—the Minnie Foster of twenty years before. It was a dingy red, with wooden rungs up the back, and the middle rung was gone, and the chair sagged to one side.

31   "How did she—look?" the county attorney was inquiring.

32   "Well," said Hale, "she looked—queer."

33   "How do you mean—queer?"

34   As he asked it he took out a notebook and pencil. Mrs. Hale did not like the sight of that pencil. She kept her eye fixed on her husband, as if to keep him from saying unnecessary things that would go into that notebook and make trouble.

35   Hale did speak guardedly, as if the pencil had affected him too.

36   "Well, as if she didn't know what she was going to do next. And kind of—done up."

37   "How did she seem to feel about your coming?"

38   "Why, I don't think she minded—one way or other. She didn't pay much attention. I said, 'Ho' do, Mrs. Wright? It's cold, ain't it?' And she said, 'Is it?'—and went on pleatin' at her apron.

39   "Well, I was surprised. She didn't ask me to come up to the stove, or to sit down, but just set there, not even lookin' at me. And so I said: 'I want to see John.'

40   "And then she—laughed. I guess you would call it a laugh.

41   "I thought of Harry and the team outside, so I said, a little sharp, 'Can I see John?' 'No,' says she—kind of dull like. 'Ain't he home?' says I. Then she looked at me. 'Yes,' says she, 'he's home.' 'Then why can't I see him?' I asked her, out of patience with her now. ''Cause he's dead,' says she, just as quiet and dull—and fell to pleatin' her apron. 'Dead?' says I, like you do when you can't take in what you've heard.

42   "She just nodded her head, not getting a bit excited, but rockin' back and forth.

43   "'Why—where is he?' says I, not knowing *what* to say.

44   "She just pointed upstairs—like this"—pointing to the room above.

45   "I got up, with the idea of going up there myself. By this time I—didn't know what to do. I walked from there to here; then I says: 'Why, what did he die of?'

46   "'He died of a rope round his neck,' says she; and just went on pleatin' at her apron."

47   Hale stopped speaking, and stood staring at the rocker, as if he were still seeing the woman who had sat there the morning before. Nobody spoke; it was as if every one were seeing the woman who had sat there the morning before.

48   "And what did you do then?" the county attorney at last broke the silence.

49   "I went out and called Harry. I thought I might—need help. I got Harry in, and we went upstairs." His voice fell almost to a whisper. "There he was—lying over the—"

50   "I think I'd rather have you go into that upstairs," the county attorney interrupted, "where you can point it all out. Just go on now with the rest of the story."

51   "Well, my first thought was to get that rope off. It looked—"

52   He stopped, his face twitching.

53   "But Harry, he went up to him, and he said, 'No, he's dead all right, and we'd better not touch anything.' So we went downstairs.

54   "She was still sitting that same way. 'Has anybody been notified?' I asked. 'No,' says she, unconcerned.

55   "'Who did this, Mrs. Wright?' said Harry. He said it businesslike, and she stopped pleatin' at her apron. 'I don't know,' she says. 'You don't *know?*' says Harry. 'Weren't you sleepin' in the bed with him?' 'Yes,' says she, 'but I was on the inside.' 'Somebody slipped a rope round his neck and strangled him, and you didn't wake up?' says Harry. 'I didn't wake up,' she said after him.

56   "We may have looked as if we didn't see how that could be, for after a minute she said, 'I sleep sound.'

57   "Harry was going to ask her more questions, but I said maybe that weren't our business; maybe we ought to let her tell her story first to the coroner or the sheriff. So Harry went fast as he could over to High Road—the Rivers's place, where there's a telephone."

58   "And what did she do when she knew you had gone for the coroner?" The attorney got his pencil in his hand all ready for writing.

59   "She moved from that chair to this one over here"—Hale pointed to a small chair in the corner—"and just sat there with her hands held together and looking down. I got a feeling that I ought to make some conversation, so I said I had come in to see if John wanted to put in a telephone; and at that she started to laugh, and then she stopped and looked at me—scared."

60   At the sound of the moving pencil the man who was telling the story looked up.

61   "I dunno—maybe it wasn't scared," he hastened; "I wouldn't like to say it was. Soon Harry got back, and then Dr. Lloyd came, and you, Mr. Peters, and so I guess that's all I know that you don't."

62   He said that last with relief, and moved a little, as if relaxing. Every one moved a little. The county attorney walked toward the stair door.

63   "I guess we'll go upstairs first—then out to the barn and around there."

64   He paused and looked around the kitchen.

65   "You're convinced there was nothing important here?" he asked the sheriff. "Nothing that would—point to any motive?"

66   The sheriff too looked all around, as if to re-convince himself.

67   "Nothing here but kitchen things," he said, with a little laugh for the insignificance of kitchen things.

68   The county attorney was looking at the cupboard—a peculiar, ungainly structure, half closet and half cupboard, the upper part of it being built in the wall, and the lower part just the old-fashioned kitchen cupboard. As if its queerness attracted him, he got a chair and opened the upper part and looked in. After a moment he drew his hand away sticky.

69   "Here's a nice mess," he said resentfully.

70   The two women had drawn nearer, and now the sheriff's wife spoke.

71   "Oh—her fruit," she said, looking to Mrs. Hale for sympathetic understanding. She turned back to the county attorney and explained. "She worried about that when it turned so cold last night. She said the fire would go out and her jars might burst."

72   Mrs. Peters's husband broke into a laugh.

73   "Well, can you beat the women! Held for murder, and worrying about her preserves!"

74   The young attorney set his lips.

75   "I guess before we're through with her she may have something more serious than preserves to worry about."

76   "Oh, well," said Mrs. Hale's husband, with good-natured superiority, "women are used to worrying over trifles."

77   The two women moved a little closer together. Neither of them spoke. The county attorney seemed suddenly to remember his manners—and think of his future.

78   "And yet," said he, with the gallantry of a young politician, "for all their worries, what would we do without the ladies?"

79   The women did not speak, did not unbend. He went to the sink and began washing his hands. He turned to wipe them on the roller towel—whirled it for a cleaner place.

80   "Dirty towels! Not much of a housekeeper, would you say, ladies?"

81   He kicked his foot against some dirty pans under the sink.

82   "There's a great deal of work to be done on a farm," said Mrs. Hale stiffly.

83   "To be sure. And yet"—with a little bow to her—"I know there are some Dickson County farm-houses that do not have such roller towels." He gave it a pull to expose its full length again.

84   "Those towels get dirty awful quick. Men's hands aren't always as clean as they might be."

85   "Ah, loyal to your sex, I see," he laughed. He stopped and gave her a keen look. "But you and Mrs. Wright were neighbors. I suppose you were friends, too."

86   Martha Hale shook her head.

87   "I've seen little enough of her of late years. I've not been in this house—it's more than a year."

88   "And why was that? You didn't like her?"

89   "I liked her well enough," she replied with spirit. "Farmers' wives have their hands full, Mr. Henderson. And then—" She looked around the kitchen.

90   "Yes?" he encouraged.

91   "It never seemed a very cheerful place," said she, more to herself than to him.

92   "No," he agreed; "I don't think any one would call it cheerful. I shouldn't say she had the homemaking instinct."

93   "Well, I don't know as Wright had, either," she muttered.

94   "You mean they didn't get on very well?" he was very quick to ask.

95   "No; I don't mean anything," she answered, with decision. As she turned a little away from him, she added: "But I don't think a place would be any the cheerfuler for John Wright's bein' in it."

96   "I'd like to talk to you about that a little later, Mrs. Hale," he said. "I'm anxious to get the lay of things upstairs now."

97   He moved toward the stair door, followed by the two men.

98   "I suppose anything Mrs. Peters does'll be all right?" the sheriff inquired. "She was to take in some clothes for her, you know—and a few little things. We left in such a hurry yesterday."

99   The county attorney looked at the two women whom they were leaving alone there among the kitchen things.

100   "Yes—Mrs. Peters," he said, his glance resting on the woman who was not Mrs. Peters, the big farmer woman who stood behind the sheriff's wife. "Of course Mrs. Peters is one of us," he said, in a manner of entrusting responsibility. "And keep your eye out, Mrs. Peters, for anything that might be of use. No telling; you women might come upon a clue to the motive—and that's the thing we need."

101   Mr. Hale rubbed his face after the fashion of a show man getting ready for a pleasantry.

102   "But would the women know a clue if they did come upon it?" he said; and, having delivered himself of this, he followed the others through the stair door.

103   The women stood motionless and silent, listening to the footsteps, first upon the stairs, then in the room above them.

104   Then, as if releasing herself from something strange, Mrs. Hale began to arrange the dirty pans under the sink, which the county attorney's disdainful push of the foot had deranged.

105   "I'd hate to have men comin' into my kitchen," she said testily—"snoopin' round and criticizin.'"

106   "Of course it's no more than their duty," said the sheriff's wife, in her manner of timid acquiescence.

107   "Duty's all right," replied Mrs. Hale bluffly; "but I guess that deputy sheriff that come out to make the fire might have got a little of this on." She gave the roller towel a pull. "Wish I'd thought of that sooner! Seems mean to talk about her for not having things slicked up, when she had to come away in such a hurry."

108   She looked around the kitchen. Certainly it was not "slicked up." Her eye was held by a bucket of sugar on a low shelf. The cover was off the wooden bucket, and beside it was a paper bag—half full.

109   Mrs. Hale moved toward it.

110   "She was putting this in there," she said to herself—slowly.

111   She thought of the flour in her kitchen at home—half sifted, half not sifted. She had been interrupted, and had left things half done. What had interrupted Minnie Foster? Why had that work been left half done? She made a move as if to finish it,—unfinished things always bothered her,—and then she glanced around and saw that Mrs. Peters was watching her—and she didn't want Mrs. Peters to get that feeling she had got of work begun and then—for some reason—not finished.

112   "It's a shame about her fruit," she said, and walked toward the cupboard that the county attorney had opened, and got on the chair, murmuring: "I wonder if it's all gone."

113   It was a sorry enough looking sight, but "Here's one that's all right," she said at last. She held it toward the light. "This is cherries, too." She looked again. "I declare I believe that's the only one."

114   With a sigh, she got down from the chair, went to the sink, and wiped off the bottle.

115   "She'll feel awful bad, after all her hard work in the hot weather. I remember the afternoon I put up my cherries last summer."

116   She set the bottle on the table, and, with another sigh, started to sit down in the rocker. But she did not sit down. Something kept her from sitting down in that chair. She straightened—stepped back, and, half turned away, stood looking at it, seeing the woman who had sat there "pleatin' at her apron."

117   The thin voice of the sheriff's wife broke in upon her: "I must be getting those things from the front room closet." She opened the door into the other room, started in, stepped back. "You coming with me, Mrs. Hale?" she asked nervously. "You—you could help me get them."

118   They were soon back—the stark coldness of that shut-up room was not a thing to linger in.

119   "My!" said Mrs. Peters, dropping the things on the table and hurrying to the stove.

120   Mrs. Hale stood examining the clothes the woman who was being detained in town had said she wanted.

121   "Wright was close!" she exclaimed, holding up a shabby black skirt that bore the marks of much making over. "I think maybe that's why she kept so much to herself. I s'pose she felt she couldn't do her part; and then, you don't enjoy things when you feel shabby. She used to wear pretty clothes and be lively—when she was Minnie Foster, one of the town girls, singing in the choir. But that—oh, that was twenty years ago."

122   With a carefulness in which there was something tender, she folded the shabby clothes and piled them at one corner of the table. She looked up at Mrs. Peters, and there was something in the other woman's look that irritated her.

123   "She don't care," she said to herself. "Much difference it makes to her whether Minnie Foster had pretty clothes when she was a girl."

124   Then she looked again, and she wasn't so sure; in fact, she hadn't at any time been perfectly sure about Mrs. Peters. She had that shrinking manner, and yet her eyes looked as if they could see a long way into things.

125   "This all you was to take in?" asked Mrs. Hale.

126   "No," said the sheriff's wife; "she said she wanted an apron. Funny thing to want," she ventured in her nervous little way, "for there's not much to get you dirty in jail, goodness knows. But I suppose just to make her feel more natural. If you're used to wearing an apron—. She said they were in the bottom drawer of this cupboard. Yes—here they are. And then her little shawl that always hung on the stair door."

127   She took the small gray shawl from behind the door leading upstairs, and stood a minute looking at it.

128   Suddenly Mrs. Hale took a quick step toward the other woman.

129   "Mrs. Peters!"

130   "Yes, Mrs. Hale?"

131   "Do you think she—did it?"

132   A frightened look blurred the other thing in Mrs. Peters's eyes.

133   "Oh, I don't know," she said, in a voice that seemed to shrink away from the subject.

134   "Well, I don't think she did," affirmed Mrs. Hale stoutly. "Asking for an apron, and her little shawl. Worryin' about her fruit."

135   "Mr. Peters says—." Footsteps were heard in the room above; she stopped, looked up, then went on in a lowered voice: "Mr. Peters says—it looks bad for her. Mr. Henderson is awful sarcastic in a speech, and he's going to make fun of her saying she didn't—wake up."

136   For a moment Mrs. Hale had no answer. Then, "Well, I guess John Wright didn't wake up—when they was slippin' that rope under his neck," she muttered.

137   "No, it's *strange*," breathed Mrs. Peters. "They think it was such a—funny way to kill a man."

138   She began to laugh; at sound of the laugh, abruptly stopped.

139   "That's just what Mr. Hale said," said Mrs. Hale, in a resolutely natural voice. "There was a gun in the house. He says that's what he can't understand."

140   "Mr. Henderson said, coming out, that what was needed for the case was a motive. Something to show anger—or sudden feeling."

141   "Well, I don't see any signs of anger around here," said Mrs. Hale. "I don't—"

142   She stopped. It was as if her mind tripped on something. Her eye was caught by a dish-towel in the middle of the kitchen table. Slowly she moved toward the table. One half of it was wiped clean, the other half messy. Her eyes made a slow, almost unwilling turn to the bucket of sugar and the half empty bag beside it. Things begun—and not finished.

143   After a moment she stepped back, and said, in that manner of releasing herself:

144   "Wonder how they're finding things upstairs? I hope she had it a little more red up there. You know,"—she paused, and feeling gathered,—"it seems kind of *sneaking*; locking her up in town and coming out here to get her own house to turn against her!"

145   "But, Mrs. Hale," said the sheriff's wife, "the law is the law."

146   "I s'pose 'tis," answered Mrs. Hale shortly.

147   She turned to the stove, saying something about that fire not being much to brag of. She worked with it a minute, and when she straightened up she said aggressively:

148   "The law is the law—and a bad stove is a bad stove. How'd you like to cook on this?"—pointing with a poker to the broken lining. She opened the oven door and started to express her opinion of the oven; but she was swept into her own thoughts, thinking of what it would mean, year after year, to have that stove to wrestle with. The thought of Minnie Foster trying to bake in that oven—and the thought of her never going over to see Minnie Foster—.

149   She was startled by hearing Mrs. Peters say: "A person gets discouraged—and loses heart."

150   The sheriff's wife had looked from the stove to the sink—to the pail of water which had been carried in from outside. The two women stood there silent, above them the footsteps of the men who were looking for evidence against the woman who had worked in that kitchen. That look of seeing into things, of seeing through a thing to something else, was in the eyes of the sheriff's wife now. When Mrs. Hale next spoke to her, it was gently:

151   "Better loosen up your things, Mrs. Peters. We'll not feel them when we go out."

152   Mrs. Peters went to the back of the room to hang up the fur tippet she was wearing. A moment later she exclaimed, "Why, she was piecing a quilt," and held up a large sewing basket piled high with quilt pieces.

153   Mrs. Hale spread some of the blocks on the table.

154   "It's log-cabin pattern," she said, putting several of them together. "Pretty, isn't it?"

155   They were so engaged with the quilt that they did not hear the footsteps on the stairs. Just as the stair door opened Mrs. Hale was saying:

156   "Do you suppose she was going to quilt it or just knot it?"

157   The sheriff threw up his hands.

158   "They wonder whether she was going to quilt it or just knot it!"

159   There was a laugh for the ways of women, a warming of hands over the stove, and then the county attorney said briskly:

160   "Well, let's go right out to the barn and get that cleared up."

161   "I don't see as there's anything so strange," Mrs. Hale said resentfully, after the outside door had closed on the three men—"our taking up our time with little things while we're waiting for them to get the evidence. I don't see as it's anything to laugh about."

162   "Of course they've got awful important things on their minds," said the sheriff's wife apologetically.

163   They returned to an inspection of the blocks for the quilt. Mrs. Hale was looking at the fine, even sewing, and preoccupied with thoughts of the woman who had done that sewing, when she heard the sheriff's wife say, in a queer tone:

164   "Why, look at this one."

165   She turned to take the block held out to her.

166   "The sewing," said Mrs. Peters, in a troubled way. "All the rest of them have been so nice and even—but—this one. Why, it looks as if she didn't know what she was about!"

167   Their eyes met—something flashed to life, passed between them; then, as if with an effort, they seemed to pull away from each other. A moment Mrs. Hale sat there, her hands folded over that sewing which was so unlike all the rest of the sewing. Then she had pulled a knot and drawn the threads.

168   "Oh, what are you doing, Mrs. Hale?" asked the sheriff's wife, startled.

169   "Just pulling out a stitch or two that's not sewed very good," said Mrs. Hale mildly.

170   "I don't think we ought to touch things," Mrs. Peters said, a little helplessly.

171   "I'll just finish up this end," answered Mrs. Hale, still in that mild, matter-of-fact faction.

172   She threaded a needle and started to replace bad sewing with good. For a little while she sewed in silence. Then, in that thin, timid voice, she heard:

173   "Mrs. Hale!"

174   "Yes, Mrs. Peters?"

175   "What do you suppose she was so—nervous about?"

176   "Oh, *I* don't know," said Mrs. Hale, as if dismissing a thing not important enough to spend much time on. "I don't know as she was—nervous. I sew awful queer sometimes when I'm just tired."

177   She cut a thread, and out of the corner of her eye looked up at Mrs. Peters. The small, lean face of the sheriff's wife seemed to have tightened up. Her eyes had that look of peering into something. But next moment she moved, and said in her thin, indecisive way:

178   "Well, I must get those clothes wrapped. They may be through sooner than we think. I wonder where I could find a piece of paper—and string."

179   "In that cupboard, maybe," suggested Mrs. Hale, after a glance around.

180   One piece of the crazy sewing remained unripped. Mrs. Peters's back turned, Martha Hale now scrutinized that piece, compared it with the dainty, accurate sewing of the other blocks. The difference was startling. Holding this block made her feel queer, as if the distracted thoughts of the woman who had perhaps turned to it to try and quiet herself were communicating themselves to her.

181   Mrs. Peters' voice roused her.

182   "Here's a bird-cage," she said. "Did she have a bird, Mrs. Hale?"

183   "Why, I don't know whether she did or not." She turned to look at the cage Mrs. Peter was holding up. "I've not been here in so long." She sighed. "There was a man round last year selling canaries cheap—but I don't know as she took one. Maybe she did. She used to sing real pretty herself."

184   Mrs. Peters looked around the kitchen.

185   "Seems kind of funny to think of a bird here." She half laughed—an attempt to put up a barrier. "But she must have had one—or why would she have a cage? I wonder what happened to it?"

186   "I suppose maybe the cat got it," suggested Mrs. Hale, resuming her sewing.

187   "No, she didn't have a cat. She's got that feeling some people have about cats—being afraid of them. When they brought her to our house yesterday, my cat got in the room, and she was real upset and asked me to take it out."

188   "My sister Bessie was like that," laughed Mrs. Hale.

189   The sheriff's wife did not reply. The silence made Mrs. Hale turn round. Mrs. Peters was examining the birdcage.

190   "Look at this door," she said slowly. "It's broke. One hinge has been pulled apart."

191   Mrs. Hale came nearer.

192   "Looks as if some one must have been—rough with it."

193   Again their eyes met—startled, questioning, apprehensive. For a moment neither spoke nor stirred. Then Mrs. Hale, turning away, said brusquely:

194   "If they're going to find any evidence, I wish they'd be about it. I don't like this place."

195   "But I'm awful glad you came with me, Mrs. Hale." Mrs. Peters put the birdcage on the table and sat down. "It would be lonesome for me—sitting here alone."

196   "Yes, it would, wouldn't it?" agreed Mrs. Hale, a certain determined naturalness in her voice. She had picked up the sewing, but now it dropped in her lap, and she murmured in a different voice: "But I tell you what I *do* wish, Mrs. Peters. I wish I had come over sometimes when she was here. I wish—I had."

197   "But of course you were awful busy, Mrs. Hale. Your house—and your children."

198   "I could've come," retorted Mrs. Hale shortly. "I stayed away because it weren't cheerful—and that's why I ought to have come. I"—she looked around—"I've never liked this place. Maybe because it's down in a hollow and you don't see the road. I don't know what it is, but it's a lonesome place, and always was. I wish I had come over to see Minnie Foster sometimes. I can see now—" She did not put it into words.

199   "Well, you mustn't reproach yourself," counseled Mrs. Peters. "Somehow, we just don't see how it is with other folks till—something comes up."

200   "Not having children makes less work," mused Mrs. Hale, after a silence, "but it makes a quiet house—and Wright out to work all day—and no company when he did come in. Did you know John Wright, Mrs. Peters?"

201   "Not to know him. I've seen him in town. They say he was a good man."

202   "Yes—good," conceded John Wright's neighbor grimly. "He didn't drink, and kept his word as well as most, I guess, and paid his debts. But he was a hard man, Mrs. Peters. Just to pass the time of day with him—." She stopped, shivered a little. "Like a raw wind that gets to the bone." Her eye fell upon the cage on the table before her, and she added, almost bitterly: "I should think she would've wanted a bird!"

203   Suddenly she leaned forward, looking intently at the cage. "But what do you s'pose went wrong with it?"

204   "I don't know," returned Mrs. Peters; "unless it got sick and died."

205   But after she said it she reached over and swung the broken door. Both women watched it as if somehow held by it.

206   "You didn't know—her?" Mrs. Hale asked, a gentler note in her voice.

207   "Not till they brought her yesterday," said the sheriff's wife.

208   "She—come to think of it, she was kind of like a bird herself. Real sweet and pretty, but kind of timid and—fluttery. How—she—did—change."

209   That held her for a long time. Finally, as if struck with a happy thought and relieved to get back to everyday things, she exclaimed:

210   "Tell you what, Mrs. Peters, why don't you take the quilt in with you? It might take up her mind."

211   "Why, I think that's a real nice idea, Mrs. Hale," agreed the sheriff's wife, as if she too were glad to come into the atmosphere of a simple kindness. "There couldn't possibly be any objection to that, could there? Now, just what will I take? I wonder if her patches are in here—and her things."

212   They turned to the sewing basket.

213   "Here's some red," said Mrs. Hale, bringing out a roll of cloth. Underneath that was a box. "Here, maybe her scissors are in here—and her things." She held it up. "What a pretty box! I'll warrant that was something she had a long time ago—when she was a girl."

214   She held it in her hand a moment; then, with a little sigh, opened it.

215   Instantly her hand went to her nose.

216   "Why—!"

217   Mrs. Peters drew nearer—then turned away.

218   "There's something wrapped up in this piece of silk," faltered Mrs. Hale.

219   "This isn't her scissors," said Mrs. Peters in a shrinking voice.

220   Her hand not steady, Mrs. Hale raised the piece of silk. "Oh, Mrs. Peters!" she cried. "It's—"

221   Mrs. Peters bent closer.

222   "It's the bird," she whispered.

223   "But, Mrs. Peters!" cried Mrs. Hale. "*Look* at it! Its neck—look at its neck! It's all—other side *to*."

224   She held the box away from her.

225   The sheriff's wife again bent closer.

226   "Somebody wrung its neck," said she, in a voice that was slow and deep.

227   And then again the eyes of the two women met—this time clung together in a look of dawning comprehension, of growing horror. Mrs. Peters looked from the dead bird to the broken door of the cage. Again their eyes met. And just then there was a sound at the outside door.

228   Mrs. Hale slipped the box under the quilt pieces in the basket, and sank into the chair before it. Mrs. Peters stood holding to the table. The county attorney and the sheriff came in from outside.

229   "Well, ladies," said the county attorney, as one turning from serious things to little pleasantries, "have you decided whether she was going to quilt it or knot it?"

230   "We think," began the sheriff's wife in a flurried voice, "that she was going to—knot it."

231   He was too preoccupied to notice the change that came in her voice on that last.

232   "Well, that's very interesting, I'm sure," he said tolerantly. He caught sight of the birdcage. "Has the bird flown?"

233   "We think the cat got it," said Mrs. Hale in a voice curiously even.

234   He was walking up and down, as if thinking something out.

235   "Is there a cat?" he asked absently.

236   Mrs. Hale shot a look up at the sheriff's wife.

237   "Well, not *now*," said Mrs. Peters. "They're superstitious, you know, they leave."

238   She sank into the chair.

239   The county attorney did not heed her. "No sign at all of any one having come in from the outside," he said to Peters, in the manner of continuing an interrupted conversation. "Their own rope. Now let's go upstairs again and go over it, piece by piece. It would have to have been some one who knew just the—"

240   The stair door closed behind them and their voices were lost.

241   The two women sat motionless, not looking at each other, but as if peering into something and at the same time holding back. When they spoke now it was as if they were afraid of what they were saying, but as if they could not help saying it.

242   "She liked the bird," said Martha Hale, low and slowly. "She was going to bury it in that pretty box."

243   "When I was a girl," said Mrs. Peters, under her breath, "my kitten—there was a boy took a hatchet, and before my eyes—before I could get there—" She covered her face an instant. "If they hadn't held me back I would have"—she caught herself, looked upstairs where footsteps were heard, and finished weakly—"hurt him."

244   Then they sat without speaking or moving.

245   "I wonder how it would seem," Mrs. Hale at last began, as if feeling her way over strange ground—"never to have had any children around?" Her eyes made a slow sweep of the kitchen, as if seeing what that kitchen had meant through all the years. "No, Wright wouldn't like the bird," she said after that—"a thing that sang. She used to sing. He killed that too." Her voice tightened.

246   Mrs. Peters moved uneasily.

247   "Of course we don't know who killed the bird."

248   "I knew John Wright," was Mrs. Hale's answer.

249   "It was an awful thing was done in this house that night, Mrs. Hale," said the sheriff's wife. "Killing a man while he slept—slipping a thing round his neck that choked the life out of him."

250   Mrs. Hale's hand went out to the birdcage.

251   "His neck. Choked the life out of him."

252   "We don't *know* who killed him," whispered Mrs. Peters wildly. "We don't *know*."

253   Mrs. Hale had not moved. "If there had been years and years of—nothing, then a bird to sing to you, it would be awful—still—after the bird was still."

254   It was as if something within her not herself had spoken, and it found in Mrs. Peters something she did not know as herself.

255   "I know what stillness is," she said, in a queer, monotonous voice. "When we homesteaded in Dakota, and my first baby died—after he was two years old—and me with no other then—"

256   Mrs. Hale stirred.

257   "How soon do you suppose they'll be through looking for the evidence?"

258   "I know what stillness is," repeated Mrs. Peters, in just that same way. Then she too pulled back. "The law has got to punish crime, Mrs. Hale," she said in her tight little way.

259   "I wish you'd seen Minnie Foster," was the answer, "when she wore a white dress with blue ribbons, and stood up there in the choir and sang."

260   The picture of that girl, the fact that she had lived neighbor to that girl for twenty years, and had let her die for lack of life, was suddenly more than she could bear.

261   "Oh, I *wish* I'd come over here once in a while!" she cried. "That was a crime! That was a crime! Who's going to punish that?"

262   "We mustn't take on," said Mrs. Peters, with a frightened look toward the stairs.

263   "I might 'a' *known* she needed help! I tell you, it's *queer*, Mrs. Peters. We live close together, and we live far apart. We all go through the same things—it's all just a different kind of the same thing! If it weren't—why do you and I *understand*? Why do we *know*—what we know this minute?"

264   She dashed her hand across her eyes. Then, seeing the jar of fruit on the table, she reached for it and choked out:

265   "If I was you I wouldn't *tell* her her fruit was gone! Tell her it *ain't*. Tell her it's all right—all of it. Here—take this in to prove it to her! She—she may never know whether it was broke or not."

266   She turned away.

267   Mrs. Peters reached out for the bottle of fruit as if she were glad to take it—as if touching a familiar thing, having something to do, could keep her from something else. She got up, looked about for something to wrap the fruit in, took a petticoat from the pile of clothes she had brought from the front room, and nervously started winding that round the bottle.

268   "My!" she began, in a high, false voice, "it's a good thing the men couldn't hear us! Getting all stirred up over a little thing like a—dead canary." She hurried over that. "As if that could have anything to do with—with—My, wouldn't they *laugh*?"

269   Footsteps were heard on the stairs.

270   "Maybe they would," muttered Mrs. Hale—"maybe they wouldn't."

271   "No, Peters," said the county attorney incisively; "it's all perfectly clear, except the reason for doing it. But you know juries when it comes to women. If there was some definite thing—something to show. Something to make a story about. A thing that would connect up with this clumsy way of doing it."

272   In a covert way Mrs. Hale looked at Mrs. Peters. Mrs. Peters was looking at her. Quickly they looked away from each other. The outer door opened and Mr. Hale came in.

273   "I've got the team round now," he said. "Pretty cold out there."

274   "I'm going to stay here awhile by myself," the county attorney suddenly announced. "You can send Frank out for me, can't you?" he asked the sheriff. "I want to go over everything. I'm not satisfied we can't do better."

275   Again, for one brief moment, the two women's eyes found one another.

276   The sheriff came up to the table.

277   "Did you want to see what Mrs. Peters was going to take in?"

278   The county attorney picked up the apron. He laughed.

279   "Oh, I guess they're not very dangerous things the ladies have picked out."

280   Mrs. Hale's hand was on the sewing basket in which the box was concealed. She felt that she ought to take her hand off the basket. She did not seem able to. He picked up one of the quilt blocks which she had piled on to cover the box. Her eyes felt like fire. She had a feeling that if he took up the basket she would snatch it from him.

281   But he did not take it up. With another little laugh, he turned away, saying:

282   "No; Mrs. Peters doesn't need supervising. For that matter, a sheriff's wife is married to the law. Ever think of it that way, Mrs. Peters?"

283   Mrs. Peters was standing beside the table. Mrs. Hale shot a look up at her, but she could not see her face. Mrs. Peters had turned away. When she spoke, her voice was muffled.

284   "Not—just that way," she said.

285   "Married to the law!" chuckled Mrs. Peters's husband. He moved toward the door into the front room, and said to the county attorney:

286   "I just want you to come in here a minute, George. We ought to take a look at these windows."

287   "Oh—windows," said the county attorney scoffingly.

288   "We'll be right out, Mr. Hale," said the sheriff to the farmer, who was still waiting by the door.

289   Hale went to look after the horses. The sheriff followed the county attorney into the other room. Again—for one final moment—the two women were alone in that kitchen.

290   Martha Hale sprang up, her hands tight together, looking at that other woman, with whom it rested. At first she could not see her eyes, for the sheriff's wife had not turned back since she turned away at that suggestion of being married to the law. But now Mrs. Hale made her turn back. Her eyes made her turn back. Slowly, unwillingly, Mrs. Peters turned her head until her eyes met the eyes of the other woman. There was a moment when they held each other in a steady, burning look in which there was no evasion nor flinching. Then Martha Hale's eyes pointed the way to the basket in which was hidden the thing that would make certain the conviction of the other woman—that woman who was not there and yet who had been there with them all through that hour.

291   For a moment Mrs. Peters did not move. And then she did it. With a rush forward, she threw back the quilt pieces, got the box, tried to put it in her handbag. It was too big. Desperately she opened it, started to take the bird out. But there she broke—she could not touch the bird. She stood there helpless, foolish.

292   There was the sound of a knob turning in the inner door. Martha Hale snatched the box from the sheriff's wife, and got it in the pocket of her big coat just as the sheriff and the county attorney came back into the kitchen.

293   "Well, Henry," said the county attorney facetiously, "at least we found out that she was not going to quilt it. She was going to—what is it you call it, ladies?"

294   Mrs. Hale's hand was against the pocket of her coat.

295   "We call it—knot it, Mr. Henderson."

Credits

Chapter 1

"The Ultimate in Diet Cults: Don't Eat Anything at All" from the Bay Area Institute. Reprinted with permission.

Chapter 8

"College for Grown-Ups" by Mitchell L. Stevens, from *The New York Times*, December 11, 2014. Reprinted by permission.

Chapter 9

"So What's So Bad About Being So-So?" by Lisa Wilson Strick. First appeared in *Woman's Day* Magazine, April 14, 1984. Copyright © 1984 by Lisa Wilson Strick. Reprinted by permission of the author.

Chapter 10

"To Bid the World Farewell" from *The American Way of Death* by Jessica Mitford. Reprinted by permission of The Estate of Jessica Mitford. Copyright 1963, 1978 by Jessica Mitford, all rights reserved.
"Preparing for the Job Interview: Know Thyself" by Katy Piotrowski. Reprinted by permission.

Chapter 11

"Grant and Lee: A Study in Contrasts" by Bruce Catton. Copyright © U.S. Capitol Historical Society, all rights reserved. Reprinted with permission.
Samuel Clemens, "Two Ways of Knowing a River."

Chapter 12

"The Munchausen Mystery" by Don R. Lipsitt from *Psychology Today*, February 1983. Reprinted with permission from Psychology Today Magazine. Copyright © 1983 Sussex Publishers, Inc.

Chapter 13

"The Plot Against the People" by Russell Baker from *The New York Times*, June 18, 1968. Copyright © 1968 The New York Times Co. Reprinted by permission.
"What Is Really in a Hot Dog" from www.sixwise.com.

Chapter 14

"Why Are Young People Ditching Cars for Smartphones?" by Jordan Weissmann, August 7, 2012, *The Atlantic*. Reprinted by permission of the author.

Chapter 15

"Mandatory voting won't cure dismal turnout: Our View" by the Editorial Board of *USA Today*, April 5, 2015.

"Required voting yields benefits: Opposing view" by Thomas E. Mann, April 5, 2015.

Chapter 16

"Pretty Girl" by Rick Bragg. The Daily South column at *Southern Living*, May 6, 2014. Time Inc. Lifestyle Group. Reprinted with permission.

Chapter 17

"Don't Mess with Auntie Jean" by Jada F. Smith, from *The New York Times*, March 14, 2015. Reprinted with permission.

Chapter 18

Lahey, Jessica. "Why Parents Need to Let Their Children Fail." 29 Jan. 2013. *The Atlantic*. Reprinted by permission of the author.

Chapter 20

Photo on pages 459 and 469: P. Ekman & W. Friesen, "Unmasking the Face," 2nd Edition 1984. Used by permission of Ekman.

Chapter 22

Kate Chopin, "The Story of an Hour."

Walt Whitman, "When I Heard the Learn'd Astronomer."

"Geraldo No Last Name" from *The House on Mango Street*. Copyright © 1984 by Sandra Cisneros. Published by Vintage Books, a division of Random House, Inc., and in hardcover by Alfred A. Knopf in 1994. Reprinted by permission of Susan Bergholz Literary Services, New York, NY and Lamy, NM. All rights reserved.

"Those Winter Sundays." Copyright © 1966 by Robert Hayden, from *Collected Poems of Robert Hayden* by Robert Hayden, edited by Frederick Glaysher. Used by permission of Liveright Publishing Corporation.

"The Road Not Taken" by Robert Frost © 1916, 1969 by Henry Holt and Company, Copyright 1944 by Robert Frost. Reprinted by permission of Henry Holt and Company, LLC.

Chapter 27

"Black Men in Public Space" first appeared in *Ms.* Magazine, 1986. Brent Staples writes editorials on politics and culture for *The New York Times* and is the author of the memoir *Parallel Time: Growing Up in Black and White*. Reprinted by permission of the author.

Mark Forsyth, "Rhetorical Reasons That Slogans Stick," from *The New York Times*, November 13, 2014. Reprinted with permission.

Shadee Ashtari, "A Look into the 'Double Lives' of America's Homeless College Students," From *The Huffington Post* December 26, 2014. Reprinted with permission.

Index